William Gearing, George Geeves

The history of the Church of Great Britain from the birth of Our Saviour untill the year of Our Lord 1667

William Gearing, George Geeves

The history of the Church of Great Britain from the birth of Our Saviour untill the year of Our Lord 1667

ISBN/EAN: 9783337273316

Printed in Europe, USA, Canada, Australia, Japan

Cover: Foto ©Lupo / pixelio.de

More available books at **www.hansebooks.com**

THE HISTORY OF THE CHURCH OF Great Britain,

FROM THE ▓▓▓ of our SAVIOUR, untill the Year of our LORD, 1667.

With an exact Succession of the Bishops, and the memorable Acts of many of them.

TOGETHER

With an Addition of all the Eng▓▓▓ Cardinals; and the several Orders of English Mon▓▓ Friars, and Nuns, in former Ages.

Historia vitæ nostræ Magistra. Bodin.

LONDON,
Printed for *Philip Chetwin*, and to be Sold by most Book-sellers, 1674.

Honoratiſſimis.

D$^{no.}$ *HENRICO TVLSE* Æquiti
Aurato : Senatori, & Vicecomiti *Londonenſi*.

Jacobi Reading. } { Richardo How.
Petro Rich. } { Johanni Shorter.

In Agro Surrienſi Armigeris:

Viris ſummi Candoris : Pietatis ac Literarum fautoribus: hunc Librum in perpetuum obſervantiæ Teſtimonium D. D. D.

G. G.

TO THE
READER.

Here is no greater Priviledge bestowed by the Lord upon one Nation above others, than in the free use of the Sacred Scriptures and Ordinances: Israel had much advantage above the Gentiles, chiefly, or principally, because unto them were committed the Oracles of God, the word of grace, the Covenant of life and peace, Rom. 3. 2. S. Paul elswhere reckoning up the Priviledges of Israel, mentioneth this in several expressions as a prime Priviledge; The Covenants, the giving of the Law, and the Promises, Rom. 9. 4. all which are comprehended under the Oracles, and word of God. So saith the Psalmist, Psal. 147. 19, 20. He sheweth his word unto Jacob, his statutes and his judgements unto Israel: he hath not dealt so with any nation; and as for his judgements they have not known them. He make's no mention of the Tabernacle, or Temple, the Ark of the Covenant, the altar of burnt-offering, the golden altar of incense, the Ordinance of Circumcision, &c. though in these they were priviledged above other Nations; but he singleth out this as a prime priviledge,

To the Reader.

ledge, that he shewed them his word, his statutes and judgements.

How deeply then is this nation of ours (even England) indebted to God, to whom the Lord hath committed his holy Oracles! how much are we bound to him for this unspeakable gift! And herein the singular goodness of God to this nation is much to be observed, not onely in visiting it with the Gospel for these last hundred years and more, but also in giving it the light of the Gospel very early, even in the Apostles dayes. Divers Writers of good credit do testifie, that even in those dayes the Britan's in our Isle did consent to Christian Religion, and pulickly professed it in their Churches, as well as other parts of the World.

Theatr. Magn. Brit.

The Authors of the Theatre of Great Britain, speaking of the Antiquity of the Christian Faith in Britain, testifie in this manner. As we have searched the first foundation of our Faith, so neither want we Testimonies concerning the continuance of the same in this Land until following Posterities; although the injury of Time and War have consumed many Records: for the Britan's that were daily strengthened in their received Faith by the Doctrine of many Learned and godly Men, left not their First-love with the Church of Ephesus, but rather took hold of the Skirts, as the Prophet speaketh, Zech. 8. 23. until the Tortures of Martyrdom cut them off by death. And those Fathers, even from the Disciples themselves, held a Succession in Doctrine (notwithstanding some Repugnancy was made by the Pagans) and Preached the Gospel with good success, even till the same, at length, went forth with a bolder countenance by the favourable Edicts of Adrian, Antoninus Pius, and Marcus Aurelius, Emperours of Rome, as Eusebius hath Noted, and in Britain was established by King Lucius; so called, as some Learned Men have observed, because a Prince of great lustre and glory; the Light of the Gospel breaking forth in this our Isle in such a perspicuous manner by his Conversion,

Euseb. Eccl. Hist. l. 4. c. 9.

To the Reader.

version; that all Christian Churches took notice thereof: Of whom a great Antiquary thus speaketh,

Lucius in Christum credit, Christoq; dicatas
Ecclesias dotat, distinctas ordinat urbes.

Vsserius. de Brit.Ecclef. Primord. p.56.

Geoffery *of* Monmouth *tells us that King* Lucius *being Baptized together with his Subjects, destroyed the Temples of Idols, and Dedicated them to the onely living God, enlargeing and augmenting them. Bishop* Godwin *saith, we have great cause with all thankfulness to Celebrate the Memory of that Excellent Prince King* Lucius, *by whom God did not onely bless this Land with so clear knowledge of the truth, but in such sort did it, as thereby He hath purchased unto the same the Title of* Primogenita Ecclesiæ, *the most Antient, and first begotten of all the Churches in the world: for that although Christ was Preached elsewhere privately in many other Nations long before the time of King* Lucius, *yet of all Nations* Britain *was the first that with publick approbation of Prince and State received the Profession of Christian Religion. Of the Teachers of those times* John Bale *hath these verses,*

Godwin de converf. Britan.

Sic ut erat Celebris, &c.

As were the *Britan's* famous for their Zeal,
   To Gentile Gods, whilst such they did adore:
So when the Heavens to Earth did Truth reveal,
   Blest was that Land with Truth, and Learnings store.
Whence British Plains and Cambreas desart-ground,
   And *Cornwal's* Crags with glorious Saints abound.

The common consent of our Protestant Writers is, that in this time I now speak of, and from the beginning of Christianity *here,* Britain *never wanted Preachers of the true Faith. And when the persecuting* Emperour's *Reigned, and persecution raged, not onely in the Eastern parts, but in* Italy, France,

To the Reader.

France, *and other Countreys in the Continent near unto us; this our Island (as another world) was almost quite free thereof, both before and after, until the nineteenth year of* Dioclesian, *in which there was a general persecution of* Christians, *(as* Gildas, *and others after him do witness) in that it ever had Kings not so depending on the persecuting Emperours; and so far from the Name and Nature of persecutors, that they ever were friends and favourers of* Christians. *And for this cause many that were persecuted for* Christianity *in other Countries, fled hither for refuge, where for themselves they might more quietly enjoy the Liberty of their Conscience and Religion; and for others desirous to be instructed in the Truth thereof, and not kept back with such terrours of persecution, as in other Countries, they might with more confidence and boldness, and with great hope of fruit and encrease* Preach *and* Teach *it unto them. This was a preparative to a more general Conversion of this Nation to* Christianity *which followed afterwards. This Island was also the more quiet, in respect of the situation, remote distance, and separation from the rest of the chief commanding places of the* Roman Empire.

Gild.lib.de ex-
cid. & conqu.
Britan.

The Name [England] *some derived from the manner of the situation of this Island in the* West *and* North : *for that* Eng, *in the Antient Teutonick Tongue, as well as in the Modern, doth signifie narrow, strait, or a nook. And a* Portugal *alluding thereunto hath this verse,*

Anglia terra ferax & fertilis Angulus Orbis,
Insula prædives, quæ toto vix eget orbe.

A fruitful Angle, [*England*] Thou,
Another world art said :
An Island rich, and hast no need
of other Countrie's aid.

And although after this, many errours in Doctrine, and corruptions in Worship crept in more and more into our Church, and

To the Reader.

and the Pope *encroaching by degrees, the* Churches *of* God *in this Land did much degenerate: as they did in other Nations, so that in Proceſs of time the whole world wondered after the* Beaſt, *and they* Worſhipped *the* Beaſt, *ſaying, who is like unto the* Beaſt? Revel. 13.3,4. *Yet even in the darkeſt times, when our Church ſuffered the greateſt Ecclipſe, when her Silver was become Droſs, and her Wine was mixed with Water, it pleaſed* God *then to raiſe up ſome eminent Perſons to ſtand up for the Defence of the Truth in this Nation, and to diſcover the impoſtures of the Church of* Rome. *Yea, how many were there that ſuffered Martyrdom for the Goſpel here in* England, *who deteſted Image-worſhip, and other abominations in the dayes of King* Henry *the fourth, King* Henry *the fift, and others afterward, long before* Luther *was born. Theſe and the like in other Nations may be called the forlorn Hope, who did* obequitare Antichriſti caſtra, & ad pugnam elicere, *advance up to, and ride round about the camp of* Antichriſt, *and provoke him to the main-fight.*

What wonderfull deliverances hath God *wrought for this Church and Nation in ſeveral ways? When King* Henry *the eighth did renounce the* Pope's *Supremacy what plots were framed by diverſe Princes againſt this Land to ruine it, and how gratiouſly did the Lord protect his people here from ſuch a ſtorm, though then he had but a very little flock in this place?*

When Queen Mary *matched with* Philip *of* Spain, *in what apparent danger was this Land to fall into miſerable ſervitude and bondage under the Iron-yoak of the* Spainard's, *which diverſe nations that have been ſubject to them have found intolerable? The blind and bloody zeal of Queen* Mary *was likely to have rooted out all the plants of God's right hand in this Land, and ſo to have baniſhed hence the true Church and Goſpel of* Chriſt, *and ſo to have ſhut this Kingdom out of the bounds of the Church. There was great*

B *expectation*

To the Reader.

expectation of Issue by that Marriage between the Spanish *Prince and Queen* Mary, *who Her self also was a* Spaniard *by the Mother's side : and Solemn Forms of Thanksgiving and Prayer were made for Her Conception and safe delivery : and besides an Act passed in Parliament, that if Queen* Mary *died in Child-bed*, King Philip *should have the Government of this Land during the Child's Nonage : and if these things had succeeded, into what misery might this Land have fallen ? And (besides) had an Issue of that Marriage lived to Reign over* England, *together with other Dominions of the* Spaniard, *what had* England *been, but an Inferiour Tributary Province to be Governed as it pleased the* Spanish *Nation, even as was attempted in the Low-Countreys with Devilish cruelties ? to say nothing of their horrible Massacres in the* West-Indies. *But here see the wonderful goodness of God, who dwelt in the midst of this Church as a Refuge. All this was prevented : Queen* Marie's *supposed Conception vanished, She was soon taken away by death, and* King Philip *of* Spain *had no longer any Interest in* England.

Mason confecr.
Epif. Angl.

Queen Elizabeth, *a Nourfing-mother to this Church Succeeded. She was born* September *the seventh,* 1533. *One calleth Her* Angliæ Delitias, Europæ Sydus, Mundi Phœnicem, &c. *the joy of* England, *the Star of* Europe, *the* Phœnix *of the World : a Glass of God's Providence, and the Mirrour of His Mercy. And (as if the Devil had presaged, what a scourge She would prove to the* Roman *greatness, and suggested it to* Pope Clement the seventh) *he is said to have made a Peremptory Decree against Her, whilst She was in Her Mother's belly. This Pope himself being the Bastard of* Julian de Medicis *a* Florentine, *he avowed to make Her illegitimate, and uncapable of the Crown. The like did* Pope Paul *the third attempt, viz. To make that* Royal Princess *illegitimate when She was but two years Old. But as the Lord blessed Her then, so he did wonderfully preserve her all her Sister's Reign, when many plots were laid to take away her life. But (as* Seneca *told.*

To the Reader.

told Nero) it was impossible for him to kill that man that must be his heir; so it was impossible for the malice of hell to accomplish the death of the Lady Elizabeth, whom the only-wise God had appointed to be her Sister's Heir. So great a Reformation She wrought in England, that one saith of it, The Gospel had a swift passage here by diligent Preaching, by Printing good Books, by translating the holy Scriptures into the Vulgar Tongue, by Catechizing youth, by publick disputations, by recording the Martyrs, such a thing, as even the former age had even despaired of, the present age admireth, and the future shall stand amazed at. It is evident, that the Almighty God, who delighteth to shew his power in Weakness, was pleased in this Renowed Queen and her brother King Edward, to let the world see what great things he was able to effect by a Child and a Woman. *Ecclesiæ Anglicana reformationem desperasset ætas præterita, admiratur præsens, obstupescet futura. Scul. tet. Annal.*

But what a multitude of plots were contrived for the destruction of Queen Elizabeth, when the next heir to the Crown was a Papist, and an enemy to the truth of Christianity, and married to the Prince of France; so that had these plots succeeded, England, in all probability, had been subjected to France in point of Civil Government, and to the Roman power in matters of Religion. Admire again the singular goodness of God in protecting Queen Elizabeth: and whilst the enemies of the Church were seeking ruine in the destruction of Her Royal Person; the French King that had Married the next heir to the English Crown, dieth and leaveth her a Widow without Issue, and she not many years after became a prisoner.

So eminent was Queen Elizabeth, that Thuanus, a professed Roman Catholick (but very ingenious) said, he heard the old Dutchess of Guise (whose sons were of the greatest Enemies that Queen Elizabeth had) to say, that she was fælicissima & gloriosissima fæmina, a most happy and a most glorious Woman. We know who made her to differ, and that she had not any thing which she had not received from above, therefore let us give the praise of all to God, who appointed her (I am

B 2

To the Reader.

am perſwaded) to build the old waſt places, to raiſe up the foundations of many generations: ſhe found the Kingdom weak, ſhe left it ſtrong: ſhe found it poor, ſhe left it rich: they that were enemies to her and the Goſpel which they profeſſed and maintained, were mighty, and likely to oppoſe, viz. the French and Spaniards. They that were friends (as the Proteſtants in France and the Netherlands) were weak, and needed her help. But the Lord of Hoſts made her a terrour to his and her enemies, and a ſuccour to all his people at home and abroad. And (it ſeemeth) the Lord began betimes to cauſe his terrour to fall upon the Adverſaries: for the Council of Trent ended in a very few years after ſhe began her Reign; and a motion was made, that the Heads, or chief of the Proteſtants, ſhould be excommunicated, and in particular Queen Elizabeth. But the Emperour Ferdinand ſent them a meſſage to cool their heat, and wrote to the Pope and the Legates, that if the Council would not yield that fruit as was deſired, that they might ſee an union of all Catholicks to reform the Church, at the leaſt they ſhould not give occaſion to the Proteſtants to unite themſelves more, which they would do in caſe they proceeded againſt the Queen of England: for undoubtedly they would by that means make a general league againſt the Catholicks, which would bring forth great inconveniences. And his admonition was ſo effectual, that the Pope deſiſted in Rome, and revoked the Commiſſion given to the Legats in Trent.

Hiſt. Concil.
Trid. lib. 8.

About that time Chriſtianity began to dawn in the Kingdom of Ireland, and ſuddenly after the Kingdom of Scotland embraced the Goſpel of Chriſt, and Queen Elizabeth is made Inſtrumental that way, who ayded the Reformed party in Scotland with great ſupplies of men and money againſt the Pope's faction both of French and Scotch.

The Goſpel did ſo prevail in France alſo at that time, and the Proteſtants grew ſo numerous and conſiderable, the Queen-Mother, who was an enemy, yet ſeemed to temporize, and ſpeak them fair; and wrote to the Pope for Reformation of
divers

To the Reader.

divers abuses to give them content: insomuch that a Learned man, then living in Germany, *(though born in* Italy*) breaketh out in an Epistle to his friend,* Totus terrarum orbis parturit Christum.

But now let us mark how the enemies of the Churches peace raged in the dayes of Queen Elizabeth: *what hideous and damnable treasons did they commit, and how did they thirst after the Royal blood of that peerless Princess? And when the* Lord *had confounded their plots, how did they seek to overwhelm and swallow us up with the power of* Spain *in the year,* 1588. *But after that in despite of the* Pope *and his Adherents that Noble Queen was carried to her grave in peace, full of dayes, riches, and honour, and her Successour both in her Kingdom and Religion was established in his Throne; how did these Romish Cannibals seek to exceed themselves in wickedness and horrible cruelty? they sought at one blow (as it were) to cut off the neck of this Church and State. A* French *Historian speaking of the bloody Massacre, saith,* Wise men which were not addicted to the Protestants part, seeking all manner of excuse for that fact, did notwithstanding think, that in all Antiquity there could not be found an example of like cruelty. *But the* English *Powder-plot doth so far exceed the* French *Massacre, that there is no degree of comparison. This cannot be paralelled. It was of such a transcendency (saith* M. Mason*) that all the Devils may seem to have holden a black Convocation in* Hell, *and there to have concluded such a Sulphurious and Acherontical device, as was never heard of since the world began. That wicked Popish crew being made drunk with the cup of spiritual fornications, held forth unto them by the Whore of* Babylon, *with unspeakable fury and madness did violate the Sacred Lawes, and break the strongest bands of common humanity; and meant to have represented a shadow of* Hell, *and* Hellish-*malice here upon earth, far exceeding the wickedness of* Kain *their Elder-brother, and exceeding all examples of Treason, Cruelty, and Murther, Except that of* Judas.

Thuan.Hist. lib. 54. *Anno* 1572.

The

To the Reader.

The Pope and Court of Rome, *who were wont to account England* Puteum inexhauſtum, *a well never drawn dry, whilſt they had the drawing of it, now ſeeing the golden ſprings like to run low, or rather to run another way, and not to empty themſelves in their Ciſterns; they, like* Balaam *loving the Wages of unrighteouſneſs, were Raging mad, and cared not how much of the beſt Blood in the Land were ſpilt, ſo that it might make way for them again to the* Engliſh *gold. But the greater their rage was, the greater was God's mercy: the greater the danger, the greater the deliverance. The Lord was known by executing judgement; and thoſe wicked wretches were ſnared in the work of their own hands.*

Now let us conſider what we were before the Chriſtian Religion was firſt known to this Nation. What were the Britains *but* Pagans *and Barbarous people? Yea, we read, that from the firſt ſubmiſſion of the* Britans *to the* Romans, *that Ambaſſadours came from* Britain *to* Rome, *ſwearing Fealty in the Temple of* Mars, *offering gifts in the Capitol to the gods of the* Romans. *And for the* Saxons, *they were at firſt no better than the* Britans: *the* Saxons *were a* Dutch *and Pagan-nation, and ſerved* Saturn, Jupiter, *and* Mercury, *till they were converted to the Faith of* Chriſt, *and renounced their Idols to ſerve the true and living God.* Earcombent *Reigning in Kent, after the death of his father King* Ethelbald, *is ſaid to be the firſt of* Engliſh Saxon *Kings, that commanded Idols to be deſtroyed in his whole Kingdom, about the year of* Chriſt. 640.

2. *Conſider we the Apoſtaſie of our forefathers in adhereing to the Roman faction, and then the renewed Apoſtaſie at the death of King* Edward *the ſixth, together with our unworthy and unfruitful walking under the Goſpel, ſince the reſtoring of it by Queen* Elizabeth.

3. *Conſider likewiſe the mighty out-ſtretched Arm of God in protecting his Church, and in preſerving the truth of Religion among us ſtill, notwithſtanding the plots, deſigns, and contri-*
vances

To the Reader.

vances of *Satan* and his *Instruments*, and the many Enterprizes of the *Papal* power ever since the days of K. *James:* the great droves of *Sectaries* swarming like *Locusts* since our late unhappy Wars, who seemed to be Spirited and acted by the *Jesuites*; their crying down *Magistracy* and *Ministry*, notwithstanding all which the *Christian Religion* hath prevailed against all its *adversaries*. The consideration of all these things may give us ground of hope, that God will still vouchsafe to dwell with his *Antient Inheritance:* and therefore we may confidently commend the care of this Church (*his old habitation*) to himself, who (*I trust*) will never suffer the Devils *Instruments* to ruine his *palace*, and to pull down the place of his *Antient possession*.

THE

HISTORY
OF THE
CHURCH
OF
Great Britain.

CENTURY I.

Jesus Chrift the Son of God, the true Prince of Peace, was born in *Bethlehem-Judah*, of the Virgin *Mary*, in the 42 year of the Reign of *Auguſtus Cæſar* the Roman Emperour, under the 194 Olympiad, in the XIX year of the Reign of *Kymbeline* King of *Britain*.

Divers Writers of note do tell us, that the Gofpel was preached and received in this Land, even in the days of the Apoſtles. *Baronius*, and the Learned Archbiſhop *Uſher* tell us, that St. *Peter* came into *Britain* in the twelfth year of the Emperour *Nero*, and ſtaid a long time here, many being by him illightned. *Nicephorus* ſaith, that *Simon Zelotes* carried the Doctrine of the Gofpel unto the Weſtern Sea, and to the *Britannick* Iſlands. The Learned Archbiſhop *Matthew Parker*, Biſhop *Godwin*, Mr. *Camden*, and others do aſſert, that St. *Paul* himſelf, that great Apoſtle of the *Gentiles*, Preached the Gofpel to this Iſland after his enlargement from his firſt captivity at *Rome*; where, ſome ſay, he continued Preaching five years. And this (ſay they) he did at the inſtigation of *Claudia*, a Noble *Britiſh* Woman. *Gildas*, our own Countrey-man, *Polydor Virgil*, Mr. *Fox*, Sir *Henry Spelman*, and many others tell us, that *Joſeph* of *Arimathea*, that Holy Man, after he had buried the body of Chriſt in his own Tomb, came into this Iſland, and Preached the Goſpel here, being ſent

Baron. *Annal.* Tom.1. An.61. Uſſer *de Brit.* Eccleſ.primord. c.1.p.7.Parker *de antiq. Eccl.* Britan.p.2,3. Fox Act. & Monum. vol.1. Sir H. Spelm. Concil. Tom. 1. Per Joſephum Evangelii lumina primum in Britania accenſa eſſ. Georg.Major.

B hither

The History of

hither by *Philip* and *James* the Apostles. That he was in this Land, is confirmed not onely by divers Histories, but also by Antient Monuments. *Baleus* alledgeth many other witnesses.

It doth not appear, that the first Preachers of the Gospel in *Britain* did so much as touch at *Rome*, much less that they received any command, or commission thence to convert *Britain*, which should lay an Eternal obligation of gratitude on this Island to the Sea of *Rome*. Insomuch that *Parsons* himself flyes at last to this slight and slender shift. That albeit St. *Joseph* came not immediately from *Rome*, yet he taught in this Island the *Roman* Faith, whereof St. *Paul* hath written to the *Romans* themselves, *that your Faith is spoken of through the whole World*, Rom. 1. 8. Hereby the Jesuite hopes to keep on foot the engagement of this Island to *Rome*, for her first conversion. But why should he call the Christian Religion the *Roman* Faith, rather than the Faith of *Jerusalem*, or the Faith of *Antioch*, seeing it issued from the former, and was received and first named in the latter City, before any spark of Christianity was kindled at *Rome*, as Dr. *Fuller* well observeth.

Fuller. church Histor. lib. 1.

Cent. II.

WE read, that the Gospel in our Land had the countenance of publick Authority through the gratious providence of God very early. A Learned Writer speaking of the dignity of this Nation, saith, *That of all the Provinces of the Roman Empire* (yea it seemeth of the whole World) *this Island of Great Britain did first receive the Gospel by publick Authority.* *Lucius* King of *Britain* was the first Christian King we read of in Ecclesiastical Stories: He embraced the Faith about an hundred and fifty years after the death of Christ. It is said of this King *Lucius*, that at first he shewed himself an enemy to the Christians: but observing the holiness of their lives, he was enclined to embrace the Christian Faith, but was held off for a time, partly by the Heathenish superstition of his Ancestors wherein he had been bred up; and partly because he found the Christians reputed infamous by the *Romans*, then the Lords of a great part of the World, under whom (it seemeth) he was a tributary King: but being afterward informed, that many of the Nobles or Senators of the *Romans* had embraced the Christian Religion, he made an open profession of it, and made a notable reformation in his Dominions. Moreover, he being much taken with the Miracles which he beheld truly wrought by pious Christians, was the more drawn to embrace their Religion, and sent *Elvanus* and *Meduinus*, men of known Piety and Learning in the Scriptures to *Eleutherius* Bishop of *Rome*, with a Letter, requesting several things of him; but principally that he might be instructed in the Christian Faith. *Eleutherius* returneth him this Answer,

Omnium Provinciarum primula Britannia publicitus christi nomen recepit. Sabel. *Enn.*7. l. 5.

the Church of GREAT BRITAIN.

fwer, *That having received in his Kingdom the Law and Faith of Christ, and having now the Old and New Testaments, he should by a Council of his Realm take Laws from thence to govern thereby; That he was the Vicar of God in his Kingdomes; That the People and Nations of the Kingdom of Britain were His, even His children; That such as were divided, he should gather them together unto the Law of Christ his holy Church, unto peace and concord; and should cherish, maintain, protect, govern, and defend them,* &c.

Holinsh. descr. of Brit. c. 7. Annals of England, by John Stow.

When Christian Religion first was publickly received and established in this Land by King *Lucius*, here were then of Heathen institution, eight and twenty *Flamines*, and three *Archflamines*. The places of the *Flamines*, the King turned to so many Bishopricks; the places of the *Archflamines*, to so many Archbishopricks; the one at *London*, translated afterward to *Canterbury*; the other at *York*; the third at *Caerleon* in *Wales*, where seaven of those Bishopricks, with this Archbishoprick were remaining when *Austin* the Monk came into *England*: Here were Temples also builded for the worship of Paynim-gods, of which he made Churches for the service of Jesus Christ. *Thomas Rudbourn* a Monk of *Winchester*, *Moratus* an old British Writer, and others testifie, that *Denotus* was Bishop of *Winchester*; and all the possessions of the Pagan *Flamines* there, were conferred upon him and his Clergy, which were so ample, that even about the City all the Lands, within twelve miles of it on all sides, were belonging unto it, containing in number 32 Villages. And thus the *Britains* had for their greatest glory, the happiness to see and enjoy the first Christian Prince in the World.

It is reported, that King *Lucius* was the Founder of St. *Peter's* Church at *Cornhil* in *London*, placing therein one *Thean* an Archbishop, and that the Metropolitan See continued in a succession of Archbishops there about 400 years, until the coming of *Austin* the Monk, who translated the Archbishop's seat from *London* to *Canterbury*. In that Church was a Table, wherein is written, that King *Lucius* founded the same Church to be an Archbishop's See, and that it so endured the space of 400 years. There are the name of these Archbishops of *London*, *Thean*, *Elvanus*, *Cadar*, *Obinus*, *Conan*, *Paladius*, *Stephen*, *Iltut*, *Theodwyn*, or *Dedwin*, *Thedrid*, *Hilary*, *Restitutus*, *Guertelinus*, or *Guitelinus*, *Fastidius*, *Vodinus*, *Theonus*, &c.

Elvanus built a Library near St. *Peter's* Church in *Cornhil*; he was a Godly, Learned and Grave Man, brought up in the School of *Joseph* of *Arimathea*, and Converted many of the *Druydes* to the Christian Faith. Bishop *Godwin* saith, That the Archbishoprick of *York* was founded *Anno* 180. by King *Lucius* also, who placed *Sampson* there. King *Lucius* also founded the Academy of *Bangor* in the favour of good Arts and Learned Men. He built the chief Cathedral Church in *Glocester*: The Church dedicated to St. *Mary* in *Glastonbury*: A Chappel in ho-

nour

nour of Christ in *Dover* Castle: A Church in *Canterbury*, afterwards dedicated to St. *Martin*. King *Lucius* died and was buried at *Gloucester*.

Cent. III.

Gildas in Epist. de excid. Britan.

BUT Christianity in *Britain* was not buried in the grave of King *Lucius*: Witness *Gildas*, whose words are a clear evidence of the constant continuing of the Christian Faith in *Britain* from the first Preaching thereof. *Christs precepts* (saith he) *though they were received, but lukewarmly of the Inhabitants, yet they remained entirely with some, less sincerely with others, even untill the nine years of Persecution under Dioclesian.*

Tertul. adverf. Judæos. c. 7.

Origen in Luc. c. 1. Homil. 6.

Cent. 3. c. 2. col. 6.

To the Authority of *Gildas* we may add the Testimony of two Fathers, both flourishing in this Century, *Tertullian* and *Origen*; *Tertullian* saith, *Britannorum inaccessa Romanis loca, Christo vero subdita:* There are places of the *Britains* which were unaccessible to the *Romans*, but yet subdued to Christ. *Origen* in like manner, *Virtus Domini Salvatoris cum his est, qui ab orbe nostro in* Britannia *dividuntur:* The power of God our Saviour is even with them. which in *Britain* are divided from our World. The *Magdeburgenses*, compilers of the General Ecclesiastical History, speaking of the Churches through *Europe* in this Age, thus express themselves: Then follow the Isles of the Ocean, where we first meet with *Britain*, *Mansisse & hac ætate ejus Insulæ Ecclesias, affirmare non dubitamus*: We doubt not to affirm, that the Churches of that Island did also remain in that Age.

Gildas modestly renders the reason; why so little is extant of the *British* History of this Age. *Scripta patriæ, Scriptorum monumenta, siquæ fuerint, aut ignibus hostium exusta, aut civium exulum classe longius deportata, non comparent*: The Monuments (saith he) of our Countrey, or Writers (if there were any) appear not, as either burnt by the fire of enemies, or transported far off by our banished Countreymen.

Gild. Epist. f. 63.

The Christians of *Britain* celebrated the Passover upon the fourteenth day of the Moon of *March* precisely, contrary to the constitutions of the *Roman* Church: which sheweth, they were not brought to Christian Religion by the *Roman* Church. And *Gildas* saith, *That the Britains used great solemnity in their Ordination of Ministers, and had other Prayers, Lessons, and Chapters, than are used in the* Roman *Church.*

Britain remained under the Domination of the *Romans*, Pagans, as their supream Lords, till the year of Christ 286. in *Dioclesian's* time, when the *Roman* Senate sent *Caransius* to repress the incursions of Barbarous Nations. But *Caransius* made a League with the *Britains*, expelled the

Romans

The Church of Great Britain.

Romans, and made himself King: And from that time, sometimes the *Romans* prevailing, sometimes the *Natives*, *Britain* was but weakly possessed by the *Roman* Empire.

Cent. IV.

SO the Gospel flourished in this Land, and they that professed it escaped the Persecutions raised by the Heathen Emperours of *Rome*, all except the last under *Dioclesian*, which extended to *Britain*; and St. *Alban* is noted to be the *Proto-Martyr* of *Britain*, who suffered death for Christ's sake with invincible Courage and Resolution, about the year of Christ 305. He was a wealthy Inhabitant of *Verolamcester*, and a Citizen of *Rome*, for so *Alexander Necchám* reports him. Necchám, in his Poem on Verulam.

Hic est Martyrii roseo decoratus honore
Albanus, Cives, Inclyta Roma, tuus.

Here *Alban*, *Rome*, thy Citizen renown'd,
With rosie grace of Martyrdom was crown'd.

Alban was a *Britain* by Parentage, a *Roman* by Priviledge; naturally a *Britain*, naturalized a *Roman*. Immediately followed the Martyrdom of *Amphibalus* a Preacher of *Caer-leon* in *Wales*, who not long before was fain to fly from persecution into the Eastern parts of this Island, and was entertained by *Alban* at his house in *Verulam*, who was instructed by *Amphibalus* in the Christian Faith: he was cruelly put to death by the Pagans in a Village called *Redburn*, three miles from *Verulam*. Besides *Amphibalus*, suffered *Aaron* and *Julius*, two substantial Citizens of *Caer-leon*, and then *Socrates* and *Stephen*, and *Augulius* Bishop of *London*, then called *Augusta*, with multitudes both of Men and Women in sundry places (faith *Beda*) as shortly after no less than a thousand Saints suffered death at *Litchfield*, whereupon the place was called another *Golgotha*, or field of blood: In memory whereof the City beareth for Armes to this day a field surcharged with dead bodies.

Afterwards it pleased God to put a period to his Servants sufferings, and to the rage of their Enemies; for when *Dioclesian* and *Maximian* had layed down the Ensignes of Command, *Constantius Chlorus* was chosen Emperour in these Western Provinces of *France*, *Spain*, and *Britain*, whose cariage towards Christians *Eusebius* thus describeth; τὰς ὑπ' αὐτὸν θεοσεβεῖς ἀβλαβεῖς φυλάξας, that he preserved such Religious people as were under his command without any hurt or harm: So that under him the Church in these parts had a breathing-time from Persecution. *Constantius* died, and was buried at *York*, who bequeathed the Empire

to *Constantine* his eldest Son by *Helen* his former Wife. That *Constan-*
tine was a *Britain*, is shewn by *Eumenius Rhetor*, who, in his Oration
made to *Constantine* himself, makes therein an Apostrophe to *Britain*,
O fortunata, & nunc omnibus beatior terris Britannia. *quæ* Constantinum
Cæsarem primâ vidisti! O happy *Britain*, and blessed above all other
Lands, which didst first behold *Constantine* Cæsar. There is another Testimony of His of like nature: *Liberavit Pater* Constantius Britannias *ser-*
vitute: Tu etiam Nobiles, illic oriendo, fecisti: Your Father *Constantius*
did free the *British* Provinces from slavery, and you have Ennobled them
by raking thence your original: It is said of him, that he was born,
made King, and Emperor first in *Britain*.

Constantine being now peaceably seiled in the Imperial Throne, there
followed a sudden and great alteration in the World, Persecutors turning Patrons of Religion: The Gospel formerly a Forrester, now became a Citizen; and leaving the Woods wherein it wandered; Hills and
holes where it hid it self before, dwelt quietly in populous places. The
stumps of ruined Churches lately destroyed by *Dioclesian*, grew up into
beautiful buildings; Oratories were furnished with pious Ministers,
and they provided of plentiful maintenance, through the liberality of
Constantine.

The most avouchable evidence of Christianity flourishing in this Island
in this Age, is produced from the Bishops representing *Britain*, in the
Councils. 1. Of *Arles* in *France*, called to take cognizance of the cause
of the Donatists, where appeared for the *Britains*, *Eborius* Bishop of *York*,
Restitutus Bishop of *London*, *Adelfius* Bishop of the City called the
Colony of *London*, which some count *Colchester*, and others *Maldon*
in *Essex*, *Sacerdos* a Priest, both by his proper Name and Office, *Ar-*
minius, a Deacon, *Anno* 313. In the Synod of *Nice* held in *Bithy-*
nia, *Anno* 325. *British* Bishops were present, being summoned to
suppress Arianism, and to establish an uniformity of the observation of
Easter, as *Athanasius*, and *Hilary* Bishop of *Poictiers* do testify. At the
Council of *Sardis* in *Thracia*, called by *Constantius* and *Constans*, Sons to
Constantine the Great, were present the Bishops of *Britain*, who concurred with the rest to condemn the Arrians, and acquit *Athanasius*. The
British Bishops were also present at the Council of *Ariminum* assembled
in *Italy*.

Theodoret tells us, that he wrote an Epistle to all Churches concerning
the Council of *Nice*, wherein he saith, there were then many Churches
in *Britain*, &c. About the year 360. *Hilary* Bishop of *Poictiers*, among
diverse others dedicated his Book, *De Synodis fidei Catholicæ contra Aria-*
nos, to the Bishops of the Provinces of *Britain*, during his exile for the
Orthodox Faith, commending them for their constancy in the profession
of that Faith. And by the testimony of *Athanasius*, it appeareth, that
the *Britains* then had not onely Churches professing the Orthodox Faith,
but

but Bishops famous for their Piety and Learning, summoned to forreign Councils in remote parts for debating and deciding the highest Articles of the Christian Faith.

In the year 383. *Maximus* a Christian, and Orthodox Prince governed *Britain*: for then all that part of the Island which was subject to the Romans, was Christian. Not long after the Empire being fallen in the West, and torn by the Gothes, Francs, Vandals, and Burgundians, the Romans forsook the Isle of *Britain*, which moved the Natives to commit the Kingdome to one *Constantine* a *Britain*, as one descended from their Nation, and a Christian vertuous man.

About the year 400. *Chrysostome* gives this testimony concerning the Britains Embracing of the Gospel *Nam et Britannia, Insula extra hoc mare sita, et qua in ipso oceano sunt, vertutem verbi senserunt (sunt etiam illic fundatæ Ecclesiæ &c.) Illius inquam verbi, quod turc dictum, quod et in omnium animabus, inque omnium labiis plantatum.* Which he seconded in another Sermon of the Feast of Pentecost.

Du Moul. *resp. ad Card-du Perron. lib.* 7 *ca.* 5.

Chrysost. *oper toms.*

CENT. V.

ABout the year 412 *Pelagius* (born in *Britain*) began to broach his Heresies publickly. The same day whereon *Pelagius* was born in *Britain* St. *Augustine* was also born in *Africk*: divine providence so ordering it that the poison and the Antidote should be Twins in a manner in respect of the same time as Dr. *Fuller* well observeth. In the year 446. the *Pelagian* Heresie spread over *Britain*: and the British Churches being defiled thereby, King *Vortigern* for the maintaining the truth, sent for *German* Bishop of *Auxerre*, and *Lupus* Bishop of *Troys* in *Champagne* out of *France*, men famous for their doctrine and counsel, who refuting this Heresie, gained unto themselves a reverent esteem among the Britains; but chiefly *German*, who in a Chappel neer unto St. *Albans* did openly out of the pulpit preach God's word sincerely to the people. This conference was held at St. *Albans*, even where at this day a small Chappel is extant to the honour of St. *German*.

Germanus having baptized multitudes of Pagan converts in the river *Alen*, marched with an Army of them against the Pagans whom he found in the North-East of *Wales*. Here he chose an hollow dale surrounded with hills, near the Village, called at this day by the English, Molo by the British Guidcrue in *Flintshire*, where the field at this day retains the name of Mæs Garmon or *German's* field. Here *Germanus* placed his men in ambush, with instructions, that a Signal given, they should all shout *Hallelujah* three times with their might; which all was done accordingly. Hereat the Pagans without striking a stroak confusedly ran away, and many were drowned for speed in the river *Alen*. After this victory *Germanus* prepared for his return.

Usser *de Brit. Eccles. primord.* p. 333.

After

After *Germanus* and *Lupus* were returned home into their native countrey, *Pelagianism* began to sprout again in *Britain*: and after three years *Germanus* came again, with *Severus* into *Britain*, and the *Pelagian* Heresie was again condemned in a second Synod, having been before condemned in a Synod at *London*. *Germanus* having setled *Baitain* in good order, returned to his own countrey, where he presenly died after his return: and by God's blessing on his endeavours, that Heresie was so cut down in *Britain*, that it never generally grew up again.

About the year 453. *Hengist* Caprain of the *Saxons*, who came to help the *Britans* against the *Scots* and *Picts*, who having married his own daughter to *Vortigern* had murthered his sovereign Lord *Constans*, and invaded his Crown: being called in for his help, came with diverse ships of stout *Saxon* Souldiers, who under pretence of protecting them from the *Picts*, intended to plant themselves in the North part of *Britain*, which when the *Britans* saw, and fearing their own ruin, they desired the King that he would drive them out of his Kingdome. The Nobles also of his Realm did inveigh much against the King's marriage with a Pagan Woman.

Whereupon *Anno* 454. they utterly deserted King *Vortigern*, and unanimously chose *Vortimer*, his son, to be their King, who, following their counsel, began to expell the Barbarians, and chasing them as far as the *Derwent*, he slew many of them: *Vortigern* also fled with them. But in the year 460 Prince *Vortimer* died, being poisoned by *Rowen* his Mother in law, with whom the hope of the *Britains* was extinguished. Hereupon *Hengist* returning into *Britain* with new forces, treacherously slew most of the British Nobles at a pretended Treaty for peace between both Nations. And the Saxons being enemies to Christian Religion, and bent upon the possession of such a fruitful Countrey, exercised great cruelty upon the Inhabitants, destroyed Churches and all Ecclesiastical things, burnt the holy Scriptures, flew the Ministers in the Churches, endeavouring to supplant Christian Religion. *Vortigern* had before caused *Vodinus* Arch-Bishop of *London* to be put to death, because he reproved him for calling in the Saxons, and marrying a Pagan Woman: and now *Theanus* Bishop of *London*, and *Thaodiceus* Bishop of *York* with others were forced to fly into remote places for the preservation of their lives.

Thus God sent down his heavie judgements upon the *Britains* for their Sins, as *Gildas* writeth, *Britones propter avaritiam & rapinam Princîpum, propter iniquitatem & injustitiam Judicum; propter desidiam praedicationis Episcoporum, propter luxuriam & malos mores populi perdidisse patriam:* that is, the *Britans* for the covetousness and oppression of the Princes, for the iniquity and injustice of the Judges, for the negligent preaching of the Bishops, for the luxury and evil manners of the people, lost their Countrey. After many battles with the *Britains*, the Pagans surprised a great part of this Island.

Then

the Church of Great Britain.

Then the *Britains* sent Ambassadors into the lesser *Britain* to *Aurelius Ambrosius*, and *Uter-Pendragon* his brother, desiring them to take the government of *Britain* upon them (of which they were right heires) and to expell the Saxons, and King *Vortigern*. Hereupon they came with many armed souldiers. Then the *Britains* set up *Aurelius* to be their King, who marched first against *Vortigern* to his Castle *Genorinm* in *Wales*, where he had fortified and immured himself; but *Aurelius* burnt the castle, and King *Vortigern* in it. After this *Aurelius* fought many battles with the *Saxons* in the years 485. 487, 488. and at last overcame them. *Aurelius* was one composed of valour and Religion, wholly employing himself in time of peace, to raise new Churches, repair old, and endow both." At this time there was an Academy of learned men under *Dubritius* neer the river *Wye* in *Monmouth-shire*. This *Dubritius* taught many scholars for seven years together in humane and divine learning; among whom the chiefest were *Theliau*, *Sampson*, *Vbelin*, *Merchiguin*, *Elquored*, &c. at *Dubritius* removed to *Werwick*, a village two miles from *Cardigan*, and from thence to *Moch-Rhos*.

Johan. Timnuthenf. *in ejus vita.*

The *Britains* being involved in perpetual Warrs with the *Scots*, *Picts*, *Normans*, *Saxons*, the Christian *Britains* were at last, by force and fraud, undermined, and driven out of their native soil into *Britain* in *France*, and into *Wales* and *Cornwall*: yet then was the Gospel preserved in those corners, where the remainder of the *Britains* (those antient Inhabitants of this land) remains unto this day. Paganism was again planted in this land, and an Heptarchy was established, this land being divided into seven Kingdomes.

The first was the Kingdome of *Kent*, which began *Anno* 457. under King *Hengist*. The second of the South-*Saxons*, comprising *Sussex* and *Surrey*. This Kingdome began under King *Ella*, *Anno* 491. and was the weakest of all the seven, affording few Kings, and fewer actions of moment. The third was of the East-*Saxons*, comprehending *Essex*, *Middlesex*, and part of *Hartford-shire*. This Kingdome began in *Erchenwin* about the year 527. The fourth of the East-Angles, containing *Norfolk*, *Suffolk*, *Cambridg-shire*, with the Isle of *Ely*, and part of *Bedford-shire*. It began *Anno* 575. under King *Vlfa*, and lay most exposed to the cruelty of the *Danish* incursions. The fifth of *Mercia*, so called, because it lay in the midst of the Island, being the merches or limits on which all the residue of the Kingdomes did bound and border. It began *Anno* 582. under King *Cridda*, and contained the Countries of *Lincoln*, *North-hampton*, *Rutland*, *Huntingdon*, *Buckingham*, *Oxford*, *Worcester*, *Warwick*, *Darby*, *Nottingham*, *Leicester*, *Stafford*, and *Chester*: besides part of *Hereford* and *Salop* (the remnant whereof was possessed by the *Welch*) *Gloucester*, *Bedford*, and *Lancaster*. The sixt of *Northumberland*, whereunto belonged whatsoever lieth between *Humber* and *Edenborough Frith*. It was subdivided sometimes into two Kingdomes,

C of

of *Bernicia*, and *Deira*. The latter confisted of the remainder of *Lancashire*, with the entire Counties of *York*, *Durham*, *Westmerland*, and *Cumberland*. *Bernicia* contained *Northumberland* with the South of *Scotland* to *Edenborough*: But it was not long before both were united under King *Ida*. The seventh of the West Saxons, who possessed *Hantshire*, *Berk-shire*, *Wilt-shire*, *Somerset*, *Dorset* and *Devon-shire*; part of *Cornwall* and *Gloucester-shire*. This Kingdom began *Anno* 519. under *Cerdicus*: This Heptarchy was at last swallowed up in the West Saxons Monarchy.

But to return to the *British* Church, and the year of our Lord 449. wherein the Irish St. *Patrick* is notoriously reported to have come to *Glastonbury*, where he lived 39 years as Abbot of that place. And so great was the credit of St. *Patrick* at *Glastonbury*, that after his death and burial there, that Church that formerly was dedicated to the Virgin *Mary* alone, was in after-ages joyntly consecrated to her and St. *Patrick*.

About the year 495 *Cerdicus* (who was afterwards first King of the West Saxons) having overcome the *Britains* at *Winchester*, killed all the Monks belonging to the Church of St. *Amphibalus*, and turned the same into a Temple of Idolatry. *Aurelius Ambrosius* was poisoned in the year 498. and his Brother *Uter-Pendragon* took upon him the Government of this Realm.

CENT. VI.

MOst miserable at this time was the *British* Common-wealth, crouded up into barren Corners, whil'ft their Enemies the Pagan *Saxons* possessed the East and South, if not the best part of the Island. *Pen-dragon* dying, the Nobles and Bishops of *Britain* set up his Son *Arthur*, being about 16 years of age, to be King of *Britain*, in the year 516. Of whom one writeth thus, *Cultum Religioni pene debitum in Civitatibus, & viris, & oppidis, reformavit: Ecclesias à Pagana Gente destructas vel dirutas reparavit: & in eis Res & Episcopos cum Clericorum officiis, prout locorum dignitas cogebat, devoto Religionis studio ordinavit. Vigente adhuc post* Germani Episcopi labores, *qui ob id in Britanniam bis venerat, Pelagiana labe, ac desperato pene remedio.* David *ex universa Gemis Synodo Præsul constitutus An.* 519. *diutina prædicatione disceptationibus publicis eandem profligavit, atque aream Ecclesiæ purgavit.* David was Unckle to King *Arthur*; he privately studied the Scriptures ten years, before he would presume to Preach, and always caryed the Gospels about him. He kept a Synod against the Pelagian error (which was now revived in *Britain*) and confirmed many wavering Souls in the Faith. The main body of the *British* Church was at this time in *Wales*, where *Bangor* on the North, and *Caerleon* (on *Usk* in *Monmouth-shire*) in the South, were the two

eyes

the Church of Great Britain. 11

eyes thereof for Learning and Religion. *Caerleon* had in it the Court of King *Arthur*, the See of an Archbishop, a Colledge of 200 Philosophers, who therein studied Astronomy, and was a populous place of great extent, though at this day reduced to a small Village. By leave obtained from King *Arthur*, *David* removed the Archiepiscopal seat from *Caerleon* to *Meneva*, now called St. *David's* in *Pembrook*-shire, in which exchange (saith *Fuller*) his devotion is rather to be admired, than his discretion to be commended, leaving a fruitful soyl for a bleach barren place; though the worse it was, the better for his purpose, being a great promoter of a Monastical life. *Girald.Cambr.*

In those days such was the correspondency between the greater and lesser *Britain*, that they seemed to possess Learned Men in common betwixt them.

About the same time flourished *Cadocus*, Abbot of *Llancanvan* in *Glamorgan* shire, Son of the Toparch of that Countrey: He retained part of his paternal principality in his hand, whereby he daily fed 300 of Clergy-men, Widdows, and poor People, besides guests and visitants daily resorting to him. Wilful poverty *then* was not by vow entailed upon Monastical life.

Iltutus followed him, a profound Scholar, who at *Llaniltut* in *Glamorgan* shire Preached God's Word, and set up a Colledge of Scholars, himself leading a single life. *Sampson*, Scholar to *Iltutus*, succeedeth, made Bishop at large, *sine titulo*. In that Age all Bishops were not fixed to the Chair of a peculiar Church, but some might sit down in any vacant place for their Cathedral, and there exercise their Episcopal Authority, provided it were without prejudice to other Bishops: This *Sampson* being afterwards made Archbishop of *Dole* in *French-Britain*, *Balcus* saith, *That he caried away with him the Monuments of* British *Antiquity*. *Fullers Church Hist.*

Patern for three and twenty years was a constant Preacher at *Llanpatern* in *Cardigan* shire.

St. *Petrock* comes next, one of great Piety and painfulness in that Age, Captain of the Cornish Saints. Then lived St. *Teliau*, who was Scholar to *Dubritius*, and succeeded him in the Bishoprick of *Landaff*, a pious Preacher, and zealous reprover of the Vices of that time. About the year 560 flourished *Congel* Abbot of *Bangor*, who much altered the discipline of that Monastery. *Kentigern*, the famous Bishop of *Elwy* in *North-Wales*; St. *Asaph* was his successor in the same place, in whose mouth this sentence was frequent; *Such who are against the Preaching of God's Word, do envy the salvation of mankind.*

About the year 596. Pope *Gregory* I. sent *Augustine* a *Benedictine* Monck, a subtil and industrious Man, into this Land, to work two ends; the one to reduce the Christians of this Isle to the Form and Service of the *Romish* Church; the other, to draw (if he could) some of those

C 2 Pagan

Pagan Kings to the Chriftian Religion. *Auguftine* with *Melitus*, and forty more of his Companions, fent to Preach the Gofpel in *Britain*, landeth at *Thanet* in *Kent*: *Ethelbert* was then King of *Kent*, and a Pagan, yet had he Married *Bertha*, Daughter to the King of *France*, a Chriftian Woman, to whom he permitted the free ufe of her Religion, allowing her both *Luidhard*, a Bifhop for her Chaplain, and an old Church in *Canterbury* (formerly dedicated by the *Romans* to St. *Martin*) to exercife her Devotion therein.

Auguftine with his followers (having obtained leave from King *Ethelbert*) advanced unto *Canterbury*, to the forefaid Church of St. *Martin*: Here they lived fo Pioufly, Prayed fo fervently, Fafted fo frequently, Preached fo conftantly, and wrought Miracles (as it is faid) fo commonly; that *Ethelbert* was perfwaded by Queen *Bertha* to embrace the Chriftian Religion, and was Baptized, whofe example multitudes of Pagans followed: There were in one day about ten thoufand Men Baptized, befides Women and Children, in a River. The Water being hallowed by *Auguftine*, he commanded the People to go in by couples, and one to Baptize the other, in the name of the Trinity. Thus *Auguftine* carieth away the credit of all that came after him, becaufe the Primitive planter of the Gofpel among the Saxons, and *Kent* was converted to Chriftianity; yet far more than half of the Land lay fome years after in the darknefs of Paganifm, which others afterwards illightened with the beams of the Gofpel. Mean time the poor Chriftian *Britains* living peaceably at home, there enjoyed God, the Gofpel, and their Mountains; not caring for the Ceremonies *A la mode*, brought over by *Auguftine*.

CENT. VII.

About the year 601. Pope *Gregory* I. fent two Archbifhops Palls into *England*, the one for *London*, the other for *York*: The former of thefe Cities had been honoured with an Archbifhop's See fome hundred years fince King *Lucius*; but at the Inftance of *Auguftine*, and by a new order of the forefaid *Gregory*, this Pall fent to *London*, was removed thence to *Canterbury* (whereof *Auguftine* was made Archbifhop) and there fixed and confirmed: *Canterbury* was the place wherein Chriftianity was firft received by the *Saxons*, and is therefore honoured to perpetuate the memory thereof; and *London* muft hereafter be contented with the plain feat of a Bifhop.

Then *Auguftine* by the aid of *Ethelbert* King of *Kent*, called a Council of *Saxon* and *Britifh* Bifhops to meet in the confines of the *Mercians* and Weft *Saxons*, in the borders of *Worcefter* and *Hereford-fhires*, under an Oak, knowing that the Pagan *Britains* performed their fuperftition under an Oak, in fome imitation, and yet a correction of their Idolatry,

the Church of GREAT BRITAIN.

try, as Sir *Henry Spelman* sheweth. But this Synod proved ineffectual; the *British* Bishops, and many very Learned Men (far differing from *Romish* Priests) rejected his Traditions which he brought from *Rome*, and would not admit thereof, detested his Pride, renounced his Authority, and would not accept of him for their Archbishop, as he desired to be; and for the space of an hundred years at least, refused to communicate with those that had received the same. And then the Bishops and Churches of *Scotland* joyned with the *Britains* against those new observations which the same *Augustine* brought from *Rome*. At that time there were 1200. Monks at the Monastery of *Bangor* in *Wales* (not Popish Monks, and idle Belly-gods, but) all living with the labour of their hands; and bestowing the time of rest from their labours in Prayer and Meditation on the Scriptures. Over that Church, at *Austin's* coming, was *Dinochus* a Learned Man, who, when *Austin* required the *British* Bishops to be subject to his *Romish* Authority, convinced them by diverse Arguments, that they did not owe him any such subjection; whereat *Augustine* being highly offended, is said to have spoken these words, *Quod si pacem cum fratribus accipere nollent, bellum ab hostibus forent accepturi: & si Nationi Anglorum noluissent viam vitæ prædicare, per horum manus ultionem essent mortis passuri:* that if they would not accept of peace with their Brethren, they should receive War from their Enemies; and seeing they would not joyn with him in Preaching the way of life to the *Saxons*, they should feel the force of their Enemies Sword: And some Writers say, that he stirred up *Ethelfred* King of *Northumberland* against them, who, with an Army of Infidels, cruelly and unmercifully slew them, who came forth to him in their shirts to entreat for mercy, fifty onely escaping.

Sir H. Spelm. *in concilii*. Geoffry of Monmouth, *calling the* Britains *the* Lord's flock, faith, Grex Domini rection ordinem tonc— bar. Galf. Monxm. lib. 11 c. 12.

But their innocent blood went not long unrevenged, for we read, how three *British* Princes, viz. *Blederic*, Duke of *Cornwall*, *Margaduc* Duke of South *Wales*, and *Cadwan* Duke of North *Wales*, gave Battel to the *Northumberlanders*, as they were invading *Wales*, and not onely dangerously wounded the foresaid *Ethelfred* their King, but also discomfited his Army, and slew ten thousand and sixty of his Souldiers; forcing him at last to Articles of composition, that he should confine himself within his own Countrey, North of *Trent*, and leave all *Wales* to be entirely and peaceably enjoyed by the *Britains*, the true owners thereof.

Nicol. Trivet.

Here we are to take our farewell of the *British* Church, for some hundreds of years, wanting instructions concerning the remarkable particulars thereof, saith Dr. *Fuller* in his Church History of *Britain*.

Let us now return to our *Augustine*, who all this while was very industrious, and no less successful in converting the *Saxons* to the Christian Faith, insomuch that a certain Author reporteth, how in the River *Swale* near *Richmond* in *Yorkshire*, *Augustine* in one day Baptized above
ten

ten thousand: but *Bede* makes no mention at all hereof, and ascribeth this numerous baptizing to *Paulinus* Bishop of *York* many years after. In that age nothing was used with Baptism, but Baptism, the word and the water made the Sacrament. At *Corn* in *Dorset-shire Austin* destroyed the Idol of *Heale*, or *Æsculapius*, which the *Saxons* formerly adored.

Sebert King of *Essex* (Nephew to *Ethelbert* King of *Kent* by *Ricula* his sister) embraced the Faith, with all his Kingdome, by the Ministry of *Mellitus*, whom *Augustine* ordained Bishop of *London*: making also one *Justus* a Roman Bishop of *Rochester*.

Bed.*Eccl.Hist.* *Augustine* died, and was buried in the Northern part of the new
li. 2. ca. 3. Church in *Canterbury*, dedicated to *Peter* and *Paul*. *Bede* saith this inscription was written upon his Monument. Here resteth Lord *Augustine*, the first Archbishop of *Canterbury*, who being in times past sent hither by blessed *Gregory* Bishop of the *Roman* City, *and supported by God with the working of Miracles, brought King* Ethelbert *and his Country from the Worshiping of Idols to the faith of Christ , and the daies of his Office being finished in peace, he died the seventh of the Calends of June, the same King reigning.* But in this Epitaph one thing is wanting, and that mainly material, namely the year that he did.

After the death of *Augustine*, *Laurentius* a *Roman* succeeded him, whom *Augustine* in his life-time ordained in that place. King *Ethelbert*, having reigned fifty six, and been a Christian one and twenty years, died, and was buried nigh to Queen *Bertha* (who died a little before him) in the Porch of St. *Martins* Church in *Canterbury*; which fabrick with some other Churches, by him were beautifully built and bountifully endowed.

After the death of *Ethelbert* Anno 616. *Eadbald*, his son and the sons of *Sebert* King of the East-*Saxons*, succeeding them, refused to be baptized, or imbrace the Christian faith, professed and set up Idolatry, expelled their Bishops, driving them out of this land into *France*, til at last King *Eadbald* being converted to Christianity by *Laurentius* Archbishop of *Canterbury*, presently began to take care of the affaires of the Church, and at the desire of *Laurentius*, *Justus* and *Mellitus*, returned again into *England*. *Rochester* readily received their Bishop, but *London* refused to entertain good *Mellitus*, who led a private life in *London*, til that after the death of *Laurentius*, he succeeded him in the Church of *Canterbury*. Five years sate *Mellitus* in *Canterbury*, after whose death *Justus* Bishop of *Rochester* succeeded him, and had his Pall solemnly sent him by Pope *Boniface*.

Ethelfred being slain by the *Britains*, *Edwin* succeedeth him, and was setled in the general government of the *Saxons*; who by the perswasion of *Paulinus* embraced and professed the Christian Religion, destroyed the Temples, Altars and Images of their Idol-Gods, and was, with
all

The Church of Great Britain.

all his Nobles and much people, baptized in the City of *York*, by *Paulinus Anno* 627.

About this time Pope *Boniface* V. directed diverse Epistles to *England*, wherein were many passages fighting against Christ's satisfaction.

A few years after the conversion of the East-Angles was advanced by King *Sigebert*, and after the death of *Earpwald*, his successor in the Kingdome. *Bede* gives him this character, that he became *vir Christianissimus & Doctissimus*, being assisted by the preaching of *Felix*, a Monk of *Burgundy*, he converted his Subjects to Christianity. This *Felix* was made the first Bishop of *Dunwich* in *Suffolk*, a place formerly furnished with fifty and two Churches, and hath scarce two now remaining, the rest being swallowed up by the Sea. This *Sigebert* is generally reputed the founder of the University of *Cambridge*.

Edwin fell out with *Cadwallan*, King of the *Britains*, and slew many thousand Christian *Britains* in battle, putting him and the rest to flight. *Anno* 633. After the victory *Edwin* led his Army through the Provinces of *Britain*, burning their Cities, and wasting their Colonies, and brought those Provinces under his subjection, chasing *Cadwallan* into *Ireland*. But *Cadwallan* returning from thence with ten thousand men, assisted by *Penda* King of *Mercia*, wasted the Countrey of King *Edwin*. Both these Kings at last met in a field called *Heath-field*, where *Edwin* was slaine, and his whole Army overthrown: *Cadwallan* slew both the Sons of King *Edwin*, and for a whole year destroyed the Provinces of the *Northumbrians*. After the death of *Edwin*, his whole kingdome relapsed to Paganism; and *Paulinus*, Arch-Bishop of *York*, taking with him Queen *Ethelburga* sister to *Eadbald* King of *Kent*, returned into *Kent*, and there became Bishop of *Rochester*.

After the death of King *Edwin*, his Kingdome of *Northumberland* was divided into two parts, both petty Kingdomes. *Osrich*, Cousin-German of King *Edwin*, was King of *Deira*; and *Eanfrith* the eldest son of *Ethelfred*, was King of *Bernicia*. They were both Christians, but became Apostates, and were slain by *Cadwallan* in the first year.

Oswald the second son of *Ethelfred*, succeeded unto them, and overthrew *Cadwallan*. Bishop *Aidan* converted *Oswald*, which King disdained not to preach, and expound to his Subjects and Nobles in the English tongue, that which *Aidan* preached to the *Saxons* in the *Scottish* tongue. By the Ministry of *Aidan* (the first Bishop of *Linsfarn*) was the Kingdome of *Northumberland* recovered from Paganism. *Aidan* parted all that was given him, by the King or Potent men, among the poor: and ceased not to go from town to town, and from house to house, not on horsback, but on foot, always catechizing, whether he met with rich or poor: if they were Pagans, he instructed them; if they were Christians, he confirmed them in the faith; and exhorted unto the works of Piety and Charity, especially to read the Scriptures diligently,

Usher's *Relig. of the antient Irish.* p. 115.

Petry. *Church hist. cent.* 7.

ly; he died *Anno* 651. From *Northumberland* the word of God was spread among many others of the *Saxon* Kingdomes.

The Scotch, that professed no subjection to the Church of *Rome*, were they that sent preachers to the conversion of these Countries; and ordained Bishops to govern them, as *Aidan* forementioned, *Finan*, and *Colman*: for the East *Saxons Cedd*, and for the *Mercians Diuma*: for the paucity of Priests (saith *Beda*) constrained one Bishop to be appointed over two people. *Finan* converted the Kingdomes of the East *Saxons*, and *Mercia*. Pope *Honorius* sent *Birinus* unto the West-*Saxons*, who by his preaching converteth many, and among the rest *Kyngils*, the West-Saxon King, whom he Baptized. *Oswald*, King of *Northumberland* was present at that time, and was first God-father, then father in law to King *Kyngils*, to whom he gave his Daughter to Wife.

Dorchester, an old City in *Oxford-shire*, was made the seate of *Birinus* his Bishoprick. *Sussex*, and the Isle of *Wight* also were converted. About this time *Honorius*, Arch-Bishop of *Canterbury*, divided *England* (so much thereof as was Christian) into Parishes. *Anno* 640. the first lent began in those parts of *England*, which obeyed the *Roman* celebration of Easter.

Oswald, King of *Northumberland*, fighting at *Maserfield* (since *Oswastrey* in *Shrop shire*) against *Penda* the Pagan Prince of *Mercia*, was overthrown, slain, and his Bodie most barbarously abused and chopped in pieces. *Oswy* his younger brother recovered his Kingdome after one year; and buried his head in the Church-yard of *Lyndesar*.

Sigebert was perswaded by his Monks to enter into a Cloister: his end was lamentable: for when he had given over his Kingdome to his Cousin *Egrick*, the forenamed *Penda* entred his Kingdome with an Army: his subjects forced him to go into the field, where both he and *Egrick* were slain. Others say, he was murdered by two Villains.

Penda, Prince of *Mercia*, having married *Alfreda*, Daughter of *Oswy*, King of *Northumberland*, renounced *Paganism*, embraced Christianity, and propogated it in his Dominions. Indeed; *Penda* his father, that persecutor of piety, was yet alive (and survived two years after) permitting an Heathen till death, but mollified to permit a toleration of Christianity in his Subjects.

From *Colmkil* (as a most famous Seminary of learning) at that time, sprang forth those, who not onely did resist the beginnings of Anti-Christian pride at home, and in our neighbour-Country, but they sowed the seed of the Gospel in other Nations. Such was that famous *Rumold*, who was called *Mechlinensis Apostolus*. *Gallus* brought *Helvetia* from *Paganism*, as *Pappas* witnesseth, built sundry Monasteries there. *Columban*, a man of excellent holiness and learning, lived sometime in *Bangor*, and thence went into *Burgundy*, where he began the Monasterie *Luxovien*, and taught the Monks, of his own Country especially, to live by the

The Church of Great Britain.

the works of their own hands. Alſo becauſe he rebuked *Theodorick* for his leacherous life, he was forced to flie, and viſited ſundry parts of *Germany*: thence he went into *Italy*, and began another Abby on the *Appennine* Hills beſide *Bobium* in *Tuſcany*. *Levin* alſo turned many to the faith about *Ghent* and *Eſca*. *Platina in Bonifacio quarto.*

Furſeus, and his brother *Fullan*, with two Presbyters, *Gobban* and *Dicul*, obtained land from *Sigebert* King of *Eſſex*, and built the Abby of *Cnobſherburg*: and paſſing into *France*, he began the Abby at *Latiniae*, where he died. *Diuma* was ordained firſt Biſhop of *Mercia*, where he converted many to the Faith, in the reign of the Chriſtian *Penda*: and for his rare gifts the Biſhoprick of *Middleſex* was committed to his charge, unto whom ſucceeded *Cella* a *Scot*. Alſo *Florentius* went to *Argentine*, or *Strausburg*, and was the firſt Biſhop thereof: he opened the firſt School in *Alſatia* about the year 669. *Kilian*, the firſt Biſhop of *Wortsburg*, did firſt inſtruct the people of Eaſt-*France*, in the Chriſtian Faith. *Anno.* 668. *Colonat* a Prieſt, and *Thomas* a Deacon, followed him in all his Travels. *Burcard* ſucceeded, to whom King *Pippin* gave a Dukedome: and from thence among all the Biſhops of *Germany*, onely the Biſhop of *Wortsburg* carieth a Sword and Prieſts Gown in his badge. Unto theſe *Scots John Pappas* joyneth ſome *Britans*, as *Willibrod* Reformer of *Friſia*; and two brethren *Evaldi*, the one Sirnamed the Black, the other the White. *John Pappas* ſaith they converted the *Weſtphalians* to the Chriſtian Faith, and ſuffered Martyrdome near *Bremen*. *John Bale* ſheweth their Death.

Pope *Agatho* ſent *John* (the Arch-chaunter of St. *Peters* in *Rome*) into *England*, to compoſe the difference betwixt *Honoricus* and *Wilfrid* the two Archbiſhops, and withal to deliver them the Acts of Pope *Martin* the firſt, and to teach them to ſing the Liturgy according to the cuſtom of *Rome*—— *Benedictus Biſcopius*, a Nobleman of *England*, went to *Rome* in the ſervice of the Church; and brought many Books into the Monaſteries of *Tinmouth*, and *Wirmouth*. The firſt Glaſs in this Iſland is ſaid to be his gift.

Mark what *Beda* ſaith of the cuſtom in thoſe dayes: Then they never came into a Church, but onely for hearing the Word, and Prayer [no word of the Maſs] the King would come with five or ſix, and he ſtayed till the Prayer was ended. All the care of theſe Doctors was to ſerve God, not the World; to feed Souls, not their own Bodies: wherefore in thoſe dayes whereſoever a Clerk or Monk did come, he was received as a Servant of God: If he were ſeen journeying, they were glad to be ſigned with his Hand, or bleſſed with his Mouth, and they gave good heed unto the words of his Exhortation. And on the Lord's day they came in Flocks to the Church or Monaſteries, not to refreſh their Bodies [nor to hear Maſſes] but to hear the Word; and if any Prieſt entred into a Village, incontinently all the People would aſſemble, being deſirous

sirous to hear the Word of Life; for neither did the Priests go into Villages upon any other occasion, except to Preach, or visit the Sick, or to feed Souls. At that time the Clergy and Monks in *England* had liberty to Marry.

Then *Theodorus*, who succeeded *Deus-dedit*, Bishop of *Canterbury*, brought many Books thither, erecting a well-furnished Library, and teaching his Clergy how to make use thereof. He rigorously pressed Conformity to *Rome*, in the observation of *Easter*; and to that purpose a Council was called at *Hartford*; here *Easter* was setled according to the *Romish* Rite. In this Synod nine other Articles were concluded of, as *Stapleton* hath thus Translated them out of *Bede*.

Lib. 4. c. 5.

I. That no Bishop should have ought to do in another's Diocess, but be contented with the charge of the people committed unto him.

II. That no Bishop should any-wise trouble such Monasteries as were Consecrated, and given to God, nor violently take from them ought was theirs.

III. That Monks should not go from one Monastery to another, unless by the leave of their own Abbot; but should continue in the obedience which they promised at the time of their conversion, and entrance into Religion.

IV. That none of the Clergy, forsaking his own Bishop, should run up and down where he lists; nor when he came any whither, should be received without Letters of Commendation from his Diocesan, &c.

V. That such Bishops and Clerks as are strangers, be content with such Hospitality as is given them, and that it be lawful for none of them to execute any Office of a Priest, without the permission of the Bishop in whose Diocess they are known to be.

VI. It hath seemed good to us all, that a Synod and Convocation should be Assembled once a year, on the first day of August, at the place called Closeshooh.

VII. That no Bishop should ambitiously prefer himself above another, but should all acknowledge the time and order of their consecration.

VIII. That the number of the Bishops should be encreased, the number of Christian folk daily waxing greater.

IX. That no man commit Advoutry, nor Fornication; that no man forsake his own Wife, but for onely Fornication, as the holy Gospel teacheth. And if any Man put away his Wife, being lawfully married unto him, if he will be a right Christian Man, let him be joyned to none other; but let him so continue, still sole, or else be reconciled again to his own Wife.

This Synod *Stapleton* calleth, *the first of the English Nation*, that is, whose Canons are completely extant.

The-

The Church of Great Britain.

Theodorus Archbishop of *Canterbury* envyed *Wilfrid* Bishop of *York*, and endeavoured, that the Diocess of *York* might be divided; whereat *Wilfrid* being offended, goes to *Rome*, and in his passage thither, by a Tempest he is cast on the Shoar of *Freezland* in *Belgia*, where the Inhabitants (as yet Pagans) were by his Preaching converted to Christianity. Returning into *England*, he returned not unto *York*, but stayed in the Pagan Kingdom of the South *Saxons*, who also by God's blessing on his endeavours were perswaded to embrace the Christian Faith. These South *Saxons* (of all the seven Kingdomes) were the last that were converted to Christ, and yet their Countrey was next in situation unto *Kent*, where the Gospel was first planted. Indeed *Edilwalck* their King was a little before Christened by the perswasion of *Wolpher* King of *Mercia* (who was his God-father, and at his Baptizing gave him for a gift the Isle of *Wight*, & *Provinciam Meanvarorum in Gente occidentalium Saxonum*) but his Countrey still remained in Paganism. And although *Dicul* a Scot, with six others, had a small Monastery at *Bosenham* in *Sussex*, yet they were more careful of their own safety, than of their Neighbours conversion. *Wilfrid* builded an Abbey in *Selsey* in *Sussex*, he taught the South *Saxons* the craft of fishing.

Cedda the Bishop of West *Saxons* died, and his Deacon *Wenfrede* was his successor: Soon after this time died *Wina* Bishop of *London*, after whom was Bishop *Erkenwald*, who founded the Monasteries of *Chertsey* in *Surrey*, and *Barking* in *Essex*. But that of *Chertsey* was thrown down by the *Danes*, and re-edified by *Edgar* King of *England*.

Then *Theodorus* kept a Synod or Council of Bishops at *Hatfield*, by authority of which Council he divided the Province of *Mercia*, that *Sexwolphus* then ruled alone, into five Bishopricks; that is, one to *Chester*, the second to *Worcester*, the third to *Lichfield*, the fourth to *Cedema* in *Lindsey*, and the fifth to *Dorchester*.

Cadwallader, the last King of *Wales*, wearied out with Wars, Famine and Pestilence, left his own Land, and with some small treasure fled to *Alan*, King of *Little Britain*: He was the last King of the stock of *Britains*. After he had reigned three years he went to *Rome*, and there died, and was buried in the Church of St. *Peter*, with this Epitaph upon his Tomb.

Culmen opus sobolem pollentia regna triumphos,
Eximias proceros mœnia castra lares,
Quæq; patrum virtus, & quæ congesserat ipse,
Cadwald armipotens, linquit amore Dei.

The which verses are thus Englished by *Fabian*.

Fabian's Chr. part. 5.

Abounding riches, kinred, triumph assured,
Plenteous wealth, with clothes richly dyght,
Houses, Castles, and Towns strongly mured,
And other honours which by his Parents Might,
And his own, this Martial vertuous Knight,
Cadwald the strong, descended of Knight's blood.
For Christ's love renounced all his good.

About the year 692. *Ina* King of the West *Saxons*, set forth his Saxon Laws, translated into English by Mr. *Lambert*; he enacted many Laws, viz. *De regula vivendi Ministrorum Dei; de Infantibus baptizandis; de censu Ecclesiæ, &c.*

Anno 694. a great Council was held at *Becanceld* by *Withred* King of *Kent*, and *Bertuald* Archbishop of *Britain*, wherein many things were concluded in favour of the Church. Five Kentish Abbesses, namely *Mildred, Ethelred, Æte, Wilnolde*, and *Herefwide*, were not onely present, but subscribed their names and crosses to the Constitutions concluded therein. And we may observe, that their subscriptions are placed, not onely before and above all Presbyters, but also above *Botred* a Bishop present in this Council. There was likewise a Council held at *Berghamsteed* by *Withred* King of *Kent*: Then Bishop *Wilfrid* was removed to *York* again, where he continued not long, and being thence expelled again, he was for a time made Bishop of *Leicester*.

Cent. VIII.

Wilfrid was troubled by the Archbishop of *Canterbury*, he appealeth to *Rome*, and is acquitted; he is at last restored, and died in peace in the LXXVI. year of his age, having been 45. years a Bishop, and was buried in his Monastery at *Rippon*.

Camden's Brit. in Wilts. shire.

The Bishoprick of *Sherborn* having been taken out of the Bishoprick of *Winchester* by King *Ina*, *Adelme* his Kinsman was made first Bishop thereof. This *Adelme* was the first of our English Nation, who wrote in Latine, and the first that taught our English Nation to make Latine verse, according to his promise.

*Primus ego in patriam mecum, modo vita superfit,
Aonio rediens deducam vertice Musas.*

the Church of Great Britain.

If life me laſt, that I do ſee
That native ſoil of mine,
From *Aon* top I'l firſt with me
Bring down the Muſes nine.

He wrote many Books; one of Virginity, another of the Celebration of *Eaſter*: And about this time the Libraries of Monaſteries began to be repleniſhed with Books, many being written in that Age.

In this age there were many Saints (ſuch as they were) of Royal, or Noble extraction: of theſe Noble Saints, St. *Guthlake*, a Benedictine Monk, was the firſt *Saxon* that profeſſed an Eremetical life in *England*; he was a Monk in the Abbey of *Repyndon*, and the third year after he went to *Crowland*, that is, the raw or crude Land, a fenny place in *Lincoln-ſhire*, and there led for a while an *Anchoret's* life, and there finally was buried; in which Iſle and place of his burying, was built a fair Abbey.

About the year 709. a Synod was aſſembled at *Alncester* in *Worcester-ſhire*, to promote the building of *Eveſham* Abbey; which was done accordingly, and the ſame was bountifully endowed by *Offa*, and other Mercian Kings, with large revenues: And not long after, another Synod was called at *London*, to introduce into *England* the doctrine of Image-worſhip, now firſt beginning to appear in the publick practice of it.

Now alſo flouriſhed another Noble-born Saint, *viz.* *John* of *Beverley*, Archbiſhop of *York*, a Learned Man, and who gave the education to one more Learned than himſelf, I mean, *Venerable Bede*, who acknowledgeth, that he received the order of Prieſthood from him.

About this time it was faſhionable for Kings and Queens in *England*, to renounce the World, and turn Monks and Nuns, commonly in Convents of their own Foundation: but they had an high opinion to merit Heaven thereby.

Among the *Saxon* Princes who thus renounced the World, in this and the next Century, theſe nine following were the principal.

1. *Kinigilſus*, King of Weſt Saxons.	4. *Edbertus*, King of Northumberland.	7. *Offa*, King of Eaſt Saxons.
2. *Ina*, King of Weſt Saxons.	5. *Ethelred*, King of Mercia.	8. *Sebbi*, King of Eaſt Saxons.
3. *Ceololfus*, King of Northumberland.	6. *Kenred*, King of Mercia.	9. *Sigebert*, King of Eaſt Angles.

Ina builded the Abbey at *Glaſtonbury* in the 32 year of his Reign; Sir H. Spelm. beſides his bounty to other Churches, he beſtowed on the Church of *in conciliis...* *Glaſtonbury*, two thouſand ſix hundred pounds weight, in the Utenſils thereof, of maſſy Gold and Silver: He was the firſt King of this Land, that

that granted a penny out of every fire-houfe in *England* to be paid to the Court of *Rome*, which was called long after *Rome-fcot*, or *Peter-pence*, and was to be paid on St. *Peters* day. After this he went to *Rome* in Pilgrimage, in the fellowfhip of poor Men, and there built a School for the *Englifh*, and a Church adjoyning to it to bury their dead.

But *Winnifrid*, an Englifh Man, about this time converted to Chrift the Provinces of *Franconia* and *Haffia* in *Germany*.

About the fame time flourifhed *Bede*, a Presbyter in the Monaftery of *Weremouth*, near *Durham*; he was born at *Girwy*, now in the Bifhoprick of *Durham*, brought up by St. *Cuthbert*, and was the profoundeft Scholar of his Age, for Latine, Greek, Philofophy, Hiftory, Divinity, Mathematicks, Mufick, and what not? Homilies of his making were read in his life-time in the Chriftian Churches, a dignity afforded to him alone. He wrote the Ecclefiaftical Hiftory, and dedicated it to *Ceolwolfus* King of *Northumberland*: He is generally firnamed *Venerable*, and is ftill accounted worthy of that Title: He was credulous in believing of falfe Miracles, and flipped into fome corruptions of the times, as Chrifm and Confeffion; yet, even in thefe, he differed from the latter times. In the Articles of pofitive Doctrine he was clear: He did obferve and deplore the growing corruptions of the Church; for in an Epiftle to *Ecbert* he did not approve the fpecious and fpacious buildings of Monafteries; and elfe-where, he faith, *Let the Reader behold with tears a thing worthy of tears, how far the Church flideth daily into a worfe, or (to fpeak moderately into a weaker eftate.* He wrote many Books, as *John Bale* teftifieth: He lived 72 years, and died *Anno* 734.

At that time began the general vicioufnefs of the *Saxons*, occafioned by the uncleannefs of *Ethelbald*, King of *Mercia*, whofe unlawful luft made no difference of Places, or Perfons, Caftles, or Cloifters: Then *Boniface* an Englifh Man, having boldly reproved *Ethelbald*, for Adultery, and Tyranny, was forced, by that King (who fought his life) to fly to *Rome*, from whence *Gregory* the fecond, Bifhop of *Rome* fent him into *Germany* to convert the *Saxons*. He caufed the Monaftery of *Eulda* to be built, in favour of the Englifh, and was flain at *Borna*, being Bifhop of *Mentz*.

Afterwards *Ethelbald* reformed himfelf; and not onely fo, but with *Cuthbert* Archbifhop of *Canterbury*, called a Council at *Cliffe* in *Kent*; the Acts of this Synod were 31 Canons, four whereof I fhall fet down, as being the chief.

I. That the *Priefts* learn, and teach to know the *Creed*, *Lord's Prayer*, and words of *Confecration in the Euchariſt*, in the *Englifh Tongue*.
II. That the *Lord's* day be honourably obferved.
III. That the fin of drunkennefs be avoyded, efpecially in the *Clergy*.
IV. That Prayers be publikely made for Kings and Princes.

King

the Church of Great Britain.   23

King *Ethelbald*, and *Offa* were prefent; and they two, with many Dukes and Counts, confirm the Decrees with their fubfcriptions.

About the year 755 *Kenulphus*, King of Weft *Saxons* conferred large priviledges on the Monaftery of *Abbingdon* in *Bark-fhire*. *Anno* 758. Bodies were firft brought to be buried in Churches, which by degrees brought in much fuperftition.

In the year 789 the *Danes* firft invaded *England* with a confiderable Army. The landing of thefe *Danes* in *England* was ufhered with many fad Prognofticks: Stars were feen ftrangely falling from Heaven, and fundry terrible flames appeared in the Skies: Serpents were feen in *Suffex*, and blood reigned in fome parts of this Land. *Lindesfern*, or *Holy Ifland*, was the firft that felt the fury of thefe Pagans, but foon after no place was fecure from their cruelty.   *Danes their firft arrival in England.*

At this time the Archbifhoprick of *Canterbury* was in part removed to *Lichfield*, by reafon of the Puiffance and Ambition of *Offa*, King of *Mercia*, commanding in chief over *England*. *Ethelbert*, King of the Eaft *Saxons*, went to Marry the Daughter of *Offa*, and *Offa* perfidioufly caufed him to be murdered: After which he gave the tenth part of all that he had unto the Church, and feveral Lands to the Church of *Hereford*; and then he went to *Rome*, and there confirmed and enlarged, to Pope *Adrian*, the gift of *Peter-pence*. Then was the corps of St. *Alban* in pompous manner taken up, enfhrined, and adored by the fpectators: *Offa* being at *Rome*, procured the Canonization of St. *Alban*, the abfolution of his own fins, and many murders, and vifited and endowed the Englifh Colledge there; and then returning home, he Founded the Monaftery of St. *Albans*, beftowing great Lands and liberties upon it, as freeing it from the payment of *Peter-pence*. Epifcopal jurifdiction, and the like. Next year *Offa* died, and was buried at *Bedford*.

Then flourifhed *Alcuinus*, or *Albinus*, Scholar to *Venerable Bede*, and Tutor to *Charles* the Great, who in an Epiftle written to him, calleth him Mafter; of whom *Trithemius* give's this character, *Vir in divinis Scripturis eruditiffimus, & infecularium literarum peritia nulli fuo tempore fecundus*. He oppofed the Canons of the fecond *Nicene* Council, wherein the Superftitious adoration of Images was enjoyned: He wrote divers Books againft the Errors of *Felix* and *Eliphant*: *Felix* in reading them, wrote a Recantation to the Presbyters and Deacons of his Church: His Books *de Trinitate* are written fo clearly, that *Sixtus Senenfis* faith, they were written by *John Calvin*, and publifhed in the name of *Alcuinus*; but Dr. *James* faith, that ancient Copies thereof were in the Prince's library at St. *James*, and they were Printed at *Lions*, *Anno* 1525. when *Calvin* had not begun to write.   R. Hoveden *Anna!. part. 1.*

Egbert, King of the Weft *Saxons* in the year 800. having vanquifhed, *Mercia*, *Kent*, *Effex*, and *Northumberland*, made himfelf fole Monarch of *England*, and fixed the fupreme Sovereignty in himfelf and pofterity.   Tho. Cooper.

For

For, though afterward there continued some petty Kings, as *Kenulph*, King of *Mercia*, &c. yet they shined but dimly, and in the next Age were utterly extinguished: *Egbert* commanded this Land to be called *Anglia*, and the Inhabitants *Angles*, or English Men.

Cent. IX.

ANno 801. the Archbishoprick was restored to *Canterbury*, at the instance of *Kenulph*, King of *Mercia*. Then *Ethelard* the Archbishop called a Synod at *Clivesho* in *Kent*, where, by power from the Pope, he riveted the Archbishoprick into the City of *Canterbury*. The subscriptions in this Council were the most formal and solemn of any so Antient. There was likewise at *Celichyth* an eminent Council, under *Wolphred* (who succeeded *Ethelard*) Archbishop of *Canterbury*.

King *Egbert* was now in the exaltation of his greatness; but the *Danes* beat the *English* in a Naval fight at *Carmouth* in *Dorset-shire*, which proved fatal to our Nation. Hence forward these Pagans setled themselves in some part of the Land.

Anno 837. *Ethelwolph*, his Son, succeeded his Father *Egbert* in the Throne; a valiant and devout Prince, though much molested by the *Danes* all his life-time.

About the year 855. *Ethelwolph* King of the West *Saxons*, summoned a Parliament of his Princes, Nobles, and Bishops at *Winchester*, in the midst of the *Danish* Wars and Invasions, to consult with them, how he might pacifie God's wrath against him, and his Realm? And by their advise and assent granted the Tithes, or tenth part of all his Lands to God and his Ministers, free from all secular services and exactions, great and small, that they might the more freely pour out their prayers to God for him and his Realm. He subjected the whole Kingdom to the payment of Tithes; he was the first-born Monarch of *England*. Indeed before his time there were Monarchs of the *Saxon* Heptarchy, but not successive, and fixed in a Family, but fluctuating from one Kingdom to another. *Egbert*, Father to this *Ethelwolph* atchieved and left this Monarchy to this his Son; not *Monarcha factus*, but *natus*, and so in unquestionable Power to make this Act obligatory over all the Land, saith *Fuller*.

King *Ethelwolph* the next year went in Pilgrimage to *Rome*, and confirmed, unto the Pope, his Predecessors grant of *Peter-pence*, and (besides) bestowed upon him the yearly Revenue of three hundred Marks, thus to be expended.

1. To maintain Candles for St. *Peter*, one hundred Marks.
2. To maintain Candles for St. *Paul*, one hundred Marks.
3. For a free Largess to the Pope, one hundred Marks.

After

the Church of Great Britain.

After the Death of King *Ethelwolph*, and his two Sons *Ethelbald* and *Ethelbert*, succeeding him, this Land was in a sad condition, though in a worse estate under the reign of his third Son, being harassed by the *Danes*. About sixty years since the West *Saxons* had subdued the other six Kings of this Nation, yet so, that they still continued Kings, but Homagers to the West *Saxon* Monarchy. They beholding *Ethelred* the West *Saxon* King, embroiled with the invasion of the *Danes*, they not onely lazily looked on, but secretly smiled at this sight. Thus the height of the *Saxon* pride and envy, caused the breadth of the *Danish* power and cruelty.

Anno 870. the *Danes* made an inrode into *Lincoln-shire*, where they met with stout resistance: The Christians had the better the first day, wherein the *Danes* lost three of their Kings, buried in a place thence called *Trekingham*; so had they the second day till at night breaking their Ranks to pursue the *Danes* in their dissembled flight, they were utterly overthrown.

Theodore Abbot of *Crowland*, hearing of the *Danes* approach, Shipped away most of his Monks, with the choycest Relicks and Treasures of his Convent, and cast his most pretious Vessels into a Well in the Cloister. The rest remaining were at their morning praiers, when the *Danes* entring Slew

Theodore the Abbot on the high Altar.
Asher the Prior in the Vestiary.
Lethwin the Sub-prior in the Refectory.
Pauline and *Herbert* in the Quire.
Wolride the Torch-bearer in the same place.
Grimketule, & *Agamund*, each of them an 100 years old in the Cloisters.

Then the *Danes* marched to *Medamstead* (since called *Peterbrough*) where finding the Abby-gates locked against them, they resolved to force their entrance, in effecting whereof *Tulba*, Brother to Count *Hubba*, was wounded almost to death with a stone cast at him. *Hubba* enraged hereat, killed Abbot *Hedda*, and all the Monks, being fourscore and four, with his own hand. Then was the Abby set on fire, which burned fifteen daies together, wherein an excellent Library was consumed. Having pillaged the Abby, and broke the Tombs and Coffins of many Saints there enterred, these *Pagans* marched forward into *Cambridge-shire*, and passing the river *Nine*, two of their waggons fell into the water, wherein the cattle which drew them were drowned, much of their rich plunder lost, and more impared.

The *Danes* spared no Age, Sex, condition of people. They wasted *Cambridge*, burnt the (then) City of *Thetford*, forced *Edmond*, King of the East-Angles, into his Castle of *Framlingham*. They took him, and
because

because he would not deny Christ, they tyed him unto a Tree, and shot at him till he died. Then they cut of his head, and cast it among the bushes. His own Subjects buried him both head and body at *Hatsedon*, which from thence was called, St. *Edmonds-bury*. There after-ages shrined, sainted, and adored his Reliques. King *Erbelbert* behaved himself bravely in nine Battles with various success against the *Danes*, and the more he slew, the more they grew, which went peer his heart, therefore he withered away in the flower of his age, desiring rather to encounter death than the *Danes*, according to the observation of the English Historian, that the *Saxon* Kings in this age, *magis optabant honestum exitum, quam acerbum Imperium.*

Guliel. Malmesbur. de Gestis Regum Anglor. lib. 2.

In this sad condition God sent *England* a deliverer, namely King *Alfred*, or *Alured*, fourth son of *Ethelwolph* by the Lady *Osburgh*. He was born in *England*, bred in *Rome*, where, by a *Prolepsis*, (saith *Fuller*) he was anointed King by Pope *Leo* (though then but a private Prince, and his three elder brothers alive) *in auspicium futuri regni,* in hope that hereafter he should come to the Crown. The *Danes* at his coming to the Crown, had *London*, many of the in-land, more of the maritime Towns, and *Alfred* onely three effectual Shires *Sommerset*, *Wiltes* and *Dorset*: yet by God's blessing on his endeavours, he got to be Monarch of all *England*.

Anno 872.

In the beginning of his reign, he was sorely distressed by the *Danes*, and one of his greatest Courts for residence, was an Island, now known by the name of *Athelney* in the County of *Sommerset*, in the Saxon tongue called *Æthelingarg* that is, *Nobilium Insula*, so termed by reason of the Kings abode, and the concourse of his Nobles unto him : in this place he lived poorly disguised in a Cow-herds house. Being excellent In Musick and Songs, he oftentimes in the habit and posture of a common Minstril, did insinuate himself in the *Danish* Camp, where his plausible cariage and skill gained a freedome of access and passage in the company of their Princes at banquets, and other meetings; and thereby he discovered their conditions, and all their martial counsels and designes. He returneth to his comfortless company, and unmasking himself and the *Danish* delignes, cheereth them up, and with a refreshed Power and strength suddenly issued forth, and gave a fierce assault upon the secure *Danes*: he slew multitudes of them, and enforced the remainder to a shameful flight for the safe-guard of their lives. In this Isle *Alfred* had built a kind of Castle, or Fortress, to receive him and his Nobles upon return from their Sallies and Encounters during his Wars in those parts.

About a year after that memorable overthrow, *viz*. Anno 879. in a Battel at *Kinwich* in *Devon-shire*, *Halden*, and some of the chief Leaders of the *Danes*, received their death's wound, and ended their lives; hereupon the daunted and dispersed *Danes* humbly present their termes of Peace to King *Alfred* with Pledges and Hostages, that they would either

the Church of GREAT BRITAIN.

either depart the Land, or become Christians, which was accepted by him. *Guthrun*, their new King, upon the death of their other Leaders with thirty Noble-men, and almost all his People, received Baptism in the new Castle of *Athelney*, where King *Alfred* was Godfather to him, and gave him the name of *Athelstane*; and upon a confederation between them, *Alfred* did assign unto him the Provinces of the *East-Angles*, and *Northumberland*; *Ut eas sub fidelitate Regis jure hæreditario foveret, quas pervaserat latrocinio*; that he might enjoy that by right, which before he usurped by rapine: and unto the new-baptized Nobles, he gave many large and rich gifts. This truce, or league, was about the ninth year of his Reign, and thus beginneth, *Fadus*, quod Aluredus, *& Gy-* thrudus, *Reges, ex sapientum* Anglorum, *atque eorum omnium, qui orientalem incolebant* Angliam *consulto fecerunt, in quod præterea, singuli non solum de seipsis, verumetiam de natis suis, ac nondum in lucem editis (quotquot saltem misericordiæ divinæ aut Regiæ velint esse participes) juraverunt.* That is, they did by a solemn Oath ratifie this League, as well for themselves as for those that were then born, and unborn, that would be partakers of mercy from God or the King. *Lamb. Archai: fol. 49.*

Then having set bounds to his Dominions, certain Comitial Lawes and Ordinances were made between them, enlarged and amplified by their Senators. Before all things they proposed and preferred the strict and holy worshipping of Almighty God, and abandoning all barbarous Idolatry, next, they took care for the Enacting, Registring, and Enrolling of Moral Laws, for containing of Subjects in their several duties, and due obedience, and therefore they first decreed, *That the peace of the Church within her Walls (as it was then delivered by the hand of King* Alfred*) should be piously and inviolably observed.* They proceeded to the promotion and propagation of the Christian Faith, and the abolition of all Paganism, and Heathenish Rites; for coercion of Clearks, and Men in Holy Orders, if they committed any Perjury, Fornication, or other Offences, or were unconformable in the celebration of Festival-days, times of Abstinence, or other Orders and Injunctions of the Church; prohibiting Merchandising, and secular Negotiations upon the Lord's day. In all which the Impositions of Penalties and Punishments upon an *English* Man, and a *Dane*, were differenced one from the other. They also provided for the exilement of Witches, Wizzards, common Strumpets, and other lewd Creatures; with other good Laws for avoiding of Homicides, and for preservation of Peace and Government, and maintenance of each Man's right of property in this their National commixture.

This adjured League quieted the Civil discords of the *Danes* and *Saxons* for the space of four years, until the twelfth year of *Alfred's* Reign: And afterwards the continual inrode of the stragling unbaptized *Danes* issuing out of *France*, and other places (who vexed that Eastern part of the Land) molested this good King untill his Death.

E 2   This

This King divided his moveables into equal portions; the one he appointed for uses Secular, and divided it into three parts, one for his Family, another for building of new Works, and a third he reserved for strangers: The other half he dedicated unto uses Ecclesiastical, and divided it into four portions; one for relief of the Poor, another to Monasteries, the third to the Schools in *Oxford*, where he had erected a School for Grammar; another for Philosophy, and a third for Divinity; whereas before they had neither Grammar nor Sciences, because Pope *Gregory* I. gave in command, that *Britain* should have no Schools, for fear of Heresies, but onely Monasteries. The Regents in the University, and Readers in the Divinity-School, were *Neoth*, a worthy Divine, and *Grimbald*, well-skilled in Divinity: In Grammar and Rhetorick, the Learned *Asserius*, who wrote the life of this King: In Logick, Musick and Arithmetick, the Reader was *John*, a Monk of St. *Davids*: In Geometry and Astronomy, read *John* a companion of *Grimbald*, a Man Witty and Learned; at which Lectures, this famous King *Alfred* was present. He gave many pensions to Scholars, Learned Men in all Arts, to instruct his Subjects in Religion, and all kinds of Learning: He contributed much to the relief of distressed Churches without his Realm: He protected his Realm from oppression and injustice by his Sheriffs, Justices, and other Officers, whose proceedings he frequently examined, punishing them severely when they had judged, or injured others contrary to Law, out of Malice, Corruption, or Partiality: He divided the Day and Night into three parts; one eight hours he allowed himself for Eating, Drinking, Sleeping and Recreation; another eight hours he spent in hearing Causes, and in doing Justice; and the rest of his time spent in Prayer, Reading the Scriptures, Meditation, and other pious Exercises. And for the instructing his Subjects in the Holy Scriptures, he began to Translate the *Psalmes* of *David*, himself, into the *English* Tongue, but being prevented by Death, did not finish it: He gathered Psalmes and Prayers together into a little Book, which he called a Manual, or Hand-book, which he always caried about him. He was the first lettered Prince in this Kingdom, since it had it's denomination of *England*; and was disciplined under the care of *Plegmundus*, a Man of eminent Parts and Learning, who was born in *Mercia*, and from the solitary life of an Heremite in the Isle of *Chester*, was called to be Tutor to this Noble Prince. A little after his Inauguration to the Kingdom, he had the comfortable service and attendance of *Werefridus* (who was consecrated Bishop of *Worcester* on *Whitsunday*, Anno 872.) for at his command he Translated the Dialogues of *Gregory*, out of the Latin into the Saxon or English Dialect: he had all the helps, advice, and instructions of *Plegmundus*, his Tutor, who was afterward Consecrated Archbishop of *Canterbury*. *Asserius* (as himself affirmeth) abode with the King in his Court by the space of eight Moneths before his return into *Wales*,

Bish. Godwin. Catal.

Wales, in which time he conſtantly read divers Books unto him : for it was his cuſtom both day and night, amidſt all other impediments both of Mind and Body, to be ever verſed in reading Books himſelf, or hearing them read by others.

This unparallelled King died, *Anno* 900. after he had reigned 29 years and ſix moneths, having fought 56 Battels with the Pagan-*Danes*. His Epitaph is the Epitome of his life, which the happineſs of thankful times have dedicated to him as a Monument of his eternal fame, and here followeth out of the Works of a Modern Chronographer.

> *Nobilitas inimica tibi probitatis honorem,*
> *(Armipotens* Alfred *) dedit probitasque laborem,*
> *Perpetuumque labor nomen: immixta dolori*
> *Gaudia ſemper erant, ſpes ſemper mixta timori,* &c.

   Engliſhed by Mr. *Flemming*.

 Nobility by birth to thee,
  (O *Alfred*) ſtrong in Armes.
 Of goodneſs hath thy honour given,
  And honour toilſome harmes.
 And toilſome harmes an endleſs name,
  Whoſe joyes ere alwayes mixt
 With ſorrow, and whoſe hope with fear
  Was evermore perplext.
 If this day thou waſt Conqueror,
  The next day's War thou dread'ſt:
 If this day thou waſt Conquered,
  To next day's War thou ſpread'ſt
 Whoſe cloathing wet with a daily ſwet,
  Whoſe blade with bloody ſtain,
 Do prove how great a burden 'tis
  In Royalty to reign.
 There hath not been in any part
  Of all the World ſo wide
 One that was able breath to take,
  And troubles ſuch abide,
 And yet with Weapons weary would
  Not Weapons lay aſide.
 Or with the Sword the toilſomneſs
  Of Life by Death divide.
 Now after labours paſt of Realm
  And Life (which he did ſpend)

Chrift is to him true quietnefs,
And Scepter voyd of end.

In this King's reign flourifhed *Johannes Scotus*, *Erigena*, (with addition fometimes of *Sophifta*) born in *Ireland*, for diftinction from a former born at *Melrofe*, and another in the XIII. Century, born in *Duns*, otherwife called *Subtilis*: he was a man of pregnant Judgement, wondrous Eloquence; and (in thofe days) rare knowledge of the Greek, Chaldean, and Arabian Languages. He wrote a Book, *De corpore & fanguine Domini*, againft the Opinion of Carnal prefence, which was condemned at the Synod of *Vercelles*. *Bellarmine* faith, *This man was the first, who wrote doubtingly of this matter*: He was the Counfellor to King *Alfred*, and Teacher of his Children, afterwards he retired to the Abbey at *Malmesbury*, where his difciples Murthered him with their Pen-knives, being enticed thereunto by the Monks, becaufe he fpake againft the carnal prefence, and was accounted a Martyr, as was recorded by *William* of *Malmesbury*, *de geft. Reg. Ang. lib.* 2. *cap.* 4.

Bellarm. de Ecclef.lib.1.c.1.

Zepper. de Calum.haeref. baptizat.

CENT. X.

AT this time there was no Bifhop in all the Weft parts of *England*: Pope *Formofus*, being offended hereat, interdicted, King, and Kingdom. But *Pleigmund* Archbifhop of *Canterbury* pofted to *Rome*, informing the Pope, that *Edward* (called the Elder, the Son of King *Alfred*) had, in a late fummoned Synod, founded fome new, and fupplied all old vacant Bifhoprickes; and carying with him *honorifica munera*, the Pope turned his curfe into a bleffing, and ratified their election.

The names of the feven Bifhops which *Pleigmund* confecrated in one day, were, *Fridftan* Bifhop of *Winchefter*, *Werftan* of *Shireburn*, *Kenulph* of *Dorchefter*, *Beornege* of *Selfey*, *Athelme* of *Wells*, *Eadulfe* of *Crediton* in *Devon*, and *Athelftan* in *Cornwall* of St. *Petrocks*: Thefe three laft Weftern Bifhops were in this Council newly erected.

A Synod was called at *Intingford*, where *Edward* the elder, and *Guthurn* King of the *Danes*, in that part of *England*, which formerly belonged to the Eaft *Angles*, onely confirmed the fame Ecclefiaftical conftitutions which King *Alured* had made before.

King *Edward* remembring the Pious example of his Father *Alfred* in founding of *Oxford*, began to repair and reftore the Univerfity of *Cambridge*; for the *Danes*, who kept the Kingdom of the Eaft *Angles* for their home, had banifhed all Learning from that place.

Joh. Roffius in lib. de Regib.

This King *Edward* the elder, expelled the *Danes* out of *Effex*, *Mercia*, and *Northumberland*. At that time the authority of invefting Bifhops, and other Ecclefiaftical Benefices, as alfo of prefcribing Lawes unto Church-

The Church of Great Britain.

Church-men, as well as unto the Laity, was in the power of the King, not of the Pope: but the Pope would be medling in such matters by way of Confirmation.

Athelstan, his Son, succeeded King *Edward*, being much devoted to St. *John* of *Beverley*, on whose Church he bestowed large priviledges. Many Councils were kept in this King's Reign at *Excester*, *Feversham*, *Thunderfield*, and *London*: But one held at *Greatlea* is of greatest account for the Lawes therein enacted; especially that concerning the payment of Tithes, which is thus Written; *I Athelstan King, by advice of Viselm my Archbishop, and of other Bishops, command all the Prelates of my Kingdom, in the name of our Lord, and of all the Saints, that first of all they, out of my own things, pay the Tithes unto God, as well of the living Beasts, as of the Corn of the ground; and the Bishops to do the like in their property, and the Presbyters. This I will, that Bishops, and other Head-men declare the same unto such as be under their subjection,* &c. He ordained, that in every Burrough all measures and weights should be confirmed by the Bishop's advice and testimony. About that time *Hoel* King of *Wales*, made a Law, That no Church-man should be a Judge in Civil affairs. *Spelman. in Concil. p.* 405.

Now St. *Dunstan* appeareth in Court, born at *Glastonbury*, of Noble Parentage, yea Kinsman remote to *Athelstane* himself: His eminencies were Painting and Graving; an excellent Musician, and an admirable worker in Brass and Iron. After a while he is accused for a Magician, and banished the Court. But after the Death of King *Athelstane*, he was re-called to Court in the Reign of King *Edmond*, *Athelstan*'s brother, and flourished for a time in great favour; but his old crime of being a Magician, and a wanton with Women, being laid to his charge, he is re-banished the Court.

But King *Edmond* being slain by one *Leoff* a Thief, *Edred* his Brother succeeding to the Crown, *Dunstan* is made the King's Treasurer, Chancellor, Councellor, Confessor: Secular Priests were thrust out of their Convents, and Monks substituted in their rooms.

But after *Edred*'s death *Dunstan* falls into disgrace with King *Edwin*, his Successor, and being expelled the Kingdom, flieth into *Flanders*. Mean-time all the Monks in *England* of *Dunstan*'s plantation, are rooted up, and Secular Priests set in their places.

Soon after many commotions happened in *England*, especially in *Mercia* and *Northumberland*. King *Edwin* died in the flower of his age.

Edgar succeedeth him, and recalls *Dunstan* home, who hath two Bishopricks given him, *Worcester* and *London*. King *Edgar* gave over his Soul, Body, and Estate, to be ordered by *Dunstan*, and two more (then the Triumvirate who ruled *England*) viz. *Ethelwald* Bishop of *Winchester*, and *Oswald* afterward Bishop of *Worcester*. This *Oswald* was the man, who procured, by the Kings Authority, the ejection of all secular Priests out of *Worcester*: which Act was called *Oswald*'s Law. In that Age *Fuller* Church History.

Dunstan

Antonin. hift. *Dunstan* being made Archbishop of *Canterbury*, Secular Priests were
lit. 19. part. 3. thrown out, and Monks every where fixed in their rooms. Many did
id. 3. dispute, and preach against *Dunstan*. And *Alfred* Prince of *Mercia*
took part with the Priests.

    Fuller makes mention of a fair and authentick guilded Manuscript, wherein he stileth himself God's Vicar in *England*, for the ordering Ecclesiastical matters, a Title which at this day the Pope will hardly vouchsafe to any Christian Prince.

    Hoel-Dha then held a National Council, for all *Wales*, at *Ty-quin*; or the White House. The Canons therein were wholly in favour of the Clergy; enacting this amongst the rest, *That the presence of a Priest and a Judge constitute a legal Court, as the two persons only in the* Quorum *thereof.* There were then seven Episcopal Seats in *Wales*. 1. *S. Davids.* 2. *Ismael.* 3. *Degenium.* 4. *Usyl.* 5. *Teylaw.* 6. *Teuledauc.* 7. *Kenew.*

    King *Edgar* died peaceably, leaving his Crown to *Edward* his Son, w'om (being under Age) he committed to the tuition of *Dunstan*. In this King's reign three Councils were successively called, to determine the difference between Monks and Secular Priests. The first was at *Winchester*, where the Priests being outed of their Convents, earnestly pressed for restitution. *Polydor Virgil* writes, that in the Synod it was concluded, that the Priests should be restored. But a voice was immediately heard from the wall (as coming from a Crucifix behind *Dunstan*) saying, *They think amiss that favour the Priests*. That was received as a Divine Oracle, and the Priests were secluded from their Benefices and Monasteries.

    A second Council was called at *Kirtlington* (now *Catlage* in *Cambridgeshire*) but to little effect. The same year a third Council was called at *Calu* in *Wilt-shire*, hither came Priests and Monks in great numbers. *Beornelm*, a Scottish Bishop, defended the cause of the Priests with Scripture and Reason. But on a sudden *Dunstan* by his Art caused the
catal. list. Beams or Joists of the Room where they were assembled to break and
writ. fall: many were wounded; most of the Secular Priests were slain, and buried under the ruines thereof: only *Dunstan* was safe with his Chair that was fixed on a Pillar. So the controversie was ended with devilish cruelty. It appears not what provision was made for these Priests when ejected.

    King *Edward* went to *Corff-Castle*; where at that time his Mother-in-Law with her Son *Egelred* lay; and by her contrivance he was barbarously murthered as he was drinking on Horse-back, and was buried at *Wareham*: and *Ethelred*, *Edward*'s half-brother, succeeded him in the Throne.

    Dunstan died, and was buried on the South-side of the high Altar in the Church of *Canterbury*. After his death, the Monks were cast out

of

of the Convent of *Canterbury*, by reason of their misdemeanours.

Siricius, the next Archbishop of *Canterbury*, endeavoured the re-expulsion of the Priests, which by *Elfrick* his Successor was effected. By him a Sermon was appointed to be read publickly on *Easter-day* before the Communion. The same Author hath two other Treatises; one directed to *Wolfsin* Bishop of *Shirburn*, and another to *Wulfstan* Bishop of *York*, about the Sacrament.

Soon after, the *Danes* by a firm Ejection outed the Monks, before they were well warm in their Nests: Their fury fell more on Convents than Castles. *England* for these last sixty years had been freed from their cruelty, which now returned more dreadful than ever before. These *Danes* were also advantaged by the unactiveness of King *Ethelred*, who with ten thousand pounds purchased a present Peace with the *Danes*. The multitude of Monasteries invited the Invasion, and facilitated the Conquest of the *Danes* over *England*.

Holy Island was forsaken by the fearful Monks, affrighted with the approach of the *Danes*: and *Alhunus*, the Bishop thereof, removed his Cathedral and Convent to *Durham*, an Inland place of more safety. The *Danes* having received and spent their Money, invaded *England* afresh, according to all Wise mens expectation.

Cent. XI.

IN the beginning of this Century certain *Danes* fled into a Church at *Oxford*, hoping the Sanctity thereof (according to the devout Principles of that Age) would secure them. But by command from *King* *Ethelred*, they were all burned in the place, whose blood remained not long unrevenged. The Danish fury fell fiercest on the City of *Canterbury* with fire and sword, destroying eight thousand people therein. *Swanus* the *Dane* tithed the Monks of S. *Augustine*'s Abbey, killing nine by cruel torment, and keeping the tenth alive for slaves. They slew there of Religious men, to the number of nine hundred. And when they had kept the Bishop *Elphege* in strait prison the space of eight months (because he would not agree to give them three thousand pounds) after many villanies done unto him, at *Greenwich* they stoned him to death. Next year a nameless Bishop of *London* was slain by them; and a great part of the City of *London* was wasted with fire. The *Danes* burnt *Cambridge* to ashes, and harassed the Country round about.

King *Ethelred* sent his Wife *Emma*, with his two Sons, *Alfred* and *Edward*, to *Richard* Duke of *Normandy*, which was Brother to the said *Emma*, with whom also he sent the Bishop of *London*, whither also himself went, after he had spent a great part of the Winter in the Isle of
F *Wight*.

Wight, whither he was chased of the *Danes*. *Swanus* hearing that *Egelred* was departed out of the Land, imposed great Exactions upon the people; and among other he required a great sum of money of S. *Edmond*'s Lands, which the people there claiming to be free of all King's tribute, denied to pay. Hereupon *Swanus* entred the Territory of St. *Edmond*, and wasted the Countrey, threatening to spoil the place of his burial. The men of the Countrey fell to fasting and prayer, and soon after *Swanus* died suddenly, crying and yelling among his Knights. In fear whereof *Canutus*, his Son and Successor, ditched the Land of St. *Edmond* with a deep Ditch, and granted to the Inhabitants thereof great Immunities, quitting them from all Tribute, and after builded a Church over the place of his Sepulture, ordained there an House of Monks, and endowed them with rich possessions. After that time, the Kings of *England* when they were crowned, sent their Crowns for an offering to St. *Edmond*'s Shrine, and redeemed them afterward with a condign price.

After the death of *Egelred*, great contention was in *England* for the Crown: some were for *Edmond Ironside* the Son of *Egelred*, and some for *Canutus*. After many bloody Fights, both parties agree to try the quarrel betwixt them two only: in sight of both Armies they make the Essay with Swords and sharp strokes: in the end upon the motion of *Canutus* they agree, and kiss one another, to the joy of both Armies, and they covenant for parting the Land during their lives, and they lived as Brethren. Within a few years a Son of *Edrik* Duke of *Mercia* killed *Edmond* traiterously, and brought his two Sons unto *Canutus*, who sent them to his Brother *Swanus*, King of *Denmark*, willing him to dispatch them. But he abhorring such a fact, sent them to *Solomon* King of *Hungary*, who married *Edwyn* to his Daughter, and soon after died. *Edward* married *Agatha* the Daughter of the Emperour *Henry* the Third.

Swanus King of *Denmark* died; and that Land fell to *Canutus*, who anon after sailed thither, and took the possession, and returned into *England*, and married *Emma*, late Wife of *Egelred*, and by her had a Son called *Hardiknout*. He assembled a Parliament at *Oxford*, wherein was agreed, that *English* men and *Danes* should hold the Laws made by King *Edgar*, as most just and reasonable: He established Laws Ecclesiastical, as well as Civil. *Canutus* went on pilgrimage to *Rome*, and there founded an Hospital for English Pilgrims: He shrined the body of *Bernius*, and gave great Lands to the Cathedral Church of *Winchester*: He builded St. *Bennet*'s in *Norfolk*, which was before an *Hermitage*. Also St. *Edmond's-bury*, which King *Athelstane* ordained before for a Colledge of Priests, he turned to an Abbey of Monks of Saint *Bennet's* Order.

The Church of Great Britain.

Two of his Sons succeeded him, first his base Son, called, from his swiftness, *Harold, Harefoot*, a man of a cowardly disposition. He reigned but four years, and the Kingdom fell to *Hardiknout* King of Denmark, his Brother, who when he had reigned two years, being drunk at *Lambeth*, suddenly was stricken dumb, and fell down to the ground, and within eight dayes after died without issue of his Body. Thus ended the Danish Kings: which *Danes* had vexed and wasted the Land two hundred fifty five years.

When *England* was freed from the *Danes*, they sent into *Normandy*, inviting over *Edward* the Confessor, and brother to King *Edmond*   He was crowned *Anno* 1045. In his time was the Law made which concerned the King's Oath at Coronation. *Mathew Paris* describes the Manners of the Countrey at his coming thus, *The Nobles were given to gluttony and leachery: they went not to Church in the morning, but only had a Priest, which made haste with the Mass and Mattens in their chambers, and they heard a little with their ears. The Clergy were so ignorant, that if any knew the Grammar, he was admired by them: most men spent nights and dayes in carousing.* In his dayes *England* injoyed *Halcion* dayes, free from Danish invasions.

The Ecclesiastical Laws, made by this King in his reign, were.

I. *That every Clerk and Scholar should quietly enjoy their goods and possessions.*
II. *What solemn Festivals people may come and go of, without any Lawsuits to disturb them.*
III. *That in all Courts where the Bishop's Proctor doth appear, his case is first to be heard and determined.*
IV. *That guilty folk flying to the Church should there have protection, not to be reproved by any, but the Bishop and his Ministers.*
V. *That Tithes be paid to the Church of Sheep, Pigs, Bees, and the like.*
VI. *How the Ordal was to be ordered for the trial of guilty persons by fire and water.*
VII. *That Peter-pence, or Rome-scot, be faithfully paid to the Pope.*

This King is reported to have entailed (by Heaven's Consort) an hereditary vertue on his Successors the Kings of *England* (only with this condition, that they continue constant in Christianity) to cure the King's Evil.

In this King's reign lived *Marianus Scotus*, that wrote much of the deeds of the Kings of *England*.

The History of

King *Edward* died childless. *Harold* the Son of Earl *Godwin* succeeded him. Indeed the undoubted right lay in *Edgar Atheling*, Son to *Edward* the Outlaw, Grandchild to *Edmond Iron-side* King of *England*. But he being young and tender, and of a soft temper, and *Harold* being rich and strong in *K*nights, the Nobles chose *Harold* to be their *K*ing. As soon as he was crowned, he established many good Laws, especially such as were for the good of the Church, and for the punishment of evil-doers.

Harold was slain in a battel near *Hastings* in *Sussex*, and *William* Duke of *Normandy* obtained the Crown of *England* by conquest: within a few years he made a great alteration in *England*: the most part of his Knights and Bishops were *Normans* ; and many English with *Edgar* fled into *Scotland*, where King *Malcolm* had married *Edgar*'s Sister *Margaret*. They incited *Malcolm* to invade *England*, and he entred into the North part. At last a peace was concluded, and a Mark-stone was set up in *Stanmoor*, as the mark of both Kingdoms, with the Pourtraict of both Kings on the sides of the Stone.

Although then corruptions crept into the Church by degrees, and divine worship began then to be clogged with superstitious Ceremonies, yet that the Doctrine remained still entire in most material points, will appear by an Induction of the dominative Controversies, wherein we differ from the Church of *Rome*, as *Fuller* in his Church-History of *Britain* hath observed.

I. *Scripture generally read.*

Bed. Eccl. hist.
lib. 3. ca. 5.

For such as were with the holy Bishop *Aidan*, either Clergy, or Laity, were tyed to exercise themselves in reading the holy Word, and in singing of Psalms.

II. *The Original preferred.*

Caradoc. in
Chron. of
Cambridge.

For *Ricemath* a *Britain*, a right learned and godly Clerk, Son to *Sulgen*, Bishop of St. *David*'s, flourishing in this Age, made this Epigram on those who translated the Psalter out of the Greek, so taking it at the second hand, and not drawing it immediately from the first vessel.

Ebreis nablam custodit litera signis,
Pro captu quam quisque suo sermone latino
Edidit, innumeros lingua variante libellos
Ebreumque jubar suffuscat nube latina, &c.

This Harp the holy Hebrew Text doth tender,
Which, to their power, whil'st every one doth render

the Church of Great Britain. 37

In Latine tongue with many variations,
He clouds the Hebrew rays with his tranflation.
Thus liquors when twice fhifted out, and pour'd
In a third veffel, are both cool'd and fowr'd.
But holy *Jerome* Truth to light doth bring,
Briefer and fuller fetcht from the Hebrew Spring.

III. *No Prayers for the dead in the modern notion of Papifts.*

For though we find prayers for the dead, yet they were not in the nature of propitiation for their fins, or to procure relaxation from their torments: but were only an honourable commemoration of their memories, and a Sacrifice of thankfgiving for their falvation.

IV. *Purgatory then not perfected, though newly invented.*

For although there are frequent Vifions and Revelations in this Age pretended, thereon to build Purgatory (which had no ground in Scripture) yet it ftood not then as now it ftands in the Romifh belief.

V. *Communion under both kinds.*

For *Bede* relateth, that one *Hildmer*, an Officer of *Egfride* King of *Northumberland*, entreated our *Cuthbert* to fend a Prieft that might minifter the Sacrament of the Lord's Body and Blood unto his Wife, that then lay a dying. And *Cuthbert* himfelf immediately before his own departure out of this life, received the communion of the Lord's Body and Blood. So that the Eucharift was then adminiftred entire, and not maimed as it is by the Papifts at this day. And though the word *Mafs* was frequent in that Age, yet was it not known to be offered as a propitiatory Sacrifice for the quick and dead.

King *William* to teftifie his thankfulnefs to God for his Victory, founded in that place *Battel-Abbey*, endowing it with Revenues, and large immunities: The Abbot whereof (being a Baron of Parliament) carried a pardon in his prefence, who cafually coming to the place of execution, had power to fave any Malefactor. The Abby-Church was a place of fafety for any Fellon or Murtherer. Here the Monks flourifhed in all abundance till the dayes of *Henry* the Eighth.

Then *Dooms-day* Book was made, containing an exact furvay of the Houfes and Lands in the Kingdom, which took up fome years before it was compleated.

King *William* called a Council of his Bifhops at *Winchefter*, wherein he was perfonally prefent, with two Cardinals fent from *Rome*. Here
Stigand

Stigand Archbishop of *Canterbury* was deposed, and *Lanfrank* a *Lombard* substituted in his room.

Sir *John Davys* in his *Irish* report.

A learned Lawyer hath observed, that the first encroachment of the Pope upon the Liberties of the Crown of *England*, was made in the time of King *William* the Conqueror. For the Conqueror came in with the Pope's Banner, and under it won the battel, which got him the Garland, and therefore the Pope presumed he might boldly pluck some flowers from it, being partly gained by his countenance and blessing.

Although this politick Prince was complementally courteous to the *See of Rome*; yet 1. He retained the ancient custom of the *Saxon* Kings, investing Bishops and Abbots by delivering them a Ring and a Staff, whereby without more ado they were put into plenary possession of the power and profit of their place. He said, *He would keep all Pastoral Staves in his own hand.*

2. Being demanded to do Fealty for his Crown of *England* unto Pope *Gregory* the Seventh, he wrote thus unto him, *That he would not do Fealty unto the Pope, because neither had he promised it, nor did he find his Predecessors had performed it.*

3. This King would in no wise suffer any one in his Dominion to acknowledge the Bishop of *Rome* for Apostolical without his command; or to receive the Pope's Letters, except first they had been shewed unto him. And although the Archbishop of *Canterbury* by his own Authority might congregate Councils, and sit as President therein: yet the King permitted him to appoint or prohibit nothing, but what was according to his own will; and what the King had ordained before.

4. The King suffered no Bishop to excommunicate any of his Barons, or Officers, for Adultery, Incest, or any such hainous crime, except by the King's command, first made acquainted with the same.

This King gave unto the Bishops an entire Jurisdiction by themselves to judge all causes relating to Religion, for before that time the Sheriff and Bishop kept their Court together. He granted the Clergy throughout *England* Tithes of Calves, Colts, Lambs, Milk, Butter, Cheese, Woods, Meadows, Mills, &c.

Then *Thomas* a *Norman* was preferred to the Archbishoprick of *York*. Betwixt *Lanfrank* Archbishop of *Canterbury*, and this *Thomas*, there grew great contention for the Oath of Obedience, but in the end, *Thomas* subscribed obedience to the other. Then it was decreed, that *York* for that time should be subject to *Canterbury* in matters appertaining to the Church: so that wheresoever within *England* the Archbishop of *Canterbury* would hold his Council, the Bishops of *York* should resort thither with their Bishops, and be obedient to his Decrees Canonical.

Then were divers Bishops Seats altered from Villages to great Cities; as of *Stalsey* to *Chichester*: out of *Cornwall* to *Exeter*: from *Wells* to *Bath*;

The Church of Great Britain.

Bath; from *Shirburn* to *Salisbury*; from *Dorchester* in *Oxford-shire* to *Lincoln*; from *Lichfield* to *Chester*; which Bishoprick of *Chester*, *Robert*, then Bishop, reduced from *Chester* to *Coventry*.

At this time several Liturgies were used in *England*, which caused confusion, and much disturbed mens devotions. A brawl happened betwixt the *English* Monks of *Glastonbury*, and *Thurstan* their *Norman* Abbot, in their very Church, obtruding a Service upon them which they disliked: eight Monks were wounded, and two slain near the steps of the high Altar. This ill accident occasioned a settlement, and uniformity of Liturgy all over *England*: for hereupon *Osmund* Bishop of *Salisbury*, devised that form of Service, which hereafter was observed in the whole Realm. Henceforward the most ignorant Parish-Priest in *England* understood the meaning of, *Secundum usum Sarum*; that all Service must be ordered, *According to the course and custom of* Salisbury *Church*. An uniformity of Liturgy all over *England*.

King *William* brought many *Jews* into *England* (for before his reign I find none in this Land) from *Roan* in *Normandy*; and setled them in *London*, *Norwich*, *Cambridge*, *Northampton*.

In the dayes of *Lanfrank*, *Waltelm* Bishop of *Winchester*, had placed about forty Canons instead of Monks; but it held not, for *Lanfrank* cast out secular Priests, and substituted Monks in their rooms. He also contested with *Odo* Bishop of *Bayeux* (though half-Brother to King *William*, and Earl of *Kent*) and in a legal Trial regained many Lordships, which *Odo* had unjustly invaded.

Although in this King's time there was almost no English-man that bare Office of honour or rule, yet he favoured the City of *London*, and granted them the first Charter that ever they had, written in the Saxon tongue, and sealed with green Wax, expressed in eight or nine lines.

King *William* died in *Normandy*, and *William Rufus*, his second Son, was crowned King of *England*. He began very bountifully; to some Churches he gave ten Marks, to others six, to every Countrey-Village five shillings, besides an hundred pounds to every County to be distributed among the poor. But afterward he proved very parcimonious, though no man more prodigal of never performed Promises. *Anno* 1088.

This year died *Lanfrank* Archbishop of *Canterbury*, after whose death the King seized the profits of that See into his own hand, and kept the Church vacant for some years. He kept at the same time the Archbishoprick of *Canterbury*, the Bishopricks of *Winchester* and *Durham*, and thirteen Abbies in his hand, and brought a mass of Money into his Exchequer. All places which he parted with, was upon present payment. He quarrelled with *Remigius* Bishop of *Lincoln*, about the founding of his Cathedral, and forced him to buy his peace. And without a sum of Money paid to the King, *John* Bishop of *Wells* could not remove his Seat to *Bath*.

King

King *Rufus* coming to *Glocester*, fell very sick: hereupon he made *Anselm* (the Abbot of *Beck* in *Normandy*) one of eminent learning, and strictness of life, Archbishop of *Canterbury*. The King soon after sent to him for a thousand pounds, which *Anselm* refused to pay.

Herbert Bishop of *Thetford* founded the Cathedral at *Norwich*.

Then *Herbert*, Bishop of *Thetford*, removed his Episcopal Seat from *Thetford* to *Norwich*, where he first founded the Cathedral. Then died *Wolstan* Bishop of *Worcester*, an English-man born, a mortified man.

Near this time began the holy War. *Robert* Duke of *Normandy*, to fit himself for that Voyage, sold his Dukedome to King *William Rufus* for ten thousand Marks. To pay this money King *Rufus* laid a grievous Tax over all the Realm, extorting it with such severity, that the Monks were fain to sell the Church-plate, and very Chalices, for discharging thereof. And when the Clergy desired to be eased of their burdens; *I beseech you* (said he) *have ye not Coffins of gold and Silver for dead mens bones?* intimating, that the same Treasure might otherwise be better employed.

At this time there was contention at *Rome* between two Popes, *Urban* and *Clement* the Third. *Rufus* took part with *Clement*; but *Anselm* stuck to *Urban*, and required of the King leave to fetch his Pall of *Urban*. All the rest of the Bishops were against him. Mean-while the King had sent two Messengers to the Pope for the Pall, who returned, and brought with them *Gualter* Bishop of *Alban*, the Pope's Legate, with the Pall to be given to *Anselm*. Which Legate so perswaded the King, that *Urban* was received Pope through the whole Land. But afterwards grew great displeasure betwixt them, so that *Anselm* went to appear to *Rome*, where he remained in exile; and the King seized all his Goods and Lands into his own Coffers. *Urban* gave unto *Anselm* the Archbishops Pall, thereby voiding the Investiture which he received from King *William*, and obliging him there-after to depend on him: as also he did, whereat the King incensed, interdicted to *Anselm* his entry into *England*, confiscated the Lands of the Archbishoprick, and declared, that his Bishops held their Places and Estates merely from him, and were not subject unto the Pope for the same. To which all the Bishops of *England* subscribed: neither did any of them contradict it, but the onely Bishop of *Rochester*, as a Suffragan to the Archbishop of *Canterbury*.

By the intervention of Friends *Anselm* made his peace: But being returned into *England*, he soon after began to disswade the Clergy from receiving Investitures from the King; wherefore he was forced again to fly out of the Kingdom, and his estate was again seized upon and confiscated, of which he had obteined restitution at his return.

King *William* the Conqueror had made the new-forrest in *Hant-shire*, with a great devastation of Towns and Churches, the place (as *Fuller* saith) being turned into a Wilderness for Men, and a Paradise for Deer.

Deer. King *Ruffus* hunting in this Forreſt, was here ſlain by the glancing of an arrow, ſhot by Sir *Walter Tirrell*, and was buried at *Wincheſter*. He gave to the Monks, called *De Charitate*, the great new Church of S. *Saviours* in *Bermondſey*, with the Manor thereof, as alſo of *Charleton* in *Kent*.

Henry Beaucleark his Brother, ſucceeded him in the throne, being one of the profoundeſt Scholars, and moſt politick Princes in his generation. To ingratiate himſelf to the Engliſh, he inſtantly and actually repealed the cruel Norman Lawes, the good and gentle Laws of King *Edward* the Confeſſor he reduced, with correction of them: *Anſelm* from exile was ſpeedily recalled, and to his Church, Lands, and Goods, was fully reſtored. The late King's extorting Publicanes (whereof *Ranulph Flambard*, Biſhop of *Durham*, the principal) were impriſoned, the Court-corruption reformed; Adultery (then grown common) ſeverely puniſhed.

Cent. XII.

King *Henry* was Married to *Mawd*, Daughter to *Malcolm* King of *Scots*, who lived ſometime as a Nun under the tuition of *Chriſtian* her Aunt, Abbeſs of *Wilton*: She was Siſter to *Edgar Atheling*, and Grand-child of *Edmond Iron-ſide*, whereby his Iſſue might merely be both of the Engliſh Blood, and of the Ancient Saxon Kings.

Anſelm ſummoneth a Council at *Weſtminſter*, where firſt he Excommunicated all Married Prieſts, half the Clergy at that time being Married, or the Sons of Married Prieſts: he alſo inhibited all Lay-men to hear their Maſſes. He alſo deprived many great Prelates of their promotions, becauſe they had accepted their Inveſtitures from the King, which was done by receiving of a Paſtoral Staffe and a Ring, an Ancient rite, teſtifying that their Donation was from their Sovereign: in which number were the Abbots of *Ely*, of *Romſey*, of *Perſhore*, of St. *Edmonds*, of *Taveſtock*, *Peterborough*, *Burch*, *Bodiac*, *Stoke*, and *Middleton*: for which his boldneſs, and for refuſing to Conſecrate certain Biſhops advanced by the King, great contention fell betwixt them: and *Anſelm* appealed to Pope *Paſchal*, and ſoon after fled to *Rome*. Hereupon the King enjoyned *Gerard* Archbiſhop of *York* to Conſecrate *William* of *Winchester*, *Roger* of *Hereford*, &c. But *William* Biſhop of *Wincheſter* refuſed Conſecration from the Archbiſhop of *York*, and reſigned his Staff and Ring back again to the King as illegally from him. This diſcompoſed all the reſt.

But not long after by the mediation of Friends the King and *Anſelm* are reconciled; the King diſclaiming his right of Inveſtiture. And now *Anſelm* who formerly refuſed, conſecrated all the Biſhops of vacant Sees. Then did *Anſelm* forbid the Prieſts Marriage. But *Anſelm* died before

before he could finish his project of Priests divorces. His two next Successors, *Rodulphus* and *William Corbel*, went on vigorously with the design, but met with many and great obstructions: Other Bishops found the like opposition, but chiefly the Bishop of *Norwich*, whose obstinate Clergy would keep their Wives in defiance of his endeavours against them. But they were forced to forgo their Wives. Among those Married Priests there was one *Ealphegus* flourishing for Learning and Piety; he resided at *Plymouth* in *Devon-shire*

To order the refractory Married Clergy, the Bishops were fain to call in the aid of the Pope. *John* Bishop of *Cremona*, an Italian Cardinal, did urge the single Life of the Clergy, and said, *It is a vile crime, that a Man rising from the side of his Concubine, should consecrate the Body of Christ.* The same Night he was taken in bed with a Whore, after he had spoken those words in a Synod at *London*. The thing was so notorious, that it could not be denied, saith *Matthew Paris*. This much advantaged the reputation of Married Priests: The King taking a fine of Married Priests, permitted them to enjoy their Wives.

About this time the old Abbey of *Ely* was advanced into a new Bishoprick, and *Cambridge-shire* assigned for it's Diocess, taken from the Bishoprick of *Lincoln*. *Spaldwick* Manor in *Huntington-shire* was given to *Lincoln*, in reparation of the jurisdiction taken from it, and bestowed on *Ely*. One *Hervey*, who had been banished by the *Welch* from the poor Bishoprick of *Bangor*, was made the first Bishop of *Ely*. King *Henry* bestowed great Priviledges upon that Bishoprick.

Hervey, the first Bishop of *Ely*.

Then *Bernard*, Chaplain to the King, and Chancellor to the Queen, was the first *Norman*, made Bishop of St. *Davids*; who soon denied subjection to *Canterbury*, and would be an absolute Archbishop of himself: But *William* Archbishop of *Canterbury*, aided by the Pope, at last forced the Bishop of St. *Davids* to a submission.

King *Henry* died at the Town of St. *Denys* in *Normandy* of a surfeit by eating of Lampreys. He was buried at *Reading* in *Bark-shire* in the Abbey that himself had there founded and endowed with large possessions.

Stephen, Earl of *Bologn*, hearing of King *Henrie*'s Death, hasteth over into *England*, and seizeth on the Crown. He was Son to *Adela*, Daughter to King *William* the Conqueror; but *Mawd* first Married to *Henry* the Emperor of *Germany*, was the undoubted heir of the Crown. She was constantly called the Empress after the Death of the Emperor, though Married to *Geoffery Plantagenet*, her second Husband. Unto her all the Clergy, and Nobility had sworn fealty in her Father's life-time.

William Archbishop of *Canterbury*, notwithstanding his Oath to *Mawd*, solemnly Crowned *Stephen*, shewing himself thereby perjured to his God, disloyal to his Princess, and ingrateful to his Patroness, by whose special favour he had been preserved. The rest of the Bishops (to their shame) followed.

The Church of Great Britain.

followed his example, hoping to obtain from an Usurper, what they could not get from a Lawful King, traiterously avowing, That it was baseness for so many, and so great Peers to be subject to a Woman.

King *Stephen* sealed a Charter at *Oxford*, *Anno* 1136. the Tenor whereof is, *That all Liberties, Customs, and Possessions granted to the Church, should be firm and in force; That all Persons and Causes Ecclesiastical, should appertain onely to Ecclesiastical Judicature; That none but Clergy-men should ever intermeddle with the Vacancies of Churches, or any Church-mens goods; That all bad usages in the Land touching Forrests, Exactions*, &c. *should be utterly extirpate, the antient Laws restored*, &c. Speeds Chron.

The Clergy perceiving that King *Stephen* performed little of his large promises to them, were not formerly so forward in setting him up, but now more ready to pluck him down, and sided effectually with *Mawd* against him. *Stephen* fell violently on the Bishops, who then were most powerful in the Land: He imprisoned *Roger* Bishop of *Sarisbury*, till he had surrendered unto him the two Castles of *Shirburn*, and the *Devizes*, for the which *Roger* took such thought, that he died shortly after, and left in ready Coin forty thousand Marks, which after his Death came to the King's Coffers: he also uncastled *Alexander* of *Lincoln*, and *Nigellus* of *Ely*, taking a great Mass of Treasure from them. The Dean and Canons of *Pauls*, for crossing him in the choice of their Bishop, tasted of his fury, for he took their *Focarias*, and cast them into the Tower of *London*, where they continued many dayes, till at last their liberty was purchased by the Canons at a great price. *Roger Hoveden* tells us plainly, that these *Focariæ* were those Canons Concubines. See here the fruit of forbidding Marriage to the Clergy, against the Law of God and Nature.

Albericus, Bishop of *Hostia*, was sent by Pope *Innocent* into *England*, called a Synod at *Westminster*, where 18 Bishops, and thirty Abbots met together. Here was concluded, *That no Priest, Deacon, or sub-deacon, should hold a Wife or Woman within his House, under pain of degrading from his Christendom, and plain sending to Hell. That no Priest's Son should claim any Spiritual Living by heritage. That none should take a Benefice of any Lay-man. That none should be admitted to Cure, which had not the letters of his Orders. That Priests should do no bodily labour. And that their Transubstantiated God should dwell but eight dayes in the Box, for fear of worm-eating, moulding, or stinking.* In this Synod *Theobald*, Abbot of *Becco* was chosen Archbishop of *Canterbury*, in the place of *William* lately Deceased. Fuller.Church History.

The most considerable Clergy-man of *England* in this Age, for Birth, Wealth, and Learning, was *Henry* of *Blois*, Bishop of *Winchester*, and Brother to King *Stephen*. He was made by the Pope his Legat for *Britain*.

In this Council, where *William* of *Malmesbury* was present, there were three parties assembled with their attendance.

1. *Roger* of *Sarisbury*, with the reft of the Bishops, grievously complaining of their Castles taken from them.
2. *Henry* Bishop of *Winchester*, the Pope's Legat, and President of the Council: with *Theobald* Archbishop of *Canterbury*, pretending to Umpire matters moderately.
3. *Hugh* Archbishop of *Roan*, and *Aubery de Vere* (Anceftor to the Earl of *Oxford*) as Advocate for King *Stephen*.

This *Aubery de Vere* was Learned in the Laws, being charactered by my Author, *Homo causarum varietatibus exercitatus*, a man well versed in the windings of Causes. This Synod brake up without any extraordinary matter effected: For soon after Queen *Mawd* came with her Navy and Army out of *Normandy*, which turned Debates into Deeds, and Consultations into Actions.

There were many Religious Foundations built and endowed in the troublesom Reign of King *Stephen*; not to speak of the Monastery of St. *Mary de Pratis* founded by *Robert* Earl of *Leicester*, and many others of this time; the goodly Hospital of St. *Katherines* nigh *London*, was founded by *Mawd*, Wife to King *Stephen*. So stately was the Quire of this Hospital, that it was not much inferior to that of St. *Pauls* in *London*, when taken down in the dayes of Queen *Elizabeth*, by Doctor *Thomas Wilson*, the Master thereof, and Secretary of State: Yea King *Stephen* himself erected St. *Stephen*'s Chappel in *Westminster*. He built also the Ciftertians Monastery in *Feversham*, with an Hospital near the West-gate in *York*.

The King earnestly urged *Theobald* Archbishop of Canterbury to Crown his Son *Eustace*. But *Theobald* stoutly refused, thou.. proscribed for the same, and forced to fly the Land, till after some time he was reconciled to the King. *Eustace* the King's Son died of a Frenzy, as going to plunder the Lands of *Bury-Abbey*. Hereupon an agreement was made between King *Stephen*, and *Henry* Duke of *Normandy*, Son of *Mawd* the Empress, the former holding the Crown during his Life, and after his Death setling the same on *Henry*, his adopted Son and Successor.

Platina in Adriano. IV. At this time *Nicholas Breakspear*, an English-man, born near *Uxbridge*, came to be Pope, called *Adrian* the fourth; he was not inferior to *Hildebrand* in Pride. Shortly after he had Excomunicated the Emperor, he walked with his Cardinals, to refresh himself, in the Fields of *Anagnia*; and coming to a Spring of Water he would taste of it; and with the Water a Fly entreth into his Throat, and choaketh him. In the latter end of his Dayes he was wont to say, *There is not a more wretched Life than*

to

the Church of Great Britain. 45

to be Pope. To come into the seat of St. Peter by Ambition, is not to succeed Peter in Feeding the Flock, but unto Romulus in Paracide; seeing that Seat is never obtained without some Brother's Blood.   Matth. Paris.

King *Stephen* died, and was buried with his Son and Wife at *Feversham* in *Kent*, in a Monastery which himself had Erected. At the Demolishing whereof, some to gain the Lead wherein he was wrapped, cast his Corpse into the Sea.

King *Henry* the second succeeded him; a Prince Wise, Valiant, and generally Fortunate. He presently chose a Privy-Counsel of Clergy and Temporalty, and refined the Common Laws: yea toward the latter end of his Reign began the use of our Itinerant Judges. He parcelled *England* into six divisions, and appointed three Judges to every Circuit. He razed most of the Castles of *England* to the ground, the Bishops being then the greatest Traders in those Fortifications.

He disclaimed all the Authority of the Pope, refused to pay *Peter-pence*, and interdicted all Appeals to *Rome*. At that time *Philip de Brok*, a Canon of *Bedford*, was questioned for Murther; he used reproachful speeches to the King's Justices, for which he was Censured; and the Judges complained unto the King, that there were many Robberies, and Rapes, and Murthers, to the number of an hundred, committed within the Realm by Church-men.

Thomas Becket, Doctor of Canon-law, was by the King made Lord Chancellor of *England*. Four years after upon the Death of *Theobald*, *Becket* was made by the King Archbishop of *Canterbury*.

Anno 1160. Thirty Teachers come from *Germany* into *England*, and taught the right use of Baptism, and the Lord's Supper, &c. and were put to Death. Then *John* of *Sarum*, and others, taught, that the Roman Church was the Whore of *Babylon*. Some were burnt with an hot Iron at *Oxford*, that dissented from the Roman Church.

The King Commanded that Justice should be executed upon all Men alike in his Courts: but *Thomas Becket* would have the Clergy (so offending) judged in the Ecclesiastical Court, and by Men of their own Coat. This Incensed the King against him. To retrench these enormities of the Clergy, the King called a Parliament at *Clarendon* near *Sarisbury*, to confirm the Antient Laws and Customs, to which *Becket* with the rest of the Bishops consented and subscribed them; but afterwards recanting his own Act, renounced the same.

The same year the King required to have punishment of some misdoings among the Clergy. The Archbishop would not permit; and when he saw (in his judgement) the Liberties of the Church trodden under Foot; he without the King's knowledge took Ship, and intended toward *Rome*; but by a contrary Wind he was brought back. Then he was called to account for his Receipts, that came to his hand while he was High-Chancellor. He appealeth to the See of *Rome*; and, under pain

of

of Excommunication, forbad both Bishops and Nobles to give Sentence against him, seeing he was both their Father and their Judge. Nevertheless they, without his consent, gave Sentence against him. Then he, seeing himself forsaken of all the other Bishops, lifted the Cross which he held in his Hand aloft, and went away from the Court; and the next day got him over into *Flanders*, and so to the Pope.

Matthew Paris hath many Letters betwixt the Pope and this King, and the King of *France*, and sundry Bishops of *France* and *England*, for reconciliation betwixt the King and the Archbishop, who abode seven years in exile. *Thomas Becket* quarrelled with *Roger* Archbishop of *York* for presuming to Crown *Henry* the King's Son (made joint-King in the Life of his Father) a priviledge which *Becket* claimed as proper to him alone. He solemnly resigned his Archbishoprick to the Pope, as troubled in Conscience, that he had formerly took it as illegally from the King; and the Pope again restored it to him, whereby all scruples in his mind were fully satisfied.

But afterward by the Mediation of the French King, *Becket* had leave given him to return into *England*; howsoever the King still retained his Temporals in his Hand, on weighty considerations, namely to shew their distinct Nature from the Spirituals of the Archbishoprick, to which alone they Pope could restore him.

Thomas returning into *England* Excommunicateth all the Bishops, which had been at the Coronation of the young King. The King sent, and required him to absolve them, seeing what was done to them, was done for his Cause: but *Thomas* refuseth.

The next year after, he Excommunicated solemnly the Lord *Sackvill* appointed by the King, Vicar of the Church at *Canterbury*, because he did derogate from the rights of the Church to please the King. He also Excommunicated one *Robert Brook* for cutting off an Horses tail, that carried Victuals to the Archbishops House.

The King being then in *Normandy*, grieved very sore before his Servants at the insolent cariage of *Thomas Becket*. This moved Sir *Richard Breton*, Sir *Hugh Morvil*, Sir *William Tracey*, Sir *Reginald Fitz-Urse*, to return into *England*; and coming to *Canterbury*, they found the Archbishop in Cathedral Church, at three a Clock in the After-noon, and calling him Traytor to the King, they slew him, and dashed his Brains upon the floor. His last words when he died, were, *I commend my self and God's Cause unto God, and to the blessed* Mary, *and to the Saints Patrons of this Church, and to St.* Denis.

Here see the lightness of the People; for the same Men that detested the pride of that *Thomas*, began to Worship him after his Death. Thus they sang of *Thomas Becket*.

Th

Tu per Thomæ sanguinem quem pro te impendit,
Fac nos Christe scandere quo Thomas *ascendit.*

By the Blood of *Thomas*, which for Thee he did spend,
Make us O Christ to climb whither *Thomas* did ascend.

Multitudes of People flocked to *Canterbury* yearly, especially on his Jubile, or each fifty years after his enshrining; an hundred thousand of English and Forreigners repaired thither. The Revenues of peoples Offerings amounted to more than six hundred pounds a year. Before *Becket*'s Death, the Cathedral in *Canterbury* was called *Christ-Church*, it was afterward called the Church of St. *Thomas*; though since by the demolishing of *Becket*'s shrine, the Church hath recovered it's Antient name.

King *Henry* protested himself innocent from the Death of *Thomas Becket*, yet was he willing to undergo such a penance as the Pope would impose. The Pope made him buy his Absolution at a dear rate. He enjoyned him to suffer Appeals from *England* to *Rome*; to quit his Rights and Claim to the Investitures; to keep two hundred Men of Armes in pay for the Holy War; of which pay the Popes Assignes were to be the Receivers; and that in *England* they should celebrate the Feast of that glorious Martyr St. *Thomas* of *Canterbury*. The words of the Bull are these, *We strictly charge you, that you solemnly Celebrate every year the Birth-day of the glorious Martyr* Thomas, *sometime Archbishop of* Canterbury, *that is, the day of his passion, and that by devout Prayers to him, you endeavour to merit the remission of your sins.*

To make the satisfaction compleat, King *Henry* passeth from *Normandy* into *England*, stayeth at *Canterbury*, strippeth himself naked, and is whipped by diverse Monks, of whom some gave him five lashes, some three.

Concerning which penance *Machiavel* speaks thus in the first Book of the Hostory of *Florence*; *These things were accepted by* Henry, *and so great a King submitted himself to that judgement, to which a private man in our dayes would be ashamed to submit himself.* Then he exclaimeth, *So much things that have some shew, are more dreaded afar off, than near hand*: Which he saith, *Because at the same time the Citizens of* Rome *expelled the Pope out of the City with disgrace, scorning his Excommunication*. This was done in the year of our Lord 1170. as appeareth by these Verses.

Le quali cose furono da En-
rico accettate,
et sotto- Messe
fi à quel giudi-
cio un tanto
Reche hoggi un
huomo privato
si vergogna-
rebbe sottometersi
&c. Tanto le
cose che paiono
sono più da di-
costo chi d' ap-
presse timute.

Anno Milleno, Centeno, Septuageno,
Anglorum *primas, corruit ense* Thomas.

In

In the year 1179. *Lewis* King of *France*, who had entertained *Thomas* at *Sens*, paffed over into *England* to Worfhip him, and made his Devotions to his Relicks. Then *Richard* Prior of *Dover*, who divided *Kent* into three Archdeaconries, was made Archbifhop of *Canterbury*. *Fabian* faith, *He was a man of evil living, and wafted the goods of the Church inordinately.*

Fabian. in Henry 2.

A Synod was called at *Weftminfter*, the Pope's Legat being prefent thereat, where was a great Contention between the two Archbifhops of *Canterbury* and *York* for Precedency; words begat blowes, and the Archbifhop of *Canterbury*'s party pulled *York* from his Seat to the ground, and tore his Cafule, Chimer, and Rochet from his Back; and put the Legat in fuch fear, that he ran away. The next day after *York* Appealeth to *Rome*. Here the Pope interpofed, and to end old divifions, made a new diftinction, Entitling *Canterbury*, Primate of all *England*; and *York*, Primate of *England*.

King *Henry* died at *Chinon* in *Normandy*, and was buried with very great Solemnity in the Nunnery of *Font-Everard* in the fame Countrey, a Religious Houfe of his own Foundation and Endowment. At that time were many Married Priefts in *Britain*.

His Son, *Richard* the firft, firnamed *Coeur de Lyon*, fucceeded him, and on *September*. 3. was crowned at *Weftminfter* of *Baldwin* Archbifhop of *Canterbury*. Then this King ordained the City of *London* to be ruled by two Bailiffs. The two firft Bailiffs were *Henry Chornhil*, and *Richard Fitz-River*. In the time of the Coronation of the King, multitudes of the Jews in this Land were deftroyed.

The King in part of fatisfaction for his trefpafs againft his Father (for Queen *Elianor* and his Sons had fided with the King of *France* againft him) agreed with *Philip* the French King to take upon them the recovery of the Holy Land. King *Richard* gave over the Caftles of *Barwick* and *Roxburgh* to the Scottifh King for the fum of ten thoufand pounds. He paffed away the Earldom of *Northumberland* unto *Hugh Pudfey* Bifhop of *Durham* for a great fum of Money for term of life; fcoffing, that he had made a young Earl of an old Bifhop. Befides, by the command-ment of Pope *Clement* the third, a tenth was exacted of the whole Realm

Fabian Chron.

The King fet over the Realm as principal in his abfence, the Bifhop of *Ely* his Chancellor, and the Bifhop of *Durham*; whom he ordained to be Chief Juftice of *England*. *Ely* to have cuftody of the Tower, with the overfight of all other parts of the Land on this fide *Humber*: and *Durham* to have charge over all other his Dominions beyond *Humber*. The Pope alfo made *William* Bifhop of *Ely* his Legate through all *England* and *Scotland*.

Fox. Acts and Monuments.

As for Men and Souldiers, the Prelates, Friars, and other Preachers, had ftirred up innumerable by their manifold exhortations (the Archbifhop

The Church of Great Britain. 49

bishop of *Canterbury* having travelled through *Wales* in Person for that purpose) in Pulpits and private Conferences. Then King *Richard* (with some of our English Nobility, who adventured their Persons in the Holy War) crossed the Seas into *France*, to *Philip* King thereof. After some necessary stayes, having passed the River *Rhene* at *Lions*, they parted company: *Philip* marching over the *Alpes* into *Italy*, and King *Richard* to the Sea-side at *Marsilia*, there to meet with his Navy. King *Richard's* Fleet of Ships being not come, he embarked himself in twenty hired Galleys, and ten great Busses (a kind of Shipping then peculiar to the Mediterranean Seas) and set Sayl toward *Messana* in *Sicily*, the Rendezvouz of both the Kings and their Armies. In which passage King *Richard* lying at Anchor (on occasion) in the mouth of the River *Tiber*, not far from *Rome*, *Octavianus* the Bishop of *Hostia* repaired unto him, desiring him in the Pope's name, that he would visit his Holiness: which the King denied to do, alleadging that the Pope and his Officers had taken 700 Marks for Consecration of the Bishop of *Mains*, 1500 Marks for the Legative power of *William* Bishop of *Ely*; but of the Archbishop of *Burdeaux* an infinite sum of Money; whereupon he refused to see *Rome*.

King *Richard* studying to fit himself for the great attempt he had in hand, called before him his Archbishops and Bishops, that accompanied him, into a Chappel at the House where he was lodged, where he made a penitent confession of his sins, humbly Praying to God for Mercy, and them (as his subordinate Ministers) for Absolution: and God (saith *R. Hoveden*) respected him with the eyes of Mercy, so that from thenceforth he feared God, eschewing evil, and doing good.

King *Richard* sent for *Joachim*, Abbot of *Calabria*, a Man of great Learning and Understanding in the Scriptures, who at his coming he heard expounding the Apocalypse of St. *John*, touching the afflictions of the Church, and the state of Antichrist, which (saith he) was then born, and in the City of *Rome*, of whom the Apostle said, *He should exalt himself above all that is called God.*

Afterwards, at the siege of *Acres*, or *Ptolemais* in *Palestine*, *Radulphus de alta ripa*, Archdeacon of *Colchester* ended his Life; there also died *Baldwin* Archbishop of *Canterbury*, and *Hubert Walter* Bishop of *Sarisbury* (afterward Archbishop of *Canterbury*) was a most active Commander there, besides many more of the eminent Clergy engaged in that service. *William* Bishop of *Ely* playd *Rex* in the King's absence, abusing the Royal Authority committed to him. *Acres* was delivered to the King's of *England* and *France*, who divided the spoil of that City betwixt them.

King *Richard* after this and many other notable Archievements in *Palestine*, at his return from thence, was taken Prisoner by *Leopald* Duke of *Austria*, and detained by him with hard and Unprince-like usage:

H whil'st

whil'ft the English Clergy endeavoured the utmost for his enlargement. His fine was an hundred and fifty thousand Marks, to be paid, part to the Duke of *Auſtria*, part to *Henry* VI. Emperor of *Germany*: Hubert Archbiſhop of *Canterbury* with much diligence perfected the work, and, on his ranſom paid, King *Richard* returned into *England*.

Hubert Walter, Archbiſhop of *Canterbury*, had almoſt finiſhed a fair Covent for Monks at *Lambeth*, begun by *Baldwin*, his Predeceſſor, but upon the petitions of the Monks of *Canterbury* to the Pope (contrary to the King's and Archbiſhop's deſire) the Covent at *Lambeth* was utterly demoliſhed.

As this *Richard*, was the firſt of the Engliſh Kings, who bare Armes on his Seals; ſo was he the firſt who carried in his ſhield *Three Lions Paſſant*, born ever after for the Regal Armes of *England*. This King's daily exerciſe after his return was to riſe early, and not to depart from the Church, till Divine Service were finiſhed. Moreover, he bountifully relieved every day much Poor, both in his Court and Towns about, and reſtored Gold and Silver to ſuch Churches from which to pay his ranſom they had been taken away.

The Biſhop of *Beavois* being alſo an Earl of the Royal Blood, and the eleventh Peer of *France*, valiantly fighting againſt *John* the King's Brother, was taken Armed at all points, and bravely mounted: on whoſe behalf the Pope (upon the Biſhop's humble ſuit, pleading the Clergy's immunity) wrote ſomewhat earneſtly to King *Richard*, to ſet his very dear Son (for ſo he called the Biſhop) at liberty. The King in a pleaſant manner cauſed the Habergeon and Curaſſes of the Biſhop to be preſented to the Pope, with this queſtion (alluding to that of *Jacob*'s Children to their Father, concerning *Joſeph*'s Garment) *Vide an haec ſit filii tui tunica, an non?* See whether this be thy Son's coat or not? Whereupon the Pope replied, *That he was neither his Son, nor the Son of the Church, and therefore ſhould be Ranſomed at the King's will; becauſe he was rather judged to be a ſervitor of* Mars, *than a Souldier of Chriſt*. Whom the King of *England* handled ſharply.

Anno 1199. One *Thyrical*, an Engliſh-man was in a rapture carried in the night to Purgatory, of which S. *Nicholas* is Governor, where alſo he ſaw the mouth of Hell, whence a ſtinking ſmoak iſſued out, which (as it was revealed to him) came out of Tithes detained, or ill paid, becauſe there thoſe Men were horribly puniſhed, who had ill-paid the Tithes due to the Church. This is related by *Mat. Paris*, a Monk of St. *Albans*, ſuperſtitious according to the Age that he lived in. Then alſo came the Minorite Friars into *England*; their Order being but lately inſtituted.

King *Richard* laying Siege to a Caſtle called *Chaluz* belonging to the Viſcount of *Limoges*, was ſhot into the Arm by a poiſoned Arrow, whereupon the Iron remaining and feſtering in the wound, the King within nine dayes after died, having firſt forgiven the Souldier before his Death.

King

When the Minorite Friars came into England.

the Church of Great Britain.

King *John* was Crowned in *Westminster-Abbey, June* 9. 1199. and was Sworn by *Hubert,* Archbishop of *Canterbury, Quod sanctam Ecclesiam, & ejus ordinatos diligeret; & eam ob incursione malignantium indemnem conservaret; & dignitates illius bona fide; & sine malo ingenio servaret illasas,* as *Roger Hoveden* expresseth it. This Archbishop, with all the Bishops, Abbots, Nobles, present at, and consenting to this Oath, and doing Homage and Fealty to him. The 13th of *June* following, he was solemnly Divorced, in *Normandy,* in the presence of three of his Norman Bishops, from the Duke of *Gloucester's* Daughter. *Unde magnam summi Pontificis* Innocentii *tertii, & Curiæ* Romanæ *indignationem, præsumens temere contra leges & canones dissolvere, quod eorum fuerat authoritate colligatum,* as *Radulphus de Diceto* informs us. But he soon after was Married to *Isabel,* sole Daughter and Heir of the Earl of *Anvolesme,* who was Crowned Queen, *Octob.* 8. by Archbishop *Hubert;* this Pope and Cardinals, not daring to question, or null his Marriage.

Cent. XIII.

King *John* being no sooner possessed of the Realm of *England,* but in the very first year of his Reign, evidenced to all the World his Ecclesiastical Sovereignty, both by ratifying, protecting, enlarging the Ecclesiastical as well as Temporal Liberties, Priviledges, Churches, Chappels, Tithes, Lands, Possessions, granted by his Ancestors to several Archbishopricks, Bishopricks, Monasteries in *England, Ireland, Normandy,* by sundry Charters, using this expression in the Prologue of Confirmation to the Monastery of *Cirencester. Johannes Dei gratia,&c. Quoniam Honori nostro condecens, & saluti nostræ necessarium, loca sancta & religiosa, quæ ab Avo patris nostri Rege* H. *primo sunt fundata, & a Rege* H. *secundo patre nostro confirmata, defendere, custodire, & amplificare. Inde est, quod Deo & Sanctæ Mariæ de* Cirencest. *& Canonitis Regularibus ibidem Deo servientibus, damus & concedimus. Dat. per manum* H. Cant. *Archiep.Cancel.nostri apud sag.*7. *die* Aug. *An. Regni nostri* 10. Which prologue he likewise used in other of his Charters. K. *John* also authorized *Hubert* Archbishop of *Canter.* to make a Will, which he could not then Legally do without his Royal Licence.

Prynne's history of Popes Usurpations. *lib.* 5, *ch.* 1.

In the year 1177. no less then 30 Nuns of the Abby of *Ambresbury,* were accused, and convicted at one time for their incontinency, to the dissolution and infamy of their Order, whereof they had been publikely defamed; whereupon King *Henry* the 2d. *Expulsis sanctimonialibus be Abbatia de* Ambresbury, *propter incontinentiam, & per alios domos Religiosos distributis* ; expelling the Nuns from this Abbey for their incontinency, distributed them throughout other Religious Houses, in stricter custody (by way of penance) and gave it to the Abbess and Nuns of *Font-Everoit,* for a perpetual possession, who sending a Covent of Nuns thither from *Font-Everoit, Richard* then Archbishop of *Canterbury,* inducted them into the Abbey of *Ambresbury*, on the firſt of *June*, King *Hen*. 2. *Bartholomew*, Biſhop of *Exceſter*; *John* Biſhop of *Norwich*, and many other of the Clergy and People being then preſent. And by his Charter, *Anno* 1179. confirmed the Lands of this Abbey to them with many liberties, and that by the advice and conſent of the Archbiſhop of *Canterbury*, and many other Biſhops, Great Men, and Barons of the Realm. King *John* in the firſt year of his Reign, by his Charter reciting all the premiſes in the Prologue, confirmed this Charter of his Father, ratified theſe Nuns deprivations and impriſonments in other Monaſteries for their incontinency, with conſent of his Biſhops, Nobles, and requeſt of Pope *Alexander*, transferring this Abbey, and all Lands thereto belonging, from one rank of Nuns to another; takes both theſe Nuns, Perſons, Lands, into his Royal protection, as if they were his own Demeſnes, grants them ſeveral Tithes, Churches, large Priviledges; and prohibits, that none of his Officers or Subjects ſhould diſturb them therein, nor implead them, but in the preſence of himſelf and his heirs. The ſame firſt year of King *John*'s Reign, the Abbot of *Weſtminſter* dying, the Monks by the King's Licenſe elected *Ralph Arundel* Prior of *Harle* for their Abbot, unto which the King gave his Aſſent. Whereupon he was conſecrated Abbot; no Biſhops, Abbots, Priors, or other Eccleſiaſtical Perſons being elected to any Dignities, but by the King's previous Licenſe, and ſubſequent Aſſent to the Perſon elected, who might approve or reject him at his Royal Pleaſure.

This King ratified the Charter of K. *Richard*, touching the exchange, between Archbiſhop *Hubert*, and the Biſhop and Monks of *Rocheſter*, of the Manor of *Lambath* for other Lands, and the Clauſe therein; authorizing the Pope, Archbiſhop of *Canterbury*, Biſhops and Clergy of *England*, to Excommunicate the infringers thereof. Beſides, he appropriated ſeveral Parochial Churches in perpetuity to the Biſhoprick of *Coventry* and *Litchfield*; converted other Parochial Churches into Prebendaries, and ratified the Orders made by Biſhop *Hugh* for the better regulation of that Church by two Charters. The like Charter of confirmation of Churches, Tithes, and Liberties, he made to the Biſhop of *Exeter*, and his Succeſſors, the ſame year. In the ſecond year of his Reign, the Dean and Chapter of *Lexoven*, within this King's hereditary Dominions in *France*, preſuming to elect a Biſhop without his conſent, ſent a Prohibition to them, to preſerve this Antient right of the Crown deſcended to him from his Anceſtors. The ſame year this King by his Charter commanded all Clerks, then Impriſoned for offences throughout *England*, to be delivered to *Hubert* Archbiſhop of *Canterbury*, upon his demand of them. Likewiſe he granted a Charter to the Biſh. of *Norwich*, to recover all Lands and Tenements belonging to that Biſhoprick, unjuſtly alienated by his Predeceſſors.

The ſame year *Geoffery Plantaginet*, Archbiſhop of *York*, King *John*'s baſe Brother, obſtructed the Levying of Carvage (demanded and granted to the King by common conſent paid by all others) on the Demeſn Lands

Chart. 1. *Johan.*
Regis part. 2.
n. 147. & *n.* 25.

The Church of Great Britain.

Lands of his Church, or Tenants, beating the Sheriff of *York's* servants, excommunicating the Sheriff himself by name, with all his Aiders, and interdicted his whole Province of *York* for attempting to levy it. Whereupon the King much incensed, summoned him to answer these high contempts, his not going over with him into *Normandy* when summoned; and also to pay him three thousand Marks due to his Brother King *Richard*; and by his Writs commanded all the Archbishop's servants, wherever they were found to be imprisoned, as they were, for beating the Sheriff's Officers, and denying to give the King of the Archbishops Wine, passing through *York.*; summoned *Geoffery* into his Court to answer all these contempts; and issued Writs to the Sheriff of *York-shire* to seize all his Goods, Temporalties, and to return them into the Exchequer, which was executed accordingly. The King and Queen repairing to *York* the next Mid-lent, the Archbishop made his peace with the King, submitting to pay such a Fine for his offences, as four Bishops, and four Barons elected by them, should adjudge, and absolved *William de Stutvil* the Sheriff, and *James de Poterna*, whom he had excommunicated, and recalled his former Interdict.

The same year there fell out a great difference between this Archbishop, the Dean and Chapter of *York*, and the Archdeacon of *Richmond*. The Præcentor's place at *York* falling void, the Dean and Chapter would not suffer him to present *Ralph de Kyme*, his Official, to it, but themselves gave it to *Hugh Murdac*, Archdeacon of *Cleveland*, the day after he had given it to *Kyme*. And when the Achbishop would have put him into the Præcentor's Stall, the Dean told him, *It belonged not unto him to put any man into a Stall, neither shall you therein place him, because we have given it by Authority of the Council of* Lateran. Whereupon when the Archbishop could not have his will, he excommunicated *Murdac*; he likewise injured *Honorius* Archdeacon of *Richmond*, by challenging to himself the Institutions of Churches and Synodals, against the ancient Dignities and Customs of the Archdeaconry, which the Archbishop pretended *Honorius* had resigned and confirmed to him by his Charter, which he denied. The Dean and Chapter, and *Honorius*, severally complained of these injuries to the King, who thereupon issued two Writs for their relief.

R. *Hoveden Annal. part. poster. p.* 817.

This *Honorius*, Archdeacon of *Richmond*, complained to the Pope as well as the King, of the injurious encroachments of this Archbishop, who suspended some of his Clerks, interdicted some Churches within his Archdeaconry, and excommunicated the Archdeacon, all which the Pope in a special Letter requires him to retract as null and void. He also sent three Epistles more: the first to the Dean and Chapter of *York*; the second to the Bishop of *Ely*, and Archdeacon of *Northampton*; the third to King *John* himself, to defend *Honorius* his rights, against the Archbishop's injuries and encroachments.

The Pope also wrote a menacing Letter to the Archbishop; but he was no way daunted at it, but proceeded still against *Honorius*, till restrained by the King's Writs, Appeals being but then in their infancy; and that not as to a supreme judicature, but only by way of complaint, as a voluntary perswading Arbitrator, and that by the King's licence first obtained, as learned Sir *Roger Twisden* truly observes.

An Historical Vindication of the church of England in point of Schism.

The same year *Hubert* Archbishop of *Canterbury*, intending to celebrate a Council at *Westminster*, without the King's special Writ, thereupon (the King being then in *Normandy*) *Geoffery Fitz-Peter*, Earl of *Sussex*, being then Chief Justice of *England*, sent a Prohibition to inhibit it; yet the Archbishop held the Council wherein he made and promulged several Decrees, *Statuens ea a suis subditis inviolabiliter observari*.

But those Decrees made concerning Procurations, Fees for Orders, Institutions, Inductions, Licences of Ministers, &c. were not esteemed obligatory, nor were they regarded. *Lyndwood*, *Aton*, and most Histories, take no notice of them, because made against the King's Prohibition.

The third year of King *John*, *Gilardus*, Archdeacon of *Brecknock*, pretending himself to be elected Bishop of St. *Davids* in *Wales* with the King's consent, by provision from Pope *Innocent* the Third, intruded himself into the possession of the Temporalties thereof, and likewise endeavoured to make it an Archbishoprick.

About that time a certain number of *Greeks* came from *Athens* into *England*, and asserted, that the *Latins* had erred from the way of Truth in the Articles of Christian Faith; and they would shew the right way by invincible Arguments, which all should receive if they will be saved. This was reported unto King *John*: He answered, *Our Faith is grounded upon the Authority of Christ and the Saints, and I will not suffer that it be tossed with disputes and janglings of men; nor will we change the certainty for uncertainty, let me hear no more of you*: So they departed.

Gilardus had procured Pope *Innocent's* Procuration and Provision to elect him Bishop of St. *Davids*, at which King *John* (though then in *Normandy* with his Queen) was much incensed, and sent out four successive Writs and Proclamations, directed to all the Clergy and Laity both of *England* and *Wales* in general, and the Chapter of St. *Davids* in special, strictly enjoyning them all to oppose and resist *Gilardus* his rash attempts and innovations against Him, to their power, according to their Allegiance; and no wayes to aid or countenance him therein, by advice or otherwise, it being unjust to do it.

Giraldus, notwithstanding all his pretended submission to the Archbishop, proceeding afresh in the Court of *Rome* to obtain his ends; thereupon the King issued out a severe Proclamation against him, as a publick Enemy and disturber of the Peace of his Kingdom.

In

the Church of Great Britain.

In the same year Pope *Innocent* takes upon him (upon pretext of necessity for relief of the holy Land) only to advise and recommend to all the Prelates of the holy Church the levying of the fortieth part of their Estates and Benefices, and in what manner to levy it, not absolutely to impose it to their prejudice. Whence *Matthew Westminster* thus expresseth it : *Ad instantiam Innocentii Papæ, data est quadragesima pars redditum omnium Ecclesiarum ad subsidium terræ promissionis.* Therefore a free Gift, not an imposed Tax. Neither would the King of *England* or *France* suffer it to to be levyed in their Realms by the Pope's Authority, but only by their Royal Order, Grant, and Assent thereto. But no Archbishop or Bishop did put this in execution.

The same year the King licensed *Peter Builler* by Charter to enter into what Religion he pleased. *Rex, &c. Omnibus, &c. Sciatis nos dedisse licentiam* Petro Builler *transferendi se ad quam voluerit Religionem, & inde has literas nostras patentes ei rei relinquimus in testimonium. Teste me ipso apud* Barnevil, 29 *die* Octobris.

The French King perfidiously breaking his Truce with King *John*, made in the first year of his reign, to carry on that War, he not only demanded a supply of Moneys from his Nobility and Clergy, but likewise from the *Cistercian Abbots*.

The same year the Church and City of *Rhoan* being consumed with fire, King *John* granted them his Letters Patents for a liberal contribution throughout all *England*, toward the repair of that Church, principally for the Virgin *Maries* sake, to whom it was dedicated, then adored more than God himself. This is the first Patent of such a Collection that we have yet met with.

Pious this King was in offering one ounce of Gold to God every Lord's-day and Holy-day, which the Archbishop of *Canterbury* then offered and disbursed for him, or claimed as his Fee, being allowed it in the Exchequer upon his account.

In the fourth year of King *John*, some Irish Bishops and Archdeacons, Suffragans to the Archbishop of *Dublin*, endeavoured, without this King's precedent License and Assent, to elect an Archbishop, and get him confirmed at *Rome* by the Pope, against the King's Right and Dignity. Whereupon he entred an Appeal against them before himself, to Preserve his Right and Dignity therein.

The same year there being many contests between the Dean and Canons, and *Geoffry* Archbishop of *York*, who by his Archiepiscopal authority and violence, did much oppress them : the King upon their complaint, by his Authority and Letters Patents granted them a Protection against Him and his Instruments.

In the fifth year of King *John*, *Godfrid* Bishop of *Winchester* deceasing, *Petrus de Rupibus*, a Knight and great Souldier, *Vir equestris ordinis*, *& in rebus bellicis eruditus procurante Rege* Johanne, being chosen

to

to the Bishoprick, succeeded him; who going to *Rome*, *Vbi magnis ze-niis liberaliter collatis ad Ecclesiam Wintoniensem, maturavit Episcopus consecrari.*

This year the Men of *Holderness* refusing to pay their *Traves* due to St. *John* of *Beverly* out of their Ploughed-lands to the Farmer of them, as they did to the Provost and Chapter before; the King issued out a Writ to the Sheriffs of *York* to seize the Persons and Goods of those the Provost and Chapter should excommunicate, and detain them till payment, since He and his Tenants duly paid them out of his and their Demesnes.

In the sixth year of King *John*, the Bishop, Dean, and Chapter of *Durham*, the Dean and Chapter of *York*, with sundry other Deans and Chapters, Abbots and Priors within the Province of *York*, to prevent the unjust arbitrary Excommunications, Suspensions, and Interdicts of *Geoffry* Archbishop of *York*, against their own Tenants, Lands and Possessions, by reason of some differences between them concerning their Jurisdictions and Ecclesiastical Priviledges; which they complained the Archbishop invaded, appearing before the King at *York*, did there in the King's own presence appeal him before the See of *Rome*, prefixing a certain day, to which the King by his Letters Patents gave his Royal Testimony and Assent, they not daring to appeal without his Licenfe.

About two years after King *John* and his Nobles meeting at *Winchester*, placing his hope and strength in his Treasures, required and received through all *England* the thirteenth part of all Movables and other things, as well of the Laity as of all other Ecclesiastical Persons and Prelats, all of them murmuring at it, and wishing an ill event to such rapines, but not daring to contradict it. Only *Geoffry* Archbishop of *York* openly contradicting it, privily departed from *England*, and in his recess, *Anathematis sententia innodabit*, actually excommunicated all Men, especially within his Archbishoprick, making this rapine, and levying this Tax, and in general all Invaders of the Church or Ecclesiastical things, for non-payment of this Tax, wherewith this King was so highly offended, that he seized his Temporalities, and banished him the Realm till his death about seven years after.

Anno 1205. died *Hubert* Archbishop of *Canterbury*. Before his body was yet committed to the earth, the younger sort of the Monks elected *Reginald* their Superiour, and placed him in the Metropolitan See, without the King's Licenfe and knowledge: who being sent unto by the elder sort of Monks, requiring his gracious Licenfe to chuse their Archbishop, consented thereunto, requiring them also instantly at his request, that they would elect *John Grey*, Bishop of *Norwich*, into that See; which they also did. And the King sent to the Pope to confirm it. The two Suffragans of *Canterbury* not being made acquainted with the matter, sent speedily to *Rome*, to have both the Elections stopped, where-upon

the Church of Great Britain.

upon arose a great tumult: for the Pope condemning both their Elections, created *Stephen Langton* with his own hand in the high Church of *Viterbo*. Upon which occasion the King banished sixty four of the Clergy and Monks of *Canterbury* out of the Land, and sharply expostulated with the Pope, for that he had chosen *Stephen Langton*, a Man brought up long among his Enemies in *France*; besides the derogation to the Liberties of his Crown; threatening, except he would favour the King's liking of the Bishop of *Norwich*, he would cut off the trade to *Rome*, and the profits that came thither from the Land. The Pope writeth, in the behalf of *Stephen Langton*, a froward and arrogant Letter, and not long after sendeth a commandment and charge into *England* to certain Bishops, that if the King would not yield, they should Interdict his Realm. For the execution whereof four Bishops were appointed, viz. *William* Bishop of *London*, *Eustace* Bishop of *Ely*, *Mauger* Bishop of *Worcester*, and *Giles* Bishop of *Hereford*, who pronounced the general Interdiction through the Realm of all Ecclesiastical service, saving Baptism of Children, Confession and the Eucharist to the dying in case of necessity. No sooner had they interdicted the Kingdom, but they with *Joceline*, Bishop of *Bath*, as speedily, as secretly, fled out of the Land. And the King took all the possessions of those Bishops into his hands. He also proclaimed, that all those that had Church-living, and went over the Sea, should return at a certain day, or else lose their Livings for ever: and charged all Sheriffs to enquire, if any Church-man received any Commandment that came from the Pope, that they should apprehend them, and bring them before him, and also take into their hands for the King's use, all the Church-lands that were given to any man by the Archbishop *Stephen*, or by the Priors of *Canterbury* from the time of the election of the Archbishop.

England remained under the Interdict six years, three months and an half, whereby not only the King and his Court, but also all the people of *England*, who had nothing to do with that Quarrel, were Excommunicated. In that long time how many thousands of men died in *England*, who by the *Rules* of the *Roman* Church, and by the Pope's Judgment, are eternally damned? and that but for a Quarrel between the King and the Pope about some Investitures of Churches, and Collations of Benefices, and Money-matters.

Then (saith *Mathew Paris*, who was an eye-witness of all that disorder) *All the Sacraments of the Church ceased in England, saving only the Confession, and the Communion of the Host in the last necessity, and the Baptism of Infants. The dead bodies were carried out of the Towns, as if they had been the bodies of Dogs, and buried by the High-wayes, and in Ditches, without Prayers, and without service of Priests. By the same Interdict all Masses, Vespers, all publick Service and ringing of Bells was forbidden; and the Kingdom was exposed to rapine and prey, and given to*

Matth. Paris.

For Acts and Monuments.

any

any that would conquer it. Only the King was not excommunicated by name, but that was done the next year after.

Next, Pope *Innocent* depofed King *John* from the Kingdom of *England*, and abfolved the *Englifh* from the Oath of their Allegiance, and commanded *Philip Auguft* King of *France*, that for the remiffion of his fins he fhould invade the Kingdom of *England* with force of Arms, giving to thofe that fhould follow the King in that Conqueft, the pardon of all their fins, and the fame Graces and Pardons, as to them that vifit the holy Sepulchre. Whereupon the faid King *Philip*, partly to obtain the remiffion of his fins, partly to make himfelf Mafter of *England*, raifed a mighty Army, whilft *Innocent* was ftirring up the *Englifh* to rife againft their King.

This moved King *John* to humble himfelf under the Pope, and to receive fuch Conditions as liked him beft. The Conditions were,

That the King fhould yield unto the Pope the whole right of Patronage of all the Benefices of his Kingdom.

That to obtain Abfolution of his fins, he fhould pay to the Clergy of Canterbury, *and to other Prelates, the fum of eight thoufand pounds* Sterling

That he fhould fatisfie for the damages done to the Church according to the Judgment of the Pope's Legat.

That the faid King fhould refign his Crown into the Pope's hand, with his Kingdoms of England *and* Ireland; for which Letters were formed and given to *Pandulphus* the Pope's Legat.

King John being informed that his Archbifhops, Bifhops and Clergy, intended to hold a Council at St. *Albans* by the command of Pope *Innocent* the Third, about the payment of *Rome-fcot* againft cuftom, and fundry other unufual Exactions, to the great deftruction of the whole Realm, upon complaint thereof by his Nobles and People, iffued out a Prohibition to them, exprefly forbidding them upon their Allegiance, not to hold any Council there, by the Popes or any other Authority, nor to confult or treat of thofe things, nor to act or ordain any thing againft the cuftom of the Realm, as they tendered his Honour, or the tranquillity of the Kingdom, until he conferred with the general Council of his Realms about it.

Thomas Sprot. Speed's Hiftory, p. 572. During this Interdict, *Alexander Cementarius*, Abbot of the *Benedictines* at *Canterbury*, *Vir corpore Elegantiffimus, facie Venerabilis, literarum plenitudine imbutus, ita ut Parifiis celebris haberetur*, 𝔐𝔞𝔤𝔦𝔰𝔱𝔢𝔯 𝔢𝔱 𝔑𝔢𝔠𝔱𝔬𝔯, 𝔢𝔱 𝔏𝔢𝔠𝔱𝔬𝔯 in 𝔗𝔥𝔢𝔬𝔩𝔬𝔤𝔦𝔞, was fent by King *John* unto *Rome*, where he openly pleaded and fomented the King's Caufe againft the Pope. He maintained there, *That there is no Power under God, higher than a King*; and *That the Clergy fhould not have Temporal government*. He

proved

The Church of Great Britain.

proved thefe two Articles by Scripture and Reafon, and by teſtimony of *Gregory* the Firſt in an Epiſtle to *Auguſtine* Biſhop of *Canterbury*. He wrote three Books againſt the Popes Uſurpations and Power, *viz. De Ceſſione Papali, De Eccleſiæ poteſtate, De poteſtate Vicaria*, in defence of his Sovereign King *John*; for which his Loyalty he was afterwards, by the Pope's Power, deprived of all his Benefices by *Pandulphus* the Pope's Legat (after King *John*'s furrender of his Crown) and enforced to beg his Bread.

Anno 1209. in the tenth year of King *John*, Henry *Fitz-Alan* was ſworn firſt Mayor of London, and *Petty Duke*

King *John* having ſeized and detained in his hands the Temporalties of the Archbiſhoprick of *Armach* in *Ireland*, for that the Biſhop was elected without his Licenſe, againſt his Will and Appeal, two Monks coming to him, proffering him three hundred Marks in Silver, and three Marks a year in Gold, for to have the Lands, Liberties, and Rights thereof, he by his Writ returned them to his Chief Juſtice there, to do what was fitting in it

with *Thomas Neal* ſworn for Sheriffs: And *London-bridge* began to be built with Stone; and St. *Saviours* in Southwark the ſame year.

John Reumond coming from *Rome* to lay claim to a Prebendary in *Haſtings*, fued to the King for his Licenſe and ſafe conduct to come into and return from *England*, which he granted upon this condition, that upon his arrival he ſhould give ſecurity, that he came hither for no ill to the King, nor for any other buſineſs but that Prebendary. The like Licenſe he granted to *Simon Langton* the Archbiſhop's Brother, upon the ſame and ſtricter conditions.

King *John* ſent a memorable Letter to the Pope by ſpecial Meſſengers, to claim and juſtifie this ancient and undoubted Right which He and his Royal Anceſtors enjoyed, to provide and prefer Archbiſhops and Biſhops to the See of *Canterbury*, and all other Cathedrals, atteſted by the Letters of the Biſhops of *England*, and other credible perſons, deſiring him to preſerve the rights of the Church and Realm of *England* entire and inviolable by his Fatherly proviſion.

Then the King entred into a League with *Otho* the Emperour, and forced *John* King of *Scots*, who received his fugitive Subjects, and harboured them in his Kingdom, to ſend to him for peace, to pay him eleven thouſand Marks to purchaſe his peace with him, and to put in Hoſtages for his fidelity without any Fight between them. Yea, the the *Welch-men* themſelves, formerly rebellious, ſoon after his return from *Scotland*, voluntarily repaired to him at *Woodſtock*, and there did homage to him.

Mr. Wiſmirſt.

After which, *Anno* 1211. he entring into *Wales* with a great Army as far as *Snowdown*, *Reges omnes & Nobiles ſine contradictione ſubjugavit, de ſubjectione in poſterum obſides viginti octo ſuſcepit, & inde cum proſperitate ad Albani Monaſterium remeavit*, *Lewellin* Prince of *North-Wales* being enforced to render himſelf to mercy, without any Battel at all.

When

When the Pope's Absolution of the Nobles and all other Subjects from the King's Allegiance would not shake his magnanimous resolution, nor his Peoples loyalty; the Pope's Legats, *Pandulphus* and *Durance*, forged new devises to effect their designs by fraud and terror; to which purpose they procured sundry Letters from divers Quarters to be brought unto him, whilst he sate at dinner at *Nottingham*, intending to set upon the *Welch-men* with a potent Army (whom they had stirred up to rebel against him, and invade *England*) to divert him from his design; all to this effect, *That there was a secret Plot laid to destroy him.* He marched to *Chester*, where he met with new Letters to the like effect; which caused him to dismiss his Army, and design against the *Welchmen*.

Pry'ur's Histo-
ry. Book 3.
ch. 3.

Besides, the Popish Priests set up one *Peter* an Hermite, a counterfeit Prophet, to terrifie the King, and alienate the peoples hearts from him by his false Prophesies. This counterfeit Sooth-sayer prophesied, *That King* John *should reign no longer than the Ascension-day, within the year of our Lord,* 1213. which was the fourteenth from his Coronation; and this (he said) he had by Revelation.

When the *Ascension-day* was come; the King commanded his Regal Tent to be spread abroad in the open field, passing that day with his noble Council and Men of Honour, in the greatest solemnity that ever he did before, solacing himself with musical Songs and Instruments, most insight of his trusty Friends. This day being past in all prosperity and mirth, the King commanded, that *Peter* the Hermite, that false Prophet, should be drawn, and hanged like a Traitor.

Now behold the misery of King *John*, perplexed with the *French* King's daily preparation to invade *England*, assisted by many English male-contents, and all the exil'd Bishops. Hereupon he sunk on a sudden beneath himself, to an act of unworthy submission and subjection to the Pope. For on *Ascension-Eve*, *May* 15. being in the Town of *Dover* (standing as it were on tiptoes, on the utmost edge, brink, and label of that Land, which now he was about to surrender) *King* John by an Instrument, or Charter sealed, and solemnly delivered in the presence of many Prelats and Nobles, to *Pandulphus* the Pope's Legat, granted to God and the Church of *Rome*, the Apostles *Peter* and *Paul*, and to Pope *Innocent* the Third and his Successors, the whole *Kingdom* of *England* and *Ireland*. And took an Estate thereof back again, yielding and paying yearly to the Church of *Rome* (over and above the *Peter-pence*) a thousand Marks *Sterling*, viz. seven hundred for *England*, and three hundred for *Ireland*. In the passing hereof, the King's Instrument to the Pope was sealed with a Seal of Gold; and the Pope's to the *King* was sealed with a Seal of Lead. This being done, the King took the Crown off his Head, and set it upon *Pandulphus* his Knees (at whose feet he also laid his Scepter, Robe, Sword and Ring, his Royal Ensigns,

Fuller's
Church History. Book 3.

as

as *John de Serres* relates) and thefe words faid he in hearing of all the great Lords of *England*. *Here I refign up the Crown and the Realm of England into the hands of Pope* Innocentius *the Third, and put me wholly in his mercy, and in his ordinance.* Then *Pandulph* received the Crown of King *John*, and kept it five dayes in his hands, and confirmed all things by his Charter.

Now the Pope's next defign was, how to take off, and pacifie the *French* King from his intended Invafions, and fo fent the Archbifhop and his Confederates into *England*, there to infult over King *John*, as they had done abroad.

Next year the Interdict was taken off the Kingdom, and a general joy was over the Land.

The feventeenth of *Auguft* following the exiled Bifhops landed at *Dover*, and were conducted in State to the King at *Winchefter*: the King's extraordinary humbling to, and begging pardon of them, proftrating himfelf to the ground at their feet, and their infolent carriage toward him, is related by *Matthew Paris*...

The next day after their coming to *Winchefter*, the King iffued out Writs to all the Sheriffs of *England*; to enquire of their damages. There were other Writs fent to the Kings Judges, to proceed in the faid Inquifition.

After this general compliance with them, the King conceiving he had given them full content, and fetled all things in peace, refolved to pafs with an Army into *Picardy*, whither the Nobles refufed to follow him. In the mean time the Archbifhop, Bifhop, Nobles, meeting at Sr. *Albans* about the damages to be reftored by the King to the Prelates, during their exile, fell to demand the confirmation of their Liberties, granted by his Grandfather King *Henry* the firft, which the King condefcended unto.

Soon after the Archbifhop caufed all the Bifhops, Abbots, Priors, Deans, and Nobles of the Realm to meet together at *London*, upon pretext of fatisfying his and the exiled Bifhops damages, but in verity to engage in a new Rebellion againft the Crown, and confer it on *Lewis* the *French* King's Son, as they did in the conclufion, under pretence of demanding the confirming the Charter and Liberties granted by King *Henry* the firft, there produced by the Archbifhop, which the King had but newly ratified at St. *Albans*.

Pandulphus, befides his former infolencies, endeavoured to wreft out of the King's hand, the power of imprifoning Clerks for Fellonies, that fo they might be at his own difpofal, and act any villanies with impunity.

King *John* being thus diftreffed, fent a bafe and unchriftian-like Ambaffage to *Admiralius Murmelius*, a Mahometan, King of *Morocco*, then very potent, and poffeffing a great part of *Spain*; offering him, if

he

he would send him succour, to hold the Kingdom of *England* as a Vassal from him, and to receive the Law of *Mahomet*, saith *Matthew Paris*. The *Moor* offended at his offer, told the Ambassadours, *That he lately had read Paul's Epistles, which for the matter liked him well, save only that Paul had renounced that Faith, wherein he was born, and the Jewish profession.* Wherefore he slighted King *John* as one devoid both of piety and policy, who would love his liberty, and disclaim his Religion. A strange tender, if true.

Modò irspexi libram in Græcosscriptum, cujdam Græci sapientis, & christiani, nomine Pauli; cujus alius & vivox mihi maxime complacent & accepto. Unum mihi displicet, quòd in urge job quà natus ist non stetit; sed ad alia tàquam transfuga, & inconstans avolvit.

But Mr. *Prynne* proveth it to be a most scandalous malitious forgery of this Monk of St. *Albans* against the King for sequestring that Abbey. *Philip* King of *France*, together with his Son *Lewis*, and his Proctor, and all the Nobles of *France*, Anno 1216. with his own mouth protested against this Charter and resignation to *Walo* the Pope's own Legat, (when purposely sent to them by Pope *Innocent*, to diswade them from invading *England* , as being then St. *Peter*'s Patrimony) not only as null, void in it self for several Reasons, but of most pernitious example.

King *John* out of his piety, to prevent profanations of the Lord's-day, removed the Market of the City of *Exeter* from the Lord's-day, whereon it was formerly kept, to the Monday.

This King to ingratiate himself with the Romish Cardinals and Court, granted them annual Pensions out of his Exchequer, the Arrears whereof he ordered to be satisfied in the first place, and likewise gave Benefices or Prebends to their Nephews and Creatures. Moreover to gratifie *Stephen Langton*, his great Enemy, he granted the Patronage of the Bishoprick of *Rochester* to him and his Successors: and to the Bishop of *Ely* he granted the Patronage of the Abbey of *Torney*.

Mr. *Prynne*, who kept the Records of the *Tower*, tells us, that upon strictest search he could find no payment of the foresaid Annuity, or Oblation to Pope *Innocent* by King *John* himself who granted it, but only for one year before hand, when he sealed his Charter, who dying about three years after, during which time his Kingdom was infested with Civil War; between him and his Barons, invaded by *Lewis* of *France*, who was made King by the Barons in his stead; his Lands, Rents seized, his Treasure exhausted, and the People every where miserably plundered; it is probable that there neither was nor could be expected any other punctual payment of it.

The Pope and his Legat *Nicholas*, having in a manner bereaved King *John* of his Regal Dignity, and Authority, began forthwith to play *Rex*: they usurped the Sovereign Authority both in Church and State, presenting to all Bishopricks, Abbies, Spiritual promotions, and Benefices then void, without the Patrons consent, by way of Provision and Collation, to the prejudice of the Crown, and enthralling of the Church

Matth. Paris. Hist. Anglic. p. 237, 238.

of *England*, not vouchsafing to consult either with the King himself, the Archbishop, or Bishops concerning their disposal.

This was the very original of Pope's Provisions, and disposals of Bishopricks, Abbies, with all sorts of Spiritual promotions and Benefices in *England*: no Pope presuming to confer any Bishoprick, Benefice, or Prebendary, in *France*, or *England*, *Usque ad tempora Domini Innocentii tertii, qui primus assumpsit sibi jus istud in tempore suo*, as the *French* Agent remonstrated to Pope *Innocent* the Fourth. These Provisions soon overflowed the Church of *England* (and *France* too) for many succeeding Ages, notwithstanding all oppositions and complaints against them. Which the Archbishop and Bishops foreseeing, perceiving withall the Legat more ready to gratifie the King and his Clerks in the disposal of Bishopricks and Ecclesiastical preferments than themselves, meeting together at *Dunstaple*, drew up an Appeal against his proceedings, which he slighting and sending to *Rome* by *Pandulphus*, together with King *John*'s Charter, so highly magnified the King, and made such complaints to the Pope against the Archbishop and Bishops, as frustrated their Appeal.

King *John* having satisfied and secured the damages of the Exiled Bishops and Monks before the Interdict released, according to his agreement; other Abbots, Priors, Clergy-men and Lay-men repaired to the Legat, craving full satisfaction also for their damages, sustained by the King's proceedings during the Interdict, though never insisted on before.

The King issued out two Writs on behalf of the Archbishop of *Canterbury*, and the Bishop of *Lincoln*, to restore them to the possession of their Temporalties in the Cinque-ports, and other places. Yet on the contrary, all the Bishops and Clergy-men, who faithfully adhered to the King, and communicated with him, or any other excommunicated person, or received any Benefices from them during the Interdict, were by these Prelates (now made their Judges) and Pope's censures, ordered to be suspended from all their Ecclesiastical Offices, Benefices, Preferments, and ordered to appear personally at *Rome* before the Pope, to be examined, ere their Suspensions released, except only such as had given satisfaction to the Church for this offence.

The turbulent Archbishop stirred up the Barons to a new Insurrection, against the King, about their Liberties, who coming all to the King after *Christmas*, *Anno* 1215. demanded the confirmation of their Charter, who craved time to advise thereon till after *Easter*, the Archbishop and two more becoming his Sureties, that then he should give satisfaction to all of them. The Barons against the time, rather preparing themselves for a Battel, than Conference with the King, assembled together at *Stamford* with a mighty Army, having Archbishop *Stephen* their principal Abettor, who yet seemed to side with the King, and was most assiduous

ous about him. The Barons marching as far as *Brackley*, the King sent the Archbishp to treat with them, who brought back a Schedule of their claimed Liberties, with this Message, *That if he presently confirmed them not to them by his Charter, they would force him to it, by seizing all his Castles and Provisions.* Whereupon the King replied, *Why do they not also demand the Kingdom?* swearing *never to enslave himself, to such a concession.* The Archbishop returning with this peremptory Answer, the Barons forthwith seized *Bedford-Castle*, and were admitted into *London*, the Citizens siding with them. Whereupon the King appointed to treat with them at *Running-mead*, whither the Barons came with armed multitudes from all parts of the Realm, where after some parley, the King granted them their desires, not only for their Liberties specified in *Magna Charta*, and *Charta Forresta*, which he then sealed, and by his Writs commanded to be put in due execution, but also that twenty five Peers elected by them (to whom all were sworn to obey) should force the King to observe these Charters (if ever he receded from them) by seizing all his Castles. *Juratum est a parte Regis; Quod* Anglicana Ecclesia libera sit, &c. It was sworn on the Kings part, that the Church of *England* is free, and all men of our Kingdom, have and do hold all the foresaid Liberties, Rights and Customs, well and peaceably, freely and quietly, fully and wholly to themselves and their Heirs, &c. All the Barons and Commons of the Realm then and afterwards taking the same Oath. The Archbishop and Barons thrust into this new Charter many Articles and Clauses, for their own, the Churches, and Pope's advantage, not extant in the Charter of King *Henry* the First, as may be seen in *Matthew Paris* his History.

This Charter (though it saved a great part of the King's Prerogative to petition him and his Heirs for Licenses to elect, and for his Assent) gave a great wound to his Ecclesiastical Supremacy; and made all Chapters, Covents, Bishops, Monks, yea Popes and their Agents to slight his Regal Authority and Licenses too, insomuch that he could prefer no person to any Bishoprick, Monastery, or elective Dignity, but whom the Electors pleased to make choice of.

King *John* withdrawing and obscuring himself from his Bishops and Barons in the Isle of *Wight*, sent Messengers secretly to *Rome*, to complain and appeal to the Pope against their Treasons, Rebellions, and the Charters forcibly extorted from him, whilst under the Pope's protection, who thereupon vacated the Charters.

Then the Archbishop to demonstrate his gratitude to King *John*, for the Patronage and Royalty of the Bishoprick of *Rochester*, newly conferred on him and his Successors, delivered up *Rochester* Castle, with all the Ammunition therein to the Barons. King *John* after three months siege took it, by force, out of the Barons hands, who proceeding in their Rebellions against the King, the Pope excommunicated them. The Pope's
Agents

Agents gave the Archbishop a personal command to execute the Excommunication, which he delayed to do, whereupon they suspended him.

King *John* complained to the Pope of the Barons obstinacy, and how the Archbishop refused to Excommunicate them. Soon after there was a General Council held at *Rome*, to which the Archbishop was summoned, and there suspended from his Archbishoprick upon the King's complaints against him. When this suspension of the Archbishop was executed, the Pope commanded all his Suffragans and Subjects to disobey him, till by his humiliation, and giving sufficient caution for his future deportment, he should demerit it. A just retaliation inflicted by God's providence on this Arch-enemy to King *John*.

The Archbishoprick of *York* becoming void, the King, by his Letters Patents, granted the Chapter of *York* a Licence to elect a new Archbishop, in the presence of five Commissioners therein specially named, and with their consents, to prevent the Election of *Simon Langton*, the Archbishop's Brother, this being the first Licence after his forecited Charter to the Archbishop and Bishops, for the freedom of Elections. After which the King sent his Patent of Appeal to the Chapter of *York*, in general termes, not to Elect any Person for their Archbishop, suspected to be an enemy to him, to avoid all misconstructions of his former Charter for freedom of Elections. He also secretly prohibited them to Elect *Simon Langton* by name, to whom he would never give his Royal Assent.

This Chapter, notwithstanding the King's and Pope's Inhibition likewise, to gratifie *Stephen* Archbishop of *Canterbury*, Elected *Simon Langton*, his Brother, Archbishop of *York*. And the Canons of *York* appearing in the Council at *Rome*, justified their Election, and presented *Simon Langton* to the Pope for their Archbishop Elect, and pressed his Confirmation of him.

The Covent and Monks of *Durham* affronted King *John* in the Election of their Bishop, whereupon he was enforced to make use of the Pope's and Legate's power, and yet could not effect his ends. But the Pope obtains His, to dispose of all Elections and Bishopricks at his pleasure.

The same year the King, with some strugling, procured *R. de Marisco*, to be Bishop of *Winchester*. Yet we find not, in any of our Historians, that he was ever Consecrated Bishop of *Winchester*, notwithstanding his Election, and the King's approbation, and Letters to the Pope's Legate on his behalf; so that, he miscarried in this design, as he did in that of *Hugh Foliot* to St. *Davids*. Neither did he succeed in his recommendation of three several Persons to the Prior and Covent of *Ramsey*.

Then the Monks of *Glastonbury* prevailed, with Money, to have their Abbey severed from the Bishoprick of *Bath* and *Wells*, and to be governed

K by

by an Abbot as formerly, parting with no less than four Manors, and the Patronage of six Benefices to *Joceline* Bishop of *Bath* and *Wells*, and his Successors, by way of composition, to obtain this disunion.

Then the Pope exempted King *John's* Chappels from Episcopal Excommunication and Jurisdiction, without the Pope's special command, which by the Lawes of the Realm were exempted from them long before.

The Barons and the *Londoners* slighted the Pope's Excommunication, and so doth *Lewis* of *France*, the Inhibition of the Pope and his Legate, not to invade *England*. In the mean time *Lewis* his Proctors at *Rome* pleaded, that King *John* had no good Title to the Crown of *England*, shewing *Lewis* his Title thereunto: which put Pope *Innocent* to a great dilemma. But the Pope himself became King *John's* Advocate, as well as Judge, not as King of *England*, but onely because he was his Vassal.

Then was *England* miserably wasted by *Lewis* and his Army in the East and South, and by King *John* in the West and North, whereupon forty of the Barons became sensible of their error in rejecting King *John*, and in calling in and Crowning *Lewis* for their King; and being likewise informed by Viscount *Melun* on his death-bed, upon his Salvation, That *Lewis*, and XVI. others of his chief Barons and Earls, whereof himself was one, had taken an Oath, 𝕮𝖍𝖆𝖙 𝖎𝖋 𝖊𝖛𝖊𝖗 𝖙𝖍𝖊 𝕮𝖗𝖔𝖜𝖓 𝖔𝖋 England 𝖜𝖊𝖗𝖊 𝖖𝖚𝖎𝖊𝖙𝖑𝖞 𝖘𝖊𝖙𝖑𝖊𝖉 𝖔𝖓 𝖍𝖎𝖘 𝖍𝖊𝖆𝖉, 𝖍𝖊 𝖜𝖔𝖚𝖑𝖉 𝖈𝖔𝖓𝖉𝖊𝖒𝖓 𝖙𝖔 𝖕𝖊𝖗𝖕𝖊𝖙𝖚𝖆𝖑 𝕰𝖝𝖎𝖑𝖊 𝖆𝖑𝖑 𝖙𝖍𝖊 𝕰𝖓𝖌𝖑𝖎𝖘𝖍 𝖜𝖍𝖔 𝖓𝖔𝖜 𝖆𝖉𝖍𝖊𝖗𝖊𝖉 𝖙𝖔 𝖍𝖎𝖒 𝖆𝖌𝖆𝖎𝖓𝖘𝖙 𝕶𝖎𝖓𝖌 John, 𝖆𝖘 𝕿𝖗𝖆𝖎𝖙𝖔𝖗𝖘 𝖙𝖔 𝖙𝖍𝖊𝖎𝖗 𝕷𝖆𝖜𝖋𝖚𝖑 𝕾𝖔𝖛𝖊𝖗𝖊𝖎𝖌𝖓, 𝖆𝖓𝖉 𝖜𝖔𝖚𝖑𝖉 𝖆𝖈𝖙𝖚𝖆𝖑𝖑𝖞 𝖊𝖝𝖙𝖎𝖗𝖕𝖆𝖙𝖊 𝖆𝖑𝖑 𝖙𝖍𝖊𝖎𝖗 𝖐𝖎𝖓𝖉𝖗𝖊𝖉: advising them timely to prevent their miseries, and lock up his words under the Seal of secrecy; thereupon addressed themselves with their Letters of submission to King *John*, but before these Letters were delivered, or any Answer returned, the King was poisoned by one *Simon* a Monk of *Swinshed*-Abbey in *Lincoln-shire*, of which poison he died. When he saw his Death approaching, he with penitent Confession of his sins, and great Devotion, received the holy Eucharist, having the Abbot of *Croxton* both for his Bodily and Ghostly Phisitian; and then not onely forgave all his Mortal Enemies, but also sent Command to *Henry* his Son to do the like, to whom he caused all present to Swear Fealty, and sent Letters to all his Officers abroad to assist him. After which he commended his Soul to God, and his Body to be interred in the Church of *Worcester*: Where he was afterwards solemnly buried near the Body of Bishop *Wolston*.

In this year 1216. flourished *Walter Mapez*, Archdeacon of *Oxford*, a very Witty Man, who in his Verses, painted forth in lively Colours

the

The Church of Great Britain.

the Life of the Pope, the Affections and Rape of the Court of *Rome*, the Excess and Pride of the Popish Prelates, as may be Read in his Book, Entitled, *Diverse Poems of the corrupt state of the Church*. He composed a Treatise, Entitled, *Apocalypsis Pontificis Goliath*, by which name he signified, that Antichrist was revealed in the Pope. Also *Prædicationem Goliath*; and other Treatises against the Pope and his Court, and of the dayes of the Court of *Rome*. *Giraldus Cambrensis* mentioneth him in his Mirror of the Church, and saith, *That he was a Man in that Age in great estimation*.

His Poetical description of the City, Popes, and Court of *Rome*, I shall here set down.

Roma caput mundi, sed nil caput mundum:
Quod pendet a Capite, totum est immundum.
Trahit enim vitium primum & secundum;
Et de fundo redolet, quod est juxta fundum.

Roma capit singulos, & res singulorum,
Romanorum Curia non est nisi forum:
Ibi sunt venalia jura Senatorum,
Et solvit contraria, copia nummorum.

In hoc consistorio si quis causam regat,
Suam vel alterius, hic inprimis legat:
Nisi det pecuniam, Roma totum negat;
Qui plus dat pecunia, melius allegat.

Romani capitulum habent in decretis,
Ut potentes audiant manibus repletis.
Dabis, aut non dabitur, petunt quando petis,
Qua mensura seminas, eadem tu metis.

Munus & petitio currunt passu pari,
Opereris munere, si vis operari.
Tullium nec timeas, si velit causari,
Munus Eloquentia gaudet singulari.

Nummis in hac Curia non est qui non vacet.
Crux placet, Rotunditas placet, totum placet,
Et cum ita placeat, & Romanis placet,
Ubi munus loquitur, & lex omnis tacet.

Cum ad Papam veneris, habe pro constanti:
Non est bonus Pauperi, soli favet danti.

Et

Et si munus præstitum non sit aliquanti,
Respondet hic tibi sic, non est mihi tanti.

Papa quærit, Chartula quærit, Bulla quærit,
Porta quærit, Cardinal quærit, Cursor quærit:
Sed si dares omnibus, at uni deerit ;
Totum mare salsum est, tota causa perit.

About that time *Nigellus Vvreker*, a Learned Monk at *Canterbury*, wrote a Book, *De abusu rerum Ecclesiæ*, and sent it to *William*, Bishop of *Ely*, Chancellor of *England*. In this Book he not onely rebuked him, but all Teachers under the Pope's Tyranny: becaufe they committed the Cure of Souls unto Children, Belly-gods, and defpifers of the Sacred Word

Henry the third of that name, fucceeded his Father King *John*, being about ten years old, and was Crowned at *Glocefter* by a part of the Nobility and Clergy (upon the perfwafion of *William* Earl *Marefhall*, Earl of *Pembrook*, a Nobleman of great Authority) the reft fiding with the French *Lewis* : within little more than a twelve Moneth he recovered the entire poffeffion of his Kingdom.

In Whitfun-week the Pope's Legate encouraged the King's Army to fight the French King's Forces at *Lincoln*: and after a fharp conflict they routed the Barons and *Lewis*'s Forces, flew and took many of them Prifoners, with the lofs onely of three Men, and took the City of *Lincoln*, with all the Treafure and baggage of the Enemy. The King's Ships watching the French Fleet at Sea, tranfporting Souldiers and fupplies unto *Lewis*, took *Euftachius* a Monk, their Admiral, Prifoner, whofe Head the King's Brother *Richard* cut off with his Sword, defpifing the great fum of Money which he proffered for his Ranfom. Soon after which defeats by Land and Sea, both Parties had a conference at *Stanes*, and came to an Agreement, *Septemb.* 3. and *Lewis* fhamefully departed this Realm.

But notwithftanding this Agreement with the Barons, yet the Pope's Legate exempted all the Bifhops, Abbots, and Clergy, out of this Act of pacification, for their contempt of the Pope's Authority, that he might difpofe of their Ecclefiaftical promotions and Benefices to his Inftruments, and put them to exceffive fines at the prefent, to fill the Pope's and his own Coffers.

Clauf. Anno 1.
H.3. m. 21, &
Pat. 1. H. 3.
m. 16. in tus.

This Legate *Gualo* did bear chief fway in the King's Council, and the King fealed fome Letters Patents ; *Sigillis venerabilium Patrum, Domini Gualonis Sancti Martini Presbyteri Cardinalis, Apoftolicæ sedis Legati, & Domini Petri Wintonienfis Epifcopi* ; and fent them abroad under their Seals, in the firft year of his Reign, becaufe as yet he had no Seal.

The Canons of *Carlisle* contemning both the Pope's and his Legates Authority and Censures, contumaciously celebrating Divine Service and Sacraments, notwithstanding their Interdicts, adhering and Swearing Fealty to the King of Scots, King *Henrie's* and the Pope's declared enemy; yea electing an interdicted Clerk for their Bishop, against the King's and Legate's Wills, and dividing the Revenues of the Bishoprick among themselves.

The King's Council thereupon sent an Epistle to Pope *Honorius* the third, (who succeeded *Innocent* the third that year) in the King's name, totally to remove these Schismatical Canons, and place Prebends in their rooms, to augment the Bishop's Revenues, which were small, and displace the intruded Bishop. Upon which Letter the Pope ordered *Gnalo* his Legate, by the King's Royal assent, to constitute *Hugh* Abbot of *Beaulieu*, Bishop of *Carlisle*.

In the second year of King *Henry* III. the Archbishop of *Dublin* in *Ireland*, and other Bishops there, Usurping upon the King's Crown and Temporal Courts, presumed to hold pleas, in their Courts Christian, of Lay fee, whereupon there issuing Prohibitions, from the King's Court, to stay these Suits, they proceeded contemptuously notwithstanding, upon which there issued out a Writ of Attachment against them, to appear before the chief Justice of *Ireland*, to answer the contempt.

In the third year of King *Henry* the third, the Bishoprick of *Leifmore* (united formerly to the Bishoprick of *Waterford*, by the Pope's Legate in *Ireland*, while the Bishop was in *England*, at the Consecration of the Bishop of *Carlisle*) *Macrobius* a Canon of *Leifmore*, procuring an election from the rest of the Canons, pretending the See to be then void, obtained the Legate's and King's Royal assent to the Election and Restitution of the Temporalties; whereof the Bishop of *Waterford* complaining to the King, the King nulled that election, and commanded the Bishop to be put in possession of his Temporalties.

The Bishop of *Ely* going into *France*, after *Lewis* his return thither, reported King *Henry* to be dead, and laboured to stir up a new War against him: whereupon the King wrote to the Pope to deprive him, and bestow his Bishoprick (by provision) upon some other: in which Letter the King acknowledgeth the Pope's great favours and assistance to him during his Infancy, puts himself and his Realms under the protection of his wings, and (by way of Complement) stiles them the Patrimony of the Church of *Rome*, to gain the Pope's readier protection and assistance in his Suits, and Wars.

In the fourth year of his Reign, King *Henry*, taking notice of diverse Usurpations upon the right of his Crown in *Ireland*, by Covents, Deanes, and Chapters, electing Abbots and Bishops as they became void, and the chief Justices approving them without his Privity, Licence, or Royal assent, he issued out a Writ to his chief Justice of *Ireland* to reform and prevent this dangerous Usurpation for the future. This year the Earl of *Albemarle* refusing to deliver up, to the King, some of his Castles and Lands committed to his custody, for which he was Excommunicated by the Bishop of *Norwich*, and the Pope's Legate, thereupon the King issued out a prohibition to all his Barons and Subjects in *Lancashire*, and five Counties more, not to Aid him or his complices, but to avoid them as Excommunicated Persons, till they had submitted to the King.

Ecclesiastical Censures were then commonly inflicted in that Age for Temporal Offences and Rebellions, to reduce Men to obedience to the King, as well as to the Church and Pope. At last the Earl came to the King under the conduct of *Walter* Archbishop of *York*, and by the mediation of *Pandulphus* the Legate, was reconciled to him.

Anno Domini 1221. The King being under the Wardship of *Peter* Bishop of *Winchester*, was, on *Whitsunday*, Crowned the second time at *Winchester* by *Stephen* Archbishop of *Canterbury*.

Soon after which there being a difference concerning the Bishoprick of *Ely*, between *Galfridus de Burgo*, Archdeacon of *Norwich*, and *Robert* of *York*, the Pope at last nulled both their Elections, and conferred the Bishoprick upon *John* Abbot of *Fontain*, who was Consecrated at *Westminster*.

The translation and enshrining of *Thomas Becket*.

The same year and day, *Hugh* Bishop of *Lincoln* was Canonized a Saint, by the procurement of the Archbishop. He likewise caused his Predecessor *Thomas Becket*, to be Translated, Enshrined, and Adored with great Solemnity. Most of the English, many of the French Archbishops, Bishops, Abbots, Priors, Clergy, and of other Countries, were, by the Archbishop's invitation, present at *Thomas Becket's* Translation.

The King by the Legat's, and his Council's advice, changed the Heathenish, and long-continued Trials in criminal Causes by Fire and Water, into other ways of Trial, and Punishments, by Imprisonment or abjuring the Realm.

Benedict Bishop of *Rochester*, *Richard* Bishop of *Sarum*, *Hugh* Bishop of *Lincoln*, *William* Bishop of *Bath* and *Glastonbury*, *Richard* Bishop of *Durham*, *Henry* Abbot of *Ramsey*, and other Clergy-men, were all made Justices Itinerants this year.

Henry Bishop of *Landaff* dying, thereupon *Pandulphus*, the Pope's Legate, conferred it upon *William* Prior of *Goldcliff*.

William de Marisco Bishop of *London*, of his own accord resigning his Bishoprick, *Eustachius de Faucumberge*, then Treasurer of the Exchequer, was chosen Bishop of *London*, whose Election was confirmed by the Legate *Pandulphus*. This Legate sent a Letter to *Peter* Bishop of *Winton*, and *Hugh de Burgh*, to prohibit and suppress the Usury of the

the Church of Great Britain. 71

the Jews, taken from Christians, and to stay a Suite brought by a Jew against the Abbot and Covent of *Westminster* before the Justices of the Jews, wherein he exacted usury from them, to the great scandal of Christianity, and the King's dishonour, and to joyn some discreet Persons with the Sheriff in each County for the collection of *Amerciaments*, to prevent their Malice and Extortions.

About this time was taken an Impostor at *Oxford* having five wounds in his Body and Members, &c. in his Side, Hands and Feet, who counterfeited himself to be Christ, with two Women his followers, counterfeiting themselves to be the Virgin *Mary*, the Mother of Christ, and *Mary Magdalen*. They were immured together with him without any Victuals, and starved to Death.

Then was a Council held at *Oxford* under Archbishop *Stephen*, where many Constitutions were made, most of them being very useful to reform Extortions, Abuses, Procurations in Visitations, the taking of any Fees for Letters of Order, Funerals, or Administring any Sacrament, as also against Pluralities, Non-residence, and other abuses of Clergymen.

Soon after this, the Archbishop and the Bishop of *Lincoln*, commanded, by their Injunctions, *That none should sell any victuals to the Jews, nor have any communion with them*; of which the Jews complaining, the King issued a Writ to the Majors of *Canterbury*, *Oxford*, and *Norwich*, to countermand the Bishop's Injunctions, that all should sell victuals and other necessaries to them, and that they should imprison every one refusing to do it, till further order.

Then the Prior of St. *Patrick* of *Dune* in *Ireland*, sent a Petition to the King to grant him and others some small Cell to reside in, in *England*, their Houses in *Ireland* being frequently burnt in the Wars, for St. *Patrick's*, and other Irish Saints sake, whose Relikes he then sent to the King for a present.

The King to satisfie the Archbishop, wrote a Letter to the Pope, to give way for the return of his Brother *Simon Langton* into *England*, out of which he was formerly banished (as well as Excommunicated, and deprived of all his Eccleliastical Benefices) for adhering to *Lewis*, and contemning the Pope's Excommunications. But we find not, that the Pope consented to this request.

Our Kings by reason of their manifold Affairs in the Court of *Rome*, relating to the Pope and other Forreign States, usually constituted, sometimes general, otherwise special Proctors, by their Letters Patents, to implead and defend in their Names and Rights, all matters there depending for or against them, of which there are many different Formes in our Records.

King *Henry* standing in need of a subsidy from the Bishops and Clergy, Pope *Honorius* thereupon sent his Bull to the Archbishops, Bishops, Abbots,

bots, Priors, and Clergy, entreating them to grant him a competent subsidy, to be disposed of by common consent onely, for publick benefit of the Realm, leaving the grant free to the Bishops and Clergy to impose and proportion it.

This year (*sc.* 1225.) the Archbishop of *Canterbury*, and his Suffragans, instead of granting the King a subsidy, or punishing leacherous Clearks, passed severe Decrees against their Concubines onely, principally intended against the Wives of Clergy men, whom they stiled Concubines in that Age.

The Bishop of *Cork* in *Ireland*, having obtained the King's Royal assent, at the Pope's request, to be Archbishop of *Cassel*, taking a journey to *Rome* to procure it, received his Writ for the restitution of his Temporalties after his return.

Then the Pope dispatched *Otto* his Legate into *England*, with Letters to the King, for his own filthy lucre. The King assembling a Parliamentary Council of his Nobles and Prelates, *Otto* read the Pope's Letters and Proposals, wherein the detestable Avarice, Extortion, and Rapine of the Pope and Court of *Rome* were clearly discovered, related by *Matthew Paris*.

Matth. Paris. Hist. Angl.

Otto pursuing his Rapines in *England*, by exacting Procurations from the Clergy, was by the Archbishop's means suddenly recalled thence, by the Pope, to his great discontent: and the prosecuting the Pope's former proposals committed to the Archbishop.

This year Pope *Honorius* the third, sent his Bull to *Geoffry de Lizimaco* the King's sworn Vassal, absolutely subverting all Papal dispensations with Subjects just Oaths to their Sovereignes. The Pope also sent prohibitory Letters to the King of *England*, to stop his intended Military Voyage into *France*, to recover his just Rights. Then the King paid ten thousand Marks, being all the Arrears of the sum granted by King *John* to the Pope by his Charter.

Godwin. Catal. of Bish. p. 515. 516.

Richard de Marisco, Bishop of *Durham*, dying suddenly at *Peterborough-Abbey*, as he was posting to *London* with a great troop of Lawyers, to prosecute his Suits against the Monks of *Durham*; thereupon they bestowed this Epitaph upon him.

Culmina qui cupi	⎫		Laudes pompasque siti	⎫	
Est sedata si	⎬		Si me pensare veli	⎬	
Qui populos regi	⎬ tis		Memores super omnia si	⎬ tis.
Quod mors immi	⎬		Non parcit honore poti	⎬	
Vobis præposi	⎬		Similis fueram, bene sci	⎬	
Quod sum vos eri	⎭		Ad me currendo veni	⎭	

Upon his Death there grew a great difference between King *Henry* the third, and the Monks of *Durham*, about the election of a Successor.

There

There was an Appeal about this Election, pending before the Archbishop of *York*, before whom the King constituted his Proctor by Patent. But after two years expensive contests, the Monks election of *William* Archdeacon of *Worcester*, a Man Learned and honest, faith *Matthew Paris*, was cancelled at *Rome*; *Luke* the King's Chaplain put by; and *Richard* Bishop of *Salisbury* Elected Bishop by the Pope's favour; the Pope onely gaining by such contests.

The Emperor *Frederick* the third, being justly incensed with the publication of divers Libellous, and Scandalous Excommunications of Pope *Gregory* IX. against him, in *England*, and all other Kingdoms and Churches, endeavoured to vindicate himself and his innocency against the Pope's calumnies, by dispatching Letters into all parts, and particularly into *England*. These proceedings of the Pope against the Emperor, so exasperated the Citizens of *Rome*, that they expelled the Pope from the City, and chafed him to *Perusium*.

Anno 1228. died *Stephen Langton* Archbishop of *Canterbury*, after whose death there grew a new contest between the King and Monks of *Canterbury*, about the Election of a new Archbishop. The Monks chose *Walter de Heveshám*, a Monk, whom the King refused to allow of, resolving to make *Richard*, his Chancellor, Archbishop. *Walter* posting to *Rome* to get Confirmation and Consecration from the Pope, and the King's Proctors there excepting against him, pressing the vacating of his Election, and making *Richard* Archbishop, with much importunity; they could not prevail with the Pope or Cardinals to stop *Walter's* Confirmation, or promote *Richard*, till they had promised, in the behalf of the King, unto the Pope, the tenths of all things moveable, from both his Kingdomes of *England* and *Ireland*. Whereupon the Pope and Cardinals forthwith vacated *Walter's* Election, for his insufficiency, and made *Richard* Archbishop. So the Pope got two years payment of his annual pension, granted by King *John*, and a Tenth in promise.

Yet where the King gave his Royal assent to Bishops duly Elected by his License; where there was no competition, the Pope interposed not.

This Archbishop *Richard* going to *Rome*, to complain against the King, that all affairs of his Kingdom were disposed by the counsel of his chief Justice *Hubert*, when he had there accomplished his designes against the King, was presently taken away by sudden Death.

Then the King issued out a prohibition to the Monks of *Canterbury*, not to do any thing prejudicial to the rights of his Crown, nor to elect any Person Archbishop, without his special License, nor to send any Monks to *Rome* by the Pope's command, to Elect an Archbishop there. The Monks in pursuance of this Prohibition by the King's License, elected *John* their Prior Archbishop, whom the King by his Letters Patents

tents approved, desiring the Pope to confirm him, and likewise made new Proctors in the Court of *Rome* concerning this Election. And the King to promote his Affairs the better in the Court of *Rome*, granted Annuities to some Cardinals to obtain that justice from them by such Pensions, which he could not procure without them. But yet the Pope vacated this second election as well as the first. Hereupon the Monks proceed to a third election; but this third Person was also cashiered by the Pope. This See continued three years after *Richard's* death, and *Edmond* being nominated Archbishop by the Pope, who sent him a Pall, was consecrated by *Roger* Bishop of *London* in *April*, *Anno* 1234. the King being present with thirteen Bishops, in *Christ-Church Canterbury*.

Fuller Church-Histor. *lib.*3.¶ In the year 1232. the Caursines first came into *England*, proving the bane of the Land. These were *Italians* by birth, terming themselves the Pope's Merchants, driving no other Trade than letting out of Money, great Banks whereof they brought into *England*, differing little from the *Jews*, save that they were more merciless to their Debtors. Now because the Pope's Legat was altogether for ready Money, when any Tax by Levy, Commutation of Vows, Tenths, Dispensations, &c. were due to the Pope, from Prelates, Convents, Priests, or Lay-persons, these Caursines instantly furnished them with present Coin upon their solemn Bonds and Obligations. These Caursines were generally hated for their Extortions. *Roger Black*, that learned and pious Bishop of *London*, once excommunicated these Caursines for their oppression: but they appealing to the Pope, their good friend, forced him after much molestation to desist.

These Caursines were commonly known by the name of *Lombards*, from *Lombardy*, the place of their nativity, in *Italy*. And although they deserted *England* on the decaying of the Pope's power and profit therein; yet a double memorial remaineth of them: one of their Habitation, in *Lombard-street* in *London*: the other of their Employment; a *Lombard* unto this day signifies a Bank for Usury, or Pawns, still continued in the Low-countries and elsewhere. See here the Pope's hypocrisie, forbidding Usury, as a sin so detestable, under such heavy penalties in his Canon Law, whilst his own Instruments were the most unconscionable practisers thereof, without any controul.

*Elius Rubeus in Semidali. Lib.*2.*c.*3.& 4. *Elias Rubeus*, an English-man, wrote a Book, wherein he said, *That the Monks had converted Religion into superstition, making salvation to consist in things, of themselves, vain and indifferent: that there was no kind of men more blind in concupiscence, or infamous for uncleanness, than the Popish Clergy,* &c.

Certain years after, one *Laurence*, an English-man, in a Sermon of his, admonished the Church, *That a great danger hung over her head by the Monks, that they were seducers, and the Ministers of Anti-christ.*

Matthew

the Church of GREAT BRITAIN.

Matthew Paris informs us, That *Hubert de Burgo*, Anno 1232. being chief Justice of *England*, the King's principal faithful Counsellor, the greatest opposer of the Pope's Usurpations and Extortions, was, by the power of the Pope, and of *Peter* Bishop of *Winchester*, suddenly removed from all his Offices, and impeached of several Crimes, some of them amounting to high Treason. *Hubert*, to prevent the rage of his Enemies, fled to the Church of *Merton*, and there took Sanctuary. Whence the King commanded the Mayor of *London* by his Letters (the *Londoners* being his mortal Enemies) to pull him out forcibly, and bring him to him alive or dead. Which the Mayor and Citizens readily undertaking, and marching thither with great Forces, the King, by the advice of the Earl of *Chester*, suddenly countermanded them thence to their great discontent. After which *Godfry* of *Cranecumb* (whom the King sent to apprehend him, in *Essex*, with three hundred men armed) finding the Chappel doors shut, violently brake them open, apprehended *Hubert*, and carried him thence, bound with cords, a prisoner to the Tower of *London*.

This breach of Sanctuary being made known to *Roger* Bishop of *London*, (whose Diocess it was) he tells the King, that if the Earl were not restored to the Chappel, he would excommunicate all the Authors of that outrage. The Earl is accordingly restored, but the Sheriffs of *Essex* and *Hertford* at the King's command, with the Powers of their Countreys, besiege the Chappel so long, that at last the Earl was compelled to come forth, and render himself, bearing his affliction patiently. *Hubert* is again imprisoned in the Tower. Nothing could appease the King's Ire, but that Mass of Gold and other Riches, which the Knights Templers had in their custody, upon trust, which *Hubert* willingly yielded up. This mollified the King's mind toward him. Hereupon he had all such Lands granted unto him, as either King *John* had given, or himself had purchased. There undertook for him as Sureties, the Earls of *Cornwall*, and *Warren*, *Marshal* and *Ferrars*; and himself was committed to the Castle of *Devizes*, there to abide in free Prison under the custody of four Knights, belonging each of them to one of these four Earls. Afterwards, though he was restored to the King's favour, yet upon new accusations of his Enemies, he was condemned to give to the King *Blanch* Castle, *Grosmount* in *Wales*, *Skenefrith*, and *Hafield*, and then also was deprived of Title of Earl of *Kent*. *Speed's Histor. in H. 3.*

King *Henry* erected a special Church, House, and form of Government for the Jews converted to the Christian Religion.

The Bishops meeting together at *Glocester*, Anno 1234. the King, being jealous, that they intended to consult of some other things, prejudicial to his Crown, State and Dignity, sent a Writ of Prohibition to them, not to treat of any thing of this nature. After this, the King and Bishops meeting at a Conference at *Westminster*, the King charged
some

some of the Bishops with a design to deprive him of his Crown, which they denied; whereupon one of them, in a great rage, excommunicated all those who raised such a report of them.

Clauſ. 18. H.3. Memb. 16.

Then the King commanded all common Whores and Concubines of Priests, to be imprisoned, and banished out of the University of *Oxford*, by his temporal Officers; unless they had Lands therein, and by Oath and other security have good assurance for their chast and honest demeanour for the future, and not to resort to Clerks Lodgings.

If a Clerk, or Beneficed person were indebted to the King, or incurred his just displeasure, the King commanded the Bishop of the Diocess to sequester all his Ecclesiastical Benefices, till his debt was satisfied, his displeasure remitted, and the sequestration discharged by special Writ.

The Pope was grown so proud in this Age by his Usurpations, that he would not vouchsafe to hear and admit the King's Proctors and Agents, sent to *Rome* upon his urgent Affairs, without most humble suits and supplications in his Letters of credence and procurations.

The King made a Remonstrance to the Pope of the several injuries done to him by the Earl of *Britain*, in seizing on his Castles, and revolting to the King of *France*; desiring the Pope by his Ecclesiastical censures to compel him to restore his Castles to him. The Pope instead of excommunicating this treacherous Earl, sent for him to *Rome*, and made him General of the *Croſſadoes* by Sea and Land against the *Grecians*.

The Pope commanded *Peter* Bishop of *Winchester* to assist him both with his purse and advice in his Military affairs against the *Grecians* and *Romans*.

The Pope, as he encroached upon the election and confirmation of the Archbishops and Bishops of *England*, so did he likewise upon the election and confirmation of Abbots, who must go to *Rome* to attend his pleasure for their approbation and confirmation, as in the case of the Abbot of St. *Albans* doth appear. The Pope condescended to the Abbot's election, but upon this condition, that he should take an express Oath of Fealty to the Pope and Church of *Rome*, and his Successors, prescribed in his Bull, directed to the Bishops, which Oath suddenly tendered to him, by way of surprise, he took publickly, before the Covent, and all the Clergy and People, at his Consecration and Instalment, related by *Matthew Paris*, a Monk of this Monastery.

Matth. Paris. p. 599.

This new Oath of Allegeance to the Pope and See of *Rome*, being the highest encroachment upon the King's Rights and Prerogative, making all who take it the Pope's Subject, and Vassals, not the King's, was concealed both from the King and Abbot, till the very nick of his Consecration and Benediction, for fear it should be opposed and refused.

The Prior of the preaching Friers presuming to arrest and imprison some persons in *York-shire*, pretended to be Heretical, when he had no legal

The Church of Great Britain.

legal power to arrest or imprison such, the King thereupon issued a Mandate to the Sheriff of *York-shire*, to arrest and imprison all Heretical persons, till his further order therein,

Anno 1236. the Archbishop of *Canterbury* being sued by the Prior and Monks of *Canterbury*, for certain Advousons of Churches, Possessions, Rents, and Services in the Ecclesiastical Court, by authority of the Pope's Letters, despising the remedy of the King's Court, where they ought to sue for them, thereupon the King issued forth his prohibition to the Archbishop, prohibiting him, in his Faith and Allegeance to him, not to answer them in that Court, it being prejudicial to his Crown and Dignity, &c. *Pryn. clauf.2c. H. 3. m. 12. dorso.*

The King by several Writs of Prohibition countermanded the Pope's own Bulls and Delegates, as contrary to the Rights and Dignities of his Crown, and prohibited their proceedings, which gave some check to his Usurpations of this Kind.

The King's Clerks and Houshold Chaplains in those dayes wearing long Hair and Peruwigs, thereupon the King to reform this abuse, issued out a Writ to *William de Perecat*, authorizing and strictly commanding him to cut their Hair, and pull off their yellow Peruwigs, under pain of being shaven and polled himself. *Pat. 21. H. 3. m. 3. dorso. Long Hair and Peruwigs forbidden in the clergy.*

The Monks and Converts of the *Cistercian* Order, contrary to their Vows and Rules, becoming common Merchants, buying, and selling again, Wools and Skins, to the prejudice of other Merchants, and scandal of their Profession, the King, for redress thereof, issued out a Writ of Prohibition to all the Sheriffs of *England*, to seize the Goods and Moneys of those Monks and Converts, to his use, who should offend therein.

There being a great difference between the Bishop of *Clochor* in *Ireland* and the Archbishop of *Armagh*, and their Tennants, concerning injuries and grievances touching their Churches; the Archbishop of *Armagh* procuring the King's Letters to his Chief Justice by misinformation, whilst he was excommunicated; the King thereupon revoked his former Letters, and commanded his Chief Justice in *Ireland*, to hear and determine the Controversies between them.

Upon the death of *Richard* Bishop of *Durham*, the King upon the Petition of the Prior and Convent, granted his Licenfe to elect a new Bishop. The Bishop of *Norwich* dying this year, the Monks elected *Simon*, their Prior, for their Bishop, whom the King disapproving, made a special Proctor against him before the Archbishop to hinder his confirmation, and to appeal against him to the See of *Rome*, if it were expedient, where he likewise constituted his Proctor.

Then the Pope upon the King's request, under a pretext to rectifie some of those abuses (against which there was an universal complaint) sent *Ottobone*, his Legat, into *England*, who soon proclaimed himself a ravening Wolf, as well as his Predecessors,

Then

Then was a Council called by the Pope's Legat unto St. *Paul's* Church in *London*, where most of the Prelates, Abbots and Priors assembled together. The Canons that were made and promulged in this Council who so please, may peruse at leisure in *Matthew Paris*, and in *Johannes de Aton*, his *Constitutiones legitimæ Ecclesiæ, totiusque Ecclesiæ* Anglicanæ, *ab Legatis à latere summorum Pontificum collectio, fol.* 1. *ad* 121. with his Glofs upon them. The first Canon was for the Dedication and Consecration of Churches, many Cathedral as well as Parish-churches being then unconsecrated. The second and third concerning Ecclesiastical Sacraments and Baptism. Others concerning the covetousness of Priests, their hearing Confessions, the qualities of such as were to be ordained; their Farmers and Vicars, Presentations to Churches; not dividing one Church into more; the Residence of Bishops and Priests; Pluralities; the Habit of Clerks, clandestine marriage of Priests, Priests Concubines; their Sons succession in their Benefices; their Judges, Procurations, undue, unjust Citations; Exactions by Procurations, Registers; abuses by Proctors and Ecclesiastical Judges; and an Oath to be prescribed to them, to prevent the like abuses for the future. In this Council this Legat introduced the use of Oaths in Ecclesiastical Courts and Causes, never formerly used in *England*, by colour whereof other Oaths were introduced by the Popish Prelates, against the Laws and Customs of the Realm, till the King, by his Prohibition, restrained these Usurpations.

The first use of Oaths in Ecclesiastical Courts in England.

Then was a private Letter sent from *Rome* to the Pope's Legat in *England*, advising him to moderation, to prevent a total rejection of the Pope and See of *Rome*.

In the 22th year of *Henry* the Third, the Greek Churches renounced all obedience to, and communion with, the Church of *Rome*: which made the Pope and his Court fear the like Schism and revolt in *England*, occasioned by the Legat's violent Extortions, and advancement of Strangers to Benefices; whereupon he intended to recal him thence to prevent these ill consequences; but the Legat loth to depart, prevailed with the King and others to sollicit the Pope for his continuance in *England*, upon pretence of publick good.

This year there happening a difference between the King and Monks of *Durham* about their Bishop elect, whom the King would not approve, he thereupon issued his Letters Patents to the Archbishop of *York*, appointing his Proctors to appeal to the See of *Rome* against this election, only for delay to preserve his right.

After the death of *Henry de Sandford*, Bishop of *Rochester*, the Monks of *Rochester* elected *Richard Windeley*, a learned Man, for their Bishop, who being presented by the Monks to *Edmond* Archbishop of *Canterbury* for his confirmation, he refused to admit him, *Unde Monachi Domini Papæ presentiam appellarunt.* Upon this Appeal the Pope gave Judgment

for

for the Monks againſt the Archbiſhop, and condemned him in coſts of ſuit, confirming their election in deſpite of the Archbiſhop, with whom the Pope was very angry for oppoſing his intolerable exactions in *England*, whereupon this Biſhop Elect was confecrated at *Canterbury* in St. *Gregory*'s Church by the Archbiſhop, the Biſhop of *London* and other Biſhops.

Then the Monks of *Coventry* choſe *Nicholas de Fernham* for their Biſhop, who refuſed to accept thereof: whereupon at laſt they choſe *Simon de Pateſhul*, who accepted it.

The Pope having excommunicated the Emperour *Frederick*, *Otto*, the Pope's Legat, was very diligent to ſee the Pope's ſcandalous Excommunications and Bulls againſt him publiſhed throughout all *England*.

In the twenty fourth year of the Reign of King *Henry* the Third, the Monks of *Cambridge* having apprehended an Heretick (as he was called) the King thereupon iſſued forth a Precept to the Sheriff of *Cambridge*, to bring this Heretick before him, at *Weſtminſter*, to be examined, and diſpoſed of as he ſhould direct. Who he was, and what his Hereſies were, *Matthew Paris* tells us, ſaying, *He was a man of an honeſt and ſevere life; and that he openly aſſerted, that* Pope Gregory *was not the Head of the Church, but there was another Head of the Church; that the Church was profaned, the Devil was let looſe; the Pope was an Heretick: that* Gregory, *who was called Pope, had defiled the Church, and the world too. This and divers other things of like nature, he ſpake, before the Pope's Legat, in the hearing of many.*

Pope *Gregory* before his death, to carry on his Wars againſt the Emperor *Frederick*, *Anno* 1240. intended by way of proviſion to confer all the Benefices in *England* (eſpecially of the Clergy) on the Sons of *Romans*, and other Forreigners, upon condition to aſſiſt him againſt the Emperour, ſending his Bull to three Biſhops, to confer no leſs than three hundred of the next Benefices, that fell void within their Dioceſs, on theſe Aliens.

Anno 1241. *Otto*, the Pope's Legat, having long pillaged the Realm and Church of *England*, was ſent for the third time by the Pope. And the King to oblige the Legat, as well to promote his Affairs at *Rome*, as in *England*, before his departure hence, Knighted and conferred an Annual penſion on his Nephew, feaſted the Legat publickly at *Weſtminſter*, and placed him at the feaſt in his own Royal Throne, to the great offence of his Nobles and Subjects.

Edmond Archbiſhop of *Canterbury* deceaſing, the King commended *Boniface* (his Queen's Uncle, a Forreigner, and every way unfit for ſuch a truſt) to the Monks of *Canterbury*, to ſucceed him, whom they accordingly elected.

There being a great conteſt between the King, and the Prior and Monks of *Winchester*, about the election of their Biſhop, they electing firſt
William

William de Raley, Bishop of *Norwich*, whom the King and Pope opposing, thereupon they Elected *Ralph Nevil*, whose election was likewise vacated. After which they Elected the Bishop of *Norwich* again, whose election was suddenly made, and quickly confirmed at *Rome*. Yet the King commanded the Major of *Winchester* to forbid the new Bishop entrance into the City; which he did; who thereupon Excommunicated him for his labour, and interdicted the whole City. The King thereupon so persecuted the Monks, that he imprisoned diverse of them, and forced the Bishop to fly the Realm, and pass into *France* for a season.

Matth. Westm.

Then there arose a new contest, between the Archbishop and Monks of *Canterbury*, about Jurisdiction and Visitation, wherein they Excommunicated one the other; and yet slighted these their mutual Anathemae's, as ridiculous nullities.

The King being in *France*, sent his Writ to the Archbishop of *York*, then *Custos Regni*, to confer Benefices that should fall void on such Clerks of His, who, to their great danger and expence, continued with him, and incurred many various casualties, in his services, beyond the Seas, commanding them all in general, and one of them onely in special, by Name, to be first provided for in this kind.

Anno 1246. *Boniface* Archbishop of *Canterbury*, upon a feigned pretext, that his Church of *Canterbury* was involved in very great debts by his Predecessor, but in truth by himself, to carry on Forreign Wars, and gratifie the Pope, procured, from Pope *Innocent*, a grant of the first years Fruits of all Benefices, that should fall void within his Diocess for seven years space, till he should raise out of them the sum of ten thousand Marks, besides two thousand Marks yearly out of the Bishoprick. This Grant of first-fruits of Benefices to *Boniface*, made way for Popes appropriating first-fruits, and Annats to themselves soon after.

N. B.

About this time was *Edmond* Archbishop of *Canterbury* Canonized for a Saint by the Pope, to gratifie the King, and facilitate the imposing and levying of his Papal exactions upon the Clergy and Realm.

The Bishops and Clergy of the Province of *Canterbury*, to avoid the turbulent visitation and exactions of Archbishop *Boniface*, made a Tax and Collection to defray the expenses of their Appeals and oppositions against him in the Court of *Rome*.

Some Abbots and Convents perceiving that *Robert Grosthed*, and other Bishops, intended to vex and oppress them, by their new powers to visit them, derived from the Pope, combined together to make a common purse to oppose and withstand them by Appeals to the Pope; whom they hoped would back them for Money, as the Bishops combined together to withstand the Archbishop's Visitation in his Province.

Not-

Notwithstanding this combination, the Bishop of *Lincoln*, proceeded to visit both the Monasteries and Nunneries in his Diocess, with great severity and Tyranny.

But although *Robert Grosthed* at first was a great stickler for the Pope, and an oppressor of the Nobility and Laity of his Diocess, with his Visitations, appeals to *Rome*, and Excommunications; yet afterwards he opposed the Pope's Provisions directed to him, for which the Pope suspended him from his Bishoprick: Whereupon he sent a notable Letter to Pope *Innocent*, rendring him the reasons why he was not bound to obey his unjust Letters and Provisions, as most contrary to the Doctrine and Practice of Christ and his Apostles, tending to the ruine of Peoples Souls; and that no Bishop or other Person was bound to obey any of the Pope's Mandates as Apostolical, but what were warranted by the Doctrine and Practice of Christ and his Apostles. The Letter is to be seen at large in Mr. *Prynne's* late History of Pope's Usurpations, &c. *Tom.2.*

A little before his death, this *Robert Grosthed* called some of his Clergy to him, and by strong reasons and arguments informed them, *That the Pope was Antichrist, because he was a destroyer of Souls,* &c. *Matthew Paris* gives this character of him; *Migravit ab hujusmode mundi, quem nunquam dilexit, exilio, sanctus* Lincolniensis *Episcopus,* Robertus *secundus, apud* Bugedonam, *manerium suum, in nocte sancti* Dionysii, *Papæ & Regis Redargutor manifestus, Prælatorum corrector, Monarchorum corrector, Presbyterorum director; Clericorum instructor, Scholarium sustentator; Populi prædicator; Incontinentium persecutor; Scripturarum sedulus perscrutator diversarum;* Romanorum *malleus & contemptor; in mensa refectionis corporalis dapsilis, copiosus & civilis, hilaris & affabilis: in mensa vero spirituali devotus, lacrymosus & contritus: in officio Pontificali sedulus, venerabilis, & indefatigabilis.*

He died *Anno* 1253. Of which year *Matthew Paris* gives this Character, Transsit igitur annus ille Papæ Papalibus augurialis. The Pope being much incensed against *Grosthed*, wrote a Letter to the King of *England*, to cause his bones to be digged up, and to be cast out of the Church: whereupon the Bishop's ghost appeared unto him that night, expostulated with him, pricked him in the side, and haunted him till his death.

Vide Ranulph Cistrens. Polychron. lib. 7. c 1. 36. & Henr. de Knighton de eventib. Angliæ. Lib. 2. c. 35.

The Canons of *Lincoln* chose *Henry* of *Lexinton* to succeed him, who was then Dean of the Church of *Lincoln*; the King approved of his Election, being Consecrated soon after by Bishop *Boniface* beyond the Seas.

Then the King issued out a Writ to the Bishop of *Chichester* to publish throughout his Diocess the priviledges he had granted to all such, who should cross themselves for the holy Land, being the same in termes with those, the year before, sent to the Archbishop of *York* to publish, the Writ running in the same forme.

M

In the 38.h. year of King *Henry* the third, the Archbishops and Bishops having agreed to grant the King a Difme toward the relief of the holy Land, by advice of the King's Council in Parliament; appointed it to be collected by the Bishops of *Norwich* and *Chichester*, and Abbot of *Westminster*, for which they assigned them an annual stipend. In *August* following, the King issued forth Patents to the Archbishops, Bishops, Abbots, &c. in *Ireland*, specially to promote this Croysado and Difme in *Ireland*, and to assist those sent thither to promote it, whereof one was the Pope's Subdeacon.

The King being in *France*, issued his precept to the Barons of the Exchequer, to issue Moneys for the repair of the Church of *Westminster*, which he intended to have consecrated before his voyage to the holy Land.

Wykes's Hist. Tom. 2.   He issued Writs to enquire of the real values of the Manors, Lands, Rents, and Revenues of Religious persons (in nature of Doomsday Book) that he might the better improve them when they fell into his hand by vacancies, or deaths of Abbots and Priors, towards the debts he contracted by his forreign Wars.

Matth. Paris, Hist. Angl. p.   *Matthew Paris* tells us, of strange forgeries and devices set on foot by the Pope and his Agents, to oppress the Clergy of *England*, and involve them in bonds and debts to the Pope and King (who served each others turns) and that by the treachery of the Bishop of *Hereford* and and others to ingratiate themselves with both. And the Bishop of *Hereford* and *Rustand*, the Pope's Legate, oppressed the Clergy of *England* that year 1254. and great complaints were made against them.

The King being unable by his absence to be personally present at the Feast of St. *Edward* at *Westminster*, which he annually consecrated, constituted several persons to solemnize this Feast, and make Offerings, Processions, and give almes in his stead, and commanded the Parishoners of St. *Margaret*, and the *Londoners* to go to *Westminster* in Procession with Wax Tapers, and other formalities for the honour of this Saint and holy-day.

The King in the 39th. year of his Reign sent a pious Writ to the Cistercians and other Abbots in their general Assembly, to make a special devout Prayer unto God for him, his Queen and Children.

The Bishop Elect of *Winton* having forcibly and unjustly by his power deprived the Prior of *Winton*, and thrust another into his place without his due Election, the deprived Prior thereupon Appealed to the Pope and Court of *Rome*, where he expected to be restored with great confidence: but to shew how much more prevalent Money then was in that corrupt Court than Justice; this intruder was confirmed, and he returned after great expence frustrate of his expectation, having some Manors assigned him for his support during life, out of which the Pope had an annual pension of 365. Marks to support his Table.

The

The Jews of *Lincoln* having crucified a Christian Child, to the great dishonour and disgrace of Jesus Christ, the King appointed special Justices, diligently to enquire of, and severely to punish, this grand offence, by his Patent and Commission.

The King this year, fearing some designs against him from *Rome*, issued a Writ to the Barons and Bailiffs of *Dover*; and to the Wardens of the Cinque-ports, not to permit any Clerks to pass out of their respective Ports beyond the Seas, unless he would first take an Oath, that if he went to the Court of *Rome*, he should demand nor require nothing against the King's Crown and Dignity, nor the Pope's grant or Ordinance concerning the Realm of *Sicily*. And the King, by his Letters Patents, constituted two distinct Proctors in the Court of *Rome*, concerning the affairs of the Kingdom of *Sicily*, and other occasions there to be transacted.

The Pope had a greater share in the Disme than the King, who could dispose of none of it, but by His and *Rustand's* consents. He likewise issued his Mandate to the Sheriff of *Kent*, to provide a speedy passage at *Dover* for *Rustand* the Pope's Agent, and to defray the charges of it, which should be allowed him.

The King understanding the Archbishop's and Bishops designs, intended to be prosecuted in a Council of the Bishops of his Province, which Archbishop *Boniface* had convocated, against his Crown, Dignity, Courts, Judges, &c. Prohibited him and them to meet therein; under pain of forfeiting their Temporalties. The Archbishop and Bishops, notwithstanding these Writs, met and proceeded in their Convocation, in a very presumptuous manner, as those fifty Articles then drawn up, and tendered to the King, and their Papal decrees in pursuit of them, will most evidently demonstrate. They were tendered to the King, by the Archbishops and Bishops, for which they resolved to contend to the uttermost.

These Constitutions are collected and Printed in *John de Aton*, quoting *Lindewood*, who cites and glosseth upon most of them under several Titles, in the Margin of every one of them, where you may peruse them with his Canonical gloss. These were made *Anno Dom.* 1261.

What Procurations the Archbishop of *Messana* (arrived in *England* this year, as the Pope's Legate) exacted and extorted from the Bishops and Abbots with great violence, and what injuries the Archbishop of *Canterbury* did to the Bishop of *Rochester*, you may read in *Matthew Paris*.

The King and his Council resolving to banish the *Poictovin* Clergymen out of the Nation, and not to imprison them in *England*, issued a Writ to the Constables of the Castles of *Winton* and *Dover*, of the banishment and transportation of the Archdeacon of *Winton*, out of the Realm, and to see he carried away no Moneys with him.

84 The History of

In the 42 year of this King, the Friers Minorites sent a Petition to King *Henry* to confirm their intrusion, into St. *Edmonds*, by his second Charter, not deeming the Pope's Bull they had got sufficient, which the Abbots and Monks contemned and set at naught.

The King to satisfie the Pope's demands, and the easier to get in the Dismes the Pope had granted him to gain *Sicily*, which the Archbishop, Bishops, and Religious Persons in *England* refused to pay, assigned thirty thousand Marks thereof to the Pope.

Godfry de Kimeton, Dean of *York*, was elected Archbishop of that See, and forced to travel to *Rome* for his Confirmation.

Fulco Bishop of *London* died of the Plague, and *Wengham* then Chancellor of *England*, notwithstanding his insufficiency, and want of learning and Knowledge, in Divinity, procured Letters Patents from King *Henry* by advice of his Council (in imitation of the Pope's Commendae's, then grown very common) to hold and retain all his former Ecclesiastical Dignities and Benefices, whereof the King was Patron, together with his Bishoprick, for so long time as the Pope should please to grant him a dispensation: whose dispensation alone would not bar the King to present to those Dignities and Benefices, being all void in Law, by making him a Bishop. He had the like Patent to retain his Benefices and Ecclesiastical preferments in *Ireland*. This is the first Patent of a *Commenda retinere*, granted by the King to any Bishop Elect, saith Mr. *Prynne*, being made by the advice of his Lords and Judges, which makes it more considerable.

The first Patent of a Commenda retinere, granted by the King to any Bishop elect.

The King in the 44th year of his Reign, issued a Writ to the Barons of *Dover*, and other Ports, to search for, and apprehend, all Italian Clerks and Lay-men, and all others that should bring any Bulls from *Rome*, prejudicial to him and his Realm, and not to permit any to arrive with Horse and Armes in the Realm, without his special License; and to arrest all such as should there Land, till they received further order from him.

The Bishop of St. *David's* and his Clerks complaining to the King how much the priviledges of their Churches, Monasteries, Houses, Goods, and Persons, were violated in *Wales*, in an hostile manner, throughout his Diocess, issued out a Writ and Prohibition to his Officers for their future protection and indemnity against such injuries and oppressions.

Boniface, Archbishop of *Canterbury*, being an Alien, and forced to fly out of the Kingdom by the Barons, was, upon a Treaty between the King and his Barons, permitted to return into *England* upon certain conditions.

The King and the Barons having by common consent, entred into Articles of Agreements under their hands, and referred themselves therein to the determination of the French King, or the Pope's Legate; the

King

King thereupon conſtituted three Proctors, to conclude and conſent on his behalf, to whatever ſhould be therein agreed, ſubmitting himſelf to the Legate's Eccleſiaſtical Cenſures and Excommunication to compell him to the performance thereof.

During the Wars between the King and his Barrons, diverſe Vicars and Parſons deſirous to reſide upon their Cures, ſo as they might be protected from violence therein, the King thereupon granted protections to thoſe who deſired them.

An *Oxford* Jew, having in contempt of Chriſt and Chriſtian Religion, in a ſolemn Proceſſion there held by the Univerſity, caſt down and broken the Crucifix carried before them, and eſcaping; and the Jews not producing his Body as the King ordered them; the King thereupon commanded the Sheriff of *Oxford*, by ſeveral Writs to ſeize the Bodies and Goods of all the Jews in *Oxford*, till they gave ſufficient ſecurity, at their proper coſts, to erect a beautifull high Marble Croſs, with the Images of Chriſt on the one ſide, and the Virgin *Mary* with Chriſt in her Armes on the other ſide, curiouſly and decently guilt, and the cauſe thereof engraven on it, in the place where the offence was committed, calling the Major of the Town and Cofferers of the Jews to his aſſiſtance; and till they made and delivered to the Proctors of the Univerſity another portable Croſs of Silver handſomly guilded, with a Spear as large as that carried before the Archbiſhop to be carryed before the Maſters and Scholars of the Univerſity in their future proceſſions. And becauſe diverſe Jewes, to prevent it, had ſecretly convayed away their goods to others, to enquire diligently after ſuch goods and ſell them, that the work might be ſpeedily effected before St. *Edwards* Feaſt.

The Money hereupon being levyed of the Jews, to make theſe Croſſes, and the King being informed, that the Marble-croſs could not be erected in the place preſcribed, without damage and prejudice to ſome Burgeſſes of *Oxford*, whereupon they purpoſed to erect it juſt over againſt the Jews Synagogue there: The King and his Council conceiving that place inconvenient, ordered it to be ſet up within the place of *Merton* Colledge, near the Church; and the other portable Croſs to be delivered to the Scholars thereof, to be kept in their Houſe, and carried in Proceſſions of the Univerſity, as aforeſaid.

Of the Diſmes granted to the King by the Pope, the King had uſually the leaſt ſhare; the Pope, the Cardinals, and Legates, ſwallowing up the greateſt part of them, as the Learned Archbiſhop *Matthew Parker* hath obſerved. *Parker. Antiqu. Eccleſ. Britan. p. 194.*

Boniface, the Military Archbiſhop of *Canterbury*, died beyond the Seas, *Anno Dom.* 1271. when he had reaped the profits of that See, and pillaged that Province twenty ſix years, ſix moneths, and ſixteen dayes; moſt of which he ſpent in Wars and negotiations beyond the Seas, and never Preached one Sermon all that time, for ought we find. That year

year there was so great an inundation of Rain at *Canterbury*, such Lightening and Tempest, as had not been seen nor heard for a long time: The Thunder was dreadful, and continued a whole day and night, and such an inundation of Water followed, that it overthrew Stones, Vines, and Trees, Cattel were drowned; and much Corn spoiled; and the City was so over-flown, that Men nor Horses could pass. After this Flood, there followed a great Famine, and the Plague swept away many in the City and Countrey round about.

Mr. *Fox* relates, That a little before King *Henry*'s death, there fell out a controversie between the Monks and Citizens of *Norwich*, about certain Tallages and Liberties, that after much altercation and wrangling words, the furious rage of the Citizens so much encreased, that they set upon the Abbey and Priory, and burned both the Church and Bishop's Palace. At the last King *Henry* calling for certain of his Lords and Barons, sent them to *Norwich*, that they might punish, and see Execution done on the chiefest Malefactors; some of them were condemned and burnt; and some were drawn by the heeles with Horses through the Streets of the City, and so in much misery ended their lives. King *Henry* having in his company the Bishop of *Rochester*, and the Earl of *Glocester*, followed his Justice *Thomas Trivet* to *Norwich*. The Bishop having Excommunicated all who consented to this wickedness, and the Judge Executed the nocent; the King condemned the Town in three thousand Marks of Silver, to be paid by a day, toward the repairing of the Church so burnt, and also to pay one hundred pounds in Silver, toward the repair of a Cup arising to twenty pounds in Gold. He returning thence towards *London*, fell grievously sick at the Abbey of St. *Edmonds* in *Suffolk*, where after he had in a Religious manner acknowledged his sins, he rendered up the same to his Redeemer, when he had reigned fifty six years and twenty dayes.

A Prince (writes *Speed*) whose devotion was greater than his discretion, as we see, in permitting the depredation of himself, and his whole Kingdom, by Papal overswayings.

After the Death and Funeral of King *Henry* (who was Buried at *Westminster* Church, Founded and almost finished by him) Prince *Edward* his Son, being at that time in the holy Land, where he obtained many notable Victories against the *Saracens*. Who thereupon suborned an Assassinate to kill him, under pretext of delivering a Message to him from the *Soldan* of *Babylon*, who stabbed him into the Body with a poisoned Knife, to the hazard of his Life; his Nobles notwithstanding his remote absence, were so Loyal as to Proclaim him King, and Swear Fealty and Allegiance to him, as their Sovereign Lord. They sent out Writs whereby they Proclaimed the King's peace: They first of them were directed to all the Sheriffs of *England*, to Proclaim in their respective Counties,

Thomas Walsingham.
Matth. Westm.

The Church of Great Britain.

Counties: the other to the King's chief Justice of *Ireland*, to be there Proclaimed, who, with others, was authorized likewise to receive the Fealty, as well of all the Archbishops, Bishops, Abbots, Clergy, as Nobles and other Lay-subjects in *Ireland*, due unto him as their King and Sovereign Lord.

In the third year of this King's Reign *Walter de Merton*, Bishop of *Rochester* and Chancellor of *England*, finished the Colledge of his own Name in *Oxford*. This *Walter de Merton*, was one of the Guardians of the Realm in the King's absence.

A Writ was issued to *Lewellin* Prince of *Wales*, requiring an Oath of Fealty from him to King *Edward*, as his Sovereign Lord; and two Abbots thereby made Commissioners to receive his Oath, who refused to appear, or give any answer to them. The Abbots made a special return of their proceedings therein to the Lord Chancellor.

The first thing this King and his Council did, was to make a publick Declaration and Protestation against Pope *Clement* the fifth, his late Usurpation, who a little before King *Henry* his death, had, by his Papal Provisions, conferred the Bishoprick of *Wintou* on *John de Pontissera*, and the Archbishoprick of *Canterbury* upon *Robert Kilwardby*, without the King's precedent Licence, or Monks Election: rejecting *William de Chilenden* (duly Elected by the Monks of *Canterbury* by King *Henry's* Licence) that so he might Usurp the disposal of all other Bishopricks by these and other former like Presidents.

After the death of Pope *Clement* the fourth, the See of *Rome* continuing void for two years and ten moneths, by reason of the Cardinals discord about a Successor: at last they Elected *Theobald* Archdeacon of *Leige*, Pope; who was with King *Edward* the first, in the holy Land: of him these two Verses were made.

Papatum munus tenet Archidiaconus unus,
Quem Patrem Patrum fecit discordia fratrum.

Prince *Edward* in his return from the holy Land, repaired to this new Pope's Court, his late Chaplain, and fellow-souldier, who, at his request, Excommunicated the Murderers of his kinsman *Henry*, Son and heir to the King of *Germany*, at *Viterbium*, and disinherited some of them by his Imperious Decree, till they should come personally to *Rome*, to purge themselves, or submit to his absolute order in all things.

This new Pope *Gregory*, sent a special Nuncio into *England*, under pretext to compel all Ecclesiastical Persons to pay two years Dismes of their Temporalties, and Ecclesiastical Livings; to the King and his Brother, but in truth to himself, who converted most of it to his own use: whereupon sundry of the Abbots and Clergy of the Realm refused to

pay

pay the premised Disme, notwithstanding the Pope's Nuncio's Excommunications denounced against them, contemning his Ecclesiastical Censures: whereupon the *Nuncio* wrote to the Chancellor to command the Sheriffs to assist the Collectors of it by their secular power, and levy it by force where there was need. Hereupon the Chauncellor issued Writs to all the Sheriffs of *England*, and some others, to assist the Collectors accordingly.

It seems the Bishop of *Winton* compounded, and paid a fine of five hundred Marks for his two years Dismes to the Pope's Collector.

At the same time the King wanting Moneys, appointed special Collectors of the Arrears due upon the Dismes granted to his Father, by the Pope, towards the relief of the holy Land.

A new Archbishop of *Dublin*, being elected the second year of this King's Reign, who resided with the Queen of *Scots* in *Scotland*, the King, at her special request, granted him, this priviledge, to make Attorneys to appear for him in all his Courts, and to exempt him from all Amercements, for not appearing personally in them.

Pope *Gregory* the tenth, usurping the Emperor's Sovereign authority, of Summoning general Councils, sent forth general Letters through every Nation, concerning the gathering together a Council, on *May* the first, at *Lyons*. Whence it was said of him.

Gregorius denus, Colligit omne genus.

Claus.2. Ed.1. m.13.dorso.

What Archbishops, Bishops, Abbots, and Clergy-men repaired to this Council by the King's special Licence, who constituted Attorneys and Proxies for them in the King's Courts, to sue and be sued, during their absence, may be seen in the Records mentioned by Mr. *Prynne*.

King *Edward* the first, himself sent four special Proctors to this General Council, to propound, assent, or dissent unto in his Name and behalf, whatever they or either of them should deem fit or expedient. A clear evidence, that He and his Proxies had an affirmative and negative voice in General Councils.

Matthew Westminster renders us an account of the proceedings in this Council, and of the Greek Emperors, Patriarcks, and Bishops acknowledgement of the Supremacy of the Pope and Church of *Rome*, over all other Prelates and Churches, as an Article of their Faith, which they never before assented to.

The Executors of *John Maunsel* Treasurer of *York*, having, by his last Will, assigned to the Vicars of St. *Peter's* in *York*, a Messuage of His in *York*, to maintain an Anniversary for his Soul, of which they were afterwards dispossessed by others; the King upon complaint thereof, issued a Writ of Inquisition, to examine the truth thereof, and restore the said Messuage to the Vicars, to maintain the Anniversary for the salvation of *John Maunsel's* soul. The

The next year the King issued Commissions for the apprehending some vagrant and Apostate Friers of the Order of St. *Augustine*, who had deserted their Houses and Order, to the prejudice of their Souls, and scandal of their Order.

King *Edward* the first, made at *Westminster* at his first Parliament General, after his Coronation, on *Easter*-Monday in the third year of his Reign, many excellent useful Statutes, some of them relating to the Priviledges and Jurisdiction of the Clergy, controlling some Canons of the Pope, formerly used to the obstruction of publick Justice. *Vide Cokes 2. Instit.p.156, 157.*

Soon after the Council of *Lions*, Pope *Gregory* the tenth, sent *Reymund de Nogeriis*, his Chaplain, as his Nuncio into *England*, *Wales*, *Scotland*, and *Ireland*, for certain affairs of the Church, especially to demand and receive from the King eight years Arrears of the annual Tribute, and *Peter-pence*, then due to the Church of *Rome*.

The Abbot and Covent of *Feversham* being greatly indebted to Merchants and others (by their expences at *Rome*, and Papal exactions) the King to preserve Them and their House from ruine, took them, and all their Lands, Moneys, Goods, into his Protection, and committed them to the management of certain persons for discharge of their debts, and necessary support. The like Protections were granted, in the same form, to the Abbot and Covents of *Bordesley* and *Byndon* the same year; and to the Prior and Covent of *Thornholm*; but the custody of them, their Lands and Goods, to other Persons.

The Chalices, Books, Ornaments, Goods and Lands of the Hermitage near *Cripple-gate*, *London*, being usually imbezilled for want of good Government and Regulation, the King being Patron thereof committed it to the care and Government of the Lord Major of *London*, for the time being.

The Chancellor and University of *Oxford*, having at their proper costs founded a Chappelry in the Church of St. *Maries*, in the midst of the Town, to pray for the safety of the King, his Queen, and Children, Ancestors; and all their Benefactors; the King highly commending their Piety therein, and endeavouring to promote it, wrote to all the Archbishops and Bishops of *England* and *Ireland*, to grant some special Indulgences to all who should resort to this Chappelry to hear Mass or Prayers.

The King upon the Petition of the Prior and Covent of *Bath*, and of the Dean and Chapter of *Wells*, granted his Licenfe to them to elect a new Bishop, that See being then void. Upon this Licenfe they Elected *Robert Burnel*. This Bishop soon after his Consecration, to end the frequent Controversies between the King, Abbots of *Glastonbury*, and Bishops of this See, by consent of the Dean and Chapter of *Wells*, and of the Prior and Covent of *Bath*, exchanged the Patronage of the Abbey of *Glastonbury*, and some other rights therein granted to him by former Kings Patents,

Patents, for the City of *Bath*. In purſuit and execution of which exchange, the King iſſued two Patents to the Citizens of *Bath*, and others, to make Livery and Seiſin thereof to the Biſhop.

 The King gave Licenſe, upon the Petition of the Dean and Chapter of *Hereford*, to Elect a new Biſhop in the place of *John Breton* after his Deceaſe: and confirmed their Election of *Thomas de Cantilupo*, and reſtored the Temporalties to him after his Confirmation by the Archbiſhop of *Canterbury*, without the Pope's approbation or privity.

Pat. 3. Edw. 1.

 This King in the fourth year of his Reign, to prevent the ruine of the Abbey of *Redding*, iſſued Patents of protection, and regulation of the expences of it, and of the Cell belonging to it, founded by his Anceſtors, committing it's Revenues to certain perſons to defray the Debts thereof.

 In the fifth year of his Reign he iſſued a Commiſſion, to enquire of all Chriſtians, who uſed uſury in *London* and elſe-where, and puniſh them according to Law, by ſeizing their Goods, as a thing unbeſeeming Chriſtians and Chriſtianity.

 About the ſame time *Walter Broneſcomb*, Biſhop of *Exeter*, and his Officials, cited ſundry of the King's Subjects, and Officers, into his Eccleſiaſtical Courts for Debts and Chattels, that concerned not Matrimony or Teſtament, and for Treſpaſſes, Free-holds, and other things, of which they had no legal juriſdiction, Excommunicating, and putting them to pecuniary Redemptions, and grievous penalties, and withall exacted illegal Oathes and obligations from them: the King upon the complaints of *Edmond*, Earl of *Cornwall*, and his Officers, and of the whole County of *Cornwall*, of theſe his exorbitances, iſſued a ſpeedy Commiſſion, in the ſixth year of his Reign, to ſome Judges, to enquire of, hear and determine theſe his Exorbitancies and Uſurpations, before whom he was Proſecuted at the King's Suite, to his dammages of 10000 *l*. which the Biſhop denying in ſome ſort, appealed to the King, Pope, and Court of *Rome*, from the King's Juſtices: for which his high affront to the King's Crown and Dignity, he was adjudged undefended, ordered to ſatisfie the King his ten thouſand pound dammages; and likewiſe to anſwer his contempt for this his enormous Appeal to the Pope, in affront of the King's Crown and Dignity, before the King and his Council.

Godwin. Catal. of Biſh. *p. 326, 327.*

 In the nineth year of King *Edward* the firſt, *John Peckham*, Archbiſhop of *Canterbury*, held a Council at *Lambeth* with his Suffragans, of which *Thomas Walſingham*, and others, render us this account. *Frier John Peckham, Archbiſhop of Canterbury, leaſt he might ſeem to have*

Frater Johan. Peckham, Cantuarienſis Epiſcopus ne

nihil feciſſe videretur convocat Concilium apud Lambeth, in quo non Evangelii Regni Dei prædicationem impoſuit, ſed Conſtitutiones Othonis & Ottobonis quondam Legatorum in Anglia *innovans, juſſit eas ab omnibus ſervari, &c.* Thomas Walfingham *in* Edw. 1.

done

done nothing, calleth a Council at Lambeth, in which he imposed not the Preaching of the Gospel of the Kingdom of God, but innovating the Constitutions of Otto and Ottobon, sometimes Legates in England, commanded them to be observed of all. Moreover, he made sixteen Ecclesiastical Laws, which are contained among the Provincial Constitutions.

The King suspecting the Archbishops and Bishops Loyalty, and proceedings in this their Council, sent a Writ to them, strictly commanding them upon their Oaths of Fealty they had all taken, to be faithful to him, and defend his Crown and Royal Dignity in all things, to their Power; to observe this their Oath therein with all diligence, and not to act, agitate, or assent to any thing against him, or the ancient Rights of the Crown enjoyed by his Progenitors, under pain of losing all their Temporalties.

But how far this Archbishop and his Suffragans were from obeying this Royal Mandate, will appear by the Prologue to their Canons and Constitutions made therein, wherein they highly extol *Thomas Becket*, as a most glorious Martyr, for opposing the antient Rights of the Crown, as inconsistent with the Churches pretended Liberties, and revived and confirmed the Constitutions of Archbishop *Boniface* and his Suffragans, (against which the King had solemnly Appealed to the Pope, as prejudicial to the Rights, Priviledges, Customs, Liberties of his Crown) by several Canons made therein, and the Excommunications re-published in it: but more especially by the Archbishop's insolent Epistle to the King, in answer to this his Royal Inhibition and Mandate sent unto them. *Vide Pryn. in Edw. 1.*

Archbishop *Peckham* (*Magnus & robustus Antichristi satelles*, as *John Bale* not improperly stiles him) in his Epistle to the King, justifies what they had done: wherein he advanceth the Ecclesiastical and Papal Jurisdiction, Power, Laws, Canons, far above the Regal, to which all Princes and Temporal Laws ought to submit.

Sundry Canons and Converts of the Order of *Sempingham*, this year, turning Apostates, and deserting their Houses in diverse Priories of that Order, to the scandal of their Profession, the King upon complaint issued a Writ to apprehend and punish them for it, and to deliver such of them who were then apprehended, to those of that Order to be chastised.

The King to prevent the imbezilling of the Rents, Chalices, Books, Vestments, Images, Relikes, Charters, and Bulls of the Hermitage by *Criple-gate*, granted the custody thereof, in his Name, to the Constable of the Tower for the time being. *Pat. 9. Edw. 1.*

This year the King recited and confirmed the antient Charter of King *John* to the Nuns of *Ambresbury*.

The King to advance Learning, and for the good of the Church, Priesthood, and Common-wealth, gave his Royal assent for translating the Friers of the Hospital of St. *John* in *Cambridge*, into a Colledge of Scholars, after the pattern and Rules of *Merton* Colledge in *Oxford*.

The Archbishop this year, to supply, his occasions, entred into several recognizances to the Bishops of *Bath*, and of *Coventry* and *Litchfield*, two wealthy Prelates and great Usurers.

Pope *Nicholas* the third deceasing, *Anno* 1280. and Pope *Martin* the fourth succeeding, he in the first year of his Papacy sent two Friers into *England*, intending by his Agents, and Forreign Merchants, to export or return out of *England* the six years Dismes therein collected, and retained for Aid of the holy Land, granted in the general Council of *Lyons*, and convert them to his own or other uses; King *Edward* upon notice hereof, to reserve the Moneys for his Brother's expedition to the holy Land, and supply the present exigences for defence of the Kingdom, issued out a Writ to prohibit Merchants, or others, under pain of loss of Life and Member, and all their Goods and Chattels, to export or convay the said Dismes, or any part thereof, out of the Realm, and to imprison all such who did the contrary, to the Pope's great disappointment.

In the tenth year of King *Edward* the first, Pope *Martin* sent a Bull to the King, to require his Favour to, and Protection of the Monks of the Order of *Cluny*, whose piety he highly extolled.

The King now and then during the vacancy of Bishopricks, disposed of some of their Stocks to others.

The Bishoprick of *Durham* becoming void by the death of *Robert de Insula*, *Anthony Beck* being elected Bishop by the King's Licence, and Confirmed and Consecrated Bishop thereof by *Wickwane* Archbishop of *York*, in St. *Peter's* Church of *York*, the King, Queen, and most of the Nobles of *England* being present; the King issued out Writs for the restitution of his Temporalties; and the stock thereon, which he bought of the King.

Pat.11.E.1.

Richard Swinfeld being elected and Confirmed Bishop of *Hereford*, by the King's Licence and assent, he issued a Writ to restore his Temporalties.

John Peckham, Archbishop of *Canterbury*, resolved to visit all his Provinces more accurately, and punish offenders more severely than in former times, to prevent all obstructions by Appeals to *Rome*. In this Visitation (saith Mr. *Prynne*) he domineered over his whole Province, and subjugated it to his arbitrary Power, which none of his Predecessors had attempted, much less effected, till then. Having visited *England*, he passed by *Chester* into *Wales*, *Anno* 1284. to reform the state of the Church. In this Visitation be made and published a Decree, what Ornaments of Churches the Parishoners should provide and pay for, and what the Priests or Incumbents.

Vide Spelm. Concil. Tom. 2. p. 343.

King

King *Edward* in the twelfth year of his Reign iſſued Warrants for the payment of two years Arrears of 1000 Marks for *England* and *Ireland*, granted by King *John*, then due and demanded by the Pope; as likewiſe for payment of ſeveal arrears of penſions he had granted to Cardinals and others.

The Archbiſhop of *Canterbury*, having interdicted ſome of the Tenants belonging to the Abbey of *Fiſcan* in *England*, the Abbot thereupon Appealed to *Rome* againſt him, and likewiſe to the King againſt this oppreſſion, deſiring his favour, that no Proceſs might iſſue out of his Court againſt them, and that he might conſtitute Attorneys in this Caſe, ſince he could not come into *England* without great damage to his houſe.

The King this year conſtituted a ſpecial Proctor for three years, by Patent, to defend the Rights and Liberties of his free Chappels and Crown, againſt all Papal and Epiſcopal invaders and oppoſers of them.

The King ſeizing the Advouſons of ſeveral Churches in *Wales*, as forfeited by their Patrons Rebellions againſt him, gave them to the Biſhop of St. *David*'s, with power to appropriate them to his Church of St. *David*'s, and *Lekadeken* (*Lancaden*) and make, or annex them to Prebendaries there. Hereupon the Biſhop of St. *Davids*, by his Charter, with conſent and approbation of the King, and his Dean and Chapter, made and erected a new Collegiate Church of Canons in *Lan Caden* in *Wales*, conſtituted ſeveral Canons and Prebendaries therein, annexing and appropriating the forecited Churches thereunto, the Patronages whereof were granted him by the King, who ſet his Seal to the Biſhop's Charter, and ratified it with his own Charter, to make it valid in Law.

In the year 1285. a Parliament at *Weſtminſter* laid down the limits, and fixed the boundaries, betwixt the Spiritual and Temporal juriſdictions.

The King having totally ſubdued the Welſh, the Archbiſhoprick of *York* becomming void, by the death of *William Wickwane* Archbiſhop thereof, the King applied the profits thereof during the vacancy, towards the building of Caſtles in *Wales*, to ſecure it.

This year *Stephen* Biſhop of *Waterford*, was made chief Juſtice of *Ireland*.

In the fifteenth year of this King, *Henry de Branceſton* was elected and confirmed Biſhop of *Sarum*. The King granted and confirmed to the Biſhop of *Bangor*, and his Succeſſors, all the Rights, Liberties, Poſſeſſions, and Cuſtomes, they had formerly uſed and enjoyed.

In the ſixteenth year of this King's Reign, *Gilbert de Sancto Leofardo*, was elected, and confirmed Biſhop of *Chicheſter*, by the King's Royal aſſent.

This year there was a great conteſt between the Archbiſhop of *Canterbury*, and the Abbot of St. *Auguſtines*, about the carrying up his croſs.

Firſt,

The History of

Firſt, The Abbot oppoſed the bearing up his own Croſs before him in the Monaſtery of St. *Auguſtines*, even within his own *Metropolis* and See of *Canterbury*, when ſpecially ſent for thither to dine with the King.

Secondly, Obſerve the Archbiſhop's pride and obſtinacy, in refuſing to ſubſcribe ſuch a Letter, as the King directed, to reconcile this difference, and preſerve the Abbot's Privildges, or repair to the King, without his Croſs carried before him; together with his malice againſt the Abbot and Covent; for not admitting him to carry up his Croſs within their Monaſtery.

Pat. 17. *Ed.* 1. Biſhop *Godwin* obſerves, That from the year 1284. the See of *Salisbury* had five Biſhops within the ſpace of five years, whereof *William de Comer* (as he ſtiles him) was the fourth. But Mr. *William de Corner* was his name, as the King's Writ for reſtoring of his Temporalties, together with the Patent of the King's Royal aſſent to his election, aſſure us.

The King having Conquered *Wales*, confirmed all the antient Rights, Liberties, Poſſeſſions, and Cuſtomes of the Church of *Aſaph*, to the preſent Biſhop and his Succeſſors, which they formerly uſed and enjoyed, and that he might freely make his Teſtament.

Pope *Nicholas* the fourth, being ſetled in his Pontifical Chair, in the firſt year of his Papacy, ſent a Bull to King *Edward* the firſt, to demand five years Arrears of the Annual penſion of one thouſand Marks, granted by King *John*. The King hereupon, the better to promote his couſin *Charles* to the Realm of *Sicily*, and expedite his own affairs in the Court of *Rome*, concerning a diſpenſation for his Son, to Marry the heir of the Crown of *Scotland*, and other buſineſs touching *Gaſcoign* and *France* (for which he had then ſent ſpecial Ambaſſadors to *Rome*, with Letters both to the Pope and Cardinals) iſſued a Writ for the payment of theſe five years Arrears accordingly. Mr. *Prynne* ſaith, *That this was the laſt payment made by King* Edward *the firſt, of this Annual penſion*.

The Pope upon receipt hereof, granted a diſpenſation to the King's Son, Prince *Edward*, to Marry with the heir of the Crown of *Scotland*, thereby to unite theſe two Crowns and Kingdomes, and prevent the long bloody Wars between them, though within the prohibited degrees of Conſanguinity.

King *Edward*, upon the receipt of this Diſpenſation, ſent Letters and Proxies to *Ericus* King of *Norway*, and likewiſe to the Guardians of the Realm of *Scotland*, to conſummate this Marriage, upon diverſe Articles and agreements.

King *Edward* likewiſe to perfect the Marriage between his Son, Prince *Edward*, and *Margaret* Queen of Scots, with the general approbation of the Keepers, Nobles, and Natives of that Realm, granted and ratified

The Church of Great Britain.

fied to the Nobles and People of *Scotland* diverse Articles, agreed on by special Commissioners sent on both sides, and approved by him, by Letters, under his great Seal, which he took an Oath to observe, under the penalty of forfeiting one hundred thousand pounds to the Church of *Rome*, towards the holy Wars, and subjecting himself to the Pope's Excommunication, and his Kingdom to an Interdict, in case of Violation, or Non-performance, as the Patent attesteth, enrolled both in French and Latine.

*Pat.*8. *Edw.*1. *m.* 8.

The King, after this, appointed the Bishop of *Durham*, to be this Queen *Margaret*'s, and his Son Prince *Edward*'s, Lieutenant in *Scotland*, for the preservation of the Peace and Government thereof. At which time he and his Son likewise constituted Proctors to Treat with the King of *Norway* in his, and his Son *Edward*'s, Name, concerning his Sons Marriage, and Espousals, with his Daughter *Margaret* Queen of *Scotland*. To facilitate this Marriage, the Bishop of *Durham*, at the King's request, obliged himself to pay four hundred pounds by the year, to certain persons in *Norway*; to discharge which annuity, the King granted him several Manors amounting to a greater value.

But the sickness and death of this Queen, in her voyage toward *Scotland* and *England*, frustrated this, much desired, Marriage between Prince *Edward* and her, and raised new questions between the Competitors for the Crown.

Thomas Walsingham saith, *That about this time (the Pope requiring it) the Churches of* England *were taxed according to their true value, to raise his Dismes and exactions higher.*

In the same year 1290. the King, out of his zeal to Christian Religion, banished all the Jews out of *England*, by a publick Act in Parliament, and Confiscated all their Houses and Lands, for their Infidelity, Blasphemy, Crucifying of Children, in contempt of Christ Crucified, and clipping of his Coyn. In *August* they were commanded to depart the Land, with their Wives and Children, between that time and the Feast of all Saints, with their moveable Goods.

The Jews banished out of *England* by Act of Parliament.

Their number was said to be sixteen thousand five hundred and eleven; they were banished, never to return again into *England*.

There hapning many contests between the Bishop of *Lincoln*, and the Masters and Scholars of the University of *Oxford*, concerning the Presentation and Confirmation of their Chancellor, whether he ought to come out of the University in Person to the Bishop; or to be admitted by his Proxies: the King by his Prerogative to advance Learning, and settle Peace between them, made a friendly accord for the future.

Pope *Nicholas* preferring his own lucre, and favour of King *Edward* and his Chaplains, before God's Service, or Peoples Souls, against sundry Canons, Licensed twenty of the King's Clerks imployed in his

service,

service, which he should nominate to be Non-residents from their Ecclesiastical Benefices for ten years space.

This year the King confirmed the grant of several Tithes, Churches, and Advousons, formerly made by *Robert de Candos* to the Monastery of *Bek* and *Goldclive*.

Then *Peter de Divion*, Abbot of *Rewley*, an Alien, born in *France*, and most Abbots and Priors that were Aliens, took an Oath, and gave sufficient Pledges for their Fidelity and true Allegeance to the King in that Age (especially in time of War) and not to send the Goods of their Monasteries out of the Realm, which they frequently did to the Kingdoms prejudice. The *K*ing issuing a *Dedimus potestatem* to the Abbot of *Thame* to take this Oath of *Peter de Divion*, the Abbot endorsed this return thereon.

Ego Frater Johannes, Abbas de Thame, virtute istius Mandati, recepi Sacramentum Dom. Petri de Divione, Abbatis de Regali loco juxta Oxon. apud Oxon. Dominica in festo Apostolorum Simonis & Judæ : & etiam recepi Manucaptores *ipsius Domini Petri Abbatis de Regali loco, viz. Johannem de Doclynton Majorem Villæ Oxon. Johannem de Crokesford Juniorem; Ricardum Cary, Johannem de Fallee, & Johannem le Peyntour, Burgenses dictæ Villæ Oxon. Qui conjunctim & divisim manuceperunt dictum Dom. Petrum Abbatem de Regali loco, quod idem Abbas bene & fideliter erga dominum Regem se habebit ; & omnia alia in Brevi isto contenta perficiet & observabit.*

The *K*ing granted two hundred pounds to the Pope's Chaplain in *Scotland* for his expences, pains, and labour therein taken in the service of Queen *Margaret* deceased.

The same year *William de Luda* was elected and confirmed Bishop of *Ely*. This year the *K*ing gave several sums of Money to buy Books and Ornaments for Religious Houses, that were burnt in *Gascoign* and *England*.

The *K*ing converted the Profits of the Archbishoprick of *York* (then void) to the repairing and building the Castle of *Carnarvan* in *Wales*, after his Conquest thereof.

Parker de Antiqu. Eccles. Anglic. f.205. Anno 1290.

Matthew Parker, Archbishop of *Canterbury*, storieth, that *John Peckham*, Archbishop of *Canterbury*, this year, after the visitation and subjugation of his whole Province, summoned a Council of his Clergy at *Reding*, wherein he propounded the drawing of all causes concerning Advousons, meerly belonging to the King's Temporal, to their Ecclesiastical Courts, and to cut off all Prohibitions to them from the King's Courts in personal Causes. Which the King hearing of, expresly commanded them by special Messengers, to desist from it, whereupon this Council was dissolved.

In the nineteenth year of *K*ing *Edward* the First, Queen *Eleanor* deceasing in *December*, the King thereupon out of his devotion (according to

The Church of Great Britain.

to the practice of that blind Age) on *January* the fourth, issued a Writ to all the Religious Houses and Monks of *Cluny* in *England*, to sing Masses and Prayers for her Soul, to purge it from all the remaining spots of sin, and to certifie him the number of the Masses they would say for her, that proportionably he might thank them.

William Thorn saith, that the Prior of *Christ-church* in *Canterbury* granted to the King, in the Feast of the Translation of St. *Edward*, fifty Hymns, and two thousand three hundred and fifty Masses for the Souls of his Progenitors, and Queens of *England*, as a great extraordinary Liberality and Spiritual Alms. The Abbot of *Condam* also sent a Letter to the King, to inform him, what Prayers, Masses, and Anniversaries, He, and his Monastery, had ordered for the Queens speedy translation to Heavenly Joyes.

Anno 1292. died *John Peckham*, Archbishop of *Canterbury*, and Pope *Nicholas* also died, who sate four years, one month, and eighteen dayes, after whose death, one delivered this Verse for an Epitaph.

Gloria, laus, speculum fratrum Nicolae Minorum,
Te vivente vigent, te moriente cadunt.

The Frier Minors pride, insolency, and avarice was great while they lived, who were both of their Order. Archbishop *Peckham*'s death this year, put a period to the Contests between him, and the Abbot of St. *Augustines*.

King *Edward* in the twentieth year of his Reign, out of his blind devotion, and love to his late deceased Consort, Queen *Eleanor*, instituted a solemn Anniversary to be kept for her every year, issuing sums of Money, and granting several Manors, and Lands to the Abbot and Covent of *Westminster* for that end, wherein he prescribed how many Tapers, and of what weight, they should find; how many and what Masses, Dirges, Pater-nosters, Ave-Maries they should sing; and what Alms they should distribute to the poor for her Soul; obliging the Abbot, Prior, and Monks by a solemn Oath duly to perform the same, under pain of forfeiting all their Goods, Chattels, and the Lands thus given to them for this end. *Claus. 20. Edw. 1.*

Anthony, Bishop of *Durham*, erecting the Parish-Churches of *Chester*, and *Langechester*, which were very rich and large, into a Deanary and seven Prebendaries, for the advancing of God's Service, and the good of the peoples Souls, and obliging the Dean and Prebends by Oath, to personal Residence thereon, and discharge of their duties and God's Service therein, according as he had prescribed by his Ordinances and Charters. The King to promote God's Service, and the good of his Peoples Souls, ratified the Bishop's Ordinances by two Charters which recite them, warranting the division of great and rich Parishes and Bishopricks

O into

into many; and obliging the Dean, Prebends, Ministers, Chaplains thereof, by Oath, to personal Residence, and discharge of their Duties, and Divine offices therein.

John Lythgraines, and *Alice* his Wife, erecting a Chappel and Chauntry to the Virgin *Mary* in their Manor of *Lasingby*, consisting of one Master and six Chaplains, to sing Mass for their Souls, and the Souls of their Ancestors, and of King *Edward* and his Heirs, of the present Bishop of *Durham* and his Successors, and of all faithful Souls deceased, prescribing an Oath to them of perpetual Residence, and discharge of the particular Divine Services, and trusts reposed in them, procured the King to ratifie this. his Charter, by his Royal Charter enrolled in the Tower.

Chart. 20 E.I. 1. n. 5.

King *Edward* the First, in the twenty one year of his Reign, as Superiour Lord of *Scotland* in that Age, exercised a Soveraign Authority, in and over the King, Clergy, and Kingdom of *Scotland*, in Causes and Inheritances which concerned the Church, Clergy, or Religious Persons, as well as in Secular mens cases, notwithstanding any Pretences, or Appeals to *Rome*, where Justice was delayed, or refused to them by the King of *Scots*, whereof there are sundry Presidents in the Patent, and Plea-Rolls of *Scotland* in this and succeeding years.

Vid. Godw. Catal. p. 427.

Robert Winchelsey, Archbishop of *Canterbury*, was no sooner consecrated at *Rome*, but he procured a Bull from Pope *Celestine* the Fifth, by his Papal provision to confer the Bishoprick of *Landaff* (which had been void for nine years space, and thereby devolved to the Pope by lapse, as he pretended) on any Person he should think meet for that employment. Whereupon, without the King's previous Authority, he conferred it, by way of provision, upon *John de Monmouth*. Yet the King was not forward to restore the Temporalties of the Archbishoprick of *Canterbury* to this Archbishop, or of *Landaff* to *John de Monmouth*, thus intruded into it against his Prerogative, but detained them near two years after in his hands as vacant, receiving the profits, and presenting to the Benefices belonging to them.

Upon the death of *Robert Burnel*, Bishop of *Bath* and *Wells*, the King's Chancellor, *William de Marchia* (then Treasurer of *England*) was elected to succeed him in that Bishoprick.

This year *John de Langton* succeeded *Robert Burnel* in the Chancellors Office of *England*.

Matth. Westm.

The King in the twenty two year of his Reign, notwithstanding a Subsidy granted to him, wanting Moneys, searched all the Monasteries and Churches throughout *England*, where any Moneys were deposited by Religious persons or others, and forcibly carried it away to supply his occasions, by the advice of his Treasurer *William de Marchia*, Bishop of *Bath* and *Wells*.

The

the Church of GREAT BRITAIN.

The same year the King granted Protections to divers Abbots and Clergy-men, who aided him with their Contributions against the *French*. He also desired the assistance of their devout Prayers unto God for a blessing upon him and his Military Forces, in defence of his Inheritance against their armed Powers, as appears by his Writs, under his Privy Seal, issued to his Bishops, and other Religious persons.

John Duke of *Brabant* (the King's dear Friend and Kinsman) dying this year, the King issued Writs to all his Bishops, and sundry Abbots and Priors, to make Prayers, and chaunt Masses for him, according to the superstition of that Age.

Then the Roman See (through the Cardinals divisions) continuing void about three years and three months after the decease of Pope *Nicholas* the Fourth, the Cardinals at last elected *Peter de Murone*, an Hermite, and Monk of the Order of St. *Benedict*, whom they named *Celestine* the Fifth. He, during his short continuance in the Papacy, granted our King *Edward* the First a Disme for seven years from all the Clergy of *England*, out of zeal to the relief of the Holy Land. But his Wars with the *French*, *Welch-men* and *Scots*, wasted all these Dismes. Pope *Celestine* in the month of *September* created twelve Cardinals, among whom were two Hermits. But the Cardinals being weary of this precise, reforming Pope, perswaded him to resign his Papacy, as being unfit to manage it without the Churches ruine, and his own destruction. So after he had sate five months and seven dayes, he resigned the Papacy. Then *Benedict Cajetan*, his grand Counsellor, was chosen Pope, and called by the name of *Boniface*. How unsutable, yea contradictory, his actions were to both his good names, he immediately discovered, which occasioned this Distich to be made of, and applied to him.

Audi, tace, lege, bene dic, bene fac Benedicte,
Aut hæc perverte, male dic, male fac, Maledicte.

Celestine returned to his Cell, from whence *Boniface* drew him forth, and cast him into a close Prison, where he abode till his death; whence it is reported, that *Celestine* prophecied of him,

Ascendisti ut Vulpes, Regnabis ut Leo, Morieris ut Canis,

Thou hast ascended into the Papacy like a Fox, thou shalt reign like a Lion, and die like a Dog: and so it came to pass.

This Pope *Boniface* by his Bull having appropriated the Church of *Wermington* to the Abby of *Peterburgh*, whereof they had the Patronage, the King authorized them accordingly to appropriate it to them and their Successors, against him and his Heirs; notwithstanding the Statute of *Mortmain*.

This Pope sent two Cardinal Legats *a latere*, first to the King of *France*, and from him to the King of *England*, then engaged in Wars against each other, under a specious pretext of mediating a Truce between *England* and *France*: but instead thereof these Cardinals did twice prey upon the *English* and *Irish* Churches and Clergy, and transported their Treasure into *France*, to enrich themselves and the King's Enemies there.

Then King *Edward* sent Writs to his Archbishops, Bishops, Abbots, and others, to make Prayers, sing Masses, and do other Works of Piety for the Soul of his Brother *Edmond*, and after that of *Margaret* Queen of *France*, according to the superstition of that Age.

Tho. Walsingh.
Hist. Angl.
p. 84.

In the twenty fourth year of King *Edward*'s Reign, there arose a great Sedition and Combat between the Scholars and Townsmen in the University of *Oxford*, wherein many were slain on both sides, and the Goods of the Scholars plundered and carried away: upon complaint whereof to the King by the Scholars, he sent his Justices thither to punish the Malefactors, and repair the Scholars damages.

King *Edward* strenuously opposed Pope *Boniface*'s Anti-monarchical Constitution, against demanding or imposing Subsidies on the Clergy. *Robert Winchelsey*, Archbishop of *Canterbury*, was stout in the prosecution of the Popes Bull which he had procured for it: for which all his Temporalties were seized; and he being forced to hide his head, and reduced to great extremities, was restored to the King's favour by the earnest mediation of his Suffragan Bishops on his behalf. Whereupon the King issued out Writs to restore his Temporalties, with all his Oxen, Goods, and Chattels formerly seized, in the state now they were.

In the twenty fifth year of this King's Reign, *Henry de Newark* being elected Archbishop of *York*, and his election approved by the King, his Proctors sent to *Rome*, procured the Pope's confirmation of his election, together with a License to be consecrated in his own Church at *York* by the Bishop of *Durham*. The King, upon the receipt of the Pope's Bull, issued a Writ for the restitution of his Temporalties.

Pope *Boniface* having confirmed the election of *David Martyn* to the Bishoprick of St. *Davids* in *Wales*, the King upon notice given accepted thereof.

The Bishoprick of *Ely* becoming void by the death of *William Luda*, the minor part of the Chapter elected *John* their Prior, but the better *John de Langten*, the King's Chancellor. The King confirmed the election of his Chancellor.

Anno Reg. 26.

The King, by his Prerogative, having granted a License to the Bishop of *Coventry* and *Litchfield*, to hold the Hospital of St. *Leonards* in *York*, in *Commenda* with his Bishoprick during his life, out of his free Gift; and special Grace, confirmed it by his Patents, so as this Dispensation should not prove prejudicial to him or his Heirs.

The

The Church of Great Britain.

The Monks of *Battel-Abbey*, by ancient Charters, having the custody of the Abby and Lands, during the vacancy upon their Abbot's death, the King issued a Writ to restore them to their custody.

Mr. *Prynne* observeth, and relateth diverse things of this year.

1. That the Contests between the Archbishop, Abbots and Monks of *Canterbury, about Exemptions, Priviledges, and Jurisdictions, was a great cause of advancing the Pope's usurped Jurisdiction over them both, and over the Rights, Prerogative of the Crown and Church of* England.

2. The Pope's Insolency in exempting the Abbots, and Monks of Canterbury, *and all their Lands, Hospitals, Churches, Impropriations, Priests, Tenants, from all Archiepiscopal, and other Ecclesiastical Jurisdiction, and subjecting them solely to the See of* Rome; *as likewise in subjecting the Archbishop of* Canterbury, *the Bishops of* London *and* Rochester, *to the commands and censures of the Abbots of* Westminster, Waltham, *and* St. Edmond.

3. The pride of the Abbots in erecting Deanaries, Officials, Ecclesiastical Consistories, and in prescribing Oaths of Canonical obedience upon the Priests and Curats of their Churches belonging to their Monastery.

4. The strange injustice and contradiction of Popes Bulls, nulling, repealing each other by Non obstantes, with all former Priviledges granted by themselves, and Contracts made or ratified by others through bribery and corruption.

Prynne's Hist. of Popes Usurpations, Tom. 3.

Cent. XIV.

IN the beginning of this Century King *Edward* the First waged cruel Wars against the *Scots*. Then Pope *Boniface* the Eighth sent his Letters to the King, to quit his claim to *Scotland*, to cease his Wars, and release his Prisoners of the *Scotch* Nation, as a people exempt, and properly belonging to his own Chappel. He grounded his Title thereunto, because (it was said) *Scotland* was first converted, by the Relicks of S. *Peter*, to the unity of the Christian Faith. Hereupon King *Edward* called a Council of his Lords at *Lincoln*, where he returned a large Answer to the Pope's Letter, endeavouring by evident Reasons, and ancient Precedents to prove his propriety in the Kingdom of *Scotland*. This was seconded by another from the English Peerage, subscribed with all their hands; declaring that the King ought by no means to answer in judgment in any case, or should bring his Rights into doubt, and ought not to send any Proctors or Messengers to the Pope, &c. The Pope foreseeing the Verdict would go against him, wisely non-suited himself.

Fox Acts and Monum. lib. 1. p. 444, 445.

Then Pope *Boniface* sent forth a Declaration in favour of the Archbishop, and proceeded so violently against the Abbot, Monks, and their Adherents,

Chron. Its", Thorn. col. 1997. ad 2003.

Adherents, by Excommunications, Interdicts, &c. that he enforced them to submit, and sue unto him for Absolution, and a friendly agreement between them.

After the death of *Henry de Newark*, *Thomas Corbridge* being elected Archbishop of *York*, repaired to *Rome* for his Confirmation, where he was forced to resign his right of Election into the Pope's hands, and to receive the Archbishoprick from him by way of provision, who thereupon not only confirmed, but consecrated him Archbishop at *Rome*, and gave him his Pall; and the King restored his Temporalties upon receipt of the Pope's Bull.

Thomas Stubs tells us of an high Contest that happened soon after betwixt the King and him, about the Chappel of St: *Sepulchres* in *York*, for which the King seized his Temporalties, and detained some of them till his death, for obeying the Pope's Provision and Commands before the King's Writ, in refusing to admit his Clerk to this Chappel, and to remove the Pope's Clerk, whom he had placed therein by his Papal Provision. This Archbishop's Liberties in *Beverley* were seized into the King's hands, *Anno* 29. of his Reign, for a contempt committed by him in the King's presence.

The King's Daughter *Mary*, being a Nun, professed at *Ambresbury*, the King granted her forty Oaks each year, twenty tun of Wines, and several Manors of above the value of two hundred pounds a year, for her maintenance.

In the thirtieth year of the Reign of King *Edward*, the French King *Philip*, with all the Peers, Earls, Barons, Archbishops, Bishops, Abbots, Priors, Clergy, Univerfity of *Paris*, and the Cities and Commonalty of *France*, did Appeal, and Article against Pope *Boniface* the Eighth his Person, Crimes, Interdicts, Excommunications, to the next General Council, in the ruffe of his Papal pride, as a most detestable Heretick, Simoniack, Adulterer, Sorcerer, and Monster of Impiety: and soon after seized, imprisoned, and brought him to a shameful Tragical end. The particular Articles are recorded by Mr. *Fox*. Of this Pope a certain Verlifier wrote thus.

For Acts and Monuments. Vol. I. p. 450, 451.

Ingreditur Vulpes, Regnat Leo, sed Canis exit.
Re tandem vera, si sic fuit ecce chimera.

Alter vero sic.

Vulpes intravit, tanquam Leo Pontificavit ;
Exiit utque Canis, de divite factus inanis.

Then

the Church of Great Britain.

Then was the Bishop of *Ostia* created Pope, and called *Benedict* the Eleventh: Of whom one saith,

A te nomen habe, bene dic, bene fac, Benedicte :
Aut rem perverte, maledic, malefac, Maledicte.

The Archbishop of *Canterbury*, *Robert Winchelsey*, having plotted Treason, with some others of the Nobility, against the King, projecting to depose him, and set up his Son *Edward* in his Room, lurked in a Covent at *Canterbury*, till fourscore Monks were, by the King's Command, thrust out of their places, for relieving him out of their Charity, and were not restored till the Archbishop was banished the Kingdom.

In the year 1305. the King sent a Letter to the Pope for the Canonizing of *Thomas de Cantelupe*, late Bishop of *Hereford* deceased, famous for sundry Miracles (as was suggested) that so he and his Realm might enjoy the benefit of his Intercession for them in Heaven, according to the Superstition of that blind Age.

After the death of Pope *Benedict*, Pope *Clement* was no sooner elected, and enthroned in *France*, but he began to exercise his new Rapines in *England*, by complying with King *Edward*, in granting him a two years Disme from his Clergy for his own use, though pretended for the aid of the Holy Land, that himself might more easily exact the First-fruits of vacant Ecclesiastical Benefices to fill his own Coffers, though out of his Dominions. Which occasioned these Satyrical Verses to be made of him and the King this year:

Ecclesia navis titubat, Regni quia navis
Errat, Rex, Papa, facti sunt unica Capa.
Hoc faciunt do, des, Pilatus hic, Alter Herodes.

This is the first president of any Pope's reserving, or exacting Annates, or First-fruits of all Ecclesiastical Dignities, and Benefices throughout *England*, extant in our Histories : which, though reserved but for two years by this Pope at first, grew afterwards into custom by degrees, both in *England* and elsewhere.

<small>When First-fruits were first brought into *England*.</small>

As this Pope thus introduced these First-fruits into *England*, so he likewise frequently sent abroad his Bulls of Provisions for Ecclesiastical Benefices and Promotions therein for his Favourites and Clerks, which were then void, or should afterwards fall void by death, or otherwise.

Manifold were the Cautions inserted into Pope's Provisions for poor Clerks, though Learned and Honest, which must be confined to an Archbishop's Living in one Diocess of small value, and those not formerly granted to any others; and they bound to personal residence thereon;

when

when as others, that were rich, and more able to pay great sums for them, were not clogged with so many Cautions. Many Instruments, under the hands of publick Notaries, these poor Clerks must procure, with vast follicitation, travel, and expence, before they get the least hopes of enjoying any small Prebend, or Benefice, by Popes Bulls, and yet, in fine, not enjoy actual possession of them. Many of the Pope's Provisions to every small, as well as great, Prebendary, nor Benefice, were granted to several persons, in possession, or expectacy, by sundry Bulls at once, contradicting, repealing each other by *Non obstantes*, engendring infinite Suits, and Appeals in the Pope's Court, to the great vexation of the Patrons, Provisors, and other Competitors, and neglect of the Peoples souls, during such Contests concerning them.

The King granted the Tithes and Appropriations of all his new *Assarts* within his Forrest of *Deane*, which were extraparochial to the Bishop of *Landaff*, to augment his small Bishoprick, and maintain a Chauntry in the Church of *Newland*. The like Grant the King made this year of extraparochial Tithes, within the Forrest of *Sherwood*, to the Prior of *Felley*. The King likewise ordered the Tithes of, all his Mills in *Holderness* to be paid to the Parsons of all Parish-churches, wherein they were, as the Nobles and others there used to pay them.

Then the King (according to the manner of that Age) commanded Prayers and Masses to be made for the Soul of *Joan*, late Queen of *France*, and for *Blanch*, late Dutchess of *Austria*, deceased.

In *Scotland* there arose a great Rebellion through the treachery of the perjured Arcbbishop of St. *Andrews*, the Bishop of *Glasgo*, and Abbot of *Schone*, who confederating with *Robert Brus*, Earl of *Carrick*, and others of the Scottish Nobility, resolved to make and Crown *Robert* King of *Scotland*: who being opposed therein by *John Gomyn* his Cousin-German, a man of great power in *Scotland*, he set upon and murdered the said *John Comyn* in the Church of *Dunfrees*, and was soon after crowned King by the premised Bishops and Abbot.

Pope *Clement* the Sixth, being informed of this murder of *John Comyn* by King *Robert*, ordered the Archbishop of *York*, and Bishop of *Carlisle* to excommunicate him, and his Complices, with sound of Bells and Candles in all places of *England*, *Scotland*, *Ireland*, *Wales*, and elsewhere (though without their Diocess) and to Interdict all their Lands and Castles, till they should submit themselves. This Bull was executed accordingly.

King *Edward* sent a great and strong Army into *Scotland* against *Robert Brus*. And *Aymery de Valence*, Earl of *Penbrook*, put to flight King *Robert*, took his Wife, his Brother *Nigellus*, and others: but himself escaped into the utmost Isles of *Scotland*. The Earl of *Athol* was put to death at *London*; and *Nigellus* at *Barwick*. The Bishops of St. *Andrews*, and *Glasgo*, and the Abbot of *Scone*, were put in Iron chains, and

The Church of Great Britain.

and kept close prisoners in *Porchester-castle*. King *Robert* was brought to such misery, that he was sometime naked, and hungry, without meat or drink, save only water and roots of Herbs, and his life alwayes in danger.

Robert Brus came forth at length out of the *Scottish* Islands, with such forces as he had gotten together, taking the Castles of *Carrick*, *Innerness*, and many other.

To put an end to all which trouble, King *Edward* appointed a great Host to attend him at *Carlisle*, three weeks after *Midsummer-day*. There he held his last Parliament, wherein the State got many Ordinances to pass, for reformation of the abuses of the Pope's Ministers, and his own former exactions, wringing from the elect Archbishop of *York*, in one year, nine thousand five hundred Marks. And *Anthony*, Bishop of *Durham*, to be made Patriarch of *Jerusalem*, gave the Pope and his Cardinals mighty sums. The Pope required the Fruits of one years revenue, of every Benefice that should fall void in *England*, *Wales*, and *Ireland*, and the like of Abbies, Priories, and Monasteries.

Daniel's Chron. in Edw. 1

King *Edward* in *July* enters *Scotland* with a fresh Army, and dyes at *Burgh* upon Sands, having reigned thirty four years, seven months, aged sixty eight.

This King had founded the Abbey of *Val-royal*, in *Cheshire*, for the *Cistercians*, and by Will bequeathed thirty two thousand pounds to the Holy Land. He was obedient, not servile to the See of *Rome*.

Edward the Second, his Son, called of *Caernarvan*, succeeded in the Kingdom, in *July* 1307. He soon caused *Walter de Langton*, Bishop of *Chester*, Treasurer of *England*, and principal Executor of the last Will of the deceased King, to be arrested by Sir *John Felton*, Constable of the Tower, and imprisoned in *Wallingford-castle*, seizing upon all his Temporalties, till afterwards, by means of the Papal authority, he was restored, and they were seemingly reconciled. The Bishop's crime was a good freedom which he used in the late King's dayes, in gravely reproving this Prince for his misdemeanours, and shortening his wast of coin by a frugal moderation. All the Bishop's Goods he gave to *Piers Gaveston*, makes a new Treasurer of his own; removes most of his Father's Officers, and all without the advice and consent of his Council.

The King was married to *Isabel*, Daughter of *Philip* the fair, King of *France*, which was performed magnificently at *Boleign*. *Piers Gaveston* was the King's great Favourite, who filled the Court with Buffoons, Parasites, Minstrels, Stage-players, and all kind of dissolute persons.

King *Edward* the Second, by Letters to the Pope, requested, that *Robert Winchelsey* might be restored to his Archbishoprick, which was done accordingly; though he returned too late to Crown the King,

P   which

which solemnity was performed by *Henry Woodlock*, Bishop of *Winchester*.

<small>The Order of the Knights Templars abolished throughout Christendom.</small> Shortly after his Coronation, all the Knights Templers throughout *England* were at once arrested, and committed to prison. In the General Council of *Vienna*, this Order was utterly abolished through Christendom. The French King caused fifty four, of that Order, together with their great Master, to be burnt at *Paris*: And the Pope and Council annexed their possessions to the Order of the Knights Hospitallers, called commonly Knights of the *Rhodes*. But in *England* the Heirs of the Donors, and such as had endowed the Templars here with Lands, entred upon those parts of the ancient Patrimonies, after the dissolution of the Order, and detained them, until not long after they were by Parliament wholly transferred unto the Knights of Saint *John* of *Jerusalem*.

<small>Guy, Earl of *Warwick* surpriseth *Piers Gaveston*, and causeth him to be beheaded.</small> *Guy*, Earl of *Warwick*, surprised *Gaveston*, carried him to his Castle of *Warwick*, where in a place called *Blacklow* (afterwards *Gaveshead*) his head was stricken off, at the commandment, and in the presence of the Earls of *Lancaster*, *Warwick*, and *Hereford*.

A great Battel was fought, between the *English* and *Scots*, at *Bannocksborough*. There perished in this Battel *Gilbert Clare*, Earl of *Gloceſter*, *Robert* Lord *Clifford*, the Lord *Tiptoft*, the Lord *Marſhal*, the Lord *Giles de Argenton*, the Lord *Edmond de Maule*, and seven hundred Knights, Esquires, and Gentlemen of Quality; of common Souldiers ten thousand. There were taken prisoners, *Humphry Bohun*, Earl of *Hereford*, *Ralph de Montholmere* (who married *Joan de Acres*, Countess Dowager of *Oxford*) with many others. The Earl of *Hereford* was exchanged for King *Robert*'s Wife, who was all this while detained in *England*.

This disaster was attended with Inundations, which brought forth Dearth; Dearth Famine; Famine Pestilence, all which exceeded any that ever before had been known.

Anno 1313. died *Robert Winchelsey*, Archbishop of *Canterbury*, in whose room *Robert Cobham* was elected by the King and Church of *Canterbury*. But the Pope did frustrate that election, and placed *Walter Reynold*, Bishop of *Worcester*.

About this time died Pope *Clement*, and *John* XXII. succeeded, who sent two Legats from *Rome*, under pretence to make agreement between the King of *England* and the *Scots*. They, for their charges, required of every Spiritual person four pence in every Mark, but all in vain: for the Legats, as they were in the North parts, about *Derlington*, with their whole Family and Train, were robbed and spoiled of their Horses, Treasure, Apparel, and whatsoever else they had, and so retired back again to *Durham*: thence they returned to *London*, where they first excommunicated all those Robbers. Then for supply of those losses they received.

The Church of Great Britain.

ceived, they exacted of the Clergy, to be given unto them eight pence in every Mark. But the Clergy would only give them four pence in every Mark: So they departed to the Pope's Court again. This King *Edward* refused to pay the *Peter-pence*.

In the time of this King the Colledge in *Cambridge*, called *Michael-houfe*, was founded by Sir *Henry Staunton* Knight.

King *Edward* the Second builded two Houses in *Oxford* for good Letters, *Orial* Colledge, and St. *Mary Hall*.

England may dare all Christendom besides, to shew so many eminent School-Divines, bred within the compass of so few years. And a forreign Writer saith, *Scholastica Theologia, ab Anglis, & in Anglia fumpsit exordium, fecit incrementum, pervenit ad perfectionem.*

Of these School-men *Alexander Hales* leads the way, Master to *Thomas Aquinas*, and *Bonaventure*. He was in the time of *Henry* the Third. At the command of Pope *Innocent* the Fourth, he wrote the Body of all School-Divinity in four Volumes.

Roger Bacon succeeded him, who lived in the time of King *Edward* the First; he was excellently skilled in the Mathematicks.

The next was *Richard Middleton*, entitled *Doctor Fundatissimus*.

Then flourished *John Duns Scotus*, in the time of *Edward* the Second: he was Fellow of *Merton-colledge* in *Oxford*. He was called *Duns* by abbreviation for *Dunensis*, that is, born at *Donn*, an Episcopal See in *Ireland*.

In this King's Reign *Walter Stapleton*, Bishop of *Exeter*, founded and endowed *Exeter-colledge* in *Oxford*.

It is charged on this King *Edward* the Second, that he suffered the Pope to encroach on the Dignity of the Crown. His Father had recovered some of his Priviledges from the Papal usurpation; which, since, his Son had lost back again.

About that time an English Hermite preached at *Paul's* in *London*, *That some Sacraments that were then in use in the Church, were not of Christ's Institution*; therefore he was committed to prison.

King *Edward* went into *Scotland* with another great Army: King *Robert* thought so great an Army could not long continue, therefore he retired into the High-lands. King *Edward* wandred from place to place, till many died for hunger, and the rest returning home half starved. *James Douglas* followed the English, and slew many of them; and King *Edward* himself hardly escaped. Then a Peace was concluded at *Northampton*, Anno 1327. *That the Scots should abide in the same estate, as in the dayes of King* Alexander *the Third; the English should render all subscriptions and tokens of bondage, and have no Land in* Scotland, *unless they shall dwell in it*.

In *England* the two *Spencers* ruled all things, till the Queen and her Son (who politickly had got leave to go beyond the Seas) returned into *England*, with a Navy and Army, landing in *Suffolk*: She denounced open war against her Husband, unless he would presently conform to her desires. The young *Spencer* was taken with the King at the Abby of *Neath*, and is hanged on a Gallows fifty foot high. Many Persons of Quality were sent down to the Parliament, then sitting, to King *Edward*, to *Kenelworth-castle*, to move him to resign the Crown, which at last he sadly surrendered; and Prince *Edward*, his Son, is crowned King.

The late King is removed from *Kenelworth* unto *Barkley-castle*, where he was barbarously butchered, being struck into the Postern of his Body with an hot Spit, as it is commonly reported.

Among the Clergy, besides *Walter Stapleton*, Bishop of *Exeter*, whose head the *Londoners* caused to be smitten off at the *Standart* in *Cheapside*; only *John Stratford*, Bishop of *Winchester*, heartily adhered to him. *Robert de Baldock*, though no Bishop, yet as a Priest, and Chancellor of *England*, may be ranked with these, who attended the King, and was taken with him in *Wales*, Hence he was brought up to *London*, and committed to *Adam Tarlton*, Bishop of *Hereford*.

Many of the Bishops ungratefully sided with the Queen against her Husband, and their Sovereign. *Walter Reynolds*, Archbishop of *Canterbury*, led their Van, preferred to that See at the King's great Importunity, and by the Pope's power of Proviſion.

Henry Burwash, Bishop of *Lincoln*, lately restored to the favour of King *Edward*: yet no sooner did the Queen appear, in the field, with an Army against him, but this Bishop was the first who publickly repaired to her.

Adam Tarlton, Bishop of *Hereford*, was the grand contriver of all mischief against the King. Witness the Sermon preached by him at *Oxford* before the Queen (then in hostile pursuit against her Husband) taking for his Text the words of the Son of the sick *Shunamite*) *my Head, my Head*. Thence he urged, *That a bad King (the distempered Head of a State) is past cure*. His writing was worse than his preaching: for when such Agents, set to keep King *Edward* in *Berkley-castle*, were (by secret order from *Roger Mortimer*) commanded to kill him, they by Letters addressed themselves for advice to this Bishop (then not far off at *Hereford*) craving his counsel what they should do in so difficult and dangerous a matter. He returned unto them a ridling Answer unpointed, which carried in it Life and Death, yea Life or Death, as variously construed.

Life

Life and Death.

To kill King Edward *you need not to fear it is good.*

Life.

To kill King Edward *you need not, to fear it is good,*

Death.

To kill King Edward *you need not to fear, it is good.*

The Body of King *Edward,* without any Funeral Pomp, was buried among the *Benedictines* in their Abbey at *Glocester.*

Edward of *Windsor,* called King *Edward* the Third. being scarce fifteen years of age, took the beginning of his Reign on *January* the twentieth; his Throne was established upon his Fathers ruine. Upon *Candlemas-day* he received the Order of Knighthood by the hands of the Earl of *Lancaster,* while his depofed Father lived; and within five dayes after he was Crowned at *Westminster,* by *Walter,* Archbishop of *Canterbury.* *Anno* 1327.

Twelve men were appointed to manage the Affairs of the Kingdom during the King's minority: the Archbishop's of *Canterbury* and *York*: the Bishops of *Winchester, Hereford,* and *Worcester*; *Thomas Brotherton* Earl *Marshal,* *Edmond* Earl of *Kent*, *John* Earl *Warren*, *Thomas* Lord *Wake*, *Henry* Lord *Piercy*, *Oliver* Lord *Ingham*, and *John* Lord *Ross:* but the Queen, and *Roger* Lord *Mortimer,* usurped this charge.

Adam Tarlton was accused of Treason in the beginning of the Reign of this King, and arraigned by the King's Officers, when in the presence of the King he thus boldly uttered himself.

My Lord the King, with all due respect unto your Majesty, I Adam,. an humble Minister, and Member of the Church of God, and a consecrated Bishop, though unworthy; neither can, nor ought to answer, unto so hard Questions, without the connivance and consent of my Lord Archbishop of Canterbury, *my immediate Judge under the Pope, and without the consent of other Bishops who are my Peers.*

Three Archbishops were there present in the place, *Canterbury, York,* and *Dublin,* by whose Intercession *Tarlton* escaped at that time. Not long after he was arraigned again at the King's Bench: whereupon the foresaid Archbishops set up their Crosses, and with ten Bishops more, attended

attended with a numerous Train of well-weaponed Servants, advanced to the place of Judicature. The King's Officers frighted at the sight, fled away, leaving Bishop *Tarlton* the prisoner alone at the Bar: whom the Archbishops took home into their own custody, denouncing a Curse upon all such who should presume to lay violent hands upon him.

The King offended hereat, caused a jury of Lay-men to be impannelled, and to enquire according to form of Law, into the Actions of the Bishop of *Hereford*. This was the first time that ever Lay-men passed their verdict upon a Clergy-man. These Jurors found the Bishop guilty, whereupon the King seized his Temporalties, proscribed the the Bishop, and despoiled him of all his moveables. But afterwards he was reconciled to the King, and by the Pope, made Bishop of *Winchester*, where he died.

The former part of this King's Reign affordeth but little Church-history, as wholly taken up with his Atchievements in *France* and *Scotland*, where his success by Sea and Land was to admiration. He had both the Kings he fought against, viz. *John de Valois* of *France*, and *David* King of *Scotland*, his prisoners, at one time, taken by fair Fight in open Field.

There was granted to the King of *England*, for these Wars, a Fifteenth of the Temporalty, a Twelfth of Cities and Boroughs, and a Tenth of the Clergy, in a Parliament holden at *London*. And afterwards in a Parliament at *Northampton* there was granted him, a Tenth peny of Towns and Boroughs, a Fifteenth of others, and a Tenth of the Clergy. All such Treasure as was committed to Churches throughout *England* for the holy War, was taken out for the King's use in this.

The next year after, all the Goods of three Orders of Monks, *Lombards*, *Cluniacks*, and *Cicestercians*, are likewise seized into the King's hands, and the like Subsidy as before, granted at *Nottingham*. Now the Caursines, or *Lombards*, did not drive so full a trade as before: whereupon they betook themselves to other Merchandise, and began to store *England* with Forreign Commodities, but at unreasonable rates, whilst *England* it self had as yet but little and bad Shipping, and those less employed.

About this time the Clergy were very bountiful in contributing to the King's necessities, in proportion to their Benefices. Hereupon a Survay was exactly taken of all their Glebeland, and the same (fairly engrossed in Parchment) was returned into the Exchequer, where it remaineth at this day, and is the most useful Record for Clergy-men (and also for Impropriators as under their claim) to recover their right.

*Fuller.*Church History.

It was now complained of, as a grand grievance, that the Clergy engrossed all places of Judicature in the Land. Nothing was left to Laymen,

the Church of Great Britain.

men, but either Military commands, as *General*, *Admiral*, &c. or such Judges places, as concerned onely the very letter of the Common Law, and those also scarcely reserved to the Students thereof. As for Ambassies into Forreign parts, Noblemen were employed therein: when *Expence*, not *Experience* was required thereunto, and *Ceremony* the substance of the Service: otherwise when any difficulty in Civil Law, then Clergy-men were ever entertained. The Lord Chancellor was ever a Bishop, yea, that Court generally appeared as a Synod of Divines, where the Clerks were Clerks as generally in Orders. The same was also true of the Lord Treasurer, and Barons of the Exchequer.

Robert *Eglesfield*, Chaplain to Queen *Philippa*, Wife to King *Edward* the third, founded a Colledge on his own ground in *Oxford*, by the name of *Queens Colledge*; and diverse Queens have been nursing Mothers to this Foundation, as Queen *Philippa*, Wife to King *Edward* the third; Queen *Elizabeth*, Wife to King *Edward* the fourth; Queen *Mary*, Wife to King *Charles*; and our Virgin Queen *Elizabeth*.

In the mean time the Pope bestirred him in *England*, while the King was busied about his Wars in *France*: so that before Livings were actually void, he pre-provided Incumbents for them. But at last the King looking into it, this *Statute of Provision* was made, whereby such forestalling of Livings to Forreigners was forbidden.

Another cause of the King's displeasure with the Pope, was, that when the Pope created twelve Cardinals at the request of the King of *France*, he denied to make one at the desire of the King of *England*.

The Papal party (notwithstanding this Law of Provision) strugled for a time, till the King's Power overswayed them. Indeed this grievance continued, all this, and most of the *next* King's Reign, till the Statute of *præmunire* was made: and afterward the Land was cleared from the encumbrance of such provisions.

Three years after the Statute, against the Pope's Provisions, was made, the King presented unto the Pope *Thomas Hatlif*, to be Bishop of *Durham*, one who was the King's Secretary, but one void of all other Episcopal qualifications. However the Pope confirmed him, and being demanded why he consented to the preferment of so worthless a person, he answered, that *rebus sic stantibus*, if the King of *England* had presented an Ass unto him, he would have confirmed him in the Bishoprick.

In this King's Reign were diverse Learned Men in *England*, *John Baconthorp*, a Man of a very low stature, of whom one saith,

Ingenio

The History of

Baleus in ejus vita.

Ingenio magnus, Corpore parvus erat.

His wit was Tall, in Body small.

Coming to *Rome*, he was hissed at in a publick Disputation, for the badness, forsooth, of his Latin and pronunciation: but indeed, because he opposed the Pope's power in dispensing with Marriages contrary to the Law of God. He wrote on the Sentences, where he followeth the truth in many things; especially he refuteth the subtilties of *John Scotus*, as *Baptist Mantuan* hath marked.

*Iste tenebrosi damnat vestigia Scoti,
Et per sacra novis it documenta viis.
Hunc habeant quibus est sapientia grata, redundat
Istius in sacris fontibus omne sophos.*

Joh. Bale. Cent.4.Sect.82. He wrote *De dominio Christi*, where he proveth, that the highest Bishop in every Kingdom should be in subjection to Princes.
Richard Primate of *Ireland* (*alias Armachanus*) was his Disciple, and taught the same Doctrine: he Translated the Bible into Irish. He discovered the hypocrisie of Friers, in that though they professed poverty, yet they had stately Houses like the Palaces of Princes, and more costly Churches than any Cathedral; richer Ornaments than all the Princes, &c.

Wiliam *Ockham* an English Man sided with *Lewis* of *Bavaria* against the Pope, maintaining the Temporal Power above the Spiritual. He was forced to fly to the Emperor for his safety. He was a Disciple of *John Scotus*, but became Adversary of his Doctrine. He was the Author of the Sect of *Nominales*. He was a follower of Pope *Nicholas* the fourth, and therefore was Excommunicated by Pope *John*. This *Ockham* was *Luther*'s chief School-man, who had his Works at his finger's end.

Robert *Holcot* was not the meanest among them, who died of the Plague at *Northampton*, just as he was reading his Lectures on the seventh of *Ecclesiasticus*.

About that time a Book was written in English, called, *The complaint and prayer of a Plough-man*. The Author of it is said to have been *Robert Langland*, a Priest. After a general complaint of the Iniquity of the time, the Author wrote zealously against Auricular Confession, as contrary to Scripture, and profit of the publick, and as a device of man: against the Simony of selling Pardons: against the Pope as the Adversary of Christ. He complaineth of the unmarried Priests committing wickedness, and by bad example provoking others; of Images in Churches

The Church of Great Britain.

Churches as Idolatry; of falſe Paſtors, which feed upon their flocks, and feed them not, nor ſuffer others to feed them. He wrote alſo againſt Purgatory.

In this King's Reign were diverſe Archbiſhops of *Canterbury*. I will begin with *Simon Mepham*, made Archbiſhop in the firſt year of his Reign.

John Stratford was the ſecond, Conſecrated firſt Biſhop of *Winchester*.

The third was *Thomas Bradwardine*, Fellow of *Merton* Colledge in *Oxford*, and afterwards Chancellor of *London*, and commonly called *The profound Doctor*. He had many diſputes with the School-men againſt the errors of *Pelagius*, and reduced all his Lectures into three Books, which he entitled, *De cauſa Dei*. He was Confeſſor to King *Edward* the third. He died a few Months after his Conſecration.

Simon Iſlip was the fourth, he founded *Canterbury* Colledge in *Oxford*. This Colledge is now ſwallowed up in *Chriſt-Church*.

Simon Langham is the fifth, much meriting by his Munificence to *Weſtminſter-Abbey*.

William Witleſee ſucceeded him, famous for freeing the Univerſity of *Oxford* from the Juriſdiction of the Biſhop of *Lincoln*, formerly the Dioceſan thereof.

Simon Sudbury was the laſt Archbiſhop of *Canterbury* in this King's Reign.

In his Reign alſo flouriſhed *Nicholas Trivet*, a black Frier, born in *Norfolk*, who wrote two Hiſtories, and a Book of Annals. *Richard Stradley*, born in the Marches of *Wales*, a Monk and a Divine, who wrote diverſe excellent Treatiſes of the Scriptures. *William Herbert*, a Welchman, who wrote many good Treatiſes in Divinity. *Thomas Wallis*, a Dominican Frier, and a writer of many excellent Books. *Walter Burley*, a Doctor in Divinity, who wrote many choiſe Treatiſes in Natural and Moral Philoſophy. *Roger*, a Monk of *Cheſter*, and an Hiſtoriographer. *John Burgh*, a Monk, who wrote an Hiſtory, and alſo diverſe Homilies. *Richard Aungervil*, Biſhop of *Durham*, and Lord Chancellor of *England*. *Richard Chicheſter*, a Monk of *Weſtminſter*, who wrote a good Chronicle, from the year 449. to the year 1348. *Matthew Weſtminſter*, who wrote the Book, called, *Flores Hiſtoriarum*. *Henry Knighton*, who wrote an Hiſtory, entitled, *De geſtis Anglorum*. *John Mandevil* Knight, Doctor of Phyſick, a great Traveller; and Sir *Geoffry Chaucer*, the *Homer* of our Nation. [Sir *Rich. Baker's Chron.*]

About the fortieth year of his Reign, there was a Prieſt in *England*, called *William Wickham*, who was great with King *Edward*, ſo that all things were done by him, who was made Biſhop of *Wincheſter*.

Towards the latter end of this King's Reign aroſe *John Wickliff*, a Learned Divine of *Oxford*, who did great ſervice to the Church in promoting

moting Reformation, and in opposing Papal power, for he wrote sharply against the Pope's authority, the Church of *Rome*, and diverse of their Religious Orders. Certain Divines, and Masters of the University entertained his Doctrine, *viz.* *Robert Rigges*, Chancellor of the University, together with the two Proctors, and many others. He not onely Preached this Doctrine in *Oxford*, but also more publickly in *London* : At the Court before the King himself, the Prince of *Wales*, his Son, *John* Duke of *Lancaster*, the Lord *Clifford*, the Lord *Latimer*, and others : likewise the Lord *Montacute*, who defaced Images throughout all his Jurisdiction ; and *John* Earl of *Sarum*, who at the point of death refused the Popish Sacrament, with diverse others of the chiefest Nobility, the Major of *London*, with diverse other worthy Citizens, who many times disturbed the Bishop's Officers, who were called for the suppressing of *Wickliff*.

This Man being much encouraged by the Duke of *Lancaster*, and Sir *Henry Piercy*, Marshall, went from Church to Church Preaching his Opinions, and spreading his Doctrine ; whereupon he is cited to answer before the Archbishop, the Bishop of *London*, and others, in St. *Paul's London*. At the day appointed, the Duke of *Lancaster*, and the Lord Marshall, go to conduct him : there the Archbishop and Bishop declared the Judgement of the Pope concerning *Wickliff*'s Doctrine. The Archbishop sent *Wickliff*'s Condemnation to *Robert Rigges*, Chancellor of the University of *Oxford*, to be divulged. *Rigges* appointed them to Preach that day, whom he knew to be the most zealous followers of *Wickliff* ; and among others he ordered one *Philip Rippinton*, a Canon of *Leicester*, to Preach on *Corpus-Christi* day, who concluded his Sermon with these words : *For speculative Doctrine* (saith he) *such as is the Sacrament of the Altar, I will set a bar on my lips, while God hath otherwise instructed, or illuminated the hearts of the Clergy.*

King *Edward* the third, died *June* 21. *Anno* 1377. in the sixty fift year of his Age, when he had Reigned fifty years four Months, and odd dayes, whose Body was solemnly buried at *Westminster*. *Richard* the second, born at *Burdeaux*, the Son of *Edward*, called, *The black Prince*, being but eleven years old, succeeded his Grandfather in the Kingdom.

In the first year of his Reign Pope *Gregory* sendeth his Bull, by the hands of one *Edmund Stafford*, directed to the Chancellor and University of *Oxford*, rebuking them sharply for suffering so long the Doctrine of *John Wickliff* to take root.

At the same time also he directed Letters to *Simon Sudbury*, Archbishop of *Canterbury*, and to *William Courtney*, Bishop of *London*, with the Conclusions of *John Wickliff* therein enclosed ; commanding them to cause the said *Wickliff* to be apprehended, and cast into prison, and that

the

the Church of Great Britain.   115

the King and the Nobles of *England* should be admonished by them, not to give any credit to the said *John Wickliff*, or to his Doctrine, in any wise.

Wickliff was summoned personally to appear before the Archbishop, and the rest of the Bishops, at his Chappel at *Lambeth*. He came accordingly: when in comes a Gentleman and Courtier, named *Lewis Clifford*, on the very day of examination, commanding them not to proceed to any definitive sentence against the said *Wickliff*. The Bishops affrighted, proceeded no farther: onely the Archbishop summoned a Synod at *London*, in which he made four Constitutions, three whereof concerned Confession, grown now much into disuse by *Wickliff*'s Doctrine. *Linwood's provinc. lib. 5. fol. 183.*

The Popish Bishops and Monks obtained of King *Richard*, that *Wickliff* should be banished out of *England*. He therefore repairing into *Bohemia*, brought a great Light to the Doctrine of the *Waldenses*, where *John Husse*, being but yet a young man, had diverse Conferences with him about diverse divine matters   But at length he was recalled home again from Exile; and the year before he died, he wrote a Letter to *John Husse*, Encouraging him to be *strong in the grace that was given to him, to fight as a good Souldier of Jesus Christ, both by word and work, Doctrine and conversation*, &c. *John Husse* hereby took heart very daringly, in the University Church at *Prague*, to inveigh against the overflowing abominations of the times; and not onely at *Prague*, but throughout the whole Kingdom of *Bohemia*, did he Preach against them. The same year *Jerome* of *Prague* returning out of *England*, and carrying *Wickliff's* Books with him, rooted up the [then] prevailing error with the like boldness in the Schools, as *John Husse* did in the Church. *Comen. histor. Sclavon. Ecclis.*

Wickliff died the last of *December* 1387. and was buried in his Church of *Lutterworth* in *Leicester-shire*.

In the second year of the Reign of King *Richard* the second, a Parliament was called at *Westminster*, where the Laity moved, *That no Officer of the Holy Church should take pecuniary sums, more or less, of the people, for correction of sins; but onely enjoyn them Spiritual penance, which would be more pleasing to God, and profitable to the Soul of the offender.* The Clergy stickled hereat, for by this craft they got their gain. But here the King interposed, *That Prelates should proceed herein as formerly, according to the Lawes of the Holy Church, and not otherwise.* Yea, diverse things passed in Parliament in favour of the Clergy. As, *Ex Rotulis in Turri Lond.*

That all Prelates and Clerks shall from hence-forth commence their Suits against Purveyors and Buyers disturbing them (though not by way of crime) by actions of Trespass, and recover treble damages.

Also, *That any of the King's Ministers arresting people of the Holy Church, in doing Divine Service, shall have imprisonment, and thereof*

Q 2   *be*

be ransomed at the King's will, and make gree to the parties so arrested.

In the Parliament held at *Glocester* the same year, the Commons complained that many Clergy-men, under the notion of *Sylva cædua, lopwood*, took Tithes even of Timber it self: requesting, that in such cases, Prohibition might be granted, to stop the proceedings of *Court Christian*. But this took no effect. Then the Archbishop of *Canterbury* inveighed as bitterly, of the Franchises infringed of the Abbey-Church of *Westminster*; wherein *Robert de Hanley* Esquire, with a Servant of that Church, were both horribly slain therein, at the High Altar, even when the Priest was singing high Mass, and pathetically desired reparation for the same. Complaints were also made against the extortion of Bishops Clerks; to which (as to other abuses) some general Reformation was promised.

In the next Parliament called at *Westminster*, one of the greatest grievances of the Land was redressed, namely, Forreigners holding of Ecclesiastical Benefices; for many Italians had the best livings in *England* by the Pope collated on them: yea many great Cardinals resident at *Rome*, were possessed of the best Prebends and Parsonages in the Land, who generally farmed out their places to Proctors their own Conntreymen; and by this means the wealth of the Land leaked out into Forreign Countries, to the great impoverishing of this Land. Therefore the King and Parliament now enacted, *That no Aliens should hereafter hold any such preferments, nor any send over unto them the Revenues of such Benefices.*

Sir. *Rich. Baker's* Chron. in *Rich.* 2.

Then burst forth the dangerous rebellion of *Wat Tyler*, and *Jack Straw*, with thousands of their wicked company, who burnt the *Savoy*, the Duke of *Lancaster's* house: from the *Savoy* they went to the Temple, where they burnt the Lawyers lodgings, with their Books and Writings: also the house of St. *Johns*, by *Smithfield*, they set on fire, which burned for seven days together. Then came they to the Tower, where the King was lodged, where they entred, and finding there *Simon Sudbury*, Archbishop of *Canterbury*, and Lord Chancellor, and Sir *Robert Hales* Lord Treasurer, they led them to the Tower-hill, and there in most cruel manner struck off their Heads, as also of diverse others. Neither spared they Sacred places, for, breaking into the Church of the *Augustine* Friars, they drew forth thirteen Flemmings, and beheaded them in the open Streets, as also, seventeen others out of other Churches. They committed outrages afterwards at St. *Albans*, cancelling the antient Charters of the Abbots and Monks there. At the same time there were gathered together in *Suffolck* to the number of fifty thousand, by the instigation of one *John Wraw*, a lewd Priest. These destroyed the Houses of the Lawyers; they beheaded Sir *John Cavendish* the Lord Chief Justice of *England*, and set his Head upon the Pillory in St. *Edmunds-bury*.

Then

The Church of Great Britain.

Then *Henry Spencer*, the valiant Bishop of *Norwich*, gathered together a great number of Men Armed, with which he set upon the Rebels, discomfited them, and took *John Littester*, and their other Chieftaines, whom he caused all to be Executed: and by this means the Countrey was quieted, *Jack Straw*, *John Kirkby*, *Alane Tredder*, and *John Sterling*, lost their Heads; *Wat Tyler* was slain by *William Walworth* Lord *Mayor* of *London*. These had to their Chaplain a wicked Priest, called *John Ball*, who counselled them to destroy all the Nobility and Clergy, so that there should be no Bishop in *England*, but one Archbishop, which should be himself: and that there should not be above two Religious persons in one house; and their possessions should be divided among the Lay-men, for the which Doctrine they held him as a Prophet. But he was executed at St. *Albans*. *Stowes Chro. in Rich. 2.*

William Wickham about this time finished his beautiful Colledge in *Oxford*, called *new Colledge*, which giveth the Armes of *Wickham, viz.* two *Cheverons* betwixt three Roses, each Cheveron alluding to two beams fastned together (called couples in building) to speak his skill in Architecture. There is maintained therein, a Warden, seventy Fellows, and Scholars, ten Chaplains, three Clerks, one Organist, sixteen Choristers, besides Officers and Servants of the Foundation, with other Students, being in all one hundred thirty five.

Within few years after the same Bishop finished the Colledge at *Winchester*, wherein he established one Warden, ten Fellows, two Schoolmasters, and seventy Scholars, with Officers and Servants, which are all maintained at his charge: out of which School he ordained should be chosen the best Scholars always to supply the vacant places of the Fellows of this Colledge.

Anno 1391. There was a Synod in *England*, which (because many were vexed for causes which could not be known, at *Rome*) ordained, *That the authority of the Pope of Rome should stretch no farther than to the Ocean Sea; and that who so Appealed to Rome, besides Excommunication, should be punished with loss of all their goods, and with perpetual imprisonment.*

Then came the Parliament wherein was Enacted the Statute, called the Statute of *Præmunire*, which gave such a blow to the Church of *Rome*, that it never recovered it self in this Land. The Statute of *Mortmain* put the Pope into a sweat, but this put him into a Fever. That concerned him onely in the Abbies, his darlings; this touched him in his person. *The Statute of Præmunire.*

About this time died that faithful, Learned, and aged Servant of God, *John de Trevisa* born at *Crocadon* in *Cornwal*, a Secular Priest, and Vicar of *Berkley*, painful in Translating the Old and New Testament into English, with other great Books.

The

The History of *William Swinderby* Priest in the Diocess of *Lincoln*, whereunto he was forced by the Friars: the Process of *John Tresnant*, Bishop of *Hereford* (into whose Diocess he removed) had against him, in the cause of Heretical pravity, as the Papists call it: the Articles that were exhibited against him, with his protestation and answer to the same. The Process against *William Swinderby*, with his answer and declaration to certain Conclusions: the Bishop's sentence against him, and his Appeal from the Bishop to the King with the causes thereof, together with *Swinderby*'s letter to the Parliament, may be read at large in Mr. *Fox* his Acts and Monuments of the Church.

Then were there Articles exhibited against *Walter Brute*, of the Diocess of *Hereford*, a Lay-man and Learned, touching the cause of Heresie, as they called it, unto the Bishop of *Hereford*; his examination and answer is also largely described by Mr. *Fox*.

Fox in *Ric.* 2.

Then were there two Bulls sent out by Pope *Boniface* the ninth, one against the Lollards; another to King *Richard* the second. Queen *Anne* Wife, to King *Richard*, at the same time had the Gospels in English, with four Doctors upon the same.

King *Richard* wrote a notable Letter to the Pope, wherein he sheweth, That the election of the Pope was not as before, comparing the Popes to the Souldiers that crucified Christ. That Secular Princes are to bridle the outrages of the Pope; and seemeth to Prophecy of the desolation of the Roman Pope.

King *Richard* was not long after deposed, and barbarously murdered at *Pomfret-castle*. In the time of the conspiracy against King *Richard*, among all the Bishops, onely *Thomas Merks* Bishop of *Carlisle* was for him. For, when the Lords in Parliament, not content to depose King *Richard*, were devising more mischief against him, up steps the foresaid Bishop, and thus expresseth himself.

> *There is no man here worthy to pass his sentence on so great a King, as to whom they have obeyed as their lawful Prince, full two and twenty years. This is the part of Traitors, Cut-throats, and Thieves: None is so wicked; none so vile, who though he be charged with a manifest crime, we should think to condemn before we heard him. And you, do ye think it equal to pass sentence on a King anointed and Crowned, giving him no leave to defend himself? How unjust is this? But let us consider the matter it self. I say, nay openly affirm, that* Henry Duke *of* Lancaster *(whom you are pleased to call your King) hath most unjustly spoiled* Richard *(as well his Sovereign as ours) of his Kingdom.*

More would he have spoken, but the Lord Marshal enjoyned him silence: and the other Bishops said, he discovered (having been a Monk) more

The Church of Great Britain.

more Covent-devotion, than Court-discretion, in dissenting from his Brethren: yet at that time no punishmet was imposed upon him. But the next year 1400. when some discontented Lord's arose against King *Henry* the fourth, this Bishop was taken prisoner, and judicially arraigned for high Treason, for which he was condemned, and sent to St. *Albans* The Pope gave unto him another Bishoprick in *Samos*, a Greek Island. But before his translation he died.

Cent. XV.

King *Henry* the fourth, held a Parliament at *Westminster*, during which *Thomas Arundel* Archbishop of *Canterbury* had convocated a Synod, which was held in St. *Paul*'s Church, to whom the King sent the Earls of *Northumberland*, and *Westmorland*, who declared to the Clergy, That they were from the King to acquaint them, that the King resolved to confirm all their Priviledges unto them, and to joyn with them as they should desire him, in the punishment of all Hereticks, and opposites to their Religion received: for which so doing he craved but their supplications to God for him and his posterity, and prosperity of the Kingdom, which was by all there present religiously promised.

Trussel in vit. Henrici. IV.

In the second year of his Reign, King *Henry* ordained, *That if any person should obtain from the Bishop of Rome, any provision, to be exempt from obedience Regular or Ordinary; or to have any Office perpetual in any House of Religion, he should incur the pains of* Præmunire. He also gave authority unto Bishops and their *Ordinaries*, to imprison and fine all Subjects who refuse the Oath *ex Officio*. In the same Parliament it was ordained, *That all Lollards* [*that is, those who professed the doctrine which* Wickliff *had taught.*] *should be apprehended; and if they should remain obstinate, they should be delivered to the Bishop of the Diocess, and by him unto the secular Magistrate to be burnt.* This Act was the first in this Island for burning in case of Religion, and began to be put in execution, Anno 1401.

The Statute made, pro Hæretico comburendo.

The first on whom his cruel Law was hanselled, was *William Santre*, formerly Parish-priest of St. *Margaret* in the Town of *Lyn*, but since of St. *Ositb* in the City of *London*. It seemeth, he had formerly abjured those Arcticles (for which he suffered death) before the Bishop of *Norwich*. Therefore he was first adjudged to be degraded and deposed, which was in order, as followeth.

From

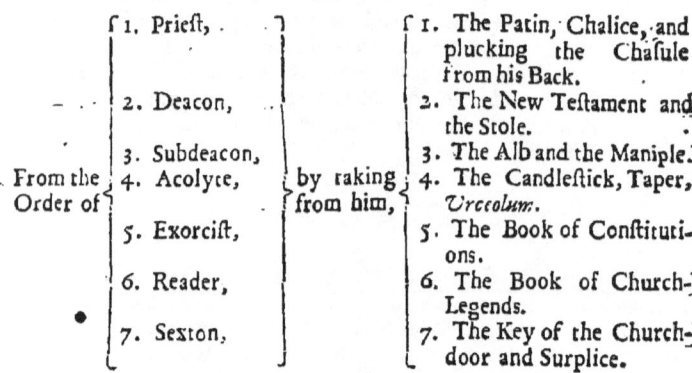

.How many steps are required to climb up to the top of Popiſh Prieſthood! how many trinkets muſt be had to compleat a Prieſt? and here we behold them ſolemnly taken aſunder in *Sautres* degradation. And now he no longer Prieſt, but plain Lay-man, with the Tonſure on his crown raſed away, was delivered to the Secular Power, with this complement worth the noting. *Beſeeching the Secular Court, that they would receive favourably the ſaid* William *unto them thus recommitted.* But ſee their hypocriſie; The Popiſh Biſhops at the ſame time (for all their fair language) called upon the King to bring him to ſpeedy execution.

Hereupon the King in Parliament iſſued out his Warrant to the Mayor and Sheriff of *London*, that the ſaid *William*, being in their cuſtody, ſhould be brought forth into ſome publick place within the liberty of the City, and there really to be burnt to the great horrour of his offence, and manifeſt example of other Chriſtians; which was done accordingly.

After this, *Richard Scroop*, Archbiſhop of *York*, with the Lord *Moubray*, Marſhall of *England*, gathered together a great company againſt King *Henry*, in the North Countrey, to whom was adjoyned the ayd of the Lord *Bardolf*, and *Henry Piercy*, Earl of *Northumberland*. They drew up ten Articles againſt the ſaid King, and faſtened them upon the doors of Churches and Monaſteries, to be read of all men in Engliſh. The Earl of *Northumberland*, and the Lord *Bardolf* were ſlain in the field, fighting againſt the Kings part, *Anno* 1408. But the Archbiſhop of *York*, and the Lord *Moubray* were taken and beheaded.

Anno 1409. *Thomas Badby*, a Tailor, was by *Thomas Arundel* Archbiſhop of *Canterbury*, condemned for the Teſtimony of the truth. He was

was brought into *Smithfield*, and there being put into an empty barrel, was bound with Iron bars fast to a stake, and dry wood put to him, and so burned.

Some Professors of the Gospel at that time did shrink back, as *John Purvey*, who wrote many Books in defence of *Wickliff*'s Doctrine, and among others a Commentary upon the Apocalypse, wherein he declareth the Pope of *Rome* to be that great Antichrist. He recanted at *Paul*'s Cross. *John Edwards* Priest revoked at the *Green-yard* at *Norwich*. *Richard Herbert*, and *Emmot Willy* of *London*, and *John Beck* also at *London*. *John Seynons* of *Lincoln-shire* revoked at *Canterbury*.

Then was *William Thorp* examined before the Archbishop of *Canterbury*, who rehearsed his belief before the Archbishop; afterwards he was committed to close Prison, where he was so straitly kept, that either he was secretly made away, or else there he died by sickness. *John Ashton* also, another follower of *Wickliff*, who, for the same Doctrine of the Sacrament held by *Thorp*, was committed to close Prison, after he was condemned, where he continued till his death.

Philip Rippington was made Bishop of *Lincoln*, who of a Professor, became a cruel Persecutor of the Gospel.

Synods of the Clergy were very frequent in this King's Reign; but most of these were but Ecclesiastical meetings for secular Money.

Sir *John Tiptoff* (made afterwards Earl of *Worcester*) put up a Petition to the Parliament touching Lollards, which so wrought on the Lords, that they joyned in a Petition to the King, that they and every of them be taken, and put in Prison, without being delivered in Bail, or otherwise, except by good and sufficient mainprise, to be taken before the Chancellor of *England*, &c.

The Popish Clergy had gained Prince *Henry* (set as a Transcendent by himself in the Petition) to their Side, entring his youth against the poor *Wickliffists*: and this earnest engaged him to the greater Antipathy against them, when possessed of the Crown.

A Petition was put up in the Parliament, That the King might enjoy half of the profits of any Parson's Benefice, not resident thereon: whereunto the King answered, That Ordinaries should do their duties therein, or else he would provide further remedy, or stay their pluralities.

The ninth year of the King's Reign, the Commons desired of the King, That none presented be received by any Ordinary, to have any Benefice, of any Incumbent, for any cause of privation, or inhabitation, whereof the Process is not founded upon Citation made within the Realm: and also that such Incumbents may remain in all their Benefices, untill it be proved by due Inquest in the Court of the King, that the Citations whereupon such privations, and inhabitations are granted, were made within the Realm: and if such Ordinaries do, or have presented, or others do present to the contrary, that then they and their Procurators, &c. incur the pain contained in the Statute made against Provisoe's, *Anno* 13. *Ric.* 2.

Also that no Pope's Collector should from thence-forth levy any Money within the Realm, for first Fruits of any Ecclesiastical dignity, under pain of incurring the Statute of Provisoe's.

The Commons in the same Parliament put up a Bill to the King to take the Temporalties out of the Hands of the Spiritualty, which amounted to three hundred and two and twenty thousand Marks by the year.

Then came the Cardinal of *Burges* into *England*, being sent from the Colledge of Cardinals, to inform the King and Clergy of the unconstant dealing of Pope *Gregory*.

Anno 1409. Stowes Chro. in *Henry* 4. After the Feast of the *Epiphany*, the Archbishop of *Canterbury* Convocated an Assembly of the Clergy at *London*, to chuse meet persons to go to the General Council holden at *Pisa*: whereunto were chosen *Robert Holam*, Bishop of *Salisbury*; *Henry Chifely*, Bishop of *St. Davids*, and *Thomas Chillindon*, Prior of *Christ-Church* in *Canterbury*: and the King had sent before, Sir *John Colvil* Knight, and *Nicholas Rixton* Clerk, with letters to be given to them. A letter also was sent unto the Pope, wherein the King chargeth him with Perjury.

At *Pisa* there assembled a great number of Cardinals, Archbishops, Bishops, and Mitred Prelates, who elected a new Pope, *viz. Alexander the fifth* (a man trained up at *Oxford*) rejecting the two other Schismatical Popes, *Gregory* and *Benedict*.

Thomas Arundel, Archbishop of *Canterbury*, came with a Pompous train to *Oxford*. His intent was Juridically to visit the University, expecting to be solemnly met, and sumptuously entertained according to his place and dignity. But *Richard Courtney*, the Chancellor of *Oxford*, with *Benedict Brent*, and *John Birch*, the two Proctors, denied the Archbishop entrance into the University under the notion of a Visitor. The Archbishop angry at the affront, fairly retreated, *re infecta* to *London*.

King *Henry* at the joynt instances of both parties, summoned them to *Lambeth*, to hear and determine the Controversie: where the King pronounced sentence on the Archbishop's side. Afterward the King confirmed the same, with the consent of the Lords and Commons in Parliament; as in the Tower-Rolls doth plainly appear.

The King though courteous, was not servile to the Pope, and the Clergy terrified with the wavering doubtfulness of the King, granted him a tenth every year for diverse years.

Fuller.Church Hist. of *Brit*. King *Henry* the fourth, is not observed (as all English Kings before and after him) to have erected and endowed any one entire house of Religion,

Religion, as first or sole-founder thereof, though a great Benefactor to the Abby of *Leicester*, and Colledge of *Fothringhay* in *Northamptonshire*. His picture is not so well known by his Head, as his Hood, which he weareth upon it in an odd fashion peculiar to himself. He died *Anno* 1413.

Henry the fifth, his Son, succeeded in the Kingdom. An universal Synod of all the Bishops and Clergy was called at *London*, where, among other weighty matters, it was determined, That the day of St. *George*, and also of St. *Dunstan*, should be a double Feast in holy Church.

At the Petition of the Commons in Parliament, to the King, all Irish begging Priests, called **Chambercakyns**, were ordered to depart the Realm by *Michaelmas* following, upon pain of loss of goods, and imprisonment during the King's pleasure. *Rotul. in Tirri Lond.*

In the beginning of this King's Reign arose Sir *John Oldcastle*, who Married *Joan de la Pole*, Baroness of *Cobham*, the Lord whereof he became: a Man (saith one) *Regi propter probitatem, charus & acceptus*, in great favour with King *Henry* the fifth, for his honesty, and likewise renouned for his valour, and great skill in feats of Armes: who sent into the Diocesses of *London*, *Rochester*, and *Hereford*, some to publish the truth of the Gospel, without the leave and Licence of the Ordinaries, who were especially in their Sermons to confute the Doctrine of Transubstantiation, the Popish Sacrament of Penance, Peregrinations, worshipping of Images, the Keys usurped by the Church of *Rome*. *Camd. Brit. in Kent.*

At that time there reforted to the Synod in *London*, twelve Inquisitors for Heresie, whom they appointed at *Oxford* the year before, to search out for Hereticks, withall *Wickliff*'s Books; who brought two hundred forty six Conclusions; which they had collected as Heresies out of the said Books.

The Names of the Inquisitors, were these; *John Witnam*, a Master in *New Colledge*. *John Langdon*, Monk of *Christ-church* in *Canterbury*. *William Ufford*, Regent of the *Carmalites*; *Thomas Clayton*; Regent of the *Dominicks*; *Robert Gilbert*, *Richard Enthisdale*, *John Luck*, *Richard Sindisham*, *Richard Fleming*, *Thomas Rotborn*, *Robert Rouberry*, *Richard Grafdale*; who all concluded, that the chief favourers of *Wickliff*'s Doctrine, were to be first dealt against. The Lord *Cobham* was complained of by the General Proctors, to be the chief, principal abettor of suspected Preachers, contrary to the mind of the Ordinaries, and to have assisted them by force of Armes.

The King sent for the Lord *Cobham*, and when he was come, he admonished him secretly to submit himself to his Mother the holy Church: Unto whom he made this Answer.

You most Worthy Prince. (saith he) *I am always ready to obey, forasmuch as I know you a Christian Prince, and the Minister of God, bearing the Sword to the punishment of evil doers, and safeguard of them that do well: Unto you* (*next unto my eternal God*) *owe I most reverence, and submit thereunto* (*as I have done ever*) *all that I have either of Nature or Fortune, ready at all times to fulfill whatsoever You in the Lord command me. But as touching the Pope, and his Spiritualty; I owe them neither Suit nor Service, forasmuch as I know him by the Scriptures to be the Great Antichrist, the Son of Perdition, the open Adversary of God.*

The King having heard this, would talk no longer with him, but utterly left him: And the Archbishop resorting to the King, he gave him authority to Cite him, Examine, and Punish him according to their Decrees.

The Archbishop Cited him to appear before him at the Castle of *Leeds* in *Kent,* and because he appeared not, he Excommunicated him. Then the Lord *Cobham* wrote a draught of the Confession of his Faith, and Sealed it with his own Hand, in which he answered the four chiefest Articles that the Archbishop laid against him; and that done, he took the Copy with him, and went therewith to the King, who would not receive it, but commanded it to be delivered to those who should be his Judges. Then he desired in the King's presence, that an hundred Knights and Esquires might be suffered to come, as upon his Purgation, which he knew would clear him of all Heresies.

Moreover, he offered himself, after the Law of Armes, to fight for Life, or Death, with any man living, Christian, or Heathen, in the quarrel of his Faith, the King's Majesty and the Lords of his Council excepted: and furthermore protested, *That he would obey all manner of Laws agreeable to the Word of God :* yet for all this, the King suffered him to be summoned personally in his own Privy-chamber.

Joh. Capgrave. lib. 2. de nobi- lib. Henrici.

He appeared before the Archbishop sitting in the Chapter-house of *Pauls,* with *Richard Clifford,* Bishop of *London, Henry Bullinbrook,* Bishop of *Winchester.* He professed, *That the Pope was true Antichrist, That he is his Head, and that the Popish Bishops were his Members; the Friars his Tayl. And as touching the other Points* (saith he) *they are Ordinances of the Church of* Rome, *made against the Scriptures, after it grew rich, and the poison had dispersed it self therein, and not before.* Another Annalist saith, That he had openly said in Parliament, that it would never be well in England, till the Pope's power were banished beyond the Seas.

The Church of Great Britain.

The Archbishop read a Bill of Condemnation against him, after which Bill read, the Lord *Cobham* said with a cheerful countenance, *Though you judge my Body, which is but a wretched thing, yet I am sure ye can do no harm to my Soul, no more than Satan could do to the Soul of* Job. *And as concerning these Articles, I will stand to them to the very death by the grace of my eternal God.* And after a short instruction to the people, he fell down upon his Knees, holding up his Hands and Eyes to Heaven, *And prayed God to forgive his Prosecutors.* The Lord *Cobham* was condemned to dye, being led back to the Tower, he escaped out of the Tower, and fled into *Wales*, where he continued by the space of four years.

In *January* 1414. Sir *Roger Acton* Knight, Mr. *John Brown*, and *John Beverley* a Minister, suffered Martyrdom in the Fields of St. *Giles*, with thirty six more. Some say, that Sir *Roger Acton* was hanged naked at *Tyburn*, saving that certain parts of him were covered, and after certain dayes, a Trumpetter of the King's, called *Thomas Cliffe*, got leave of the King to take him down, and bury him.

The next Month after the Execution of these Men, died *Thomas Arundel* Archbishop of *Canterbury*, famished to Death, not for want of Food, but of a Throat to swallow it: such the swelling therein, that he could neither speak nor eat for some days.

After him succeeded *Henry Chichely*, whose mean birth interrupted the chain of Noble Archbishops, his two Predecessors and Successors being Earls Sons by Extraction. Although many Laws had been made against the Pope's usurped Authority in bestowing Ecclesiastical preferments by way of Provision; yet durst not this man consent unto his election made by the Covent of *Canterbury*, but committed the matter unto the Pope's determination, who first pronounced the election of the Monks void, and then bestowed the Archbishoprick upon him. Godwin's Cath. of Ellh.

The same year the King began the Foundation of two Monasteries: one of the Friars observants on the one side of *Thames*; and the other on the other side of the same River, called *Shene*, and *Sion*, dedicated unto the Charter-house Monks, with certain Nuns of St. *Briget*, to the number of sixty, dwelling within the same precinct: so that the whole number of these, with Priests, Monks, Deacons, and Nuns, should equal the number of thirteen Apostles, and seventy two Disciples. These were to eat no Flesh, to touch no Money, to wear no Linnen.

The King held a Parliament at *Leicester*, in which the Commons put up their Bill again, which was put up, *Anno* 11. *Henry* the fourth, that the Temporalties wasted so disorderly by the Clergy, might be converted to the use of the King, and of his Earls, and Knights, &c. In fear of which Bill, the Clergy put him upon a long War with the French, offering to him in behalf of the Clergy, great and notable sums, by reason whereof the Bill was put off again. The

The Archbishop, *Henry Chichley*, condemned *John Claydon's* Books, and condemned him, and shortly after he was burnt in *Smithfield* with *Richard Turning*, Baker, *Anno* 1415.

The next year the said Archbishop, in his Convocation holden at *London*, made sharper Constitutions, than were before, against the *Lollards*. There two Priests, noted for Hereticks, were brought before the Bishops, the one *John Barton*, the other *Robert Chappel*. *Barton* was committed to *Philip*, Bishop of *Lincoln*, to be kept in prison, till otherwise it were determined. *Chappel* submitted himself, and with much ado received pardon: and was (in stead of penance) enjoyned certain Articles to publish at *Paul's Cross*.

Then divers persons were forced to abjure, as *John Tailer* of the Parish of St. *Maries* at *Quern*, *William James* Physitian, who had long lain in prison. *John Gourdley* of *Lincoln-shire*, a learned man, *John Duerfer*, *Katherine Dertford*, the Parson of *Higley* in *Lincoln-shire*, named Mr. *Robert*, *William Henry of Tenterden*; *John Gaul*, a Priest of *London*, *Richard Monk*, Vicar of *Chesham* in *Lincoln-shire*, with divers others.

During the time of the Provincial Convocation, Pope *Martin* had sent to the Clergy of *England* for a Subsidy to maintain the Pope's Wars against the *Lollards* of *Bohemia*. Another Subsidy was demanded to persecute *William Clerk*, Master of Arts in *Oxford*, who sailing out of *England*, was at the Council of *Basil* disputing on the *Bohemians* side. A third Subsidy was also required, to persecute *William Ruffel*, Warden of the *Grey-Friers* in *London*, who was fled, having escaped out of prison.

Ralph Mungin, Priest, refusing to abjure, was condemned to perpetual prison. The recantation of *Thomas Granter*, and *Richard Monk*, Priests, was read openly at *Paul's Cross*, after which *Granter* was put to seven years imprisonment, under the custody of the Bishop of *London*. *Edmond Frith* recanted, who was Butler to Sir *John Oldcastle*.

Besides these, many other *Wicklivites* were sore vexed in *Kent*, in the Towns of *Romney*, *Tenterden*, *Woodchurch*, *Cranbrook*, *Staplehurst*, *Bennenden*, and *Rolvenden*; where Men and their Wives, and whole Families were driven to forsake their Houses, and Towns, for fear of persecution. Among whom were *William White*, and *Thomas Greenfted*, Priests, *Bartholomew Chronemonger*, *Joan Waddon*. *Joan* his Wife, *Thomas Evernden*, *Stephen Robins*, *William Chineling*, *John Tame*, *John Facolin*, *William Somer*, *Marian* his Wife, *John Abraham*, *Robert Munden*, *Laurence Cook*: which persons, because they appeared not, were excommunicated by the Archbishop.

The Lord *Cobham*, having lived four years in *Wales*, and being at last discovered, was taken by the Lord *Powis*: yet so, that it cost some blows and blood to apprehend him, till a Woman at last with a stool broke

The Church of Great Britain.

broke the Lord *Cobham*'s legs, whereby being lame, he was brought up to *London* in an Horse-litter. At last he was drawn upon an Hurdle to the Gallows, and there was hanged and burnt.

In the ninth year of King *Henry* the Fifth, he suppressed the French Houses of Religious Monks and Friars, and such like, in *England*, because they spake ill of the King's Conquest over *France*. Their Lands were given by him, and King *Henry* the Sixth, to Monasteries, and Colledges of learned men. *Stow's Chrol; in Hen. 8.*

King *Henry* died in *France*, and was brought over, and buried at *Westminster*,

This King ordained the King of Heraulds over the English, which is called *Garter*.

In this King's Reign *Richard Fleming*, Bishop of *Lincoln*, founded a Colledge, named *Lincoln--colledge* in *Oxford*.

King *Henry* the sixth, an Infant of eight months old, succeeded his Father in the Kingdom of *England*, Anno 1422.

In the eighth year of his Age he was crowned at *Westminster*, and in the tenth year crowned King at *Paris*; Cardinal *Henry*, Bishop of *Winchester*, being present at them both.

The Clergy had then a strong party in the Privy Council, *viz.*

1. *Henry Chicheley*, Archbishop of *Canterbury*.
2. *John Kemp*, Bishop of *London*.
3. *Henry Beauford*, Bishop of *Winchester*, lately made Cardinal.
4. *John Wackaring*, Bishop of *Norwich*, Privy-seal.
5. *Philip Morgan*, Bishop of *Worcester*.
6. *Nicholas Bubwith*, Bishop of *Bath* and *Wells*, Lord Treasurer.

In the first year of this King's Reign, was burned a faithful Witness of God's Truth, *William Tailor*, a Priest, under *Henry Chicheley*, Archbishop of *Canterbury*, March 1. Anno 1422.

In the year 1424. *John Florence*, a Turner, appeared before *Will. Bernam*, Chancellor to the Bishop of *Norwich* being accused for holding and teaching divers Heresies. But being threatened, he submitted himself, and abjured: and for his penance he was whipped three Sundayes, in a solemn procession, in the Cathedral Church of *Norwich*, before all the people. The like also was done about his Parish-church of *Shelton* three other several Sundayes, he being bare-headed, bare-footed, and bare-necked, after the manner of a publick Penitentiary, his body being covered with a canvas shirt and breeches, carrying in his hand a Taper of a pound weight.

In the same year *John Goddesel* of *Dickingham*, Parchment-maker, abjured and was set at liberty till the year 1428.

Richard

Richard Belward of Erisam sware, that he would neither teach nor assist any against the Church of Rome, and was dismissed.
The like happened to *Hugh Pie*, Chaplain of *Ludney*.

In the year 1428. King *Henry* the Sixth sent down Letters of Commission to *John Exeter*, and *Ja olet Germain*, keeper of the Castle of *Colchester*, for the apprehending of *William White* Priest, and others suspected of Heresie. *John Exeter* attached six persons in the Town of *Bungay*, in the Diocess of *Norwich*, and three of them were committed to the Castle of *Fremingham*, belonging to the Duke of *Norfolk*, namely *John Waddon* of *Tenterden* in *Kent* ; *Bartholomew Monk* of *Ersham*, and *William Skutt*.

In the Towns of *Beckles*, *Ersham* and *Ludney*, a great number both of Men and Women were cast into prison, and after their abjuration brought to open shame in Churches and Markets by the Bishop of *Norwich*, and his Chancellor *William Bernham*, *John Exeter* being Register : so that within the space of three or four years about one hundred and twenty Men and Women were examined, and suffered great vexation for the profession of Christian Faith. Some taken upon suspition only, more easily escaped, as *Robert Skirring* of *Harlstone*, *William Skirring*, and some others. Some were burned, among whom special mention is made of these three, *Father Abraham* of *Colchester*, *William White*, and *John Waddon*, Priests. The residue abjured, and suffered penance, as *John Beverley*, *J. Wardon*, *John Capper*, Vicar of *Tunstal*, with more than threescore others. They had their Doctrine from *William White* who was a Scholar and follower of *John Wickliff*.

An. 1428. Such was the Spleen of the Council of *Sienna*, as they not only cursed the memory of *John Wickliff*, as dying an obstinate Heretick, but ordered, that his bones should be taken out of the ground, and thrown far off from any Christian burial. In obedience hereunto, *Richard Fleming*, Bishop of *Lincoln*, Diocesan of *Lutterworth*, sent his Officers to ungrave him accordingly, who took his bones out of the grave, and burnt them to ashes, and cast them into *Swift*, a neighbouring Brook running hard by.

Anno 1430. R. *Hovedon*, a Wool-winder, and Citizen of *London*, was burnt at the Tower-hill for the Doctrine of *Wickliff*. The year following *Thomas Bagley*, a Priest, Vicar of *Monenden* besides *Malden*, was condemned of Heresie at *London*, about the midst of *Lent*, degraded, and burned in *Smithfield*.

At St. *Andrews* in *Scotland*, Anno 1431. *Paul Craw* was burnt for *Petries church Hislory.* denying that the substance of the Bread and Wine are changed in the Eucharist ; or that Confession is necessary to be made unto Priests, or Prayers unto Saints departed. At his condemnation they put a Bull of Brass in his mouth, to the end he should not speak unto the people, nor tell for what he was burnt.

Henry

The Church of Great Britain.

Henry Beauford, Bishop of *Winchester*, Cardinal *Sancti Eusebii*, was by consent of Parliament made one of the King's Council, with this condition, that he should make a protestation to absent himself from the Council, when any matters were to be treated betwixt the King and Pope. The Cardinal took the Protestation, and promised to perform it. *Ex Archivis Turris Lond.*

The Clergy complained to the King in Parliament, that their Servants, which came with them to Convocations, were often arrested, and they prayed that they might have the same Priviledge, which the Peers and Commons of the Kingdom have, which are called to Parliament, which was granted accordingly.

Great at this time was the want of Grammar-schools, and the abuse of them that were even in *London* it self, it being pænal for any (to prevent the growth of *Wicklivism*) to put their Children to private Teachers. Hence it was, that some hundreds were compelled to go to the same School, where (to use the words of the Records) *The Masters waxen rich in money, and Learners poor in cunning.* Whereupon this grievance was complained of by four eminent Ministers in *London*, viz.

Mr.
{ *William Lichfield*, Parson of *Alhallowes* the Great.
{ *Gilbert*, Parson of St. *Andrew's Holborn*.
{ *John Cote*, Parson of St. *Peter's Cornhil*.
{ *John Neele*, Master of the House of St. *Thomas Acre's*, and Parson of *Colchirch*.

To these it was granted, by the advice of the Ordinary, or Archbishop of *Canterbury*, to erect five Schools (*Neele* having a double License for two places) in their respective Parishes. Know, that the House of St. *Thomas Acre's* was where *Mercers* Chappel standeth at this day.

Then was the Lady *Eleanor Cobham* (so called from the Lord *Cobham*, her Father, otherwise *Eleanor Plantagenet* by her Husband, *Humfry* Duke of *Glocester*) and *Roger Only*, Priest, her Chaplain, condemned: the Dutchess (after solemn penance, and carrying a Taper barefoot at *Paul's* Cross) to perpetual banishment, for plotting with *Only* (say *Hall* and *Fabian* in their Chronicles) an abominable Necromancer) with three others, by Witchcraft to destroy the King, so to derive the Crown to her Husband, who was next Heir in the line of *Lancaster*: And *Roger Only* was burned. But the main cause of their condemnation was for the profession of the Truth, although Treason was pretended against them. *Polydor Virgil* makes no mention thereof, otherwise quick-sighted enough in matters of this nature.

At this time *William Heiworth* sate Bishop of *Coventry* and *Lichfield*, being translated thither from being Abbot of St. *Albans*.

S   At

At this time *William Lynwood* finished his industrious and useful Work of his Constitutions. He was bred in *Cambridge*, first Scholar of *Gonvil*; then Fellow of *Pembrook-hall*. His younger years he spent in the Law, afterwards he became Keeper of the Privy-seal unto King *Henry* the Fifth, who employed him in an Embassie into *Spain* and *Portugal*, which he exactly performed. After the King's death he re-assumed his Official's place of *Canterbury*, and then at spare hours collected and digested the Constitutions of the fourteen latter Archbishops of *Canterbury*, from *Stephen Langton* unto *Henry Chichley*, unto whom he dedicated the Work, a worthy Work, highly esteemed by forreign Lawyers, his Comment thereon is a Magazine of the Canon Law. It was printed at *Paris*, *Anno* 1505. (but at the cost and charges of *William Bretton*, an honest Merchant of *London*) revised by the care of *Wolfangus Hippolita*, and prefaced unto by *Iodocus Badius*. This *Linwood* was afterwards made Bishop of St. *Davids*.

Anno 1434. began the active Council of *Basil*; to which our Ambassadors were to represent both their Sovereign, and the English Nation, where they were received with honour and respect. This was a troublesome Council, and continued seventeen years. In this Council it was concluded (as before at *Constance*) that the General Councils were above the Pope. Fourteen Ambassadors were sent from the King unto *Basil*. One Earl (not that he was to vote in the Council, but only behold the transactions thereof) *viz*. *Edmond*, Earl of *Morton*. Five Bishops, *viz*. *Robert*, Bishop of *London*, *Philip*, Bishop of *Lisieux*; *John*, Bishop of *Rochester* *John*, Bishop of *Baieux*, and *Bernard*, Bishop of *Aix*. Two Abbots, *Nicholas*, Abbot of *Glaston*, *William*, Abbot of *St. Maries* in *York*. One Prior, *William*, Prior of *Norwich*. Two Knights, *Henry Broumfleet*, and *John Colvil*. Mr. *Thomas Brown*, Doctor of Laws, Dean of *Sarum*. *Peter Fitz-Maurice*, D. D. and Mr. *Nicholas David*, Archdeacon of *Constance*, and Licentiate in both Laws.

John, Bishop of *Rochester*, here mentioned, was *John Langdon*, intruded by the Pope into that Bishoprick, to the prejudice of the Archbishop of *Canterbury*. But he was indeed a Learned man, and died this year in his Ambassy at *Basil*. This Council deposed Pope *Eugenius*, and substituted in his room *Amideus*, the most devout Duke of *Savoy*, who was called *Felix* the Fifth, and was crowned in the City of *Basil*.

Anno 1437. *Henry Chichley*, Archbishop of *Canterbury*, founded a Colledge in *Oxford*, by the name of *All-souls*, for a Warden, and forty Fellows: which number, by Statute, was never to be augmented, or impaired; and all void places (by death or otherwise) once in a year to be supplied. Six years did he survive the first founding of this Colledge. He founded another Colledge in *Oxford*, called *Barnard-colledge*, suppressed by King *Henry* the Eighth, and renewed by Sir *Thomas White*, who named it St. *Iohn's-colledge*, one of the fairest of the University.

This

The Church of Great Britain.

This Archbishop bestowed much money in repairing the Library at *Canterbury*, and then replenished the same with a number of goodly Books. He gave unto his Church many rich Ornaments and Jewels of great price, and built a great part of the Tower, called *Oxford-tower*, in the said Church. He founded a goodly Colledge, and an Hospital, at *Higham-ferries*, where he was born, for eight secular Priests, Fellows, four Clerks, and six Choristers: it was so endowed, as at the suppression of the same, it was valued at 156 pounds *per annum*. The Hospital was for poor people likewise liberally endowed.

Goodwin's Catal. of Bishops.

Iohn Stafford, Son unto the Earl of *Stafford*, succeeded in the place of *Henry Chichley* deceased. Pope *Eugenius* the Fourth translated him from *Bath* and *Wells*.

About the year 1446. King *Henry* the Sixth founded *Eaton* Colledge, incorporate by the name of *Præpositi & Collegii Regalis, Col. Beatæ Mariæ de Eaton juxta Winsor*.

This Colledge consisteth of one Provost, Fellows, a School-master and Usher; besides many Oppidanes maintained there at the cost of their Friends. This *Eaton* is a Nursery to *King's-colledge* in *Cambridge*.

Humfry, Duke of *Glocester*, the King's Uncle, at a packt Parliament at *Bury*, was condemned of High-treason, and found dead in his Bed, not without rank suspition of cruel practices upon his person. He gave to the Library in *Oxford* many pretious voluminous Manuscripts. He was buried in St. *Albans*, to which Church he was a great Benefactor.

The same month, with the Duke of *Glocester*, died *Henry Beaufort*, Bishop of *Winchester*, and Cardinal. He was a man of such Wealth, that at once he lent King *Henry* the Fifth twenty thousand pounds, who pawned his Crown to him. He built the fair Hospital of St. *Cross*, near *Winchester*.

The Clergy moved in vain against the recalling of the Statute of *Præmunire*.

About the year 1453. began the broyls to break out out between the two Houses of *Lancaster* and *York*, so mutually heightened, that scarce a County betwixt *York* and *London*, but a set Battel hath been fought therein, besides other Counties in the Marches of *Wales*: besides many other Skirmishes (Corrivals with Battels) so that such, who consider the blood lost therein, would admire *England* had any left. And such as observe how much it had left, would wonder it had any lost.

In the midst of these Civil wars, *William*, Sirnamed *Patin* from his Parents, but *Wainfleet*, from the place of his Nativity, now Bishop of *Winchester*, founded the fair Colledge, dedicated to *Mary Magdalen*, in *Oxford*, for one President, forty Fellows, thirty Demies, four Chaplains, eight Clerks, and sixteen Choristers. This *William Wainfleet* first founded *Magdalen-hall*, hard by, and afterwards undertook

S 2 and

and finished this most stately piece of Architecture. There is scarce a Bishoprick in *England*, to which this Colledge hath not afforded one Prelate at the least, doubling her files in some places. At this day (besides those forementioned) there are one Schoolmaster and an Usher, three Readers, *viz.* of Divinity, Natural and Moral Philosophy, besides divers Officers and Servants of the foundation, with other Students, being in all two hundred and twenty.

Iohn Kemp, Archbishop of *Canterbury*, built the Divinity-School in *Oxford*, and *Paul's* Crofs.

King Henry being conquered in a fatal Battel at *Touton* in *Nottinghamshire*, fled with his Queen into *Scotland*, and to make himself the more welcome, resigned *Berwick* to the King thereof. *Edward*, Duke of *York*, reigned in his stead. This King's Reign affordeth very little Church-story. This good was done by the Civil Wars, it diverted the Popish Prelates from troubling the *Lollards*.

Thomas Bourchier (Son unto *Henry Bourchier*, Earl of *Essex*) Archbishop of *Canterbury*, kept a Synod of his Clergy at *London*. The Parliament sitting at the same time bestowed many priviledges on the Clergy.

In the time of this Archbishop, *Raynold Peacock*, Bishop of *Chichester*, was afflicted by the Popish Prelates for his Faith and profession of the Gospel, after he had laboured many years in translating the Holy Scriptures into English. He was accused and convicted for holding and publishing certain Opinions, at that time held Heretical, which at last openly at *Paul's* Crofs he revoked, but was notwithstanding deprived of his Bishoprick; only a certain Pension was assigned him to live on in an Abby, where soon after he died.

Sir *Rich. Baker's* Chron.

Fox Acts and Monuments Luke 8. 3.

About the year 1465. there was here in *England* one *Thomas Holden*, a *Carmelite* Friar, who preached in *Michaelmas* Term at *Paul's* Crofs in *London*, *That our Lord Iefus Chrift was in poverty, and did beg in the world*. A manifest untruth! For great is the difference betwixt begging, and taking what the bounty of others doth freely confer, as our Saviour did from such who *did minifter unto him of their fubftance* : This Sermon caused a great stir. The principal Champions on both sides, whose Pens publickly appeared, were

For *Mendicants*.

1. *Henry Parker*, a *Carmelite*, bred in *Cambridge*, living afterward in *Doncafter-Covent*, imprisoned for preaching.

2. *Iohn Milverton*, bred in *Oxford*, Carmelite of *Briftol*, being excommunicated by the Bishop of *London*, and appealing to the Pope, found no favour, but was kept three years captive in St. *Angelo*.

Againft

the Church of GREAT BRITAIN.

Againſt *Mendicants*.

1. *Thomas Wilſon*, Doctor of both Laws, and ſay ſome, Dean of S. *Paul's*, a zealous Preacher and Diſputant.
2. *William Ivy*, Canon of S. *Paul's*, who wrote in the Defence of *Richard Hill*, Biſhop of *London*, who Impriſoned two Mendicants for their proud Preaching.

But after *Pope Paul* the ſecond had interpoſed herein, concluding that this ought to be declared in all places for a dangerous Doctrine, and worthy to be trodden down under all mens feet, the controverſie ceaſed.

At this time *George* Nevil, brother to *Richard* Nevil, the Great Earl of *Warwick* that ſet up and pulled down Kings at his pleaſure, was Archbiſhop of *York*. He was famous for a prodigious feaſt made at his Inſtallation, unto which he invited, as Gueſts, all the Nobility, moſt of the prime Clergy, many of the Great Gentry of the Land. The Bill of Fare may be read in Biſhop *Godwins* Catalogue of Biſhops. Seven years after, King *Edward* ſeized on all his Eſtate, to the value of twenty thouſand pounds, among which he found ſo rich a Mitre, that he made himſelf a Crown thereof. The Archbiſhop he ſent over priſoner to *Callis*, where he was kept bound in exreme poverty, juſtice puniſhing his former prodigality. He was afterwards reſtored to his Liberty and Archbiſhoprick, but went drooping till the day of his death. It added to his ſorrow, that the Kingdom of *Scotland*, with twelve Suffragan Biſhops therein (formerly ſubjected to his See) was now, by *Pope* *Sixtus*, freed from any further dependance thereon; S. *Andrews* being advanced to an Archbiſhoprick, and that Kingdom in Eccleſiaſtical matters made entire within it ſelf : whoſe Biſhops formerly repaired to *York* for their conſecration.

Scotland freed from the See of York.

Anno 1473. in *Auguſt*, *John Gooſe*, ſole Martyr in this King's Reign, was condemned and burned at *Tower-hill*. This man, when ready to ſuffer, deſired meat from the Sheriff which Ordered his Execution, and had it granted unto him. *I will eat* (ſaith he) *a good competent dinner, for I ſhall paſs a ſharp ſhower, ere I come to Supper.*

King *Edward* IV. died *April* 9. 1483. In his Reign flouriſhed *Thomas Littleton*, a Reverend Judge of the Common-pleas, who brought a great part of the Law into method, which lay before confuſedly diſperſed, and his book called *Littletons Tenures*. Then *John Harding* Eſquire wrote a Chronicle in Engliſh verſe. *John Fortescue* a Judge, and Chancellor of *England*, wrote divers Treatiſes concerning the Law, and Politick Government. *Rochus*, a *Charter-houſe* Monk, born in *London*, wrote divers Epigrams. *William Caxton* alſo wrote a Chronicle.

Miſerable.

Miserable King *Edward* v. ought to have succeeded his Father, but he, by the wicked practice of his Unckle *Richard* Duke of *Glocester*, chosen Protector, was quickly made away. The Protection of the young King's Person was by the last King appointed to Earl *Rivers* the Queen's brother, and by the mother's side Unckle to the said Prince, who kept his Residence and Court at *Ludlow*. The Queen with the Earl *Rivers*, her brother, and with her Son *Richard* Lord *Gray*, and other Friends, being guarded with a strong power of Armed men and Souldiers, intended to bring the Young King from *Ludlow* to *London* to be Crowned. But the Duke of *Glocester* wrought so cunningly with the Queen, that she dispatched messengers to her Brother and Son, who (though unwilling) upon her request were perswaded to Disband and Cashier all their Souldiers: and attended only with their own Menial Servants, they set forward, with the Young King towards the Queen. They came to *Northampton*; and soon after the Dukes of *Glocester* and *Buckingham* dismounted themselves in the Earls Inn, being accompanied with great store of resolute attendants. There they surprized the Earl *Rivers*, committed him to safe Custody. Then the two Dukes rode to *Stony-stratford*, where the King then was. There they seized on *Richard* Lord *Grey*, the King's half-brother, and on Sir *Richard Vaugham*, and some others, all which they sent under a strong guard to *Pomfret-castle*, where without any judicial sentence, or legal trial, they were beheaded upon the same day that the Lord *Hastings*, (who conspired in that action with the two Dukes) lost his head.

*Mart.*Chron. in *Edw.*v.

The Queen with the rest of her Children enters the Sanctuary at *Westminster*. The young King is brought to *London*, and the Duke of *Glocester* by the contrivement of the Duke of *Buckingham* is made Protector of the King and Kingdom, by the Decree of the Councel-Table: and now he wickedly plotteth to make away the young King and his Brother, and in order thereunto he laboureth first to get into his hands the Duke of *York*, the King's brother; And to that end the Archbishop of *Canterbury* was employed with instructions to procure the Queen to part with her younger son, to accompany the elder. The Protector having gotten both the brothers into his hand, causeth them within few days in great pomp and State to be convayed through *London* to the Tower. The Sunday following he caused Doctor *Shaa* at *Paul's* cross to blazon the Honourable birth and parentage of the Protector, to relate his vertues, to commend his valour, to weaken the Fame and Honour of the deceased King *Edward*; by reason of his lascivious wantonness with *Shore's* wife and others, to bastardize all his Children; because the King was in the person of *Richard* Earl of *Warwick* (before his said marriage) affianced unto the Lady *Bona*, sister to the wife of the *French* King. He also accused the Protector's own mother of great incontinency. When King *Edward*, and *George* Duke of *Clarence* were

were begotten. Then setting forth the worthiness of the Protector, he supposed, that the people could not chuse but receive him for their King.

Pynkney the Provincial of the *Augustinian* Friars, who in the same place used so loud adulation, lost his credit, conscience, and voice altogether. These two were all of the Clergy, who engaged actively on his party.

His Coronation was performed with more pomp than any of his Predecessors. Soon after followed the murther of King *Edward*, and his Brother *Richard*, Duke of *York*.

After this bloody act, having visited his Town of *Glocester*, which he endowed with ample Liberties and Priviledges, he took his journey towards *York*. At a certain day appointed the whole Clergy assembled in Copes richly vested, and so went about the City in Procession, after whom followed the King with his Crown and Scepter, apparrelled in his Circot Robe Royal, accompanyed with many of the Nobility of the Realm: after whom marched in order Queen *Anne*, his wife, Crowned, leading in her left hand Prince *Edward* her Son, having on his head a demy-crown appointed for the degree of a Prince. The Northern people hereupon extolled and praised him far above the Stars. After this glorious pomp, and a solemn feast, having done all things discreetly, he returned by *Nottingham*, and afterwards came to *London*, whom the Citizens more for fear than love, received in great Companies. Now King *Richard* made good Laws in that sole Parliament kept in his time. He began to found a Colledge of an hundred Priests, which foundation with the founder shortly had end. He built a Monastery at *Middleham* in the North, and a Colledge at *Alhallows Barking* hard by the Tower: and endowed *Queens-Colledge* in *Cambridge* with five hundred marks of yearly revenue. Soon after the Duke of *Buckingham* requireth the Earldom of *Hereford*, and the Hereditary Constableship of *England*, laying title to them by discent. The King rejected the Duke's request with many spiteful and minatory words. *Buckingham* storms thereat, and withdraws to *Brecknock* in *Wales*, with his Prisoner *John Morton* Bishop of *Ely* (committed to him by the King on some distast) who tampered with him about the marriage of *Henry* Earl of *Richmond* with the eldest daughter of King *Edward* IV. But the Duke was surprized by King *Richard*, and beheaded before this marriage was compleated. More cunning was Bishop *Morton* to get himself over into *France*, there to contrive the union of the two Houses of *York* and *Lancaster*.

In the year 1485, *Henry* Earl of *Richmond* landeth with small Forces at *Milford-Haven*. From *Milford* he marcheth North-East through the bowels of *Wales*, and both his Army and the fame thereof encreased by marching. Into *Leicester-shire* he came, and in the navel

Sir *Th. Moores* History of King *Rich.* 3.

thereof

thereof is met by King *Richard.* The next day the Armies joyned in battel. The scales of Victory seemed for a long time so equal, that none could discern on which side the beam did break. At length the coming in of the Lord *Stanley* with three thousand fresh men, decided the controversie on the Earl's side. King *Richard* fighting valiantly in the midst of his enemies was slain, and his Corps were disgracefully carried to *Leicester,* without a rag to cover his nakedness. The Crown ornamental being found on his head, was removed to the Earl's, and he Crowned in the field, and *Te Deum* was solemnly sung by the whole Army. The body of King *Richard* lay for a spectacle of hate and scorn by the space of two days bare, and uninterred. At last without solemn funeral pomp, scarce with ordinary solemnity, by the charity of the Gray-friers he was inhumed in their Monastery there.

King *Henry* VII. coming to *London* the Mayor and Companies received him at *Shoreditch,* whence with great Honourable attendance, and Troops of Noblemen and persons of quality he entred the City, himself not being on horseback, or in any open Chair, or Throne, but in a close Chariot, as one that chose rather to keep State, and strike a reverence into the people, than to fawn upon them. He went first into S. *Paul's* Church, where he made offertory of his Standards, and had *Orizon,* and *Te Deum* again sung, and went to his lodging prepared in the Bishops palace.

Lord *Verul.*
Histor. of
Henr. VII.

Thomas Bourchier, Cardinal, and Archbishop of *Canterbury,* Crowned the King on the last of *October.* At which day for the better security of his person the King did institute a band of fifty Archers under a Captain to attend him, by the Name of *Yeomen of his Guard.* The Archbishop also Married King *Henry* to the Lady *Elizabeth,* eldest daughter to King *Edward* the fourth. And then having sate in a short Synod at *London* (wherein the Clergy presented their new King with a tenth) died, having sate in his See two and thirty years.

He gave to the University of *Cambridge* an hundred and twenty pounds, which was joyned with another hundred pound; which Mr. *Billingforth* (Master of *Bennet-Colledge*) had some years before given to the said University.

John Morton, born at S. *Andrews Milbourn* in *Dorset-shire,* succeeded him in the See at *Canterbury.* He was formerly Bishop of *Ely;* and appointed by King *Edward* IV. one of the Executors of his will, and on that account hated of King *Richard* the third, the Executioner thereof. He was (as aforesaid) imprisoned, because he would not betray his trust, fled into *France* and returned, and was justly advanced by King *Henry,* first to be Chancellor of *England,* and then to be Archbishop of *Canterbury.* He was also created Cardinal of S. *Anastasius.*

Now

The Church of Great Britain.

Now began the Pope to be very busie by his Officers to collect vast summs of money in *England*, presuming at the King's connivance therear, whom he had lately gratified with a needless dispensation, to legitimate his marriage with the Lady *Elizabeth*, his Cousin so far off, that it would half pose a Herauld to recover their kindred.

The Pope in favour of the King, and indeed of equity it self, ordered concerning Sanctuaries.

1. That if any Sanctuary man did by might, or otherwise, get out of Sanctuary privily, and commit mischief and trespass, and then come in again, he should lose the benefit of Sanctuary for ever after. *Lord Verul. in Henry VII.*

2. That howsoever the Person of the Sanctuary-man was protected from his Creditors, yet should not his goods out of Sanctuary.

3. That if any took Sanctuary for cause of treason, the King might appoint him keepers to look to him in Sanctuary.

The King Confined the Queen Dowager (his wives mother) to a Religious house in *Bermondsey*, because three years since she had surrendered her two daughters out of the Sanctuary at *Westminster* to King *Richard*.

A Synod was holden by Archbishop *Morton* at *London*, wherein the Luxury of the *London* Clergy in Cloathes, with their frequenting of Taverns was forbidden: Such Preachers also were punished, who inveighed against Bishops in their absence. *John Giglis*, an *Italian*, about this time employed by the Pope, got an infinite mass of money, having power from the Pope to absolve people from all crimes whatsoever, saving smiting of the Clergy, and conspiring against the Pope. This *Giglis* gat for himself the rich Bishoprick of *Worcester*. Yea, in that See four *Italians* followed each other, *Antiq. Brit. pag. 298.*

1. *John Giglis.*
2. *Silvester Giglis.*
3. *Julius Medices*, afterwards Pope *Clement* VII.
4. *Hieronymus de Negutiis*.

The Pope gave power to Archbishop *Morton*, to visit all places formerly exempt from Archiepiscopal jurisdiction; and to dispence his pardons where he saw just cause. Hereupon *Rochester-bridge* being broken down, the Archbishop bestowed Remission from Purgatory; for all sins whatsoever committed within the compass of fourty dayes, to such as should bountifully contribute to the building thereof.

King *Henry* VII. desired much that King *Henry* VI. might be Canonized. But Pope *Alexander* III. delayed, and in effect denyed the King's desire herein. The reason given by Mr. *Camden*, was the Pope's Covetousness, who demanded more than thirfty King *Henry* would allow. This King removed the Corps of *Henry* VI. from *Chertsey* in Surrey, *Camd. Brit. in Surry.*

T

Surrey, where it was obscurely interred to a place of greater note, viz. Windsor Chappel.

But the Saintship of *Anselm* Archbishop of *Canterbury* was procured by Archbishop *Morton* on cheaper terms.

King *Henry* was submissive to Pope for his own ends, never servile. The deserving Clergy he employed in State affairs more than his Nobility. To the vitious Clergy he was very severe, ordaining that Clerks Convict should be burnt in the hand, both that they might taste a Corporal punishment, and carry a brand of infamy.

To the *Lollard's* (so godly men were called) he was more cruel than his Predecessors: for he not only in the beginning of his Reign connived at the cruel persecutions which *John* Halse Bishop of *Coventry* and *Litchfield* raised against them, but in the middle and towards the latter end of his Reign he appeared very bloody to them. An Aged old man was burnt in *Smithfield*, and one *Joan Boughton* widow, mother to the Lady *Young* (who was afterward Martyred) she being fourscore years of Age, was burnt for an Heretick. In the year 1497. *Janu.* 17. being Sunday; *Richard Milderal*, and *James Sturdy* bare faggots before the Procession of S. *Paul's*, and after stood before the Preacher in the time of his Sermon. And the Sunday following stood other two men at *Paul's* Crofs all the Sermon-time; one garnished with painted and written papers, the other having a Faggot on his neck. Upon Passion Sunday one *Hugh Glover* bare a Faggot before the Procession of S. *Paul's*, and after with the Faggot stood before the Preacher all the Sermon-while. And on the next Sunday following four men stood, and did their open penance at *Paul's* Crofs, and many of their books were there burnt before them.

Anno 1498. The King was in *Canterbury*, where was an old Priest so resolute in his opinions, that none of the Clergy there could convince him of the contrary. Some say the King, by what Arguments we know not, converted this Priest, and then presently gave Order he should be burnt.

About this time *William Smith*, Bishop of *Lincoln*, began the foundation of *Brason-nose* Colledge in *Oxford*. The work was after his death accomplished by *Richard Sutton* Esquire. It maintaineth a Principal, twenty Fellows, besides Scholars and Officers of the Foundation in all amounting to one hundred eighty six.

In the year 1499. a constant Martyr of Christ, named *Babram*, was burnt in *Norfolk*.

In the year 1500. died *John Morton* Archbishop of *Canterbury*, at his Manour of *Knoll*. He gave much to good uses, and was very bountiful to his Servants.

CENT.

Cent. XVI.

HEnry *Dean* succeeded in the place of Archbishop *Morton* deceased, and sate but two years in that See. His Pall was sent unto him by *Hadrian de Castello* the Pope's Secretary, and delivered by the Bishop of Coventry in these words: *Ad honorem Dei omnipotentis, & B. Mariæ Virginis, ac Bb. Petri, & Pauli Apostolorum, & D. N. Alexandri P. VI. & S. Romanæ Ecclesiæ, necnon & Cantuariensis Ecclesiæ tibi Commissæ, tradimus pallium de corpore B. Petri sumptum, plenitudinem viz. Pontificalis officii; ut utaris eo infra Ecclesiam tuam certis diebus qui exprimuntur in privilegiis ei ab Apostolica sede concessis.* Having received his Pall, he was to take his Oath unto the Pope, which I will set down once for all.

Ego Henricus Archiep, Cantuar' ab hac hora in antea fidelis & obediens ero B. Petro Sanctæque Apostolicæ Romanæ Ecclesiæ, & Domino meo Alexandro P. VI. suisque successoribus canonice intrantibus. Non ero in Consilio aut consensu, vel facto, ut vitam perdant vel membrum, seu capiantur mala captione, Concilium vero quod mihi credituri sunt, per se aut nuntios ad eorum damnum me sciente nemini pandam Papatum Rom. & Regalia S. Petri, adjutor ero eis ad retinendum & defendendum, salvo ordine meo, contra omnem hominem Legatum sedis Apostolicæ ineundo & redeundo honorifice tractabo, & in suis necessitatibus adjuvabo. Vocatus ad Synodum veniam, nisi præpeditus fuero Canonica præpeditione. Apostolorum limina Rom. Curiæ existente citra Alpes singulis annis, ultra vero montes singulis Bienniis visitabo, aut per me, aut per meum Nuntium, nisi Apostolica absolvar licentia. Possessiones vero ad mensam mei Archiepiscopatus pertinentes non vendam neque donabo, neque impignerabo, neque de novo infeudabo, vel aliquo modo alienabo inconsulto Romano Pontifice, sicut me Deus adjuvet, &c. he enjoyed his honour but two years, and left it to *William Warham*. Archbishop *Dean* bequeathed to his Church a Silver Image of fifty one ounces weight, and appointed five hundred pounds to be bestowed on his funerals. He built the most part of *Oxford-house*, and made the Iron-work upon the coping of *Rochester-bridge*.

Buckinghamshire a small County, had more Martyrs in it before *Luther*'s time, than all the Kingdom besides. *William Tylsworth* was burnt at *Amersham* (the Rendezvous of God's children in those dayes) and *Joan* his only daughter, and a faithful woman was compelled with her own hand to set fire to her dear Father. At the same time more than sixty Professors did bear Faggots for their penance, and were enjoyned to wear on their right sleeves for some years after, a square piece of cloth, as a badge of disgrace to themselves, and difference from others,

Godwins Catal. of Bishops

others. And a new punishment was found out of branding them in the cheek. The manner thus, Their necks were tyed fast to a post with towels, and their hands holden that they might not stir, and so the hot Iron was put to their cheeks whether branded with L. for *Lollard* or H: for Heretick, I am not certain; but this is sure, *they bare in their bodies the marks of the Lord Jesus*. Father *Reive*, though branded at that time, did afterwards suffer at a stake. One Father *Roberts* was burned at *Buckingham*. Father *Rogers* was in the Bishop's prison fourteen weeks together, and was so pinched with cold, hunger, and Iron, that after his coming out of prison he was so lame in his back, that he could never go upright; as long as he lived.

*A*1. 1506. *Thomas Chafe* of *Amersham*, (was after other sore afflictions) strangled in the prison at *Wooburn*, who to cover their cruelty gave it out that he had hanged himself, and in colour thereof caused his body to be buried by the High-way's side, with a stake knockt into his grave. One *Thomas Novice* was burnt at *Norwich*, Anno 1507. and *Laurence Gleft* at *Sarum*, at whose burning *William Ruffel* was burnt in the Cheek.

After this a Godly-woman was burnt at *Sadbury* by the Chancellor of *Gloccfter*, Doctor *Whittington*, after she was burned, as the people were returning homeward, a Bull brake loose from a Butcher that was in hand to have killed him, and singled out Doctor *Whittington* from all the Company; and (hurting neither old nor young) took him alone, gored him thorough and thorough, carrying his guts upon his horns all the streets over, to the great amazement of the people.

All the Arrears of mony due to the Pope for pardons in the year of *Jubilee*, five years since were fully collected, and safely returned to *Rome* by the Popes Officers: the money which was sent last thither, came soon enough to be received there. This payment was the last in this kind which *Rome* did generally receive out of *England*. Mean-time the King did share with the *Pope*, to connive at the rest, he had a part allowed to him.

Sir *Rich*. Ba-
ker's Chron.

King *Henry* VII. died of a Consumption at his palace of *Richmond*, *April* 22. 1508. Of our own Country there lived in his time, *George Ripley*, a Carmelite Friar of *Boston*, who wrote divers Treatises in the Mathematiques. *John Roufe*, born in *Warwickshire*, a diligent searcher of Antiquities.

Thomas Scroop entred into diverse Orders of Religion, and after withdrew himself to his house, where for twenty years he lived the life of an Anchoret; and after coming abroad again was made a Bishop in *Ireland*, and went to *Rhodes* in Ambassage; from whence being returned he went barefooted up and down in *Norfolk* teaching the ten Commandments, and lived till near an hundred years old. Now also lived Robert

The Church of Great Britain.

bert Fabian, a Sheriff of *London*, and Hiftoriographer. *Edmond Dudley*, who wrote a book Entitled, *Arbor Reipublicæ*. *John Bockingham*, an Excellent School-man. And *William Blackney* D.D. a Carmelite Friar, and a Necromancer.

Henry VIII. fucceeded his Father. On *June* 3. He was Married to the Lady *Katherine* Dowager, formerly wife to his brother Prince *Arthur* deceafed. *Pope Julius* by his difpenfation, removed all obftructions, againft the Laws of God or man, hindering or oppofing the said Match.

Cruelty still increafed on the poor *Lollards* (as they were called) after abjuration forced to wear the fafhion of a Faggot wrought in thread, or painted on their fleeves as long as they lived, it being death to put on their clothes without that cognizance. Their cafe was fad, if they put it off, they muft be burned, if they put it on, they muft be ftarved; for none generally would fet them on work that wore that badge. On this account were *William Sweeting*, and *James Brewfter* re-imprifoned. In vain did *Brewfter* plead, that he was commanded to leave off his badge, by the Controller of the Earl of *Oxford*'s houfe. And as little did *Sweeting*'s plea prevail, that the Parfon of *Mary Magdalen*'s in *Colchefter*, caufed him to lay his faggot afide. Soon after they were both burnt together in *Smithfield*, Anno 1511.

One *John Brown*, who had born a faggot before in the days of King *Henry* the Seventh, was burned at *Afhford* in *Kent* for the Profeffion of the Truth, condemned by Archbifhop *Warham*, firft having had his Feet burned to the Bones, to compel him to deny the Truth.

Richard Hunn, a wealthy Citizen of *London*, imprifoned in *Lollards* Tower, for adhering to *Wickliff*'s Doctrine, had his neck therein fecretly broken. To cover their cruelty, they gave it out, that he hanged himfelf on *December* 20. 1514. the dead Body of the faid *Richard Hunn* was burnt in *Smithfield* Sixteen days after he was murdered. But the matter having been fully examined by the Council and Judges, and Juftices of the Realm, it was evidently proved, that Dr. *Horfey* the Chancellor, *Charles Jofeph* the Sumner, and *John Spalding* the Bel-ringer had committed the Murder.

Thomas Man and *John Stileman*, were alfo burned in *Smithfield*. *Thomas Man* confeffed, he had converted Seven hundred from Popery to the Truth. *Robert Cofin* was alfo condemned, and burned at *Buckingham*, for holding againft Pilgrimages, Confeffion to Priefts, and Worfhipping of Image. *Chriftopher Shoomaker* was burned at *Newbery* upon the like account.

Cardinal *Bainbrigg*, Archbifhop of *York*, being then at *Rome*, was fo highly offended with *Rivaldus de Modena*, an Italian, his Steward, that he cudgelled him: but being foon after poifoned, his Body was buried in the Englifh Hofpital at *Rome*.

Richard

Fuller. Church Hist.

Richard Fox, Bishop of *Winchester*, Founded and Endowed *Corpus Christi-Colledge* in *Oxford*, bestowing thereon Lands to the yearly value of Four hundred and one pounds, eight shillings and two pence. There are maintained in it a President, Twenty Fellows, Twenty Scholars, Two Chaplains, Two Clerks, and Two Choristers, besides Officers and Servants of the Foundation, with other Students. *Hugh Oldham*, Bishop of *Exeter*, was a great Benefactor to this Colledge.

Pirries Chur. Hist.

Anno 1519. died *John Colet* at *Shene* in *Surrey*, he had learned humane Sciences at home, and travelled into *France* and *Italy*: when he returned, he studied the Scriptures, and expounded St. *Paul*'s Epistles publickly at *Oxford*. *Henry* the Seventh promoted him to the Deanry of *Pauls* : He professed to distast many things that he had heard in *Sorbon*. He called the Scotists men without judgement, and the Thomists arrogant. He said, *He reaped more fruit by the Books which the Doctors of Sorbon called Heretical, than by their Books that were full of divisions and definitions, and were most approved of them.* He never married, and yet regarded not Monks without Learning. In his Sermons he said, *Images should not be Worshipped, and Clerks should not be Covetous.* Two Friars, viz. Bricot and *Standish* accused him for Heresie unto *Richard Fitz-James* Bishop of *London*; and He unto the Archbishop first, and then unto King *Henry* the Eighth. But both the King and the Archbishop became his Patrons. He was the eldest, and sole surviving child of Sir *Henry Collet* Mercer, twice Lord Mayor of *London*; who with his ten Sons and as many Daughters, were depicted in a Glass-window on the Northside of St. *Anthonie's* (corruptly St. *Antlin's*) to which Church he was a great Benefactor. His Son *John* Founded the Free-School of St. *Pauls*; in it are One hundred fifty and three Scholars, whereof every year some appearing most pregnant, have salaries allowed them for Seven years, or untill they get better preferment in the University, or in the Church. *William Lily* was the first School-master thereof, by *Colet*'s own appointment. An excellent Scholar, born at *Odiam* in *Hamp-shire*, and afterward he went on Pilgrimage to *Jerusalem*. In his return through *Italy*, he applyed himself to his Studies. His Teachers and Instructers were *John Sulpitius*, and *Pomponius Sabinus*, two eminent Criticks. Returning home into his native Countrey well accomplished with Latin, Greek, and all Arts and Sciences, he set forth a Grammar, which still goes under his Name, and is generally taught over all *England*.

Stow's Survay, p. 265.

Anno 1517. *Luther* wrote against Popish Indulgences, shewing the abuses of them.

King *Henry* the Eighth, set forth a Book against *Luther*, endeavouring the Confutation of his Opinions, as novel and unsound. To requite his pains, the Pope honoured him and his Successors with a specious Title, *Defender of the Faith*. *Luther* sharply answered that Book.

Cardinal

The Church of Great Britain.

Cardinal *Wolsey* was now the Pope's *Legat de latere*, by vertue whereof he visited all Churches and Religious houses, even the Friars observants themselves, notwithstanding their stoutness and stubbornness that first opposed him. Papal and Royal power met in him, being the Chancellor of the Land; and keeping so many Bishopricks in *Commendam*, his yearly income is said to equal, if not exceed, the Revenues of the Crown.

Being to found two Colledges, he seized on forty small Monasteries, turning their Inhabitants out of House and home, and converting their means principally to a Colledge in *Oxford*. This alienation was confirmed by Pope *Clement* the Seventh, so that in some sort the Pope may thank himself for the demolishing of Religious houses in *England*.

His Colledge in *Oxford* did thrice change it's name in seven years, first called Cardinals Colledge, then King's Colledge; and at last *Christ-church*, which it retaineth at this day.

King *Henry* took just offence that the Cardinal set his own Arms above the King's on the Gate-house, at the entrance into the Colledge. There have been maintained in this Colledge, one Dean, eight Canons, three publick Professors of Divinity, Hebrew, and Greek, sixty Students, eight Chaplains, eight Singing-men, an Organist, eight Choristers, twenty four Almes-men: at this present Students of all sorts, with Officers and Servants of the Foundation, to the number of two hundred twenty three.

John Higdon, first *Dean* of this Colledge, was a great Persecutor of Protestants, *viz*.

John Clark,	+ *John Fryer*,	*William Betts*,	Such whose names are noted with a Cross, did afterwards turn zealous Papists.
John Frith,	*Goodman*,	*Lawney*,	
Henry Sumner,	+ *Nicholas Harmar*,	*Richard Cox*,	
Baley,	+ *Michael Drumme*,	*Richard Taverner*.	

All these were for their Religion imprisoned in a deep Cave under ground, where the Salt-fish of the Colledge was kept. Some of them died soon after with the stench thereof, and others escaped with great difficulty. *Taverner* was well-skilled in Musick, on which account he escaped, though vehemently accused; the Cardinal pleading for him, that he was but a Musitian, though afterward he repented to have set Tunes to so many Popish ditties.

The example of *Wolsey*'s haughtiness, made the English Clergy so proud and insolent, that their labours formerly applyed to the studies of moral vertues, and of Divinity, were now employed to devise curious fashions in their behaviour, in their apparrel, and in their diet.

Martin's Chr. in Henry 8.

In

In the fifteenth, sixteenth, and seventeenth year of King *Henries* Reign, this proud Cardinal (under colour of the King's partaking with the Emperor in his Wars against the French King) of his own authority, and wi hout the King's commandement, granted forth Commissions, under the Great Seal of *England*, into every Shire and Province of the Kingdome, and directed them unto the chiefest men. And therein every man was required to depose the true value of their Estates; and then of every fifty pounds there was demanded four shillings in the pound. And in *London* he made himself the chief Commissioner; The like Commissions he granted forth against all the Clergy of the Land, of whom he demanded four shillings in the pound of all their livings.

These things grieved the Clergy and Common People at the heart. The Cardinal perceiving this, recalled those Commissions, and sent forth others, which also being not endured, the King by his Letters directed into every County, commanded a present cessation of all executions of the said Commissions, and protested they were granted forth without his knowledge or consent. But, if they would by way of a Benevolence, of their own accord, enlarge themselves towards him, he would take it as an infallible proof of their love toward him.

The Cardinal now resolved to revenge himself on the Emperor *Charles* the Fifth, for not doing him right, and improving his power in preferring him to the Papacy, according to his promises, and intends to smite *Charles* through the sides of his Aunt, *Katharine*, Queen of *England*, endeavouring to alienate the King's affections from her. *Wolsey* now put this scruple into the head of Bishop *Longlands*, the King's Confessor, and he insinuated the same into the King's Conscience. King *Henry* greedily resented the motion; and principles of pure Conscience puts him upon endeavours of a divorce.

The business is brought into the Court of *Rome*, there to be decided by Pope *Clement* the Seventh. But the Pope at this time was a prisoner to the Emperor, who constantly kept a guard about him: Yet after some delay, the Pope dispatched a Commission to two Cardinals, *Wolsey* and *Campegius*, an Italian, to hear and determine the matter at *London*. The Pope draws back the cause unto himself, and the King being impatient, having the consent of both Universities, as also of that of *Paris*, he forsaketh *Katharine*, and marrieth *Anna Bolen*, Anno 1533.

And in the year 1534. he denieth obedience to the Pope, and chargeth all his Subjects, that they send no Money unto *Rome*, nor pay *Peter-pence* unto any of the Collectors, which vexeth the Roman Court.

Then he published an Edict; whereby he declares himself under Christ, *The supreme Head of the Church of* England, and chargeth upon pain of Death, that no man ascribe any Power to the Pope within

England,

the Church of Great Britain.

England, and commandeth all the Collectors of *Peter-pence* to be gone. These things were confirmed by the Parliament, who also enacted, That the Archbishop of Canterbury should invest all the Bishops of England, and that the Church-men shall pay to the King yearly one hundred and fifty thousand pounds for defence of the Kingdom.

Wolsey was accused in Parliament for exercising his power Legantine without leave, to the prejudice of the King's Crown and dignity. Mr. *Cromwel*, Servant to the Cardinal, being a Burgess, defendeth his Master: yet were all his goods of inestimable value confiscated to the King, and he outed of most of his Ecclesiastical promotions. His enemies get the King to command him away to *York*, leaving him the whole revenues of *York*-Archbishoprick (then worth little less than four thousand pounds yearly) besides a large pension paid him out of the Bishoprick of *Winchester*.

As he was preparing there in a Princely Equipage for his Installation, he is Arrested by the Earl of *Northumberland*, by Commission from the King, in his own Chamber at *Cawood*.

By slow and short Journeys he setteth forward toward *London*, and coming to *Leicester* he died, where he was obscurely buried.

Then *John Fisher*, Bishop of *Rochester*, was imprisoned for refusing the Oath of Supremacy. The Clergy in the Province of *York* did a long time deny the King's Supremacy. *Edward Lee*, Archbishop of *York*, fomented this difference. He was a virulent Papist, one that wrote against *Erasmus*, and a persecutor of Protestants, witness *John Bale*, Convented before him for suspition of Heresie, who in vain pleaded Scripture, in his own defence, till at last he casually made use of a distinction out of *Scotus*, which the Archbishop more valued, than all which he had before more pertinently alledged out the Old and New Testament.

The King wrote a fair and large Letter to the Convocation of *York*, claiming nothing more than what Christian Princes in the Primitive times assumed to themselves in their own Dominions, so that it seems he wrought so far on their affections, that at last they consented thereunto.

Soon after the Clergy in the Convocation so submitted themselves to the King, that each one severally promised, *in verbo Sacerdotis*, never henceforth to presume to Alledge, Claim, or put in ure any new Canons, unless the King's most Royal assent might be had unto them; and soon after the same was ratified by Act of Parliament.

After the Statute of *Præmunire* was made (which did much restrain the Papal power, and subject it to the Laws of the Land) Archbishops called no more Convocations by their sole and absolute command, but

U   at

at the pleasure of the King, as oft as his necessities and occasions with the distresses of the Church did require it. Yea now their meetings were by vertue of a Writ or Precept from the King.

For, it was Enacted in the Parliament of the twenty fifth, of *Henry* the Eight, *That all Convocations shall be thenceforth called by the King's Writ; and that in them nothing shall be promulged or executed without his Highness Licence; under pain of imprisonment of the Authors, and Mulct at the King's will.* And that his Highness shall, at his pleasure, appoint thirty two men, to survay the said Canons or Constitutions, for the Confirmation or Abolition of the same.

L. *Herbert's* Hist. of *Hen.* 8.

And as concerning Appeals, they shall be made from inferiour Courts to the Archbishop's, and for lack of Justice there, to the King's Majesty in his Court of Chancery.

Bishop *Fisher* was Arraigned of high Treason, I will insert the Sting of the indictment out of the Original.

Diversis Domini Regis veris subditis, falsè, malitiosè, & proditoriè loquebatur, & propalabat, viz. The King owre Soveregin Lord is not Supreme Hed yn erthe of the Cherche of *England. In dicti Domini Regis immund. despect. & vilipendium manifest.*

Of this he was found Guilty, had Judgement, and was remanded to the Tower.

The King by the advice and consent of the Clergy, in Convocation, and Great Council in Parliament, resolved to reform the Church, under his inspection from gross abuses crept into it.

Thomas Hitten, a Preacher at *Maidstone,* for the Testimony of the Truth, after long Torments and sundry imprisonments, by *William Warham* Bishop of *Canterbury,* and *John Fisher,* Bishop of *Rochester,* was burned at *Maidstone* for the Testimony of the Truth; *Anno* 1530.

In the year 1531. *Thomas Bilney* of *Cambridge,* Professor of both Laws, converted *Thomas Arthur,* and Mr. *Hugh Latimer,* then Crossbearer at *Cambridge,* on procession days. Afterwards *Bilney* recanted, but for the space of two years after his abjuration, *Bilney* lived in great anguish of mind: and repenting, Preached publickly the Doctrine which he before abjured. He was afterwards taken, condemned, and burned without *Bishops-gate,* in a low Valley, called the Lollards pit, under St. *Leonard's* Hill.

Going to Execution, one of his friends wished him to stand sure and constant: to whom he answered, *That whatsoever storms he passed in this venture, yet shortly after, my Ship,* saith he, *shall be in the Haven.*

There

The Church of Great Britain.

There came forth in print a Book called, *The Supplication of Beggars*, made by *Simon Fish*, which Book, the Lady *Anna Bolen* delivered to the King, who gave him his protection. Sir *Thomas Moor* wrote an Answer to that Book, under the Title of, *Poor silly Souls pewling out of Purgatory*; to which *John Frith* made a pithy and effectual Reply.

Tindal's Translation of the New Testament came forth in English.

Richard Bayfield suffered for the truth, and was burned in *Smithfield*. He was sometime a Monk of *Surrey*, and converted by Doctor *Barnes*. After him *John Tewksbury* was burned in *Smithfield*.

Valentine Freese, and his Wife, gave their Lives at one Stake for the testimony of the Truth.

Afterwards, the Bishops, which had burned *Tindal's* Testaments, were enjoyned by the King to cause a new Translation to be made, but they did nothing at all. And on the contrary, the Bishop of *London* caused all the translations of *Tindal*, and many other Books which he had bought, to be burnt in *Paul's* Church-yard.

James Bainham, a Gentleman of the Middle-Temple, was put in a Prison in Sir *Thomas Moore's* House, and whipped at a Tree in his Garden, called *The tree of Truth*, and was by him afterward sent to the Tower to be racked: by racking he was lamed, because he would not accuse the Gentlemen of the Temple of his acquaintance, nor shew where his Books lay. He abjured, had his liberty, but he asked God and the world forgiveness, before the Congregation in those dayes, in a Warehouse in *Bow-lane*. And immediately the next Sunday after, he came to St. *Austin's*, with the New Testament in his hand in English; and the obedience of a Christian-man in his bosom, and there with tears declared before the people, that he had denied God, and prayed the people to forgive and beware of his weakness. He was shortly after apprehended, and committed to the Tower of *London*, and after three appearances, he was condemned, and burnt in *Smithfield*. *Fox Acts and Monuments.*

About this time *John Benet*, a Tailor, was burnt at the *Devizes* in *Wilt-shire*, for denying the Sacrament of the Altar.

In the year 1532. *Robert King*, *Nicholas Marsh*, and *Robert Gardiner*, men of *Dedham*, and one *Robert Debnam*, had overthrown and burned the Rood of *Dover-court*, ten miles from *Dedham*: for which fact, half a year after, they were hanged in Chains. *King* at *Burchet* in *Dedham*, *Debnam* at *Cattaway-causey*, *Marsh* at *Dover-court*. *Gardiner* escaped and fled.

Many Images were cast down, and destroyed in many places. As the Crucifix by *Coggeshal* in the High-way. St. *Petronel* in the Church of Great *Horksleigh*; St. *Christopher* by *Sudbury*; St. *Petronel* in a Chappel by *Ipswich*: Also *John Seward*, of *Dedham*, overthrew a Cross in *Stoke-park*, and took two Images out of a Chappel in the same Park, and cast them into the water.

U 2 *John*

John Frith, who was first a Student in *Cambridge*, and afteward one of those whom Cardinal *Wolsey* gathered together to furnish his new Colledge, was condemned by the Bishop of *London*, and was burnt in *Smithfield*. Great was his learning, gravity and constancy, though but six and twenty years of age. With *Frith* was *Andrew Hewet* burned, after he had given testimony to the truth.

Thomas Benet, a Schoolmaster, of fifty years of age, born in *Cambridge*, was burned at *Exeter*. Divers others were condemned to perpetual prison.

During the time of Queen *Anne*, no great persecution, nor abjuration was in the Church of *England*.

Sir *Thomas Moore*, Doctor *Nicholas Wilson*, and Bishop *Fisher*, refused the Oath to the Act of Succession, made *Anno* 1534. and Sir *Thomas Moor*, and Doctor *Wilson*, were also sent to the Tower. The Doctor dissembled the matter, and so escaped, but the other two remained obstinate.

On *November* the third this Parliament was again assembled, in which the Pope and Cardinals with his Pardons and Indulgences, were wholly abolished: to the abolition of which, and to the ratifying of the King's Title of Supreme Head, *Stephen Gardiner* gave his Oath; so did *John Stokesley*, Bishop of *London*, *Edward Lee*, Archbishop of *York*, *Cuthbert*, Bishop of *Durham*, and all the rest of the Bishops in like sort: to this Title also agreed the sentence of the University of *Cambridge*. *Edmond Bonner*, then Archdeacon of *Leicester*, was also of the same judgment.

To this also agreed the whole Clergy of the Church of *England*, and subscribed with the hands of the Bishops, and other learned Men, to the number of forty six Doctors of Divinity, and of both Laws.

Polydor Virgil, who being sent into *England*, had been the Pope's Collector General of the *Peter-pence*, exacting them in the notion of a Rent and Tribute due to the Pope his Master, was made Archdeacon of *Taunton*, and Dignitary of the Cathedral Church of *Wells*, on the Quire whereof he bestowed Hangings flourished with the Lawrel-tree, and wrote upon them.

Sunt Polydori munera Virgilii.

He wrote a Latin History of *Britain*, until the year of our Lord 1533. out of many rare Manuscripts which he had collected together.

Anno 1533.   *John Fisher*, Bishop of *Rochester*, was beheaded, soon after the Pope had made him Cardinal of St. *Vitalis*. He was Chaplain and Confessor to the Lady *Margaret*, Countess of *Richmond*, at whose Instance, and by whose advice, she founded, and endowed *Christ's* and St. *John's* Colledge in *Cambridge*. He died in the seventy seventh year of his Age, on *June* 22.

Sir

the Church of Great Britain. 149

Sir *Thomas Moor* was beheaded the next month after Bishop *Fisher*, and was buried at *Chelsey*. He was a great Enemy to the Protestants.

On *June* the eighth began a Parliament, which was dissolved on *July* the eighteenth following. A parallel Convocation began the day after, wherein the Lord *Cromwel*, Prime Secretary, sate in State above all the Bishops, as the King's Vicar, or Vicegerent General in all Spiritual matters. *Deformi satis spectaculo* (saith Bishop *Godwin*) *indocto Laico cætui Præsidente Sacratorum Antistitum, omnium, quos ante hæc tempora Anglia unquam habuisset, doctissimorum.* But the Lord *Cromwel* had in Power and Policy what he wanted in Learning. In that Convocation the said Lord tendered unto them an Instrument to be publickly signed by all the Convocation, concerning the nullity of the King's Marriage with the Lady *Anna Bolen*. Some ten days before Archbishop *Cranmer* had pronounced it invalid, frustrate, and of none effect at *Lambeth*. No particular cause is specified in that sentence. Sure I am, there is no dashing on the credit of the Lady, nor any the least insinuation of unchastity in that Instrument. *Præclara Domina, & Serenissima Regina*, being the worst Titles that are given her therein. King *Henry* got her Divorce confirmed both by Convocation and Parliament. She was beheaded *May* 19: 1536. The King on the next day was married to the Lady *Iane Seymour*.

Godwin's Annals. *Anno* 1536.

Soon after by little and little began the ruine of the Abbeys and Religious Houses, for all Religious Houses, whose possessions in yearly revenue exceeded not the sum of two hundred pounds, were suppressed and dissolved, and all their Sites and Possessions whatsoever were given for ever to the King. The Clergy also at the same time, of their own accord, and to insinuate themselves into grace and favour with the King, composed and published in printed Books, certain Articles, for the ordering and governing of the Church, in which mention was made of three Sacraments only, and the rest of them (which former times did superstitiously receive and maintain) were left out of the said Books.

These proceedings of the King and Clergy against the Pope and Holy Church, were so generally disliked by the rude and ignorant people, that they openly affirmed, that the King's Council irreligiously directed him amiss, and that the temporizing Clergy of the Land practised by all means possible, to extinguish all Devotion, and utterly to subvert all the ancient Rites, Ceremonies, and commendable Government of the Church. And the unruly people in *Lincoln-shire*, to the number of twenty thousand, assembled themselves in Arms, taking upon themselves to frame better Orders for the governing of the Church and Commonwealth. But the King approaching near them with an Army, they ran away, and Doctor *Mackarel*, their Ring-leader, with some others, were shortly after apprehended and executed.

Then

Then there arose another Insurrection in the North, and the number of those Rebels exceeded the number of forty thousand men, who termed themselves, *The holy Pilgrims*, who intended nothing, but the establishing of true Religion, and the reformation of great abuses, which defaced the Government of the Church. The King's Army drawing near (upon the faithful promise of the Dukes of *Norfolk*, and *Suffolk*, that commanded his Army, that the King should pardon them) the Rebels left the field, and quietly departed to their own houses.

Now the King waxed more absolute in his Government, especially concerning his Clergy, and the ordering of the Church.

William Tindal, who translated the New Testament in English, and the five Books of *Moses*, with many other godly Works, was burned at the Town of *Filford* in *Flaunders*, by vertue of the Emperor's Decree, made in the Assembly at *Ausburgh*. He was first strangled, and after consumed with fire. At the Stake he cried with a loud voice, *Lord open the King of England's eyes*.

The King began with a little Book of Articles, for the instruction of the people, bearing this Title, *Articles, devised by the King's Highness, to establish Christian quiet and unity among the people*. It contained the Creed, three Sacraments, Baptism, the Eucharist, and Penance, how Images might safely be worshipped, and how Saints departed ought to be reverenced; that the Parsons should teach their people, that Christ is their only Mediator, and how the Ceremonies of holy Water, holy Bread, Candles, &c. should without superstition be used. It took away also the abuses which arose upon the imagination of Purgatory, as Masses for Souls departed, Pardons, &c. Not long after these Articles, certain other Injunctions were also given out about the same year: whereby a number of Holy-dayes were abrogated, especially such as fell in Harvest-time. Other Injunctions were also given out by the King concerning Images, Relicks, and blind Miracles: for abrogating of Pilgrimages. Also for the Lord's Prayer, Creed, and ten Commandements, and the Bible to be done into English.

Anno 1538, the Parsons of Churches, and the Parishes together, were bound to provide in every Parish Church a Bible in English. Also for every Parishioner to be taught by the Minister, to understand and say the Lord's Prayer and Creed in their own vulgar tongue, with other necessary Injunctions, as for the free preaching of the Word of God, against Images, Pilgrimages, Avies, Suffrages of Saints, &c. and for a Register-book to be kept in every Church.

This year was Friar *Forrest* burned quick, hanging in Chains in *Smithfield*, for denying the King's Supremacy: with this *Forrest* was *Darvel Gatheren*, an abominable Idol of *Wales*, burned.

The First-fruits Office first set up in *London*.

Great was the King's profit at this time from the Office for the receipt of Tenths and First-fruits, which was now first set up in *London*. Such moneys

the Church of GREAT BRITAIN. 151

moneys were formerly paid to the Pope, who had his Collectors in every Diocess, which sometimes by Bills of Exchange, but generally in *specie* (to the great impoverishing of the Land) yearly returned the Tenths and First-fruits of the English Clergy to *Rome*.

The Pope being now dead in *England*, the King was found his Heir at Common Law, as to most of the power and profit the other had usurped. But now as the Clergy had changed their Landlord, so their Rents were new rated, Commissioners being employed in all Counties (the Bishop of the Diocess being alwayes one of them) to value their yearly Revenue, that so their Tenths and First-fruits may be proportioned accordingly. These Raters were the chiefest in all Counties under the degrees of Barons.

These Commissioners were impowred by the King, to send for the Scribes and Notaries of all Bishops and Archdeacons, to swear the Receivers, and Auditors of Incumbents, to view their Register-books, Easter-books, and all other Writings, and to use all other wayes to know the full value of Ecclesiastical preferments, with the number and names of persons enjoying the same. They were to divide themselves by *Three* and *Three*, allotting to every number so many Deaneries, and to enquire the number and names of all Abbies, Monasteries, Priories, Brotherships, Sisterships, Fellowships, *&c.* Houses Religious and Conventual, as well *CHARTER-HOUSE* as others (these *Carthusians* being specified by name, because pretending priviledge of Papal exemption) and meeting together to certifie into the Exchequer (at the time limited in their Commission) the true value of such places or preferments. *Fuller*.Church history.

This work took up some years in the effecting thereof; *Devon-shire* and *Sommerset* were done in the twenty seventh; *Stafford-shire*, and many other Counties, in the thirty fourth year of King *Henry* the Eighth, and most of *Wales* not till the Reign of King *Edward* the Sixth. In *Ireland* the Commissioners found the work so troublesome, that they never came into the County of *Kerrey*, the South-West extremity of that Island, so that the Clergy thereof are put into their Benefices without any payments. But in *England* all were unpartially rated, and Vicaridges valued very high, according to their present Revenue, by personal Requisites. In that Age he generally was the richest Shepherd that had the greatest Flock, where Oblations from the living, and Obits for the dead (as certainly paid as predial Tithes) much advanced their Income. In consideration whereof Vicaridges (mostly lyinig in Market-Towns and populous Parishes) were set very high, though soon after those obventions sunk with superstition. And the Vicars, in vain, desired a proportionable abatement in the King's Books; which once drawn up, were no more to be altered. *Item ibid.*

Now Queen *Mary* did by Act of Parliament, exonerate, acquit, and discharge the Clergy from all First-fruits.

As

As for Tenths, the same Statute ordered them to be paid to Cardinal *Pool*, who from the same was to pay the Pensions allowed to Monks and Nuns by her Father at the dissolution of Abbeys: yet so, that when such persons, who were but few and aged, (all named in a Deed indented) should decease, all such payments of the Clergy, reserved *Nomine Decima*, should cease, and be extinct for ever.

Vide Statut.
1 Eliz. cap. 4.
But her Sister, Queen *Elizabeth*, succeeding her, was exact to have her Dues from the Clergy. Sir *Christopher Hatton*, who was Master of this *First-fruits Office*, was much indebted to her for Moneys received. All which Arrears her Majesty required so severely and suddenly from him, that the grief thereof cost him his life. I say, this Queen, in the first of her Reign, resumed First-fruits and Tenths, only with this case, to Parsonages not exceeding ten Marks, and Vicaridges ten pounds, that they should be freed from First-fruits.

In the months of *October* and *November*, *Anno* 1538. the Abbeys and Monasteries in *England* were dissolved. *Cromwel* being made General Visitor, employed *Richard Layton*, *Thomas Lee*, *William Detre*, Doctors of the Law, Doctor *John London*, Dean of *Wallingford*, with others, giving them instruction, in eighty six Articles, for visiting Monasteries every where, by which they were to enquire into the government, behaviour, and education of the persons of both Sexes: to find out all their offences, and to this purpose give them encouragements, to accuse both their Governors, and each other. To command them to exhibit *Lord Herbert* their *Mortmains*, Evidences, and Conveyances of their Lands: to produce their Plate and Money, and give an Inventory thereof.
in vit. Henr. 8.

The King also gave forth Injunctions to be observed, some tending to the establishing of his Supremacy : Some touching the good Government of the Houses.

As that no Brother go out of the Precinct.
That there be but one entrance.
That no Woman frequent the Monks, nor any Man the Nuns, &c.
And some for Education :
As that a Divinity-lecture be every where read and frequented.
That the Abbot daily expound some part of the Rule of their Order, shewing yet, that these Ceremonies are but Introductions to Religion, which consisteth not in Apparel, shaven Heads, &c. but in purity of mind.
That none shall profess, or wear the Habit, till twenty four years of age.
That no feigned Relicks, or Miracles be shewed : no Offerings to Images, &c.

Lee, and the rest at their return, gave that account of their feigned Miracles and Relicks, as well as sinful and sluggish life of the Religious Orders, as not only *Cromwel* said, their Houses should be thrown down

to

The Church of Great Britain. 153

to the foundation; but the whole Body of the Kingdom, when it was published to them, became so scandalized thereat, as they resolve, if the King ever put it into their hands, to give remedy thereunto. Yet were not all alike criminal, for some Societies behaved themselves so well, as their life being not only exempt from notorious faults, but their spare times bestowed in writing Books, Painting, Carving, Graving, and the like Exercises, their Visitors became Intercessors for them. But these being not many, were at last involved in the common fate.

Not long after this, the King caused all Colledges, Chantries, and Hospitals, to be visited, not omitting to take a particular survey of all the Revenues and Diguities Ecclesiastical within his Kingdom; which was returned to him in a Book, to be kept in the Exchequer.

Then King *Henry* sent *Fox*, Bishop of *Hereford*, to the Protestant Princes in *Germany*, assembled at *Smalcald*, to exhort them to an unity in Doctrine, wherein he offered his assistance by conference with their Divines.

Immediately after the ruine of Monasteries, in the Month of *November* followed the condemnation of *John Lambert*, that faithful Servant of Christ. On a set day *Lambert* was brought forth, where he had not only the King's fierce countenance against him, but also ten Disputers against him, from twelve of the clock till five at night, among which were the Archbishop, *Stephen Gardiner*, C. *Tunstal*, Bishop of *Durham*, and *J. Stokesley*, Bishop of *London*. Through *Winchester's* perswasion, to gratifie the people, the King himself condemned *Lambert*, and commanded *Cromwel* to read the Sentence. He was burned in *Smithfield*, where he suffered most horrible torments before he expired.

The King, after the burning of many Images, caused the bones of *Thomas Becket*, Archbishop in the time of *Henry* the Second, to be burned. He also seized on that immense Treasure and Jewels that were offered to his Shrine; there being few, since the time of *Henry* the Second, that passed to *Canterbury*, that did not both visit his Tomb, and bring rich Presents to it. Among which there being one Stone eminent, which, it was said, *Lewis* the Seventh, coming hither on Pilgrimage from *France*, Anno Dom. 1179. bestowed: Our King wore it in a Ring afterwards.

The number of Monasteries, first and last, suppressed in *England* and *Wales*, were (as Mr. *Camden* accounts them) six hundred forty five; whereof these had voices among the Peers. The Abbot of St. *Albans*, declared the first Abbey of *England* : St *Peters* in *Westminster*, St. *Bennet* of *Holm*, *Berdsey*, *Shrewsbury*, *Crowland*, *Abingdon*, *Evesham*, *Glocester*, *Ramsey*, St. *Maries* in *York*, *Tewksbury*, *Reading*, *Battel*, *Winchcomb*, *Hide* by *Winchester*, *Cirencester*, *Waltham*, *Malmesbury*, *Thorney*, St. *Augustine* in *Canterbury*, *Selby*, *Peterborough*, St *John's* in *Colchester*, *Coventry*, *Tavestock*.

Camd. Brit.

Of Colledges were demolished, in divers Shires, ninety. Of Chauntries, and Fire-chappels, two thousand three hundred seventy four; and Hospitals one hundred and ten; the yearly value of all which were, one hundred sixty one thousand, one hundred pounds, being above a third part of all our spiritual Revenues, besides the money made of the present stock of Cattle and Corn, of the Timber, Lead, Bells, &c. and lastly, but chiefly of the Plate and Ornaments, which was not valued, but may be conjectured by that one Monastery of St. *Edmond's-bury*, whence was taken five thousand Marks of Gold and Silver, besides Stones of great value.

L. Herbert's Hist. of Hen. 8.

But the King not only augmented the number of the Colledges and Professors in his Universities, but erected, out of the Revenues gotten hereby, divers new Bishopricks, whereof one at *Westminster*, one at *Oxford*, one at *Peterborough*, one at *Bristol*, one at *Chester*, and one at *Glocester*; all remaining at this day, save that at *Westminster*: which being revoked to its first Institution, by Queen *Mary*, and *Benedictines* placed in it, was, by Queen *Elizabeth* afterward, converted to a Collegiate-church, and a School for the teaching and maintenance of young Scholars. Besides many of the ancient Cathedral-churches, formerly possessed by Monks only, were now supplied with Canons, and some new ones erected and endowed; the Revenues allotted by the King to those new Bishopricks, and Cathedrals, amounting to about eight thousand pounds *per Annum*. Besides, the King in demolishing the Abbies, did not only prefer divers Learned men which he found there, but took special care to preserve the choicest Books of their well-furnished Libraries, wherein *John Leland*, a curious searcher of Antiquities, was employed.

Martin's Chronic. in Hen. 8.

These Houses, Sites, Possessions, were by the Parliament setled on the King, who (to prevent the future restoring of them back again to their former uses) exchanged them liberally for other Lands with the Nobles and Gentry of his Realm, many of whose Estates at this day do wholly consist of Possessions of that nature, or else are greatly advanced by those Lands.

A Match being made up betwixt King *Henry*, and the Lady *Anne* of *Cleeve*, by the Lord *Cromwel's* contrivance, many Dutch-men flocked into *England*, whose heads were busied about points of Divinity, whilst their hands were busied about their Manufactures. Soon after they broached their strange Opinions, being branded with the general name of *Anabaptists*.

Stow's Chron. p. 575.

This year 1529. their name first appears in our English Chronicles: for I read, that four *Anabaptists*, three Men, and one Woman, all Dutch, bear Faggots at *Paul's* Crofs, and three dayes after a Man and Woman, of their Sect, were burnt in *Smithfield*.

the Church of GREAT BRITAIN.

The King liked not *Anne* of *Cleeve*, who was a very vertuous Lady, but in her countenance not well composed, fair, nor lovely. Some feminine impotency was objected against her, though only her precontract with the Son of the Duke of *Lorrain* was publickly insisted on, for which, by Act of Parliament now sitting, she was solemnly divorced. And the Bishops and Clergy of this Land, in their solemn Convocation, published an authentical Instrument in writing, under the Seals of the two Archbishops, *That the King's Marriage with the said Lady* Anne *of* Cleve *was void, and of none effect.*

From thenceforth the King frowneth upon the Lord *Cromwel*.

Then the six Articles, called by some, *The bloody Statute*, by others, *The Whip with six strings*, by the perswasion of Bishop *Gardiner* (in defiance of Archbishop *Cranmer*, and the Lord *Cromwel*, opposing it) was enacted, being

I. That in the Sacrament of the Altar, after Consecration, no substance of Bread or Wine remaineth, but the natural Body and Blood of Christ.
II. That the Communion in both kinds is not necessary, ad salutem, by the Law of God to all persons.
III. That Priests, after Orders received, may not marry by the Law of God.
IV. That Vows of Castity ought to be observed.
V. That it is meet and necessary, that private Masses be admitted and continued in Churches.
VI. That Auricular confession must be frequented by people, as necessary to Salvation.

The Lord *Cromwel* was soon after arrested, and ten dayes after his Arrest, he was attainted of High-treason in Parliament, and he, with the Lord *Hongerford*, the next week after, was beheaded on *Tower-hill*.

After the execution of the Lord *Cromwel*, the Parliament still sitting, a motly Execution happened in *Smithfield*: three Papists hanged by the Statute, for denying the King's Supremacy, *viz*.

>*Edward Powel.*
>*Thomas Abley.*
>*Richard Fetherston.*

And as many Protestants burned at the same time and place, by vertue of the six Articles, *viz*.

>*Robert Barnes*, Doctor of Divinity.
>*Thomas Gerard,*} Batchelors of Divinity.
>*William Jerom,*}

The History of

This was caused by the difference of Religions in the King's Privy Council, wherein the Popish party called for the execution of these Protestants, whilst the Protestant Lords in the Council, cried as fast, that the Laws might take effect upon the Papists.

A Statute made for the recovery of Tithes. 32 Hen. 8. c. 7.
In the Parliament a Statute was made, commanding every man, *Fully, truly, and effectually to divide, set out, yield, or pay all and singular Tithes and Offerings, according to the lawful customs and usages of the Parishes and places where such Tithes, or Duties, shall grow, arise, come, or be due.* And remedy is given for Ecclesiastick persons before the Ordinary; and for Lay-men, that claimed appropriated Tithes by grant from the Crown, in the secular Courts, by such Actions, as usually Lay-possessions had been subject to. This Statute, in favour of Lay-impropriators, was beneficial to the Clergy, to recover their Predial Tithes at Common Law.

A Statute also was made, *That it was lawful for all persons to contract marriage, who are not prohibited by the Law of God*: for after the time of Pope *Gregory*, other Popes did not only forbid the marriage of Cousin-Germans, but other degrees farther off, thereby to get money for Dispensations.

This Law came seasonably to comply with King *Henry*'s occasions, who had the first-fruits thereof, and presently after married *Katherine Howard*, Cousin-german to *Anna Bolen*, his second Wife, which by the Canon-law formerly was forbidden, without a special Dispensation first obtained.

In the third Session of the Convocation at St. *Paul*'s several Bishops were assigned to peruse several Books of the Translation of the new Testament. *Cranmer* stickleth for the Universities approbation.

The Parliament, *Anno* 1544. mitigated the six Articles; for it was required, that all Offenders should first be found guilty by a Jury of twelve men, before they should suffer.

Anno 1545. began the last Parliament in this King's Reign, wherein many things of consequence were enacted.

1. Against Usury.
2. For Tithes in *London*.
3. For an exchange of Lands betwixt the King's Majesty, and *Thomas Cranmer*, Archbishop of *Canterbury*, *Robert Holgate*, Archbishop of *York*, and *Edmond Bonner*, Bishop of *London*; which the King annexed to the Dutchy of *Lancaster*.
4. An Act for union of Churches, not exceeding the value of six pounds.
5. That Doctors of the Civil Law might exercise Ecclesiastical jurisdiction.

At this time also, by the King's command, were the Stews suppressed.

The

The Favourers of the truth among the Noblemen were, the Earl of *Suffolk*, Viscount *Beauchamp*, Viscount *Lisle*, Lord *Russel* Treasurer, Lord *Awdley* Chancellor, Lord *Paget*, and *Sadler*, and *Thomas Cranmer* Archbishop of *Canterbury*. *Fox. Acts and Monuments.*

The Patrons of Popery were, the Bishop of *Winchester* and *Durham*, the Duke of *Norfolk*, and Earl of *Southampton*, *Anthony Brown*, *William Pawlet*, *John Baker*, *Richard* Chancellor of the Augmentation, *Winckfield* Vice-chancellor.

Four and twenty were Executed for Traitors, in the time of King *Henry*, for the cause of Supremacy.

Adam Damlip, who before had escaped, and lay hid in the West-countrey, teaching a School about a year or two, by the miserable Inquisition of the six Articles, was again taken and brought up to *London*, where he was by *Stephen Gardiner* commanded to the Marshal-sea, and after two years space he was Condemned and Executed for Treason. One *Henry* was burnt at *Colchester*, and one *Kerby* at *Ipswich*, for the Testimony of the Truth.

In the year 1546. in *June*, *Anne Ashcough*, alias *Kyme*, Daughter of Sir *William Ashcough* of *Kelsey* in *Lincoln-shire*, of the age of 25. years, whose Wit, Beauty, Learning and Religion, procured her much esteem on the Queens side of the Court, and as much hatred from the Popish Bishops, was burned for the profession of the Truth, in *Smithfield*, with three men, *Nicholas Belevian*, Priest of *Shrop-shire*, *John Lacels*, Gentleman of the houshold of King *Henry* the Eighth, and *John Adams* a poor Tailor of *London*. Her several examinations penned by her self are extant in Mr. *Fox*.

Then began the troubles of Queen *Katherine Parr*, whom the King had married some two years since. She was one of great piety, beauty, and discretion: next to the Bible, she studied the King's disposition, observing him to her utmost: yet sometimes she would presume to discourse with the King about points of Religion, defending the Protestant Tenets by Scripture, and sometimes would hold up the King very close hard at it. This displeased him, who loved loosenes and liberty in his Clothes, Arguments, and Actions, and was quickly observed by *Gardiner*, and others, the Queen's enemies.

Hereupon *Gardiner* drew up Articles against her, and got them subscribed with the King's own hand, to send her to the Tower. But Chancellor *Wriothesley* put the paper of those Articles in his own bosom, which casually fell out, was taken up by one of the Queen's Servants, and brought to the Queen, who on her sickness and submission to the King, obtained his Pardon, Signed and Sealed unto her with many kisses and embraces. And her enemies that came to attach her, were sent back with the Taunts and Threats of the enraged King against them. King *Henry* made his Will, and died a moneth after, and was buried at *Windsor*. After

The History of

Sir John Hayward's Hist. of K. Edw. 6.

After the Death of King *Henry*, succeeded King *Edward* his Son, being scarce ten years old, full of as much Worth as the model of his Age could hold. He attained not onely commendable Knowledge, but speech in the Greek, Spanish, and Italian Languages, having always great Judgment in measuring his Words by his Matter; his Speech being alike, both fluent and weighty, such as best beseemed a Prince. As for Natural Philosophy, Logick, Musick, Astronomy, and other Liberal Sciences; his perfections were such, that the great Italian Philosopher *Cardan*, having tasted him by many Conferences, seemed to be astonished between admiration and delight, and divulged his abilities to be miraculous.

These his acquirements, by industry, were very much enriched and enlarged by many excellent Endowments of nature; for in disposition he was mild, gratious, and pleasant, of an heavenly wit; in Body beautiful, but especially in his Eyes, which seemed to have a Starry livelinefs and lustre in them. Generally he seemed to be, as *Cardan* reported of him, *A Miracle of Nature*.

Because he was young, he was committed to sixteen Governours, the Lord *Edward Seimour*, Duke of *Sommerset*, his Unckle, was assigned unto him Protector, by whose endeavour the six bloody Articles forementioned were abolished.

This King restored the holy Scriptures in the English Tongue, he abolished Masses, and such as were banished were received home, as *John Hooper*, *Miles Coverdale*, &c. He changed most part of the Bishops of Diocesses, and compelled dumb Priests to give place to those that would Preach: he suppressed Idolatry, restored the Gospel and worship of God, encouraged Godly Preachers, sent for Eminent Men, both for Learning and Piety, from beyond the Seas, to Teach in both Universities, viz. *Peter Martyr* in *Oxford*, and *Martin Bucer*, and *Paulus Fagius* in *Cambridge*, and was a Refuge to all the Godly that fled for Religion out of other Countries; and therefore is called by *Melchior Adam*, *Summa spei Princeps, qui omnibus piis & doctis, Polonis, Germanis, Gallis, Scotis, Italis, Hispanis, hospitium & patrocinium dederat*: A Prince of singular hope, who gave protection and entertainment to all Godly and Learned Men, *Polonians, Germans, French, Scots, Italians, Spaniards*. In consideration whereof an eminent Martyr in Queen *Maries* days, in an effectionate Speech of His, before a Popish Persecutor, cried out, *Blessed be God for King* Edward.

Melch. Adam. in vit. Germ. Theolog.

This King was much enclined to Clemency, especially in matters of Blood, and most especially if it were for Religion, insomuch, that albeit he was greatly affected to that Religion wherein he had been brought up, yet none were executed in his time for other Religion, but onely two blasphemous Hereticks, *Joan Butcher*, and *George* a Dutch-man. And when

the Church of Great Britain.   159

when *Joan Butcher* was to be burned, all the Council could not procure him to set his hand to the Warrant: wherefore they employed *Thomas Cranmer*, Archbishop of *Canterbury*, to deal privately with him for his subscription. But the King remained firm in resolution, affirming, *That he would not drive her headlong to the Devil*. The Archbishop was violent both by persuasions and entreaties: and when with meer importunity he had prevailed, the King in subscribing his name said, *That he would lay all the charge thereof upon the Archbishop before God*.

Then the Professors of the Gospel were in all places relieved, and many Prisoners appointed to die, were enlarged and preserved: Onely *Thomas Dobby*, Fellow of St. *John's* in *Cambridge*, committed to the Counter in *Bred-street*, and condemned for speaking against the Masse, died of a natural death in Prison; his speedy death prevented the pardon which the Lord Protector intended to send him.

The Lord Protector ordered all in Church and State. The King in his protection, took speedy order for Reformation of Religion, and having chosen Wise, and Learned, Men to be his Commissioners in that behalf, divided them into several Dioceses, to be visited, appointing likewise unto every company one or two Godly Learned Preachers, to instruct the people at every Session in the true Doctrine of the Gospel. To those Commissioners were delivered thirty six Injunctions, and Ecclesiastical Laws, which they should enquire of, and also command in his Majesties name and behalf, all tending to the abolishing of Popish superstition, and establishing the Truth of the Gospel.

Besides which general Injunctions, for the estate of the whole Realm, there were also certain others particularly appointed for the Bishops onely; whereby they were enjoyned to see the other put in Execution; besides others which did more particulary confirm them. These Injunctions may be seen at large in the first Edition of the *Acts and Monuments* (fol. 684.) and you may read them in a smoother Abstract in *Fuller's* Church History. Some Homiles were left with the Parish-Priests, which the Archbishop had composed, not onely for the help of unpreaching Ministers; but for the regulating and instructing even of the Learned Preachers. Besides the points contained in the said Injunctions, the Preachers, above mentioned, were more particulary instructed to perswade the people from Praying to the Saints, from making Prayer for the Dead, from Adoring of Images, from the use of Beads, Ashes and Processions, from Mass, Diriges, Praying in unknown Languages, and from other such like things, whereunto long custom had brought a Religious observation.

All which was done to this intent, That the people in all places being prepared by little and little, might with more ease and less opposition, admit the total alteration in the face of the Church, which was intended in due time to be introduced.

Fuller. Church History, p.372, 373.

Dr. P.Helyns History of K. Edw. 6.

While

While these Commissioners were occupied abroad, the King desiring a Reformation, appointed a Parliament, *Novemb.* 4. in the first year of his Reign, *Anno* 1547. wherein all Acts made before against the Professors of the Truth were Abrogated. In the same Parliament also it was Decreed, *That the Sacrament should be ministred to all under both kinds.* Then also were Candles on *Candlemas-day* forbidden, and Ashes on *Ash-wednesday*, according to the Popish custom.

About the same time also all Images were taken away in most places of the Kingdom.

The first who declared his averseness to the King's proceedings, was Dr. *Stephen Gardiner*, Bishop of *Winchester*, who stomaching his being left out of the list of the Council, appeared more Cross to all their doings than others of his Order: for which being brought before their Lordships, they sent him Prisoner to the Fleet.

Albeit *Edmond Bonner*, Bishop of *London*, at first seemed to comply, yet at length he bewraied himself, by suffring daily to be Sung the Apostles Mass, and our Ladies Mass, &c. in diverse of his Chappels in *Pauls*, cloaking them with the name of the Apostles, and our Ladies Communions, whereof the Council being informed, caused him to reform the abuse.

Sir *Anthony Cook*, and Sir *John Goodsale*, Knights; *John Goodsal*, and *Christopher Nevinson*, Doctors of the Laws, and *John Madew*, Doctor of Divinity, the King's Commissioners, called before them the said *Edmond Bonner*, *John Royston*, *Polydor Virgil*, and many others of the Dignitaries of the said Cathedral, to whom the Sermon being done, and their Commission openly read, they ministred the Oath of the King's Supremacy, according to the Statute of thirty one of King *Henry* the eighth, requiring them withal to present such things as needed to be reformed. Which done, they delivered to Bishop *Bonner* a Copy of the Injunctions forementioned, together with the Homilies set forth by the King's authority, received by him with protestation, *That he would observe them, if they were not contrary to the Law of God, and the Ordinances of the Church.* But afterwards he revoked his protestation, and humbly submitted himself to his Majesties pleasure. Yet for a Terror to others, Bishop *Bonner* was committed to the Fleet.

During the short time of his restraint (*viz. Septemb.* 18.) the Litany was Sung in the English Tongue in St. *Paul's* Church, between the Quire and the High Altar, the Singers kneeling half on the one side, and half on the other. And the same day the Epistle and Gospel was also read at the High Mass in the English Tongue. And in *November* next following (Bishop *Bonner* being then restored to his former liberty) the Image of Christ, then called *the Rood*, and all other Images in that Church, as also in all the other Churches of *London* were taken down. And in speeding of this work, as Bishop *Bonner*, together with

the

the Church of GREAT BRITAIN.

the Dean and Chapter, did perform their part in the Cathedral of St. *Paul*; so *Bellaffere*, Archdeacon of *Colchefter*, and Doctor *Gilbert Bourn* (being at that time Archdeacon both of *London* and *Effex*) were no lefs diligent in doing the like in all the Churches of their refpective Jurifdictions, according to the charge impofed upon them by his Majeftie's Vifitors.

The firft Tranflation of the Bible was fet forth in the Reign of King *Henry* the Eighth, *Anno* 1541. with a Grave and Pious preface of Archbifhop *Cranmer*, and Authorized by the King's Proclamation, Dated *May* 6. Seconded alfo with Inftructions from the King. It was called the Bible of the greater Volume. Few Countrey-parifhes could go to the coft of them, though Bifhop *Bonner* caufed fix of them to be chained in the Church of St. *Pauls* in convenient places.

The fecond Tranflation of the Bible was fet forth in the Reign of King *Edward* the Sixth, and not onely fuffered to be read by particular perfons, but ordered to be read over yearly in the Congregation, as a principal part of Divine Service. Two Editions there were thereof, one fet forth 1549. the other 1541. but neither of them divided into verfes.

The third Tranflation of the Bible was fet forth in the fecond year of Queen *Elizabeth*. The laft Tranflation was again reviewed by fome of the moft Learned Bifhops (appointed thereunto by the Queen's Commiffion) whence it took the name of the Bifhops Bible, and by the Queens fole commandment Reprinted. [Extant in Sir *Tho.Cotton*. Library.]

Then diverfe Proclamations were iffued out in the King's name, relating to Ecclefiaftical matters, in the four firft years of his Reign, among which there was a Proclamation inhibiting Preachers, *Anno fecundo, Edwardi fexti*, whereof this was the occafion. Certain Popifh Preachers, difaffected to the King's Government, in their Sermons declared, *That the King intended to lay ftrange exactions upon the people*. To prevent further mifchief, the King ordered by Proclamation, *That none fhould Preach except Licenfed under the Seals of the. Lord Protector, or Archbifhop of* Canterbury. At this time many Popifh Pulpits founded the Alarum to *Kets* Rebellion, and the *Devon-fhire* Commotion.

There was alfo a Proclamation for the payment of the late Incumbents of Colledges, and Chanteries lately diffolved.

Anno 3. *Edwardi fexti*, A Proclamation alfo for the Inhibition of Players, *Aug*. 6.

The Parliament not long before, paffed an Act for Election of Bifhops, and what Seals and ftyles fhould be ufed by Spiritual perfons: in which it was Ordained.

That Bifhops fhould be made by the King's Letters Patents, and not by the election of the Deans and Chapters.

Y   That

That all their Processes and Writings should be made in the King's name onely, with the Bishops Teste added to it, and sealed with no other Seal but the King's, or such as should be authorized and appointed by him. The Intent of the Contrivers of this Act (saith Dr. *Heylin*) was to weaken the authority of the Episcopal Order, by forcing them from their strong-hold of Divine Institution, and making them no other than the King's Ministers onely. And of this Act such use was made, that the Bishops of those times were not in a capacity of conferring Orders, but as they were thereunto impowered by special Licenfe. The Tenour whereof was (if *Sanders* may be believed) in these words following, viz.

Heyl'in Hist. Edw. 6.

The King to such a Bishop, Greeting. Whereas all and all manner of Jurisdiction, as well Ecclesiastical as Civil, flows from the King, as from the Supreme Head of all the Body, &c. We therefore give and grant to Thee full Power and Licenfe, to continue during our good pleafure, for holding Ordination within thy Diocefs of N. and for promoting fit perfons unto holy Orders, even to that of the Prieft-hood.

Queen *Mary* caufed this Act to be repealed in the firft year of her Reign, leaving the Bishops to depend on their former Claim, and to Act all things which belonged to their Jurifdiction in their own Names, and under their own Seals, as in former times. In which eftate they have continued without any legal interruption from that time to this.

Doctor *Nicholas Ridley* was promoted to the See of *Rochefter*, to which he had been nominated by King *Henry* the Eighth, a man of great Learning, and well-ftudied in the Fathers, and an excellent Preacher. Doctor *Barlow* was preferred to the Bishoprick of *Bath and Wells*.

The Commiffioners authorized to take away Images out of Churches, were in many places entertained with contempt and railing, and the farther they went from *London* the worfe they were handled: one of them called *Body*, as he was pulling down Images in *Cornwal*, was ftabbed in the body by a Prieft.

Many there were that then cried down all the obfervations of Days and Times, and particularly of keeping *Lent*: complaint whereof being made by Bishop *Gardiner* in a Letter to the Lord Protector, a Proclamation was fent out commanding all people to abftain from Flefh in the time of *Lent*, and the King's Lenten dyet was fet out, and ferved as in former times.

Hugh Latimer having by the power of *Cromwel*, and his favour with the King, been made Bishop of *Worcefter*, Anno 1535. continued in that See, till on the firft of *July* 1539. he chofe rather to refign the fame, than

The Church of Great Britain.

than to have any hand in passing the six Articles, then agitated in the Convocation, and confirmed by Parliament: full eight years he betook himself to the retiredness of a private life. On New-years day he Preached his first Sermon at *Pauls* Cross (the first I mean after his re-admission to his former Ministry) and two Lords-days after again in the same place, and on *January* 25. Such multitudes flocked to hear his Sermon, that being to Preach before the King the first Friday in *Lent*, a pulpit was placed in the King's privy Garden, where he might be heard of four times as many Auditors, as could have thronged into the Chappel. Which as it was the first Sermon that was Preached in that place, so afterward a fixed and standing Pulpit was erected for the like occasions, especially for Lent-sermons on the Sundays in the Afternoon, and hath so continued ever since till these latter times.

At the return of the King's Commissioners, dispatched throughout the Realm, to take a Survay of all Colledges, Free-chappels, Chanteries, and Brotherhoods, in the first place (as lying nearest) came in the free Chappel of St. *Stephen*, originally founded in the Palace at *Westminster*, and reckoned for the Chappel Royal of the Court of *England*. The whole Foundation consisted of thirty eight persons, *viz*. one Dean, twelve Canons, thirteen Vicars, four Clerks, six Choristers, besides a Verger, and one that had the charge of the Chappel. This Chappel hath been since fitted, and employed for an house of Commons in all times of Parliament.

At the same time also fell the Colledge, commonly called St. *Martins le Grand*, near *Aldersgate* in *London*: the King gave the same, with the Liberties and precincts thereof to the Church of *Westminster*. These two, *St. Stephen's* and *St. Martin's*, were the richest of all the rest.

Then the Lord Protector being unfurnished of a Palace proportionable to his Greatness, doubted not to find room enough upon the dissolution of the Bishoprick of *Westminster* lately erected, to raise a Palace equal to his vast designs. Which coming to the ears of *Benson*, the last Abbot, and first Dean of *Westminster*, he was willing to preserve the whole, by parting for the present with more than half of the estate belonging to it. And thereupon a Lease is made of seventeen Mannors, and good Farmes, lying almost altogether in the County of *Glocester*, for the Term of ninety nine years, which was presented to the Lord *Thomas Seymor*, to serve as an addition to his Mannor of *Sudley*. Another present of almost as many Mannors, lying in the Counties of *Glocester*, *Worcester*, and *Hereford*, was made for the like Term to Sir *John Mason*, for the use of the Lord Protector, which after the Duke's fall came to Sir *John Bourn*, principal Secretary of Estate, in the time of Queen *Mary*. The Mannor of *Islip* was also put into the scale, conferred upon that Church by King *Edward* the Confessor, to which two hundred Tenants owed their soile and service, and being one of the best-wooded things in those parts of the Realm;

was

was to be granted also without impeachment of waste, as it was accordingly. Thus *Benson* saved the Deanery, but fell into great disquiet of mind, and died a few moneths after. To whom succeeded Doctor *Cox*, being then Almoner to the King, Chancellor of the University of *Oxford*, and Dean of *Christ-Church*.

Latimer. Ser. p. 38. 71, 91, 114.

Bishop *Latimer* in his printed Sermons complaineth, *That the Gentry at that time invaded the profits of the Church, leaving the Title onely to the Incumbent; and that Chantery Priests were put by them into several Cures, to save their pensions; that many Benefices were laid out in Fee-farmes, and for making of Gardens: and finally, that the poor Clergy being kept to some sorry pittances, were forced to put themselves into Gentlemens houses, and there to serve as Clerks of the Kitchin, Surveyours, Receivers,* &c. All which Enormities, were generally connived at by the Lords and others, who onely had the power to reform the same, because they could not question those who had so miserably invaded the Churches patrimony, without condemning of themselves.

Stephen Gardiner, Bishop of *Winchester*, having long lain Prisoner in the Fleet was enlarged, and permitted to return to his Diocess, where contrary to the promise made at his enlargement, he shewed himself cross to the King's proceedings in case of Images and other things, that he was sent Prisoner to the Tower, where he abode till he was set at liberty by Queen *Mary*.

Notwithstanding the King's great care to set forth one uniform order of Administring the holy Communion in both kinds, yet among the inferior Priests and Ministers of Cathedral and other Churches in this Realm, there arose variety of Factions in Celebrating the Communion Service, and Administration of the Sacraments, and other Rites of the Church. Some followed the Order of the King's proceedings: others patchingly used some part of them onely: but many causelesly contemning them all, would still continue in their former Popery. Moreover, many of those who had been licensed, appeared as active in Preaching against the King's proceedings, as any of the unlicensed Preachers had been found to be. Which being made known to the King, and the Lords of the Council, it was advised, that a publick Liturgy should be drawn, and confirmed by Parliament, which was done, *An.* 1548. and in the next year a penalty was imposed by Act of Parliament on such who should deprave, or neglect the use thereof.

The King caused those Godly Bishops, and other Learned Divines (whom he had formerly imployed in drawing up the order for the holy Communion) to frame a publick Liturgy, containing the order of Morning and Evening Prayer, together with a Form of Ministring the Sacraments, and for the celebrating of all publick Offices in the Churches.

This was done acccordingly: Some exception being taken at it by Mr. *Calvin* abroad, and some zealots at home, the Book was brought

under

under a review, and by Statute in Parliament, it was appointed, it should be faithfully perused, explained, and made fully perfect.

And here take notice, that those who had the chief stroke in this Affair, were before-hand resolved, that none but English Heads or hands should be used therein. *Calvin* offered his assistance to Archbishop *Cranmer*, as himself confesseth, but he refused the offer. And though it was thought necessary, for the better seasoning of both Universities in the Protestant Reformed Religion, that *Martin Bucer*, and *Peter Martyr*, two eminent Divines of Forreign Churches, should be invited to come over, yet had the Liturgy passed the approbation of the King and Council, if not both Houses of Parliament before their coming. Which being finished, they all subscribed it, except Doctor *Day*, Bishop of *Chichester*.

Then in Parliament it was enacted, that all such positive Lawes and Ordinances, as prohibited the marriages of Priests, and pains and forfeitures therein contained, should be repealed.

In this Parliament also it was enacted, that no person should from thence-forth take, or carry away any Tithe or Tithes which had been received or paid within the space of fourty years next before the date thereof, &c. under the pain or forfeiture of the Treble value of the Tithes so taken or carried away. To which a clause was also added, enabling the said Parsons, Vicars, &c. to enter upon any man's Land for the due setting out of his Tithes, and carrying away the same without molestation.

There also passed another Act for Abstinence from flesh upon all such days, as had been formerly taken and reputed for fasting-dayes, *viz*. fall Fridays and Saturdays in the year, the time of Lent, the Ember-dayes, the Eves or Vigils of such Saints, as had been anciently used for Fasts by the Rules of the Church. On *Septemb*. 5. 1548. Doctor *Farrar's* was consecrated Bishop of S. *Davids*, as Doctor *Heylin* noteth, and not in the year 1547. as Mr. *Fox* makes it, nor in 1549. as Bishop *Godwin* saith.

The Lord Protector pulled down two Churches, two Chappels, and three Episcopal Houses for the materials of the building of his new intended Palace, called *Sommerset-house*.

About this time there arose a sort of men, who were termed Gospellers, against whom Bishop *Hooper* inveigheth, in the Preface to his Exposition on the ten Commandments. Some Anabaptists also discovered themselves. Some of the Chiefs of them were convented before the Archbishop of *Canterbury*, and the Bishop of *Westminster*, Doctor *Cox* Almoner to the King and others: and being convicted of their errours, some of them were dismissed only with an Admonition, some sentenced

to

to a Recantation, and others, among which I find one *Champney's*, condemned to bear their Faggots at St *Paul's* Cross.

Then brake forth two dangerous Rebellions, one in *Devonshire*, the other in *Norfolk*. That of *Devonshire* was found to be chiefly raised in maintenance of their old Religion. On *Whitsun-Munday*, being next day after the first exercising of the publick Liturgy, some few of the Parishioners of the Parish of *Sampford-Courteney*, compelled their Parish-Priest, who is supposed to have invited them to that compulsion, to let them have the Latine Mass as in former-times. These being seconded with many others, *Henry Arundel*, Esquire, Governour of the Mount in *Cornwal*, *Winslade* and *Cossin*, Gentlemen, headed them. The seditious exceeding the number of ten thousand, march in a full Body to *Exeter*. They sent their demands to the King, among which one more specially concerned the Liturgy. It was demanded by the Rebels, That forasmuch as we constantly believe, that after the words of Consecration spoken by the Priest being at Mass, there is very really the Body and Blood of our Saviour Jesus Christ, God and man, and that, no substance of Bread and Wine remaineth after, but the very self-same body that was born of the Virgin *Mary*, and was given upon the Cross for our Redemption; Therefore we will have Mass Celebrated as it was in times past without any man Communicating with the Priests, forasmuch as many presuming unworthily to receive the same, put no difference between the Lord's body, and other kind of meat, &c.

To which demand of theirs the King thus answered, viz. that for the Mass I assure you, no small study nor Travel hath been spent, by all the Learned Clergy therein; and to avoyd all contention, it is brought even to the use that Christ left it, as the Apostles used it; as the Holy Fathers delivered it: indeed somewhat altered from that to which the Popes of *Rome*, for their lucre, had brought it. And although (saith he,) you may hear the contrary from some Popish evil men; Yet we, on our Honour assure you, that they deceive, abuse you, and blow these opinions into your Heads to finish their own purposes. But this answer satisfying not, they marched with all their forces to the siege of *Exeter*, carrying before them in their march the Pix or Consecrated Host under a Canopy, with Crosses, Banners, Candlesticks, Holy-bread, and Holy-water, &c. But the Lord *Gray* and the Lord *Russel* with forces conjoyned, so strongly charged the Rebels, that they bear them out of their works; and then forced them with great slaughter to raise their siege. After the like success in some following fights, the Lord *Russel* enters that City on *August* 6. where he was joyfully received by the half-starved Citizens. *Miles Coverdale* gave publick thanks to God for the Victory, in the view of *Exeter*, and soon after was made the Bishop thereof.

Arundel,

Arundel, *Berry*, *Wihflade*, and *Coffin* were sent to *London*, and there executed. Six Popish Priests were hanged, and the Vicar of *S. Thomas* (one of the Grand Incendiaries) hanged on the top of his own Steeple, apparrelled in his Popish Weeds, with his Beads at his Girdle.

The *Norfolk* Rebellion brake forth on *June* 20. and that especially for a grievance about Enclosures. The Rebels had gotten one *Robert Ket*, a rich *Tanner* of *Wimondham* for their Leader, and were grown to a Body of twenty thousand, seating themselves at *Moushold* near *Mount Surrey*, where they carried a face (as it were) of Justice and Religion; for they had one *Coniers*, an idle fellow, to be their Chaplain, who read solemn Prayers to them Morning and Evening, Sermons also they had often. And as for Justice, they had a bench under a Tree (which Tree was called by them, and so hath ever since been called, *the Tree of Reformation*) where *Ket* usually sate, and with him two Companies of every Hundred, whence their Companies had been raised, to hear complaints, and give judgement. They sent certain complaints to the King, requiring he would send a Herrald to them to give them satisfaction. The King returned this answer, that in *October* following he would call a Parliament, wherein their complaints should be heard, and their grievances should be redressed, requiring them in the mean time to lay down Arms, and return to their houses, and thereupon granting them a general pardon. But this not satisfying the seditious, hereupon they first assaulted the City of *Norwich*, took it, and made *Thomas Cod* the Mayor of *Norwich* attend them as their servant. At length He and others of the Gentry detained Prisoners in *Ket*'s Camp, were admitted to the Counsels of the Rebels for the better credit thereof.

Doctor *Matthew Parker* (afterward Archbishop of *Canterbury*) getting up into *the Oak of Reformation*, Preached to the Rebels of their Duty and Obedience, where his life was in danger, many Arrows being shot at him. *Conyers* set the *Te Deum*, during the singing whereof the Doctor withdrew, and went to his own house.

William Par Marquess of *Northampton*, with the Lords *Sheffield* and *Wentworth*, Sir *Anthony Denny*, Sir *Ralph Sadler* and other persons of Honour, is sent to quell this Rebellion. But success failed them: the Lord *Sheffield* was barbarously butchered, Sir *Thomas Cornwallis* taken prisoner, and the City fired by the Rebels, but the clouds melting into tears pittying the Cities calamity, quenched the flames, and the Marquess quitting the service, returned to *London*.

Then was *John Dudley*, Earl of *Warwick* sent to undertake the task, and was attended by the Marquess of *Northampton*. Coming to *Norwich* he easily entred the City, and entertained the Rebels with many Sallies with various success, but generally the Earl of *Warwick* came off with the better.

The Rebels deserted *Moushold-hill*, and came down into *Duffing-dale*.

Here

Here their superstition fancied themselves sufficiently fenced by the vertue of an old prophecy.

Hob, Dick, and Hick, with Clubs, and Clouted Shun.
Sall fill up Dussindale with blood of slaughtred bodies soon.

In this place was a bloody battel: two thousand of the Rebels were slain in the fight and chase, the Residue of them scattered all over the Countrey: the Principals of them taken, and Executed: *Robert Ket* hanged on *Norwich-Castle*, *William* his brother, on the Top of *Wimondham* steeple, nine of his followers on as many boughs of the Oak where Ket held his Courts. On *August* xxix. a solemn thanksgiving was made to God for their deliverance, in the City of *Norwich*, and is Annually observed. As for the Rebellion at the same time in *York-shire*, it was soon quelled on the Execution of *Omler* and *Dale*, the chief promoters thereof.

These things quickned the Lords of the Council to a sharper course against all those whom they suspected not to advance the publick Liturgy. Among whom none was more distrusted than Bishop *Bonner* of *London*, who is commanded to attend the Lords of the Council on *Aug.* 11. by whom he was told, that by his negligence not only many people within his Diocess forgat their duty to God in frequenting the Divine Service than by Law established, but divers others despising the same, did in secret places often frequent the Popish Mass. Therefore he is commanded to Preach against the Rebels at *Paul's* Cross on *Septemb.* 1. and there to shew the unlawfulness of taking Arms on pretence of Religion. But on the Contrary, he spent most part of his Sermon in maintenance of the Cross, Carnal and Papistical presence of Christ's body and bloud in the Sacrament of the Eucharist: complaints whereof being made, a Commission is Issued out to the Archbishop of *Canterbury*, the Bishops of *Rochester* and *Peterborough*, Sir *Thomas Smith*, and Doctor *May*, before whom he was convented at *Lambeth*, where after many shifts on his part, and much patience on theirs, he is taken *pro confesso*, and in the beginning of *October* deprived of his Bishoprick. To whom succeeded Doctor *Nicholas Ridley*, Bishop of *Rochester*.

There passed an Act of Parliament in the following Session (which took beginning *Novemb.* 4.) for taking down of such Images, as were still remaining in the Churches, as also for the bringing in of all Antiphonaries, Missals, Breviaries, Offices, Horaries, Primars and Processionals, with other Books of false and superstitious worship. The Tenour of which Act signified to the Subject by the King's Proclamations, and seconded by the Missives of Archbishop *Cranmer* to the Suffragan Bishops, requiring them to see it diligently put in execution. Also the Bishops were required to punish all those that refused to give

to

the Church of Great Britain.

to the charge of bread and wine for the Communion. Now was there no further opposition against the Liturgy by the Romish party during the rest of the King's Reign.

But then there started up another faction, as opposite to the publick Liturgy, as were those of *Rome*. The Archbishop and the rest of Prelates which co-operated with him in the work of Reformation, were resolved now to go forwards with a Reformation in point of Doctrine. And therefore Letters were directed by Archbishop *Cramner* to *Martin Bucer* and *Peter Martyr*, two eminent Divines. *Martyr* came over in the end of *November*, and having spent sometime with the Archbishop in his house at *Lambeth*, was dispatched to *Oxford*, where he was made the King's Professour for Divinity, and about two years after made Canon of *Christ-Church*. His readings were so much disliked by some of that University, that a publick disputation was shortly had betwixt him, and some of those that disliked his doings, about some points in the Sacrament. Doctor *Cox*, Chancellour of the University, assisted by Mr. *Morrison* a right learned man, being Moderators, declared that *Martyr* had sufficiently answered all Arguments which were brought against him by *Chadsey* the chief of the opponents, and the rest of those who disputed with him. *Heylin's Hist. Edw. VI.*

Bucer came not over till *June*, and, being, here receives letters from *Calvin*, by which he was advised to take heed of his old fault (for a fault he thought it) which was to run a moderate course in his Reformations. The first thing that *Bucer* did after his coming hither, was to acquaint himself with the English Liturgy, translated for him into Latine by *Alexander Alesius*, a Learned *Scot*, and generally well approved of by him, as to the main Frame and Body of it. Of this he gives an account to *Calvin*. Having received a courteous entertainment from the Lord Protector, and being heartily well-commed by Archbishop *Cranmer*, he is sent to take the Chair at *Cambridge*. But he had not held that place long, when he left this life, deceasing on *January* 19. *Anno* 1550. to the great loss and grief of that University. *Mediis consistiis vel Authorem esse vel Approbatorem, Calvin. Epist. ad Bucer.*

Calvin writes to the Protector to this effect, That the Papists would grow more insolent every day than other unless the difference were composed about the Ceremonies. But how? not by reducing the Opponents to Conformity, but by encouraging them rather in their opposition.

John Rogers, Lecturer in S. *Paul's*, and *John Hooper* Vicar of S. *Sepulchres* were founders of Non-conformity. This *John Hooper* was bred in *Oxford*, well-skilled in Latine, Greek, and Hebrew, and afterwards travelled over into *Switzerland*. He was preferred to be Bishop of *Glocester* by the favour of his Patron, *John* Earl of *Warwick*, afterwards Duke of *Northumberland*. The Founders of Nonconformity.

But when *Hooper* came to be consecrated Bishop of *Glocester*, he scrupled

scrupled the wearing of certain Episcopal Ornaments (Rochet, Chimere, Square Cap, &c.) producing a letter from the Earl of *Warwick*, that he might be favourably dispensed with therein. The King also thirteen dayes after wrote to Archbishop *Cranmer* to the same effect. All would not do, Resolute Bishop *Ridley* stood stiffly to his tackling, and here was bandying of the businefs betwixt them, and arguments urged on both sides. The Earl of *Warwick* deserted his Chaplain, and *Hooper* was sent to prison, and kept sometime in durance, till he condescended to conform himself in his habit, and so was consecrated Bishop of *Glocester*. After this, *Hooper* bare a great grudge against *Ridley*, who enforced him thereunto: but God's providence sanctified their sufferings afterwards into an agreement. We must not forget, that this earnest contest was not about the vocation, but about the vestments of Bishops. Thus we have the first beginning of that opposition, which hath continued ever since against the Liturgy, &c. and other Rites and Usages of the Church of *England*.

About this time *John a Lasco*, free Baron of *Lasco* in *Poland*, with his Congregation of *Germans* and other strangers, took Sanctuary this year in *England*, hoping that here they might enjoy that liberty of conscience, and safety for their goods and persons, which their own Countrey had denyed them. The King gratioufly vouchsafed to give them both entertainment and protection: assigned them the west part of the Church, belonging to the late diffolved house of *Augustine-friars* for the exercise of Religious Worship, made them a Corporation, consisting of a Superintendent, and four other Ministers, with power to fill the vacant places by a new Succeffion, whenfoever any of them should be voyd by death or otherwife, the parties by them chosen to be approved by the King and Council. He commanded the Lord Mayor of *London*, the Aldermen and Sheriffs thereof, as also the Archbishop of *Canterbury*, and all other Bishops of this Realm not to diftrub them in the free exercise of their Religion and Ecclefiaftical Government, although they differed from the government and forms of Worship eftablished in the Church of *England*. All which he granted by his Letters Patents. This *John a Lasco* quickly publisheth a book, Entitled, *Forma & Ratio totius Ecclefiaftici Minifterii*, wherein he maintains the use of sitting at the Holy Communion, contrary to the cuftom of the Church of *England*, to the encouragement of those who impugned her Orders. A controverfie moved by Bishop *Hooper* touching the Episcopal Habit, was prefently propagated among the reft of the Clergy touching Caps and Surplices. And in this quarrel *John a Lasco* engageth, countenancing those that refused to wear them, and Writing to *Martin Bucer*, to declare against them. But that Moderate and Learned Man severely reprehended him, and folidly answered all his Objections. Which being sent to him in the way of letter, was afterward Printed and disperfed

for

the Church of Great Britain.

for keeping down that opposite humour. This controversie was countenanced by *Peter Martyr*, for besides his judgement which he gives of these things in some of his Epistles about things of this nature, he hath told us of his own practice in one of his Epistles, Dated at *Zurick*, *Novemb*. 4. 1559. being more than five years after he had left this Kingdom. That he had never used the Surplice, when he lived in *Oxford*, though he were then a Canon of *Christ-church*, and frequently present in the Quire. While this controversie was on foot between the Bishops and the Clergy, *John Rogers* (one of the Prebends of S. *Paul's*, and Divinity Reader of that Church then newly return'd from beyond the Seas) could never be perswaded to wear any other than the round cap when he went abroad. And being further pressed unto it, he thus declared himself: That he would never agree to that point of Conformity, but on this condition, that if the Bishops did require the Cap and Tippet, &c. then it should also be declared, that all Popish Priests (for a distinction between them and others) should be constrained to wear upon their sleeves a Chalice with an Host upon it. Nay, such peccancy of humour began then to break out, that it was Preached at *Pauls* Cross by one *Steven*, Curate of *Katherine Cree-Church*, That it was fit the names of Churches should be altered, and the names of the dayes in the Week changed; that Fish-dayes should be altered, and the Lent kept at any other time, except onely between *Shrovetide* and *Easter*. *John Stow* saith, that he had seen the said *Steven* to leave the Pulpit, and Preach to the People out of an high Elm, which stood in the midst of the Church-yard, and that being done, to return into the Church again. *Stow's* Chro. Edw. VI.

The wings of Episcopal Authority had been so clipped, that it was scarce able to fly abroad: the sentence of Excommunication had not been in use since the first year of this King; which occasioned not onely these disorders among the Ministers of the Church but also tended to the great encrease of vitiousness in all sorts of men. So that it was not without cause that it was called for so earnestly by Bishop *Latimer* in a Sermon Preached before the King. Bring into the Church of *England* (saith he) the open Discipline of Excommunication, that open sinners may be stricken withal.

Then upon the Complaint of *Calvin* to Archbishop *Cranmer*, and *Peter Martyr's* bemoaning the miserable condition of the Church for want of Preachers, it was ordained by the advice of the Lords of the Council, that of the King's six Chaplains, which attended in Ordinary, two of them should be always about the Court, and the other four should travel in Preaching abroad. About this time Sermons at Court were encreased also.

Then followed the taking down of Altars by publick Authority. This being resolved on, a Letter cometh to Bishop *Ridley* in the name

Z 2 of

of the King, subscribed by *Sommerset*, and other of the Lords of the Council, concerning the taking down of Altars, and setting up Tables in the stead thereof. He appointed the form of a right Table to be used in his Diocess, and caused the wall standing on the back-side of the Altar in the Church of *S. Paul's* to be broken down for an example to the rest. No universal change of Altars was there into Tables in all parts of the Realm, till the repealing of the first Liturgy, in which the Priest is appointed to stand before the midst of the Altar in the Celebration; and the establishing of the second, (in which it is required, that the Priest shall stand on the North-side of the Table) had put an end to the Dispute.

About this time *David's* Psalms were Translated into *English* metre, by *Thomas Sternhold*, Esq; and of the Privy Chamber to King *Edward* the sixth, *John Hopkins*, *Robert Wisdon*, &c. and generally permitted to be Sung in all Churches.

Bishop *Gardiner* having been a Prisoner in the Tower almost two years, the Lord Treasurer, the Earl of *Warwick*, and some others are sent with certain Articles Signed by the King and Lords of the Council unto him. According to the tenour hereof; he is not only to testifie his consent to the establishing the Holy-dayes and Fasting-days by the King's Authority, the allowance of the publick Liturgy, and the abrogating of the Statute for the six Articles, but to subscribe the confession of his fault in his former obstinacy, after such form and manner as was there required. To which Articles he subscribed, but refused to put his hand to the said Confession.

Then a Book of Articles is drawn up, containing all the alteration made by the King and his Father, as well by Act of Parliament as their own injunctions, of all which doings he is required to signifie his approbation; to make Confession of his fault with an acknowledgment that he had deserved the punishment which was laid upon upon him: but no such submission and acknowledgment being made as was required, on *Feb.* 14, 1550, he was deprived, and so remitted to the Tower.

Notwithstanding this severity, yet some of the Bishops were so stiff in their old opinions, that neither terrour nor perswasions could prevail upon them, either to approve of the King's proceedings, or otherwise to advance the King's commands. And some complyed so coldly with the King's commands, as that they were laid open to the spoil, though not to the loss of their Bishopricks: of which last sort were *Kitching* Bishop of *Landaff*, *Salcot* Bishop of *Salisbury*, and *Sampson* of *Coventry* and *Lichfield*; *Heath* of *Worcester*, *Voysie* of *Exeter*, *Day* of *Chichester*, and *Tonstal* of *Durham* would not any way comply. *Voisy* made such havock of his Lands, before he was brought under a deprivation, that he left but seven or eight of the worst mannours, and those let out into long Leases and those charged with pensions, and not above

two

Heylin.Hist.
Edw. VI.

The Church of Great Britain. 173

two houses, both bare and naked. He was deprived a few moneths after *Gardiner*, but lived to be restored again (as *Gardiner* also was) in the time of Queen *Mary*. *Day* and *Heath* were both deprived, *October* 10. and were both restored in Queen *Maries* Reign. *Tunstal* was cast into the Tower, *December* 20. and was there kept until the dissolution of his Bishoprick by Act of Parliament.

To *Gardiner*, in the See of *Winchester*, succeeded Doctor *John Poynet*, Bishop of *Rochester*. To *Voisy*, in the See of *Exeter*, succeeded Doctor *Miles Coverdale*, one who had formerly assisted *Tyndal* in translating the Bible into English, and for the most part lived at *Tubing*, an University belonging to the Duke of *Saxony*, where he received the degree of Doctor. *Scory* being Consecrated Bishop of *Rochester*, in the place of *Poynet*, on the thirtieth of *August*, in the next year following, succeeded *Day* of *Chichester*. Of which Bishoprick he was deprived in the time of Queen *Mary*, and afterwards preferred by Queen *Elizabeth* to the See of *Hereford*, in which place he died. The Bishoprick of *Worcester* was given in *Commendam* to Bishop *Hooper*.

The Princess *Mary*, having been bred up in the Romish Religion, would not change her mind. And although the King and the Lords of his Council, wrote many Letters to her, to take off those affections which she bear to the Church of *Rome*, yet she keeps up her Mass, with all the Rites and Ceremonies belonging to it, and suffers divers persons (besides her own domestick Servants) to be present at it. By the Emperor's mediation, her Chaplains were permitted to celebrate the Mass, but with this Restriction, that they should do it in her presence only. For the transgression of which bounds, *Mallet* and *Barkley*, her two Chaplains were imprisoned.

Then a Plot is laid to convey the Princess *Mary* out of the Realm by stealth ; but the King being secretly advertised of the design, puts a stop thereunto. She is brought to the King, and appointed to remain with him, but none of her Chaplains permitted to have any access unto her.

And notwithstanding the mediation of the Emperor in her behalf, and his threatening War, in case she were not permitted the free exercise of her Religion, and although the Lords of the Council generally seemed very inclinable thereunto, yet the King would not be perswaded thereunto. And when the Archbishop of *Canterbury*, and the Bishop of *London*, sent by the Lords to the King, used divers Arguments to perswade him, he declared a Resolution rather to venture life, and all things else that were dear unto him, than to give way to any thing, which he knew to be against the Truth. Then the King burst forth into a flood of tears, and the Bishops, on sight thereof, wept as fast as He.

The Bishops thereupon withdrew, admiring at such great Abilities in so young a King, and blessed God for giving them a Prince of such eminent piety.

Then

Then the reviewing the Liturgy, and the compoſing of a Book of Articles, were brought under conſideration: This laſt for the avoiding diverſities of Opinions, and for the eſtabliſhing conſent touching true Religion, the other for removing ſuch offences as had been taken by *Calvin*, and his followers, at ſome parts thereof. The Liturgy, ſo reviewed, was ratified by Act of Parliament in the year following. By the learned Writings of *Eraſmus* and *Melancthon*, together with the *Auguſtan* Confeſſion (a Book of Articles being thought neceſſary to be compoſed) the Compoſers of thoſe Articles were much directed, uſing them as ſubſervient Helps to promote the ſervice.

Now followed the fatal Tragedy of the Duke of *Sommerſet*, and we muſt recoyl a little to fetch forward the cauſe thereof. *Thomas Seymour*, Baron of *Sudely*, and Lord Admiral, the Protector's younger Brother, had married the Lady *Katherine Par*, the Relict of King *Henry* the Eighth. A conteſt aroſe between their Wives about place. The Women's diſcords derived themſelves into their Husbands hearts: whereupon, not long after, followed the death of the Lord *Thomas Seymour*, arraigned for deſigning to tranſlate the Crown to himſelf.

Soon after the Lords of the Council accuſe the Protector of many high offences; his greateſt Enemy and Accuſer was *John Dudley*, Earl of *Warwick*. Hereupon he was impriſoned at *Windſor*, yet he was acquitted, though outed his Protectorſhip, reſtored, and continued Privy Counſellor. But after two years and two months his Enemies aſſault him afreſh. He was indicted of Treaſon and Felony: he was condemned for Felony, by a new made Statute, for plotting the death of a Privy Counſellor, namely, the Earl of *Warwick*. Here a ſtrange overſight was committed, that he craved not the benefit of the Clergy, which could not legally be denied him. Not long after he was beheaded on Tower-hill, with no leſs praiſe for his piety and patience, than pity and grief of the beholders.

In the beginning of the year 1551. happened a terrible Earthquake at *Croydon*, and ſome other Villages thereabouts, in the County of *Surrey*. Afterwards ſix Dolphins were taken up in the *Thames*, three at *Queenborough*, and three near *Greenwich*, the leaſt as big as any Horſe. Their coming up ſo far, beheld by Stateſ-men, as a preſage of thoſe ſtorms and Tempeſts, which afterwards befel this Nation in the death of King *Edward*, and the tempeſtuous Reign of Queen *Mary*. But the ſaddeſt preſage of all was, the breaking out of a Diſeaſe, called the Sweating-ſickneſs, appearing firſt at *Shrewsbury*, on *April* 15. and afterwards ſpreading by degrees over the Kingdom; wherewith, if any man were attacqued, he died, or eſcaped, within nine or ten hours: if he ſlept (as moſt perſons deſired to do) he died within ſix hours: if he took cold, he died within three hours.

Sir

Sir *Michael Stanhop*, Sir *Thomas Arundel*, Sir *Ralph Vane*, and Sir *Miles Partridge*, were arraigned, and condemned to dye. The two first were beheaded, and the two last hanged, at what time they solemnly protested, (taking God to witness) that they never practised Treason against the King, &c. *Vane* adding, after all the rest, that his Blood would make the pillow of the Earl of *Warwick* (lately made Duke of *Northumberland*) uneasie to him.

Then fifty six Articles are drawn up against *Robert Farrars*, Bishop of St. *Davids*, and a Commission issued *March* 9. to enquire into the merit of those Articles charged against him: on the return whereof he is indicted of a *Præmunire* at the Assizes at *Carmarthen*, committed thereupon to prison, where he remained all the rest of King *Edward*'s time; never restored to liberty till he came to the Stake in Queen *Maries* Reign.

On the twenty ninth of *January*, 1552. The Bishoprick of *Westminster* was dissolved by the King's Letters Patents, by which the County of *Middlesex*, which had before been laid unto it, was restored unto the See of *London*.

The Book of Articles made in the Synod at *London*, may be truly said to be the work of that Convocation, though many Members of it never saw the same till the Book was published: in regard (as Mr. *Philpot* saith) *that they had a Synodical Authority, to make such spiritual Laws, as to them seemed to be necessary or convenient, for the use of the Church.* Moreover the Church of *England*, for the first five years of Queen *Elizabeth*, retained these Articles and no other, as the publick Tenents of the Church in point of Doctrine; which she had not done, had they been commended to her by a less Authority than a Convocation. These Articles were confirmed and published for such, by the King's Authority, as appears further by the Title in due form of Law. And so it is resolved by *Philpot*, in behalf of the Catechism which came out, *Anno* 1553. with the approbation of the said Bishops and learned Men. *Fox* Acts and Monuments. *fol.* 1282. *Regiâ authoritate in lucem editi.*

The Liturgy being setled and confirmed in Parliament, was by the King's command translated into French, for the use of the Isles of *Guernsey* and *Jersey*, and such as lived within the Marches and command of *Calais*. But no such care was taken for *Wales*, till the fifth year of the Reign of Queen *Elizabeth*, nor of the Realm of *Ireland* from that time to this, as Doctor *Heylin* observeth.

Then that which concerns as well the nature, as the number of such Feasts and Fasts, as were thought fit to be retained, were determined and concluded on by an Act of Parliament. Which Statute (though repealed in the first of Queen *Mary*, and not revived till the first year of the Reign of King *James*, yet) in effect it stood in force, and was more punctually observed in the time of Queen *Elizabeth*'s Reign, than after the reviving of it.

Tho

The next care was, that Confecrated places fhould not be profaned by fighting and quarrelling, as they had been lately fince the Epifcopal Jurifdiction, and the ancient Cenfures of the Church were leffened in Authority and reputation.

This Parliament ending on *April* 15. the Book of Common-prayer was printed and publifhed, which had been therein authorized. And the time being come which was fet for the officiating it, there appeared much alteration in the outward folemnities of Divine fervice, to which the people had formerly been fo long accuftomed. For by the Rubrick of that Book, no Copes, or other Veftures were required, but the Surplice only, whereby the Bifhops muft forbear their Croffes, and the Prebends of St. *Paul*'s leave off their Hoods. To give a beginning hereunto, Bifhop *Ridley*, then Bifhop of *London*, did the fame day officiate the Divine fervice of the Morning in his Rochet only, without Cope or Veftment: he preached alfo at St. *Paul's* in the afternoon, the Lord Mayor, Aldermen, and Companies in their beft Liveries in their Companies being prefent at it, the Sermon tending (for the moft part) to the fetting forth the faid Book of Common-prayer, and to acquaint them with the Reafons of fuch alterations as were made therein. On the fame day the new Liturgy was executed alfo in all the Churches of *London*. Not long after, the upper Quire in St. *Paul*'s Church, where the high Altar ftood was broken down, and all the Quire thereabout, and the Communion-table was placed in the lower part of the Quire, where the Minifter fang the daily Service.

Then publick care was had for the founding and eftablifhing of the new Hofpital in the late diffolved Houfe of *Gray-Friers* near *Newgate* in *London*, and that of St. *Thomas* in the Borough of *Southwark*: of which ye are to know, that the Church belonging to the faid Houfe, together with the Cloyfters, and almoft all the publick building which ftood within the liberties and precincts thereof, had the good hap to efcape that ruine, which generally befell all other Houfes of that nature. And ftanding undemolifhed till the laft times of King *Henry*, it was given by him, not many dayes before his death, to the City of *London*, together with the late diffolved Priory, called *Little St. Bartholomews*. In which Donation there was reference had to a double end: The one for the relieving the poor out of the Rents of fuch Meffuages and Tenements, as in the Grants thereof are contained and fpecified. The other for conftituting a Parifh-church in the Church of the faid diffolved *Grey-friers*, not only for the ufe of fuch as lived within the precincts of the faid two Houfes, but for the Inhabitants of the Parifh of St. *Nicholas* in the Shambles, and of St. *Edwin's*, fituate in *Warwick-lane*, near *Newgate-market*. Which Churches, with all the Rents and profits belonging to them, were given to the City at the fame time alfo, and for advancing the fame ends, together with five hundred Marks *per annum* for ever: The Church of

the

the Gray-friers to be from thence-forth called *Christ-church*, founded by King *Henry* the Eight. All which was signified to the City, in a Sermon Preached at *Paul's* Cross, by the Bishop of *Rochester*, on *January* 13. being but a fortnight before his death: Mass was said in this Church by the Parishioners that resorted to it according to the King's donation. After which (in the first year of King *Edward*) followed the taking down of the said two Churches, and building several Tenements on the ground of the Churches and Church-yards, the Rent whereof to be employed about the further maintenance and relief of the Poor, Living and Loytering, in and about the City.

But these things being not sufficient to carry on the work to the end desired, it hapned that Bishop *Ridley*, Preaching before King *Edward*, insisted much upon some constant course for relief of the poor: which Sermon wrought so far upon him, that having sent for the Bishop, he gave him great thanks for his good Exhortation, whose advice was, that Letters should be written to the Lord Mayor and Aldermen. By whom it was agreed, that a general contribution should be made by all rich and well-affected Citizens, toward the advancement of a work so necessary for the publick good. Every man subscribed according to his ability, and Books were drawn in every ward of the City, containing the sum of that Relief which they had contributed: Which being delivered to Sir *Richard Dobbs*, Lord Mayor of *London*, were by him tendred to the King's Commissioners, *February* 17. The buildings in the Gray-friers were forthwith repaired: The like reparation was also made of the ruinous buildings belonging to the late dissolved Priory of St. *Thomas* in *Southwark*, which the Citizens had then newly bought of the King, to serve for an Hospital for such Sick, Wounded, and Impotent persons, as were not fit to be intermingled with the sound: on *November* 23. the Sick and Maimed people were taken into the Hospital of St. *Thomas*; and into *Christ-church* Hospital, to the number of four hundred Children; all of them to have Meat, Drink, Lodging and Clothes, at the charge of the City; till other means could be provided for their maintenance.

On *April* 10. this King gave for ever to the City his Palace of *Bridewel* (erected by King *Henry* the Eighth) to be employed for such Vagabonds and thriftless poor, as should be sent thither to receive chastisement, and be forced to labour. He caused the Master and-Brethren of the Hospital in the *Savoy*, founded by King *Henry* the Seventh, to resign the same into his hands, with all the Lands and Goods thereunto belonging: out of which he presently bestowed the yearly rent of seven hundred Marks, with all the Beds, Bedding, and other Furniture found therein toward the maintenance of the said Work-house, and the Hospital of St. *Thomas* in *Southwark*; The Grant whereof he confirmed by his Letters Patents, adding thereunto a Mortmain for enabling the City to

A a purchase

purchase Lands to the value of four thousand Marks *per annum*, for the better maintenance of those and the other Hospitals. Thus he was entitled to the Foundation of *Bridewel*, St. *Bartholomews*, and St. *Thomas*, without any charge to himself.

Nothing else memorable about this time, but the coming of *Cardan*, the death of *Leland*, and the preferment of Doctor *John Tailor* to the See of *Lincoln*.

Then for raising Money, a Commission was speeded into all parts of the Kingdom, under pretence of selling such of the Lands and Goods of Chanteries as remained unsould, but in plain truth (saith Dr. *Heylin*) to seize upon all Hangings, Altar-clothes, Fronts, Parafronts, Copes of all sorts, with all manner of Plate, which was to be found in any Cathedral or Parochial Church. Certain Instructions were likewise given to the Commissioners, by which they were to regulate themselves in their proceedings. This was done generally in all parts of the Realm, into which the Commissioners began their Circuits in the moneth of *April*; which general seizure being made, they were to leave one Chalice, with certain Table-clothes for the use of the Communion-table, as the said Commissioners should think fit; the Jewels, Plate, and ready Money, to be delivered to the Master of the King's Jewels, in the Tower of *London*; the Copes of cloth of Gold, and Tissue to be brought into the King's Wardrobe; the rest to be turned into ready Money, and that Money to be paid to Sir *William Peckham* the King's Cofferer, for the defraying the charges of his Majestie's houshold.

But some there were, who were as much before hand with the Kings Commissioners in embezeling the Plate, Jewels, and other Furnitures, as the Commissioners did intend to be with the King, in keeping all or most part to themselves.

The King grew Sick, and weak in Body, in which Estate Duke *Dudley* so prevailed upon him, that he consented to a transposition of the Crown, from his natural Sisters, to the Children of the Dutchess of *Suffolk*.

His dying Prayer, as is was taken from his mouth, was in these words following.

Lord God, deliver me out of the miseries of this wretched and sinful life, and take me among thy chosen. Howbeit, not my will, but thy will be done, Lord, I commit my Spirit to Thee. O Lord, thou knowest, how happy it were for me to be with Thee; yet for thy chosens sake send me life and health, that I may truly serve Thee. O my Lord God, bless thy people, and save thine inheritance. O Lord God, save thy chosen people of England. *O my Lord God, defend this Realm from Papistry, and maintain thy true Religion, that I*

and

and my people may truly praise thy Name for Jesus Christ his sake.

Thus endeth the Reign of that good King *Edward* the Sixth, sufficiently remarkable for the progress of Reformation, but so distracted unto Sides and Factions, that in the end the King himself became a prey to the strongest party, which (saith Dr. *Heylin*) could not otherwise be safe but in his destruction, contrived on purpose (as it was generally supposed) to smooth the way to the advancement of the Lady *Jane Gray* (newly married to *Guilford Dudley*, fourth Son to Duke *Dudley*) to the Royal Throne.

King *Edward* being dead, the Princess *Mary* hearing of her Brothers death, and knowing her own right, writeth to the Lords of the Council, and challengeth them for their doing, making her claim to the Crown. To whom the Council writeth again, as to a Subject, requiring her to rest so contented: The Lady *Jane* was on the same day that these Letters were dispatched, brought by Water to the Tower, attended by a Noble Train of both Sexes, from *Durham-house* in the *Strand*, where she had been entertained, as part of *Dudley's* Family, ever since her Marriage : When she came into the presence of the two Dukes, her Father and Father in Law, it was signified to Her by the Duke of *Northumberland*, that the King was dead, and that he had declared her for his next Successor in the Crown. After a pithy speech, the poor Lady found her self in a great perplexity. But being wearied at last with their importunities, and overcome by the entreaties of her Husband whom she dearly loved, she submitted unto that necessity which she could not vanquish.

Hereupon the two Dukes, with all the rest of the Lords of the Council, swore Allegiance to her. And on the same day about five a Clock in the afternoon, they solemnly caused her to be Proclaimed Queen of *England, France* and *Ireland*, &c. in many of the principal Streets of *London*; and after by degrees, in most of the chief Cities, Towns, and places of greatest concourse. In which Proclamation it was signified, *That by the Letters Patents of the late King* Edward, *the Lady* Jane Gray, *eldest Daughter to the Dutchess of* Suffolk, *had been declared, to be his true and lawful Successor to the Crown of* England, *the same to be enjoyed after her decease by the heirs of her Body*, &c. Which Proclamation, though it was published in the City with all due solemnities, and that the concourse of the people was great, yet their acclamations were few.

The next day the Lords were advertised, that many persons of quality were drawn together at *Kenning-hall* Castle in *Norfolk*, to offer their service and assistance to the Princess *Mary*; as the Earl of *Bath*, Sir Tho-

was Wharton, Son of the Lord *Wharton*, Sir *John Mordant*, Son of the Lord *Mordant*, Sir *William Drury*, Sir *John Shelton*, Sir *Henry Beddingfield*, Sir *Henry Jerningham*, Sir *John Sulierd*, Mr. *Richard Higham* of *Lincolns-Inne*. It was advertised also, that the Earl of *Sussex*, and his Son, were coming towards her with their Forces. Therefore they perswade Duke *Dudley* to take the conduct of some Forces, that might scatter those small companies before they grew unto an Head. Swelled with vain-glory, he suffered himself to be entreated to an action of such fame and merit, as that which they presented to him. So the Duke with the Marquess of *Northampton*, the Lord *Gray*, and divers others of note, on *July* 14. 1553. set forward with eighth thousand Foot, and two thousand Horse. The Duke's March was slow. In the mean time, *Edward Hastings*, the Earl of *Huntingdon's* Brother, having an Army of four thousand Foot, committed to him by the Duke of *Northumberland*, left his party, and went to the Lady *Mary*. And six great Ships which lay before *Yarmouth* to intercept her, if she should attempt to fly, now at the perswasion of Mr *Jerningham*, came to her aid. Upon news hereof, the Lords themselves assembled at *Baynards* Castle: first the Earl of *Arundel*, then the Earl of *Pembrook*, fell to Invectives against *Northumberland*, and then all the Lords consenting with them, they called for the Lord Mayor, and in *London* Proclaimed the Lady *Mary* Queen. She was also Proclaimed by divers other Lords and Knights in divers other Counties; which the Duke (being then at *Bury*) hearing of, he returneth to *Cambridge*, and there himself Proclaimeth the Lady *Mary* Queen: but the next morning he was arrested by *Henry Fitz-Alan*, Earl of *Arundel*, by Order from Queen *Mary*.

Together with the Duke, his three Sons, *John*, *Ambrose*, and *Henry*, the Earl of *Huntingdon*, Sir *Andrew Dudley*, the two *Gates*, Sir *Thomas Palmer*, and Doctor *Sands*, were committed to the Tower: and the next day the Marquess of *Northampton*, the Lord *Robert Dudley*, and Sir *Robert Corbet*. Before which time, the Duke of *Suffolk*, entring his Daughter the Lady *Jane's* Chamber, told her, she must now put off her Royal robes, which she willingly did.

Doctor *Nicholas Ridley*, Bishop of *London*, was also sent to the Tower, on *July* 27. Sir *Roger Cholmley*, Chief Justice of the King's Bench; and Sir *Edward Mountague*, Chief Justice of the Common-Pleas; the Duke of *Suffolk*, were sent also to the Tower; Sir *John Cheek*, on the morrow after, bringing up the Reer: But the Duke of *Suffolk* (Father to the Lady *Jane*), was released within three days after.

The Duke of *Northumberland*, together with *John* Earl of *Warwick*, his eldest Son, and *William*, Marquess of *Northampton*, were brought to their Trial, on *August* 8. before *Thomas* Duke of *Norfolk*, then sitting as Lord High Steward in *Westminster* Hall: they all confessed the Indictment.

Indictment, and received Judgment in the ufual form. The like Judgement paffed on the morrow after, on Sir *John Gates*, Sir *Henry Gates*, Sir *Andrew Dudley*, and Sir *Thomas Palmer*. The Duke was on *Auguſt* 22. beheaded, and profeſſed himſelf a Papiſt at his death, whoſe Recantation the Papiſts publiſhed abroad with great rejoycing, with him died alſo Sir *John Gates*, and Sir *Thomas Palmer*: which *Palmer* confeſſed the Faith he learned in the Goſpel, and lamented that he had not lived more as became the Goſpel.

The Queen had diſſolved her Camp at *Farmingham*, confiſting of fourteen thouſand men, and prepared for her journey toward *London*. Being met on the way by the Princeſs *Elizabeth*, her Siſter, attended with a thouſand Horſe, ſhe entred *London* on the third of *Auguſt*. Taking poſſeſſion of the Tower, ſhe was firſt welcommed thither by. *Thomas*, the old Duke of *Norfolk*, *Anne* Dutcheſs of *Sommerſet*, Edward Lord *Courtney*, eldeſt Son to the late Marqueſs of *Exceter*, and Dr. *Stephen Gardiner*, Biſhop of *Wincheſter*, all which ſhe lifted from the ground, called them her Priſoners, gratiouſly kiſſing them, and reſtoring them ſhortly after to their former liberty. Taking the Great Seal from Dr. *Goodrick*, Biſhop of *Ely*, within two days after ſhe gave it for the preſent to Sir *Nicholas Hare*, whom ſhe made Maſter of the Rolls, and afterwards committed it together with the Title of Lord Chancellor to the ſaid Biſhop of *Wincheſter*, then actually reſtored to that See.

Having performed the obſequies of her Brother, on the ninth and tenth, ſhe removes her Court to *Whitehal*; on *September* ſhe paſſeth thence to the Tower by Water, attended by her Siſter, and a great Train of Noble Ladies, and made her return through the principal Streets of the ſame City, on the laſt of the ſame moneth, in a moſt ſtately manner: and the next day proceeded in like pomp to the Abbey-Church at *Weſtminſter*, where ſhe was met by the Silver Croſſes, and eighty Singing-men, all in rich Coaps (ſo ſudden a recruit was made of theſe ſacred Veſtments) among whom went the new Dean of *Weſtminſter*, Dr. *Weſton*, and diverſe Chaplains of her own, each of them bearing in their handſome enſign or other. After them marched ten Biſhops (which were all as remained of her perſwaſion) with their Miters, rich Coaps, and Croſier-ſtaves. The Sermon was preached by Doctor *Day*, whom ſhe had reſtored to the See of *Chicheſter*. The ſolemnity of the Coronation was performed by the Biſhop of *Wincheſter*, the new Lord Chancellor. *Cranmer*, Archbiſhop of *Canterbury*, being then committed to the Tower. Till this time none was more dear to her than her Siſter, the Lady *Elizabeth*, but after her Coronation ſhe eſtranged her ſelf from her.

Dr. *P. Heylins* Hiſtory of Queen *Mary*.

She preferred *Henry Ratcliff*, Earl of *Suſſex*, to the ſociety of the Garter, which honour ſhe conferred on his Son *Thomas* after his deceaſe;

and

and to be covered in her presence at all times and places, according to the custom of the Grandees in the Realm of *Spain*. She also advanced the Earl of *Arundel*, to the Office of Lord Steward. She made Sir *Edward Hastings* Master of the Horse, and Knight of the Garter, and afterwards Lord Chamberlain of the Houshold, and Lord *Hastings* of *Loughborough*. She honoured Sir *John Williams*, with the Title of Lord *Williams* of *Thame*. She preferred Sir *Henry Jerningham*, to be Captain of her Guard: and afterwards Sir *Thomas Tresham* was created Lord Prior of the Order of St. *John* of *Jerusalem*. She preferred her old Servants, *Hopton*, her old Chaplain, to the See of *Norwich*, *Rochester*, to be Comptroller of her Houshold, *Inglefield* to be Master of the Wards, and *Walgrave* to be Master of the Wardrobe.

Sir *John Gage* (a zealous Papist) was made Lord Chamberlain of her Houshold, when she came first to the Tower. Bishop *Bonner* was discharged of the Marshalsey, and Bishop *Tunstal* from the King's Bench, within two days after. *Bonner* is restored to his See of *London*, and *Tunstal* to *Durham*; and an Act of Parliament procured for the restoring of the Church of *Durham* to all its Lands, and Jurisdictions, of which it stood divested by the late Act of Dissolution, made in the last year of the deceased King.

Coverdale was displaced from the See of *Exeter*, *Scory* from that of *Chichester*, and *Hooper* from the Commendatory of the See of *Worcester*: to which Sees *Voisy*, *Day*, and *Heath*, were again restored. The like course also followed for the depriving of all Deans, Dignitaries, and Parochial Ministers, who had succeeded into any of those preferments, during the Reign of the two last Kings.

Doctor *Cox* was on *August* 5. brought to the Marshalsey, and spoiled of his Deaneries of *Christ-church* and *Westminster*, to make room for Doctor *Richard Marshal* in the one, and Doctor *Hugh Weston* in the other.

Peter Martyr coming from *Oxford* to *London*, where for a time he was commanded to keep his House, but was soon after suffered to return into his own Countrey.

A Letter was sent at the same time to the Mayor of *Coventry*, to set at liberty *Hugh Simons*, if he would recant his Sermon, or else to stay him.

A little before Mr. *Bradford*, Mr. *Vernon*, and Mr. *Beacon*, Preachers, were committed to the Tower: A Letter was sent to the Sheriffs of *Buckingham* and *Bedford*, for the apprehending Mr. *Fisher*, Parson of *Amersham*: Another Letter was sent to the Bishop of *Norwich*, not to suffer any to Preach or Expound openly the Scriptures, without special Licence from the Queen. Mr. *John Rogers*, Preacher, was confined to his own house.

Hooper

the Church of Great Britain.

Hooper and *Coverdale* being cited to appear before the Lords of the Council, did appear. *Hooper* was committed to the Fleet, and *Coverdale* commanded to attend the pleasure of the Lords.

Fisher of *Amersham*, and *Hugh Sanders*, Vicar of St. *Michaels* in *Coventry*, appeared also before the Council.

Hugh Latimer appeared also, and was committed to the Tower.

Doctor *Bourn*, Archdeacon of *London*, Preaching at *Pauls* Cross, in favour of Bishop *Bonner* (there present at the Sermon) inveighed against some proceedings in the time of the late King *Edward*, : which so incensed the people, that a great tumult arose upon it, some pelting with Stones; others crying aloud, *Pull him down*; and one (who could never be known) flinging a Dagger at his Head, which after was found sticking in a post of the Pulpit. The Preacher with difficulty was secured in a School adjoyning : By reason of which tumult the Lords of the Council with the Lord Mayor and Aldermen, took order, that every Housholder should cause their Children and Apprentices to keep their own Parish-churches upon Holidays : order was taken for preventing the like Tumult on the Sunday following. A Sermon was Preached at the Cross by Doctor *Watson*, who (afterwards was Bishop of *Lincoln*) : for whose security many Lords of the Council were there present, and *Jerningham*, Captain of the Guard with two hundred of his Yeomen, standing round about the Pulpit with their Halberts.

Then care was taken, that nothing should be Preached in private Churches, contrary to the Doctrine which was, and should be Taught at the Cross, by them which were appointed to it. It was further ordered, that every Alderman in his Ward should send for the Curates of every Church within their Liberties, and warn them not onely to forbear Preaching themselves, but also not to suffer any other to Preach, or make any open reading of Scripture in their Churches, unless the said Preachers were severally Licensed by the Queen.

For eight weeks after the Proclaiming of *Mary* Queen, Protestantism and Popery were together set on foot, the former hoping to be continued, the latter labouring to be restored. Seeing by the fidelity of the *Norfolk* and *Suffolk* Protestant Gentry, the Queen was much advantaged for the speedy recovering of her *Right*, they conceived, that as she by them had regained the Crown, so they under her should enjoy their Consciences. The Papists put their Ceremonies in execution, presuming on the Queens private practice, and publick countenance.

The Queen on *August* 18. puts forth a Proclamation, declaring her self for the Popish Religion, which she resolves to observe for her self, wishing her Subjects to follow her example; yet that she mindeth not to compel any thereunto, until such time as further order by common Assent may be taken therein : forbidding all her Subjects to move Seditions

ons at their perils; and the Printing of any Book, Rhyme, Enterlude, or Treatife, without her fpecial Licenfe for the fame: and likewife to Preach, or by way of reading in Churches, or other publick or private places (except in Schools of the Univerfities) to Interpret or Teach any Scripture, or any points of Doctrine concerning Religion.

Hereupon many of the people in divers places, received their old Religion; erected again their Altars, and ufed the Mafs, and Latin Service, as was wont to be in King *Henrie*'s time.

In *Cambridge* the Vice-chancellor chalenged one *Peirfon*, on *Octob*. 3. for officiating the Communion, in his own Parifh Church, in the Englifh Tongue: and on the 26. difplaced Doctor *Madew*, Mafter of *Clareball*, for being Married. In like manner, fome of the Popifh party in King's Colledge, on the 28th of the fame moneth, officiated the Divine Service in the Latin Tongue.

At *Oxford*, *John Jewel* was chofen to pen the firft gratulatory Letter to the Queen, in the name of the Univerfity, an Office impofed on him by his Enemies. Doctor *Trefham*, a Van-currier, before authority, repaired the great Bell in *Chrift-church* and named it *Mary*.

Harley, Bifhop of *Hereford*, and *Taylor* of *Lincoln* (two of the laft of King *Edward*'s Bifhops) were prefent at the opening of the Parliament, *Octob*. 10. But no fooner was the Mafs begun (though not then reftored by any Law) than they left the Church. For which the Bifhop of *Lincoln*, being firft examined, and making profeffion of his Faith, prevented the malice of his enemies by a timely Death. And *Harley* (upon information of his Marriage) was prefently excluded from the Parliament-houfe, and not long after from his Bifhoprick alfo.

Hereupon Bifhop *Barlow* of *Wells*, and *Scory* of *Chichefter*, paffed beyond the Seas, followed not long after by Bifhop *Poinet* of *Winchefter*.

On *November* 3. Archbifhop *Cranmer* was arraigned at the *Guildhall* in *London*, with the Lord *Guilford Dudley*, the late Queen *Jane*, his Wife, and others, all of them being attainted and condemned of Treafon.

After *Peter Martyr* had quit the Realm, his Wive's Body having been buried in the Church of St. *Fridefwid*, was afterward by publick order taken out of the Grave, and buried in a common dunghill.

John a Lafco, was forced to diffolve his Congregation, and He with his Strangers to quit the Countrey: The like haft made the French Proteftants alfo. At which time many of the Englifh (as well Students as others) departed alfo. The principal of thofe were *Katherine*,

the

the last Wife of *Charles Brandon*, Duke of *Suffolk*, Robert Berty Esq; Husband to the Dutchess, the Bishops of *Winchester* and *Wells* (as before was said) Sir *Richard Morison*, Sir *Anthany Cook*, and Sir *John Cheek*, Doctor *Cox*, Doctor *Sands*, and Doctor *Grindal*.

The News of Queen *Maries* succeeding her Brother to the Crown of *England*, posted to *Rome*, and was very welcome to Pope *Julius* the Third, because it gave him some assurance of his re-admission into the Power and Jurisdiction of his Predecessors in the Realm of *England*; in pursuance of which hopes, it was resolved, that Cardinal *Pool* should be sent Legate into *England*, who being of the Blood-royl, and a man of eminent Learning and of exemplary life, was looked on as the fittest Instrument to reduce that Kingdom.

The Parliaments first Act was to take away all Statutes passed by the two last Kings, wherein certain Offences had been made High Treason; and others brought within the compass of a *Præmunire*. This was done especially for *Pool*'s security; that neither He by exercising his authority, nor the Clergy by submitting to it, might be entangled in the like snare, as Cardinal *Wolsey*, and the whole Clergy of his time had before been caught.

Then an Act was passed for repealing certain Statutes of King *Edward*: thereby they took away all former Statutes for administring the Sacraments in both kinds, for establishing the first and second Liturgy, &c. In a word! by this one blow the Queen cut down all that had been done in the Reformation in seven years before. And then for want of Canonical Ordination on the one side, and under colour of Uncanonical Marriages on the other, there was presently such a remove among the Bishops and Clergy, as it is not any where to be paralelled in so short a time.

An Act was passed likewise, Entitled, *An Act against offenders of Preachers*, &c which two Acts were seconded by the Queen, with two Proclamations, *December* 5. By one of which it was declared, that all Statutes made in the time of the late King *Edward*, which concerned Religion, were repealed by Parliament: and therefore that the Mass should be said as formerly, to begin on the twentieth of that moneth. And by the other it was commanded, that no person should dare from thenceforth to disturb any Priests in saying Mass, or executing any other Divine Office. Accordingly the Mass was publickly officiated in all parts of the Kingdom, and so continued during the Reign of the Queen without interruption.

Another Act was passed, wherein it was Enacted, *That the Marriage between King Henry the Eighth, and Queen Katherine, his first Wife, was lawful, and to stand with God's Laws, and his Holy Word*, &c. That the Decree of Divorce heretofore passed between the said King Henry, and the said Queen, by Thomas Cranmer, Archbishop of Canterbury, should be reputed to be void and null, with a Repeal of all such Statutes, wherein the Queen had been declared to be Illegitimate.

There also past another Act, in which there was a clause for the invalidating of all such Commissions as had been granted in the time of the late Queen *Jane*, and one in confirming the Attainders of the late Duke of *Northumberland*; *Thomas* Archbishop of *Canterbury*, &c.

Together with this Parliament the Queen summoned a Convocation, that all matters of Religion might first be debated and concluded in a Synodical way, before they were offered to the Parliament. In the Writs of which Summons, she retained the Title of *Supreme Head on Earth of the Church of England*, &c. the want whereof in those of the present Parliament occasioned dispute among some of the Members; Whether they might lawfully proceed, or not, in such publick business as were to be propounded to them in that Session. The Presidentship of the Convocation was transferred upon Bishop *Bonner*, priviledged in respect of his See to preside in all such Provincial Synods, which were either held during the vacancy of the See of *Canterbury*, or in the necessary absence of the Metropolitan.

Heylin. Hist. of Q. Mary.

The lower House of the Clergy also was fitted with a Prolocutor of the same affections, Doctor *Hugh Weston*, Dean of *Westminster*, in the place of Doctor *Cox*. So partially had the elections been returned from the several Diocesses, that we find none of King *Edward*'s Clergy among the Clerks; and but six of the Deans and Dignitaries to have suffrage in the Convocation, viz. *James Haddon*, Dean of *Exeter*; *Walter Philips*, Dean of *Rochester*; *John Philpot*, Archdeacon of *Winchester*; *John Elmer*, Archdeacon of *Stow*, in the Diocess of *Lincoln*; *Richard Cheiney*, Archdeacon of *Hereford*; one more mentioned by Mr. *Fox*, without a name, joyned himself to the other five in the disputation.

The Prolocutor would admit of no more, though desired by *Philpot*, that some of the Divines which had the passing of the Book of Articles, in King *Edward*'s time, might be assembled with them in the defence thereof.

The main point in debate, concerned the manner of Christ's presence in the Sacrament: It was not denied by *Philpot*, and his Brethren, That Christ was present in the Sacrament rightly administred, according to his Institution; but onely that He was not present in the gross and carnal manner, which They of the Popish party had before subscribed unto. Six dys the disputation lasted, but to little effect. At length *Weston* put an end to the dispute, saying, *It is not the Queen's pleasure, that we should spend any longer time in these debates, and yet are well enough already: For you (*saith He*) have the Word, and we have the Sword.*

After

After the end of the Evensong on St. *Katherine's* day, *Bonner* caused the Quire of St. *Paul's* to go about the Steeple, singing with lights after the old custom. And on St. *Andrew's* day, next following, he began the Procession in Latin himself, with many Parsons and Curates, and the whole Quire, together with the Lord Mayor and divers of the Aldermen, the Prebendaries of the Church, attired in their old *gray Amises* (as they used to call them) in which manner they continued it for three days after: on *January* 14. he restored the solemn Sunday's procession about the Church, with the Mayor and Aldermen, the Preacher taking his Benediction in the midst of the Church, according to the antient custom; likewise he sent out his Mandates to all Parsons and Curates within his Diocese; for taking the names of all such as would not come the *Lent* following to Auricular Confession, and receive at *Easter*: he likewise enjoyned the blotting out of all such paintings, and sentences of holy Scripture, as had been pensiled on the Church-walls in King *Edward's* days.

Mr. *Jewel* continued some weeks in *Broad-gates* Hall, whither his Scholars repaired unto him, whom he instructed in Learning and Religion: He had not long lived there; but being perswaded by the Popish Inquisitors to subscribe, he took a pen in his Hand, and smiling said, *Have you a mind to see how well I can write?* and thereupon under-writ their Opinions. *Fuller.* Church History of Q. *Mary.*

The Papists trusted him not any whit the more for this his subscription. His life being *way-laid* for, with great difficulty he escaped into *Germany*. But on a Sunday after his Forenoon-sermon (by the advice of Dr. *Edwin Sandys*, afterwards Archbishop of *York*, Mr. *Chambers*, and Mr. *Sampson*, his bosom Friends) in the Congregation of *Franckfort*, he bitterly bewailed his fall, and heartily requested pardon from God and his people, whom thereby he had offended.

On *November* 20. the Mayor of *Coventry* sent up to the Lords of the Council, one *Baldwin Cleark*, *John Carelefs*, *Thomas Wilcocks*, and *Richard Eftlin*; *Carelefs* and *Wilcocks* were committed to the Gatehouse, and *Cleark* and *Eftlin* to the *Marshalsey*.

In the moneth of *December* the Parliament broke up, in which there was a Communication of Marriage betwixt the Emperor's Son *Philip*, and the Queen. In the mean-while Cardinal *Pool* hasteneth towards *England*. The Emperor invites him to come into *Germany* by his way, and entertains him with great shew of Honour, untill by his Ambassador he had finished a Contract of Marriage between his Son *Philip* and Queen *Mary*. *Petri.* Church Hist. Cent. 16.

This match was generally distasted. To hinder it Sir *Thomas Wyat*, a Kentish Knight, took Armes with a great party assisting him. But albeit he wanted neither, Wit, Wealth, Learning, yet all were ill-employed about him. *Wyat* demandeth the Perfon of the Queen, the Tower of *London* to be committed unto him, with power to difplace evil Counfellors; his demands were refufed with fcorn. Queen *Mary* came to *Guildhall*, and there made a long Oration, which fecured the affections of the Citizens unto her.

Wyat came up to *London*. He was taken at *Temple-bar*, carried thence be examined, and thence to the Tower to be committed. Some days after, he fuffered penitently and patiently on the Scaffold, condemning his own Act.

Of his complices were hanged fifty perfons, and four hundred more led through the City with halters about their necks to *Weftminfter*, where they were all pardoned in the Tilt-yard by the Queen.

Doctor *Crome*, for his Preaching without Licenfe on *Chriftmas* day, was committed to the Fleet; *Thomas Wotton* Efquire, was for matters of Religion committed alfo to the Fleet.

The Duke of *Suffolk*, Father to the Lady *Jane*, but lately pardoned of life in the midft of the Kentifh tumult, fecretly departeth into *Leicefter* and *Warwick-fhires*, inftigating the people to withftand the Queen's Marriage agreed upon with *Philip*. The Duke was betrayed by one *Underwood*, his Servant, in *Afhley-park*, with his Brother *John* Lord *Gray*, unto the Earl of *Huntington*, whence they were by him convayed prifoners to the Tower of *London*. This feemed to haften the death of the Lady *Jane* and the Lord *Guilford* her Husband, who were both beheaded, *February* 12. 1554. he was beheaded on a Scaffold on Tower-hill, and fhe upon the Green within the Tower. Two days before her death Mr. *Fecknam* was fent unto her, by the Queen, to reduce her to the Popifh Religion, whom fhe conftantly, and with great power of God's Spirit, refifted. Eleven days after her death, her Father the Duke of *Suffolk*, was beheaded on Tower-hill.

Spuds Chron. in Q. *Mary*.

And on *April* 23. his Brother, the Lord *Thomas Gray* fuffered death in the fame place.

Now for putting the Affairs of the Church into a pofture, Articles are fent into every Diocefe, and Letters writ unto their feveral and refpective Bifhops on the third of *March*, to fee them carefully put in execution: the fubftance whereof were,

1. *That the Ecclefiaftical Laws of King* Henry *the Eighth, fhould be put in practice, being not directly againft the Laws and Statutes of the Realm.*
2. *That no Bifhop do ufe the Claufe (in any of their Ecclefiaftical writings). Regia authoritate fulcitus.*
3. *That no Sacramentary be admitted to Benefice.*

4. *That*

the Church of Great Britain.

4. That all Bishops do labour to suppress Heresies, especially in the Clergy.
5. That they should suppress all unlawfull Books and writings.
6. The next Article was against Priests Marriages, and that such as would depart from their Wives, should be admitted to the same function.
7. That for want of Priests, one Priest should serve two places.
8. That Processions be used.
9. That Holy-days and Fasts be frequented.
10. That the Ceremonies be used, and Confirmation of Children be put in practice.

In the same moneth of *March* the Lord *Courtney* (whom the Queen at her first entry delivered out of the Tower) and the Lady *Elizabeth* also, the Queen's Sister, were both (by the suggestion of *Stephen Gardiner*, Bishop of *Winchester*) suspected to have been of *Wyat's* Conspiracy, and for the same were apprehended and sent to the Tower, although *Wyat* at his death cleared them both, as unacquainted with the matter. Many trains were laid to ensnare the Lady *Elizabeth*; And being on a time asked, what she thought of the words of Christ, *This is my Body*; whether she thought, it is the true Body of Christ? it is said, that after some pausing, she thus Answered.

> *Christ was the Word that spake it,*
> *He took the Bread, and brake it:*
> *And what the Word did make it,*
> *That I Believe, and take it.*

Sir *Richard Bakers* Chron.

One *Elizabeth Crofts*, about eighteen years old, was by practice put into a Wall (and therefore called, *The Spirit in the Wall*) who with a whistle made for that purpose, whistled out many Seditious words against the Queen, the Prince of *Spain*, the Mass, Confession, &c. for which she did Penance, standing upon a Scaffold at *Pauls* Cross, all the Sermon-time, where she made open Confession of her fault.

Queen *Mary* altereth her stile, leaving out the latter part of her Title, which is, Supreme Head of the Church of *England* and *Ireland*, because in this Parliament holden at *Westminster* in *April*, the Supremacy being given away from the Crown of *England* to the Pope, thereupon this Parcel of the Title was also taken away.

Then followed a communication between Bishop *Ridley*, and Secretary *Bourn*, Mr. *Fecknam* and others at the Lieutenants Table in the Tower, (described at large by Mr. *Fox*) touching the Sacrament.

On *April* 10. Archbishop *Cranmer*, Bishop *Ridley*, and *Latimer* were sent down to *Oxford* by the Lord *Williams* of *Thame*, there to dispute with the Divines of both Universities, about the presence, substance, and sacrifice of the Sacrament. Of *Oxford*, Dr. *Weston* prolocutor, Dr. *Tresham*, Dr. *Cole*, Dr. *Oglethorp*, Doctor *Pie*, Doctor *Harpsfield*, Mr. *Fecknam*. Of *Cambridge*, Dr. *Young* Vice-Chancellor, Doctor *Glyn*, Dr. *Seaton*, Dr. *Watson*, Dr. *Sedgwick*, Dr. *Atkinson*. The Questions whereon they should Dispute, were these, 1. Whether the natural body of Christ be really in the Sacrament after the words of Consecration be spoken by the Priest? 2. Whither any substance do remain after the words, saving the body and blood? 3. Whither the mass be a sacrifice propitiatory? The order and manner of the disputation against these three worthy Martyrs, the disordered usage of the University men, the rude tumult of the multitude, the fierceness and interruption of the Doctors, the full pith and ground of all their Arguments the Censure of the Judges, the railing Language of the Prolocutor, with his blast of triumph in the latter end, is set forth fully by Mr. *Fox*.

The disputation being ended, on *April* 20. they were again brought upon the stage, and then demanded, whether they would persist in their opinion, or else recant? And affirming that they would persist, they were all Three adjudged Hereticks, and condemned to the fire, but their execution was respited to a longer time.

May 19. the Lady *Elizabeth* was brought out of the Tower, and committed to the custody of the Lord of *Thame*, who gently entreated her: afterwards she was had to *Woodstock*, and there committed to the keeping of Sir *Henry Bennefield*, who dealt hardly with her.

Prince *Philip* arriveth at *Southampton*, *July* 20. 1554. and on the twenty third came to *Winchester*, where the Queen met him; and on the twenty fifth day the marriage between them there was openly Solemnized. At which time the Emperour's Ambassadour presented to the King a donation of the Kingdoms of *Naples* and *Sicily*, which the Emperour, his Father had resigned unto him. Which presently was signified, and the Titles of the King and Queen Proclaimed by sound of Trumpet in this following Style. Philip and Mary *by the Grace of God, King and Queen of* England, France, Naples, Jerusalem, Ireland, *Defenders of the Faith, Princes of* Spain *and* Sicily, *Archdukes of* Austria, *Dukes of* Milan, Burgundy *and* Brabant, *Counts of* Auspurg, Flanders, *and* Tirrol, &c. At the Proclaiming of which Style (which was performed in *French*, *Latine* and *English*) the King and Queen shewed themselves hand in hand, with two Swords born before them for the greater State, or in regard of their distinct capacity in the Publick Government. From *Winchester* they removed to *Basing*, and

The Church of Great Britain. 191

and so to *Windsor*, where *Philip* on *August* the fifth was Installed Knight of the Garter: On the eleventh of the same Moneth they made a Magnificent Passage through the Principal Streets of the City of *London*. The King prevailed with the Queen for discharge of such Prisoners as stood committed in the Tower, either for matter of Religion, or on the account of *Wyat's* Rebellion, or for engaging in the practice of the Duke of *Northumberland*: which was done accordingly, among which were the Arcbishop of *York*, ten Knights, and many other persons of name and quality. He also procured the enlargement of the Lady *Elizabeth*, and of the Earl of *Devonshire*, who travelled through *France* into *Italy*, and died at *Padua*, *Anno* 1556. the eleventh and last Earl of *Devonshire* of that Noble Family of the *Courtneys*.

Marriage and Heresie were the crimes of *Holgate*, Archbishop of *York*, for which being deprived during his imprisonment in the Tower, Dr. *Nicholas Heath* succeeded him in the See of *York*, and leaves the Bishoprick of *Worcester* to Doctor *Richard Pates*, who had been nominated by King *Henry* VIII. *Anno* 1534. and having spent the intervening twenty years in the Court of *Rome*, returned a true servant to the Pope. *Goodrick* of *Ely* died *April*. 10. leaving that Bishoprick to Dr. *Thomas Thurlby*, Bishop of *Norwich*. And Dr. *John Hopton* is made Bishop of *Norwich*, Doctor *Gilbert Bourn*, Archdeacon of *London*, is made Bishop of *Wells*, *Harley* of *Hereford* is succeeded by *Purefoy* of S. *Asaph*; Old *Bush* of *Bristol*, and *Bird* of *Chester* (the two first Bishops of those Sees) were deprived also. The first succeeded to by *Holiman*, once a Monk of *Reading*: the last by *Coles*, Master of *Baliol* Colledge in *Oxford*. Dr. *Randolph Bayn*, who had been Hebrew Reader in *Paris* in the time of King *Francis*, was Consecrated Bishop of Coventry and *Litchfield*.

Heylin's Hist. of Q. Mary.

The Parliament began *Novemb.* 12. where a way was opened for Cardinal *Poole's* Reception by preparing a Bill, whereby he was to be discharged of the Attainder which had passed upon him, *Anno* 1539. restored in Blood, and rendred Capable of all those Rights and Priviledges, of which he had stood possessed in this Kingdom. This Bill was quickly passed into an Act, and on *Novemb.* 24. the Cardinal came first to *London*. Then it was concluded, by both Houses of Parliament, that a petition should be made in the name of the Kingdom, wherein should be declared, how sorry they were, that they had withdrawn their obedience from the Apostolick See, and consenting to the Statutes made against it, promising to endeavour hereafter, that the said Lawes and Statutes should be repealed, beseeching the King and Queen to intercede with his Holiness for their Absolution. Then the Cardinal having read his Authority given him from the Pope, they all kneeled upon their knees; and imploring the mercy of God, received Absolution

Absolution for themselves and the rest of the Kingdom; Which Absolution was pronounced in these words

Our Lord Jesus Christ, which with his most pretious blood hath redeemed us from all our sins, &c. and whom the Father hath appointed Head over all his Church, absolve you. And we by Apostolick Authority given unto us (by the most holy Lord Pope Julius *the third, His Vicegerent here on earth) do absolve and deliver you, and every of you, with the whole Realm and the Dominions thereof, from all heresie and schism, and from every judgement, censure, and pain, for that cause incurred. And also we do restore you again unto the unity of Our Mother the Holy Church. In the name of the Father, the Son and the Holy Ghost.*

Which words of His being seconded with a loud *Amen*, by such as were present, he concluded the dayes work with a solemn Procession to the Chappel, for rendring thanks to God. Then did the Cardinal dispence with much irregularity in several persons, confirming the Institution of Clergy-men in their Benefices, legitimating the Children of forbidden Marriages, ratifying the processes and sentences in matters Ecclesiastical: and his dispensations were confirmed by Acts of Parliament. Then was *Anthony Brown*, Viscount *Montacute*, *Thursby* Bishop of *Ely*, and Sir *Edward Carn*, sent on a gratulatory Embassie to Pope *Paul* IV. to tender *England*'s thanks for the favours conferr'd thereon.

Heyl.in.Hist. of Q.Mary.

The Convocation that then was held, knew that the Cardinal was to be entreated, not to insist upon the restoring of Church-lands, rather to confirm the Lords and Gentry in their present possessions. And to that end a Petition is presented to both their Majesties, that they would be pleased to intercede with the Cardinal concerning it: Which Petition was offered to the Legate in the name of the whole Convocation by the Lord Chancellor; the Prolocutor, and six others of the Lower House. Concerning which the Legate was not ignorant, that a Message had been sent to the Pope in the name of the Parliament, to desire a confirmation of the Sale of all the Lands belonging to Abbies, Chanteries, &c. or otherwise to let him know, that nothing could be granted on his behalf. And it is likely, they received some fair promises to that effect, in regard that on New-years day next following, the Act for restoring the Pope's Supremacy was passed in both Houses of Parliament. The whole matter being transacted to the content of all parties (the poor Protestants excepted only) on *January* 25. there was a solemn procession throughout *London*, to praise God for their Conversion to the Catholick Church: wherein were ninety Crosses, an hundred and Sixty Priests and Clerks, each of them attired in his Cope, and after them eight

eight Bishops in their *Pontificalibus*, followed by *Bonner* carrying the Popish Pix under a Canopy, and attended by the Lord Mayor and Companies in their several Liveries. Which Procession being ended, they all returned to S. *Paul*'s Church, where the King and Cardinal, together with all the rest, heard Mass, and the next day the Parliament and Convocation were dissolved.

 The English Ambassadors came to *Rome* on the first day of the Papacy of *Pope Paul* IV. and in the first consistory after his Inauguration they were brought before him, who granted the pardon desired, and lovingly embraced the Ambassadors, and as an over plus, the Pope conferred the Title of King's of *Ireland* on their Majesties. In his private discourses with the Ambassadors, he said that the Church-goods ought to be wholly restored, saying also that his Authority was not such, as to profane things dedicated unto God. He also told them, that the *Peter-pence* ought to be paid as soon as might be, and that according to the custom, he would send a collector for that purpose. He closed his discourse with this, that they could not hope, that S. *Peter* would open to them the Gates of Heaven, as long as they usurped his goods on earth.

 A rumour was spread of the Queen's being with Child, and that she was quick, and thereupon Letters were sent from the Lords of the Council to *Bonner* Bishop of *London*, that prayers and thanksgivings should be made in all Churches. The Parliament also while it was sitting, passed an Act, desiring the King that if the Queen should fail, he would be pleased to take upon him the Education of the Child. Set forms of prayer were also made for her safe delivery. Great preparations were also made of all things necessary against the time of her delivery. And upon a sudden rumour of her being delivered, the Bells were rung, and Bonfires made in most parts of *London*. But it proved in fine that the Queen neither was with Childe for the present, nor had any hopes of being so for the time to come.

 A Gun was shot at one Doctor *Pendleton*, as He Preached at *Paul's* Cross, *June* 10. 1554. the pellet whereof went very neer him, but the Gunner was not to be heard of. Upon which the Queen published a Proclamation prohibiting the shooting with hand-guns, and the bearing of weapons. A little before this, some had caused a Cat to be hanged upon the Gallows, near the Cross in *Cheapside*, with her head shorn, the likeness of a vestment cast upon her, and her two feet tyed together, holding between them a piece of Paper, in form of a Wafer, tending to the disgrace of the Popish Religion. Then were some Antient Statutes revived that were made in the time of King *Richard* the second, *Henry* the fourth, and *Henry* the fifth, for the severe punishment of obstinate Hereticks, even to death it self, and an Act was passed for that purpose.

C c

Here-

Hereupon followed, that Inquisition for Blood, which raged in *London*, and more or less was exercised in most parts of the Kingdom. Mr. *John Rogers*, a Learned man, and a great companion of that *Tyndal*, by whom the Bible was translated into English in the time of King *Henry*; after whose Martyrdom, he retired to *Wittenberg* in the Dukedome of *Saxony*, where he abode till King *Edward's* coming to the Crown, and was by Bishop *Ridley* presented to the Lecture of S. *Paul's*, and made one of the Prebendaries. He was convented, and condemned, and publickly burnt in *Smithfield* on *Feb.* 4. He was the first Martyr in Queen *Mary's* dayes : On the nineth day of which moneth *John Hooper* late Bishop of *Glocester*, was burnt in that City. The like course was taken with Bishop *Farrar*, Bishop of S. *David's*, but that I do not find him restrained from speaking his mind unto the people as the other was. He was cast into prison by the Protestants in King *Edward's* days. Being continued in prison in Queen *Mary's* dayes, and called before Bishop *Gardiner*, he gave such offence, that he was sent back again to prison, and being sent back into his own Diocess, he there received the sentence of condemnation at the hand of *Morgan*, who had supplanted and succeeded him in the See of. S. *David's*. He desisted not till he had brought him to the Stake.

On *Feb.* 8. *Laurence Saunders*, an excellent preacher, was burnt at *Coventry*, where he had spent the greatest part of his Ministry. On *Feb.* 9. *Anno* 1555. Doctor *Rowland Tailor* was burned at *Hadley*; the Town whereof he was Pastor, where calling on the name of God, he endured the Torment, till one *Soice* with an Halbert struck him on the Head, that the brains fell out, and the dead Corpse fell into the fire. *Thomas Tomkins* on *March* 16. suffered in *Smithfield*. *William Hunter* an Apprentice of nineteen years of age was burnt at *Burntwood* in *Essex*.

Speeds Chron. of Q. Mary.

Within the compass of less than four years there died for the testimonial of their conscience for the truth, no less than two hundred seventy and seven persons.

In the heat of the fire were consumed five Bishops, one and twenty Divines, eight Gentlemen, eighty four Artificers, one hundred Husband-men and Labourers, twenty six Married-women, twenty widows, nine Virgins, two Boys, and two Infants, one of them whipped to death by Bishop *Bonner*, and the other springing out of his mother's womb from the stake as she burned, was by the Serjeants thrown again into the fire.

Ridley and *Latimer* were both degraded on *Octob.* 15. and brought unto the stake in the Town-ditch in *Oxford*, over against *Baliol-colledge* on the morrow after, where with great courage and constancy they endured that death, to which they had been precondemned before they were heard. *Cranmer* was a prisoner at that time in the North-gate of the

the City, called *Bocardo*, from the top whereof he beheld that most doleful Spectacle, and casting himself down on his Knees, he humbly entreated the Lord to give them strength of faith and hope, which he also desired for himself, whensoever he should Act his part on that bloody Theater.

When *Ridley* understood *Hooper* (before his Execution) to have been marked out for the slaughter, he remembred that controversie which had been between them in the time of King *Edward* about the Episcopal Habit, and thought it not enough if he left not to the world some testimony of their mutual Charity, as well as their consent in Doctrine. Concerning which he wrote to him in this manner following.

My dear brother, forasmuch as I understand by your Books, that we throughly agree, and wholly consent together in the substantial points of our Religion, against which the world now so furiously rageth, however in times past in certain circumstances of Religion your wisdom and my simplicity (I must confess) have a little jarred, each of us following the abundance of his own spirit. Now (I say) be assured, that even with my whole heart (God is my witness) in the bowels of Christ, I love you in the Truth, and for the Truth's sake which abideth in us, as I am perswaded, and by the Grace of God shall abide in us for evermore. And because the world, as I perceive, Brother, ceaseth not to play his pageant, and busily conspireth against Christ our Saviour, with all possible force and power, exalting high things against the knowledge of God: let us joyn hands together in Christ, though we cannot overthrow, yet to our power, and as much as in us lieth, let us shake those high Altitudes, not with carnal, but with spiritual weapons: and withal (brother) let us prepare our selves to the day of dissolution, by that which after the short time of this bodily affliction by the Grace of our Lord Jesus Christ we shall triumph together with him in eternal glory.

Comforted with Reciprocal Letters of this holy nature, they both prepared themselves for death, in which *Hooper* had the honour to lead the way, as hath been shewn.

It is memorable, that the same day in which Bishop *Ridley*, and *Latimer* were burnt at *Oxford*, *Stephen Gardiner* Bishop of *Winchester*, would not go to dinner till four a Clock in the afternoon, though the old Duke of *Norfolk* was come to dine with him. The reason was, because he would first hear of their being burnt. And as soon as word of that was brought unto him, he presently said, now let us go to dinner: where sitting down, and eating merrily, upon a sudden he fell into such extremity, that he was fain to be taken from the Table, and carried to his bed, where he continued fifteen dayes without voyding any thing by Urine, or otherwife, which caufed his Tongue to fwell in his Mouth. He died at *Whitehall, November* the twelfth; from whence conveyed by water to his houfe in *Southwark*, his body was firft lapt in Lead, kept for a feafon in the Church of St. *Saviours* and afterwards folemnly interred, under a fair and goodly Monument, in his Cathedral. The cuftody of the Great Seal, with the Title of Lord Chancellor, was, upon *New-years-day*, conferred upon Doctor *Nicholas Heath*, Archbifhop of *York*. But the Revenues of the Bifhoprick were appropriated to the ufe of the Cardinal-Legat. But Doctor *John White*, Bifhop of *Lincoln*, having been born at *Winchefter*, and educated in that School, of which he was afterward chief Mafter, and finally Warden of that Colledge, fo far prevailed, by his Friends at Court, that, on the promife of an annual Penfion of a thoufand pounds, to the ufe of the Cardinal, he was permitted to enjoy the Title, with the reft of the profits. But he was not actually tranflated till the next year following. *Voify*, Bifhop of *Exeter* dies, and Doctor *James Turbervil* fucceedeth him.

Thuan Hiftor. lib. 13.

Queen *Mary* caufed that claufe of Prayer [*That God would deliver the Kingdom from fedition, and tyranny of the Church of* Rome] to be blotted out of the Litany: and would not fuffer her Father's name to be mentioned in publick Prayers, becaufe he had made Apoftafie from the Church.

She reftored all Ecclefiaftical Livings, affumed to the Crown, faying, *That fhe fet more by the falvation of her Soul, than fhe did by ten Kingdoms.*

And fhortly after *John Feeknam*, late Dean of St. *Paul's*, was made Abbot of *Weftminfter*, and had poffeffion delivered him, and with him fourteen Monks received the Habit at the fame time.

Doctor *Henry Cole* was made Dean of St. *Paul's*.

Pa'er.Church Hiftery.

Befides thofe that fuffered in the flames for the Gofpel, in this Queens dayes, fixty four more were perfecuted for their Faith and Profeffion, whereof feven were whipped, fixteen perifhed in prifon, and were buried in dunghils: many lay in captivity condemned, but were releafed by the happy entrance of Queen *Elizabeth*, and many fled the Land in thofe dayes of diftrefs; among whom were many perfons of Quality, as *Katharine*, Dutchefs of *Suffolk*, laft Wife of *Charles Brandon*, Duke of *Suffolk*, with her Husband, *Richard Berty* Efquire, Sir *John Cheeke*, Sir *Richard Morifon*, of *Caifhobury* in *Hertford-fhire*, Sir *Francis Knollys*, afterwards Privy Counfellor to Queen *Elizabeth*; Sir *Anthony Cook*, Father-in-law to *Cecil*, after Lord *Burghley*, and famous for his learned Daughters; Sir *Peter Carew*, renowned for his Valour in *Ireland*, where he died, Anno 1576. Sir *Thomas Wroth*, of *Middlefex*, the Lady *Dorothy Stafford*, afterwards of the Bed-chamber to Queen *Elizabeth*, and the Lady *Elizabeth Berkley*.

Some

The Church of Great Britain.

Some of the English Exiles seated themselves at *Emden* in *East-Frizland*, a Staple Town of English Merchants. *John Scory*, late Bishop of *Chichester*, was Superintendent of the English Congregation in *Emden*.

Some setled themselves at *Weasel*, then in the Dominions of the Duke of *Cleve*, but bordering on the Low Countries in the King of *Spain*'s possession: but they quickly left this place: some of them went to *Arrow*, a small City in *Switzerland*, on the banks of the River *Arrola*, belonging to *Bern*. The most eminent English seated themselves at *Strasburgh*, as *James Haddon*, *Edwyn Sandys*, *Edmond Grindal*, *John Huntington*, *Guido Eaton*, *John Geoffry*, *John Peader*, *Thomas Eaton*, *Michael Raymuger*, *Augustine Bradbridge*, *Arthur Saule*, *Thomas Steward*, *Christopher Goodman*, *Thomas Lakin*, *Humfrey Alcocson*, *Thomas Crafton*. Some went to *Zuric*, stiled the Students at *Zuric*, viz. *Robert Horn*, *Richard Chambers*, *Thomas Leaver*, *Nicholas Carvil*, *John Mullings*, *Thomas Spencer*, *Thomas Bentham*, *William Cole*, *John Parkhurst*, *Roger Kelk*, *Robert Beaumont*, *Laurence Humfrey*, *Henry Cockcraft*, *John Pretio*.

At *Franckford* on the *Meine* was the most conspicuous English Church beyond the Seas, consisting of *John Bale*, *Edmond Sutton*, *John Makebray*, *William Whittingham*, *Thomas Cole*, *William Williams*, *George Chidley*, *William Hammon*, *Thomas Steward*, *Thomas Wood*, *John Staunton*, *William Walton*, *Jasper Swift*, *John Geoffry*, *John Gray*, *Michael Gill*, *John Fox*, *Laurence Kent*, *William Kethe*, *John Hollingham*, *John Samford*, *John Wood*, *Thomas Sorby*, *Anthony Carier*, *Hugh Alford*, *George Whetnal*, *Thomas Whetnal*, *Edward Sutton*.

Besides these (the first Founders of these Congregations) many additional persons, coming afterward out of *England*, joyned themselves thereunto.

Now followed the sad troubles of *Frankford*, rending these Exiles into divers Factions: The English had a Church granted unto them in *coparcenie* with the French Protestants, they one day, and the English another. Which was granted them with this proviso, *That they should not dissent from the French in Doctrine or Ceremony, left thereby they should minister occasion of offence.*

The English constituted their new Church, chusing a Minister and Deacons for a time, and, out of conformity to the French, abrogated many things, formerly used by them in the Church of *England*.

1. They concluded there should be no answering aloud after the Minister.
2. That the Litany, Surplice, &c. should be omitted.
3. Instead of the English Confession, they used another, framed according to the state and time.

4. The

4. The same ended, the people sang a Psalm in metre in a plain tune.
5. That done, the Minister prayed for the assistance of God's Spirit, and so proceeded to the Sermon.
6. After Sermon a general Prayer for all States, and particularly for *England* was devised.
7. Then followed a Rehearsal of the Articles of Belief, which ended, the people sang another Psalm.
8. Lastly, The Minister pronounced the Blessing, and so the people departed.

Thus setled in their Church, they write Letters to all the English Congregations at *Strasburgh, Zuric, Emden*, &c. to invite them with all convenient speed to joyn with them at *Franckford*. This occasioned several reiterated Letters from *Franckford*, requiring those of *Zurich*, to weigh the necessity of joyning themselves in one Congregation. Those of *Zurich*, by many dilatory Letters, excused themselves from coming thither. But the main reason was, those of *Zurich* were resolved to recede no whit from the Liturgy used in *England* under King *Edward* the sixth; and unless, coming thither they might be assured, they should have the full and free use thereof, they utterly refused any Communion with their Congregation.

Then came Mr. *John Knox* from *Geneva*, and was chosen by the Congregation at *Frankford* for their Pastor. At which time Mr. *Chambers*, and Mr. *Edmond Grindal*, came thither as Agents, with a Letter from the Congregation of *Strasburgh*. These made a motion, that they might have the substance of the *Common-prayer-book*, though such Ceremonies, and things, which the Country could not bear, might well be omitted. But *Knox* and *Whittingham* were as much bent against the substance of the Book, as against any of the Circumstantials which belonged to it. Hereupon *Grindal* and *Chambers* return back again to *Strasburgh*.

Knox, and others in *Frankford*, drew up, in Latin, a platform of the English Liturgy, and sent it to *Geneva*, tendring it to the judgment of Mr. *John Calvin*: who answereth, that in the English Liturgy he had observed *multas tolerabiles ineptias*, many tolerable fooleries, adding, that there wanted that purity which was to be desired in it, that it contained many Relicks of Popish dregs; that seeing there was no manifest impiety in it, it had been tolerated for a season, because at first it could not otherwise be admitted. But howsoever! though it was lawful to begin with such beggarly rudiments, yet it behoved the learned, grave, and godly Ministers of Christ, to endeavour further, and set forth something more refined from filth and rustiness.

This being sent unto *Knox* and *Whittingham*, those who formerly approved, did afterwards dislike the English Liturgy. But in the end it was

Troubles of Frankford. p. 24.

The Church of Great Britain.   199

was agreed on, that a mixt form, confisting partly of the order of *Geneva*, and partly of the Book of *England*, should be digested, and received till the first of *April*.

In this condition of affairs, Doctor *Richard Cox*, the late Dean of *Christ-church*, and *Westminster*, first School-master, and afterward Almoner to King *Edward* the Sixth, putteth himself into *Frankford*, *March* 13. accompanied with many English Exiles. Being a man of great learning, of great authority in the Church, and one that had a principal hand in drawing up the Liturgy by Law established, he could not patiently bear these innovations in it. He thereupon first begins to answer the Minister, contrary to the order there agreed on, and the next Lord's-day after causeth one of his company to go into the Pulpit, and read the Litany. Against which doings of his *Knox*, in a Sermon the same day, inveigheth most bitterly, affirming many things in the English book to be imperfect, and superstitious: for which he is both rebuked by *Cox*, and forbidden to preach. Hereupon *Whittingham* procureth an Order from the Magistrates, requiring that the English should conform themselves to the Rules of the French.

Cox his party being depressed, they accuse *Knox* to the State, for high Treason against the Emperor, in an English book of his, entitled, *An Admonition to all Christians*, first privately preached in *Buckinghamshire*, and now publickly printed to the world, wherein he called the Emperor *no less an enemy to Christ, than* Nero. Hereupon the State of *Frankford* willed *Knox* to depart the City, who on *March* 25. to the great grief of his Friends, left the Congregation, and retireth himself to *Geneva*. *Whittingham* and the rest of his party were commanded to receive the Book of *England*, against which Order *Whittingham*, for a time, opposeth, encouraged therein by *Goodman*; but finding *Cox* and his party too strong for them, they also left *Franckford* shortly after.

Then Doctor *Cox* and his Adherents proceed to elect Officers in the Congregation. Mr. *Whitebead* is chosen their Pastor, yet so, as two Ministers, four Elders, and four Deacons were joyned to assist him. And because this was then an University, as well as a Congregation, of the English, Mr. *Robert Horn* was chosen to be Hebrew Reader, Mr. *Mullings* to read the Greek Lecture, and Mr. *Trahern* the Lecture in Divinity.

Here a moderate motion was made, that the difference might be compremised, and referred to Arbitrators, which should be equally chosen on both sides.

To this Doctor *Cox* his party would in no wise consent, and lost much reputation by the refusal.

The Names of those who separated themselves from this Congregation were as followeth.

William Williams.	*John Hilton.*
William Whittingham.	*Christopher Scothow.*
Anthony Gilby.	*Nicholas Purfote.*
Christopher Goodman	*John Escot.*
Thomas Cole.	*Thomas Grafton.*
John Fox.	*William Walton.*
Thomas Wood.	*Laurence Kent.*
William Kethe.	*John Hellingham.*
John Kelk.	*Anthony Carier.*

Of these Mr. *Fox*, with a few more, went to *Basil:* the rest setled themselves at *Geneva*, where they made choice of *Knox* and *Goodman* for their constant Preachers, under which Ministry they reject the whole frame and fabrick of the Reformation made in *England*, conformed themselves wholly to the fashions of the Church of *Geneva*.

It was not long after the setling of the Liturgy at *Franckford*, before *Whitthead* left the Ministry of the English Congregation, which *Cox* obtained for Mr. *Horn.* That being done, he withdrew himself to *Strasburg*, there to enjoy the company of *Peter Martyr*, with whom he was well acquainted, while he lived in *Christ-church*.

By Doctor *Cox* his departure a new gap is open for another dissention. Some words had passed, at a Supper, between *Horn* the Pastor, and *Ashley*, a Gentleman of note, intended rather for increase of charity, than breach of friendship. *Ashley* is three dayes after cited to appear at the house of one of the Elders, to answer for some words he had spoken in contempt of the Ministry. But, from the Elders, he appeals to the Congregation, among whom he prevails so far, that they send a Message, by two of their company, to the Pastor, and Elders, to proceed no further in the cause. *Horn* being backed by *Chambers*, the publick Treasurer, excepts against this Message, as not decreed by the whole Congregation, and resolves to maintain that authority, which had been conferred on him and the rest of the Elders, *Ashley*, and his party, on the other side, protest against the Pastor and Elders, as an adverse party, and therefore not in a capacity to sit as Judges in the present case, and do consult about the making of a Book of Discipline for the curbing the exorbitant power (for so they thought it) of the Pastors and Elders. Thereupon the Pastor and Elders forsake their Offices, and on the next day of publick meeting take place among the rest as private persons. The Congregation full, but the Pulpit empty, which put the rest upon a humour of electing others to take the Pulpit charge upon them. The noise

of

The Church of Great Britain.

of thefe diforders awakens the Magiftrates, who command *Horn* and *Chambers* to forbear the Congregation until further order, and afterwards reftoring them to their former authority, by publick edict, were contradicted in it by *Afhley's* party, who, having got fome power into their hands, were refolved to hold it.

In the mean time a Book of Difcipline had been drawn, and tendred to the Congregation, according to the Rules, whereof the Supreme power, in all Eccleliaftical caufes, was put into the hands of the Congregation, and the difpofing the publick moneys committed to the truft of *Heylin's* Hift. certain Officers, by the name of Deacons. This makes the breach wider of Q. *Mary.* than before. The Magiftrates write their Letters to *Strasburg*, defiring Doctor *Cox*, Doctor *Sandys*, together with *Robert Berty* Efquire, to undertake the clofing of the prefent Rupture. To their arbitrament each party is content to fubmit the controverfie. In the end a form of Reconciliation is drawn up by fome of the *Englifh*, who really fought the peace of the Church. But thofe, who ftood for the new difcipline, refufed to fubmit themfelves to any eftablifhment, by which the power of the diffufive body of the Congregation might be called in queftion. Whereupon *Horn* and *Chambers* depart to *Strasburg*, from whence *Chambers* writ his Letters to them twice, but to no effect. They had before elected fome new Minifters, and though *Horn*, and his party, oppofed it, yet they concluded it for the prefent, and now they mean to ftand to the conclufion, let *Horn* and *Chambers* go or tarry, as beft pleafed themfelves. Such were the troubles and diforders in the Church of *Frankford*, occafioned firft by a diflike of the publick Liturgy, before which they preferred the nakednefs and fimplicity of the French and Genevian Churches, (faith Doctor *Heylin*) and afterwards continued by the oppolition made by the general body of the Congregation, againft fuch who were appointed to be Paftors and Rulers over them.

And now it is time to return to *England*, and look back upon *Cranmer*, who had been cited to the Court of *Rome* ; for nothing could be done againft the perfon of a Metropolitan, before the Pope had taken cognifance of the caufe, and eighty dayes had feemingly been given to *Cranmer*, for making his appearance in the Court of *Rome*. And though the Pope knew well enough, as well the Archbifhop's readinefs to appear before him, if he were at at liberty, as the impoffibility of making any fuch appearance, as the cafe then ftood ; yet at the end of the faid eighty dayes he is pronounced by the Pope, to be contumacious, and for his contumacy to be degraded, excommunicated, and finally delivered over to the fecular Magiftrate. According unto which Decree a Commiffion is directed unto *Edmond Bonner*, Bifhop of *London*, and *Thomas Thurlby*, Bifhop of *Ely*, to proceed in the Degradation of the faid Archbifhop, who caufed him to be degraded. After this, and before his death, great pains was taken by a Spanifh Frier, in the Univerfity, to perfwade him

him to a retraction of his former Opinions, by whom it was suggested to him, How acceptable it would be to the King and Queen, how gainful to himself, in regard both of his soul and of his temporal being, putting him in good hope, that he should not only have his life, but be restored again to his ancient Dignity, &c. if he would but subscribe his name to a piece of Paper, which was made ready for his hand.

By these and the like alluring temptations he was prevailed upon to sign the Writing, in which were briefly comprehended the chief points of Doctrine defended in the Church of *Rome*, and by him formerly condemned, both in publick and in private. But all this could not save him from being made a Sacrifice to revenge and avarice.

The Queen had still a vindicative spirit against him, for the injury which she conceived had been done to her Mother: and the Cardinal (who hitherto had enjoyed the profits of the See of *Canterbury* as an Usufructuary) was altogether as solicitous for getting a right and title to them as sole proprietary. No way to pacifie one, and to satisfie the desires of the other, but by bringing him (when he least looked for it) to the fatal Stake. And thither they brought him, and first he retracts his retraction, and after punisheth that hand which had subscribed it, by holding it forth into the flame, and suffering it to be consumed before the rest of his body had felt the fire. The residue of his body being burnt to ashes, his heart was found entire and untouched in the midst of the cinders: which possibly may serve as a witness for him, that his heart stood fast unto the Truth, though with his hand he had subscribed some Popish errors.

Cardinal *Pool* received Confecration to the See of *Canterbury*, the very next Sunday after *Cranmer's* death.

No fewer than two hundred are reported to have been burnt by bloody *Bonner*, the most eminent of all which number was Mr. *John Philpot*, Archdeacon of *Winchester*, who, though of *Gardiner's* Diocefs, was condemned by *Bonner*; *Gardiner* being well enough contented to find out the Game, and leave it to be followed by that bloody Hunter. Dr. *John Christopherson*, Bishop of *Chichester*, is recorded to have burnt ten in one fire at *Lewis*, and seventeen others at several times in sundry places, among which was *Richard Woodman*, of *Warbleton* in *Suffex*, that notable Martyr; and four at *Mayfield*, viz. *John Hart*, *Thomas Ravenfdal*, a Shoomaker, and a Collier. *Harpfield*, Archdeacon of *London*, and *Thornton*, the Suffragan of *Dover*, are said to have poured out blood like water. The same is said of *Griffin* of *Rochester*, and *Downing*, Chancellor of *Norwich*. The same character is given of Bishop *Bayn* of *Coventry* and *Litchfield*, who burned many faithful Ministers and others.

In all the Province of *York* I find none brought to the Stake but *George Marfh* of *Chester*, condemned thereto by Bishop *Coles*. Besides the

the burning of Bishop *Farrar*, at *Carmarthen*, by Bishop *Morgan*, and of *Rawlins*; and *White*, at *Cardiff*, by Bishop *Kitching* : No great cruelty seems to have been acted in the four Welsh Dioceses. In the Diocess of *Exeter*, *Wells*, *Peterborough*, and *Lincoln* (though this last the greatest in the Kingdom) I find mention but of one a piece : of two in that of *Ely*, and of no more than three apiece in that of *Bristol*, and *Sarisbury* ; for at *Newbury* were burnt that famous *Julius Palmer*, with two others. Doctor *Tunstal*, Bishop of *Durham*, was in Queen *Maries* time no great persecutor, his Bishoprick had dayes of quiet under him. When Mr. *Russel*, a Preacher was brought before him, and Doctor *Himner*, his Chancellor, would have had him examined more strictly, the Bishop stayed him, saying, *Hitherto we have had a good report among our Neighbours, I pray you bring not this mans blood upon my Head.* The Bishop of *Carlisle* also was a man of a moderate temper.

The Pope had published a Bull in print, *Anno* 1556. in which he threatened excommunication to all persons that kept any Church-lands unto themselves, as also all Princes and Magistrates, that did not put the same in execution. Which though it did not edifie much in the Realm of *England*, yet it found more obedience in that of *Ireland*, in which a Parliament being called, in *June* 1557. there passed an Act for repealing of Statutes, Articles, and Provisions made against the See of *Rome*, since the twentieth year of King *Henry* the Eighth, and for abolishing of several Ecclesiastical possessions, conveyed to the Laity, as also for the extinguishment of First-fruits and Twentieth parts (no more than the yearly payment of the Twentieth part, having been laid by Act of Parliament upon the Clergy of *Ireland*) in the first and last clause whereof, as they followed the example of the Realm of *England*, so possibly they might have given a dangerous example to it in the other point, if by the Queens death, which followed shortly after, King *Philip*, and the Popes, had not lost all their power and influence on the English Nation; by means whereof there was no farther progress in the Restitution of the Abbey-lands, no more re-edifying the old Religious houses, and no intention for the founding any new.

Cardinal *Poole*, having visited his own Diocess, and given out divers printed Articles, to shew his great care for the suppressing the growth of Heresie, sent his Commissioners to *Cambridge*, who interdicted the two Churches, wherein *Martin Bucer*, and *Paulus Fagius*, had been interred; and the Writ being taken out *de comburendo Hæretico*, and being come down, and sent to the Mayor of *Cambridge*, on *February* 6. the two dead Bodies were taken out of their Graves, and being laid in their Coffins, on mens shoulders, were carried to the Market-place with a guard of men, well armed and weaponed, chained unto several posts, as if still alive, the wood and fire put to them, and their Bodies burned, together with so many of their Books as could be gotten, which were cast into the same flames also.

Queen *Mary* now engageth in her Husband's quarrel, and King *Philip* having made up an Army of thirty five thousand Foot, and twelve thousand Horse, besides a thousand Horsemen, four thousand Footmen, and two thousand Pioners sent out of *England*, under the command of the Earl of *Pembrook*, sate down before St. *Quintin*, the chief Town of *Piccardy*. On *August* the tenth the Battels joyn, in which the French were vanquished, and their Army rouzed, the Constable of *France*, the Prince of *Mantua*, the Duke of *Montperser* and *Longueville*, with six others of the prime Nobility, and many others of less note, being taken prisoners. The Duke of *Anguien*, the Viscount *Turin*, most of the Foot-Captains, and the common Souldiers, to the number of two thousand five hundred, were slain upon the place. King *Philip* stormed St. *Quintin* on the eighteenth day. After which service, the English findi.g some neglect from King *Philip*, desired to be dismissed into their Country, which was indulged unto them. By whose dismission King *Philip* could do no action of importance in the rest of the War.

But the Queen shall pay dearly for this Victory. The English were then possessed of the Town of *Calais*, with many other Forts thereabout, as *Guisnes*, *Hames*, *Ardres*, &c. together with the whole Territory, a Town situate on the mouth of the English Chanel, opposite to *Dover*, and distant not above twenty five miles from it. King *Edward* the Third, after a Siege of more than eleven months, became Master of it, *Anno* 1347. by whom it was first made a Colony of the English Nation, and after one of the Staple-Towns for the sale of Wooll: kept with great care by his Successors, who, as long as they had it in their hand, were said to carry the Keys of *France* at their Girdle: a Town which, for more than two hundred years had been in possession of the English. The Queen had broke the peace with *France*, and taken no care to fortifie this place in this time of War. Then the Duke of *Guise*, one of the best Souldiers of that Age, now called back out of *Italy*, being informed by the Governor of *Bulloign*, that the Town was neither so well fortified, nor so strongly garritioned, but that it might easily be taken, on *New-years-day* sate down before it, and on *Twelfth-day* had it surrendred up unto him, by the Lord Deputy *Wentworth*, who had the chief government of it. *Guisnesse*, *Hames*, and all the other Forts in the County of *Oye* were reduced under the power of the French within few dayes after.

The Pope is displeased with Cardinal *Pool*, by whose perswasion, it was thought, that the Queen had broke her League with *France*, to take part with her Husband: therefore he deprives *Pool* of the Legantine power, confers the same upon Friar *Peitow*, an English-man by birth, and of good descent; whom he designs also to the See of *Sarisbury*, then void by the death of *Capon*. *Karn*, the Queens Agent with the Pope, advertiseth her of these secret practices. *Pool* layes by the Cross of his Legation

The Church of Great Britain.

Legation, and abstains from the exercise of his Bulls and Faculties. *Peitow*, the new Cardinal-Legat, puts himself on the way to *England*, when the Queen commandeth him, at his peril, not to adventure to set foot on English ground. *Peitow* died in *April* following, the rupture was made up again, and *Pool* was confirmed in the possession of his former powers. And thereupon followed the burning: divers persons in the Diocess of *Canterbury*, whereof two suffered at *Ashford*, and six in his own Metropolitan City. These Godly Martyrs, in their prayers which they made before their Martyrdom, desired God, that their blood might be the last that should be shed, and so it came to pass.

The number of prohibited Books increasing every day more and more, a Proclamation was set forth on *June* the sixth, to hinder the continual spreading of so great a mischief. Which Proclamation, though it were very smart, yet not so full of rigour as another, which came out at the burning of seven persons in *Smithfield*, published both at *Newgate*, where they were imprisoned, and at the Stake where they were to suffer, whereby it was straitly charged and commanded, *That no man should either pray for, or speak to them, or once say, God help them.* Which Proclamation notwithstanding, *Bentham*, the Minister of one of the *London* Congregations, seeing the fire set to them, turning his eyes unto the people, and cried, *We know they are the People of God, and therefore we cannot chuse but wish well to them, and say, God strengthen them.* And so he said, *Almighty God, for Christ's sake strengthen them.* With that all the people, with one consent, cried, *Amen, Amen.*

It was very admirable, that the Protestants should have a Congregation under *Bonner's* nose, yet so it was: and in one of those Congregations, whereof *Bentham* was Minister, there assembled seldom under forty, many times an hundred and more: the Ministers whereof successively were Mr. *Edward Scambler*, after Bishop of *Peterborough*, Mr. *Thomas Foule*, Mr. *John Rough* convented and condemned by *Bonner*, and burnt for the Truth. After whom followed Mr. *Augustine Bernher*, a moderate and learned man, and finally Mr. *Thomas Bentham* forementioned, who continued in that charge till the death of Queen *Mary*, and was by Queen *Elizabeth* preferred to the See of *Lichfield*, Anno 1589.

And notwithstanding all the care of the Queens Inquisitors, many good Books of true Christian Consolation, and good Doctrine, did either find some Press in *London*, or were sent over to their Brethren by such learned men as had retired themselves to their several Sanctuaries.

Then raged a contagious Fever in most parts of the Land, and no former Plague was thought to have destroyed a greater number, so that divers places were left void of Justices, and men of worth, to govern the Kingdom. At which time died also so many Priests, that a great number of Parish-Churches, in divers places, were unserved, and no Curates could be gotten for money. Much corn was also loft in the field for want of Workmen to get it in. Physitians died as well as the Patients, two of the Queens Doctors dying of it a little before the death of the Queen. It spared the Prelat no more than the Priest, infomuch, that within less than the space of twelve months almost one half of the English Bishops had made void their Sees.

Now God put an end to those calamities of his Children by the death of Queen *Mary*, who died of a Dropsie, *November* the seventeenth, 1558. Within few hours after her death, died Cardinal *Pool*, Archbishop of *Canterbury*. He procured of the Queen the Patronage of nineteen Benefices unto his See, promised, and intended, to repair the Palace at *Canterbury*. He was buried in his own Cathedral, with this short and modest Epitaph upon his plain Monument, *DEPOSITUM CARDINALIS POLI*.

The Parliament sate at Queen *Maries* death, after which they only continued so long, as joyntly and publickly to proclaim *Elizabeth* Queen, and then they were dissolved: Queen *Maries* body was enterred in the Chappel of King *Henry* the Seventh, in the Isle on the North side thereof.

ELIZABETH, the only Child then living of King *Henry* the Eighth, succeeded her Sister in the Throne, on *November* the seventeenth, *Anno* 1558. She was proclaimed by the King at Arms, first before *Westminster-hall* door, in the presence of the Lords and Commons, and, not long after, at the Cross in *Cheapside*, and other places in the City, in the presence of the Lord Mayor, Aldermen, and principal Citizens, to the great joy of all peaceable and well-affected people.

The news whereof, being brought unto her by some of the Lords, she removes from *Hatfield* on the nineteenth of that month, and with a great and royal Train sets forward to *London*. At *Highgate* (four miles from the City) she was met by all the Bishops then living, who presented themselves before her upon their knees. In which address, as she expressed no small contentment, so she gave to each of them particularly her hand to kiss, except only unto *Bonner* of *London*. At her first coming to the City, she took her lodging in the *Charter-house*, where she staid some dayes, till all things in the Tower might be fitted for her reception. Attended by the Lord Mayor and Aldermen, with a stately Train of Lords and Ladies, she entreth by *Cripple-gate* into the City, passeth along the Wall till she came to *Bishops-gate*, where all the Companies of the City, in their several Liveries waited her coming, in their proper and distinct ranks, reaching from thence until the further end of *Mark-lane*, where she was enterrained with a peal of great Ordinance from the Tower. At her entrance into which place she rendred her most humble

thanks

the Church of Great Britain.

thanks to Almighty God, for the great and wondrous change of her condition, in bringing her from being a prisoner in that place, to be the Ruler of her people, and now to take possession of it as a Royal Palace. Here she remained till *December* the fifth, then next following, and from thence removed by water to *Sommerset-house.* In each remove she found such infinite throngs of people, which flocked from all parts to see her, both by land and water, and testified their publick joy, by such loud acclamations, as much rejoyced her heart to hear, and could not but express it in her words and countenance.

As she passed through *London*, the Bible was presented to her at the little Conduit in *Cheapside*, which she received with both her hands; and kissing it, laid it to her breast, saying, *That the same had ever been her delight, and should be the rule by which she meant to frame her Government.*

She was crowned by *Owen Oglethorp*, Bishop of *Carlisle*, on *January* the fourteenth, for that the Archbishop of *York*, and the rest of the Bishops refused to perform that office, suspecting her Religion, who had been first bred in the Protestants Religion, and also for that she had very lately forbidden the Bishop, in saying Mass to lift up the Host to be adored, and permitted the Litany, with the Epistle and Gospel, to be read in the vulgar tongue.

Camden's Hist. of Q. Elizab.

For the first six weeks things stood in their former state, without the least alteration. She being now twenty five years of age, and taught by Experience and Adversity, had gathered wisdom above age; the proof whereof she gave in chusing her Counsellors, which were as follow.

Nicholas Heath, Archbishop of *York*.
William Pawlet, Marquess of *Winchester*, Lord Treasurer.
Henry Fitz-Alan, Earl of *Arundel*.
Francis Talbot, Earl of *Shrewsbury*.
Edward Stanley, Earl of *Darby*.
William Herbert, Earl of *Pembrook*.
Edward, Lord *Clinton*, Lord Admiral of the Sea.
William, Lord Howard of *Effingham*, Lord Chamberlain.

Sir *Thomas Cheiney*.
Sir *William Peter*.
Sir *John Mason*.
Sir *Richard Sackvill*.
Nicholas Wotton, Dean of *Canterbury*.

All these were Papists, and of Queen *Maries* Council.

To these she joyned of her own,

William Par, Marquess of *Northampton*.
Francis Russel, Earl of *Bedford*.
Edward Rogers.
Ambrose Cave.
Francis Knollys.
William Cecil, who had been Secretary to King *Edward* the Sixth, and soon after *Nicholas Bacon*, whom she made Lord Keeper of the Great Seal.

All these were of the Protestants Religion, and had been in no place under Queen *Mary*.

Proclamations came forth, that Preachers should abstain from questions controverted in Religion. Then care was taken for sending new Commissio's unto such Ambassadors, as resided in the Courts of several Princes, both to acquaint them with the change, and to assure those Princes of the Queen's desire to maintain all former leagues between them and the Crown of *England*.

To her Agent in the Court of *Spain*, it was given in charge, to represent to the King the dear remembrance which she kept of those many Humanities received from him in the time of her Troubles.

Instructions are sent also to Sir *Edward Karn*, the late Queen's Agent with the Pope, and now confirmed by her in the same employment, to make the Pope acquainted with the death of Queen *Mary*, and her succession to the Crown, not without some desire, that all good Offices might be reciprocally exchanged between them. But the Pope answered,

Heyl'in.Hist. of Q. Eliz. 1b. *An. Reg.* 1.

That the Kingdom of England *was held in Fee of the Apostolick See: That she could not succeed, being Illegitimate. That He could not contradict the declaration of* Clement *the Seventh, and* Paul *the Third. That it was a great boldness to assume the Name, and Government of it, without him; yet being desirous to shew a Fatherly affection, if she would renounce her pretensions, and refer her self wholly to his free disposition, He will do whatsoever may be done with the Honour of the Apostolick See.*

The new Queen having performed this office of Civility to him, as she did to others, expected no answer, nor took much thought of it when she heard it.

Many

Many who were imprisoned for Religion, she restored to liberty at her first coming to the Crown: which occasioned *Rainsford*, a Gentleman of the Court, to make a sute to her in the behalf of *Matthew, Mark, Luke* and *John*, who had been long imprisoned in a Latin Translation, that they also might walk abroad (as formerly) in the English Tongue. To whom she made answer, *That he should first endeavour to know the minds of the prisoners, who perhaps desired no such liberty as he demanded.*

King *Philip* fearing least he should lose the strength and title of the Kingdom of *England*, and that the Kingdom of *England*, *Scotland*, and *Ireland*, would by *Mary* Queen of *Scots* be annexed unto *France*, dealt seriously with Queen *Elizabeth*, about a Marriage to be contracted with her, promising to procure a special dispensation from the Bishop of *Rome*. The Queen weighing in her mind the unlawfulness of such a Marriage, puts off King *Philip* by little and little, with a modest answer, but indeed out of scruple of Conscience. And now she thought nothing more pleasing to God, than that Religion should be forthwith be altered. Thereupon the care of correcting the Liturgy, was committed to Doctor *Matthew Parker*, *Bill*, *May*, *Grindal*, *Whitehead*, and *Pilkinton*, Learned and moderate Divines, and to Sir *Thomas Smith* Knight; the matter being imparted to no man, but the Marquess of *Northampton*, the Earl of *Bedford*, Sir *John Grey* of *Pyrgo*, and Sir *William Cecil*.

A Parliament was summoned to begin on *January* 25. which opened with an Eloquent and Learned Sermon, Preached by Dr. *Cox*. In the House of Commons there were some furious Spirits, who eagerly opposed all propositions, which seemed to tend unto the prejudice of the Church of *Rome*. Of which number none so violent as *Scory*, Doctor of the Laws, and a Great Instrument of *Bonner's* Butcheries in Queen *Mary's* Reign: who being questioned for the cruelty of his Executions, declared himself to be sorry for nothing more, *That instead of lopping off some few boughes and branches, he did not lay his Ax to the Root of the Tree*: Yet passed He unpunished for the present, though Divine Vengeance brought him in the end to his just reward.

In this Parliament passed an Act for recognizing the Queen's just Title to the Crown, but without any Act for the validity of her Mother's Marriage, on which her Title most depended.

There passed an Act also for restoring the Tenths, and first Fruits, to the Crown; first setled thereon in the time of King *Henry* the Eighth, and afterwards given back by Queen *Mary* to the Pope.

They passed an Act also for the dissolution of all such Monasteries, Convents, and Religious Orders, as had been Founded and established by Queen *Mary*. By vertue of which Act Queen *Elizabeth* was repossessed of all those Lands, which had been granted by her Sister, to the

Monks of *Westminster* and *Shen*, the Knights Hospitallers, the Nuns of *Sion*, together with the Mansion houses re-edified for the Observan:s of *Greenwich*, and the Black-friers in *Smithfield*.

In passing the Act of the Supremacy there was some trouble; it seemed to be a thing even abhorrent in Nature and Polity, that a Woman should be declared to be the Supreme Head on Earth of the Church of *England*. But the Queen declined the Title of Head, and assumed the name of Governor of the Church of *England*. This Act having easily passed the House of Commons, found none of the Temporal Lords in the House of Lords to oppose it, save onely the Earl of *Shrewsbury*, and *Anthony Brown* Viscount *Montacute*. As for the Bishops, there were but fourteen, and the Abbot of *Westminster*, then alive: of whom four being absent, the rest could not make any considerable opposition.

In the Convocation of the Clergy there passed certain Articles of Religion, which they tendered to the Parliament, which were these.

I. *That in the Sacrament of the Altar, by the vertue of Christ assisting, after the word is duly pronounced by the Priest, the natural Body of Christ, conceived by the Virgin Mary is really present, under the Species of Bread and Wine, also his natural Blood.*

II. *That after the Consecration, there remains not the substance of Bread and Wine, nor any other substance, save the substance of God and Man.*

III. *That the true Body of Christ, and his true Blood is offered a propitiatory Sacrifice for the quick and dead,*

IV. *That the supreme power of feeding and governing the Militant Church of Christ, and of confirming their Brethren, is given to* Peter *the Apostle, and to his lawful Successors in the See Apostolick, as unto the Vicars of Christ.*

V. *That the Authority to handle and define such things which belong to Faith, the Sacraments, and Discipline Ecclesiastical, hath hitherto ever belonged, and onely ought to belong unto the Pastors of the Church, whom the Holy Spirit hath placed in the Church of God, and not unto Lay-men.*

This Remonstrance exhibited by the lower house of Convocation to the Bishops, was, according to their Requests, presented by *Edmond Bonner*, Bishop of *London*, to the Lord Keeper of the Broad-seal of *England* in the Parliament.

Both Universities did concur to the truth of the foresaid Articles, the last onely excepted.

the Church of Great Britain.

This Declaration of the Popish Clergy haftened the difputation appointed on the laſt of *March*, in the Church of *Weſtminſter*, wherein thefe Queſtions were debated.

I. *Whether Service and Sacraments ought to be celebrated in the vulgar Tongue?*
II. *Whether the Church hath not power to alter Ceremonies?*
III. *Whether the Maſs be a propitiatory Sacrifice for the living and the dead.*

Popiſh Difputants.

White Biſhop of *Winchefter.*
Watſon Biſhop of *Lincoln.*
Baynes Biſhop of *Coventry* and *Litchfield.*
Scot Biſhop of *CHESTER*.

Proteſtant Difputants.

John Scory late Biſhop of *Chicheſter*.
David Whitehead.
Robert Horn.
Edmond Gweſt.

Edwyn Sandys.
John Elmer.
Edmond Grindal.
John Juel.

Moderators.

Nicholas Heath, Archbiſhop of *York*, Sir *Nicholas Bacon*, Lord Keeper of the Great Seal.

Befides the Difputants, there were prefent many of the Lords of the Queens Council, with other of the Nobility, as alfo many of the lower Houfe of Parliament. For the manner of their conference, it was agreed it fhould be performed in writing, and that the Biſhops fhould deliver their Reafons in writing firſt. Many differences arofe between them, fo that the conference broke off, and nothing was determined. The Biſhops of *Lincoln* and *Winchefter* thought meet, that the Queen and the Authors of this defection from the Church of *Rome*, ſhould be Excommunicated, who for this caufe were imprifoned.

Then a Peace being made, was Proclaimed over all *England*, betwixt the Queen of *England*, the King of *France*, the Daulphin, and the Queen of *Scots*. The Parliament being diffolved, by Authority of the fame the Liturgy was forthwith brought into the Churches in the Vulgar Tongue; the Oath of Supremacy offered to the Popifh Biſhops, and others

others of the Ecclesiastical profession, which most of them had sworn unto, in the Reign of King *Henry* the Eighth. All the Bishops refused, except *Anthony* Bishop of *Landaff*.

As many as refused, were turned out of their Livings, Dignities, Bishopricks.

In the Sees of the Prelates removed were placed Protestant Bishops : *Matthew Parker* was made Archbishop of *Canterbury*, who was Consecrated by three that formerly had been Bishops, namely, *William Barlow* of *Bath* and *Wells*, *John Scory* of *Chichester*, and *Miles Coverdale* of *Exeter*. And being Consecrated himself, he afterward Consecrated *Edmond Grindal* Bishop of *London*, *Richard Cox* Bishop of *Ely*, *Edwyn Sandys* Bishop of *Worcester*, *Rowland Merick* Bishop of *Bangor*, *Thomas Young* Bishop of St. *David's*, *Nicholas Bullingham* Bishop of *Lincoln*, *John Juel* Bishop of *Salisbury*, *Richard Davis* Bishop of St. *Asaph*, *Edward Guest* Bishop of *Rochester*, *Gilbert Barkley* Bishop of *Bath* and *Wells*, *Thomas Bentham* Bishop of *Coventry* and *Litchfield*, *William Alley* Bishop of *Exeter*, *John Parkhurst* Bishop of *Norwich*, *Robert Horn* Bishop of *Winchester*, *Richard Cheiney* Bishop of *Glocester*, *Edmond Scambler* Bishop of *Peterborough*, *William Barlow* Bishop of *Chichester*, *John Scory* Bishop of *Hereford*, *Thomas Young* Archbishop of *York*, *James Pilkinton* Bishop of *Durham*, *John Best* Bishop of *Carlile*, and *William Dounham* Bishop of *Chester*.

Nicholas Heath Archbishop of *York*, lived privately many years in his Mannor of *Chobham* in *Surrey*, never restrained to any one place, and died in great favour with the Queen, who bestowed many gratious visits upon him, during his retirement. *Tonstal* of *Durham* spent the remainder of his time with Archbishop *Parker*, by whom he was kindly entertained, and honourably buried. The like civility was afforded to *Thurlby* Bishop of *Ely* in the same house, and unto *Bourn* of *Wells*, by the Dean of *Exon*, in which two houses they both died about ten years after. *White*, though at first imprisoned for his faults, after some cooling himself in the Tower of *London*, was suffered to enjoy his liberty, and to retire himself to what friend he pleased: Which favour was vouchsafed unto *Turbervil* also, who being a Gentleman by extraction wanted not friends to give him good entertainment. *Watson* of *Lincoln*, after a short restraint, spent the remainder of his time with the Bishops of *Rochester* and *Ely*; till having practised against the State, he was shut up in the Castle of *VVisbich*, where at last he died. *Oglethorp* died soon after his deprivation, of an *Apoplexy*, *Bayn* of the *Stone*, and *Morgan* in *December* following. *Pool* enjoyed the like freedom, and died in a good old age. *Christopherson* lived on his Estate. *Bonner* alone was doomed to a perpetual imprisonment; the prison proving to that wretch (saith Dr. *Heylin*) his greatest Sanctuary, whose horrid Butcheries had otherwise exposed him to the popular fury.

We

The Church of Great Britain.

We find no more to have been deprived of their preferments, than fourteen Bishops, six Abbots, Priors, and Governors of Religious Orders, twelve Deans, and as many Archdeacons, fifteen Presidents or Masters of Colledges, fifty Prebendaries of Cathedral Churches, and about eighty Parsons or Vicars. The whole number not amounting to two hundred men, which in a Realm consisting of nine thousand Parishes, and twenty six Cathedral Churches, could be no great matter.

But there was not a sufficient number of Learned men to supply the Cures, which filled the Church with an Ignorant Clergy, whose Learning went no further than the Liturgy, or the Book of Homilies, but otherwise conformable (which was no small felicity) to the Rules of the Church. And on the other side many were raised to great preferments; who having spent their time of exile in such Forreign Churches as followed the platform of *Geneva*; returned so disaffected to Episcopal Government, unto the Rites here by Law established, as not long after filled the Church with most sad disorders : On which account we find the Queens Professor in *Oxford*, among the Non-conformists, and *Cartwright* the Lady *Margaret*'s in *Cambridge*. *Whittingham* the Ring-leader of the *Franckfort* dividers, was preferred to the Deanery of *Durham* : *Sampson* to the Deanery of *Christ-church*, and within few years after turned out for a rigid Non-conformist. *Hardiman*, one of the first twelve Prebendaries of the Church of *Westminster*, deprived soon after for throwing down the Altar, and defacing the Vestments of the Church.

Dr. *P. Heylins* History of Queen *Eliz.*

Whether it were by the Pope's instigation, or by by the ambition of the Daulphin who had then Married the Queen of *Scots*, the Scottish Queen assumeth unto her self the Style and Title of Queen of *England*, quartereth the Armes thereof upon all her Plate, and in all Armories and Escutcheons as she had occasion. A folly that Queen *Elizabeth* could never forget nor forgive ; and this engaged her the more resolutely in that Reformation so happily begun. And to that purpose she sets out by advice of her Council a certain Body of Injunctions, accommodated to the temper of the present time: wherein severe course was taken about Ministers Marriages, the use of Singing, and the Reverence in Divine Worship to be kept in Churches ; the posture of the Communion-table, and the Form of Prayers in the Congregation.

By the Injunctions, she made way to her Visitation, Executed by Commissioners in their several Circuits, and regulated by a Book of Articles printed and published for that purpose. Proceeding by which Articles, the Commissioners removed all carved Images out of the Church, which had been abused to Superstition, defacing also all such Pictures, Paintings, as served for the setting forth feigned Miracles. They enquired also into the life and doctrine of Ministers, their diligence in attending their several Cures; the decency of their apparel,

Heylin's Hist. of Q. Elizab. the respect of the Parishioners toward them; the reverent behaviour of all manner of persons in God's Worship, &c. by means whereof the Church was setled and confirmed in so good an Order, that the work was made more easie to the Bishops, when they came to Govern, than otherwise it could have been.

In *London*, the Visitors were Sir *Richard Sackvil*, Father to *Thomas* Earl of *Dorset*; *Robert Horn*, soon after Bishop of *VVinchester*; Doctor *Huick*, a Civilian; and one *Salvage*, a Common Lawyer; who calling before them divers Persons of every Parish, gave them an Oath to enquire and present upon such Articles and Injunctions as were given unto them. In pursuance whereof they burnt in St. *Paul's* Church-yard, *Cheapside*, and other places of the City, all the Roods and other Images which had been taken out of the Churches. And in some places the Copes, Vestments, Altar-cloathes, Books, Banners, Sepulchres, and Rood-lofts were burned altogether.

A Peace being concluded betwixt *England* and *France*, although Queen *Elizabeth* had just cause to be offended with the young King *Francis* the Second, for causing the Queen of *Scots* his Wife, to take upon her self the Title and Armes of *England*, yet she resolved to bestow a Royal obsequy upon the King deceased, which was performed in St. *Paul's* Church on the eighth and nineth of *September* in most solemn manner.

Kellison the Jesuite, and *Parsons* from him, slaunderously affirmed, That Archbishop *Parker* was consecrated at the *Nags-head* Tavern in *Cheapside*. This slaunder was raised on this occasion: In order to his Consecration, the first thing to be done after the passing the Royal Assent for ratifying the election of the Dean and Chapter, was the confirming it in the Court of the Arches, according to the usual form in that behalf; Which being accordingly done, the Vicar General, the Dean of the Arches, the Proctors and Officers of the Court, whose presence was required at this Solemnity, were entertained at a Dinner provided for them at the *Nags-head* Tavern in *Cheapside*, for which though Archbishop *Parker* paid the shot, yet shall the Church be called to an after-reckoning. But the Records of the Archbishoprick declare, that he was Consecrated in the Chappel, within his Mannor of *Lambeth*.

Mason's Consecration of Bishops in the Church of England, lib. 3. cap. 4.

These slaunderers knew right well, that nothing did more justifie the Church of *England* in the eye of the World, than that it did preserve a Succession of Bishops, and consequently of all other sacred Orders in the Ministration; without which as they would not grant it to be a Church, so could they prove it to be none by no stronger Argument, than that the Bishops (or the pretended Bishops rather in their Opinion) were either not Consecrate at all, or not Canonically Consecrated as they ought to be.

And

the Church of GREAT BRITAIN.

And now we may behold the face of the Church of *England*, as it was first setled and established under Queen *Elizabeth*. The Government of the Church by Archbishops and Bishops. These Bishops nominated and elected according to the Statute in the twenty sixth of King *Henry* the Eighth, and Consecrated by the Ordinal, confirmed by Parliament, in the fifth and sixth year of King *Edward* the Sixth, never appearing publickly but in their Rotchets, nor Officiating otherwise than in Copes of the Altar: the Priests not stirring out of doors in their square Caps, Gowns, or Canonical Coats, nor Executing any Divine Service but in their Surplice. The Doctrine of the Church reduced unto it's antient purity, according to the Articles agreed upon in Convocation, *Anno* 1552. The Liturgy conform to the Primitive paterns. The Festivals preserved in their former dignity, observed with their distinct Offices peculiar to them; the weekly Fasts, the time of Lent, the Embring weeks, and Rogation severely kept, not now by vertue of the Statute, as in the time of King *Edward*, but as appointed by the Church in her publick Calendar before the Book of Common-Prayer. The Sacrament of the Lord's Supper celebrated in a Reverend manner, the Table seated in the place of the Altar.

Heylin. Hist. of Q. *Elizab.*

In the Court the Liturgy was officiated every day, both Morning and Evening, not onely in the publick Chappel, but the private Closet, celebrated in the Chappel with Organs, and other Musical Instruments, and the most excellent voices both of men and children that could be got in all the Kingdom. The Gentlemen and Children in their Surplices, and the Priests in Copes as oft as they attended the Divine Service at the Altar. The Altar furnished with rich Plate, two fair gilt Candlesticks with Tapers in them, and a Massy Crucifix in midst thereof: Which last remained there for some years. The antient Ceremonies customably observed by the Knights of the Garter in their Adoration toward the Altar were by this Queen retained as formerly in her Father's time. The solemn Sermons Preached upon each *Wednesday, Friday*, and *Lords-day* in the time of Lent, Preached by the choycest of the Clergy, she devoutly heard, attired in black, according to the custom of her Predecessors.

The Bishoprick of *Carlile* was first profered to *Bernard Gilpin*, Rector of *Houghton* in the North, but Mr. *Gilpin* refused the offer, not that he had any disaffection to the Office, but because he had so much kinred about *Carlile*, at whom He must either connive in many things, not without hurt to himself, or else deny them, not without offence to them. It was afterward given to Dr. *John Best*, as was shewed before. As for *Miles Coverdale*, formerly Bishop of *Exeter*, he never returned to his See, but remained a private Minister to the day of his death.

*Fuller.*Church History of *Britain*

Such

Such of the Scots as defired a Reformation of Religion, taking advantage by the Queen's abfcence, and want of power in the Queen Regent to fupprefs their practices, had put themfelves into a Body. Headed by fome of the Nobility, they take unto themfelves the name of the *Congregation*, managing their own Affairs apart from the reft of the Kingdom. They petition the Queen Regent, and the Lords of the Council, that the Sacrament of the Lord's Supper might be adminiftred in both kinds. That divine Offices might be celebrated in the vulgar Tongue, and that they might have the choice of their own Minifters. The chief of the party well backed by the common people, put themfelves into *Perth*, the news whereof occafioneth Mr. *Knox* to leave *Geneva*, and joyn himfelf to the Lords of the *Congregation*. At *Perth* he Preacheth againft Images, Idolatry, and other Superftitions of the Church of *Rome* fo bitterly, that the people in a popular fury deface all the Images in that Church, and prefently demolifh all Religious Houfes in that City. Thofe of *Couper* hearing of it, forthwith deftroyed all Images, and pulled down the Altars in that Church alfo. The like was done after his Preaching at *Craile* and St. *Andrews*, in thofe places. They burnt down the rich Monaftery of *Scone*, and ruined that of *Cambuskenneth*, demolifhed all the Altars, Images, and Covents of Religious perfons in *Sterling*, *Lithgow*, *Glafcough*, *Edenburgh*, which laft they poffefs, and put up their own Preachers into all the Pulpits of that City, not fuffering the Queen Regent to have the ufe of one Church onely for her own devotions. They alfe deprive the Queen Regent of all place and power in the publick Government. But fhe gathering Forces recovereth *Edenborough*, and the chief key of all that Kingdom garifoned by the French. In their extremity *Maitland* and *Melvin* being difpatched to the Court of *England*, imploring aid from Queen *Elizabeth*. And an Army is fent into *Scotland* of fix thoufand Foot and three thoufand Horfe, commanded by the Lord *Gray*. Some Ships were alfo fent to block up the haven, and hinder all Relief which might come by Sea to the Town of *Leith*. At length after divers Articles figned and confirmed for both Kingdoms, the French take their leave of *Scotland*, and the Englifh Army was difbanded at *Berwick*.

As the *Congregation* was by the Queen put upon a prefent confidence of going vigoroufly on in their Reformation, fo it concern'd them to proceed fo carefully in purfuance of it, as might comply with the dependance which they had upon her. Firft, Therefore they bound themfelves by their fubfcription to embrace the Liturgy, with all the Rites of the Church of *England*, which for a time remained the onely form of Worfhip for the Kirk of *Scotland*.

In the next place, They caufe a Parliament to be called in the moneth of *Auguft*: for the Boroughs there appeared the accuftomed number,

but

The Church of Great Britain.

but of the Lords Spiritual no more than six Bishops of thirteen, with thirteen Abbots and Priors: and the Temporal Lords to the number of ten Earls, and as many Barons.

Three Acts were passed to the advantage of the Reformation.

The first, was for the abolishing the Pope's Jurisdiction and Authority within the Realm.

The second, for annulling all Statutes made in former times for maintenance of Idolatry and Superstition.

The third, for the punishing the Sayers and Hearers of the Mass.

To this Parliament also some of the Ministers presented a Confession of the Faith and Doctrine to be believed and professed by the Protestants of the Kirk of *Scotland*: which being put to the Vote, was opposed but by three of the Temporal Lords. The Popish Prelates were silent in it: which being observed by the Earl Marshal, he broke out into these words, *Seeing* (saith He) *that my Lords the Bishops, who by their Learning can, and for the zeal they should have to the Truth, ought, as I suppose, to gainsay any thing repugnant to it, say nothing against the Confession we have heard, I cannot think but that it is the very Truth of God, and that the contrary of it is false Doctrine.*

The Queen was now as active in advancing the Reformed Religion in *Ireland*, as she had been in either of the other Kingdoms. A Parliament is therefore held on *January* 12. where past an Act restoring to the Crown the antient Jurisdiction over all Ecclesiastical and Spiritual Persons. By which Statute were established both the Oath of Supremacy, and the High Commission, as before in *England*. There past also an Act for the Uniformity of Common-Prayer, &c. with a permission for saying the same in Latin, in those Churches where the Minister had not the knowledge of the English Tongue. The people by that Statute are required, under several penalties, to frequent their Churches, and to be frequent at the reading the English Liturgy, which they understand as little as the Mass; by which means the Irish were kept in ignorance, as to the Doctrines and Devotions of the Church of *England*. *Heylin's Hist. of Q. Elizab.*

There also past another Statute for restoring to the Crown the first-fruits, and twenty parts of all Ecclesiastical promotions within that Realm, as also of all Impropriate Parsonages. The like Act passed for restoring all such Lands belonging to the Knights of St. *John* of *Jerusalem*. An Act was also past for the recognition of the Queen's just Title to the Crown, as before in *England*. The Queen left the prosecution of the work to her Bishops and Clergy: But they so dissipated the Revenues of their several Bishopricks, by long Leases, Fee-farmes, and plain Alienations, that to some of their Sees they left no more than a Rent of five Marks *per annum*, to others a bare yearly Rent of forty shillings, to the great dishonour of God, disservice of the Church, and the perpetual Ignominy of themselves.

Now Return we again to *England*, where we find Reverend *Jewel*, newly confecrated Bishop of *Salisbury*, to have Preached a Sermon at *Paul's* Cross, on 1 *Cor.* 11. 23. *That which I delivered to you, I received of the Lord,* &c. on *March* 30. 1560. There he published that memorable Challenge, which so much exercised the Pens and Studies of the Romish Clergy.

Bishop *Jewel's* Chalenge.

If any Learned man of our Adversaries, or all the Learned men that be alive, be able to bring any one sufficient sentence, out of any old Catholick Doctor, or Father, or General Council, or Holy Scripture, or any one Example in the Primitive Church, whereby it may be clearly and plainly proved, during the first six hundred years.

I. That there was at that time any private *Mass* in the World.
II. Or that there was then any Communion ministred unto the people in one kind.
III. Or that the People had their Common-Prayer in a strange Tongue.
IV. Or that the Bishop of Rome was then called the Head of the Universal Church.
V. Or that the People were then taught to believe, that Christ's Body is really, Substantially, Carnally, Corporally or Naturally in the Sacrament.
VI. Or that his Body is or may be in a thousand places or more at one time.
VII. Or that the Priest did then hold up the Sacrament over his head.
VIII. Or that the People did then fall down and Worship it with godly honour.
IX. Or that the Sacrament was then, and now ought to be hanged up under a Canopy.
X. Or that in the Sacrament, after the words of Confecration, there remained onely the accidents and shews, without the substance of Bread and Wine.
XI. Or that then the Priests divided the Sacrament into three parts, and afterwards received Himself all alone.
XII. Or that whosoever had said the Sacrament is a Figure, a Pledge, a Token, or a Remembrance of Christ's Body, had therefore been judged for an Heretick.
XIII. Or that it was lawful then to have thirty, twenty, &c. Masses said in one day.

XIV. Or

the Church of GREAT BRITAIN.

XIV. Or that Images were then set up in the Churches to the intent the people should worship them.
XV. Or that the Lay-people were then forbid to read the Word of God in their own Tongue.
XVI. Or that it was then lawful for the Priest to pronounce the words of Consecration closely, or in private to Himself.
XVII. Or that the Priest had then authority to offer up Christ unto his Father.
XVIII. Or to receive the Sacrament for another as they do.
XIX. Or to apply the vertue of Christ's death to any man by the means of the Mass.
XX. Or that it was then thought a sound Doctrine to teach the People, that Mass, Ex opere operato, is able to remove any part of our sin.
XXI. Or that any Christian man called the Sacrament of the Lord, his God.
XXII. Or that the People were then taught to believe, that the Body of Christ remaineth in the Sacrament as long as the Accidents of Bread and Wine remain there without corruption.
XXIII. Or that a Mouse, or any other Worm or Beast, may eat the Body of Christ.
XXIV. Or that when Christ said, Hoc est corpus meum, the word [Hoc] pointed not the Bread, but Individuum Vagum, as some of them say.
XXV. Or that the Accidents, Formes, or Shews of Bread and Wine, be the Sacrament of Christ's Body and Blood, and not rather the very Bread and Wine it self.
XXVI. Or that the Sacrament is a Token, or sign of the Body of Christ that lieth underneath it.
XXVII. Or that Ignorance is the Mother and Cause of true devotion.

The Conclusion is, That then I shall be content to yield and subscribe.

This Chalenge being published in so great an Auditory startled the English Papists both at home and abroad. The buliness was first agitated by the exchange of friendly Letters betwixt Bishop *Jewel*, and Dr. *Henry Cole*, the late Dean of St. *Pauls*; more violently followed in a Book of *Rastals*; followed therein by *Dorman* and *Marshal*: *Dorman* was well answered and foiled by *Nowel*, and the other by *Calfhil*. But the main encounter was between the Chalenger himself and Dr. *John Harding*; who had the better of the day will easily appear to any that consults their Writings: But these Discourses came not out till some years after.

Pope *Paul* the Fourth dying, Pope *Pius* the Fourth succeedeth him, who being moved to Excommunicate Queen *Elizabeth*, by the Count of

Feria,

Feria, takes a more moderate course, by sending *Vincent Parpalia*, Abbot of St. *Saviour's*, with courteous Letters unto her. *Parpalia* was instructed to offer in the Name of the Pope, That the English Liturgy should be confirmed, the use of the Communion in both kinds allowed of: And that all sentences passed, in the Court of *Rome*, against her Mother should be rescinded, upon condition she would own the Pope's Primacy, and cordially unite her self to the Catholick Church: yea some thousands of Crowns (but all in vain) were promised to the effecters thereof. But for all this the Abbot came no nearer than *Bruxels* with his Bulls and Faculties, not being suffered to set Foot on English ground.

Now another Enemy quarrels at the Rites and Extrinsecals of the Church: Those that for Religion fled to *Frankford* in Queen *Marie's* days, after her death hastened into *England*: followed not long after by the Brethren of the Separation, which retired from thence unto *Geneva*. Some Friends they had about the Queen, and *Calvin* make's use of all his power and credit, both with the Queen and *Cecil* (as appears by his Letters unto both) to advance their ends. And he was seconded therein by *Peter Martyr*. But the Queen resolved to keep up the Church in such outward splendor, as might make it every way considerable in the eye of the World: when therefore they saw the Liturgy imposed by Act of Parliament, and so many Episcopal Sees supplied with able Pastors, they began to revive the quarrels raised in King *Edward's* time, about Caps, and Surplices, &c. faith Dr. *Heylin*. And herein they were seconded (as before in King *Edward's* time) by the same *Peter Martyr*, as appears by his Letters to a nameless friend, bearing date at *Zurich*, *November* 5. 1560. to which he added his dislike in another of his Letters, touching the Cap, the Episcopal Habit, the Churche's Patrimony: the manner of proceeding to be held against Papists; the Perambulation used in the Rogation week, &c. in which his judgement was desired.

But these helps being too far off, another project was set on foot. *Gryndal*, the new Bishop of *London*, was known to have a great respect to *Calvin*; the business therefore is so ordered, that by *Calvin's* Letters to *Gryndal*, and the friends they had about the Queen, way should be given to such of the French Nation, as had repaired hither, to enjoy the freedom of their own Religion, to have a Church unto themselves, and in that Church not onely to erect the *Genevian* Discipline, but to set up a Form of Prayer (faith Dr. *Heylin*) which should hold no conformity with the English Liturgy. This was effected. And now there is another Church in *London*, as different from the Church of *England* in Government and Forms of worship, as that of *John Alasco* was in the *Augustine* Friars.

Upon

Upon the news of which succefs, divers both French and Dutch came into *England*, planted themfelves in the Sea-Towns, and openly profeffed the Reformed Religion. But fome of them proved to be Anabaptifts, and others infected with corrupt Opinions of as ill a nature; which being made known to the Queen, fhe commands them all by Proclamation to depart the Kingdom, whether they were Aliens, or naturalborn Englifh, within twenty days upon pain of imprifonment, and lofs of all their goods; yet notwithftanding many of them lurked in *England* without fear of difcovery, efpecially after the erecting of fo many French and Dutch Churches in the Maritime parts. The French and Dutch Churches in *London* were infected with their frenzies; and fuch difputes were among them on that account, that *Peter Martyr* interpofed his Authority with them, to the compofing of thofe differences which had grown among them: for which fee his Letter bearing date at *Zurich*, on *February* 15. next following after the date of the faid Proclamation (which feemeth to have been about *September* 16.) and fuperfcribed, *Unto the Church of Strangers in the City of* London.

By another Proclamation fhe labours to reftrain a facrilegious kind of people, which under pretence of abolifhing Superftition, demolifhed antient Tombs, razed the Epitaphs, and Coat-armors of moft Noble Familes, and other Monuments of venerable Antiquity, took the Bells out of Churches, and pluckt off the Lead from the Churchroofs.

The Abbey of *Weftminfter*, moft renouned for the Inauguration of the Kings of *England*, their Sepulture, and the keeping of the Regal Enfignes, fhe converted to a Collegiat Church: and there fhe inftituted a Dean, twelve Prebendaries, a School-mafter, an Ufher, forty Scholars (called the Queen's Scholars, whereof fix or more are preferred every year to the Vniverfities) Petit Canons and others of the Quire to the number of thirty, ten Officers belonging to the Church, and as many Servants belonging to the Colledge-diet, and twelve Almesmen, befides many Officers, Stewards, and Collectors for keeping Courts, and bringing in of their Revenue. The principal of which (called the *High Steward* of *Weftminfter*) hath ever fince been one of the prime Nobility. The Dean intrufted with keeping the *Regalia*, honoured with a place of neceffary fervice at all Coronations, and a Commiffioner for the peace within the City of *Weftminfter*, and the liberties of it by Act of Parliament. The Scholars annually preferred by election either to *Chrift-church* in *Oxford*, or *Trinity Colledge* in *Cambridge*. Since this new Foundation of it, it hath given breeding and preferment to four Archbifhops, two Lord Keepers of the Great Seal of *England*, twenty two Bifhops, and thirteen Deans of Cathedral-churches, befides Archdeacons, Prebendaries, and other Dignitaries in the Church to a proportionable number.

The

The death of *Francis* the second, the young King of *France*, who had married *Mary* Queen of *Scots*, encouraged the Scots to proceed boldly with their Reformation.

The Duke of *Guise* laboured with the Pope to fulminate his Excommunications against Queen *Elizabeth*, as one that had renounced his authority, apostatized from the Catholick Religion, and utterly exterminated the profession of it out of her Dominions. But the Duke sped no better in his negotiation than the Count of *Feria* did before.

About this time one *Geoffrys* was committed Prisoner to the Marshalsey in *Southwark*, and *More* to the house of Mad-men (commonly called *Bethlem*) without Bishop's-gate in *London*. *More* professed himself to be Christ: *Geoffrys* believed him to be such, and reported him so. Having remained a whole year in prison, without shewing any sign of their repentance, *Geoffrys* was whipt, on *April* 10. 1561. from the said Marshalsey to *Bethlem*, with a paper bound about his head, which signified, That this was *William Geoffrys*, a most blasphemous Heretick, who denied Christ to be in Heaven. At *Bethlem* he was whipt again in the presence of *More*, till the lash had extorted from him a confession of his damnable error. After which *More* was stript and whipt in the open Streets, till he had made the like acknowledgment, confessing Christ to be in Heaven, and Himself to be a vile, sinful man. Which being done, they were again remitted to their several prisons for their further cure.

On *June* the fourth, a lamentable fire about four a Clock in the afternoon, first shewed it self near the top of the Steeple of St. *Paul's* Church in *London*, and from thence burnt down the Spire, to the Stone-work and Bells, and raged so terribly, that within the space of four hours the Timber and Lead of the whole Church, and whatsoever else was combustible in it, was miserably consumed, to the great terror of all Beholders: Which Church said to be the largest in all the Christian World for all dimensions, contains in length seven hundred and twenty foot, in breadth one hundred and thirty foot, and in height from the pavement to the top of the roof one hundred and fifty foot. The Steeple from the ground to the Cross or Weather-cock, contained in height five hundred and twenty foot, of which the square Tower onely amounted to two hundred and sixty, the Pyramide or Spire to as many more; which Spire being raised of massy Timber, and covered over with sheets of Lead, as it was the more apt to be enflamed, so was the mischief more incapable of a present remedy.

The Queen hereupon directed her Letters to the Lord Mayor and City of *London* to take care therein. In obedience to whose Royal Pleasure the Citizens granted a Benevolence, and three Fifteens to be speedily paid, besides the great bounty of particular persons, &c. The Queen

also

also sent in a thousand Marks in ready money, and Warrants for one thousand load of Timber to be served out of Her Majesties Woods. The Clergy of the Province of *Canterbury* contributing to this work the fortieth part of their Benefices which stood charged with first-fruits, and the thirtieth part of those which had paid the same. The Clergy of the Diocess of *London* bestowed the thirtieth part of such of their livings as were under the burden of that payment, and the twentieth part of those which were not. To which the Bishop added at several times the sum of nine hundred pound one shilling eleven pence, the Dean and Chapter one hundred thirty six pound thirteen shillings four pence. By all which, and some other little helps, the work was carried on so fast, that before the end of *April* 1566, the Timber-work of the Roof was not onely fitted, but compleatly covered.

And now the Pope's Nuncio being advanced already in his way to *England*, as far as *Flanders*, expecteth the Queen's pleasure touching his admittance: for the Pope could not be taken off from sending his Nuncio to the Queen, with whom he conceived himself to stand upon termes of Amity. But the Queen persevered in her first intent, affirming she could not treat with the Bishop of *Rome*, whose authority was excluded out of *England* by consent of Parliament. The greatest obstacle to the Nuncio's coming was partly laid by the indiscretion of some Papists in *England*, and partly by the precipitancy of the Pope's Ministers in *Ireland*; for sundry ill-disposed persons upon the noise of the Nuncio's coming, not onely brake the Laws made against the Pope and his Authority, but spread abroad slaunderous reports, that the Queen was at the point to change her Religion, and alter the government of the Realm. Some also had practised with the Devil by Conjurations, Charms, and casting of Figures, to be informed in the length of her Majesties Reign. And on the other side the Pope's Legate being at the same time in *Ireland*, joyned himself to some desperate Traitors, who stirred up rebellion there, and as much as in him was had deprived the Queen of all Right and Title to that Kingdom. Upon which grounds it was carried clearly at the Council-boord against the Nuncio, notwithstanding the Interceffion of the French, the *Spaniard*, or the Duke of *Alva*.

Yet notwithstanding the Emperor *Ferdinand* sends to perswade the Queen to return to the old Religion, at least that she would set apart some Churches to the use of the Catholicks. To whom she answered, *That she had setled her Religion on so sure a Bottom, that she could not easily be changed, And for granting Churches to the Papists, it did not consist with the Polity and good Laws of the Land.*

Then divers abuses arising in the Church, Archbishop *Parker* found it necessary to have recourse unto the power which was given to him by the Queen's Commission, and by a clause of the Act of Parliament, *For the Uniformity of Common-Prayer and service in the Church*, &c. As one of the

the Commissioners for causes Ecclesiastical, he was authorized with the rest of his Associates. To reform, redress, order, correct and amend all such Errors, Heresies, Schismes, Abuses, Offences, Contempts, and Enormities whatsoever, as might from time to time arise in the Church of *England*.

And in the passage of the Act forementioned it was provided, That all such Ornaments of the Church and the Ministers thereof should be retained, as were in the Church of *England*, by Authority of Parliament, in the second year of King *Edward* the Sixth, untill further order should be taken therein from the Queen's Majesty, *&c.* And also if there shall happen any contempt or irreverence to be used in the Rites of the Church, by the misusing of the Orders of the said Book of Common-Prayer, the Queen might by the advise of the Commissioners or Metropolitan, ordain or publish such further Ceremonies or Rites, as should be most for the advance of God's glory, the edifying the Church, *&c.* Hereupon the Archbishop, by the Queen's consent, and the advice of some of the Bishops, sets forth a certain Book of Orders to be diligently observed, and executed by all persons whom it might concern.

Heylin.Hist. of Q. *Elizab. in. Reg.* 3.

In which it was provided, That no Parson, Vicar, or Curate of any exempt Church, should from thenceforth attempt to conjoyn, by solemnization of Matrimony, any not being of his or their Parish-church, without good Testimony of the Bains being ask'd in the several Churches where they dwell, or otherwise were sufficiently Licensed. That no other days should be observed as Holy-days and Fasting-days, but onely such as be expressed in the Calendar, lately set forth by the Queen's Authority. That neither the Curates or Parents of Children which are brought to Baptism, should answer for them at the Font, but that the antient use of Godfathers and Godmothers should still be retained; and that in all such Churches in which the steps to the Altar were not taken down, the said steps should remain as before they did. That the Communion-Table should be set in the said place where the steps then were, or had formerly stood: and that the Table of the Decalogue should be fixed upon the wall over the said Communion-Table.

This year the Merchants Tailors School in *London* was founded, first by the Master, Wardens, and Assistants, of the Company of Merchants Tailors, whence it had the name, and by them founded for a Seminary to St. *John's* in *Oxford*, built and endowed at the sole costs of one of their Livery. But of a far more private nature was the Foundation of another Grammar School in the Town of *Sandwich*, built at the charge of Sir *Roger Manwood*, and endowed with forty pound *per annum.*

The Council of *Trent* being now opened, it was said in that Council, that i. was good to let the Protestants alone, and not name them, alledging

ing the danger of moving ill humors in a Body which was then quiet. To give a safe conduct to the English-men, which neither They nor any of them did require, were a great indignity. They were content it should be given to the Scots, becaufe their Queen would demand it, but fo as that the demand should firft be made. But the English Proteftant Bishops would not venture themfelves into that Council on fuch weak affurance, confidering how ill the fafe conduct had been formerly kept to *John Hus*, and *Jerom* of *Prague*, at the Council of *Conftance*. And the Queen kept the Papal party fafe from gadding thither.

Then *Scipio*, a Venetian Gentleman (formerly acquainted with Mafter *Jewel*, whil'ft he was a Student at *Padua*) wrote now an expoftulating Letter unto him, being lately made Bishop of *Sarisbury*, in which he much admireth, that *England* should fend no Ambaffador, nor Letter, nor Meffage, to excufe their Nation's abfence from the General Appearance of Chriftianity in that Council, &c. Bishop *Jewel* returned him fuch an Anfwer, that neither *Scipio* himfelf, nor any other of that party durft reply upon him. The Anfwer is to be found at large at the end of the Hiftory of this Council, Tranflated by Sir *Nathanael Brent*.

At this time it was advifed, by *Lewis* Prince of *Conde*, the Cardinal *Chaftilion*, and other principal leaders of the Proteftant party in *France*, that they should put themfelves under the protection of the Queen of *England*, who had not long before fo feafonably relieved the Scots in the like diftrefs.

The Queen had been fecretly advertifed of all paffages there by Sir *Nicholas Throgmorton*, her Majeftie's Refident in that Kingdom.

It being agreed on between them, that the Queen should fupply the Prince of *Conde*, and his Affociates with a fufficient quantity of Money, Corn, and Ammunition, for the fervice of the French King, againft the practices of the Houfe of *Guife*, and that the Town of *New-haven* should be put into her Majeftie's hands, to be garrifoned by English Souldiers. Immediately a manifeft was published in the name of the Queen, wherein was declared, that she had obferved, how the Guifian Faction, in the names of the Queen-Mother of *France*, and the young King, had endeavoured to root out the Profeffors of the Reformed Religion, and what maffacres had been made at *Vaffey*, *Paris*, *Sene*, *Tholoufe*, *Bloys*, *Tours*, *Angiers*, and other places; that there were thought to be Butchered no lefs than an hundred thoufand of the natural French, between the firft of *March* and the twentieth of *Auguft* then laft paft: that with the like violence they had caufed to be fpoiled and imprifoned fuch of her Majeftie's Subjects as Traded in the Ports of *Bretaign*, and fuch as fought to preferve themfelves, to be killed, their goods and Merchandize to be feized, without charging any other crime upon them but that they were Hugonots; and that in confideration of the premifes she could do no lefs
than

than endeavour the preserving the Reformed Religion, from an universal destruction, and the maintaining her own Subjects and Dominions in peace and safety. The ayd amounting to six thousand men, was divided into two equal parts, of which the one was destined to the defence of *Roven* and *Deep*, then being in the hands of the Confederates, the other to take possession of the Town of *New-haven*, which by the Inhabitants was joyfully surrendred to the English. The Lord *Ambrose Dudley*, the eldest Son then living of the late Duke of *Northumberland*, she sent to command that place, whom on *Decemb.* 26. She had created Lord *Lisle*, and Earl of *Warwick*, where he was solemnly received with a peal of Ordnance.

A petit Rebellion hapned in *Merton-colledge* in *Oxford*. The Wardenship of that house being voyd by the death of *Gervase*, one *Man* is chosen to the place; one *Hall* and his Popish faction opposed his admission, and raised such a persecution, that it was poenal for any to be a Protestant. Archbishop *Parker* hearing of it, summoneth *Hall* to appear before him, but the seal of the citation was torn off by some of that party. Hereupon the Archbishop made a solemn visitation of that Colledge, wherein all were generally examined, *Man* confirmed Warden, *Hall* justly expelled, his party publickly admonished; the young Scholars relieved, Papists curbed and suppressed, Protestants countenanced, and encouraged in the whole University.

Now many strange whispers were abroad, and no small hopes conceived by those of the Popish faction, for suppressing the Protestants in all parts of the Kingdom, and setting up their own Religion as in former times: of the plot were. *Arthur Pool*, younger brother to *Reginald Pool* the late Cardinal Legate, and *Geoffry Fortescue*, who had married his sister, and others. The substance of their charge was, a design of levying War against the Queen, &c. with a particular intention of advancing the Queen of *Scots* to the Crown of *England*, and *Pool* himself unto the Title of Duke of *Clarence*. All which they Confessed upon the Indictment, and did all receive the sentence of death; but were all afterwards pardoned by the Queen, out of that great respect which she bare to their Royal Extraction.

Then was that elegant discourse published by Bishop *Jewel*, Entitled, The Apology of the Church of *England*, first writ in *Latine*, translated presently into *English*, *French*, *Italian*, *Dutch*, and at last in *Greek*, to the publishing whereof he was much encouraged by *Peter Martyr*, with whom he had spent the greatest part of his time when he lived in exile. But *Martyr* lived onely to see the Book which he so much longed for, dying at *Zurich* on the twelfth of *November* following, and laid into his grave by the Magistrates and people of that City with a solemn funeral.

The five Bishopricks erected by King *Henry* the eighth, were so

impo-

impoverished in this Queen's Reign that the new Bishops were necessitated to require the benevolence of their Clergy at their first coming to them, to furnish their Episcopal houses, and to enable them to maintain some tolerable degree of Hospitality in their several Dioceses.

The Parliament called *January* 12. 1562. passed an Act *for Assurance of the Queen's Royal power over all Estates and Subjects in her Dominions*. In which it was provided, That no man Residing in the Queen's Dominions, should from thenceforth either by-word or writing, &c. endeavour willingly to maintain the power and jurisdiction of the Bishop of *Rome* heretofore usurped within this Realm. It was also enacted, that none should be admitted unto Holy Orders, or to any Degree in either of the Universities, or to be Barrester, or Bencher in any of the Inns of Court, or to Practise as an Attourney, &c, till He or They should first take the Oath of Supremacy on the Holy Evangelists; with a power given to every Archbishop and Bishop within this Realm and the Dominions of the same, to Minister the said Oath to all and every Spiritual Person in their proper Dioceses, as well in places exempt as elsewhere; It had been declared by the Bishops and Clergy assembled at the same time in their Convocation, To be a thing plainly repugnant to the word of God, and the Custom of the Primitive Church, *to have publick Prayer in the Church, or to administer the Sacraments in a Tongue not understood by the People*: therefore it was Enacted, That the Bishops of *Hereford*, S. *David's*, *Bangor*, *Landaff* and S. *Asaph*, should take care for Translating the whole Bible with the Common-prayer-book, into the *Welch* Tongue: The like care was also taken for Translating the Books of Homilies.

Then were the Nine and thirty Articles (composed in the Convocation at *London*) published soon after both in *English* and *Latine* with this following Title, *viz*. Articles agreed upon by the Archbishops and Bishops of both Provinces, and the whole Clergy in the Convocation holden at *London*, *Anno* 1562. for the avoyding of Diversities of opinions, and establishing consent touching true Religion.

The 39. Articles compiled in Convocation.

These Articles came forth much about the time that the Decrees of the Council of *Trent* were published. Many of which Decrees begin with lying, and all end with Cursing, threatening *Anathema*'s to all dissenters. *Anno* 1571. the Parliament confirmed these Articles so far, that every Clerk should before *Decemb*. 25. next following subscribe the same. And hereafter every person promoted to an Ecclesiastical living, should within a time prefixed, in the time of Divine Service publickly read and profess his consent to the same, on pain of deprivation *ipso facto*, if omitted. This subscription was extended only to men of Ecclesiastical Function.

After the return of the Queen of *Scots* out of *France* into *Scotland*, Besides

Besides the Ratifying the Act of *Oblivion*, (formerly condescended to in the Treaty at *Edenburgh*) there were also past some other Acts, *viz.* one Act for repairing and upholding Parish Churches, and the Church-yards of the same for burial of the dead. Another against letting Parsonages, Gleabes, or Houses, into long Leases or Fee. But on the other side no safety or Protection could be found for the Queen's own Religion, no not so much as the Chappel Royal, or the Regal City. In contempt whereof a force was violently committed in the moneth of *August* in the Chappel of the Palace of *Holy-rood* house, where certain of the Queen's servants were assembled for their own devotions, the doors broke open, some of the Company haled to the next prison, and the rest dispersed, the Priest escaping with difficulty by a private passage, the Queen being then absent in the North.

In *France* the City and Castle of *Cane* besieged by the confederate forces both *French* and *English*, was finally surrendred to the Admiral *Chastilion* to the use of the Princes. After which followed the surrendry of *Baieux*, *Faleise*, *S. Lod's*, and divers other Towns and Castles. The Town of *Hareflew* on the *Seine* was gallantly taken by the help of the *English* of *Newhaven* on the tenth of *March*, and garrisoned by such Souldiers and Inhabitants as were sent from thence. These successes amazed the *Guisian* faction, that they agreed unto an Edict of Pacification, by the which the *French* forces were restored to the King's Favour, the Hugonots to the free exercise of their own Religion. But they must buy this happiness by betraying the *English*, whom they had brought into the Countrey, and joyn their forces with the rest to drive them out of *New-haven*, if they would not yield it on demand. The *French* closely besiege the Town, and the Plague raging sore among the *English*, they capitulate, and leave the Town to the *French* on *July* the twenty ninth, and carry the Plague with them into *England*.

Hist. Concil. Tridenr.

The Pope was so incensed against Queen *Elizabeth*, that he dispatched a commission to the Fathers of *Trent*, to proceed to an excommunication of the Queen of *England*. But the Emperour *Ferdinand* wrote Letters both to the Pope and to the Legates, in which he signified unto them, That if the Council would not yield that fruit which was desired, at least they should not give occasion to the Hereticks to unite themselves more; which certainly they would do, in case they proceeded so against the Queen of *England*, by means whereof they would undoubtedly make a league against the Catholicks. Hereupon the Pope desisted at *Rome*, and revoked his Commission sent before to the Legates at *Trent*.

The Plague brought out of *France* by the Garrison Souldiers of *New-haven*, had so dispersed it self, and made such desolation in many parts of *England*, that it swept away above twenty thousand of the City

City of *London*, which was the greatest at that time which any man living could remember. Soon after this the Queen makes peace with *France*.

Then the Queen went in progress to take the pleasures of the Countrey, and visited the University of *Cambridge*, where being with all kinds of honour received by the Students, and delighted with Comedies, Tragedies, and Scholastical disputations, she surveyed every Colledge: and in a Latine Oration takes her leave of *Cambridge*, giving them encouragement to pursue their Studies.

The *English* Bishops being impowered by their Canons, began to shew their Authority in urging the Clergy of their Dioceses, to subscribe to the Liturgy, Rites, and discipline of the Church; and such as refused the same were branded with the name of Puritans.

The Non-conformists in this Age were divided into two Ranks: some mild and moderate, contented onely to enjoy their own conscience. Others fierce and fiery, to the disturbance of Church and State, saith *Fuller*. Among the former was Father *John Fox* (for so Queen *Elizabeth* termed him) summoned to subscribe by Archbishop *Parker*. The old man produced the New Testament in Greek, To this (saith he), will I subscribe. But when a subscription to the Canons was subscribed of him, he refused it, saying, *I have nothing in the Church save a Prebend at Salisbury: and much good may it do you, if you will take it away from me.* However such respect did the Bishops (most formerly his fellow-exiles) bear to his Age, parts, and pains, that he continued in his place till the day of his death. With Mr. *Fox* we may joyn his dear friend *Laurence Humfery*, who was Regius Professor of Divinity in *Oxford*. But such was his quiet carriage, that notwithstanding his nonsubscribing, he kept his Professors place, and Deanery of *Winchester* as long as he lived.

A second sort of Non-conformists were fierce sticklers against Church-discipline, we will begin with *Anthony Gilby* bred in Christ's Colledge in *Cambridge*. His fierceness against the Ceremonies take from his own pen, *They are* (saith he) *known Liveries of Antichrist, accursed leaven of the blasphemous popish Priest-hood, cursed patches of Popery and Idolatry* &c. *William Whittingham* succeeds, who after his return from his exile in *Germany*, was made Dean of *Durham*. *Christopher Goodman* is the third, who wrote a book stuffed with much dangerous Doctrine, wherein he maintained, *that Sir Thomas Wait was no Traitor, that his cause was God's*, &c. These three (saith Mr. *Fuller*) were the Antesignani of the fierce Non-conformists: for *David Whitehead* is not mentioned with them. Yet find we none of them silenced. Onely we meet with *Thomas Sampson* Dean of *Christ-church* in *Oxford*, who was displaced out of his Deanery for his Non-conformity. This Deanery was then conferred on Dr. *Thomas Godwin*, Chaplain in Ordinary to the Queen

Queen, who was after advanced to the Bishoprick of *Bath* and *Wells*, who was Father to *Francis Godwin*, late Bishop of *Landaff*, the Author of the Catalogue of the *English* Bishops.

Bullinger and *Gualter*, two Divines of *Switzerland*, men eminent in all points of Learning being sollicited by some zealous brethren to signifie their judgement in the present controversie about the Habit of the Clergy, return an approbation of it, but send the same enclosed to *Sandy's*. *Horn*, and *Grindal*.

Now the *Queen* thought fit to make a further signification of Her Royal Pleasure, legally declared by Her Commissioners for causes Ecclesiastical, according to the Acts and Statutes made in that behalf. The Archbishop is thereupon required to consult together with such Bishops and Commissioners as were next at hand upon the making of such Rules and Orders as they thought necessary for the peace of the Church, with reference to the present estate thereof. Which being accordingly performed, presented to the *Queen*, and by her approved, the said Rules and Orders were set forth, and published in a certain Book Entitled, *Advertisements, partly for due Order in the publick Administration of the Common-prayers, and using the holy Sacraments; and partly for the Apparel of all Persons Ecclesiastical, by vertue of the Queen's Majestie's Letters Commanding the same,* January *fifteenth*, &c.

In this year 1564. died the Emperour *Ferdinand*, and Mr. *John Calvin*. What *Peter Lombard* was esteemed to be in the Schools at *Rome*, the same was *Calvin* reckoned to be in all those Churches which were Reformed according to the *Zuinglian* Doctrine in the point of the Sacrament. Yet the Royal and Prelatical Divines conceived otherwise of him (saith Dr. *Heylin*) and the learned *Adrian Seravia* (though by birth a *Dutchman*) Yet being once preferred in the Church of *England*, could not endure to be called *Calvinian*.

Hev'lin's Hist. of Q. Elizab.

About the middle of *February* the Lord *Darly* came to the Court of *Scotland*, who being not fully twenty years old, of lovely person, sweet behaviour, and a most ingenuous disposition, exceedingly prevailed in short time on the *Queen's* affections. About the middle of *July* the Marriage-Rites were celebrated in the Royal Chappel by the Dean of *Restalrig*, and the next day (the Queen having made him before Earl of *Rosse*, and Duke of *Rothsay*) the new Duke was proclaimed King by sound of Trumpet, and declared to be associated with the Queen in the publick government. The news whereof being brought unto Queen *Elizabeth*, she seemed more offended than indeed she was. But never was marriage more calamitous to the parties themselves, or more dishonourable to that nation, or finally more scandalous to both Religions: in nothing fortunate but in the birth of *James* the sixth; born in the Palace of *Edenburgh* on *July* 19. *Anno* 1566. Solemnly Crowned King of the *Scots* on the same day of the Month,

Anno.

Anno 1567. and joyfully received to the Crown of *England* on *March* 14. 1602.

Of such a temper were the devotions of the Church of *England* at this time, that generally the *English* Papists, and the Ambassadours of Foreign Princes still reforted to them. For the first ten years of Her Majestie's Reign, the Papists in general came to our Churches. In the beginning of the eleventh year of her Reign, *Cornwallis*, *Beddingfield* and *Selyard* were the first Recusants.

L. Coke's charg given at Norwich Assizes, 1606.

Now we are come to the setling the Episcopal Government by as good Authority as could be given to it by the Lawes of the Land. By a Statute made in the last Parliament for keeping Her Majestie's Subjects in their due obedience, a power was given unto the Bishops to tender and receive the Oath of Supremacy of all manner of persons residing and dwelling in their several Diocesses. *Bonner* was then Prisoner in the *Marshalsey*, which being within the Borough of *Southwark*, brought him within the Jurisdiction of *Horn* Bishop of *Winchester*, by whose Chancellor the Oath was tendred to him. On the refusal of which Oath he is Indicted at the King's Bench upon the Statute, to which he appeared in some Term in the year foregoing, and desires that Council be assigned to plead his cause. The Court assigns him *Christopher Wray*, afterwards Chief-justice of the Common-Pleas, that famous Lawyer *Edmond Ploydon*, and one Mr. *Lovelace*.

But the business came under consideration in the following Parliament; which began on *September* thirty, where the Legality of *Horn's* Episcopacy (which was objected against in the behalf of *Bonner*) was cleered by Statute, by which the Parliament did only publish, notifie, and declare the Legal Authority of the *English* Bishops, whose call and Consecration to their place was formerly performed.

In the year 1566. Queen *Elizabeth* came to *Oxford*, Honourably attended with *Robert Dudley*, lately made Earl of *Leicester*, and Chancellor of *Oxford*, the Marquess of *Northampton*, the Lord *Burleigh*, and the *Spanish* Ambassadour. She was lodged in *Christ-Church*, where many Comedies were acted before Her. Many Acts were kept before Her in Philosophy, and one most eminent in Divinity. She concluded all with a Latine Oration, which you may read in *Fuller's Church History*, as it was taken by Dr. *Laurence Humfrey*, and by him Printed in the Life of Bishop *Jewel*. Having stayed seven dayes, she took Her leave of the University.

Anno 1567. Another Generation of Active Non-conformists succeeded the former. Of these *Coleman*, *Button*, *Benson*, and *Halingham*, were the chief, inveighing against the established Church-discipline, endeavouring to conform the *English* Church in all things to that of *Geneva*. To these three more may be added, viz. *William White*, *Thomas Rowland*, *Robert Hawkins*, all Beneficed within the Diocese of *London*.

London. This year thefe three were cited to appear before *Edmond Grindal* Bifhop of *London*: one who was not very forward to prefs Conformity. The Bifhop asked them this queftion,

Have we not a godly Prince? speak, is fhe evil?

To which they made their feveral anfwers in manner following.

William White.] What a queftion is that? the fruits do fhew.

Thomas Rowland.] No, but the fervants of God are perfecuted under Her.

Robert Hawkins.] Why, this queftion the Prophet anfwereth in the Pfalms, *How can they have understanding that work iniquity, spoiling my people, and that extol vanity?*

The Queen proceeded feverely againft fome of them, commanding them to be put in prifon, though ftill their party daily encreafed.

And now to ftrengthen the Romifh party, two moft Active fugitive Papifts, *Thomas Harding*, and *Nicholas Saunders*, return into *England*. Very earneft they were in advancing the Catholick Caufe, and perverted very many to their own erroneous opinions.

A moneth or two after the Prince of *Scotland*'s baptizing, the King her Husband in the one and twentieth year of his age was in the dead time of the night, by bloody & barbarous hands, was ftrangled in his bed, and thrown forth into an Orchyard, the houfe being blown up with Gun-powder. The Queen afterwards marrieth Earl *Bothwel*, but he is forced to fly out of *Scotland*. And the Queen is thruft in prifon at *Loch-levin*. But what fhould be done with Her the Confpirators could not agree among themfelves. At length they extort from her a refignation of her Kingdom to her Son, who was fcarce thirteen moneths old. But fhe being ill-ufed at home by her own Subjects, made an efcape into *England*, and landed at *Wirkington* in *Comberland*, and the fame day wrote a letter in *French* to *Queen Elizabeth*. The Countefs of *Lenox* complaineth againft her to *Queen Elizabeth*, and befought her, that fhe might be brought to her trial for the murther of her Son. The Queen of *Scots* wrote a letter to the Pope, to manifeft her devotion to the See of *Rome*, written from *Caftle Boulton*, *Novemb.* 30. 1568.

Then *Thomas Piercy* Earl of *Northumberland*, and *Charles Nevil* Earl of *Weftmorland* brake out into open Rebellion againft the Queen. Their firft

Vid. Fuller's Church Hift. Cent. 16.

first valour was to fight against the *English* Bible and Service-book in *Durham*, tearing them to pieces. They set up Mass in most places where they came, *Richard Norton* an aged Gentleman carrying the Cross before them, and others bearing in their banners the five wounds of Christ, or a Chalice, according to their different devices. But the Earl of *Sussex* advancing out of the South with an Army to oppose them, they fled Northwards, and mouldered away to nothing. *Northumberland* fled into *Scotland*, lurked there awhile, was betrayed to Earl *Murrey*, sent back into *England*, and beheaded at *York*. *Westmorland* fled into *Flanders*, where he long lived very poor, on a small pension. Many were executed by Sir *George Bowes* Knight Marshal, in every Market-town betwixt *New-castle* and *Witherby*. *Leonard Dacres* the next year laboured to raise a New Rebellion, but by the valour and vigilancy of the Lord *Hunsdon*, his design was seasonably defeated.

Commissioners were appointed by Queen *Elizabeth* to take cognizance of the cause of the Queen of *Scots*, *Murrey* cometh to *York* being the City appointed for that purpose, and with him seven of his Inwardest friends as Delegates for the Infant-King; and for the Queen of *Scots* Delegates also appeared. After *Lidington*'s admonition to the *Scots*, and the *Scots* Protestation, the Delegates for the Queen delivered a Declaration in Writing. Some few dayes after *Murrey* the Regent, and the Delegates for the Infant-King gave in their Answer. To this the Queen of *Scots* Delegates renewing again their former Protestation, opposed their Replication. *Murrey* refuseth to yield reasons for deposing the Queen. Then were the *English* Commissioners Revoked, and their Authority abrogated to the great rejoycing of the Duke of *Norfolk*, who had ever favoured the Queen of *Scots* Title to the Succession to the Crown of *England*.

New Commissioners were appointed to hear and examine the matter: but the matter cometh to nothing. *Murrey* propoundeth to *Norfolk* a Marriage with the Queen of *Scots*, yet spreadeth rumours against her. The Queen of *Scots* was committed to the Earl of *Shrewsbury*. Queen *Elizabeth* relieveth the Protestants in *France*, Edicts being published there, whereby the exercise of the Reformed Religion was utterly forbidden, the Professors thereof removed from Publick Offices, and the Ministers of the word commanded to depart the Realm within a prefixed time. She also gratiously received the *Netherlanders*, of whom a great multitude had withdrawn themselves into *England* as into a Sanctuary, from the cruelty of the Duke of *Alva*.

John Story, Doctor of the Lawes, a great persecutor in Queen *Mary*'s dayes, being allured by a wile into a Ship, which was reported to have brought over *English* Merchandises and Heretical Books; the Master of the Ship presently set Sail, and brought him into *England*, where afterwards

Camden's Hist. of Q. Elizab.

wards he was executed as a Traytor to his Countrey, at *Tyburn*. Then were the *English* Merchants in the *Netherlands* and *Spain*, drawn into the Inquifition, and condemned to the Galleys, and their goods confifcate.

The old ftore of Papifts in *England* began now much to diminifh, prifons confumed many, Age more of their Priefts, and they had no place in *England* whence to recruit themfelves. Hereupon they refolved to erect Colledges beyond the Seas for *Englifh* youth to have their education therein. This project begun *Anno* 1569. was fo effectually profecuted, that within the compafs of fifty years nine Colledges were by them founded, and furnifhed with Students, and they with maintenance. *Doway-colledge* in *Flanders* was founded 1569. by *Philip* the fecond King of *Spain*; all the Recufants in *England* were Benefactors to it. The firft Rector was *William Allen*, afterwards Cardinal He died *Anno* 1594. The fecond *Thomas Worthington*, Rector *Anno* 1609. The third *Matthew Kellifon*, Rector 1624. Whereas the government of all other *Englifh* Colledges belongs to Jefuites; this onely is ruled by Secular Priefts.

The fecond Colledge was at *Rome*, founded *Anno* 1579. Pope *Gregory* the thirteenth exhibited maintenance, firft to fix, then to fourteen, at laft to threefcore Scholars therein, to the yearly value of four thoufand Crowns. The *Welch* Hofpital in *Rome*, founded and endowed many hundred years fince by *Cadwallader* King of *Wales* for *Welch* Pilgrims, with the Rich Lands thereof, were conferred by the faid Pope on this Colledge. Now whereas *Anno* 1576. there were but thirty old Priefts remaining in this Realm, thefe two Colledges alone within two years fent above three hundred Priefts into *England*. The firft Rector was Dr. *Maurice*. The fecond *Ferdinando*, a *Neapolitan* Jefuite. The third *Robert Parfons*. The fourth *Thomas Fitz-herbert*. 1623.

The third Colledge was founded by *Philip* the fecond, King of *Spain* at *Valladolit* in old *Caftile*. *Donna Luyfa de Caravaial*, a rich Widow Lady in *Spain*, gave all her eftate (being very great) to this Colledge, and came over into *England*, where fhe died. Father *Walpoot* by pretending to have gained Mr. *Pickering Wotton* (Son and Heir to the Lord *Wotton*) to the Romifh Church, got above five hundred pounds to this Colledge. Sir *Francis Inglefield*, Privy Counfellor to Queen *Mary*, forfaking his fair eftate in *Berk-fhire* in the firft year of Queen *Elizabeth*, was a bountiful Benefactor to this Colledge.

The fourth Colledge was of *Sivil*, founded by *Philip* the fecond, King of *Spain*, *Anno* 1593.

The fifth was at S. *Omers* in *Artois*, founded 1596. by *Philip* the fecond, who gave them a good Annuity; for whofe foul they fay every
day

The Church of Great Britain.

day a Mass, and every year an *Obitum*. Their Rector generally is a Fleming, though this Colledge be of English only.

The sixth Colledge is at *Madrid*, in new *Castile*, founded 1606. *Joseph Creswel*, the Jesuite, with money of the two Colledges of *Valladolit* and *Sivil*, bought an House here, and built a Colledge thereon.

The seventh, a Colledge of *Lovain* in *Brabant*, founded 1606. by *Philip* the third, King of *Spain*, who gave a Castle, with a Pension, to the English Jesuits, to build them a Colledge therewith.

The eighth Colledge was at *Liege* in *Lukeland*, founded 1616. The Archbishop of *Collen* (being at this time also Bishop of *Liege*) gave them a Pension to live on, and leave to build a fair Colledge here. Many of the English Nobility and Gentry, under pretence of passing to the *Spaw* to recover their healths, dropped here much of their Gold by the way.

The ninth Colledge was of *Gaunt* in *Flanders*, founded 1624. by *Philip* the Fourth, who gave them a Pension.

The Colledge of St. *Omers* generally is for Boyes to be taught in Grammar: *Rome* for Youths studying the Arts; All the rest for Men (Novices or professed Jesuits) save that *Doway* is for any, of what age or parts soever. It is incredible what a mass of money was yearly made over out of *England* for the maintenance of these Colledges: having here their *Provincials, Sub-provincials, Assistants, Agents, Coadjutors, Familiars*, &c. who collected vast sums for them.

The solemn Oath which each Student (arrived at man's estate) ceremoniously sweareth, when admitted into one of these Colledges is as followeth:

I A. B. one bred in this English Colledge, considering how great benefits God hath bestowed upon me, but then especially when he brought me out of my own Countrey so much infected with Heresie, and made me a member of the Catholick Church, as also desiring with a thankful heart to improve so great a mercy of God, have resolved to offer up my self wholly to Divine service, as much as I may, to fulfil the end for which this our Colledge was founded. I promise therefore, and swear, in the presence of Almighty God, that I am prepared, from my heart, with the assistance of Divine grace, in due time to receive holy Orders, and to return into England, to convert the Souls of my Countrey-men and Kinred, when, and as often, as it shall seem good to the Superior of this Colledge, &c.

Continuation of *Sanders de Schismat. Anglicano.* p. 115.

Now Pope *Pius* the Fifth thunders out his Excommunication against Queen *Elizabeth*, and the Hereticks (as he calleth them) adhering to her: wherein also her Subjects are declared absolved from the Oath of Allegiance, and every other thing due unto her whatsoever: and those, which from henceforth obey her, are innodated with the *Anathema*.

The news thereof flying over into *England*, variously affected the Catholicks, according to their several dispositions. *John Felton*, who fastened the Pope's Bull to the Palace of *London*, being taken, and refusing to fly, was hanged on a Gibbet before the Pope's Palace.

Then *Hugh Price*, Doctor of the Civil Law, procured the foundation of *Jesus Colledge* in *Oxford*, on a Ground where *White hall* had been formerly situated; which with Edifices and Gardens thereto belonging, being then in the Crown, Queen *Elizabeth* gave to so pious an use; and therefore is stiled the Foundress in this *Mortmain*.

In the year 1570. *Murray* sueth to have the Queen of *Scots* delivered unto him. But soon after he was shot with a leaden Bullet, beneath the Navil, at *Lithguo*, as he rode in the street. *Hamilton*, the murtherer, escaped into *France*. Then *Matthew Lenox*, the young King's Grandfather, was made Regent of *Scotland*.

Now began Popery to encrease, and the word [*Recusant*] to be born and bred in mens mouths.

A Parliament sate at *Westminster*, which acted against Papists, *That to write, print, preach, or affirm, that the Queen was an Heretick, Schismatick*, &c. *should be adjudged Treason.* Also, *That it should be, so accounted, and punished, to bring, and put in execution, any Bulls, Writings, Instruments*, &c. *from the See of* Rome *from the first of* July *following.*

A severe Act was made also against Fugitives (who being natural born Subjects of this Realm, departed the same without licence. Against Non conformists it was provided, *That every Minister should, before* December *the twenty fifth next following, in the presence of his Diocesan, or his Deputy, declare his assent to all the Articles of Religion, agreed on in the Convocation* 1562. *upon pain of deprivation on his refusal thereof.* Against covetous Conformists it was provided, *That no Spiritual person, Colledge, or Hospital shall let, lease, other than for the term of one and twenty years, or three lives; the usual rent, or more, reserved payable yearly, during the said Term.*

Now began Queen *Elizabeth's* favour to decline toward the Queen of *Scots*, principally for practising with the Pope and forreign Princes.

Anno 1571. Queen *Elizabeth* went in Royal state to see a most beautiful Burse, which Sir *Thomas Gresham* Knight, Citizen of *London*, had built for the use of Merchants, and by the voice of the Crier, and the sound of Trumpets, as it it were by way of Dedication, she named it, *The Royal Exchange.*

A little before that, *Florentine Ridolpho*, who had for the space of fifteen years exercised Merchandise at *London*, secretly conveyed Letters from the Pope to the Queen of *Scots*, wherein he promiseth all kindness, and aid for advancing the Catholick Religion, and Her, &c. *Ridolpho* also, by his own Letters apart, prayeth the Queen to acquaint the Duke of *Norfolk* with these things, &c.

Anno

the Church of GREAT BRITAIN. 237

Anno 1572. died *William Alley*, Bishop of *Exeter*, a diligent Preacher, and *John Jewel*, Bishop of *Salisbury*.

The Canons made in 1563. were not for nine years after confirmed by Act of Parliament: but now being ratified by Parliamentary Authority, the Bishops began the urging of them more severely than before; which many dissenters keep their private meetings in Woods, Fields, their Friends Houses, &c. And now *Thomas Cartwright* (chief of the Non-conformists) presents the Parliament with a Book called, *An Admonition*. This was seconded with another more importunate to the same effect. Great bandying there was of Books between two eminent Authors of opposite parties.

1. The Admonition first and second made by Mr. *Cartwright*.
2. The Answer to the Admonition by Doctor *John Whitgift*.
3. The Reply to the Answer, by Mr. *Thomas Cartwright*.
4. The Defence of the Answer, by Doctor *John Whitgift*.

This last kept the field, and received no solemn refutation.

The Non-conformists, after the dissolution of the Parliament, presumed to erect a Presbytery at *Wandsworth* in *Surrey*. Eleven Elders were chosen therein, and their Offices, and general Rules (by them to be observed) agreed upon, and described, as appears by a Bill endorsed with the hand of Mr. *Field*, Lecturer (it is supposed) of that place, but living in *London*: Mr. *Smith* of *Micham*, and Mr. *Crane* of *Roughampton*, are mentioned for approving all passages therein. This was the first-born of all Presbyteries in *England*.

The first Presbytery in *England*.

Here were two sorts of Ministers.

First Mr.
1. Field.
2. Wilcox.
3. Standen.
4. Jackson.
5. Bonham.
6. Scintloe.
7. Crane.
8. Edmonds.

Afterwards Mr.
1. Chark.
2. Travers.
3. Barber.
4. Gardiner.
5. Cheston.
6. Crook.
7. Egerton.

The former of these were principally against Ministers Habits, and the Common-prayer-book.

The latter endeavouring the modelling of a new Discipline.

But it was not long before both Streams uniting together, *Non-conformity* began to bear a great Channel in the City of *London*.

Then

Then *Rofs*, the Queen of *Scots* Ambaſſador, and the Duke of *Norfolk*, were ſent to the Tower, for plotting againſt Queen *Elizabeth*. The Duke of *Norfolk* was arraigned and condemned by his Peers, and beheaded on Tower-hill.

This year happened a cruel Maſſacre in *Paris*, the Queen of *Navar*, and all the choiceſt of the Proteſtants being bidden thither to a Marriage, between *Henry* of *Navar*, and Madam *Margarite*, the King's Siſter. No ſooner was the Marriage ſolemnized; but there followed bloody Butcherings, committed upon men of all eſtates, throughout all the Cities of *France*. And Admiral *Coligny* (the Pillar of the Reformed Church) was ſlain in his Bed on *Bartholomew-eve*.

In *November* following a new Star was ſeen in the Conſtellation of *Caſſiopeia*, which continued full ſixteen months, being carried about with the daily motion of the Heaven. *Theodor. Beza* wittily applyed it to that Star, which ſhone at the Birth of Chriſt, and to the murthering of the Infants under *Herod*, and warned *Charles* the ninth, King of *France*, who had confeſſed himſelf to be the Author of the Maſſacre at *Paris*, to beware, in this Verſe.

<small>Camden's Hiſtory of Queen Eliz.</small>

Tu Vero Herodes ſanguinolente cave.

And look thou, bloody *Herod*, to thy ſelf.

And he was not altogether deceived in his belief: for the fifth month, after the vaniſhing of this Star the ſaid *Charles*, after long and grievous pains, died of exceeding bleeding.

Now begin the Anabaptiſts to encreaſe in *England*: On *Easter-day* was diſcloſed a Congregation of Dutch Anabaptiſts, without *Aldgate* in *London*, whereof twenty ſeven were taken, and impriſoned, and four bearing Faggots at *Paul's-croſs*, ſolemnly recanted their Opinions. In the next month one Dutch-man, and ten Women, were condemned: of whom one Woman renounced her errors; eight were baniſhed the Land: Two more ſo obſtinate, that command was iſſued out for their burning in *Smithfield*, where they died in great horror, with crying and roaring.

Anno 1573. one *Peter Burchet*, who had perſwaded himſelf, that it was lawful to kill any that had oppoſed the truth of the Goſpel, drew his Dagger upon *Hawkins*, that famous Navigator, in the open ſtreet, and wounded him, ſuppoſing him to be *Hatton*, who was then in great favour with the Queen, whom he had heard to be one of the Innovators. Being caſt into the Tower of *London*, he ſlew one of his Keepers with a Billet, which he ſnatched up out of the Chimney, for which he was condemned of murther, had his right hand cut off, and nailed to the Gallows, and then he was hanged.

the Church of Great Britain.

In the year 1574. certain Ministers of *London* were deluded by a Maid, which counterfeited her self to be possessed of the Devil.

So powerful was the party of the Non-conformists grown at this time, that Doctor *Humfrey*, then President of *Maudlins*, and Mr. *John Fox* himself (both which scrupled subscription in some particulars) were deserted by them as luke-warm and remiss in the cause. *Coleman, Burton, Hallingham, Benson*, out-did all of their own Opinions. Then died *Matthew Parker*, Archbishop of *Canterbury*, an excellent Antiquary, a great Benefactor to *Bennet-colledge* in *Cambridge*, on which he bestowed many Manuscripts. *Edmond Grindal* succeeded him in his place.

Not long after died *James Pilkinton*, Bishop of *Durham*. He was (as appeareth by many of his Letters) a great conniver at Non conformity.

The same year died *Edward Deering*, an eminent Divine, born of an ancient Family in *Kent*, bred Fellow of *Christ's-colledge* in *Cambridge*, a pious and painful Preacher, but disaffected to Bishops and Ceremonies.

Rowland Jenkes, a Popish Bookseller, was indicted, at the Summer-Assizes in *Oxford*, for dispersing of scandalous Pamphlets, defamatory to the Queen and State.

Then the Queen laboureth to compound the *Netherland* differences; but it had little effect. She relieveth the Estates and the Prince of *Orange* with twenty thousand pounds of English money, upon condition they should neither change their Religion, nor their Prince, nor receive the French into the *Netherlands*.

Then one *Cutbbert Mayn*, a Priest, was drawn, hanged, and quartered at *Launston* in *Cornwal*, for his obstinate maintaining of the Papal power: and *Trugion*, a Gentleman of that Countrey, which had harboured him, was turned out of his Estate, and condemned to perpetual imprisonment.

In this year 1577. died *Nicholas Bullingham*, Bishop of *Worcester*. And the same year died *William Bradbridge*, Bishop of *Exeter*, and *Edmond Guest*, Bishop of *Salisbury*.

Anno 1579. died *Richard Cheincy*, Bishop of *Bristol*. *Robert Horn*, Bishop of *Winchester*, succeeded. *Thomas Centham*, Bishop of *Coventry* and *Litchfield*, followed him. And not long after died *Richard Cox*, Bishop of *Ely*.

Now the Sect (called *The Family of Love*) began to grow so numerous, that the Privy Council thought fit to endeavour their suppression. They perswaded their followers, *That those only were elected, and to be saved, which were admitted into that Family, and all the rest Reprobates, and to be damned: and that it was lawful for them to deny, upon their Oath, before a Magistrate, whatsoever they list.* Of this Fanatical vanity they dispersed Books among their followers, translated out of the

Dutch

Dutch Tongue into English, which they entitled, *The Gospel of the Kingdom*; *Documental Sentences*; *The Prophesy of the Spirit of Love*; *The publishing of Peace upon Earth*: The Author was *Henry Nicolas* of *Leyden*, who blasphemously said, *That he did partake of God, and God of his Humanity*. This Man came over into *England* in the Reign of King *Edward* the Sixth, joyned himself to the Dutch Congregation in *London*, where he seduced many Artificers, and silly Women, among whom two Daughters of one *Warwick*, (to whom he dedicated an Epistle) were his principal Perverts. Mr. *Martin Micronius*, and Mr. *Nicholas Charineus*, then the Ministers of the Dutch Congregation, zealously confuted his errors; but it seems their Antidotes pierced not so deep as his Poysons. The Privy Council now tendred unto them an Abjuration; but with what success we find not. The Queen commanded by Proclamation, That the Civil Magistrate should be assistant to the Ecclesiastical, for the timely suppressing of them, and that their Books should be burnt.

<small>The Abjuration may be read in *Fuller*. Church Hist. ad An. 1580.</small>

Then divers Seminary Priests were sent forth into several parts of *England* and *Ireland*, to administer (as they pretended) the Sacraments of the Romish Religion, and to preach. But the Queen, and her Council found, that they were sent under-hand, to withdraw the Subjects from their Allegiance, and Obedience, due to their Prince, to bind them, by Reconciliation, to perform the Pope's Commandements, to raise intestine Rebellion under *the Seal of Confession;* and flatly to execute the Sentence of Pope *Pius* the Fifth against the Queen.

To these Seminaries, for as much as there were sent daily out of *England*, from the Papists, very many Boys, and young Men of all sorts, and admitted into the same, making a Vow to return; and others from thence crept secretly into *England*, there came forth a Proclamation in the month of *June*, That *whosoever had Children, Pupils, Kinsmen, or others, in the parts beyond the Seas, should, after ten dayes, deliver their names to the Ordinary; and to those which returned not, they should not directly, or indirectly, supply any money. That no Man should entertain in his house, or lodge, Priests sent forth of the Seminaries, and Jesuits, or cherish and relieve them: And whosoever did the contrary, should be accounted a favourer of Rebels*, &c.

<small>Cambden's Hist. of Queen Eliz. Anno 1580.</small>

But *Robert Parsons*, and *Edmond Campian*, Jesuits, living at *Rome*, obtained of the Pope licence to come over into *England*. *Parsons* was born in *Sommerset-shire*, of *Baliol-colledge* in *Oxford*, a man of a fierce nature, and rude behaviour, he professed openly the Protestants Religion, until he was, for his dishonesty, expelled the University, then fled he to the Papists. *Campian* was born in *London*, and bred in St. *John's-colledge* in *Oxford*, one of a sweet nature, and fluent tongue. These two notably advanced the Roman cause, travelling up and down the Countrey secretly, and, to Popish Gentlemens houses, in disguised habits, bit, sometimes of Souldiers; sometimes of Gentlemen; sometimes of Ministers of the Word; sometimes of Apparitors. *Campian*, by a Writing set forth, challenged the Ministers of the English Church to a Disputation, and published a Book in Latin, of ten Reasons, for maintenance of the Doctrine of the Church of *Rome*; and *Parsons* another virulent Book, in English, against *Chark*, who had written soberly against *Campian*'s challenge. But to *Campian*'s Reasons *Whitaker* answered soundly. He was taken a year after, and put to the rack, and afterwards being brought forth to dispute, hardly maintained the expectation raised of him. *Parsons* hardly escaping at *Norwich* in *Cheshire*, politickly returneth to *Rome*.

This year *Edmond Grindal*, Archbishop of *Canterbury*, groaning under the Queens displeasure, was forbidden access to the Convocation. But a Petition was drawn up, in the name of the whole Convocation, for the restitution of the Archbishop, by *Toby Matthew*, Dean of *Christ-church*.

This Petition, after delayes, ended in a final denial; it being daily suggested to the Queen, that *Grindal* was a great Patron of Prophecyings (now set up in several parts of the Land) which, if permitted, would in fine prove the bane of the Church and State.

These Prophecyings were thus modelled.

1. The Ministers of the same Precinct, by their own appointment, met at the principal place therein.

Fuller Church Hist. An. 1580.

2. The Junior Divine went first into the Pulpit, and for about half an hour treated upon a portion of Scripture, formerly by a joynt agreement assigned unto him. After him four or five more observing their seniority, successively dilated on the same Text.

3. At last a Grave Divine made the closing Sermon, somewhat larger than the rest, praising the pains of such who best deserved it, and mildly reproving the mistakes of such of those, if any were found in their Sermons. Then all was ended (as it was begun) with a solemn Prayer. And at a publick refection of those Ministers, together (with many of the Gentry repairing to them) the next time of their meeting was appointed, Text assigned, Preachers deputed, a new Moderator elected, or the one continued, and so all were dissolved.

But some incoveniences were seen, and more foreseen, if these Prophecyings might generally take place in the Land. However the Archbishop, to vindicate himself, wrote a large Letter to the Queen. But all in vain, for the Earl of *Leicester* had so filled the Queens ears with complaints against him, that there was no room to receive his Petition. Indeed *Leicester* cast a covetous eye on *Lambeth-house*, and maliced him, because he stoutly opposed the alienating this his principal Palace.

Now began Priests and Jesuits to flock faster into *England* than ever before, having exchange of clothes, names, and professions. Hereupon

I i the

the Parliament, now met at *Westminster*, enacted severe Laws against them. *John Pain*, a Priest, was executed at *Chelmsford*, *Thomas Ford*, *John Shert*, and *Robert Johnson*, Priests, were executed at *London*.

This year died *Gilbert Berkley*, Bishop of *Bath* and *Wells*.

The Presbyterian party met at *Cockfield* (Mr. *Knewstub*'s Cure) in *Suffolk*, even sixty Ministers of *Norfolk*, *Suffolk*, and *Cambridge-shire*, to confer of the Common-prayer-book, what might be tolerated, and what refused in every point of it, apparel, matter, form, dayes, fastings, injunctions, &c. Whilst the severity of the State was at this time great against Jesuites, some lenity of course fell to the share of the Nonconformists.

The City of *Geneva* being now reduced to great extremities by the Duke of *Savoy*, *Beza* addressed himself by Letters to Mr. *Walter Travers*, one of the chief of the Presbyterian party, then Chaplain to the Lord Treasurer: in which Letter may be seen much of the secret sympathy betwixt *England* and *Geneva* about Discipline; *Geneva* helping *England* with her Prayers, *England* aiding *Geneva* with her purse.

The Duke of *Anjou* came into *England*, and was an earnest Suitor to Queen *Elizabeth*. A Book was set forth against the Marriage, entitled, *The Gulps wherein England will be swallowed by the French Marriage*. The Queen, by open Proclamation, commended the Duke of *Anjou*'s affection towards her, and the Protestants Religion, sorrowed that so great an injury was offered to so high a Prince, she condemned the Author of the Book, as a publisher of Sedition, and commanded the Book to be burnt before the Magistrates face. From this time she began to be more incensed against the *Innovators*, from whom she believed that these things proceeded. And within few dayes after, *John Stubs*, of *Lincolns-Inn*, (whose Sister Mr. *Cartwright*, formerly mentioned, had married) the Author of this Book, *William Page*, who dispersed the Copies, and *Singleton*, the Printer, were apprehended. *Stubs* and *Page* had their right hands cut off with a Cleaver driven through the wrist with the force of a Beetle, upon a Scaffold, in the Market-place at *Westminster*. The Printer was pardoned. *Stubs* having his right hand cut off, put off his hat with his left, and said with a loud voice, *God save the Queen*.

The Queen also, to take away the fear which had possessed many mens minds, that Religion would be altered, and Popery tolerated, permitted that *Edmond Campian*, Jesuite, *Ralph Sherwin*, *Luke Kirby*, and *Alexander Briant*, Priests, should be arraigned, they were condemned and executed for Treason. This was done during the abode of *Anjou* in *England*.

The Earl of *Leicester* improved his power (at this time very great with the Queen) to obtain great Liberty for the Non-conformists. Hence it was, that many Bishops active in pressing subscription in their Diocess, when repairing to Court, were checked by this great Favourite,

The Church of Great Britain. 243

rite, to their great difcouragement. Hereupon the *Brethren* (who hitherto had no particular platform of Difcipline among themfelves, as univerfally practifed by their party) began, in a folemn Council held by them, to conclude on a certain form, as may be feen in their Decrees, faithfully tranflated out of their Latin Copy. The Title thereof, *Thefe be the things that (do feem) may well ftand with the peace of the Church.*

The form of Difcipline by the Brethren confidered of in a folemn Synod with the Decrees thereof, may be read in Fuller. church Hift. Cent.16. Anno 1582.

This year died three that feemed Pillars in the Romifh Church. Frift *Richard Briftow*, born in *Worcefter-fhire*, bred at *Exeter-colledge* in *Oxford*, whence he fled beyond the Seas, and by Cardinal *Allen* was made Overfeer of the Englifh Colledge, firft at *Doway*, then at *Rhemes*. For the recovery of his health, he returned into his native Land, and died quietly near *London*.

The fecond *Nicholas Harpifield*, bred firft in *Winchefter-fchool*, then in *New-colledge* in *Oxford*, where he proceeded Doctor of Law, and after became Archdeacon of *Canterbury*: Under King *Edward* the Sixth he banifhed himfelf: Under Queen *Mary* he returned, and was advanced: Under Queen *Elizabeth* imprifoned, for denying her Supremacy. Yet fuch was his mild ufage in his Reftraint, that he wrote much therein and among the reft his *Ecclefiaftical Hiftory*. He wrote alfo fix Dialogues in favour of his own Religion. He fet it forth under the name of *Alan Cope*. Yet caufed he thefe Capital letters to be engraven at the end of his Book.

A. H. L. N. H. E. V. E. A. C.

Hereby myftically meaning.

Auctor Hujus Libri Nicolaus Harpfeldus. Edidit Vero Eum Alanus Copus.

The third *Gregory Martin*, born at *Mayfield* in *Suffex*, bred with Campian at St. *John's-colledge* in *Oxford*, Tutor to *Philip*, Earl of *Arundel*, eldeft Son to *Thomas*, Duke of *Norfolk*. Afterwards he went over beyond Sea, and became Divinity Profeffor in the Colledge of *Rhemes*, and died there.

Now as touching the Controverfie of Church-government, the Minifters of *Kent*, having been called to fubfcribe to certain Articles propounded to them by the Archbifhop of *Canterbury*, fend their Petition to the Privy Council: Subfcribed thus, *Your Honours daily and faithful Orators, the Minifters of Kent, which are fufpended from the execution of their Miniftry.*

The Lords of the Council fent this Petition, with another Bill of complaint, exhibited unto them, againft *Edmond Freak*, Bifhop of *Norwich*,

wich, unto the Archbishop of *Canterbury*. What his Answer was thereunto, may be seen at large in *Fuller*'s Church History.

Doctor *John Whitgift* was now Archbishop of *Canterbury*, Anno 1583. who wrote a Letter to the Lord Treasurer, complaining of Mr. *Beal*, Clerk of the Council, who brought these Letters to him, his insolent carriage towards him.

Now that the Presbyterian party were befriended at the Council-board, who endeavoured to mittigate the Archbishop's proceeding against them appeareth also from the Privy Counsellors Letter to the Archbishop, in favour of the Non-conformists. Signed *W. Burleigh, G. Shrewsbury. A. Warwick, R. Leicester, C. Howard, J. Croft, Ch. Hatton, Fr. Walsingham.* But albeit Sir *Cbr. Hatton* subscribed among the Privy Counsellors for moderation to Non-conformists, yet that he was a great countenancer of *Whitgift*'s proceedings against them, appeareth in an immediate Address of the Archbishop unto him. As for the Lord *Burghleigh*, he was neither so rigid, as to have Conformity prest to the height, nor so remiss, as to leave Ministers at their own liberty: He would argue the case, both in Discourse and Letters, with the Archbishop; and one Letter he wrote to the Archbishop for some Indulgence to the Ministers; Mr. *Travers* seems to have an hand in all this, who being the Lord *Burghleigh*'s Chaplain, by him much respected, and highly affected to the *Geneva* Discipline, was made the mouth of the Ministers, to mediate to his Lord in their behalf. But the Archbishop's unmoveableness appeared by his Letter sent to the Lord Treasurer, at some passages whereof he took exception, and sends a smart Letter to the Archbishop.

That which concerneth the Non-conformists therein is this.

I deny nothing that your Grace thinketh meet to proceed in, with those whom you call factions; and therefore there is no controversie between you and me, expressed in your Letter: the controversie is passed in your Graces Letter in silence, and so I do satisfie. Your Grace promised me to deal, I say only with such as violated Order, and to charge them therewith, which I allow well of. But your Grace not charging them with such faults, seeketh, by examination, to urge them to accuse themselves; and then, I think, you will punish them. I think your Grace's proceeding is, I will not say rigorous or captious, but I think it is scant charitable, &c. If I had known the fault of Brown, *I might be blamed for writing for him; but when by examination only it is to sift him with twenty four Articles, I have cause to pity the poor man.*

Your Grace's, as friendly as any

W. Burghleigh.

The

The Archbishop writes a calm Letter in anfwer to the Lord Treafurer's Letter, fending him enclofed therein certain Reafons to juftifie the manner of his proceedings, praying his Lordfhip not to be carried away, either from the caufe, or from the Archbifhop himfelf, upon unjuft furmifes, and clamours, left he be the occafion of that confufion which hereafter he would be forry for. Profeffing that in thefe things he defired no further defence, neither of his Lordfhip, nor of any other, than Juftice and Law would yield unto him.

Sir *Francis Walfingham* was a good Friend to Non-conformifts, he wrote a Letter to the Archbifhop, to qualifie him for a *Semi-Non-conformift*, one Mr. *Leverwood*.

Grindal being fenfible of the Queens difpleafure, had defired to refign his place, and confine himfelf to a yearly Penfion. This place was proffered to *Whitgift*, but he, in the prefence of the Queen, refufed it: yet what he would not fnatch, fuddenly fell into his hands by *Grindal's* death, who out of his contempt of the world, left not much wealth behind him. That little he had, as it was well gotten, was well beftowed in pious ufes in *Oxford* and *Cambridge*, with the building and endowing of a School at St. *Bees* in *Cumberland*, where he was born : yea he may be held as a Benefactor to this Nation, by bringing in *Tamarix* firft over into *England*, that Plant being very excellent in mollifying the hardnefs of the Spleen.

Now *Robert Brown*, a *Cambridge-man*, and young Student in Divinity (of whom the Separatifts in thofe dayes, and long after, were called *Brownifts*) born in *Rutland-fhire* of an ancient Family, near allied to the Lord Treafurer *Cecil*, began, with one *Richard. Harifon*, a Schoolmafter, to vent their Opinions. They fet forth Books in *Zealand*, whither they travelled. *Brown* returning home, difperfeth thefe Books all over *England*. But their Books were fuppreffed by the Queens Authority, confuted by Learned men; and two of his followers were executed one after another at St. *Edmonds-bury*. *Brown* coming to *Norwich*, there infected both Dutch and Englifh, for which he was confined.

The Lord Treafurer writes a Letter to the Bifhop of *Norwich* in his behalf. *Brown* being thus brought up to *London*, was wrought to fome tolerable compliance, and being difcharged by the Archbifhop, was by the Lord Treafurer fent home to his Father, *Anthony Brown*, at *Toletborp* in *Rutland* Efquire.. But, it feems, *Brown's* errors were fo inlaid in him, no conference with Divines could convince him to the contrary, whofe incorrigiblenefs made his own Father weary of his company.

He, and *Harifon*, inveighed againft Bifhops, Ecclefiaftical Courts, Ceremonies, Ordination of Minifters, fancying here on earth a platform of a perfect Church. Doctor *Fulk* learnedly proveth, that the *Brownifts* were, in effect, the fame with the ancient *Donatifts*.

Nicholas

Nicholas Saunders (more truly *Slanders*) died this year 1583. being starved to death among the Bogs and Mountains in *Ireland*. Near the same time one *John Lewis* was burnt at *Norwich* for denying the Godhead of Christ, and holding other detestable Heresies. At this time the Jesuites set forth many slaunderous libels against her Majesty; one of their principal Pamphlets, was *a Treatise of Schism*. *William Carter*, the Stationer, was executed at *Tyburn* for publishing it. Soon after five Seminaries, *John Fen, George Haddock, John Munden, John Nutter*, and *Tho. Hemmerford*, were hanged, bowelled, and quartered for Treason at *Tyburn*, and many others about the same time executed in other places. Yet at the same time the Queen by one Act of Grace pardoned seventy Priests, some of them actually condemned to die, all legally deserving death.

Among these were, 1. *Gasper Haywood*, Son to that eminent Epigrammatist, the first Jesuite that ever set foot in *England*.

2. *James Bosgrave*.

3. *John Hart* a zealous disputant.

4. *Edward Rushton*, an ungrateful wretch, who afterwards railed on the Queen in Print, who gave him his life.

In the year 1584. Two conferences were kept at *Lambeth*, about the Discipline and Ceremonies of the Church. For the same were the Archbishops of *Canterbury* and *York*, and *Cooper*, Bishop of *Winchester*. Unconforming Ministers against it. The Lords of the Privy Council, and some other Honorable persons, Auditors thereof. This conference effected nothing on the Disputants as to the altering their Opinions. Some of the Lords afterwards secretly acted against the Archbishop in favour of the other party.

The Archbishop now take's another course, enjoyning all admitted to the Ecclesiastical Orders and Benefices, the subscription of the following Articles.

I. *That the Queen had supreme Authority over all persons born within her Dominions, of what condition soever they were. And that no other Prince, Prelate, or Potentate, hath, or ought to have, any Jurisdiction, Civil or Ecclesiastical, within her Realms, or Dominions.*

II. *That the Book of Common-Prayer, and the Ordination of Bishops, Priests, and Deacons, containeth nothing contrary to the Word of God, but may lawfully be used; and that they will use that, and none other.*

III. *That the Articles of Religion agreed in the Synod holden at London, Anno 1562. and published by the Queens Authority they did allow of, and did believe them to be consonant to the word of God.*

Now

Now came forth the *Rhemish* Tranflation of the New Teftament, every where befpeckled with hard words, which tranfcend common capacities; taxed by our Divines as full of abominable errors.

Secretary *Walfingham* foliciteth Mr. *Thomas Cartwright* to undertake to refute this *Rhemish* Tranflation; and fent him an hundred pounds out of his own purfe, the better to enable him for the work. *Walfingham's* Letters, to *Cartwright*, were feconded by another from the Doctors and Heads of Houfes (and Dr. *Fulk* among the reft) at *Cambridge*, befides the importunity of the Minifters of *London*, and *Suffolk*, to the fame purpofe. *Cartwright* prepares for the work. But Archbifhop *Whitgift* having notice thereof, prohibiteth his further proceeding therein. *Cartwright* hereupon defifted. But fome years after, encouraged by an honourable Lord, he refumed the work, but prevented by death, he perfected no further than the fifteenth Chapter of the *Revelation*. Many years lay this worthy work neglected, and the Copy thereof Moufe-eaten in part, at laft came forth (though late *Anno* 1618. a Book to which the Rhemifts never durft return the leaft anfwer. But whilft *Cartwrights* work lay retarded, Dr. *William Fulk*, Mafter of *Pembrook-hall* in *Cambridge*, entred the lift againft the Rhemifts, and Judicioufly and Learnedly performed his undertaking therein.

This year came forth the Expofition of Mr. *Thomas Rogers*, on the Articles of the Church of *England*; not onely the two extremes, Papifts and Schifmaticks, but many Proteftants of a middle temper were offended thereat. Mr. *Rogers* his reftrictive Comment, fhut out fuch from their concurrence with the Church of *England*, which the difcreet laxity of the Text admitted thereunto.

On *November* 23. 1585. The Parliament was begun and holden at *Weftminfter*, wherein the Statute againft Jefuites and Priefts, their departing out of *England*, and not returning thither, was made, with penalty for relieving them. A Convocation was kept in St. *Pauls* Church in *London*; and from hence removed to St. *Peter's* in *Weftminfter*, where *William Redman* D. D. was chofen and prefented Prolocutor. An Affembly of Minifters met at the fame time: but the certain place of their meeting not known, being Clandeftine, Arbitrary, and changeable, as advifed by their Conveniences. Some Agents for them were all day at the door of the Parliament-houfe, and fome part of the night in the Chambers of Parliament-men, effectually folliciting their bufinefs with them.

What impreffion was made by the Agents of the Minifters, may appear by an enfuing Letter fent to her Majefty, by Archbifhop *Whitgift*, wherein he complaineth of feveral Bills that had, the day before the dating of his Letter, paffed in the Houfe of Commons, in favour of the Non-conformifts, about Marrying at all times in the year, concerning

Ecclefiaftical

Ecclesiastical Courts, and Episcopal Visitations, which (*saith he*) may reach to the overthrow of Ecclesiastical Jurisdiction, and study of the Civil Law. But the Queen would alter nothing material to Church-government.

The Parliament being dissolved, the Convocation ended the next day after, having effected nothing of moment, save that in the ninth Session thereof *John Hilton* Priest, made a solemn Abjuration of his blasphemous Heresies.

The Non-conformists now missing their mark, abated much of their former Activity; insomuch as that Mr. *Cartwright* began to make by the mediation of the Earl of *Leicester* (who now design'd to make him Master of his new-built Hospital in *Warwick*) compliance with the Archbishop, though he not over-fond of his friendship, warily kept him at distance, as appears by the Earl of *Leicester's* Letter to the Archbishop, in *Cartwright's* behalf, and the Archbishops answer thereto.

Now the Earl of *Leicester* went over into the Low Countries, commanding a great Army, with the Title of *General of the Auxiliaries of the Queen of* England; and the Non-conformists lost their best friend in Court. And afterwards the Archbishop being sworn one of the Privy Council, it fared worse with them.

Three Protestant Bishops died this year, *viz.* *Richard Curteys*, Bishop of *Chichester*; *Nicholas Robinson*, Bishop of *Bangor*; and *John Scory*, Bishop of *Hereford*. The same year also died *John Fecknam*, late Abbot of *Westminster*.

The Jesuites began now to possess their English Proselites, with high Opinions of the Spanish power, as the Nation designed by God's providence to work their restitution in *England*: and they sent into *England* (as *Pasquier* saith) one *Samier*, a man of their Society, to draw Noblemen, and Gentlemen to the Spaniards party, and to thrust forward the Queen of Scots to dangerous practices, by telling her, *That if she were refractory, neither She nor her Son should Reign*: and by exciting the *Guises* her kinsmen to new stirs, against the King of *Navar* and the Prince of *Conde*, that they might not be able to ayd her.

In the year 1586. a firm League of Amity was concluded and ratified betwixt the Queen of *England* and *James* King of *Scotland*.

A dangerous conspiracy against the Queen of *England* (begun by *John Savage*, but prosecuted by *Anthony Babington* and others) was discovered. The chief discover of this Conspiracy was one *Gifford*, a Gentleman of a good house at *Chellington* in *Stafford-shire*, not far from *Chartley*, where the Queen of Scots was kept prisoner. He was sent by the English fugitives in *France*, under the counterfit name of *Luson*, to put *Savage* in mind of the vow which he had made, to kill Queen Elizabeth

Elizabeth, and to convey Letters between them and the Queen of *Scots*. *Gifford* revealed the plot to Secretary *Walsingham*, who sent him down into *Stafford-shire* to do the work he had undertaken.

Here *Gifford* bribing the Brewer of the house where the Queen of Scots lay, so contrived the matter with him, that by a hole in the wall, in which a loose stone was put, he should give in, and receive forth Letters, the which, by Messengers purposely laid by the way, came ever to *Walsingham*'s hands, who broke them open, copied them out, and by the cunning of *Thomas Philips*, found out the meaning of the private Cyphers: and by the Art of *Arthur Gregory* sealed them up again, so neatly, that no man could have imagined them to be opened, and ever sent them to the parties to whom the superscription directed them. In like manner were the former Letters from the Queen of Scots to *Babington* intercepted; as also other Letters written at the same time to *Mendoza* the Spanish Ambassador, *Charles Paget*, the Lord *Paget*, the Archbishop of *Glasco*, and *Francis Englefied*. Then *Ballard* was apprehended. *Babington* seeks to escape, and is taken. The Queen of Scots hath her Closets broken open, and her Boxes searched. Fourteen of the Conspirators were Arraigned, Condemned of High-treason and executed. Afterwards in the Star-chamber sentence was pronounced against the Queen of Scots. And in a Parliament presently following, the Lords petition the Queen, that the sentence passed against her may presently be promulged. The King of Scots and the King of *France* sollicit for her life. But when this would not prevail, *L' Aubespine*, the French Ambassador thinks no way so effectual, for saving the Queen of Scots life, as to take away the life of Queen *Elizabeth*. The plot was discovered. And at length the Sentence against the Queen of Scots was put in execution, and she ended her doleful life at *Fothringhay* Castle. She was buried in the Quire of *Peterborough*, and Doctor *Wickham* Bishop of *Lincoln* Preached her Funeral-sermon. Some twenty yaars after King *James* caused her Corps to be solemnly removed from *Peterborough* to *Westminster*, where in the South-side of the Chappel of King *Henry* the Seventh, he erected a stately Monument to her Memory.

The Earl of *Leicester* having raised great offence, is called home again into *England* by the Queen, giveth over his Government, and the free Administration of his Government is left to the States.

Now Conformity was pressed to the height. The power of the High Commission began to extend far, and penalties to fall heavy on offenders: whereupon the favourers of Non-conformists much opposed it in their Printed Books; some questioning the Court as not warranted by Law; others taxing their proceedings, as exceeding their Commission. But the most general exception against the High Commission was this, *Fuller.Church Hist. in An. 1587.*

K k That

That proceeding, *Ex Officio mero*, by way of enquiry against such whom they suspected, they tendred unto them an Oath, which was conceived unjust, that in cases criminal a party should be forced to discover what might be penal to himself. The lawfulness of which Oath was learnedly canvassed with arguments on both sides.

Because many did question the Legality and Authority of the High Commission, Archbishop *Whitgift* so contrived the matter, that the most sturdy Non-conformists (especially if they had any visible Estates) were brought into the Star-chamber, the power whereof was above dispute; where some of them besides imprisonment, had very heavy fines imposed on them. And because most of the Queens Council were present at the Censures, this took off the *odium* from the Archbishop.

This year died Mr. *John Fox*, the Industrious compiler of the Acts and Monuments of the Church, and was buried at St. *Giles* near *Cripplegate* in *London*. It is said he foretold the destruction of the Invincible (so called) Spanish *Armado*, in the year 1588. which came so to pass though he survived not to see the performance of his own prediction.

Camd. Brit. in Kent. About this time Mr. *William Lambert* finished his Hospital at *Greenwich*, founded and endowed by him for poor people. He was the first Protestant who erected a charitable house of that nature, saith *Camden*: But King *Edward* the Sixth, founded *Christ-church* and St. *Thomas* Hospital.

Now the sticklers against the Hierarchy appeared more vigorous, though for a time they had concealed themselves.

The Parliament now sitting at *Westminster*, the House of Commons presented to the Lords a petition, complaining how many Parishes, especially in the North of *England* and *Wales*, were destitute of Preachers, and no care taken to supply them. Sixteen were the particulars, whereof the six first were against insufficient Ministers. Of all the particulars the House fell most fiercely on the debate of pluralities, and Non-residents.

The Arch-bishop pleads for Non-residency in divers cases. He affirmed (whatever was pretended to the contrary) that *England* then flourished with able Ministers, more than ever before, yea had more than all Christendom besides. The Lord *Grey* rejoyned to this Assertion, saying, That *England* had more able Ministers than all the Churches in Christendom, was onely to be attributed to God, who now opened the hearts of many to see into the truth, and that the Schools were better observed. The Lord Treasurer seemed to moderate betwixt them. Matters flying thus high, the Archbishop with the rest of the Clergy Petition the Queen: To the Petition were annexed a Catalogue of those inconveniencies to the State present, State to come, Cathedral Churches, the **Church** of GREAT BRITAIN. 250

Churches, Universities, to her Majesty, to Religion, in case pluralities were taken away. Nothing was effected in relation to this matter, but things left, *in statu quo prius*, at the dissolution of this Parliament.

This year died *Richard Barnes* Bishop of *Durham*.

In the year 1588. when there was a Treaty of Peace between *England* and *Spain*, out cometh their Invincible Navy and Army, perfectly appointed for both Elements, Land and Water, to Sayl and March compleat in all Warlike Equipage: but that great Fleet was wonderfully defeated by the English, and dissipated by stormy Winds: and many of the Spaniards were Barbarously butchered by the Irish.

For the happy success of this action Queen *Elizabeth* appointed Prayers and Thanksgivings over all the Churches in *England*: and she with a great Train of the Nobility came into St. *Pauls* Church, (where the Banners taken from the Enemy were placed in view) and therein most humble manner gave thanks to Almighty God the giver of all Victory. About this time many Papists were committed to custody in *Wisbych* Castle.

At this time many Libels flew abroad, thus named.

1. *The Epitome.*
2. *The Demonstration of Discipline.*
3. *The Supplication.*
4. *Diotrephes.*
5. *The Minerals.*
6. *Have ye any work for the Cooper.*
7. *More work for the Cooper.*
8. Martin Senior ⎱ *Mar-prelate.*
9. Martin *Junior* ⎰

The main drift of these Pamphlets was to defame the English Prelates, scoffing at them for their Garb, Gate, Apparel, Vanities of their Youth, natural Defects, and personal Infirmities. It is strange how secretly they were Printed, how speedily Dispersed, how generally Bought, how greedily Read, how firmly Believed, especially of the Common sort. Some precise men of that side, thought these jeering pens well employed: but these Books were disclaimed by the more descreet and devout sort of men.

And how highly the State distasted these Books, will appear, by the heavy censures inflicted on such as were but accessary thereunto. To pass by *John Udal* and *John Penry* Ministers accused for making some of them, together with the Printers, and *Humfry Newman* a Cobler, chief disperser of them. The Star-chamber deeply fined Sir *Richard Knightly*, and Sir   *Wigston*, for entertaining and receiving the press Gentlemen. But upon their submission they had their liberty, and were eased of their fines.

Kk 2   A

A Synod of the Presbyterians of the *Warwick-shire Classis* was called at *Coventry*, wherein the questions brought the last year from the Brethren of *Cambridge-Synod*, were thus resolved.

Bp. Bancroft's Book, called, Englands Scotizing for Discipline by practice.

I. That private Baptism was unlawful.
II. That it is not lawful to read Homiles in the Church.
III. That the sign of the cross is not to be used in Baptism.
IV. That the faithful ought not to communicate with unlearned Ministers, although they may be present at their service, &c.
V. That the calling of Bishops is unlawful.
VI. That as they deal in Causes Ecclesiastical, there is no duty belonging unto, nor any publickly to be given them.
VII. That it is not lawful to be Ordained Ministers by them, or to denounce either Suspensions, or Excommunications sent from them.
VIII. That it is not lawful to rest in the Bishop's deprivation of any from the Ministry, &c.
IX. That it is not lawful to appear in a Bishop's Court, but with protestation of their unlawfulness.
X. That Bishops are not to be acknowledged either for Doctors, Elders, or Deacons, as having no ordinary calling.
XI. That touching the restauration of their Ecclesiastical Discipline, it ought to be taught to the people as occasion shall serve.
XII. That (as yet) the people are not to be solicited (publicly) to the practice of the Discipline, (till) they be better instructed in the knowledge of it.
XIII. That men of better understanding are to be allured privately to the present embracing of the discipline, and practice of it, as far as they shall be well able, with the peace of the Church.

Likewise in the same Assembly, the aforesaid Book of Discipline was approved to be a draught essential and necessary for all times. And certain Articles (devised in approbation, and for the manner of the use thereof) were brought forth, treated of, and subscribed unto by Master *Cartwright* and others, and afterwards tendred far and near to the several Classes for a general ratification of all the brethren.

After a solemn humiliation of the Ministers at *Northampton*, one Mr. *Johnson*, formerly a Non-conformist, but afterwards falling from that side, discovered many passages to their disadvantage in the Highcommission Court.

Harion. Quodlibets.

This year also the Popish Clergy set forth a Book, called *the Admonition*, dispersed among the Papists, and much cried up. But the Spanish Navy presently miscarying after it's publishing, *Parsons* procured the whole impression to be burnt (save some few sent abroad aforehand to his friends) that it might not remain a monument of their falshood.

This

the Church of Great Britain.

This year died *Edwyn Sandys*, Archbishop of *York*, an excellent Preacher, and of a pious Life: and Dr. *Laurence Humfrey*, President of *Magdalen* Colledge.

On *September* 1. 1596. Mr. *Cartwright* was brought before the Queen's Commissioners, there to take his Oath, and give in his positive answer to divers Articles objected against him. The Articles were tendred to him in the Consistory of St. *Paul*'s before *John Elmar* Bishop of *London*, the two Lord Chief Justices, Justice *Gawdy*, Serjeant *Puckering*, (afterward Lord Keeper) and Attorney General *Popham*. The Commissioners assured him on their credits, that by the Laws of the Realm he was to take his Oath, and to answer as he was required. But Mr. *Cartwright* pleaded, That he thought he was not bound by the Laws of God so to do. Hereupon he was sent to the Fleet unto the rest of his Brethren.

Now the main pillars of the Presbyterian party, being some in Prison, more in Trouble, all in Fear, applied themselves by their secret solicitors to *James* King of *Scotland*, and procured his Letter to the Queen in their behalf. But this Letter prevailed little. But Archbishop *Whitgift*, on Mr. *Cartwright*'s general promise to be quiet, procured his dismission out of the Star-chamber and prison wherein he was confined. And henceforward Mr. *Cartwright* became very peaceable.

Then one *Hacket*, born at *Owndle* in *Northampton-shire* undertook to be a discoverer of, and Informer against Recusants, a confident Fellow, one that was great with *Wigginton* and that Faction. Always Inculcating, that some extraordinary course must be presently taken with the obstructors of the *Genevian* discipline. Once he desperatley took his dagger, and violently struck it into the picture of the Queen. He pretended also Revelations, Immediate Raptures, and Discourses with God, as also to Buffetings of Satan, attesting the truth thereof with most direful Oathes and Execrations. He railed also against Archbishop *Whitgift*, and Chancellor *Hatton*, with other privy Counsellors, pretending himself sent from Heaven to reform Church and State. He gave it out, that the principal Spirit of the Messias rested in him, and had two Attendants. *Edmond Coppinger* (the Queen's Servant, and one of good descent) for his Prophet of Mercy. And *Henry Artbington*, a *York-shire* Gentleman, for his Prophet of Judgment. These Proclaimed in Cheap-side, *That Christ was come in* Hacket, *with his fan in his hand, to purge the godly from the wicked*, &c. *They cried Repent, Repent*, &c. The next day all three were sent to *Bridewel: Hacket* was arraigned, drawn, hanged, and quartered, continuing even at his death his blasphemous assertions. *Coppinger* starved himself to death in prison, *Artbington* made his Recantation in a publick writing, and became the object of the Queen's mercy.

This

This accident was unhappily improved against the Non-conformists, and rendred them so hated at Court, that for many months together, no favourite durst present a petition in their behalf to the Queen, being loth to lose himself to save others.

Fuller. Church Hill. *Cent.* 15. l. 5.

The same day wherein *Hacket* was executed, Mr. *Stone*, Parson of *Warkton* in *Northampton-shire*, by vertue of an Oath tendred him the day before by the Queen's Attorney, and solemnly taken by him, was examined by the Examiner for the Star-chamber in *Grays* Inn, from six a clock in the morning untill seven at night, to answer unto thirty three Articles, but could onely effectually depose to some of them: but by his confession he discovereth the meetings of the Brethren, with the circumstances thereof, the Classes more formally setled in *Northampton-shire*, than any where else in *England*. When the news of Mr. *Stone's* answer was brought abroad, he was generally censured by most of his party: So that he found it necessary, in his own vindication, to impart the reasons of his Confession to such as condemned him, if not for a Traitor, at least for a coward in the cause. What satisfaction this gave to his party I know not. Certainly the Bishop till his dying day beheld him as an ingenuous man, carrying his conscience with the reason thereof in his own breast. He was permitted peaceably to possess his Parsonage (being none of the meanest) though he continued a stiff Non-conformist, onely quietly enjoying his own opinion. He died an old man at *Warkton*, *Anno* 1617.

Stone's discovery marred for the future all their formal meetings, as Classically or Synodically methodized.

Then began the foundation of an University in *Dublin* in *Ireland*. Henry *Usher*, then Archdeacon of *Dublin* (afterwards Archbishop of *Armagh*, and Unckle to *James Usher* late Archbishop thereof) took a journey into *England*, and procured the Mortmain from Queen *Elizabeth*, who graciously granted it, naming the corporation, *Collegium Sanctæ ac Individuæ Trinitatis, ex fundatione Reginæ* Elizebethæ, *juxta* Dublin. The Lord *Burgley* is appointed first Chancellor of the University. Sir *William Fitz-Williams*, Lord Debuty of *Ireland*, issued out his Letters to all the Counties in *Ireland* to advance so good a design. The Irish Papists were very bountiful thereunto. The Mayor and Aldermen of *Dublin*: Sir *Warham St. Leger*, Sir *Francis Shane*, *Robert D'eureux* Earl of *Essex*, afterwards Lord Lieutenant of *Ireland*, and second Chancellor of this University, were Benefactors to it. King *James* confirmed the revenues of this Colledge *in perpetuum*, endowing it with good Lands in the Province of *Ulster*. *Adam Loftus*, Archbishop of *Dublin*, and Chancellor of *Ireland*, was the first Master of the Colledge. Mr. *Luke Chaloner* received and disbursed the moneys, had the oversight of the Fabrick, which he faithfully procured to be finished. The first stone in this foundation was laid, *March* 13. 1591. and in the

year

year 1593. Scholars were first admitted: and the first of them *James Usher*, since Bishop of *Armagh*, that mirrour of Learning and Religion.

Now began a sad contest betwixt Mr. *Richard Hooker*, Master, and Mr. *Walter Travers*, Lecturer of the Temple. *Hooker* was born in *Devonshire*, bred in *Oxford*, Fellow of *Corpus Christi* Colledge : one of a solid Judgment, and great Reading. A great defender both by Preaching and Writing of the Discipline of the Church of *England*, yet never got (nor cared to get) any eminent dignity therein. Mr. *Travers* was bred up in *Trinity* Colledge in *Cambridge*. *Travers* travelling to *Geneva*, contracted familiarity with *Beza*, and other forreign Divines. Then returned He, and commenced Batchelor of Divinity in *Cambridge*, and after that went beyond Sea again, and at *Antwerp* was ordained Minister by the Presbytery there, where he continued some years and Preached (with Mr. *Cartwright*) unto the English Factory of Merchants, untill at last he came over into *England*, and for seven years together became Lecturer in the Temple (refusing all presentative preferment to decline subscription) and lived Domestick Chaplain in the house of the Lord Treasurer *Cecil*, being Tutor for a time to *Robert*, his Son, afterwards Earl of *Sarisbury*.

Yea now so great grew the credit of Mr. *Travers*, that (by the advice of Mr. *Andrew Melvin*) he and Mr. *Cartwright* were solemnly sent for, to be Divinity-professors in the University of St. *Andrews*. This proffer being joyntly refused, *Travers* quietly continued Lecturer in the Temple, till Mr. *Hooker* became the Master thereof. Mr. *Hooker's* voice was low, stature little, gesture none at all, standing still in the Pulpit. His stile was long and pithy, so that when the copiousness of his stile met not with proportionable capacity in his Auditors, it was unjustly censured for tedious and obscure. His Sermons were for the most part on Controversies, and deep points of School-divinity.

Mr. *Travers* his utterance was graceful, gesture plausible, matter profitable, and method plain. But these two Preachers acted with different Principles, and clashed one against another : so that what Mr. *Hooker* delivered in the Fore-noon, Mr. *Travers* confuted in the After-noon. Here Archbishop *Whitgift* interposed his power, and silenced *Travers* from Preaching in the Temple or any where else ; *Travers* Petitions the Lords of the Council : his Petition is publickly extant in Print, with Master *Hoooker's* answer thereunto. But Mr. *Travers*, notwithstanding his friends at Court, was over-born by the Archbishop.

Adam Loftus, Archbishop of *Dublin*, and Chancellor of *Ireland*, invited him over to be Provost of *Trinity* Colledge in *Dublin*. Embracing the motion, he accepted the place, and continued some years therein, till for fear of their Civil Wars he returned into *England*, and lived here many years after very obscurely.

In the year 1592. In *London* more than ten thousand died of the Plague, and among them Reverend Mr. *Richard Greenham*. He was one that always bitterly inveighed against Non-residents, he ended his days at *Christ Church* in *London*.

Mr. *Udal* was indicted, and arraigned at *Croidon*, for defaming the Queen her Government, in a Book by him written and entitled, *A Demonstration of the Discipline which Christ hath prescribed in his Word for the Government of his Church in all times and places unto the World's end.* But the mortal words (as they may be termed) are in the Preface of the Book, written, *To the supposed Governours of the Church of England, Archbishops, Bishops*, &c. and are inserted in the Body of his indictment.

To this Indictment he pleaded *Not guilty*, denying himself to be the Author of the Book. Next day he was cast by the Jury, but was remanded to the Marshalsey; *March* following he was brought again to the bar before the Judges, to whom he had privatelp presented a Petition with all advantage, but it found no entertainment, insomuch that in this moneth of *March*, he at the Assizes held in *Southwark*, was there condemned to be executed for a Felon.

Various were mens Censures on these proceedings against him. The proof was not pregnant (saith Mr. *Fuller*) and it is generally believed, that he made onely the Preface, out of which his indictment was chiefly framed) and not the body of the Book laid to his charge. But without any other sickness, save heart-broken with sorrow, he died peaceably in his bed. The Ministers of *London* flocked to his Funeral, and he was decently interred in the Church-yard of St. *George* in *Southwark*, not far from Bishop *Bonner's* grave. He was Father to *Ephraim Udal*, a pious and solid Divine, but in point of Discipline differing in Opinion from his Father.

Anno 1593. *Henry Barrow* Gentleman, and *John Greemoood* Clerk, were condemned, and executed at *Tyburn*, for writing certain Seditious Pamphlets. And not long after, *John Penry*, a Welch-man, was arraigned and condemned of Felony, at the King's Bench Bar, for being a principal penner, and publisher of a Libellous Book, called *Martin-mar-prelate*, and executed at St. *Thomas Waterings*.

Sir *John Haringt.* addit. supply to Bish. *Godwin.* p. 134.

This year Queen *Elizabeth* took her last farewel of *Oxford*, where a Divinity-Act was kept for her. Next day her Highnels made a Latin Oration to the Heads of Houses, in which she gave a check to Dr. *Rainolds* for his Non-conformity.

The same year died *John Piers*, Archbishop of *York*, highly esteemed by Queen *Elizabeth*; whose Almoner he was many years; and *John Elmar*, Bishop of *London*. He was one of a low stature, but stout spirit, a witty man, a stiff-champion of the Church-discipline, on which account none was more mocked by *Martin-mar-prelat*, or hated by Non-conformists.

the Church of GREAT BRITAIN. 257

Of the Papists died, *Anno* 1594. two principal pillars beyond the Seas: first *William Rose*, bred in *Winchester-school*, then in *New-colledge* in *Oxford*. He went to *Rome*, and there solemnly abjured the Protestant Religion: from *Rome* he removed to *Rhemes* in *France*, where he became Professor of Divinity and Hebrew in the English Colledge: He died at *Antwerp* in the fiftieth year of his Age, as he was making a Book, called *Calvino-Turcismus*, which after by his dear friend, *William Gifford*, was finished, set forth, and dedicated to *Albert* Duke of *Austria*. Cardinal *William Allen* died also the same year. The King of *Spain* bestowed on him an Abbey in the Kingdom of *Naples*, and nominated him to be Archbishop of *Machlin*: but he died, and was buried in the Church of the English Colledge at *Rome*. His loss was much lamented by the Catholicks: for he had done many good offices in composing the grudgings which began to grow between the Secular Priests and Jesuites. Untill this time the prime Catholicks in *Wisbich* Castle, had lived there in restraint, with great concord. And the Papists do brag, that then and there the English Church was most visible, untill one Father *Weston*, a Jesuite coming thither, erected a Government among them, making certain Sanctions and Orders, which all were bound to observe, claiming a superiority over all the Catholicks there. Besides those of his own society, many of the Secular Priests submitted unto him, though the greatest number and Learned sort of the Secular Priests resisted his superiority. If any Order might pretend to this Priority, it was most proper for the *Benedictines*, extant in *England* above a thousand years ago: one might admire why Father *Weston* should so earnestly desire so silly a Dominion, having his power, as well as his own person confined within the walls of *Wisbich* Castle.

Pitræus de il-lustr. Angl. Script. p. 793.

Anno 1595. Began throughout *England* the more solem and strict observation of the Lord's day, occasioned by a Book then set forth by P. *Bound*. D. D. and enlarged with additions.

Anno 1606. Hereupon the Lord's day (especially in Corporations) began to be precisely kept, people forbearing such sports as yet by Statute permitted; yet Learned men were much divided in their Judgments about the Sabbatarian Doctrines. The first that publickly opposed Dr. *Bounds* Opinions, was Mr. *Thomas Rogers* of *Horninger* in *Suffolk*, in his Preface to the Book of Articles: yet notwithstanding were these Sabbatarian Doctrines published more generally than before. The price of the Doctor's Book began to be doubled, as commonly Books are then most called on, when called in. Yea six years after *Bounds* book came forth, with enlargements publickly sould.

Now also began some Opinions about Predestination, Free-will, Perseverance, which much troubled the Schools and Pulpit. Wherein Archbishop *Whitgift* caused a solemn meeting of many Learned Divines at *Lambeth*, where (besides the Archbishop) *Richard Bancroft*,

L l Bishop

Bishop of *London*; *Richard Vaughan*, Bishop of *Bangor*; *Humfrey Tyndal*, Bishop of *Ely*; Dr. *Whitaker*, Queen's Professor in *Cambridge*, and others were assembled. These after a serious debate, resolved on the now following Articles.

Fuller.Church Hist.An.1595.

I. God from eternity hath Predestinated certain men unto life, &c.
II. The moving cause of Predestination unto life, is not Faith and good Works foreseen, &c. but onely the good will and pleasure of God.
III. There is predetermined a certain number of the predestinate, &c.
IV. Those who are not predestinated to Salvation, shall be necessarily damned for their sins.
V. A true, living, justifying Faith, &c. is not extinguished, vanisheth not away in the elect either finally or totally.
VI. A man truly faithful, i. e. such a one who is endued with justifying Faith, is certain with the full assurance of Faith of the Remission of his sins, and of his everlasting Salvation by Christ.
VII. Saving Grace is not given, granted, communicated to all men, by which they may be saved if they will.
VIII. No man can come unto Christ, Unless it shall be givenll unto him, and unless the Father shall draw him. And as men are not drawn by the Father, that they may come to the Son.
IX. It is not in the will or power of every one to be saved.

Matthew Hutton, Archbishop of *York*, did also fully and freely in his judgement concur with those Divines, as appeareth by a Letter of his sent to a most Reverend Prelate.

Mountagu in his Appeal. p. 55, 56, 71, 72.

When these Articles came abroad into the World, some had an high Opinion of them; others valued them at a low rate. Some flatly condemned both the Articles and the Authors of them. One affirmeth; that these Articles were forbidden by publick Authority, but when, where, and by whom, he faith nothing.

Forreign Divines raised, or decryed, the esteem of these Articles just as they were biassed in judgment. Some Printed, set forth, and cited them, as the sence of the Church of *England*, others as fast flighted them as the narrow positions of a few private and partial persons. Although those Learned Divines be not acknowledged as competent Judges to pass definitive sentence in those points, yet their testimony is an infallible evidence, what was the general and received Doctrine of *England*, in that Age, about the forenamed Controversies.

This

The Church of Great Britain.

This year died first Dr. *William Wickham*, bred in King's Colledge in *Cambridge*, first Bishop of *Lincoln*, after of *Winchester*. Secondly, Worthy Dr. *William Whitaker*. And among the Romanists, *Daniel Halesworth*. More infamous was the death of *Robert Southwel*, a Jesuite, who was executed for a Traitor at *London*.

In the year 1596. died Bishop *Fletcher* of *London*, who died suddenly, and *John Coldwel*, Bishop of *Sarisbury*.

About this time also died Doctor *Laurence Humfrey*, a moderate Non-conformist, Dean of *Winchester*, and Master of *Magdalen* Colledge in *Oxford*.

Master *Baltazar Zanchez*, a Spaniard, born in *Estremadura*, founded an Almes-house at *Totnam-Highcross* in *Middlesex*, for eight single people, allowing them competent maintenance.

Thomas Stapleton this year ended his life at *Lovain*: he was born at *Henfield* in *Sussex*, and was a Learned assertor of the Romish Religion.

This year also died *Richard Cosins*, Doctor of the Law, and Dean of Arches, one of the greatest Civilians which our Nation hath produced.

The death of *Robert Turner* was now much lamented by the Papists. He was born at *Barstable* in *Devonshire*, bred for awhile in *Oxford*, whence flying beyond the Seas, he became Canon of *Breslaw* in *Silesia*, and at the same time Privy Councellor to the Duke of *Bavaria*. *Ferdinand* of *Gratz* (afterwards Emperor) took him from the Duke to be his own Secretary in the Latin Tongue. He lieth buried at *Gratz* under a handsom Monument.

In the year 1599. died *Richard Hooker*, of whom largely before. He was much lamented by Protestants.

Anno 1600. died two eminent Roman Catholicks; *John Saunderson*, born in *Lancaster*, bred in *Trinity* Colledge in *Cambridge*, from whence he fled to *Cambray* in *Artois*. The other *Thomas Case* of St. *Johns* in *Oxford*, Doctor of Physick; always a Papist in heart, but never expressing the same, till a little before his Death.

Century XVII.

THe difference betwixt the *Seculars* and the *Jesuites* still continuing and encreasing, Bishop *Bancroft* afforded the *Seculars* countenance and maintenance in *London-house*, furnishing them with necessaries to write against their Adversaries, hoping the Protestants might assault the Romish cause with the greater advantage, by the breach made to their hands by the others own dissentions.

Archbishop *Whitgift* founded and endowed an Hospital at *Croydon* in *Surrey*, for a Warden and twenty eight Brethren : as also a free School with liberal maintenance for the training up of Youth.

Sir Rich. Baker's Chron.

The Queen and Her Council finding both the Jesuites and the Secular Priests dangerous to this Common Wealth both the one and the other, commandeth them to depart out of the Kingdom presently.

The last Parliament in this Queen's Reign was now begun at *Westminster*, and dissolved the Moneth next following. In this Parliament it was Enacted, That overseers of the poor should be nominated yearly in Easter-week under the Hand and Seal of two Justices of peace, and that these with the Church-wardens should take care of the poor, binding out of Apprentices, &c. As also, That the Lord Chancellor should award Commissions under the great Seal into any part of the Realm (as cause should require) to the Bishop of every Diocess, and his Chancellor, &c. to enquire by oathes of twelve men, into the misemployment of any lands or goods given to pious uses.

Francis Godwin, D. D. Subdean of *Exeter*, son of *Thomas Godwin* Bishop of *Bath* and *Wells*, was made Bishop of *Landaff*. He was born in the fourth year of Queen *Elizabeth*, and was made a Bishop within Her Reign, *Anno* 1601.

Now came forth a notable book against the Jesuites, written Scholastically by *Watson* a secular Priest, consisting of ten *Quodlibets*, each whereof is subdivided into as many Articles, which discovereth the Jesuites in their Colours.

Anno. 1602. died *Herbert Westphaling*, Bishop of *Hereford*, being the first Bishop of that foundation, a man very pious, and of such gravity, that he was scarce ever seen to laugh. There died also *Alexander Nowel*, D. D. and Dean of S. *Paul's* in *London*. He fled into *Germany* in the Reign of Queen *Mary*, and was the first of English exiles that returned in the days of Queen *Elizabeth*: an holy and Learned Man. He bestowed two hundred pound a year rent on *Brazen-nose Colledge*, wherein he was educated, for the maintenance of thirteen Students. He died at ninety years of age, a single man, fresh in

his

his youthful Learning; his eyes were not dim, nor did he ever make use of Spectacles.

Mr. *William Perkins* who was born in the first, died also in the last year of Queen *Elizabeth*. *Gregory Sayer* also, and *William Harris*, two Popish Writers, bred the one at *Cambridge*, the other at *Oxford*, died this year beyond the Seas.

At this time the City of *Geneva* was in a low estate; for the Duke of *Savoy*, addicted to the Spanish faction had banished all Protestants of his Dominions. By the Liberal example of Archbishop *Whitgift* large summes of Money were Collected, and seasonably sent over for the Relief of *Geneva*.

Queen *Elizabeth*, the mirrour of her Sex and Age, died having Reigned over this Kingdom above fourty years. Her Corps were Solemnly interred under a fair Tomb in *Westminster* Abbey.

Now the Defenders both of Episcopacy and Presbitery, with equal hopes of success, make (besides private and particular Addresses) publick and visible Applications to King *James*, the first to continue, the last to set up their Government. Dr. *Thomas Nevil*, Dean of *Canterbury* sent by Archbishop *Whitgift* to his Majesty in the name of the Bishops and Clergy of *England*, brought back a well-come answer, which was to uphold the Government of the Late Queen, as she left it setled.

Then *Watson* a Secular Priest with *William Cleark* another of his Profession, having fancied a notional Treason, impart it to *George Brook*. These break it to *Brook*'s brother; the Lord *Cobham*, to the Lord *Gray* of *Wilton*, and Sir *Walter Rawleigh* besides some other discontented Knights. *Watson* devised an Oath of secrecy for them all. The ends they propounded to themselves were to kill the King, raise Rebellion, alter Religion, and procure a Forreign invasion, &c. The treason was discovered. The two Priests alone with G. *Brook* were executed, the rest were pardoned.

No sooner was King *James* setled on the English throne, but Mr. *Cartwright* presented unto him his Latine Comment on *Ecclesiastes*: and died soon after. Mr. *Dod* Preached his funeral Sermon.

Now there being a general expectation of a Parliament to succeed; the Presbterian party went about to get hands of the Ministers to a petition which they intended seasonably to present to the King and Parliament. A conference was appointed at *Hampton-Court*, which began on *January* 14. 1603. The names of the Persons which were employed therein, are as follow.

For

For Conformity.

Archbishop of *Canterbury*, *Whitgift*.

Bishops of
- *London* — *Bancroft*.
- *Durham* — *Mathew*.
- *Winchester* — *Bilson*.
- *Worcester* — *Babington*.
- *S. David's* — *Rudd*.
- *Chichester* — *Watson*.
- *Carlile* — *Robinson*.
- *Peterborow* — *Dove*.

Deans of
- *The Chappel*.
- *Christ-Church*.
- *Worcester*.
- *Westminster*.
- *S. Paul's*.
- *Chester*.
- *Sarisbury*.
- *Windsor*.

Doctor { *Field*. *King*. }

Against Conformity.

Doctor { *Reinolds*. *Sparks*. }   Master { *Knewstubs*. *Chadderton*. }

Moderator — King *James*.
Spectators — All the Lords of the Privy Council.

On the first dayes Conference the Bishops and five of the Deans were called in severally by themselves, then the King reduceth some special points wherein he desireth to be satisfied, to three Heads.
1. Concerning the Book of Common Prayer, &c. used in the Church.
2. Excommunication in Ecclesiastical Courts.
3. The providing of fit and able Ministers for *Ireland*.

In the Common-prayer-book he required satisfaction about three things,
1. About *Confirmation*.
2. *Absolution*.
3. *Private Baptism*.

Touching

Touching *Confirmation*, he said he abhorred the abuse wherein it was made a Sacrament, or Corroboration to Baptism, As for *Absolution*, he said he had heard it likened to Pope's Pardons.

And Concerning *Private Baptism*, he would be satisfied, if called private from the place, or if so termed that any besides a Lawful Minister may Baptize, which he disliked.

Concerning excommunication he offered two things to be considered of,

1. The Matter.
2. The Persons.

For the first, whether it were executed in light Cases, which causeth the undervaluing thereof, For the persons, he would be resolved, why Chancellors and Commissaries being lay men should do it, and not rather the Bishops themselves, &c. As for providing Ministers for *Ireland*; he said he would refer it in the last dayes Conference to a Consultation.

The Archbishop of *Canterbury* answered, that Confirmation hath been used in the Catholick Church ever since the Apostles. The Bishop of *London*. That it is an Apostolical Institution, named in express words. *Heb.* 6. 2. The Bishop of *Carlile* Learnedly urged the same. And the Bishop of *Durham* urged something out of S. *Mathew*, for the Imposition of hands on Children.

The Conclusion was this, for the fuller explanation, that we make Confirmation neither a Sacrament, nor a Corroboration thereof, their Lordship should consider whether it might not without alteration, be entitled an *Examination* with a *Confirmation*.

As for *Absolution*, the Archbishop told His Majesty that it is clear from all Superstition as it is used in the Church of *England*, as will appear on the Reading both of the Confession and Absolution following it, in the beginning of the Communion-book.

Here the King perused both, liked and approved them.

The Particular and Personal Absolution in the Visitation of the sick, was also Read by the Dean of the Chappel, and approved by the King.

The Conclusion was this, That the Bishops should Consult; whether unto the Rubrick of the General Absolution, these words [*Remission of sins*] might not be added for explanation-sake.

To the point of *Private Baptism*, the Archbishop of *Canterbury* said, the Administration thereof by women and Lay-persons is not allowed in the Practice of the Church, &c. The King answered, the words of the Book cannot but intend a permission of such persons to Baptise. The Bishop of *Worcester* said, that the Compilers of the book did not so intend

tend them, as appeareth by their contrary practice. The Bishop of *London* said, those men intended a permission of private persons to baptise but in case of necessity. Here he spake much of the necessity of Baptism. The King answered, this necessity of Baptism I so understand, that it is necessary to be had, if lawfully to be had, *i.e.* Ministred by lawful Ministers, by whom alone, and no private person in any case it may be administred.

The result was this, To consult, whether in the Rubrick of Private baptism, these words [*Curate*, or *lawful Minister*] may not be inserted.

For the point of Excommunication, His Majesty propounded, whether in causes of lesser moment the name might not be altered, and the same censure retained. Secondly, whether in place thereof another coertion equivalent thereunto might not be invented. Which all sides yielded unto, and so was an end of the first dayes conference.

On Monday *January* 16. they all met in the same place with all the Deans and Doctors aforementioned (*Patrick Galloway* Minister of *Perth* in *Scotland*, admitted also to be there) and Prince *Henry* sate on a Stool by his Father. After the King had made a pithy speech to the four opposers of conformity. He willed them to begin.

Then Dr. *Rainolds* said, All things disliked, or questioned, may be reduced to these four heads.

I. *That the Doctrine of the Church might be preserved in purity according to God's word.*

II. *That good Pastors might be planted in all Churches to preach the same.*

III. *That the Church-government might be sincerely Ministred according to God's word.*

IV. *That the book of Common-prayer might be fitted to more encrease of Piety.*

For the first, he desired, that the book of Articles of Religion concluded on 1562. might be explained where obscure, enlarged where defective, *viz.* Art. 16. where it is said, *After we have received the Holy Ghost, we may depart from Grace*, Those words may be explained, with this addition, *yet neither totally nor finally*.

He propounded also, that the nine Assertions concluded on at *Lambeth*, might be inserted into the Book of Articles. Some other things also he added.

The Bishop of *London* speaks passionately against Dr. *Rainolds:* for which the King reproveth him.

As for Private Baptism, His Majesty said, he had already with the Bishops taken order for the same.

Then

the Church of Great Britain.

Then came they to *Confirmation*, And after some debate thereon betwixt Dr. *Rainolds*, and the Bishops of *London* and *Winchester*, his Majesty said, he intended not to take confirmation from the Bishops which they had so long enjoyed; seeing as great reason that none should confirm, as none should Preach without the Bishop's License.

Dr. *Rainolds* said, It were well, if this proposition might be added to the book of Articles, *The Intention of the Minister is not of the Essence of the Sacrament*. He urged again, that the nine Orthodoxal Assertions concluded at *Lambeth* may be generally received.

The King thought it unfit to thrust into the book of Articles every position Negative, which would swell the book into too great a volume. And as to the nine Assertions, his Majesty said, he knew not what they were. The Bishop of *London* told the King the occasion of them. He answered, the better course would be to punish the broachers of false Doctrine than to multiply Articles.

Then Dr. *Rainolds* requested, that one Uniform Catechism may be made, and none other generally received.

His Majesty thought the Doctor's request very reasonable, yet so, that the Catechism may be made in the fewest, and plainest affirmative terms that may be. And herein (said he) I would have two Rules to be observed. 1. That curious and deep questions be avoided in the fundamental instruction of a people. 2. That there should not be so general a departure from the Papists, that every thing should be accounted an errour wherein we agree with them.

Dr. *Rainolds* said, Great is the profanation of the Sabbath day, and contempt of your Majestie's Proclamation which I earnestly desire may be Reformed.

This motion found an unanimous consent.

Then the Doctor desired that the Bible be New Translated, &c. His Majesty answered, that he never yet saw a Bible well-translated in *English*; and he wished some special pains were taken for an Uniform Translation, which should be done by the best Learned in both Universities; then reviewed by the Bishops, presented to the Privy Council, lastly ratified by Royal Authority to be read in the Church, and none other.

Dr. *Rainolds* moved also, that unlawful and Seditious Books be suppressed. The Lord *Cecil*, that these had done much mischief, but especially one, called *Speculum Tragicum*. His Majesty said, that was a dangerous book indeed.

Concerning the planting of Learned Ministers in every Parish, His Majesty said he had consulted with his Bishops about it; whom he found willing and ready herein.

The Bishop of *London* moved, that there might be a praying Ministry among us, saying, that men now thought it is the onely duty of

M m   Ministers

Ministers to spend their time in the Pulpit. His Majesty well liked his motion. His second motion was, that until Learned men may be planted in every Congregation, Godly Homilies may be read therein. The King liked this motion, especially where the living is not sufficient to maintain a Learned Preacher. Also where were multitudes of Sermons, he would have Homilies read divers times. The Plaintiffs confessed, A Preaching Ministry is best; but where it may not be had, Godly Prayers and exhortations do much good. The Bishop's last motion was, that Pulpits may not be made pasquils, wherein every discontented person may traduce his Superiors. His Majesty approved thereof.

Then Dr. *Rainolds* came to *Subscription*, as a great impeachment to a Learned Ministry, and therefore entreated it might not be exacted as heretofore, for which many good men are kept out, though otherwise willing to subscribe to the Statutes of the Realm, Articles of Religion, and the King's Supremacy. He objected against the enjoyning of the Apocrypha Books to be read in the Church, some Chapters therein containing manifest errours repugnant to Scripture.

His Majesty said, he would not have all Canonical books read in the Church; nor any Chapter out of the Apocrypha, wherein any errour is contained.

The next scruple against Subscription was, because it was twice set down in the Common-prayer-book, *Jesus said to his Disciples*, when by the Text in the Original it is plain, that he spake to the Pharisees. His Majesty answered, let the word [*Disciples*] be omitted, and the words [*Jesus said*] be Printed in a different Character.

Mr. *Knewstubs* took exceptions at the Cross in baptism, and said, it is questionable whether the Church hath power to institute an outward significant sign. The Bishop of *London* answered, The Cross in Baptism is not used otherwise than a Ceremony.

His Majesty desired to be acquainted about the Antiquity of the use of Cross. Dr. *Rainolds* said, it hath been used ever since the Apostles time, but the question is, how Ancient the use thereof hath been in Baptism. The Bishop of *Winchester* said, in *Constantine*'s time it was used in Baptism. His Majesty replied, if so, I see no reason but we may continue it.

Mr. *Knewstubs* said, put case the Church may add significant signs, it may not add them where Christ hath already ordained them, which is as Derogatory to Christ's Institution, as if one should add to the great Seal of *England*. His Majesty answered, the case is not alike, seeing the Sacrament is fully finished, before the use of the Cross.

Mr. *Knewstubs* demanded then, how far the Ordinance of the Church bindeth without impeaching Christian Liberty? The King answered, I will have one Doctrine, one Discipline, one Religion in substance, and in
Cere-

Ceremony. Never speak more to that point, how far ye are bound to obey.

Doctor *Rainolds* wished, that the Cross (being Superstitiously abused in Popery) were abandoned, as the Brazen-serpent was stamped to powder by *Hezekiah*, because abused to Idolatry.

His Majesty answered, Inasmuch as the Cross was abused to Superstition in time of Propery, it doth plainly imply, that it was well used before. He said, he detested their courses, who peremptorily disallow of all things which have been abused in Popery, and know not how to answer the Objections of the Papists, when they charge us with Novelties, but by telling them, we retain the Primitive use of things; and onely forsake their Novel corruptions. Secondly, no resemblance between the Brazen-Serpent (a material visible thing) and the sign of the Cross made in the Air.

Thirdly, Papists did never ascribe any spiritual grace to the Cross in Baptism. Lastly, material Crosses to which people fell down in time of Popery (as the Idolatrous Jews to the Brazen-serpent) are already demolished, as you desire.

Mr. *Knewstub's* proceeded, excepting at the wearing of the Surplice, a kind of garment (said he) used by the Priests of *Isis*. His Majesty answered, he did not think till of late, it had been borrowed from the Heathen, because commonly called *a Rag of Popery*. And seeing we border not upon Heathens, &c. I see no reason (said he) but for comeliness sake it may be continued.

Dr. *Rainolds* said, I take exception at these words in Marriage, *With my body I thee worship*. His Majesty answered, I find it an usual English Term, A Gentleman of Worship: and it agreeth with the Scriptures, *Giving honour to the wife* The Dean of *Sarum* said, some take exception at the Ring in Marriage. Dr. *Rainolds* said, he approved it well enough. Then said he, some take exceptions at *the Churching of women* by the name of *Purification*. His Majesty said, I allow it very well.

Unto Doctor *Rainolds* his last exception against committing Ecclesiastical censures to Lay-chancellors, His Majesty answered, that he had conferred with the Bishops about that point, and such order should be taken therein as was Convenient.

Doctor *Rainolds* desired; That according to certain Provincial Constitutions the Clergy may have meetings every three weeks. 1. In Rural Deaneries, therein to have prophecying, as Archbishop *Grindal*, and other Bishops, desired of her late Majesty. 2. That such things as could not be resolved on there, might be referred to the Archdeacons Visitations. 3. And so to the Episcopal Synod, to determine such points before not decided.

His Majesty answered. If you aim at a Scottish Presbytery, it agreeth as well with Monarchy, as God and the Devil. Then *Jack* and *Tom*, &c. shall meet, and censure me and my Council.

Then the King asked the Doctor, whether they had any thing else to say?

He answered, No more, if it please your Majesty.

If this be all your party have to say, said the King, I will make them conform, or else I will harry them out of the Land, or do worse.

Thus ended the second dayes Conference.

The third began on the Wednesday following, many Knights, Civilians, and Doctors of the Law, being admitted thereunto, because the *High-commission* was the principal matter in debate.

His Majesty thus began I understand, that the parties named in the High-commission are too many, and too mean, and the matters they deal with, base, such as Ordinaries might censure in their Courts at home.

Archbishop of *Canterbury*.] Were not their number many, I should oftentimes sit alone. I have often complained of the meanness of matters handled therein, but cannot remedy it: for though the offence be small, that the Ordinary may, yet the Offender oft-times is so great, that the Ordinary is forced to crave help at the High-commission to punish him.

A nameless Lord said, The proceedings in that Court are like the Spanish Inquisition, wherein men are urged to subscribe more than Law requireth; and by the Oath *Ex officio*, forced to accuse themselves, being examined upon many Articles on a sudden, and for the most part against themselves.

The Lord Chancellor said, There is necessity, and use of the Oath *Ex officio*, in divers Courts and Causes.

His Majesty said, That it is requisite that fame and scandals be looked unto in Courts Ecclesiastical, and yet great moderation is to be used therein. And here he soundly described the Oath *Ex officio* for the ground thereof, the wisdom of the Law therein, the manner of proceeding thereby, and profitable effect from the same.

After much discourse between the King, the Bishops, and the Lords, about the quality of the Persons, and Causes, in the High Commission, rectifying Excommunications in matters of less moment, punishing Recusants, providing Divines for *Ireland*, *Wales*, and the Northern borders, the four Preachers were called in, and such alterations in the Liturgy were read unto them, which the Bishops, by the King's advice, had made, unto which, by their silence, they seemed to consent.

Then the King said to Doctor *Rainolds*, and his Associates, *I expect obedience and humility from you (the marks of honest and good men) and that you would perswade others abroad by your example.*

Doctor

the Church of Great Britain.

Doctor *Rainolds* answered, *We here do promise to perform all duties to Bishops, as Reverend Fathers, and to joyn with them, against the common Adversary, for the peace of the Church.*

Thus ended the three dayes Conference. Doctor *Sparks* soon after set forth a Treatise of Unity and Uniformity.

This Conference produced some alterations in the Liturgy; Womens baptising formerly frequent, hereafter forbidden; in the Rubrick of Absolution, Remission of sins inserted, Confirmation termed also an Examination of Children, and some words altered in the Dominical Gospels, with a resolution for a new translation of the Bible. Henceforward many, that wavered before, for the future quietly digested the Ceremonies of the Church.

About this time a Petition, called the Millenary Petition for Reformation, was solemnly presented to his Majesty, in the name of the Ministers of the Church of *England*, desiring Reformation of certain Ceremonies and abuses of the Church. Subscribed, *Your Majesties most humble Subjects, the Ministers of the Gospel, that desire not a disorderly Innovation, but a due and godly Reformation.* The Episcopal party gave this Petition a lash, some with their Pens, more with their Tongues. The Universities were justly netled thereat. *Cambridge* passed a Grace in their Congregation, That *whosoever, in their University, should by word, or writing, oppose the received Doctrine, and Discipline, of England, or any part thereof, should be suspended from their former, and excluded from all future Degrees.* *Oxford* followed, making a sharp and strong confutation of the Petition. After his Majesty had discountenanced it, some of the opposite party maintained, That now the property thereof was altered, from a Petition to a Libel.

Soon after died Archbishop *Whitgift* of the Palsey, and was buried at *Croidon*, the Earl of *Worcester*, and Lord *Zouch*, his Pupils attending his Herse; and Bishop *Babington* (his Pupil also) made his Funeral Sermon. *Richard Bancroft*, Bishop of *London*, brought up in *Jesus-colledge*, succeeded him in the Archbishoprick.

Now a Parliament was assembled, in which it was enacted, *That neither the King himself, nor his Successors, should be capable of any Church-land, to be conveyed unto them, otherwise than for three lives, or twenty one years.* Thus the King was pleased to bind himself for the liberty of the Church: and hereby he eased himself of many troublesome Suitors.

In the Convocation many Canons were made. A Book of Canons was compiled, not only being the sum of the late Queens Articles, Orders of her Commissioners, Canons of 1571. and 1597. which were in use before, but also many more were added. the whole number amounting unto 141 An explanation was made in one of the Canons of the use of the Cross in Baptism. Bishop *Rudd*, of St. *Davids*, opposed the Oath of Simony.

Anno

Anno 1664. the Family of Love presented a tedious Petition to King *James*, wherein, by fawning expressions, they seek to insinuate themselves into his Majesties good opinion. We find not what effect this Petition produced.

This year died two Romanists beyond Sea much lamented, one *Richard Hall*, bred in *Chrift's-colledge* in *Cambridge*, whence he ran over to *Rome*, and after died Canon and Official at *St. Omers* Cathedral. The other *Humfrey Ely*, born in *Hereford-shire*, Fellow of St. *John's-colledge* in *Oxford*; whence going beyond Sea; at *Rome* he commenced Doctor of Law, and afterwards died Professor thereof, in the University of *Ponta' Moufan* in the Dutchy of *Lorrain*.

Now the Romish Cotholicks despairing of getting any free and publick exercise of their Religion, some of them entred into a devilish Conspiracy to blow up the Parliament House with Gunpowder.

In this Plot were engaged.

Robert Catesby.
Thomas Piercy.
Sir *Everard Digby*.
Francis *Tresham*.
Thomas Winter.
John Wright.
Christopher Wright.

Ambrose Rookwood.
Robert Keys.
Robert Winter.
John Grant.
Thomas Bates, *Catesbies* man.
Guido Faux.

The principal Contriver of this Plot was *Robert Catesby*, a Gentleman of good account in *Northampton-shire*, who drew in many other Papists to assist him. *Gerard* tyeth them together with an Oath of secrecy. *Garnet* and *Tismond* encourage the design. But here an important scruple was injected, how to part their Friends from their Foes in the Parliament. Here *Garnet*, instead of untying, cut this knot asunder. That in such a case as this it was lawful to kill Friend and Foe together.

Now though these Plotters intended at last, with honour, to own the Action, when success had secured all things; yet they purposed, when the blow was first given, to father the fact upon those that were called Puritans. But for the discovery of this Plot, God's Providence so ordered it, that a Letter was framed, and sent to the Lord *Mounteagle*, brought him by one of his Footmen, which he received from an unknown man in the street, in manner following

My Lord, out of the love I bear to some of your Friends, I have a care of your preservation. Therefore, I would advise you, as you tender your life, to forbear your attendance at this Parliament: for God, and man, have

have concurred to punish the wickedness of this time. And think not slightly of this advertisement, but retire your self into your Countrey, where you may expect the event in safety: for, though there be no appearance of any stir, yet, I say, they shall receive a terrible blow this Parliament, and yet they shall not see who hurts them, This counsel is not to be contemned, because it may do you good, and can do you no harm, for the danger is past as soon as you have burnt the Letter. And, I hope, God will give you the grace to make use of it, to whose holy protection I commend you.

 The Lord *Mounteagle* communicates the Letter to the Earl of *Sarisbury*, He to the King, who on the second perusal expounded the mystical blow meant therein, must be by Gunpowder, and gives order for searching the Rooms under the Parliament House. The first search, about evening, discovered nothing but *Percie*'s Cellar full of Wood, and *Johnson* his man (under that name was *Faux* disguised) attending therein. At midnight a more strict and secret search was made by Sir *Thomas Knevet*, Gentleman of his Majesty's Privy Chamber, and others, in the Vault under the Parliament House. There was quickly discovered, a pile of fewel, faced over with Billets, lined under with thirty six Barrels of Powder, besides Iron bars to make the force of the fire more effectual. *Guido Faux* was apprehended in the outward room, with a dark Lanthorn in his hand, and three Matches ready to give fire to the Train. Mean-time *Catesby*, *Percy*, *Rookwood*, both the *Wrights*, and *Thomas Winter*, were hovering about *London*, to attend the issue of the matter. They, and their Servants, post down into the Countrey, through *Warwick-shire*, *Worcester-shire*, into *Stafford-shire*; Sir *Richard Verney*, High Sheriff of *Warwick-shire*, chased them from thence, and Sir *Robert Walsh*, Sheriff of *Worcester-shire*, overtook them at *Holbeck* in *Stafford-shire*, the House of Mr. *Stephen Littleton*, where, upon their resistance, the two *Wrights* were killed, *Rookwood*, and *Thomas Winter*, grievously wounded. *Percy*, and *Catesby*, setting back to back, fought desperately against all that assaulted them; after many Swords drawn upon them, they were both slain with one shot of a Musquet. *Francis Tresham* was taken about the Court, and sent to the Tower, where he confessed all, and within a few dayes after died of the Strangury.

 The rest were solemnly arraigned, convicted, condemned at *London*. First Sir *Everard Digby*, *Robert Winter*, *Grant*, and *Bates*, were hanged, drawn, and quartered at the West-end of St. *Paul's*. Three of them (but especially Sir *Everard Digby*) died very penitently. *Grant* expressed most obstinacy at his death.

 The next day *Thomas Winter*, *Ambrose Rookwood*, *Keys*, and *Faux*, were executed, as the former, in the Parliament-yard in *Westminster*. *Keys* followed *Grant* in his obstinacy: and *Faux* shewed more penitency than all the rest,

Fuller's Church Hist.

Jan. 30.

On *March* twenty eight following, *Henry Garnet*, Provincial of the English Jesuites, was arraigned in *Guild-hall*, for concealing the foresaid Treason, where he had judgment to be hanged, drawn, and quartered, and accordingly, on *May* the third, was drawn from the Tower to the West-end of *Paul's-church*, and there executed. At his death he confessed his fault, asked forgiveness, and exhorted all Catholicks never to plot any Treason against King or State, as a course which God would never prosper.

The memory of this deliverance was perpetuated by Act of Parliament

Anno 1605. died that Religious Prelat, *Matthew Hutton*, Archbishop of *York*; one of the last times he preached in his Cathedral was on this occasion: The Papists in *York-shire* were commanded, by the Queens Authority, to be present at three Sermons, and at the two first were so uncivil, that some of them were forced to be gagged before they would be quiet. The Archbishop preached the last Sermon most gravely and solidly, taking for his Text, *John* 8. 47. *He that is of God, heareth God's Word: ye therefore hear them not, because ye are not of God*. Not long after died *John young*, Bishop of *Rochester*, and *Anthony Watson*, Bishop of *Chichester*.

The Parliament enacted many things for the discovering and repressing of Popish Recusants. Whereof none was more effectual, than that Oath of Allegiance, which every Catholick was commanded to take. The Pope hereupon dispatched two *Breves* into *England*, prohibiting all Catholicks to take this Oath, so destructive to their own souls, and the See of *Rome*, exhorting them to suffer persecution, and manfully to endure Martyrdom. Notwithstanding all which, this Oath being tendred to, was generally taken by Catholicks, without any scruple. And particularly, *George Blackwell*, Archpriest of the English, being apprehended, and cast into prison, by taking this Oath wrought his own enlargement. This Oath was ministred immediately after the putting forth of a Proclamation, which commanded all Seminaries and Jesuits to depart the Land.

Now the Alarm being given, whether this Oath was lawful or no, both parties, of Protestants and Papists, wrote against each other. King *James* wrote an Apology for the Oath of Allegiance, together with a Premonition to all most mighty Monarchs, Kings, free Princes, and States of Christendom, effectually confuting the Pope's *Breves*. Bishop *Andrews* wrote against *Bellarmine*, Bishop *Barlow* against *Parsons*, Doctor *Morton*, Doctor *Robert Abbot*, Doctor *Buckeridge*, Doctor *Collins*, Doctor *Burrel*, Mr. *Tomson*, Doctor *Peter Du-moulin*, maintain the legality of the Oath against *Suarez*, *Eudæmon*, *Becanus*, *Coffetus*, *Peleterius*, and others.

the Church of GREAT BRITAIN.

Anno 1607. That Religious defign of King *James*, for a new Tranflation of the Bible, was now effectually profecuted; and the Tranflators being forty and feven in number, were digefted into fix companies, and feveral Books were affigned them, according unto the feveral places wherein they were to meet, confer, and confult together; fo that nothing fhould pafs without a general confent.

Weftminfter X.

The *Pentateuch*; the Story from *Joshua* to the firft Book of the Chronicles exclufively.

Doctor *Andrews*, then Dean of *Weftminfter*, after Bifhop of *Winchefter*.
Doctor *Overal*, then Dean of St. *Pauls*, after Bifhop of *Norwich*.
Doctor *Saravia*.
Doctor *Laifield*, Rector of St. *Clement Danes*: Being skilled in Architecture, his judgment was relyed on for the fabrick of the Tabernacle and Temple.
Doctor *Leigh*, Archdeacon of *Middlefex*, Parfon of *Alhallows-Barking*.
Mr. *Burley*.
Mr. *King*.
Mr. *Tompfon*.
Mr. *Bedwel*, Vicar of *Tottenham*, nigh *London*.

Oxford VII.

The four great Prophets, with the Lamentations, and the twelve leffer Prophets.

Doctor *Harding*, Prefident of *Magdalen* Colledge.
Doctor *Rainolds*, Prefident of *Corpus Chrifti* Colledge.
Doctor *Holland*, Rector of *Exeter* Colledge, and *Regius Profeffor*.
Doctor *Kilby*, Rector of *Lincoln* Colledge, and King's Profeffor.
Mr. *Smith*, after D. D. and Bifhop of *Glocefter*.
Mr. *Brett*, of *Quainton* in *Buckingham-fhire*.
Mr. *Fairclough*.

Cambridge VIII.

From the first of the *Chronicles*, with the rest of the Story, and the Hagiographa, viz. *Job, Psalms, Proverbs, Canticles, Ecclesiastes*.

Mr. *Edward Lively*.
Mr *Richardson*, after D. D. Master first of *Peter-house*, then of *Trinity* Colledge.
Mr. *Chaderton*, after D.D. and Master of *Emmanuel* Colledge.
Mr. *Dillingham* of *Christ's* Colledge.
Mr. *Andrews*, after D. D. Brother to the Bishop of *Winchester*, and Master of *Jesus* Colledge.
Mr. *Harison*, Vice-master of *Trinity* Colledge.
Mr. *Spalding*, Fellow of St. *John's* in *Cambridge*, and Hebrew Professor therein.
Mr. *Bing*, Fellow of *Peter-house* in *Cambridge*, and Hebrew Professor therein.

Cambridge VII.

The Prayer of *Manasseh*, and the rest of the Apocrypha.

Doctor *Duport*, Master of *Jesus* Colledge.
Doctor *Branthwait*, after Master of *Gonvil* and *Caius* Colledge.
Doctor *Radclyffe*, a Senior Fellow of *Trinity* Colledge.
Mr. *Ward*, after D. D. Master of *Sidney* Colledge, and *Margaret* Professor.
Mr. *Downes*, Greek Professor.
Mr. *Boys*, Fellow of St. *John's* Colledge, Parson of *Boxworth* in *Cambridge-shire*.
Mr. *Ward*, Regal; after D. D. Rector of *Bishop's Waltham* in *Hampshire*.

Oxford VIII.

The four Gospels, Acts of the Apostles, Apocalypse.

Doctor *Ravis*, Dean of *Christ-church*, after Bishop of *London*.
Doctor *George Abbot*, Master of *University* Colledge, afterwards Archbishop of *Canterbury*.
Doctor *Eedes*.
Mr. *Towpson*.
Mr. *Savile*.

Doctor

Doctor *Peryn*.
Doctor *Ravens*.
Mr. *Harmer*.

Westminster VII.

The Epistles of St. *Paul*, the Canonical Epistles.

Doctor *Barlow*, of *Trinity-hall* in *Cambridge*, after Bishop of *Lincoln*.
Doctor *Hutchinson*.
Doctor *Spencer*.
Mr. *Fenton*.
Mr. *Rabbet*.
Mr. *Saunderson*.
Mr. *Dakins*.

The King's Instructions to the Translators were these following.

I. The ordinary Bible read in the Church, to be followed, and as little altered, as the Original will permit.
II. The names of the Prophets, and the holy Writers, with the other names in the Text, to be retained as near as may be, accordingly as they are vulgarly used.
III. The old Ecclesiastical words to be kept, &c.
IV. When any word hath divers significations, that to be kept which hath been most commonly used by the most eminent Fathers, being agreeable to the propriety of the place, and the Analogy of Faith.
V. The division of the Chapters to be altered, either not at all, or as little as may be, &c.
VI. No Marginal notes at all to be affixed, but only for the explanation of the Hebrew, or Greek words, which cannot without some circumlocution, so briefly and fitly be expressed in the Text.
VII. Such Quotations of places to be marginally set down, as shall serve for the fit reference of one Scripture to another.
VIII. Every particular man, of each company, to take the same Chapter, or Chapters; and having translated or amended them severally by himself, where he thinks good, all to meet together, confer what they have done, and agree for their part what shall stand.
IX. As any one company hath thus dispatched any one Book, they shall send it to the rest, to be considered of seriously and judiciously.
X. If any company, upon the review of the Book so sent, shall doubt, or differ upon any places, to send them word thereof, note the places, and therewithall send their Reasons: to which, if they consent not, the

Fuller, Church History. *Anno* 1607.

difference to be compounded at the General meeting; which is to be of the chief persons of each company at the end of the work.

X ¹. When any place of special obscurity is doubted of, Letters to be directed by Authority, to send to any learned in the Land for his judgment in such a place.

XII. Letters to be sent from every Bishop to the rest of his Clergy, &c. to move and charge as many as, being skilful in the Tongues, have taken pains in that kind, to send his particular Observations to the company, either at *Westminster*, *Cambridge*, or *Oxford*.

XIII. The Directors in each Company to be the Deans of *Westminster*, and *Chester*, for that place; and the King's Professors in the Hebrew and the Greek in each University.

XIV. These Translations to be used, when they agree better with the Text, than the Bishops Bible ordinarily read in the Church : *Viz.* { *Tindals. Mathews. Coverdales. Whitchurch. Geneva.*

Three or four of the most grave Divines in either of the Universities, not employed in translating; to be assigned by the Vice-Chancellor; upon Conference with the rest of the Heads, to be Overseers of the Translations, as well Hebrew as Greek.

The untimely death of Mr. *Edward Lively* (much weight of the Work lying on his Skill in the Oriental Tongues) happening about this time, much retarded their proceedings.

On *May* 21. 1607. died Doctor *John Rainolds*, King's Professor in *Oxford*, and one of those Translators of the Bible. So great was his Memory, that he could readily turn to all material passages in every Leaf, Page, Volume, Paragraph, in all his voluminous Books. A man of a solid Judgment, and great Humility. His disaffection to the established Discipline was not so great, as some Bishops did suspect, or as more Non-conformists did believe. He desired the abolishing of some Ceremonies for the ease of others Consciences, to which, in his own practise, he did willingly submit, kneeling at the Sacrament, and constantly wearing Hood and Surplice. On his death-bed he desired *Absolution*, according to the form of the Church of *England*, and received it from Doctor *Holland*. Doctor *Featly* made his Funeral Oration in the Colledge, Sir *Isaac Wake* in the University.

In this year died *Richard Vaughan*, D. D. successively Bishop of *Bangor*, *Chester*, and *London* : Mr. *Thomas Brightman* died the same year. He was born in the Town of *Nottingham*, bred in *Queens* Colledge in *Cambridge*, where a constant opposition, in point of Judgment, about Ceremonies, was maintained betwixt him and Doctor *Meryton*, afterwards Dean of *York*. He died suddenly (according to his desire) and

the Church of Great Britain.

and was buried at *Haunes* in *Bedford-shire*, whereof he had been Minister fifteen years, Doctor *Bulkley* preaching his Funeral Sermon.

King *James* founded a Colledge at *Chelsey*, and bestowed on the same, by his Letters Patents, the Reversion of good Land in *Chelsey*, then in possession of *Charles* Earl of *Nottingham*. Doctor *Matthew Sutcliffe*, Dean of *Exeter*, bestowed on this Colledge,

The Farms of { *Kingston*, *Hazzard*, *Appleton*, *Kramerland*, } In the Parish of { 1. *Staverton*. 2. *Harberton*. 3. *Churchton*. 4. *Stoke-rivers*. } All in the County of *Devon*, and put together worth 300 *l.* per *Annum*.

Besides these, by his Will he bequeathed unto Doctor *John Prideaux*, and Doctor *Clifford* (as Feoffees in trust to settle the same on the Colledge) the benefit of the extent on a Statute of four thousand pounds, acknowledged by Sir *Lewis Steukly*, &c.

Here we will insert the number and names of the Provost and first Fellows.

Matthew Sutcliff, Dean of *Exeter*, Provost.
1. *John Overal*, Dean of St. *Paul's*.
2. *Thomas Morton*, Dean of *Winchester*.
3. *Richard Field*, Dean of *Glocester*.
4. *Robert Abbot*.
5. *John Spencer*.
6. *Miles Smith*.
7. *William Cevit*.
8. *John Hewson*.
9. *John Layfield*, } Doctors of Divinity.
10. *Benjamin Carrier*,
11. *Martin Fotherby*,
12. *John Boys*,
13. *Richard Bret*.
14. *Peter Lilie*.
15. *Francis Burley*.
16. *William Hellier*, Archdeacon of *Barstable*.
17. *John White*, Fellow of *Manchester* Colledge.
William Camden, *Clarenceaux*, } Historians.
John Haywood, Doctor of Law,

To promote this Work, his Majesty sent his Letters to the Archbishop of *Canterbury*, to stir up all the Clergy in his Province to contribute to so pious a Work. The Archbishop sent his additional Letter to his Clergy to the same intent: yet for all these endeavours, and Collections in all the Parishes of *England*, slow and small were the sums of money brought in to this Work. Many things obstructed those hopeful proceedings, especially the untimely death of Prince *Henry*, the chief Author of this design, as some conceived.

At this present it hath but little of the case, and nothing of the Jewel, for which it was intended. Almost rotten before ripe, and ruinous before it was finished.

Anno 1609. died *William Overton*, Bishop of *Coventry* and *Litchfield*, *Martin Heton*, Bishop of *Ely*, and *Thomas Ravis*, successively Bishop of *Glocester*, and *London*.

Anno 1610. *Gervas Babington*, Bishop of *Worcester*, ended his pious life. The same year expired Bishop *Bancroft*, Archbishop of *Canterbury*. He bequeathed his Library, the confluence of his own Collections, with his Predecessors, *Whitgift*, *Grindal*, *Parker*, to *Chelsey* Colledge: and if that took not effect, to the publick Library in *Cambridge*, where at this day they remain. *George Abbot* succeeded him in the See of *Canterbury*.

Now after long expectation, and great desire, came forth the new Translation of the Bible, most beautifully printed, by a select and competent number of Divines, appointed for that purpose; whose Industry, Skilfulness, Piety, and Discretion, hath therein bound the Church unto them in a debt of thankfulness, as Mr. *Fuller* well noteth.

The Romanists take exceptions at the several fences of words noted in the Margin. And some Brethren complained of this Translation, for lack of the *Geneva* Annotations. But those Notes could no way be fitted to this new Edition of the Bible. And as some perchance over-valued the *Geneva* Notes, out of that special love they bear to the Authors, and place whence it proceeded; so on the other side, some without cause did slight, or rather uncharitably did slander the same: for about this time (*Anno* 1611) a Doctor in *Oxford* publickly, in his Sermon at St. *Maries*, accused them as guilty of misinterpretation touching the Divinity of Christ, and his Messias-ship, as if symbolizing with *Arrians* and *Jews* against them both; for which he was afterwards suspended by Doctor *Robert Abbot*, *Propter conciones publicas minus orthodoxas, & offensionis plenas*.

Fuller. Church History. *Anno* 1611.

This year King *James* was careful for the seasonable suppression of the dangerous Doctrines of *Conradus Vorstius*. This Doctor had lived about fifteen years a Minister at *Steinford*, within the Territories of the Counts of *TESLENBURG*, *BENTHAM*, &c. the Counts whereof were the first in casting off the Romish yoke, and ever since continuing Protestants. This *Vorstius* had written to, and received Letters from certain *Samosatenian* Hereticks in *Poland*, and became infected therewith. Hereupon he set forth two Books; the one entitled, *TRACTATUS THEO-*

the Church of Great Britain.

THEOLOGICUS. DE DEO, dedicated to the Land-grave of *HESSEN*: the other *EXEGESIS APOLOGETICA*, dedicated to the States, both of them stuffed with many dangerous Positions concerning the Deity.

This Wretch debased the Purity of God, assigning him a material body, confining his Immensity, as not being every where, shaking his Immutability, as if his Will were subject to change; darkening his Omnisciency, as uncertain in future contingents, with many more monstrous Opinions. Notwithstanding all this, the said *Vorstius* was chosen by the Curators of the University of *Leyden*, to be their publick Divinity-Professor, in the place of *Arminius* lately deceased; and to that end the States General, by their Letters sent, and sued to the Count of *TECKLENBOURGH* and obtained of him, that *Vorstius* should come from *Steinford*, and become publick Professor in *Leyden*.

King *James* being this Autumn in his hunting Progress, did light upon, and perused the aforesaid Books of *Vorstius*; he observed the dangerous Positions therein, determining speedily to oppose them. Hereupon he presently dispatched a Letter to Sir *Ralph Winwood*, his Ambassador, Resident with the States, requiring him to let them understand, how highly he should be displeased, if such a Monster as *Vorstius*, should be advanced in their Church. This was seconded with a large Letter of his Majesties to the States, dated *October* the sixth, to the same effect. But the States entertain not the motion of King *James* against *Vorstius*, according to expectation. They said, *That if* Vorstius *had formerly been faulty in offensive expressions, he had since cleared himself in a new Declaration*. For lately he set forth a Book, entitled, *A Christian and modest Answer*, but he gave no satisfaction in his new Declaration.

King *James* therefore gave Instructions to his Ambassador, to make publick protestation against their proceedings, which Sir *Ralph Winwood* most solemnly performed. And after his Majesties Request, Letter, and Protestation, had missed their desired effect, he wrote in French a Declaration against *Vorstius*, which since, by his leave, hath been translated into English, among his other Works. *Vorstius* his Books were also, by the King's Command, publickly burnt at St. *Paul's-cross* in *London*, and in both Universities.

The same year, in *March*, *Bartholomew Legate*, an *Arrian*, was burnt in *Smithfield*, for denying the Deity of the Son of God, and holding that there are no Persons in the Godhead, with many other damnable Tenets.

In the next month *Edward Wightman*, of *Burton* upon *Trent*, was burnt at *Litchfield*, for holding ten several Heresies, *viz.* those of Ebion, Cerinthus, Valentinian, Arrius, Macedonius, Simon Magus, Manes, Manicheus, Photinus, and of the Anabaptists. Only a Spanish *Arrian*, who was condemned to die, was notwithstanding suffered

suffered to linger out his Life in *Newgate*, where he ended the same.

This year died *Richard Sutton*, the Founder of *Charter-house* Hospital, Esquire. The Manors which in several Counties he setled, for the maintenance of this Hospital, were these.

1. *Balsham* Mannor in *Cambridge-shire*.
2. *Blastingthorp* Mannor in *Lincoln-shire*.
3. *Black-grove* Mannor in *Wilt-shire*.
4. *Broad-Hinton* Land in *Wilt-shire*.
5. *Castle-Camps* Mannor in *Cambridge-shire*.
6. *Chilton* Mannor in *Wilt-shire*.
7. *Dunby* Mannor in *Lincoln-shire*.
8. *Elcomb* Mannor and Park in *Wilt-shire*.
9. *Hackney* Land in *Middlesex*.
10. *Hallingbury-Bouchers* Mannor in *Essex*.
11. *Missunden* Mannor in *Wilt-shire*.
12. *Much-Stanbridge* Mannor in *Essex*.
13. *Norton* Mannor in *Essex*.
14. *Salthrop* Mannor in *Wilt-shire*.
15. *South-minster* Mannor in *Essex*.
16. *Tottenham* Land in *Middlesex*.
17. *Ufford* Mannor in *Wilt-shire*.
18. *Watelscot* Mannor in *Wilt-shire*.
19. *Westcot* Mannor in *Wilt-shire*.
20. *Wroughton* Mannor in *Wilt-shire*.

Anno 1612. On *November* the sixth, died Prince *Henry* of a burning Fever. He was generally lamented of the whole Land, both Universities publishing their Verses in print.

Prince *Henry*'s Funerals are followed with the Prince *Palatine*'s Nuptials, solemnized with great state.

Anno 1613. *Nicholas* Wadham Esquire, of *Merrifield* in the County of *Sommerset*, bequeathed, by his Will, four hundred pounds *per annum*, and six thousand pounds in Money, to the building of a College in *Oxford*, leaving the care of the Whole to *Dorothy* his Wife: This year the same was finished, built in a place where formerly stood a Monastery of the *Augustine Friars*. This year *Anthony Rudd*, Bishop of St. *Davids* ended his Life.

Some three years since (on the death of King *Henry* the Fourth) *Isaac Causabon*, that learned Critick, was fetcht out of *France* by King *James*, and preferred Prebendary of *Canterbury*. Presently he wrote, First to *Fronto Duræus*, his learned Friend; then to Cardinal *Perron*, in the just vindication of our English Church.

After

the Church of Great Britain.

After these he began his Exercitations on *Baronius* his Ecclesiastical Annals, which more truly may be termed, The Annals of the Church of *Rome*. He died, and was buried in the South-Isle of *Westminster-Abby*. His Monument was erected at the cost of *Thomas Morton*, Bishop of *Durham*.

Anno 1614. Mr. *John Selden* set forth his Book of Tithes, wherein he Historically proveth, that they were payable *jure humano*, and not otherwise. Many wrote in answer to his Book.

Anno 1616. Mr. *Andrew Melvin* was freed from his imprisonment in the Tower, whither he had been committed for writing some Satyrical Verses against the Ornaments on the Altar in the King's Chappel. He afterwards became a Professor at *Sedan*, in the Duke of *Bovillon*'s Country. Here he traduced the Church of *England*, against which he wrote a Scroll of Saphicks, entitled, *TAMI-CHAMI-CATEGERIA*. When first brought into the Tower, he first found Sir *William Seymour* (afterwards Marquess of *Hertford*, and Duke of *Sommerset*,) there imprisoned for marrying the Lady *Arabella*, so nearly allyed to the Crown, without the King's consent: To whom *Melvin* sent this Distick.

> *Causa mihi tecum communis carceris, Ara*
> *Regia, Bella tibi, Regia sacra mihi.*

Anno 1615. died *Thomas Bilson*, Bishop of *Winchester*, a profound Scholar, well read in the Fathers.

Anno 1616. *Marcus Antonius de Dominis*, Archbishop of *Spalato*, came over into *England*.

The same year King *James* went into *Scotland*, with a Princely Train, to visit his native Country.

This year died Doctor *William James*, Bishop of *Durham*.

Two other prime Prelats also followed him, *viz.* Doctor *Henry Robinson*, Bishop of *Carlisle*, and *Robert Bennet*, Bishop of *Hereford*, termed (saith Mr. *Fuller*) *Eruditus Benedictus*.

Doctor *Mocket*, Warden of *All-Souls* in *Oxford*, set forth a Book in pure Latin, containing,

> The Apology of the Church of England.
> The greater and lesser Catechism.
> The nine and thirty Articles.
> The Common-prayer.
> The Ordination of Bishops, Priests and Deacons.
> The Polity, or Government of the Church of England.

He epitomized the Homilies into certain Propositions faithfully extracted. The Book fared the worse for the Author; the Author had for his

Patron the Archbishop, against whom many Bishops began then to combine. Dr. *Mocket's* Book was censured to be burnt, which was done accordingly: soon after he ended his life.

Anno 1617. died *Robert Abbot*, Bishop of *Salisbury*: he died of the Stone, and was much lamented by the University of *Oxford*.

About this time *William Perry*, a Boy dwelling at *Bilson* in *Stafford-shire*, not full fifteen years of Age, was practised on by some Jesuites (repairing to the House of Mr. *Gifford*, in that County) to dissemble himself possessed. But the Boy having gotten a habit of counterfeiting, leading a lazy life thereby, to his own ease and Parents profit, would not be undeviled by all their Exorcismes, so that the Priests raised up a Spirit which they could not allay. At last by the Industry of Dr. *Morton*, then Bishop of *Coventry* and *Litchfield*, the jugling was laid open to the World by the Boys own confession and repentance.

All this King's Reign was scattered over with Cheaters in this kind. Some Papists, some Sectaries, some neither.

Papists.

Sarah Williams.
Grace Sourbuts of *Salmisbury* in *Lancashire*.
Mary and *Amy* two Maids of *Westminster*.
Edward Hance, a Popish Priest.

No Papists.

Richard Heydock, Fellow of *New-Colledge* in *Oxford*, Preached in his dreams Latin Sermons against the Hierarchy. He recanted, and lived long after in *Sarum*, practising Physick, being also a good Poet, Limner, and Engraver.

Anne Gunter, a Maid of *Windsor*, had strange extatick phrensies, and gave out she was possessed of a Devil.

A Maid at *Standon* in *Hertford-shire*, so personated a Demoniack, that she deceived many.

The King having the last year in his progress, into *Scotland*, through *Lancashire*, observed, that by the strictness of some Magistrates and Ministers, in several places, people were hindered from their recreations on the Sunday, the Papists being thereby perswaded, that no recreation was tolerable in our Religion; whereupon the Court being at *Greenwich*, he set forth a Declaration for liberty on the Lord's day: When this Declaration came abroad, many were offended at it. But no Minister was enjoyned to read the Book in his Parish, wherewith they had so affrighted themselves.

Yet

the Church of Great Britain.

Yet many conceived, that the Declaration came forth seasonably, to suppress the endeavour of such, who now began to broach the dregs of Judaism, whereof *John Thrask* was a principal, who asserted, *That the Lord's day was to be observed with the same strictness by Christians, as it was by Jews, and that all meats drinks forbidden in the Levitical Law bound Christians to the same observance,* thereby opening the door to let in the rabble of all Ceremonies. He seduced many souls with his Tenets, and his own wife among many others. For these he was censured in the Star-chamber, but afterwards recanted his Opinions.

He afterwards relapsed, not into the same, but other Opinions. He asserted, *That one may know Another's Election:* or, *That one that is the child of God may infallibly know the Election and Regeneration of Another.* Dr. *William Sclater,* saith, *That for his outragious behaviour he received publick stigmatical punishment.*

Sclater. Exposit.in 1 Thes. ch.1. v.4.

At this time began the troubles in the Low Countries about matters of Religion, heightned between two opposit parties; *Remonstrants,* and *Contra-remonstrants.* Their controversies being chiefly reducible to five points, Of *Predestination* and *Reprobation,* of the latitude of *Christ's death;* of the *power of Man's free-will,* both before and after his *conversion;* and of the *Elect's perseverance in Grace.* To decide these difficulties, *The States of the United Provinces,* resolved to call a National Synod at *Dort,* desiring some forreign Princes to send them the aid of their Divines for so pious a Work. Especially, they requested our King of *Great Britain,* to contribute his assistance thereunto, who out of his Princely wisdom made choice of,

George Carleton, D. D. then Bishop of *Landaff,* and afterwards Bishop of *Chichester.*

Joseph Hall, D. D. then Dean of *Worcester,* and after Bishop of *Exeter* and *Norwich.*

John Davenant, D. D. then *Margaret-Professor,* and Master of *Queens* Colledge in *Cambridge.*

Samuel Ward, D. D. then Master of *Sidney* Colledge in *Cambridge,* and Archdeacon of *Taunton.*

These repairing to his Majesty at *New-market,* received Instructions from him concerning their behaviour in the Synod; on *October* 27. they came to the *Hague,* where they kissed the hand of his Excellency, *Grave Maurice,* to whom the Bishop made a short speech, and by whom they were all courteously entertained. Hence they removed to *Dort* where *November* 3. the Synod began. Every one at his first entrance taking an admission Oath. These four Divines had allowed them by the week threescore and ten pounds; weekly Intelligence was communicated to the King from his Divines.

On *December* 10. *Walter Balcanqual* B. D. and Fellow of *Pembrookhall*, came into the Synod, being added to the four Englifh Colleagues in the name of the Church of *Scotland*. Dr. *Hall* finding that Air not agreeing with his health, on his humble requeft, obtained his Majeftie's leave to return: whereupon with a Latin fpeech gravely delivered, he publickly took his folemn farewell of the Synod, and returned into his own Countrey. On *January* 7. Dr. *Thomas Goad*, Chaplain to *George* Archbifhop of *Canterbury* came into the Synod, fent thither by his Majefty of *Great Britain*.

April the twentieth, the Belgick Confeffion was brought into the Synod, containing matter both of Doctrine and Difcipline, and the publick confent thereunto was required. Here Bifhop *Carleton*, in the name of the reft, approved all the points of Doctrine. But as for matter of Difcipline, that his own Order, and his Mother-church, might not fuffer therein, and he feem by filence to betray the caufe thereof, a Proteft was entred by him as mouth for the reft, to preferve the fame. Thefe things he profeffed himfelf to have hinted, not to offend thofe Churches therewith, but to defend their own Church of *England*. To this Interpellation of the Britifh Divines, nothing at all was anfwered; And fuch as defire further fatisfaction herein, may perufe the joynt Atteftation which thofe Englifh Divines did fet forth, *Anno* 1626. to juftifie their proceedings therein.

On *April* 29. the Synod ended. The States to exprefs their gratitude, gave to the Englifh Divines two hundred pounds at their departure, to bear their charges in their return; befides a Golden Medal of good value was given to every one of them, wherein the fitting of the Synod was artificially reprefented. When their work was ended, they viewed the moft eminent Cities in the Low Countries, and at all places were bountifully received, *Leiden* onely excepted: for the Great ones of that Univerfity, at this time being Remonftrants, were difaffected to the decifions of the Synod. This gave occafion to that paffage in the fpeech of Sir *Dudley Carleton*, the Englifh Ambaffador, when in the name of his Mafter he tendred publick thanks to the *States* for their Great refpects to the Englifh Divines, ufing words to this effect, *That they had been entertained at* Amfterdam, *welcommed at the* Hague, *cheerfully received at* Rotterdam, *kindly embraced at* Utrecht, &c. *and that they had feen* Leiden.

Fuller.Church Hift. Ad. A°. 1618.

How high an efteem the *STATES GENERAL*, had of our Englifh Divines will appear by their Letters which they fent to King *James*, written in Latin. With which Letters they came over into *England*, and prefented themfelves to the King at Court, where after courteous entertaining of them, he favourably difmiffed them, Removing Bifhop *Carleton* to *Chichefter*, preferring Dr. *Davenant* to the Bifhoprick of *Salisbury*, and beftowing the Masterfhip of the *Savoy* upon *Balcanqual*.

The

The decisions of this Synod have been since approved, applauded, magnified by some; vilified, condemned by others. Of such as dislike the Synod, none falls heavier upon it, than Mr. *John Goodwin*, charging the Synodians to have taken a previous Oath to condemn the opposite party on what termes soever. *Joh. Goodwin in his Redemption Redeemed, c. 15. parag. 24.*

Mr. *Fuller* desirous to be rightly informed herein, wrote a Letter to Bishop *Hall*, who was pleased to return him this answer. *Whereas you desire from me a just relation of the carriage of the business of the Synod of* Dort, *and the conditions required of our Divines there, at, or before their Admission to that Grave and Learned Assembly; I, whom God was pleased to employ, as an unworthy Agent in that great work, and to reserve still upon Earth, after all my Reverend and Worthy Associates; do, as in the presence of that God, to whom I am now daily expecting to yield up my account, testifie to you, and (if you will) to the World, that I cannot without just indignation read that slaunderous Imputation which Mr.* Goodwin, *in his* Redemption Redeemed; *reports to have been raised, and cast upon those Divines, eminent both for Learning and Piety: That they suffered themselves to be bound with an Oath, at, or before their Admission into that Synod, to vote down the Remonstrants howsoever; so as they came deeply preingaged to the decision of those unhappy differences. All the Oath that was required of us was this, After that the Moderator, Assistents, and Scribes were chosen, and the Synod formed, and the several members allowed, there was a solemn Oath required to be taken by every one of that Assembly, which was publickly done in a grave manner, by every person in their order, standing up, and laying his Hand upon his heart, calling the great God of Heaven to witness; that he would unpartially proceed in the judgement of these Controversies, which should be laid before him, onely out of, and according to the written Word of God, and no otherwise; so determining of them, as he should find in his Conscience most agreeable to the holy Scriptures.* Which Oath was punctually agreed to be thus taken by the Articles of the States, concerning the Indiction, and ordering of the Synod, as plainly appeareth in their tenth Article; and this was all the Oath that was either taken or required, &c.

The same year died Dr. *James Mountague*, the worthy Bishop of *Winchester*, son to Sir *Edward Mountague* of *Boughton* in *Northamptonshire*, highly favoured by King *James*, preferring him to the Bishoprick first of *Bath* and *Wells*, then to *Winchester*. In *Bath* he lies buried under a fair Tomb, though the whole Church be his Monument, which his Bounty repaired.

Anno 1619. died *John Overal*, Bishop of *Norwich*, accounted one of the most Learned Controversial Divines of those days.

Anno 1620. the Protestant States of the Upper and Lower *Austria*, upon the approach of the Bavarian Army, seeing nothing but manifest ruin,

Rushworth. Histor. Collections.

ruin, renounce their Confederacy with the Bohemians, and submit to the Emperor, saving to themselves their Rights and Priviledges in Religion. And the Elector of *Saxony* assists the Emperor, and executes the Ban against the Palatine. King *James* soon after receives the news of the Palsgrave's overthrow. After the Assembly at *Segenbergh*, the *Palatine* and his Princess took their journey into *Holland*, where they found a refuge, and noble entertainment with the Prince of *Orange*. The Ambassage of *Weston* and *Conway* prevailed little. More Princes of the union reconcile themselves to the Emperor. The Imperial Protestant Towns, *Strasburgh*, *Worms*, and *Norembergh*, subscribe to conditions of Peace. The reconciled Princes and States intercede for the Elector *Palatine*, but in vain.

In *England* the Parliament petition the King for the due execution of Laws against Jesuites, Seminary Priests, and Popish Recusants.

On *July* 10. 1621. *John Williams* D. D. and Dean of *Westminster*, was sworn Keeper of the Great Seal of *England*. Then the King was sollicited from *Spain* and *Rome*, to enlarge his favours to Popish Recusants.

The House of Commons presented to the King a petition and Remonstrance, which laid open the distempers of those times, with their Causes and Cures.

They Represented to Him,

I. *The Vigilancy and Ambition of the Pope of* Rome, *and his dearest Son, the one aiming at as large a Temporal Monarchy, as the other at a Spiritual Monarchy.*

II. *The devilish Doctrines whereon Popery is built, and taught with Authority to their followers, for advancement of their Temporal ends.*

III. *The miserable estate of the professors of true Religion in forreign parts.*

IV. *The disastrous accidents to his Majestie's children abroad,* &c.

V. *The strange confederacy of Popish Princes,* &c.

VI. *The interposing of forreign Princes and their Agents in the behalf of Popish Recusants,* &c.

VII. *Their usual resort to the Houses and Chappels of forreign Ambassadors.*

VIII. *Their more than usual concourse to the City, and their frequent Conventicles and conferences there.*

IX. *The education of their Children in several Seminaries and Houses of their Religion in forreign parts, appropriated to the English fugitives.*

X. *The*

X. *The licentious Printing and dispersing of Popish and Seditious Books, even in the time of Parliament.*
XI. *The swarms of Priests and Jesuites dispersed in all parts of the Kingdom.*

From these Causes they offered to his Majesty, what dangerous Effects, they foresaw, would follow.

I. *The Popish Religion is incompatible with ours, in respect of their positions.*
II. *It draws with it an unavoidable dependancy on forreign Princes.*
III. *If once it get but a connivency, it will press for a Toleration,* &c.

Then they propounded Remedies against these, some whereof were,

That for securing the peace at home, his Majesty would be pleased to review the parts of their petition formerly delivered to him, and to put in execution, by the care of choice Commissioners to be thereunto appointed, the Laws already, and hereafter to be made, for preventing of dangers by Popish Recusants.
That the Children of the Nobility, and Gentry, of this Kingdom, and of others, suspected in their Religion, now beyond the Seas, may be forthwith called home.
That the Children of Popish Recusants, &c. be brought up during their minority with Protestant School-masters.
That his Majesty will be pleased to revoke all former Licenses for such Children to travel beyond the Seas, and not grant any such License hereafter, &c.

The House had sufficient Cause to set forth the danger of true Religion, when besides the great wound made in *Germany*, and the cruelties of the prevailing House of *Austria*, the Protestants in *France* were almost ruined by *Lewis* the Thirteenth; being now besieged in *Montauban* by the King, and in *Rochel* by Count *Soisons*, and the Duke of *Guise*. And for their Relief the King of *England* prevailed nothing by sending of Sir *Edward Herbert*, since Baron of *Cherbury*, and after him the Viscount *Doncaster*, Ambassador for Mediation.

About this time a sad misfortune befel *George Abbot*, Lord Archbishop of *Canterbury*, for shooting at a Deer with a Cross-bow in *Bramshil* Park, belonging to the Lord *Zouch*; he casually killed the Keeper. The King made choice of the Lord Keeper, the Bishops of *London*, *Winton*, *Rochester*, *St. Davids*, and *Exeter*, Sir *Henry Hobart*, Justice *Doderidge*, Sir *Henry Martin*, and Doctor *Stuart*, to inform him of the

the nature of this cause, and the scandal that might arise thereupon, whether to an Irregularity, or otherwise. However this consultation was managed, the Archbishop was not deprived. In this business, Bishop *Andrews* proved the Archbishop's great friend. The Archbishop gave twenty pound a year to the man's Widow. He kept a monethly fast on a *Tuesday*, as the day whereon this casualty befell.

About this time young *Merick Casaubon* set fort a Book in defence of his deceased Father, against *Herbert Rofwed* a Jesuite; and *Andrew Schoppius* a notorious railer, *Julius Cæsar Bulinger*, and *Andrew Eudemono Joannes*. He thought it his duty to assert his Father's memory, and to give a brief account of his life and conversation.

Upon the remove of *Richard Milborn* to *Carlile*, Doctor *William Land*, President of St. *John's* Colledge in *Oxford*, was made Bishop of S^t. *Davia's*. He founded in *Oxford* a Professor in the Arabick Tongue.

This year died *John King*, Bishop of *London*. He was sworn first Chaplain to King *James*, who commonly called him, *The King of Preachers*. And Sir *Edward Coke*, said of him, *He was the best speaker, in Star-chamber, in his time*. When Bishop of *London*, unless hindred by sickness, he omitted no Lord's day, wherein he did not visit some Pulpit in *London*, or near it. The Papists raised a false aspersion upon him, *That at his death he was reconciled to the Church of* Rome: but this was sufficiently confuted by those eye and ear-witnesses, present, at his pious departure. *George Mountain*, Bishop of *Lincoln* succeeded him in his See.

The same year died *William Cotton* Bishop of *Exeter*, whom *Valentine Carew*, Dean of St. *Paul's*, succeedeth. *Robert Townson* Bishop of *Sarisbury* dieth, whom *John Davenant* succeedeth. Therein also expired Dr. *Andrew Willet*, a man of great judgement and Industry, one that had a large soul in a narrow estate. The same year died also *Richard Parry*, Bishop of St. *Asaph*. We will conclude this year with the death of Mr. *Francis Mason*, who wrote that worthy Book, *De Ministerio Anglicano*.

Rushw. Hist. Collect.

Anno 1622. Multitudes of Priests and Popish Recusants then imprisoned, were released, which the Spaniards professed to be a great demonstration of the King's sincere affection, to confirm the amity between the Crowns. But a General offence was taken at this Indulgence to Papists.

Anno 1622.

The next year began with the end of that arrant *Apostata* in this Land, M. *Antonius de Dominis*, Archbishop of *Spalato*, and his fair riddance out of it. He had fourteen years been Archbishop of *Spalato* in *Dalmatia*, under the *State* of *Venice*, and had now been five years in *England*. Conscience in shew, and Covetousness indeed, caused his coming hither.

He

He wrote sharply against the Pope, out of a particular grudge against Pope *Paul*, who had ordered him to pay a yearly pension of five hundred Crowns out of his Bishoprick, to one *Audrentius*, a Suffragan Bishop, which this Archbishop refused to do. The matter was brought to the Court of *Rome*, where the Archbishop, angry that he was cast in his Cause, posts out of *Italy*, through *Germany* into the Low Countries, and thence came over into *England*.

Fuller. Church Hist. An.1622.

Here multitudes of people flocked to behold this old Archbishop, now a new Convert. Prelates and Peers presented him with gifts of high valuation. He was Feasted wheresoever he came, and both the Universities (when he visited them) highly honoured him. But above all King *James* was most munificent to him. The King consigned him to the Archbishop of *Canterbury* for his present entertainment, and as an earnest of his bounty, sent him to *Lambeth*, a fair Bason and Boll of Silver, which *Spalato* received with this complement, *The King of Great Britain hath sent me a Silver Bason, to wash from me the filth of the Roman Church; and a Silver Cup to mind me to drink the purity of the Gospel.*

Misit mihi Rex Magnæ Britanniæ pelvim argenteum ad abstergendam sordes Romanæ Ecclesiæ, & poculum argenteum, ad imbibendam Evangelii puritatem.

Preferment is quickly conferred upon him, as the Deanery of *Windsor*, and the Master-ship of the Hospital of the *Savoy*, with a good Parsonage at *West-Ilsey* in *Berk-shire*, being a peculiar belonging to the Episcopal jurisdiction of the Dean of *Windsor*, which Parsonage he collated on himself.

He improved the profits of his place to the utmost, and had a design to question all his Predecessors Leases at the *Savoy*, and began to be vexatious to his Tenants: for which he was gravely and sharply reproved by Dr. *King*, then Bishop of *London*. *Spalato* complained to King *James*, who in some choler said, *Extraneus, extraneus es, relinque res sicut eas invenisti*; *You are a Stranger, you are a stranger, leave things as you found them.* He would passionately perswade others unto bounty to the poor, though he would give nothing himself.

He now perfects his Books, the Collections whereof were made by him at *Spalato*. His works (being three fair Folio's, *De Republica Ecclesiastica*) give ample testimony of his abilities.

He delighted in jeering; one of his Sarcasms he unhappily bestowed on Count *Gondomar*, the Spanish Ambassador, telling him, *That three turns at* Tyburn, *was the onely way to cure his Fistula*. *Gondomar* hereupon meditates revenge, and tells King *James*, That his charity abused his judgment, in conceiving *Spalato* a true Convert, who still in heart remain'd a Roman Catholick. The Ambassador writes to the King of *Spain*, He to Pope *Gregory* the Fifteenth, that *Spalato* might be pardoned, and preferred in the Church of *Rome*, which was easily obtained. Letters are sent from *Rome* to Count *Gondomar*, written by the Cardinal *Millin*, to impart them to *Spalato*, informing him of his pardon at *Rome*, and that upon on his return the Pope would prefer him to the Bishoprick of *Salerno* in *Naples*, worth twelve thousands pounds by the year; and also that a Cardinal's Hat should be bestowed upon him. And if *Spalato* with his hand subscribed to this Letter would renounce what formerly he had Printed, an Apostolical *Breve*, with pardon, should solemnly be sent him to *Bruxels*. *Spalato* embraceth the motion, recanteth his Opinions largely, subscribes solemnly, and thanketh the Pope affectionately for his favour: *Gondomar* carrieth his subscription to King *James*, who is glad to behold the Hypocrite unmasked.

Now died *Toby Mathew*, Archbishop of *York*; presently posts *Spalato* to *Theobalds*, becomes an Earnest Petitioner to the King for the vacant Archbishoprick, and is as flatly denied. *Spalato* offended at this repulse, requests his Majesty by his Letter to grant him his good leave to depart the Kingdom. Five days after the Bishops of *London* and *Durham*, with the Dean of *Westminster*, by his Majestie's direction, repaired to *Spalato*, propounding unto Him sixteen Queries, all arising out of his own Letter, and requiring him to give the explanation of five of the most material under his hand, for his Majestie's greater satisfaction, which he did accordingly: yet not so clearly, but that it occasioned a second meeting, wherein more interrogatories were propounded unto him, to all which he gave his answers. He pretended many reasons for his return. In pursuance of which his desire, he wrote a second Letter to King *James*.

At length *Spalato* appears before the Archbishop of *Canterbury*, the Bishops of *Lincoln*, *London*, *Durham*, *Winchester*, at *Lambeth*, where the Archbishop of *Canterbury* in a long Latin Speech, recapitulated the many misdemeanors of *Spalato*, principally insisting on his changing of Religion, as appeared by his purpose of returning to *Rome*: and that contrary to the Laws of this Realm, he had held correspondency with the Pope, without the privity of the King's Majesty. To which charge when *Spalato* had made a shuffling excuse, rather than a just defence, the Archbishop in his Majestie's name commanded him to depart the Kingdom within twenty days, and never to return again. To this he promised obedience, protesting, he would ever justifie the Church of *England* for Orthodox in Fundamentals, even in the presence of the Pope, or whomsoever, though with the loss of his life.

However, he was loth to depart, and secretly deals with his Friends in the English Court, that his Majesty would permit him to stay. But in vain, and therefore within the time appointed, he went over in the same Ship with Count *Swartenzburgh*, the Emperor's Ambassador, returning hence into *Flanders*. Being come to *Bruxels*, he recants his Religion, and rails bitterly on the English Church. Here he stayed six moneths for the Pope's *Breve*, which at last was utterly denied him. Now he desperately adventures to *Rome*; barely presuming on promises, and

and the Friendship of Pope *Gregory* the Fifteenth, then Pope, formerly his Colleague, and Chamber-fellow. He lived at *Rome* not loved, and died unlamented. He was clapt into prison, his study seized on, wherein many papers were found speaking Heresie enough, his Adversaries being admitted sole Interpreters thereof. He died some moneths after, and after his death his Excommunicated Corps were put to publick shame, and solemnly proceeded against, in the Inquisition, for relapsing into Heresie since his return to *Rome*. Several Articles of Heresie are charged upon him, and he found convict thereof, is condemned to have his body burnt by the publick Executioner in the Field of *Flora*, which was performed accordingly.

<small>*Fuller*.Church Hist. Ad. An. 1622.</small>

The Spanish Match was now the Discourse general, but at last it brake off: Heaven forbidding the Banes (saith Mr. *Fuller*) even at the third and last asking thereof. King *James* falls off, and for a condition of the Marriage, demands the Restitution of the Palatinate. The Prince returns from *Spain*.

Then was there a conference entertained between Dr. *White*, and Dr. *Featly*, Protestants; Father *Fisher*, and Father *White*, Jesuites: Now hapned the fatal Vespers at *Black-friers* in *London*, Father *Drury* a Jesuite, of excellent Morals, Preached there in a great upper-room, next to the House of the French Ambassador, where three hundred persons were assembled. His Text *Matth*. 18. 32. *O thou ungratious servant, I forgave thee all the debt, because thou desiredst me, shouldst not Thou also have had compassion on thy fellow-servant?* In application whereof he bitterly inveighed against the Protestants. About the middle of his Sermon, and the day declining, on a sudden the Floor fell down where they were assembled; many were killed, more bruised, all frighted. Ninety five persons were slain, among whom Mr. *Drury*, Mr. *Rodiat*, Priests, with the Lady *Webb*, were of the chiefest note. Twenty of the poorer sort were buried hard by in one Grave, and the rest bestowed by their friends in several places of Sepulture.

Yet notwithstanding this sad Accident, the Papists were very insolent towards all true English men, the rather, because it was generally reported, That his Majesty intended a Toleration of Religion: which made the Archbishop of *Canterbury*, in a serious Letter, to present the King with his apprehensions; beseeching the King to consider, *Lest by this Toleration, and discountenancing of the true profession of the Gospel, wherewith God hath blessed us, and this Kingdom hath so long flourished under it, God's heavy wrath be not drawn upon this Kingdom*, &c. What effect this Letter took is unknown, sure it is, all mens mouths were filled with a discourse of a Toleration, for, or against it: yea the Pulpits are loud against *Toleration*.

<small>The Letter may be read at large in *Rushworth's* Collect. and *Fuller*.Church History.</small>

Now because the peoples mouths were open, and some Preachers were two busie, the King gave directions for the regulation of the Ministry, in his Letters directed to the Lord Archbishop of *Canterbury*: for many shallow Preachers handled the profound points of *Predestination*, &c. Sermons were turned into Satyrs against Papists, and Non-conformists. The King revived the primitive and profitable order of Catechizing in the after-noon. Various censures were passed on the King's Letters. But these Instructions from his Majesty were not pressed with equal rigour in all places.

Both the Palatinates were now lost, the Vpper seized on by the Emperor; the Nether by the King of *Spain*; the City of *Heidelberg* taken and plundered, and the inestimable Library of Books therein carried over the Alpes on Mules backs to *Rome*. Now those Books are placed in the Pope's *Vatican*. The Duke of *Bavaria* was invested in the upper *Palatinate*.

Anno 1624. The match with *France* was concluded, and in *November* the Articles were sworn unto by King *James*, Prince *Charles*, and the French King. The Articles for Religion were not much short of those for Spanish match.

Count *Mansfield* was at this time in *England*, and the Forces raised in the several parts of the Kingdom for the recovery of the Palatinate, were put under his command. *Dover* was the place assigned for their Rendezvous, where the Colonels and Captains were to receive their several Regiments and Companies, from the Conductors employed by those several Counties where the men were raised. These being long pent up in their Ships, suffered the want of all necessaries, by which means a Pestilence devoured many of them, so that scarce a Third part of the men were landed; the which also afterwards mouldred away, and the design came to nothing.

At this time upon the death of *William*, Titular Bishop of *Calcedon*, most of the English Secular Priests did petition the Pope, that another Bishop might be sent over into *England*, there to ordain Priests, give Confirmation, and exercise Episcopal jurisdiction. Among others *Matthew Kellison*, and *Richard Smith*, were presented. Not long after Pope *Urban* the Eighth, created *Richard Smith*, Bishop of *Calcedon*, and sent him into *England* with Episcopal Authority over the Priests within the English Dominions.

King *James*, after he had been troubled with a Tertian Fever four weeks at *Theobalds*, called unto him his onely Son, Prince *Charles*, to whom he recommended the protection of the Church of *England*, &c. and died on the seven and twentieth day of *March*. He Reigned twenty two years and three days.

The sad news of King *James* his death was brought to *Whitehall*, when Dr. *Laud*, Bishop of St. *David's*, was Preaching therein. This caused him to break off his Sermon in the midst thereof, out of civil compliance.

the Church of Great Britain.

ance with the sadness of the Congregation. And the same day was King *Charles* Proclaimed at *Whitehall*.

Shortly after, King *James* his death, Bishop *Laud* delivered to the hands of the Duke of *Buckingham*, brief memorables of the Life and Death of King *James*. On *May* fourteenth following, King *James* his Funerals were performed very solemnly in the Collegiate-church at *Westminster*. King *Charles* in his own person mournfully attended the Funerals of his Father. Dr. *Williams*, Lord Keeper, and Bishop of *Lincoln*, Preached the Sermon, taking for his Text, 2 *Chron* 9. 29. 30, and part of vers. 31. containing the happy Reign, quiet Death, and stately Burial of King *Solomon*. In this Sermon he made a parallel between two peaceable Princes, King *Solomon* and King *James*, adding, that *Solomon's* vices could be no blemish to King *James*, who resembled him onely in his choycest vertues.

Doctor *Preston* still continued, and increased in the favour of the King, and the Duke of *Buckingham*.

Then a Book came forth, called *Apello Cæsarem*, made by Mr. *Mountague*, then Fellow of *Eaton*, upon this occasion. He had lately written Satyrically enough against the Papists, in confutation of *The Gagger of the Protestants*. Now two Divines of *Norwich* Diocese, Mr. *Yates*, and Mr. *Ward*, inform against him for deserting our Cause, instead of defending it. Mr. *Mountague* in his own Vindication writes a second Book licensed by *Francis White*, Dean of *Carlile*, finished, and partly Printed in the Reign of King *James*. Many bitter passages in this his Book gave great exception.

At that time a Schedule was delivered to the Duke wherein the names of Ecclesiastical persons were written, under the letters of *O*, and *P*, *O* standing for *Orthodox*, and *P*. for *Puritans*: for the Duke commanded that the names of eminent persons to be presented unto the King should be thus digested under that partition.

Rushw. Coll. lect. An. 1629.

On Sunday *June* 12. Queen *Mary* landed at *Dover*: Next day the King coming from *Canterbury*, met her at *Dover*, Thence his Majesty conducted the Queen to *Canterbury*, and the same Evening the Marriage was there consummated. On *June* 16. the King and Queen came both to *London*. A Chappel at *Sommerset-house* was built for the Queen and her Family, with conveniences thereto adjoyning for *Capuchin* Friers, who were therein placed, and had permission to walk abroad in their Religious habits.

Then began a Parliament at *London*, wherein the first Statute agreed upon was for the more strict observation of the Lord's day. Sir *Edward Coke* went to the House of Peers with a message from the Commons, desiring their concurrence in a petition concerning Religion, and against Recusants, which being agreed to, and presented to the King, his Majesty answered, That he was glad, that the Parliament was so forward.

ward in matters of *Religion*, and assured them, they should find him as forward.

Mr. *Richard Mountague* was brought to the Bar of the Commons House, for his Book fore-mentioned, which was Printed, and dedicated to King *Charles*. But the King rescued him from the House of Commons, by taking Mr. *Mountague*'s business into his own hand. The Plague increasing in *London*, the Parliament removed to *Oxford*, where Doctor *Chalenor* died of that infection. The Parliament to prevent the growth of Popery, presented a petition to his Majesty, containing sixteen particulars, to which they received a satisfactory answer from the King.

Mr. *Mountagues* cause was recommended to the Duke of *Buckingham*, by the Bishops of *Rochester*, *Oxford*, and *St. Davids*, as the cause of the Church of *England*. They affirm boldly, that they cannot conceive, what use there can be of Civil Government in the Commonwealth, or of external Ministry in the Church, if such fatal Opinions as some are, which are opposite to those of Mr. *Mountague*, be publickly taught and maintained. But other Learned men were of a different judgement.

At *Oxford* in a late Divinity disputation held upon this Question, *Whether a Regenerate man may fall away totally and finally from Grace?* The Opponent urging the Appeal to *Cæsar*, the Doctor of the Chair handled the Appellator very roughly, saying, *That he was a man that studied phrases more than matter*; *That he understood neither Articles nor Homilies, or at least perverted both*; *That he attributed, he knew not what vertue to the sign of the Cross*; and concluded with an Admonition to the Juniors, *That they should be wary of reading that and the like Books*.

The King according to his late answer to the Parliament at *Oxford*, issued out a Commission to the Judges, to see the Law against Recusants put in Execution. This was read in all the Courts of Judicature at *Reading* (where *Michaelmas* Term was kept) and a letter directed to the Archbishop of *Canterbury*, to take special care for the discovery of Jesuites, Seminary Priests, &c. within his Province.

In this and the next year many Books from persons of several abilities and professions, were written against Mr. *Mountague*, by Dr. *Sutcliff* Dean of *Exeter*; Mr. *Henry Burton*; Mr. *Yates*, a Minister of *Norfolk*, his Book he entitled, *Ad Cæsarem ibis*. Dr. *Carleton*, Bishop of *Chichester*; *Anthony Wotton*, Divinity-professor in *Gresham* Colledge, and Mr. *Francis Rowse*, a Lay-man. His Majesty sensible of his Subjects great distast at Mr. *Mountague's* Book, resolved to leave him to stand or fall according to the justness of his Cause. The Duke imparted as much to the Bishop of St. *David's*, who conceived it of such ominous concernment, that he entred the same in his Diary, *viz*. *I seem to see a cloud*

cloud arising, and threatning the Church of England, *God for his mercy dissipate it.*

The King issued forth a Proclamation, *Whereby he commanded the return, within limited time, of all such Children of Noble-men, and other his natural Subjects, who were now breeding up in Schools and Seminaries, and other Houses of the Popish Religion beyond the Seas. That their Parents, Tutors, and Governors, take present order to recal them home, and to provide; that they return by the day prefixt, at the utmost severity of his Majestie's Justice:* He commanded further, *That no Bishop, Priest, or any other person, having taken Orders under any Authority derived from the See of* Rome, *do presume to confer Ecclesiastical Orders, or exercise Ecclesiastical Function, or Jurisdiction toward any of his Natural Subjects, in any of his Dominions,* &c.

On *Candlemas-day* King *Charles* was Crowned, Bishop *Laud* had the chief hand in compiling the form of the Coronation, and had the honour to perform this Solemnity, instead of the late Lord Keeper *Williams,* who (through the King's disfavour) was sequestred from this service, which belonged to his place, as he was Dean of *Westminster.* Dr. *Senhouse,* Bishop of *Carlile,* Preached at the Coronation. The Coronation Oath was tendred to the King by the Archbishop of *Canterbury.* The Ceremonies of the Coronation being ended, the *Regalia* were offered at the Altar by Bishop *Laud,* in the King's Name, and then reposited.

Bishop *Williams* fallen into disgrace, by the displeasure of the Duke of *Buckingham,* besought his Majesty, That he would mitigate the Duke's causeless anger towards him; and that in his absence in the Parliament, no use might be made of his Majestie's sacred Name to wound the Reputation of a poor Bishop, &c.

On *Monday, February* the sixth, began the second Parliament of the King's Reign. The House of Commons began where they left at *Oxford,* with matters of Religion and publick grievances. They made strict enquiry into what abuses had been of the King's grace, since that time, and who were the Authors and Abbettors thereof; for they had been informed of many Pardons and Reprieves to Priests and Jesuites. An Act was tendred against scandalous Ministers. It was moved, that some provision might be made against scandalous Livings, as well as against scandalous Ministers.

A Committee was named concerning Religion, and the Growth of Popery, and Mr. *Mountague's* [*Appeal to* Cæsar] was again brought in question. This Book the Commons referred to the Committee for Religion, the contents whereof were reported from Mr. *Pym* to the House, and the House passed their Votes thereupon; *That Mr.* Mountague

tague endeavoured to reconcile England to Rome, and to alienate the King's affections from his well-affected Subjects. Divers Articles were exhibited by the Commons against Mr. *Mountague*. They prayed, That the said Mr. *Mountague* might be punished according to his Demerits, and that the Book aforesaid might be suppressed and burnt.

Many resorting to hear Mass at *Durham* house, in the Lodgings of a Forreign Ambassador, the Bishop of *Durham* was required to apprehend such of the King's Subjects as should be present at the Mass, and to commit them to prison. There was also a Letter sent from the Attorney General, to the Judges of the circuits, to direct their proceedings against Recusants.

Fuller. Church Hist. *An.*1626. During the sitting of this Parliament, at the procurement of *Robert Rich*, Earl of *Warwich*, a conference was kept in *York house*, before the Duke of *Buckingham* and other Lords, betwixt Dr. *Buckeridge* Bishop of *Rochester*, and Dr. *White* Dean of *Carlile*, on the one side; and Dr. *Morton* Bishop of *Coventry* and Dr. *Preston* on the other, chiefly, *About the possibility of one elected to fall from grace*. The passages of which conference are variously reported. Soon after, a second conference was in the same place, on the same points, before the same persons, betwixt Dr. *White* Dean of *Carlile*, and Mr. *Mountague* on the one side, and Dr. *Morton* Bishop of *Litchfield*, and Dr. *Preston* on the other. But these conferences rather increased the differences, than abated them.

An old Hall in *Oxford*, formerly called *Broad-gates-Hall*, was this year turned into a new Colledge, and called *Pembrook* Colledge, partly in respect to *William* Earl of *Pembrook*, then Chancellor of the University. This Colledge consisteth of a Master, ten Fellows, and ten Scholars, with other Students and Officers to the number of one hundred sixty nine.

Now Dr. *Preston* decline's in the Duke's favour, and the Duke betakes himself to the opposit Interest. This year died *Arthur Lake*, Bishop of *Bath* and *Wells*; and *Lancelot Andrews*, who had been Dean of *Westminster*, Bishop of *Chichester*, *Ely*, and at last, of *Winchester*. Doctor *Nicholas Felton*, Bishop of *Ely*, died some days after Bishop *Andrews*.

About this time the Marshal of *Middlesex* petitioned to the Committee of the House of Commons touching his resistance in seizing of Priests goods. A Warrant was made by Mr *Attorney-General* to *John Tendring* Marshal of *Middlesex*, and all other therein named, to search the prison of the *Clink*, and to seize all Popish and superstitious matters there found. A Letter also was directed to Sir *George Paul*, a Justice of Peace in *Surrey*, to pray him to take care in expediting that service. Upon search four several Priests were found in the *Clink*, viz. *Preston*, *Candon*, *Warrington*, *Prator*. *Preston* was committed to the

Clink

Clink about sixteen years since, and discharged of his imprisonment about seven years ago, yet remained there in the Prison still, attended with two Women servants, and one Man servant, who as it was suspected, had continued with him ever since the Gunpowder-Treason. Anno 1605. He kept there by himself apart from the Keeper of the prison, and had for his lodging part of the Bishop of *Winchester's* house, into which there was a passage made through the prison-yard. There were found in his Chamber five or six Cart-loads of Books set up with shelves, as in a Library, or Book-seller's shop, supposed to be worth two thousand pounds at least: besides which it was affirmed by the Keeper of the prison, that he had a greater Library abroad. There were also found two Altars ready furnished for Mass; one more publick in an upper Chamber, the other more private, in a Study, many rich Copes, Surplices, Wax-candles, Crosses, Crucifixes very rich, Beads, Jewels, Chaines, Chalices of Silver and of Gold; five or six bags of money which were not opened, and loose money to the quantity of an hundred pound thrown up and down in his Desk; abundance of Manuscripts, and a pacquet of Letters bound up together with a thread.

Rushw. Collec. Anno 1626.

In *Candon's* Chamber was found an Altar ready furnished with many Plates, Jewels, rich Pictures and Manuscripts, Wax-candles, &c. with many Books in a Study. In another Study of his many curious Tools and Engines, three Rapiers, one Pistol, and a Fowling piece, the pictures of Queen *Elizabeth*, King *James*, Queen *Anne*, and King *Charles*. He had also in his custody all the Keeper's Warrants for committing of his prisoners, which were found in his Chamber, together with some store of Plate, which he said he kept for the Keeper's wife.

In *Warrington's* Chamber were found Books, Beads, Boxes of Oyl for extreme Unction, &c. But the wall thereof was broken down into another house adjoyning to the Prison, through which it is conceived the rest of *Warrington's* stuffe was convaied away in the Interim of the search made in the two former Chambers.

Prator was first committed to *Glocester* Gaol, but a Warrant was procured by the Papists for his remove to the *Clink*, where he was found a prisoner. But a countermand was brought from the Archbishop, and Mr. Atturney, whereby the proceeding of that business was staid, and the Marshal prohibited to remove, or take any thing, so much as a paper. The Keeper and his Wife, and the Priests did grievously threaten the Marshall and all his Assistants, with very high terms, especially with Arrests and Imprisonments for this action.

The Marshall also informed the Committee, that upon the twenty second of *March* last, by a like Warrant from the Lord *Conway*, he searched the Bishop's prison, called the *New prison* in *Maiden-lane* in *London*,

London, where he found six several Priests in several Chambers, an Altar with all furniture thereto belonging, *&c.* as much as three Porters could carry away, it being in the hands of the Lord *Conway*.

The House of Commons agreed upon a petition to his Majesty concerning Recusants, That he would give order to remove from all places of Authority and Government, all such persons, as are either Popish Recusants, or justly to be suspected. Here they named many Lords, Knights, and Esquires, in divers Counties of *England*. But this Parliament was soon after dissolved.

A general Fast was observed, *July* 5. in the Cities of *London* and *Westminster*, and places adjacent, and on the second of *August*, throughout the Kingdom, to implore a blessing upon the endeavours of the State, and the diverting of those judgments which the sins of the Land deserved and threatned.

Divers Lords of the Council were appointed to repair into their several Countries, for the advancement of a Loan to the King. This business occasioned a complaint to the Lords of the Council against the Bishop of *Lincoln*, for publickly speaking words concerning it, which was conceived to be against the King and Government. Whereupon Sir *John Lamb*, and Dr. *Sibthorp*, informed the Council to this purpose, That many were grieved to see the Bishop of *Lincoln* give place to unconformable Ministers, when he turned his back to those that were conformable, and how the Puritans ruled all with him, *&c.* The Informations given against the Bishop of *Lincoln* being transmitted to the Council-Table, were ordered to be sealed up, and committed to the custody of Mr. *Trumbal*, one of the Clerks of the Council: nevertheless the Bishop of *Lincoln* got a copy of them.

Dr. *Sibthorp* published a Sermon in Print, Preached by him at *Northampton*, *February* 22. 1626. at Lent Assizes, entitled, *Apostolick Obedience*. This Book was Licensed by the Bishop of *London*, who approved thereof. It was dedicated to the King; it was brought forth upon his Majesties Commission for raising of moneys by way of Loan.

Dr. *Roger Manwaring* promoted the same business in two Sermons Preached before the King and Court at *Whitehall*. The Papists at this time were very liberal on this occasion, that it was then said, That in the point of Allegiance then in hand, the Papists were exceeding Orthodox, and the Puritans were the onely Recusants.

1627. Archbishop *Abbot* having been long slighted at Court, now fell under the King's high displeasure, for refusing to License Dr. *Sibthorp's* Sermon forementioned, and not long after was suspended from his Office and confined to his House at *Ford* in *Kent*, and a Commission was granted to the Bishops of *London*, *Durham*, *Rochester*, *Oxford*, and
Dr.

Doctor *Laud* Bishop of *Bath* and *Wells*, to execute Archiepiscopal Jurisdiction. The occasion of this Commission was not discovered otherwise than by what was expressed in the Commission it self, *viz.* That the said *Archbishop* could not at that present in his own person attend those services, which were otherwise proper for his cognisance and jurisdiction; and which as *Archbishop* of Canterbury he might and ought in his own Person have performed and Executed.

The Archbishop for a memorial of these proceedings left to posterity a Narrative penned with his own hand. The City of *London* was filled with the report of his Confining, and divers men spake diversly of it.

The Papists in *Ireland* proffer to pay five thousand men, if they might but enjoy a toleration. But that motion was crushed by Bishop *Downham's* Sermon in *Dublin*, on *Luke* 1. 74.

After this, the King being resolved upon the calling of a Parliament, Archbishop *Abbot*, the Earl of *Bristol*, and the Bishop of *Lincoln*, notwithstanding the cloud they are under, are had in consideration by the King and Council; and Writs are Ordered to be sent unto them to sit in the House as Peers in the ensuing Parliament.

A little before the Parliament assembled, a Society of Recusants was taken in *Clarkenwel*. Divers of them were found to be Jesuites, and the house wherein they were taken was designed to be a Colledge of that Order. Among their Papers was found a Copy of a Letter written to their Father Rector at *Bruxels* discovering their designs upon this State, and their judgement of the temper thereof, with a conjecture of the success of the ensuing Parliament. *Vid. Rushw. Collects. Ad Anno 1627.*

A Parliament assembleth *March* 17. which proveth full of troubles. Money came from them heavily to the supply of the King's necessities: the rather, because they complained of Doctrines destructive to their Propriety Preached at Court. For towards the end of the Session of this Parliament Mr. *Rouse* brought in a charge against Dr. *Manwaring*, which some days after was seconded with a Declaration. He was severely censured for two Sermons he had Preached and Printed about the power of the King's Prerogative.

Four days after, it was ordered by the House of Lords against him.

I. To be imprisoned during the pleasure of the House.
II. To be fined a thousand pounds.
III. To make his submission at the Bar in this House.
IV. To be suspended from his Ministerial function three years.
V. To be disabled for ever hereafter from Preaching at Court.
VI. To be uncapable of any Secular Office.
VII. That

VII. *That his Books are worthy to be burnt, and His Majesty, to be moved that it may be so in* London.

But much of this Cenfure was remitted, in Confideration of the performance of his humble fubmiffion at both the Bars in Parliament, Where he appeared on *June* the three and twentieth following, and on his knees before both Houfes fubmitted himfelf with much outward expreffion of forrow.

1628.

On Thurfday *May* 26. 1628. ended this Seffion of Parliament; wherein divers abufes of the Lord's day reftrained. All Carriers, Carters, Waggoners, Wainmen, Drovers of Cattle, forbidden to travel therein, on the forfeit of twenty fhillings for every offence, &c. A Law was alfo made, that whofoever goeth himfelf or fendeth others beyond the feas, to be trained up in Popery, &c. fhall be difabled to fue, &c. and fhall lofe all his goods, and forfeit all his lands for life.

On *July* 20. died Dr. *Prefton* of a Confumption, and was buried at *Fawfley* in *Northampton-fhire*, Mr. *Dod* Preaching his Funeral-fermon: an Excellent Preacher; a fubtil Difputant, and good Politician. About this time *George Carleton*, that grave and godly Bifhop of *Chichefter*, ended his Pious life. He was bred and brought up under that holy man M. *Bernard Gilpin* (whofe life he wrote in gratitude to his memory.) and retained his youthful and Poetical ftudies, frefh in his old age. Mr. *Richard Mountague*, one of a differing judgement fucceeded in his See. At the fame time the Rich Parfonage of *Stanford-rivers* in *Effex* was conferred on Dr. *Manwaring*, as voyd by Bifhop *Mountague*'s preferment.

A Proclamation came forth declaring the King's pleafure for proceedings with Popifh Recufants, and directions to his Commiffioners for making Compofitions for two parts of three of their eftates, which by Law were due to His Majefty. Neverthelefs (for the moft part) they got off upon eafie terms by reafon of compofitions at undervalues. Dr. *Barnaby Potter* is now made Bifhop of *Carlile*.

This was feconded with another Proclamation, commanding, that diligent fearch be made for all Priefts and Jefuites (particularly the Bifhop of *Calcedon*) and others that have taken Orders by Authority from the See of *Rome*, that they be apprehended, and committed to the Gaol of that County where they fhall be found. *Smith* the titular Bifhop of *Calcedon* hereupon conveyed himfelf over into *France*, where he became a confident of Cardinal *Richlieu's*.

This year died *Toby Mathew* Archbifhop of *York*. *George Mountain* fucceeded him, but died a few moneths after. During the fitting of the Parliament, one Dr. *Leighton* a Scottifh man prefented a Book unto them, exciting the Parliament and people to kill all the Bifhops, and to

the Church of Great Britain.

to smite them under the fifth Rib. He bitterly inveighed against the Queen, calling her a Daughter of *Heth*, a Canaanite and Idolatress: and *Zions plea* was the specious title of his Pamphlet, for which he was sentenced in the *Star-chamber* to be whipt and stigmatized, to have his ears cropt, and nose slit; which censure was inflicted on him.

On *August* 23. 1628. The Duke of *Buckingham* was Murthered at *Portsmouth* by one Lieutenant *Felton*. After the death of the Duke, the King highly favoured Dr. *Laud* Bishop of *London*, to whom he sent many gratious messages.

Some three years since, certain Feoffees were legally setled in trust to purchase in Impropriations with their own and other well-disposed persons money, and with their profit to set up and maintain a constant Preaching Ministry in places of greatest need, where the word was most wanting. The Feoffes were twelve in number diversly qualified,

William Gouge } Doctors in Divinity.
Richard Sibbs }
Charles Off-spring.
John Davenport.
Ralph Eyre } of *Lincolns Inne*.
Sa. Brown }
C. Sherland of *Grays Inne*.
John White of the *Middle Temple*.
John Gearing }
Richard Davis } Citizens.
Geo. Harwood }
Francis Bridges }

It is incredible, what large summs were advanced in a short time toward so laudable a work.

In *March* Bishop *Davenant* preaching his course on a Sunday in *Lent* at *White-hall* before the King and Court; In his Sermon he was conceived to fall on some forbidden points, insomuch that his Majesty manifested much displeasure thereat: for which he is convented before the Council, where Dr. *Harsenet*, Archbishop of *York*, aggravated his offence. His answer was, that he had delivered nothing but the received Doctrine of our Church established in the seventeenth Article, and that he was ready to justifie the truth of what he had then taught. Their answer was the Doctrine was not gain-said, but his Highness had given Command these questions should not be debated; and therefore he took it more offensively that any should be so bold, as in his own hearing to break his Royal Commands. Here the Archbishop of *York* aggravated the offence from many other Circumstances. His Reply

was

was onely this, That he never underſtood that his Majeſty had forbid a handling of any Doctrine compriſed in the Articles of our Church, but onely railing of new queſtions, or adding of new ſenſe thereunto, which he had not done, nor ever ſhould do.

Anno 1630. died *Thomas Dove*, Biſhop of *Peterborough*. The Nonconformiſts complained of his ſeverity in aſſerting Eccleſiaſtical diſcipline. He was an aged man, being the onely Queen *Elizabeth's* Biſhop that died in the Reign of King *Charles*.

*Fuller.*Church Hiſt.*An.*1631. *Anno* 1631. began great diſcontents to grow in the Univerſity of *Oxford*. Many conceived that Innovations (defended by others for Renovations, and now onely reduced as uſed in the primitive times) were multiplied in Divine Service: Whereat offended, they, in their Sermons, brake forth into (what was interpreted) bitter invectives. Dr. *Smith* Warden of *Wadham-colledge* convented Mr. *Thorn* of *Baliol-colledge*; and Mr. *Ford* of *Magdalen* hall, as offenders againſt the King's Inſtructions, and ordered them to bring in the Copies of their Sermons. Biſhop *Laud* procured the cauſe to be heard before the King at *Woodſtock*; and 1. The Preachers complained of were expelled the Univerſity. 2. The Proctors were deprived of their place for accepting their Appeal. 3. Dr. *Prideaux* and Dr *Wilkinſon* were ſhrewdly checked for engaging in their behalf. The expulſion of theſe Preachers encreaſed the Differences in *Oxford*.

This year died that eminent Preacher Mr. *Arthur Hilderſam*. After he had entred into his Miniſtry, he met with many troubles. He was ſilenced by the High Commiſſion in *June Anno* 1590. and reſtored by the High Commiſſion in *January* 1591. He was ſilenced by Biſhop *Chaderton*. *April* 24. 1605. reſtored by Biſhop *Barlow* in *January* 1608. Silenced by Biſhop *Neile* in *November* 1611. reſtored by Dr. *Ridley June* 20. 1625. Silenced by the Court at *Leiceſter Mar.* 4. 1630. reſtored by the ſame Court 1631. He was Miniſter of *Aſhby de la Zouch* forty and three years. The ſame year died *Robert Bolton* Miniſter of *Broughton* in *Northampton-ſhire*, an Authoritative Preacher.

Now a Bill was exhibited in the Exchequer-chamber by Mr. *Noy* the Attourney-general againſt the Feoffees for Impropriations. It was charged againſt them, that they diverted the Charity wherewith they were intruſted, to other uſes. That they generally preferred Nonconformiſts to the Lectures of their erection. The Court condemned their proceedings as Dangerous to the Church and State, pronouncing the Gifts, Feoffments, and contrivances made to the uſe aforeſaid, to be illegal, and ſo diſſolved the ſame, confiſcating their money to the King's uſe.

About this time died *Samuel Harſenet* Archbiſhop of *York*. He lies buried at *Chigwel*-Church in *Eſſex*, where he built a School.

Now

Now the Sabbatarian controversie began to be revived. *Theophilus Bradburn*, a Minister of *Suffolk*, had five years before set forth a book, Entitled. *A defence of the most ancient and Sacred Ordinance of God, the Sabbath-day*. *Francis White* now Bishop of *Ely* was employed by his Majesty to confute Mr. *Bradburn*'s erroneous opinion. In the writing whereof many strict people were offended at some expressions dropping from his pen. Hereupon many Books were wrote, and controversies on this subject were multiplied. These were distinguished into three several opinions.

* *Sabbatarians.*
Moderate men.
Anti-sabbatarians.

In *Sommerset-shire* some of the Justices were offended at the keeping of *Wakes, Church-ales*, &c. on the Lord's day, which occasioned many disorders to be committed. They moved the Lord Chief-justice *Richardson*, and Baron *Denham* then in their circuit in the *Lent-vacation* to make some order therein. These in compliance with their desire, make an Order to suppress such Revels, in regard of the manifold inconveniences daily arising thereby, enjoyning the Constables to deliver a Copy thereof to the Minister of every Parish, who on the first Sunday in *Feburary*, and likewise the two first Sundays before Easter, was to publish the same every year. This was looked upon by the Bishops as an Usurpation of Ecclesiastical jurisdiction, and they therefore procured a Commission directed to the Bishop of *Bath* and *Wells*, and other Divines, and to enquire into the manner of publishing this Order, and the carriage of the Judges in the Business. Notwithstanding which, the Chief-justice at the next Assizes gave strict charge against the Revels, requiring an account of the publication and execution of the former order, punishing some persons for the breach thereof. This Order was afterward revoked, And hereupon, the Justices of that County made an humble supplication to the King for suppressing the foresaid Assemblies.

Sir *Rich.* *Baker's* Chro.

In this juncture of time a Declaration for sports on the Lord's day, published in the Reign of King *James*, was revived, and enlarged. This gave great distast to many, and some Ministers were suspended, and some deprived *ab officio & beneficio*; and more vexed in the High-commission. All Bishops urged not the reading of the Book with rigour alike, nor punished the refusal with equal severity. The thickest complaints came from the Diocess of *Norwich*, and of *Bath* and *Wells*. Much was the Archbishop's moderation in his own Diocese, silencing but three ; in whom also a concurrence of other Non-conformities) through the whole extent thereof.

Here

Here it is much to be lamented, that such who at the time of the Sabbatarian controversie were the strictest observers of the Lord's day, are now become (in another extreme) the greatest neglecters, yea contemners thereof.

Now such *Irish* Impropriations as were in the Crown, were by the King restored to the Church, to the great Diminishing of the Royal Revenue. And Archbishop *Laud* was a worthy Instrument in moving the King to so pious a work.

A Convocation (concurrent with a Parliament) was called, and held at *Dublin* in *Ireland*, wherein the Nine and thirty Articles of the Church of *England* were received in *Ireland* for all to subscribe to.

Dr. *William Juxon* Bishop of *London*, was made Lord Treasurer of *England*, whose carriage was so discreet in that place, that it procured a general love to him.

Anno 1635. Archbishop *Laud* kept his Metropolitical Visitation, and hence-forward Conformity was more vigorously pressed than before: Now many differences about Divine Worship began to arise, and many Books were written *pro* and *con*. One controversie was about the Holyness of our Churches. Another about Adoration towards the Altar. A Controversie was also started about the posture of the Lord's Boord, Communion-table, or Altar. This last controversie was prosecuted with much needless animosity. Indeed if moderate men had *had* the managing of these matters, the accommodation had been easie.

In *June* Anno 1636. Mr. *Prynne*, Dr. *Bastwick*, and Mr. *Burton*, were sentenced in the High-commission-court. Some three years since Mr. *Pyrnne* set forth a Book, called *Histrio-mastrix*, for which he was censured to lose his ears on the Pillory, and for a long-time (after two removals to the fleet) Imprisoned in the Tower: whence he dispersed New Pamphlets, against the established Discipline of the Church of *England*, for which he was indited in the Star-chamber.

Dr. *John Bastwick* set forth a Book, Entitled *Flagellum Pontificis, & Episcoporum latialium*, in a fluent Latine Style. He was accused in the High-commission, committed to the Gate-house, where he wrote a second Book, taxing the injustice of the proceedings of the High-commission, for which he was indited in the Star-chamber.

Mr. *Burton* Preached a Sermon on the last fifth of *November*. On Prov. 24. 21. *My son, fear thou the Lord and the King, and meddle not with them that are subject to change.* This Sermon was afterwards Printed, charging the Prelats for Introducing several Innovations in Divine Worship, for which as a Libel, he was indited in the Starchamber. Mr. *Prynne*'s Plea is rejected, and his answer refused; so is Dr. *Bastwick's*: and Mr. *Burton*'s is cast out for imperfect. The Censure of the Court was, that they should lose their ears in the Palace-yard

the Church of Great Britain.

yard at *Westminster*, fining them also five thousand pounds a man to his Majesty, and perpetual Imprisonment in three remote places. The Lord *Finch* added to Mr. *Prynne*'s Censure, that he should be branded in each Cheek with *S. L.* for a slanderous Libeller, to which the whole Court agreed. Two days after, three Pillories were set up in Palace-yard; or one double one, and a single one at some distance, for Mr. *Prynne*, as the chief offender. Mr. *Burton* first suffered, making a long speech in the Pillory, not entire; but interrupted with occasional expressions; His ears were cut so close, that the *Head-artery* being cut, the blood abundantly streamed down upon the Scaffold, at which he did not shrink at all

Dr. *Bastwick* succeeded him. His friends highly commended the erection of his mind over pain and shame. Others conceived, that anger in him acted the part of patience, as to the stout undergoing of his sufferings.

The Censure was with all rigour executed on Mr. *Prynne*, commended more for his kindly patience than either of his Predecessors in that place. Not long after they were removed, Mr. *Prynne* to *Carnarvan-castle* in *Wales*; Dr. *Bastwick* and Mr. *Burton*, the one to *Lancaster-castle*; the other to *Laneeston* in *Cornwal*. The two latter again were removed, one to the Isle of *Scilly*; the other to the Isle of *Gernezey*, and Mr. *Prynne* to *Mount-orguile-castle* in *Jersey*.

Next came the Bishop of *Lincoln* to be Censured in the Star-chamber. After the great Seal some ten years since taken from him, he retired himself to *Bugden* in *Huntington-shire*, where he lived very hospitably, and had great concourse. Among others, Sir *John Lamb*, Dean of the Arches, formerly a favourite of the Bishop of *Lincoln* (fetcht off from being prosecuted in Parliament, and Knighted by his means) with Dr. *Sibthorp*, *Allen* and *Burden*, two Proctors, came to visit him: and being at dinner with him there was much discourse about Non-conformists. The Bishop knowing these to be busie men in the prosecution of such, advised them to take off their heavy hand from them, informing them, that the King intended to use them hereafter with more mildness *&c.* adding that He had communicated this unto him by his own mouth.

The Bishop of *Lincoln* censured.

A few years after Sir *John Lamb* upon some difference with the Bishop, informed against him for revealing the King's secrets; whereupon an Information was put in against him in the Star-chamber, unto which Bishop *Williams* by good advice of Counsel did plead and demurre, as containing no matter fit for the Cognisance of that Court, as concerning words spoken of matters done in Parliament, and secrets pretended to be revealed by him, a Privy-counsellour, and Peer of Parliament, and therefore not to be heard but in that high Court. The Demurrer being rendred useless in the Bishop's Defence, he put in a

R r   strong

strong plea, which likewise being argued and debated in open Court, came at last to the same fate with the demurrer, as referred to Judge *Richardson*, and smothered by him in a Chamber.

This plea thus over-ruled, the Bishop put in a special answer to the Information, declaring, how all was grounded by a Combination of the persons named in the Bill, out of an intent to advance themselves, &c. To this special answer, Attourney *Noy* rejoyned in issue, admitting the Bishop to prove his special matters by his Witnesses. After a while, the Attorney being somewhat remiss in the prosecution, one *Richard Kilvert*, became the Bishop's Prosecutor, who had found out, that one *John Prigion*, a Register of *Lincoln* and *Leicester*, was a most material Witness in the Bishop's defence, the credit of whose testimony he desired to invalidate, by charging him with getting a Bastard on one *Elizabeth Hodson*. This Bastard was by the Sessions at *Lincoln*, ordered to be kept by *Prigion*, as the reputed Father thereof, but at a Sessions following, the order was reversed, and the Child fathered on one *Bourn*, and *Prigion* acquitted; and at a third Sessions it is returned upon *Prigion* again. This last Order of Sessions was again dissolved as illegal, by the Judges of the King's Bench, and *Prigion* cleared from the Child charged on him; in the doing whereof it was said, that *Powel* and *Owen*, two Agents of the Bishops, did menace, and tamper, with the Witnesses.

Hence-forward *Kilvert* let fall his first information in the *Star-chamber*, and employed all his power on the proof of *Subornation*, and therein he succeeded. The Bishop was fined eight thousand pounds, and a thousand marks to Sir *John Munson*, with *Suspension ab Officio, & Beneficio*, and to be imprisoned during the King's pleasure. All his Preferments in the Church were sequestred to the use of the King; and the Archbishop of *Canterbury*, as Archbishop of the Province, exercised all kind of Ecclesiastical Jurisdiction throughout the Diocess of *Lincoln*, not only as an Ordinary of that Diocess, but as Visitor of all those Colledges, which had any dependance on that See. At the same time were fined, with the Bishop, *George Walker*, his Secretary, *Cadwallader Powel*, his Steward, at three hundred pounds a piece, and *Thomas Lund*, the Bishop's Servant, at a thousand marks, all as Defendants in the same Cause; yet none of them was imprisoned, save *Lund* for a few weeks, and their fine never called upon to this day.

About four years after, viz. 1640. when this Bishop was fetcht out of the Tower, and restored a Peer in Parliament he therein presented several grievances, concerning the prosecution of this Cause against him. And the Parliament ordered all the Records of that Suit in the *Star-chamber* to be obliterated.

Sir *Rich. Ba-ker's Chron.* In the year 1616. King *James* had obtained an Act of the General Assembly at *Aberdeen*, for the compiling a Liturgy, which was to be first

first presented to the King, and, after his approbation, universally received throughout the Kingdom. This Book was framed, and sent up to the King, who himself perused, revised it, referring it also to the consideration of others, in whom he much confided. And after his own and their Observation, Additions, Expunctions, Mutations, &c. he returned it to *Scotland*, to be commended to that Church: but before a period was put to that business, the King died.

King *Charles* understanding his Father's intention, in composing a Liturgy for the Church of *Scotland*, ordereth the Archbishop of *Canterbury*, the Bishop of *Ely*, together with divers other Bishops of both Nations, to revise and correct (as they should think meet) the Liturgy compiled in his Father's life-time (which very little differeth from that of *England*) ordereth it to be sent to the Council in *Scotland*, to be made use of there.

1637.

On *July* twenty three, 1637. as the Dean of *Edenborough* began to read the Book in St. *Giles* his Church, a sudden uproar began by the women, and baser sort of people. The Bishop appointed to preach, goes into the Pulpit, hoping to convince them of their irreverent carriage which nothing prevailed; for they were the more insolent, flinging stools, stones, and whatever else came next to hand, at him, so that he hardly escaped with life. Divers other Churches were infested with the like fury: but by the Industry of the Archbishop of St. *Andrews*, Lord Chancellor, and other Magistrates, the tumult was appeased, some were afterwards apprehended, and endeavours made to find out the first beginner.

Lambert Wood of the Life and Reign of King Charles.

But not long after, a great concourse of people, from all parts of that Kingdom, came to *Edinborough*, which occasioned the Lords of the Council to put forth several Proclamations to prevent the like disorders, but they nothing prevailed. For, the next day, the Bishop of *Galloway*, going to the Council, was followed by a great multitude reviling him until he came to the Council-door, where he was no sooner entred, but they beset the House with very great numbers, threatening destruction to all that were within. The Council require aid of the Provost, and other Magistrates of the City, who return answer, that they were in the like danger. The tumult still increasing, they of the City were forced, for the safeguard of their own lives, to subscribe as followeth.

1. To *joyn in opposition to the Service-book, and to petition against it.*
2. To *restore* Ramsey *and* Rollock, *two silenced Ministers.*
3. To *receive in Mr.* Henderson, *formerly silenced.*

Which being signed, the Council thought was a good step to suppress the tumult. But entring into the High-street, the Lord Treasurer, and other Lords, were fresh assaulted, trodden under foot, and brought

brought back by violence to the Council-house; where being in great danger, they require aid of divers Noble-men, disaffected to the Common-prayer-book, who promised what aid they possibly could, and in the end returned home safe.

In the afternoon Proclamation was made at the Cross at *Ebenborough,* to prevent the like disorders, but to small effect: some Citizens demanding the Restitution of the Ministers, and the performance of what was subscribed.

Suddenly two Petitions were presented against the Common-prayer-book, and the Composers and Abettors of it; which Petitions were *Lamb. Wood.* sent to the King (with the narrative of the whole) who immediately *History King* sent Instructions for adjourning the Term to *Sterling,* a strong place, *Charles.* and to make Proclamation of severe penalties to be inflicted on the breakers of the peace, which was no sooner proclaimed, but the Lord *Hume, Lindsey,* and divers others, protest against it, and in contempt of Authority compell'd the Heraulds to hear the Protest, or Covenant read.

These troublesome beginnings, did afterward occasion *the solemn League and Covenant,* whereby the greatest part of the Nation united themselves to defend their Priviledges, as was pretended, and which laid the foundation of a long and woful War in both Kingdoms.

They erected a new Government among themselves, which consisted *Heylin on the* of four Tables for the four Orders of the State, *viz.* the Noblemen, *life of Arch-* Barons, Burgesses, and Ministers. These fixed themselves in *Edenb-* *bishop Laud,* rough, leaving the Lords of Council and Session to make merry at *Ster-* *part. 2.* *ling,* where they had little else to do than to follow their pleasures.

The Tables being formed, they resolved upon renewing the ancient Confession of that *Kirk,* with a Band thereunto subjoyned, but accommodated to the present occasion; which had been signed by King *James* on *January* 28. *Anno* 1580. And by this Band they entred Covenant for maintenance of their Religion then professed, and his Majesty's person; but aiming at the contrary. And to this Covenant they required an Oath of all the Subjects, which was as great an Usurpation of the Regal power, as they could take upon themselves, for confirming their own authority, and the peoples obedience, in any project whatsoever; which should afterwards issue from those Tables.

Return we now to *England,* where we shall find things in a better condition, at least to outward appearance. And now the Metropolitical visitation having been carried into all parts of the Realm of *England,* and Dominion of *Wales,* the Archbishop of *Canterbury* began to cast his eye upon the Islands of *Guernsey* and *Jersey,* two Islands lying on the Coast of *Normandy;* to the Dukedom whereof they once belonged, and in the Right of that Dukedom to the Crown of *England.* As parts of *Normandy* they were subject in Ecclesiastical matters to the Bishops of *Con-*
stance

stance in that Dukedom, and so continued till the Reformation of Religion here in *England*, and were then added to the Diocess and Jurisdiction of the Bishops of *Winchester*.

Heylin's Hist. of Archbishop Laud. Ad An. 1637.

But the *Genevian* Discipline being more agreeable to such Preachers as came to them from *France*, they obtained the exercise thereof in the eighth year of Queen *Elizabeth*, *Anno* 1565. The whole Goverment distinguished into two *Classes*, both meeting in a Synod every second or third year, according to the order of their Book of Discipline (digested by *Snape* and *Cartwright*) in a Synod held at *Guernsey*, *June* 28. 1576.

In this manner they continued till King *James* his time, when the Churches in the Isle of *Jersey*, falling into some disorder, and being under an immediate Governor, who was no great friend to *Calvin's* Platform, they were necessitated, for avoiding a great mischief, to cast themselves into the Arms of the Church of *England*.

The principal Ecclesiastical Officer, whilst they were under the Bishops of *Constance*, had the Title of *Dean*, for each Island one; the several powers, both of the Chancellor and Archdeacon, being united in his Person.

This Office is restored again, his Jurisdiction marked out, his Fees appointed, his Revenue setled; but made accountable for his Administration to the Bishop's of *Winchester*.

The English Liturgy is translated also into French, to be read in their Churches: Instructions first, and afterwards a Body of Canons framed, for regulating both Ministers and people in their several duties.

Now it was resolved, that the Metropolitical visitation should be held in each of them at the next opening of the Spring. And the Archbishop had designed a Person for his principal Visitor, who had spent some time in either Island, and was well acquainted with the Bailiffs, Ministers, and Men of special note among them. But the Affairs of *Scotland* growing worse, this Council was laid by.

But these Islands were not out of his mind. The Islanders used to breed such of their Sons, as they designed for the Ministry, either at *Saumur*, or *Geneva*, from whence they returned well-seasoned with *Calvinism*. Therefore to allure the people to send their Children to *Oxon*, or *Cambridge*, he thought of providing some preferment for them in our Universities.

It now happened, that one *Hubbard*, the Heir of Sir *Miles Hubbard*, Citizen and Alderman of *London*, died, to whom, upon an Inquisition taken after his death in due form of Law, no Heir was found, which could lay claim to his Estate. Which so unexpectedly fallen to the Crown, and being a fair Estate withall, the Archbishop perswaded his Majesty to bestow some small part thereof upon pious uses. And so much was allotted out of it, as, for the present, served sufficiently to endow three Fellowships,

ships, for the perpetual education of so many of the Natives of Guernsey and Jersey. These Fellowships to be founded in Exeter, Jesus, and Pembrook Colledges, that being disperst into several Houses, there might be an increase both of Fellows, and Revenues of the said Foundations. By means whereof he did (as Doctor Heylin observeth) both piously and prudently provide for those Islands, and the advancement of Conformity among them for the future.

It is not to be thought, that the Papists were all this while asleep. *An.* 1636. *Prancani* arriving in *England*, brought with him many pretended Relicks of Saints, Medals, and pieces of Gold, with the Pope's Picture stamped upon them, to be distributed among those of the Party, but chiefly to the Ladies of the Court, and Countrey, to whom he made the greatest part of his Applications: Then he practised upon some of the principal Lords, and used his best endeavours to be brought into the acquaintance of the Lord Archbishop of *Canterbury*. But his Grace neither liked the Man, nor the Message he came about, and admitted him neither to complement, nor communication. However! the Popish faction multiplying in some numbers about the Court, resorted more openly to the Masses at *Sommerset-house*, where the Capuchins had obtained both a Chappel and Convent. Of this none bears the blame but the Archbishop, who is traduced in Libels, and common talk, for the principal Architect in the plot, and the contriver of the mischief.

Awakened by so many Alarms, he had good cause to look about him, but more at the great noise not long after raised about the seduceing of the Countess of *Newport*, to the Church of *Rome*, effected by the practices of *Walter Mountague*, a younger Son of the Earl of *Manchester*, and the importunities of *Toby Mathews* (an undeserving Son of a worthy Father.) *Con* interposing in it as he found occasion. Wherefore he passionately besought the King, that they might be barred, either from coming into the Court at all, or to give no offence and scandal to their misbehaviours. Hereupon *Mountague*, and *Mathews*, were discharged the Court, the one betaking himself to his Countrey-practice, the other for a time to his former Travels in *France* and *Italy*.

The next year he moved for a Proclamation, for the calling in of a Popish Book, written in French by *Francis Sales*, Bishop of *Geneva*, translated into English, entitled an *Introduction to a holy life*. The Printer was thereupon apprehended, and the Translator diligently sought for to be brought to Justice. His Majesty caused the said Book to be called in, and as many as could be seized on, to be publickly burned.

But that which did most generally vindicate the Archbishop's reputation, was the enlarging and re-printing of his *Conference* with *Fisher* the Jesuite, even then when the Libellers were most fierce against him, to which he had been moved by some private friends, and afterwards advised to it by the King himself at the Council-Table.

Now

the Church of GREAT BRITAIN.

Now as he laboured by these means to preserve the Church of *England* from the growth of Popery, so he took care for preventing the subversion of it by the spreading of *Socinian* Heresies. He also procured a Decree to pass in *Star-chamber*, to regulate the Trade of Printing, and prevent all abuses of that Excellent Art to the disturbance of the Church.

Many Lecturers, who had been super-inducted into other Men's Cures, had deserted their Stations, because they would not read the Common-prayer in their Hoods and Surplices. And as for the position of the Communion-Table, it was no longer left to private Instructions, as it was at the first. It now began to be more openly avowed in the Visitation Articles of several Bishops and Archdeacons. *Heylin's Hist. of Archbish. Laud.*

The people in many trading Towns, which were near the Sea, having been long discharged of the bond of Ceremonies, no sooner came to hear of the least noise of a Conformity, but they spurn at it. And finding that they had lost the comfort of their Lecturers, and that their Ministers began to shrink at the name of a Visitation, it was no hard matter for those Ministers, and Lecturers, to perswade them to remove their dwellings, and transport their Trades.

Among the first which separated upon this account, were *Goodwyn*, *Nye*, *Burroughs*, *Bridge*, and *Symson*, who taking some of their followers with them, betook themselves unto *Holland*. *Goodwyn* and *Nye* retired to *Arnheim*, a Town of *Gelderland*; *Symson* and *Bridge* fixed at *Rotterdam*: where *Burroughs* placed himself I am yet to seek. These men embraced *Robinson's* model of Church-government in their Congregations, consisting of a co-ordination of several Churches for their mutual comfort, not a subordination of one to the other in the way of direction or command. Hence came that name of *Independents*, continued unto those among us, who neither associate themselves with the Presbyterians, nor embrace the frenzies of the Anabaptists. But *Rotterdam* grew too narrow a place for *Bridge* and *Symson*, and *Symson* was forced to leave it, and *Ward*, who succeeded him, tarried not long. More unity there was at *Arnheim*.

But the Brethren of the Separation in *England*, desiring elbow-room, cast their eye chiefly on *New-England*, a Countrey first discovered, to any purpose, by Captain *Gosnold*, *Anno* 1602. and in the next year surveyed more perfectly by some of *Bristol*; afterwards granted by King *James*, *Anno* 1606. unto a Corporation of Knights, Gentlemen, and Merchants, to be planted and disposed of for the Publick, under the direction of Chief Justice *Popham*, by whom a Colony was sent thither in the year next following, at what time they built St. *George's* Fort to secure their Haven. It never setled into form till the building of *New-Plinmouth*, *Anno* 1620. *New-Bristol*, *New-Boston*, and *New-Barnstable*, being quickly added to the other.

Do-

De Laet lib. 3. ca. 8.   De *Laet*, a good Chorographer, informeth us, in his Description of *America*, that the first Planters, and those which followed after them, were altogether of that Sect, which in *England* were called *Brownists*, many of which had formerly betaken themselves to *Holland*, but afterwards departed thence to joyn with their Brethren in *New-England*. In this estate they stood, *Anno* 1633. when *John de Laet* gave that character of them.

Whatsoever were the causes of their separation, Doctor *Heylin* saith, the crime was laid on the Archbishop of *Canterbury*: and among the Articles of his Impeachment by the House of Commons, we find this for one, *viz*. *That in his own person, and his Suffragans, Visitors, Chancellors*, &c. *he had caused divers learned, pious, and orthodox Preachers of God's Word to be silenced, suspended, deprived, excommunicated, or otherwise grieved, and vexed without any just cause*, &c. *and caused divers of his Majesties Subjects to forsake the Kingdom*. Hereupon (saith Doctor *Heylin*) so is the Judge to be accused for all those mischiefs, which the condemned Malefactors, when they once break prison, may design, and execute. And (saith my Author further) the principal Bell-weathers of these Flocks were *Cotton*, *Chauncy*, *Wells*, *Hooker*, and perhaps *Hugh Peters*.

It was once under consultation to send a Bishop over to them, for their better government, and back him with some Forces to compel, if he he were not otherwise able to perswade, obedience.

But this design was strangled in the first conception, by the violent breakings out of the Troubles in *Scotland*, where the Covenanters now began to raise Arms, levy Souldiers, invite home their Commanders abroad, impose Taxes upon the people, seize some of the King's Castles, raise Fortifications, prepare for a War, and chose old *David Lesley* for their General.

Saunderson of the Reign of King Charles.   To pacifie these distempers, *Hamilton* is designed for the King's High-Commissioner into *Scotland*. The Bishops, and others, advised the King to have delegated the Marquis of *Huntley* for his High-Commissioner, to manage the Affairs of *Scotland*. *Hamilton* trifleth away the time from *July* 32. 1637. until *June* 6. 1638. with Declarations, Proclamations, Messages, Letters, while the Scots raised Officers, Arms, Ammunition from abroad: four months more in vain Disputes, and three Journeys to the King, and back again, with the expence of so much money as might have reduced them by reward, or power. On *May* 26. he sets forward for *Scotland*, and coming to *Edenborough*, puts himself into *Holy-Rood-house*, where the first thing he did was, the waving of his attendance at the reading of the English Liturgy. Then he published the King's gratious Proclamation for the nulling of Service-book and High-Commission, promising an Assembly to be held at *Glascow*, *November* 21. 1638. and a Parliament at *Edenborough*, *May* 15. 1639. But nothing satisfied. But

But before the Assembly at *Glascow* was indicted, the Covenanters had so laid the plot, that none but those of their own party should have suffrage in it, not suffering the Archbishops and Bishops to sit as Moderators in their Presbyteries, where the Elections were to pass; and citing them to appear as Criminal persons at the said Assembly. The Archbishops, and Bishops, in the name of themselves and of all their Adherents, prepared their *declinator*, or protestation against the said *General Assembly*, and all the Acts and Conclusions of it, as being void and null in Law to all intents and purposes whatsoever: The day being come, *Hamilton* marcheth to the place appointed for the Session, in the equipage of an High-Commissioner, the Sword and Seal being carried before him, *&c.* The reading of his Commission, the putting in and rejecting of the *declinator*, the chusing of *Henderson* to be Moderator of the Assembly, the constituting of the Members of it, and some debates touching Votes and Suffrages, challenged by *Hamilton* for such as were Assessors to him, took up all their time, betwixt their first meeting and their dissolution, which was by proclamation solemnly declared on the twenty ninth of the same month.

But notwithstanding the said dissolution, the Members of the said Assembly continued their Session, and therein passed many Acts for the utter overthrow of the Polity and Government of the Church. They not only excommunicated the Bishops and their Adherents, but condemned the very Function it self to be *Antichristian*, and utterly to be abolished out of the Church. The like censure also they passed on the *Service-book* and the *Canons*, with the five Articles of *Perth*, and all the Arminian Tenets in case of Predestination, and declared all men subject to excommunication, and all other censures of the Church, who should refuse to yield obedience to all their determinations. And albeit his Majesty, by the same Proclamation, had commanded all his Subjects not to yield obedience to any of their Acts and Ordinances, yet those of the Assembly were resolved to maintain their Authority: and not only the Bishops and Clergy, but also as many of the Laity as had refused to subscribe to the Acts thereof, were deprived of their Offices and Preferments, banished their Country, and forced to fly into *England*, or other places, the King being unable to protect them from the power and malice of their Adversaries.

The King now thinks of raising an Army against the Scots: and a Loan, for the King's assistance against the Scots, is subscribed by many Lords of the Council, and Bishops, *&c.* Cardinal *Richlieu* was no small Incendiary in this business betwixt the King and Scots, who sent his Chaplain, and Almoner, Mr. *Thomas Chamberlain*, a Scotch-man, to assist the Confederates in advancing the business, and to attempt all wayes of exasperation, and not to depart from them till he might return with good news in this project.

Sir *Rich. Baker's Chron.*

About the latter end of this year died *John Spottiswood*, Archbishop of St. *Andrews*, at *London*, and was buried near unto King *James* in the Abbey-church of *Westminster*.

The King began his journey towards the North on *March* twenty seven, his Army being advanced before, the chief command whereof was committed to the Earl of *Arundel*.

The Scots presented a Petition to the King at his Camp near *Berwick*. And Commissioners being on both sides appointed, they came at last to this conclusion, on *June* 17. viz. first, That his Majesty should confirm whatsoever his Commissioner hath already granted in his Majesties name, and that from thenceforth all matters Ecclesiastical should be determined by the Assemblies of the Kirk, and all matters civil by the Parliament: and to that end a General Assembly to be indicted on the sixth of August, and a Parliament on the twentieth of the same month, in which Parliament an Act of Oblivion was to pass for the common peace and satisfaction of all parties: that the Scots, upon the publication of the accord, should within forty eight hours disband all their Forces, discharge all pretended Tables and Conventicles, restore unto the King all his Castles, Forts, and Ammunition of all sorts: the like restitution to be made to all his good Subjects of their liberties, lands, goods, &c. taken and detained from them, since the late pretended General Assembly at Glascow: that thereupon the King should presently recal his Fleet, and retire his Land-forces, and cause restitution to be made to all persons of their goods detained, and arrested, since the first of February.

But as for the proceedings of the Assembly at *Glascow*, they seem to have been left in the same condition in which they stood before his Majesties taking Arms. And the King doing nothing to the abrogating of them, when he was in the Head of a powerful Army, he could not expect, that the Scots could yield to any such abrogation, when he had no such Army to compel obedience.

And this immediately appeared on his Majesties signing the Agreement, and discharging his Army thereupon.

For the Covenanters, upon the declaration of this accord, produced a Protestation.

First, Of adhering to their late General Assembly at Glascow, and to all the proceedings there, especially the sentences of Deprivation, and Excommunication, of the sometimes pretended Bishops of that Kingdom, as they were termed.

Secondly, Of adhering to their solemn Covenant, and declaration of the Assembly, whereby the Office of Bishops is abjured.

Thirdly, That the Bishops have been malitious Incendiaries of his Majesty against this Kingdom by their wicked calumnies; and that if they return to this Kingdom, they be esteemed, and used, as accursed, &c.

Fourthly,

Fourthly, *That all the entertainers of the excommunicated Bishops should be orderly proceeded against with Excommunication, conform to the Acts and Constitutions of this* Kirk.

They continued their Meetings, and Consultations, as before they did, maintained their Fortifications at *Leith*, the Port-town to *Edenborough*, and kept their Officers and Commanders in continual pay. His Majesty hereupon sent for some of the Chiefs of them to come unto him to *Berwick*, but was refused in his Commands. The Earls of *Kinnoul*, and *Traquair*, Chief Justice *Elphinston*, and Sir *James Hamilton*, all Privy Counsellors, were pulled violently out of their Coach, on a suspition that some Bishops were disguised among them; that the King might have some cause to suspect, that there could be no safety for him in such a place, and among people so enraged, notwithstanding his great clemency toward them in the *pacification*.

In this condition of Affairs his Majesty returned toward *London* in the end of *July* 1639. leaving the Scots to play their own game as they listed; having first nominated *Traquair*, as his High-Commissioner, for managing both the Assembly and the following Parliament. *Heylin's Hist. of Archbish. Laud. part. 2.*

In the first meeting of the two, they acted over all the parts they had plaid at *Glascow*, to the utter abolition of Episcopacy, and the ruine of all that adhered to it, their actings in it being confirmed in his name by the High-Commission.

The news whereof caused the King to send for the Lord *Wentworth* out of *Ireland*, who was presently made Lord Lieutenant of *Ireland*, and not long after, with great solemnity, created Earl of *Strafford* in the County of *York*. As Lord Lieutenant he had power to appoint a Deputy, that he might the better attend the service here without any prejudice to that Kingdom: which Office he committed to *Wansford*, a *York-shire* Gentleman, whom he had took along with him into *Ireland* at his first going thither.

His Majesty was pleased to commit the conduct of the Scottish Affairs to a Juncto of three, namely, the Archbishop of *Canterbury*, the Earl of *Strafford*, and the Marquiss of *Hammilton*.

These three move his Majesty to call a Parliament: and it was concluded, that a Parliament should be called on *April* 13. 1640. In the mean time the Lord Lieutenant held a Parliament in *Ireland*, and so governed the affair, that an Army of eight thousand Horse and Foot was speedily raised, and money granted by the Parliament to keep them in pay, to furnish them with Ammunition, Arms, and all other necessaries.

And the Lords of the Council here subscribed largely for the carrying on of the War, until such time as the Parliament should convene.

The Scots being informed of the King's preparation for a War, sent the Earl of *Dumferling*, the Lord *Loudon*, Sir *William Douglas*, and Mr. *Barkham*, to represent the Affairs of their transactions, which were received by the King in a friendly manner.

Some dayes being unprofitably spent in these debates, the Archbishop, and the rest of the Committee delegated for this business, made a report of the whole business to the rest of the Council, who came to this result, *That since the Scots could not be reclaimed to their obedience by other means, they were to be reduced by force.*

Therefore the Scots as much bestirred themselves on the other side. Part of the walls of *Edenborough-castle*, with all the Ordnance upon it, had fallen down on the nineteenth of *November* last, being the Anniversary day of his Majesties birth, for the repair whereof they would neither suffer Timber, nor other Materials, to be carried to it: but on the contrary, they began to raise Fortifications against it, with an intent to block it up, and render it unuseful to his Majesties service. Neither would they suffer the Souldiers to come into the Market to recruit their victuals. They made provisions of great quantity of Artillery, Munition, and Arms, from forreign parts; laid Taxes of ten Marks in the hundred upon all the Subjects; scattered abroad many seditious Pamphlets, for justifying themselves, and seducing others; some of which were burnt, in *England*, by the hand of the Hangman; fortified *Inchgarvy*, and other places; imprisoned the Earl of *Southesk*, and other Persons of Quality, for their fidelity to the King: took to themselves the government of *Edenborough*; and employed their Emissaries in *England*, to sollicit them to aid them in maintaining the War against their Sovereign.

But their chief corespondence was with *France*, and *Ireland*. In *France* they had made sure of Cardinal *Richlieu*, who governed all Affairs in that Kingdom. In *Ireland* they had a strong party of natural Scots, planted in *Ulster* by King *James*, upon the forfeited Estates of *Tir-Owen*, *Tir-Connel*, *Odighirty*, &c. But *Wentworth* crushed them in the beginning of the combination, seizing upon such Ships and Men as came thither from *Scotland*, imprisoning some, fining others, and putting an Oath upon the rest. By which Oath they were bound to abjure the Covenant, not to aid the Covenanters against the King, nor to protest against any of his royal Edicts, as their Brethren in *Scotland* use to do: for the refusing of which Oath, he fined one Sir *Henry Steward*, and his Wife, at no less than five thousand pound apiece; two of their Daughters, and one *James Gray* of the same confederacy, at the sum of three thousand pound apiece, committing them to prison for not paying the fines imposed on them.

Some Scots having endeavoured to betray the Town and Castle of *Carick-fergus* to a Noble-man of that Countrey, the principal Conspirator was executed. Finally,

the Church of Great Britain.

Finally, The Lord Lieutenant gave a power to the Bishop of *Down* and *Connor,* and other Bishops of that Kingdom, and their several Chancellors, to attach the bodies of all such of the meaner sort, who either should refuse to appear before them upon citation, or to perform all lawful Decrees, and Orders, made by the said Bishops, &c. and to commit them to the next Gaol, till they should conform, or answer the contempt at the Council-Table. By means whereof the poorer sort became very obedient to their several Bishops.

In the mean time the Archbishop of *Canterbury* is intent on the preservation of the Hierarchy, and the Church of *England,* against the practices of the Scots, and Scotizing English: and no less busied in digesting an Apology for vindicating the Liturgy commended to the *Kirk* of *Scotland.* He took order for translating the Scottish Liturgy into the Latin Tongue, that being published with the Apology which he had designed, it might give satisfaction to the world of his Majesties Piety, and his own great care, the orthodoxy and simplicity of the Book it self, and the perverseness of the Scots in refusing all of it. Which Work was finished, and left with him: the present distemper of the times, and the troubles which fell heavily on him, putting an end to it in the first beginning.

He recommended to Doctor *Hall,* then Bishop of *Exon,* the writing of a Book in defence of *the Divine right of Episcopacy,* in opposition to the Scots and their Adherents.

Exeter having undertaken it, sent the first delineations of the Pourtracture to *Lambeth* in the end of *October,* which were generally well approved of by the Metropolitan: who having made some alterations, sent them back with many kind expressions of a fair acceptance. And such was the freedom he used in declaring his judgment in the case; and such the Authority which his Reasons carried along with them, that the Bishop of *Exon* found good cause to correct his Opinon according to the Rules of these Animadversions; agreeable unto which the Book was writ, and published not long after, under the name of *Episcopacy by Divine right,* &c.

Whilst the Archbishop laboured to support Episcopacy on the one side, some of the adverse party laboured as much to suppress it, by lopping off the branches first, and afterwards by laying the Axe to the root of the Tree. *Bagshaw,* a Lawyer of some standing, of the *Middle-Temple,* began to question the Bishop's place and vote in Parliament, their Temporal power, and the authority of the Commission. For being chosen *Reader,* by that House for the *Lent-vacation ,* he first selected for the Argument of his discoursings, the Statute of 25 *Edw.* 3. *cap.* 7. His main design was intended chiefly for the defence of such Prohibitions, as formerly had been granted by the Courts in *Westminster-hall,* to stop the proceedings of the *Court-Christian,* and specially of the High-Com-

Commission, and in the next place to deny the Authority of the Commission it self, as before was noted. Hereupon the Archbishop informs his Majesty both of the Man and of his design, how far he had gone in justifying the proceedings of the Scottish Covenanters, in decrying the temporal power of Church-men, and the undoubted right of Bishops to their place in Parliament: his Majesty hereupon gives order to *Finch*, the new Lord Keeper, to interdict all further Reading on those points. Hereupon it was soon found, that nothing could be done therein without leave from the King, and no such leave to be obtained without the consent of the Archbishop. To *Lambeth* therefore goes the Reader, where he found no admittance till the third Address, and was then told, *That he was fallen upon a Subject neither safe nor seasonable, which should stick closer to him then he was aware of.* Whereupon *Bagshaw* hasteneth out of Town.

Short view of the life and reign of King *Charles*, p. 77.

The Parliament came together on *April* 13. 1640. instead of acting any thing for his Majesties service, they were at the point of passing a Vote for blasting his War against the Scots. To prevent which, his Majesty was forced to dissolve them on *May* 5. the Convocation still continuing, who granted him a Benevolence of four shillings in the pound for all their Ecclesiastical promotions, to be paid six years together then next ensuing.

The Convocation sate after the breaking up of the Parliament. A new Commission was brought from his Majesty, by vertue whereof they were warranted to sit still, not in the capacity of a Convocation, but of a Synod, to prepare their Canons for the Royal assent thereunto. But Doctor *Brewnrigg*, Doctor *Hacket*, Doctor *Holdsworth*, Mr. *Warmstrey*, with others, to the number of thirty six (the whole House consisting of about sixscore) protested against the continuance of the Convocation. To satisfie these, an Instrument was brought into the Synod, signed with the hands of the Lord Privy-seal, the two chief Justices, and other Judges, justifying their so sitting in the nature of a Synod, to be legal according to the Laws of the Realm. Now their disjoynted meeting being set together again, they consulted about new Canons.

I shall set down the number, and titles, of the several Canons.

1. *Concerning the Regal power.*
2. *For the better keeping of the day of his Majesties Inauguration.*
3. *For suppressing of the growth of Popery.*
4. *Against Socinianism.*
5. *Against Sectaries.*
6. *An Oath enjoyned for the preventing of all Innovations in Doctrine and Government.*

7. *A*

the Church of GREAT BRITAIN.

7. *A Declaration concerning some Rites and Ceremonies,*
8. *Of preaching for Conformity.*
9. *One Book of Articles of enquiry to be used at all Parochial visitations.*
10. *Concerning the Conversation of the Clergy.*
11. *Chancellors Patents.*
12. *Chancellors alone not not to censure any of the Clergy in sundry cases.*
13. *Excommunication, and Absolution, not to be pronounced but by a Priest.*
14. *Concerning the Commutations, and the disposing of them.*
15. *Concerning some Concurrent Jurisdictions.*
16. *Concerning Licenses to marry.*
17. *Against vexatious Citations.*

The Oath it self I shall set down, as I find it in the Life of Archbishop *Laud*, written by Doctor *Heylin*, in this form following, *viz.*

I A. B. do swear, That I do approve the Doctrine, and Discipline, or Government established in the Church of England, *as containing all things necessary to salvation; And that I will not endeavour by my self, or any other, directly, or indirectly, to bring in any Popish doctrine, contrary to that which is so established. Nor will I ever give my consent to alter the Government of this Church by Archbishops, Bishops, Deans, and Archdeacons, &c: As it stands now established, and as by right it ought to stand; nor yet ever subject it to the usurpations and superstitions of the See of* Rome. *And all these things I do plainly and seriously acknowledge and swear, according to the plain and common sence and understanding of the same words, without any equivocation, or mental evasion, or secret reservation whatsoever. And this I do heartily, willingly and truly, upon the faith of a Christian. So help me God in* Jesus Christ.

Toward the close of the Convocation, Doctor *Griffith* made a motion, that there might be a new Edition of the Welsh Church-bible, some sixty years first translated into Welsh by the endeavours of Bishop *Morgan*, but not without many mistakes and omissions of the Printer. The matter was committed to the care of the Welsh Bishops, but nothing was effected therein.

Near the ending of the Synod *Godfrey Goodman*, Bishop of *Glocester*, privately acquainted the Archbishop of *Canterbury*, that he could not in his Conscience subscribe the new Canons. The Archbishop being present with the Synod in King *Henry* the Seventh his Chappel, said unto him, *My Lord of* Glocester, *I admonish you to subscribe*: and presently
after,

after, *My Lord of* Glocelter, *I admonish you the second time to subscribe:* and immediately after, *I admonish you to subscribe.* To all which the Bishop pleaded Conscience, and returned a denial. Some dayes after he was committed to the Gate-house. Soon after the same Canons were subscribed at *York*, and on the last of *June* following the said Canons were publickly printed, with the Royal assent affixed thereunto.

Fuller. Church History. ad An. 1640.

Various were mens censures upon these Canons. But most took exception against that clause in the Oath, *We will never give any consent to alter this Church-governmet,* as if the same were intended to abridge the liberty of King and State in future Parliaments, and Convocations, if hereafter they saw cause to change any thing therein. Yet others with a favourable sence endeavoured to qualifie this suspitious clause, whereby the taker of this Oath was tied up from consenting to any alteration, saying, that these words, [*We will never give any consent to alter*] are intended here to be meant only of a voluntary and pragmatical alteration, when men conspire and endeavour to change the present Government of the Church, in such particulars as they do dislike, without the consent of their Superiors.

Bishop *Goodman*, on *July* the tenth, made acknowledgment of his fault before the Lords of the Council, and took the Oath enjoyned in the sixth Canon, for preserving the Doctrines and Discipline of the Church of *England*, against all Popish doctrines which were thereunto repugnant. Upon the doing whereof he was restored, by his Majesty, to his former liberty. Yet in the time of his last sickness, it is said, that he declared himself to be a Member of the Church of *Rome*, and caused it so to be expressed in his last Will and Testament.

On *December* 27. 1639. at night, and the night following, there was such a violent Tempest, that many of the Boats, which were drawn to Land at *Lambeth*, were dashed one against the other, and were broke to pieces: and that the shafts of two Chimneys were blown down upon the roof of the Archbishop's Chamber, and beat down both the Lead and Rafters upon his Bed, in which ruine he must needs have perished, if the roughness of the Water had not forced him to keep his Chamber at *White-hall.*

Heylin's Hist. of Archbishop Laud. ad An. 1640.

A like mischance happened the same night at *Croydon* (a retiring place belonging to the Archbishop of *Canterbury*) where one of the Pinacles fell from the Steeple, beat down the Lead and Roof of the Church above twenty foot square.

But that which was more remarkable than either of these, was that which happened the same night at *Canterbury*, in the Metropolitical Church, where one of the Pinacles upon the top of the *Belfrey*-Tower, which carried a Vane with this Archbishop's Arms upon it, was violently struck down, but born a good distance from the Steeple, to fall upon the

Roof

Roof of the Cloyster, where the Armes of the Archiepiscopal See it self were ingraven in Stone: which Armes being broke to pieces by the fall of the other: on *Friday* night, *January* 24. 1639. he dreamed, that his Father (who died 46. years before) came to him, being to his thinking seemingly well and cheerful, that his Father asked him, what he did there: that after some speech, he demanded of his Father how long he would stay there; and that his Father made this answer, he would stay till he had him along with him. Which made such an *impression on him, that he thought fit to remember this in his Breviate.*

A brute being spread abroad, *That the late Parliament had been dissolved by his procurement*; a paper was pasted up at the Exchange, by *John Lilburn*, animating the Apprentices to sack his House at *Lambeth*, on the *Monday* following, and that night we was assaulted by five hundred of the Rabble, who strove to force an entrance, but were repulsed. And having fortified his House with some pieces of Canon, he with-drew to his Chamber at *Whitehall* till the Rage of the people was blown over. Some of the principal Actors in this Sedition being apprehended and committed to the Goal in *Southwark*, were forcibly delivered by others of their Accomplices, who brake open that and all other Prisons in that precinct, for which one *Benstead*, one of the Ring-leaders was retaken, arraigned, condemned, hanged, drawn and quartered, on *May* 21. Yet for all this, Libels were scattered against the Archbishop in most parts of the City. And his Majesty being then newly gone in person with an Army against the Scots, about the end of *August* a paper was dropt in *Covent-garden*, encouraging the Souldiers and Apprentices to fall upon him, yet was there no tumult raised upon it.

Then he gave order, that the High-commission should be kept at St. *Paul's*: and the Commissioners sitting there, on *October* 22. were violently assaulted by a mixt multitude of Sectaries, to the number of two thousand, crying out, *They would have no Bishops, nor High Commission.* In which tumult having frighted away the Judges, Advocates, and Officers of the Court, they brake down all the seats and benches which they found in the Consistory; so that a guard was set upon that Church, as before at *Westminster*, not onely at the next sitting of the said Commissioners, but at the first meeting of the Convocation, which soon after followed.

The Scots were now entred the Realm in hostile manner: and having put by his Majesties Forces at a place called *Newbourn*, they passed over the *Tine*, and presently made themselves Masters of the strong Town of *New-castle*, his Majesties Forces not very far distant. Many of the King's own Souldiers in their marchings through the Countrey, brake into Churches, pulled up the Rayles, threw down the Communion Tables, defaced the Common-Prayer Books, tore the Surplices, &c.

The Scots set forth a *Remonstrance*, wherein it was declared, That their Propositions and desires could find no access unto the ears of the Gratious King, by reason of the powerful Diversion of the Archbishop of *Canterbury* and the Deputy of *Ireland*, &c. who did onely side in all matters of Temporal and Spiritual Affairs, &c. This Remonstrance was seconded with another Pamphlet, called, *The Intention of the Army*. They signified therein, that they had no design to wast the goods of the People of *England*, or spoil their Countrey; but onely to become petitioners to his Majesty to call a Parliament, and to bring the said Archbishop and Lord Lieutenant to their condign punishments. And that the English might the better see whom they chiefly aimed at, a Book was published by the name of *Laudensium Autocatacrisis*, or the *Canterburians self-conviction*.

Heylin. Hist. of Archbish. Laud.

Upon this his Majesty was assaulted by a Petition from some Lords in the South, wherein complaint was made of the many inconveniences which had been drawn on this Kingdom, by the King's ingagings against the Scots, as also of the growth of Popery; of the pressing of the present payment of Ship-money; the dissolving of former Parliaments, Monopolies, Innovations, and some other grievances; among which the Canons which were made in the late Convocation, could not be omitted. For remedy whereof, His Majesty is desired to call a Parliament, &c. Subscribed by divers of the Nobility, presented to the King at *York* on *September* 3. and seconded by another from the City of *London* to the same effect.

The King therefore resolves to hold a Parliament, and on *November* 3. 1640. that long-lasting Parliament began. A Letter was writ to the Archbishop of *Canterbury*, advertising, That the Parliament of the twentieth year of King *Henry* the Eighth, which began in the fall of Cardinal *Wolsey*, continued in the Diminution of the Power and Priviledges of the Clergy, and ended in the dissolution of the Abbies and Religious Houses, was begun on the third day of *November*: and therefore that, for good-luck-sake, he would move the King to respite the first sitting of it for a day or two longer. But the Archbishop hearkned not to this advertisement, and the Parliament began at the time appointed.

On the morrow after began the Convocation at St. *Paul's* Church, handselled at their first meeting by the news of the Decease of Dr. *Neile*, Archbishop of *York*. But litle was done in this Convocation, but that a motion was made by Mr. *Warmstrey* (a Clerk for *Worcester*) That they should endeavour (according to the Levitical Law) to cover the pit which they had opened, and to prevent their Adversaries intention, by condemning such offensive Canons as were made the last Convocation. But they were loth to confess themselves guilty before they were accused.

Soon

the Church of Great Britain.

Soon after Mr. *Prynne*, Dr. *Baſtwick*, and Mr. *Burton* were diſcharged out of priſon, and brought with great Triumph into *London*. Biſhop *Williams* and Mr. *Osbaſton*, being remitted their fines, were reſtored to their Livings and Liberty. Doctor *Pocklington*, and Doctor *Bray* were cenſured; the former for Preaching and Printing, the latter for Licenſing two Books, one called *Sunday no Sabbath*: the other *The Chriſtian Alter*.

Not many days after the Earl of *Strafford* was impeached of High Treaſon, by Mr. *Pym*, in fourteen Articles. The Earl was forthwith Sequeſtred the Houſe, and committed to the Black Rod, and ſent not long after to the Tower.

December 18. Archbiſhop *Laud*, and Biſhop *Wren*, were voted by the Commons, Guilty of High Treaſon, and a charge was immediately brought in againſt Biſhop *Laud*, upon the Reading of which on *March* 1. he was ſent to the Tower.

The ſame moneth Alderman *Pennington*, with a great multitude out of *London*, petitioned the Houſe againſt Epiſcopal Government, and the Rites and Ceremonies of the Church. A Committee was appointed to conſider of matters of Religion, ſetled in the Upper Houſe of Parliament. Ten Earls, ten Biſhops, ten Barons. At the ſame time the Lords appointed a *Sub-committee*, to prepare matters fit for their cognizance (the Biſhop of *Lincoln* having the Chair in both) authorized to call together divers Biſhops and Divines, to conſult together for correcting what was amiſs, and to ſettle peace, *viz.*

The Archbiſhop of *Armagh*.	Dr. *Ralph Brownrigg*.
The Biſhop of *Durham*.	Dr. *Richard Holdſworth*.
The Biſhop of *Exeter*.	Dr. *John Hacket*.
Dr. *Samuel Ward*.	Dr. *Cornelius Burgeſſe*.
Dr. *William Twiſſe*.	Mr. *John White*.
Dr. *Robert Sanderſon*.	Mr. *Stephen Marſhall*.
Dr. *Daniel Featley*.	Mr. *Edmond Calamy*.
	Mr. *Thomas Hill*.

The place of their meeting was *Jeruſalem-chamber* in the Dean of *Weſtminſter's* houſe, where they had ſolemn debates ſix ſeveral days.

Firſt they conſult on innovations in Doctrine. Then they enquire into Preter-canonical conformity, and innovations in Diſcipline; and concerning the Common-Prayer. Laſtly, they entred on the Regulating of Eccleſiaſtical Government, which was not brought in, becauſe the Biſhop of *Lincoln* had undertaken the draught thereof, but not finiſhed it, as employed at the ſame time in many weighty matters of State. This conſultation continued till the middle of *May*. But the Bill againſt Deans and Chapters, put ſuch a diſtance between the foreſaid Divines, that never their Judgments (and scarce their persons) met after together.

The Canons made in the late Convocation were condemned in the House of Commons, as being against the King's Prerogative, the Fundamental Laws of the Realm, the Liberty and Property of the Subject, and containing divers other things tending to Sedition, and of dangerous consequence.

Many things were charged against the Archbishop by the Scots Commissioners, *viz.*

That he had pressed upon that Kirk, many Innovations in Religion, contained in the Liturgy and Book of Canons, contrary to the Liberties and Laws thereof.

That he had required *Ballentine*, Bishop of *Dumblane*, and the rest of the Bishops to be present at the Divine Service in their *Whites*, and blamed the said Bishop for his negligence in it, *&c.*

That he gave order for the taking down Stone-walls and Galleries in the Churches of *Edenborough*, to no other end but for the setting up of Altars, and Adoration toward the East.

That for their Supplicating against these Novations, they were declared Rebels in all the Parish-Churches of *England*, and a War kindled against them by his Arts and Practices.

That their Covenant by him was called ungodly, and that divers Oathes were imposed upon their Countrey-men to abjure the same.

That he in the presence of the King spared not to rail against the General Assembly held at *Glascow*, and put his hand to a Warrant for imprisoning some of those Commissioners sent from the Parliament of *Scotland*, for the Peace of both Nations.

That when the late Parliament could not be moved to assist in the War against them, he had caused the same to be dissolved, and continued the Convocation, to make Canons against them and their Doctrines, *&c.*

Such was the charge exhibited by the Scots Commissioners, in which many thought there was nothing criminal enough to deserve Imprisonment, much less to menace him with death.

The Bishop of *Ely* was impeached for many reputed misdemeanours in the See of *Norwich*. That he deprived, or banished, within the space of two years, fifty Godly, Learned, Painful Ministers. His placing the Communion-Table Altar-wise, and causing a Rayl to be set before it. The practising of Superstition in his own person, his bowing toward it; Consecrating the Bread and Wine at the West-side of the Table, with his back toward the people, and elevating the same above his Head, that the people might see it, causing the seats in all places to be so contrived,

The Church of GREAT BRITAIN.   325

trived, that the people muſt of neceſſity kneel towards the Eaſt. Appointing no Prayers to be uſed by Preachers before their Sermons, but that preſcribed by the Canon, &c.

In the midſt of theſe troubleſom times died Dr. *John Davenant*, Biſhop of *Salisbury*. A little before his death he prayed emphatically for half a quarter of an hour. Among many heavenly paſſages therein, *He thanked God for this his fatherly correction, becauſe in all his life-time he never had any one heavy affliction, which made him often much ſuſpect with himſelf, whether he was a true child of God or no.*   1641.

Deans and Chapters being now oppoſed by Parliament, the Cathedral-men endeavour to preſerve their Foundations; and by their friends obtain leave to be admitted into the Houſe of Commons, and to be heard what they could alledge in their own behalf. They made choice of Doctor *John Hacket*, Prebendary of St. *Pauls* to be the mouth for all the reſt.

He ſhewed, that to ſupply the defects of Prayer committed by private men, the publick duty thereof ſhould be conſtantly performed in ſome principal place (in imitation of the Primitive practice) and this is done in Cathedrals. He ſpake much alſo in praiſe of Church-muſick, when moderated to Edification. He took occaſion to refell that ſlaunder, which ſome caſt on Lecture-preachers, as an upſtart Corporation, alledging, that the local Statutes of moſt, or all Cathedral Churches, do require Lectures on the week-days. And in the name of his Brethren, he requeſted that Honourable Houſe, that godly and profitable Preaching might be the more exacted. Then he inſiſted on the advancement of Learning, as the proper uſe and convenience of Cathedrals, each of them being a ſmall Academy for the Champions of Chriſt's cauſe, againſt the Adverſaries, by their Learned pens. Here he proffered to prove by a Catalogue of their Names and Works, which he could produce, that moſt excellent labours in this kind (excepting ſome few) have preceeded from perſons preferred in Cathedrals: Now what a diſheartning would it be to young Students, if ſuch promotions were taken away. He alledged alſo, that the antient and genuine uſe of Deans and Chapters; was as *Senatus Epiſcopi*, to aſſiſt the Biſhop in his juriſdiction. He ſaid, that Cathedral-Churches were the firſt Monuments of Chriſtianity in *England*.   *Fuller*. Church Hiſt. *cent*. 17. *lib*. 11.

From things he paſſed to perſons, and began with the multitude of ſuch members, as had maintenance from Cathedrals, the total amounting to many thouſands; All which by the diſſolution of Deans and Chapters muſt be expoſed to poverty. Next, he inſtanced in their Tenants, who holding Leaſes from Deans and Chapters, are ſenſible of their own happineſs (as enjoying ſix parts of ſeven in pure gain) and therefore have petitioned the Houſe to continue their Antient Landlords. Moreover, ſuch Cities wherein Cathedrals ſtand (if Maritime) being

very

very poor in Trade, are enriched by the hospitality of the Clergy, and the frequent resort of Strangers unto them. Then he shewed, that divers of low degree, but generous Spirits, would labour by qualifying themselves by Industry and Vertue, to attain a share of Cathedral endowments, as the common possession of the Realm, &c. He trusted their Honours would account it reasonable, that the Clergy had in some sort a better maintenance than in neighbouring reformed Churches, and not with *Jeroboam's* Priests to be the basest of the people.

Then he instanced in some famous forreign Protestants, who had found relief by being installed Prebendaries in our Cathedral and Collegiate Churches, as Dr. *Saravia* preferred by Queen *Elizabeth*, Dr. *Casaubon* (Father and Son) by King *James*, Dr. *Primrose*, Mr. *Vossius*, in the reign of King *Charles*, and Dr. *Peter Du-Moulin*. And to destroy Deans and Chapters would highly gratifie *Rome*; for *Sanders* himself seemeth to complain, that Queen *Elizabeth* had left Provosts, Deans, Canons, and Prebendaries in Cathedral and Collegiate Churches, because he foresaw such Foundations would conduce to the stability of Religion.

He went forward to shew how such Lands paid greater sums to the Exchequer for *First-fruits*, tenths and subsidies, according to the proportion, than any other Estates and Corporations in the Kingdom. He implored to find the antient and honourable Justice of the House unto his Brethren, who were not charged, much less convicted of any Scandalous faults justly for the same to forfeit their estates. At last he set before them the Honour of God, to whose worship and service such Fabricks and Lands were dedicated, and barred all alienations with (which he said, is *termenda vox*) curses and imprecations. He minded them of the censures of *Korah* and his Complices, pronounced hallowed, because pretended to do God service therewith. He added that of *Solomon*, Prov. 20.25. *It is a snare to a man that devoureth that which is holy.* He added also that smart question of St. *Paul, Thou that abhorrest idols, dost thou commit Sacriledge?* and concluded, that on the ruines of the rewards of Learning, no structure can be raised but ignorance, and upon the Chaos of ignorance, nothing can be built but Profaneness and Confusion. This speech was generally well-resented, and wrought much on the House for the present.

In the afternoon Dr. *Cornelius Burgesse* made a vehement Invective against Deans and Chapters, &c. He aggravated the debauchedness of Singing men, not onely useless, but hurtful by their Vicious conversation: Yet he concluded with the utter unlawfulness to convert such endowments to any private person's profit.

Then was a Bill brought up from the Commons to the Lords against Bishops and Clergy-men: and it was Voted.

I. *That*

I. *That they should have no Votes in Parliament.*
II. *That they should not be in the Commission of the Peace, nor be Judges in Temporal Courts.*
III. *Nor sit in the Star-chamber, nor be Privy Counsellors.*

The last branches of this Bill passed by general consent, not above two dissenting. But the first branch was Voted by the Lords in the negative. But at last it was wholly cast out.

The Archbishop advised the drawing of a Petition to both Houses of Parliament in the name of the University of *Oxford*, not onely for the preservation of Episcopal Government, but of those Foundations, as being both the encouragements and rewards of Learning. In which petition having spoken, in few words, of the Antiquity and Succession of Bishops, from the Apostles themselves, they insist more at large upon such suggestions as might best justifie and endear the cause of Cathedral Churches. The like petition came from *Cambridge*, as much concern'd in this common cause as *Oxon*.

At a solemn Fast, not long after, the Temporal Lords took precedence of the Bishops, contrary to the custom of their Predecessors in all times foregoing: which being observed by the Lord *Spencer*, Is this, said he, *a day of humiliation, wherein we shew so great a pride, in taking place of those to whom it was allowed by all our Ancestors?*

The Bill against the High-commission Court, was the third time read in the House of Lords, and passed, which some days after was confirmed by his Majesty. The Bishop of *Lincoln* brought up a Bill to regulate Bishops and their jurisdiction. This Bill was but once read in the House, and no great matter made thereof. The Bishops that were impeached for making Canons, craved time till *Michaelmas* Term. This was vehemently opposed by some Lords, and two questions were put.

I. *Whether the Bishops should sit still in the House, though without voting (to which themselves consented) whilst the circumstance of time for their answer was in debate.*
II. *What time they should have for their answer.*

The first of these was carried for them by one present voice, and four Proxies; and for the second, time was allowed them till the tenth of *November*, and Council was permitted unto them. Bishop *Warner* of *Rochester* is chosen by joynt consent to solicit the cause, sparing neither care nor cost therein. Mr. *Chute* drew up a *Demurrer* in their behalf, that their offence in making Canons could not amount to a *Præmunire*: and now the cause sunck in silence.

But

But the main matter was, that the Bishops were denied all medling even in the Commission of preparatory examinations concerning the Earl of *Strafford*, *Causa sanguinis*; and they as men of mercy not to deal in the condemning of any person. The Bishops against the perswasions of the Lord *Kimbolton*, and the Earl of *Essex*, resolved to keep possession of their Votes, till a prevalent power outed them thereof.

No day passed, wherein some petition was not presented to the Parliament against the Bishops, who durst not come to the Parliament by Land for fear of the Apprentices, who were gathered together in great numbers to *Westminster*. The Bishops therefore intended to come to Parliament by water in Barges: but as they thought to come to Land, they were so pelted with Stones, and frighted at the sight of such a company of them, that they were rowed back, and went away to their places.

The next day twelve of the Bishops repaired to *Jerusalem* Chamber, in the Dean's lodgings, and drew up a Protestation, directed thus, *To the King's most excellent Majesty, and the Lords and Peers now assembled in Parliament*. This Instrument they delivered to Bishop *Williams*, now Archbishop of *York*, who at the next opportunity presented it to his Majesty; who wholly remitted the matter to the Parliament. The next morning a Privy Counsellor brought this Protestation into the House: and the twelve subscribers are impeached of High Treason, and Voted to be committed to the Tower, save that Bishop *Morton* of *Durham*, and Bishop *Hall* of *Norwich*, found some favour, so that they alone were sent to the custody of the Black Rod.

Now was the Bill against the Bishops sitting in Parliament brought up into the House of the Lords, and the matter agitated so eagerly on both sides. The Lord Viscount *Newark* (afterwards Earl of *Kingston*) made two notable speeches in the House, in defence of Episcopacy, which confirmed those of the Episcopal party, making the Lords very zealous in Bishops behalf. There were in the House many other defenders of Episcopacy, as *William* Lord Marquis of *Hartford*; the Earl of *South-hampton*; the Earl of *Bristol*, and the Lord *Digby* his Son; and that learned Lord, *William* Earl of *Bath*, and many other Lords voted for them.

About this time died *Richard Mountague* Bishop of *Norwich*, and Doctor *Joseph Hall* succeeded him in his See. Doctor *John Prideaux*, *Regius Professor* in *Oxford*, was made Bishop of *Worcester*. Doctor *Thomas Winniff*, Dean of St. *Pauls*, was made Bishop of *Lincoln*. Doctor *Ralph Brownrigg*, made Bishop of *Exeter*. Doctor *Henry King*, made Bishop of *Chichester*. Doctor *John Westfield*, made Bishop of *Bristol*; he died not long after. These were as likely persons to have kept up Episcopacy, if God's providence had so appointed, as any could have been culled out of *England*.

The

The Bill was again brought in against Bishops Votes in Parliament, and it was clearly carried in the Negative, that Bishops never more should Vote as Peers in Parliament. The King was very unwilling to consent to it, but at last, with much importunity, he signed the Bill, as he was, in St. *Augustines* in *Canterbury*, passing with the Queen towards *Dover*, then undertaking her voyage into the Low Countries.

1642.

Ten of the eleven Bishops formerly subscribing their Protestation to the Parliament, were after some moneths durance (upon good bale given) released. These now at liberty severally disposed themselves. Some went home to their own Diocess, as the Bishops of *Norwich*, *Oxford*, &c. The Bishop of *Durham* continued in *London*. Some withdrew themselves into the King's quarters, as Archbishop *Williams*, &c. Bishop *Wren* within few moneths after he was discharged from the Tower, was seized on by a party of Souldiers at his house at *Downham*, and brought back again to the Tower, where he continued till the end of the year 1659. As for the Archbishop of *Canterbury*, as he first took possession of that fatal lodging before any of the rest came to him, so he continued there after their dismission, without hope of finding his passage out of it by any other door than the door of death: which as he did not look for before it came; so when it came he did not fear it, saith Doctor *Heylin*.

On *October* 23. in the year foregoing, the House of Peers sequestred his Jurisdiction from him, conferring it on Sir *Nathanael Brent*, and others of his under-officers, and ordered, *That He should bestow none of the Benefices within his Gift, without acquainting them with the name and quality of the party whom he intended to prefer, leaving to them the approbation if they saw cause for it*. And on *October* 15. 1642. (for so long he remained without further disturbance) it was resolved upon the Question, That the Fines, Rents, and Profits of Archbishops, and Bishops, should be Sequestred for the use and service of the Common-wealth. On the ninth of *November* following, the Archbishop's house at *Lambeth* was forcibly possessed by a party of Souldiers, to keep it for the Publick service; and seventy eight pounds of his Rents as forcibly taken from some of his Officers, by an order under the hands of some of the Lords. But upon his petition shortly after, he had an order for securing of his Books and Goods. Another order came to bar him from any conference with any of the other prisoners; or speaking with any other, but in the presence of the Warder, who was appointed to attend him; and from having the liberty of the Tower; or from sending any of his servants into the City, but on occasion of providing victuals, and other necessaries. The Souldiers brake open the doors of his Chappel in *Lambeth* house, and began to spoil the Organs there; but their Captain put a stop to their fury. On *December* 21. his saddle-horse was seized on by order from some members in the House of Commons: and on the

Heylin. Hist. of Archbish. *Laud.*

23. Dr. *Leighton*, who had before been sentenced in the Star-chamber for his libellous Pamphlets, came with an order from that House to dispossess the Souldiers of their quarters there, and turn his House into a Prison: his Wood and Coals seized on, without any permission to make any use of them for himself. In the beginning of *May* the windows in his Chappel were defaced, and the steps torn up; his Books and Goods seized on by *Leighton*, and some others. And on the sixteenth of the same moneth he was served with an order of both Houses, debarring him from bestowing any of his Benefices, which either were or should be vacant for the time to come. And on the thirty first, an order was directed unto *Prynne* and others, to seize on all his Letters and Papers, to be perused by such as should be Authorized to that end, and purpose.

The entertaining of many petitions by the Houses of Parliament visibly tending to the abolition of Episcopal government, made it appear most necessary in the eyes of those who wisht well to it, to hasten the publishing of such petitions, as had been presented to the King in behalf thereof, and by his Majesty had been ordered to be published accordingly. Among which none did plead the cause with greater fervency, than that which was tendred in the name of the Gentry and Clergy of the Diocess of *Canterbury*. To which petition there subscribed no fewer than twenty four Knights and Baronets; Esquires and Gentlemen of note, above three hundred; Divines one hundred and eight; Freeholders and Subsidy men eight hundred: Many petitions of like nature came from other Counties, where the people were at any liberty to speak their own sence. All which, with some of those which had led the way unto the rest, were published by order from his Majesty, bearing date *May* 20. 1642. under the Title of *A collection of the petitions of divers Countries*, &c. Which petitions being drawn together, besides many which were presented after this Collection, amounted to nineteen in all, that is to say, two from the County of *Chester*, two from *Cornwall*, one from the University of *Oxford*, and another from the University of *Cambridge*; one from the Heads of Colledges and Halls. This from the Diocess of *Canterbury*; another from the Diocess of *Exeter*; one from the six Counties of *North-wales*; and one a piece from the Counties of *Nottingham, Hereford, Huntington, Somerset, Rutland, Stafford, Kent, Oxford,* and *Lancaster.*. These petitions came from thousands of the most eminent subjects of the Realm. But nothwithstanding the importunity of the Petitioners on the one side, and the moderation of the King's answer on the other, the prevailing party in both Houses had long since resolved upon the Question, which afterwards they declared by their publick Votes: for on the eleventh of *September* the Vote passed in the House of Commons, for abolishing Bishops, Deans and Chapters; celebrated by the Citizens with Bells and Bonfires, the

Lords

Lords not coming in till the end of *January*, when it paſt there alſo.

The War now begins to open. The Parliament had their Guards already, and the affront which *Hotham* had put upon the King at *Hull*, prompted the *York-ſhire* Gentlemen to become a guard to his Perſon. Both Houſes preſently Vote this to be a levying War againſt the Parliament, for whoſe defence not onely the Trained bands of *London* muſt be in a readineſs, and the Good people of the Countrey required to put themſelves into a poſture of Armes; but Regiments of Horſe and Foot are liſted, a General appointed, great ſums of money raiſed. Hereupon the King haſtens from *York* to *Nottingham*, where he ſets up his Standard, inviting all his good Subjects to repair unto him, for defence of their King, the Laws and Religion of their Countrey. And marching with great Forces he was encountred at *Edge-hill* by the Parliaments Forces, where five thouſand men on both ſides were ſlain on the place, among which was the King's General. Yet the King kept the field, and made his way open, forced *Banbury* Caſtle, and entred triumphantly into *Oxford* with an hundred and twenty Colours taken in the Fight.

The King reſolves on his advance towards *London*, and goes forward as far as *Brainford*, out of which he beats two of their beſt Regiments, takes five hundred priſoners and ſinks their Ordnance. But underſtanding that the Earl of *Eſſex* joyning with the *London-Auxiliaries* lay in way before him at *Turnham-Green* near *Chiſwick*, he retreated toward *Oxford*, where he receives Propoſitions of Peace from the Houſes of Parliament. Among which I find this for one.

> *That his Majeſty would be pleaſed to give his Royal Aſſent, for taking away ſuperſtitious Innovations; and to the Bill for the utter aboliſhing and taking away all Archbiſhops, Biſhops, their Chancellors, Commiſſaries, Deans, Subdeans, Deans and Chapters, Archdeacons, Deacons, Canons and Prebandaries; and all Chantors, Chancellors, Treaſurers, Sub-treaſurers, Succentors and Sacriſts, and all Vicars Choral and Choriſters, old Vicars, or new Vicars of any Cathedral or Collegiate Church, and all other their under-officers out of the Church of England. To the Bill againſt ſcandalous Miniſters: To the Bill againſt pluralities: And to the Bill for conſultation to be had with Godly, Religious, and Learned Divines: That his Majeſty would be pleaſed to paſs ſuch other Bills for ſetling of Church-government, as upon conſultation with the Aſſembly of the ſaid Divines ſhall be reſolved on by both Houſes of Parliament, and by them to be preſented to his Majeſty.*

Which Proposition with the rest, being presented to him on *Candlemas-day*, he referred to the following Treaty to be held at *Oxford*, but the Commissioners were so tyed to their Instructions, that nothing could be yielded by them.

Hylin. Hist. of Archbishop Laud.

But the Parliament had now entred on the Rents and profits of all the *Episcopal Sees* and *Capitular Bodies*, which were within the power of their Armies, and sequestred the Benefices of many under the common notion of scandalous Ministers: who if they had transgressed the Laws of the Realm, by the same Laws were to have been proceeded against; that so being legally deprived, the vacant Churches might be left to be filled by the Patrons with more deserving Incumbents. But this consisted not with the present design.

Most of the silenced Lecturers and Ministers, which within ten years past had left the Kingdom for Inconformity, were put into these sequestred Benefices: with which his Majesty being made acquainted, he presently signified his dislike of it by his Royal Proclamation, bearing date *May* 15. 1643.

> In which he complains, *That divers of the Pious and Learned Clergy were forced from their Cures and Habitations, or otherwise silenced, &c. for no other reason; but because (contrary to the Laws of the Land, and their own Consciences) they would not pray against Him, and his Assistants, or refused to publish any Illegal orders for fomenting the War raised against him, but conformed themselves according to the Book of Comon-Prayers, and preached God's Word according to the purity thereof, without any mixture of Sedition.* Next, *That many Factious and Schismatical persons were intruded into them, to sow Sedition, and seduce his good Subjects from their Obedience, contrary to the Word of God, and the Laws of the Land, &c. And thereupon he straitly commandeth all his good Subjects to pay their Tythes to the several and respective Incumbents, or their Assignes without guile or fraud, notwithstanding any Sequestration, pretended Orders, or Ordinances whatsoever, from one or both Houses of Parliament, &c. Requiring all Church-wardens and Sides-men to be assistant in gathering and receiving their Tythes, Rents, and Profits; and to resist all such persons (as much as in them lay) which were intruded into any of the Benefices or Cures aforesaid.*

But this rather served to declare his Majesties piety, than to stop the course of those proceedings.

Then an infamous Pamphlet is dispersed, Licensed by *John White*, Chair-man of the Committee for Religion, called, *The Committee for plundred Ministers*, under the Title of, *The first Century of Scandalous and Malignant Priests*, &c.

Their

the Church of GREAT BRITAIN.

1643.

Their Commissioners were no sooner returned from *Oxford*, but they called an Assembly of Divines by their own Authority, who met at *Westminster* in King *Henry* the Seventh his Chappel. These were of four several natures.

First, Men of Episcopal perswasion, as the most Reverend *James Usher*, Archbishop of *Armagh*: Doctor *Ralph Brownrigg*, Bishop of *Exeter*: Doctor *Westfield*, Bishop of *Bristol*: Doctor *Daniel Featly*, Doctor *Richard Holdsworth*, &c.

Secondly, Such who in their judgements favoured the Presbyterian Discipline, &c. among whom we take special notice of these.

Doctor *Hoyle* Divinity Professor in *Ireland*.

Cambridge.	Oxford.
Dr. *William Gouge* in *Black-friers*.	Dr. *William Twisse*.
Dr. *Peter Smith*.	Dr. *Cornelius Burgesse*.
Mr. *Oliver Bowles*.	Dr. *Edmond Stanton*.
Mr. *Thomas Gataker*.	Mr. *John White* of *Dorchester*.
Mr. *Henry Scudder*.	Mr. *Harris* of *Hanwel*.
Mr. *Anthony Tuckney*.	Mr. *Edward Reynolds*.
Mr. *Stephen Marshall*.	Mr. *John Maynard*.
Mr. *John Arrow-Smith*.	Mr. *Charles Herle*.
Mr. *Herbert Palmer*.	Mr. *Corbert* of *Merton Colledge*.
Mr. *Thomas Thorowgood*.	Mr. *Conant*.
Mr. *Thomas Hill*.	Mr. *Francis Cheynel*.
Mr. *Nathanael Hodges*.	Mr. *Obadiah Sedgewick*.
Mr. *John Gibbon*.	Mr. *Cartar* Senior.
Mr. *Timothy Young*.	Mr. *Cartar* Junior.
Mr. *Richard Vines*.	Mr. *Joseph Caryl*.
Mr. *Thomas Coleman*.	Mr. *Strickland*.
Mr. *Matthew Newcomen*.	Mr. *Thomas Baily*.
Mr. *Jeremiah Whitaker*.	&c.
Mr. *John Lightfoot*.	
&c.	

Thirdly, Some who formerly disliking Conformity, removed themselves beyond the Seas, now returned home at the beginning of this Parliament. These afterward proved dissenting Brethren to some transactions in the Assembly, as *Thomas Goodwin*, *Philip Nye*, *Sidrach Symson*, *Jeremiah Burroughes*, *William Bridge*.

Fourthly, Some Members of the Lords and Commons were mingled among them, and Voted joyntly in their Consultations; as the Earl of *Pembrock*,

Pembrook, the Lord *Say*: The most Learned Antiquary Mr. *Selden*, Mr. *Francis Rouse*, Mr. *Bulstrode Whitlock*, &c.

Commissioners from *Scotland* were also joyned with them, as the Earl of *Lothian*, the Lord *Lauderdale*, the Lord *Warriston*, of the Nobility; others of the Clergy, as Mr. *Alexander Henderson*, Mr. *Gelaspy*, &c.

*Fuller.*Church Hist. *Ad An.* 1643.

Doctor *Twisse* Preached the first Sermon, at the meeting of the Assembly, though the Schools, not the Pulpit, was his proper Element (witness his Controversal writings) and in his Sermon he exhorted them Faithfully to discharge their high calling to the glory of God, and honour of his Church. He much bemoaned, That the Royal Assent was wanting to give encouragement to them: yet he hoped, That by the efficacy of their fervent Prayers it might in due time be obtained, and that a happy union might be procured betwixt him and the Parliament. Sermon ended, the Ordinance was read, by which was declared the Cause, Ground, and Intent of their Convention; namely to consult with the Parliament for the setling of Religion and Church-government.

Of an hundred twenty elected, but sixty nine appeared.

And of the first of Royalists, Episcopal in their judgements, very few appeared, and scarce any continued any time in the House, save Doctor *Daniel Featly*, alledging privately several reasons for their departure.

Dr. *Twisse*, is now chosen Prolocutor, and Mr. *Henry Robrough*, and Mr. *Adoniram Bifield*, their Scribes and Notaries: And now their good success (next to the Parliament's) is publickly prayd for by the Preachers in the City, and Books dedicated unto them, under the Title of the most Sacred Assembly; and four shillings a day sallary was allowed them: and the Chamber of *Jerusalem*, the fairest in the Deans lodgings (where King *Henry* the Fourth died) was the place where these Divines did daily meet together.

His Majesty looks on this as a strange and unparallell'd encroatchment on his Royal Prerogative, to which alone the calling of such Assemblies did belong by the Laws of the Realm. And thereupon by his Proclamation of *June* 22 1643. being just ten days after the date of the Ordinance by which the Assembly was indicted. He inhibits all and every person named in that Ordinance (under several pains) from assembling together for the end and purpose therein set down, declaring the Assembly to be illegal, and that the Acts thereof ought not to be received by any of his good Subjects, as binding them, or of any Authority with them. Which Prohibition notwithstanding, most of the Members authorized by that Ordinance assembled, as was before declared.

Bibl. Regia. f. 331.

One

One of the first publick Acts which they performed, was the humble presenting of a petition to both Houses, for the appointing of a solemn Fast to be generally observed. And presently a Fast is appointed, and accordingly kept on the following *Friday*, Master *Bowles*, and Master *Newcomen*, (whose Sermons were after Printed) Preaching on the same.

The King summons the Lords and Commons to *Oxford*, to attend there on *January* 22. then next following. Being come, scarce were they setled in their several Houses, when they were entertained with an hot Alarum, made by the coming in of the Scots with a puissant Army. The Scots had thrived so well by the former service, as made them not unwilling to come under the pay of such bountiful Masters. And knowing well in what necessity their dear Brethren in *England* stood of their assistance, they were resolved to husband that necessity to their best advantage. The English must first enter into Covenant with them, for conforming of this Church with that, *&c.*

In the first branch of it, it was to be Covenanted between the Nations, *That all endeavours should be used for the preservation of the Reformed Religion in the Church of* Scotland, *both in Doctrine, Discipline, and Government ; Directory for worship and Catechizing.*

And in the second, *That in like manner they endeavour without any respect of persons, the extirpation of Popery, Prelacy, that is, Church Government by Archbishops, Bishops, their Chancellors and Commissaries, Deans, Deans and Chapters, Archdeacons, and all other Ecclesiastical Officers depending on that Hierarchy,* &c.

But by whomsoever it was framed, his Majesty saw that it aimed at the subversion of the present Government. Therefore looking on it as a dangerous combination against himself, the established Religion, and the Laws of this Kingdom, for the bringing in of Forreign Forces to subvert them all (saith Doctor *Heylin*) interdicted all his Subjects from imposing, or taking the same, as they would answer the contrary at their perils. Which Proclamation bearing date on *October* 9. came out too late to hinder the taking and enjoying of this Covenant, where the restraint thereof had been most necessary : for it had been solemnly taken by all the Members of the House of Commons, and the Assembly of Divines at St. *Margarets* in *Westminster*, on *September* 25. and within two days after it was Administred with no less solemnity to divers Lords, Knights, Gentlemen, Colonels, Officers, Souldiers, and others, residing in and about the City of *London* ; a Sermon being Preached by Mr. *Coleman*, to justifie the piety and legality of it : and finally enjoyned to be taken on the *Sanday* following, in all Churches and Chappels of *London*, within the lines of Communication ; as afterwards by all the Kingdom in convenient time. No sooner was this Covenant taken, but to let the Scots see that they were in earnest, a further impeachment,

ment, confisting of ten Articles, were prepared against the Archbishop of *Canterbury*.

In the Assembly of Divines some concurred not with the major part, and were therefore stiled, *Dissenting Brethren*, These men crave a *Toleration* to be indulged them; (who since their return out of the *Low-countries* had fallen upon gathering of Congregations in or about the City of *London*.) and they excused for being concluded by the votes of the Assembly. But the Presbyterians highly opposed their Toleration; they tax the dissenting Brethren for Singularity; and some moved their ejection out of the Assembly, except in some convenient time they would comply therewith.

The Dissenters seasonably presented an Apologetical Narrative to the Parliament, stiled by them, *The most sacred refuge or Asylum for mistaken and misjudged innocence*. Herein they petitioned pathetically for some favour, whose conscience could not joyn with the Assembly in all particulars, concluding with that pityful close, *That they pursued no other Interest or design, but a subsistence (be it the poorest and meanest) in their own land, as not knowing where else with safety, health, and livelyhood to set their feet on earth, and subscribed their names*,

   Thomas Goodwin.   *Sidrach Symson.*
                                      William Bridge.
   Philip Nye.   *Jeremiah Burroughs.*

These Petitioners found such favour with some potent persons in Parliament, that they were secured from farther Trouble, and afterwards grew able, not onely to encounter, but invade all opposers; yea to open and shut the door of preferment to others.

Dr. *William Twisse* their Prolocutor died, and Mr. *Charles Herle*, Fellow of *Excter-colledge* succeeded him in his place.

The Assembly met with many difficulties; some complained that Mr. *Selden* that Great Antiquary, advantaged by his skill in Antiquity, and the Oriental Tongues, studied rather to perplex than inform the Members thereof, as appeared by the fourteen Queries he propounded; whose intent was, to give a check to the design of those who held Presbytery to be *Jure Divino*. More trouble was caused to the Assembly by the opinions of the *Erastians*. And divers Parliament men hearing their own power enlarged thereby, made use of the *Erastians* for a check to such who pressed Conformity to the *Scotch Kirk* in all particulars.

Indeed the Major part of the Assembly endeavoured the setling the Scotch Government in all particulars: and this was laboured by the Scotch Commissioners with all Industry and probable means to obtein the same. But it could not be effected, nor was it ever setled by Act of of Parliament, who kept the coercive power in their own hands, so that the power of Excommunication was not intrusted with them, but ultimately resolved into a Committee of eminent persons of Parliament.

On *January* 10. 1644. *William Laud*, Lord Archbishop of *Canterbury*, was beheaded on Tower-hill, after he had been kept four years a prisoner in the Tower. His charge was a constructive treason under several Heads, reducible into two particulars.

I. *For endeavouring of the subversion of the Laws of the Land.*
II. *And a like endeavour to overthrow the Protestant Religion.*

His trial was at the Lords bar, and Mr. *William Prynne*, was his Prosecutor, but notwithstanding all that could be said, nothing that did amount to Treason could be proved against him. But the *Scots* who were at that time very prevalent would not be satisfied, unless he were put to death, to manifest thereby their zeal against the Episcopal Hierarchy, to usher in the Presbyterian Government; at the approaching Treaty: so that by an Ordinance of Lords and Commons he was adjudged guilty of High Treason, though at the passing thereof in the House of Peers, there were but seven present. *Heylin's Hist. of the life of K. Charles, I. pag. 113.*

In pursuance of several messages from the King for a Treaty, it was assented to by the Parliament, and at *Uxbridge* Commissioners met for the King on one part, and for the Parliament of *England*, and the Parliament of *Scotland* on the other. Master *Christopher Love* (waiting on the Parliaments Commissioners in a general Relation) gave great offence to the Royalists in his Sermon, shewing the impossibility of an agreement. With the Commissioners on both sides certain Clergy-men were sent, in their presence to debate the point of Church-government.

For the King.		For the Parliament.
Doctor { Sheldon. Steward. Benjamin Laney. Henry Hammond. Henry Ferne.	Master {	Stephen Marshal. Richard Vines.

These, when the Commissioners were at leasure from Civil affairs, were called to a conference before them. But this Treaty proved ineffectual. The King complained of what came to pass, the fruitless end of this Treaty, that his Commissioners offered full-measured reasons, and the other Commissioners have stuck rigidly to their demands, &c. The Treaty at *Uxbridge* (saith he) gave the fairest hopes of an happy *Nixon Basil. Chap. 18.*

com-

composure, had others applyed themselves to it with the same moderation as he did, he was confident the war had been ended.

To return to the Assembly, the Monuments which they have left to posterity of their meeting, are a new form of worship by the name of a *Directory*, Articles of Religion drawn up by them, and a double Catechism, one the lesser, the other the greater.

This Assembly dwindled away by degrees, though never legally dissolved. Many of them after the taking of *Oxford* returning to their own Cures, and others living in *London* absented themselves, as disliking the managing of matters.

Anno 1645. died Mr. *John Dod*, a *passive Non-conformist*, as Mr. *Fuller* calleth him, a man much esteemed among men of his own perswasion, one that loved not any one the worse for difference in judgement about Ceremonies, but all the better for their unity of affections in grace and goodness. He used to retrench some hot spirits when inveighing against Bishops, telling them how God under that Government had given a marvellous encrease to the Gospel, and that Godly men might comfortably comport therewith, under which Learning and Religion had so manifest an Improvement. He was an excellent Scholar, and an exquisite Hebrician, who with his Society and directions in one Vacation taught that Tongue unto Mr. *John Gregory*, that rare Linguist, and Chaplain of *Christ-Church*, who survived him but one year, Mr. *Dod* was buried at *Fausly* in *Northampton-shire*.

Saunderson's Hist. of King Charles.

Now comes strange news, Dr. *Williams*, Archbishop of *York*, is no less suddenly than strangely Metamorphosed from a zealous Royalist into an active Parliamentarian: and desirous to make his peace with the Parliament, he betakes himself to his house at *Purin* neer *Aberconway* in *Wales*, put a garrison therein, and fortified the same, protesting against the King's party, and disswading the County from paying Contribution to the King. And wrote to Colonel *Mitton* (of the Parliament's party) to assist him against the Lord *Byron*, who understanding of his Revolt, had sent a party from *Aber-conway* to besiege him. At length he lays siege to the Town and Castle of *Aber-conway*, reduceth them to the Service of the Parliament, & much of the Town to his own possession. Hereby he saved his estate from Sequestration. But by his last complyance he lost his old friends at *Oxford*, and in Lieu of them finding few new ones at *London*.

He expended much on the repair of *Westminster Abby-church*. And when pressed by Archbishop *Laud* to a larger contribution to S. *Paul's*, he answered *he would not rob* Peter *to pay* Paul. The Library of *Westminster* was the effect of his bounty, and so was a Chappel in *Lincoln-Colledge* in *Oxford*. At S. *John's* in *Cambridge* he founded two fellowships, built a fair Library, and furnished it with Books. To a grave Minister coming to him for Institution in a living, he thus expressed himself.

the Church of Great Britain.

himself. *I have (saith he) passed through many places of honour and trust, both in Church and State, more than any of my Order in England these seventy years before, But were I but assured, that by my preaching I had but converted one soul to God, I should take therein more spiritual joy and comfort, than in all the Honours and Offices which have been bestowed upon me.* He died on *March*. 25. 1649.

Now I will present the Reader with a list of the Principal Ordinances of the Lords and Commons which respected Church-matters, and to make this History the more entire, must go a little backward in time.

November 8. 1644.

An Ordinance of the Lords and Commons in Parliament, for the payment of Tythes by every person within the Realm of England and Wales.

December 13. 1644.

An Ordinance for the Ordination of Ministers pro tempore within the County of Lancaster, according to the Ordinance of the second of October for the Ordination of Ministers.

April 12. 1645.

An Ordinance for the Regulating the University of Cambridge, and for the removing of scandalous Ministers in the seven Associated Counties.

April 23. 1645.

An Ordinance appointing Ministers for certain Churches and Lectures, viz. Philip Goodwin to be Vicar of the Church of Watford in Hartfordshire: and to receive to himself all Tythes, Oblations, &c. thereunto belonging, during his life. And Dr. Cornelius Burgess to have yearly allowance of four-hundred pounds paid unto him by the Lord Mayor of the City of London, and the Court of Aldermen; to be paid quarterly out of the Houses, Rents, Revenues of the Dean, Dean and Chapter of the Church of S. Paul's for and during the term of his life, he performing the Lectures in the said Church, as by the Lords and Commons he was Ordered to do.

Hught's Abridgement of ordinances of Parliament. Part 2.

April 26. 1645.

An Ordinance, that no person be permitted to Preach, who is not Ordained a Minister, either in this or some other Reformed Church; except such as intending the Ministry, shall be allowed for the trial of their gifts by those who shall be appointed thereunto.

August 19. 1645.

Directions of the Lords and Commons (after advice had with the Assembly of Divines) for the electing and chusing of Ruling Elders, in all the Congregations, And in the Classical Assemblies for the Cities of London *and* Westminster, *and the several Counties of the Kingdom; for the speedy setling of the Presbyterial government.*

August 21. 1645.

Ordained, that the Knights and Burgesses of Parliament of the several Counties of England *and* Wales, *shall send Printed books of the Directory of God's Worship fairly bound up in Leather to the Committees of Parliament residing in the several Counties, who shall send or cause the same to be delivered to the several Ministers of every Parish, &c.*

October 20. 1645.

An Ordinance of the Lords and Commons, together with Rules and Directions concerning suspension from the Sacrament of the Lord's Supper, in cases of Ignorance and Scandal. Also the names of such Ministers and others, that are appointed Tryers and Judges of the Ability of Elders in the twelve Classes within the Province of London.

January 7. 1645.

An Ordinance for making Covent-garden *Parochical: and that the new erected Church within the Precinct of the said new intended Parish shall be a Parish-Church for the said Precinct, and that* William Earl of Bedford, *his Heirs and Assigns for ever shall have the Patronage of the said Church, &c.*

March

March 14. 1645.

An Ordinance for keeping of scandalous Persons from the Sacrament of the Lord's Supper, the enabling of the Congregation for the choyce of Elders, and supplying of defects in former Ordinances, and Directions of Parliament concerning Church-government.

June 5. 1646.

An Ordinance for the present setling (without further delay) of the Presbyterial government in the Church of England.

August 28. 1646.

An Ordinance for the Ordination of Ministers by the Classical Presbyters *within their respective bounds for the several Congregations in the Kingdom of England.*

January 29. 1647.

An Ordinance for the speedy dividing and setling of the several Counties of this Kingdom into distinct Classical Presbyteries, and Congregational Elderships.

February 9. 1647.

An Ordinance for Reparation of Churches, and paying of Church-duties.

April 3. 1648.

An Ordinance for union of Churches in the City of Glocester, *and maintenance for Preaching Ministers there.*

May 2. 1648.

An Ordinance for punishing Blasphemies and Heresies.

The King on *April* 17. 1646. In disguise went out of *Oxford*, attended by Mr. *John Ashburnham*, and one more. On *May* 6. His Majesty came to the *Scots* Army which occasioned the *Scotch* Commissioners to write to the Parliament about it. *May* 19. the *Scots* came with the King to *New-castle*.

As

Henderson's Hist. of King Charles p.904.

A great dispute was between the King and Mr. *Alexander Henderson* about Church-matters, where after several Discourses and meetings, many writings passed between them till *July* 16. concerning these matters by Authority of the Fathers, and Practice of the Primitive Church. His Majesty concludeth, that to him it is incredible, that any custome of the Catholick Church be erroneous, which was not Contradicted by Orthodox Learned men in the times of their first practice, as is easily perceived that these defections were which *Henderson* mentions. And finally, that albeit He never esteemed any Authority equal to the Scriptures, yet he thinks the unanimous consent of the Fathers, and the Universal practice of the Primitive Church, to be the best and Authentical Interpreters of God's word, and consequently the fittest Judges between him and *Henderson*, until better may be found. These disputes were afterwards published in Print, to the everlasting Honour of His Majesty and his Cause.

On *February* 6. 1646. the *Scots*, according to agreement, quitted *New-castle*, and the *English* possessed it. The Parliament voted the King's remove to *Holdenby-house*, with respect to the safety of His Person. And the Commissioners appointed for receiving the King's Person came to *Newcastle* on *June* 22. The King desireth two of his Chaplains to be with him, which was denied him, at which he is much troubled. His Majesty resolves to keep every Friday a day of Solemn Fasting and Humiliation.

After His Majesty had been neer five moneths at *Holdenby*, near a Thousand Souldiers commanded by Cornet *Joyce* came to *Holdenby* to the King, and told him, that they were come by command from the Army to remove him from that place. His Majesty demanded, whether they would offer any violence to his Person. They all cried, *None*. He also desired, that his Trunks and Papers might not be Riffled and tumbled. They promised to set a guard on them. Thirdly, he required such servants to attend him, against whom there was no just exceptions. They answered, he should. Lastly he desired, that nothing be imposed on him contrary to his Conscience. They answered, it was not their judgement to force any thing against Conscience upon any one, much less on His Majesty. So at one of the Clock His Majesty went along with them.

On *June* 28. 1647. His Majesty was brought to *Hatfield*, the Duke of *Richmond* attending him, and others: and from thence came to *Casam*.

At this time the Parliament was jealous of the King and the Army, lest they should treat without the consent of the Parliament. And the Army likewise devised as many jealousies and fears of a private engagement, and Subscribing in the City of *London*, and against the Army.

Then the Parliament Order their Votes of the Militia in the hands of
the

the City to be *Null*, &c. The Apprentices clamour at the Houses, and gather together in *Westminster-hall* in such multitudes, that the Commons were forced to unvote and null their last Orders.

Then the Army marcheth nearer *London*. Both Speakers and some Members fly the Army. On *August* 7. the General and the Army march in Triumph through the City. Sir *Thomas Fairfax* is made Constable of the Tower: and *Titchburn* is made Lieutenant of the Tower. The King is brought first to *Oatelands*, and afterward to *Hampton-court*, and his Children Ordered to be with him.

September 28. 1647. The Commons considered of several Propositions to send to His Majesty, That about Religion being the main thing. They also Vote, that His Majesty be desired to give His consent to such Act or Acts of Parliament, as shall be presented for setling of Presbyterian Government, according to the matter of several Ordinances of Parliament, for the Directory, or Church-government to continue for the space of three years from the time that the King shall give his consent to such Acts. They likewise voted the Common-prayer book shall not be used in Private.

November 11. 1647. the King escaped from *Hampton-court*, and left on the Table three Papers, one to the Parliament, one to the Commissioners, a third to Colonel *Whaley*.

On *October* 15. Information was brought to the House, that His Majesty was safe at the Isle of *Wight*, and had put himself into the Protection of Colonel *Hammond*, then Governour of the Island.

Come we now to the Church-part of the Treaty in the Isle of *Wight*. Here appeared of the Divines chosen by the King, *James Usher*, Archbishop of *Armagh*, *Brian Duppa* Bishop of *Sarum*, Dr. *Sheldon*, Dr. *Sanderson*, Dr. *Fern*. On the other side Mr. *Stephen Marshall*, M. *Richard Vines*, Mr. *Lazarus Seaman*, and Mr. *Joseph Caryl*, were there present by appointment of the Parliament.

All things were transacted *in scriptis*. His Majesty consulted with his Chaplains when he pleased. The King's writings were publickly read before all by Mr. *Philip Warwick*: and Mr. *Vines* read the Papers of his Fellow-divines.

As for the difference between Primitive Episcopacy and present Hierarchy, urged by the Parliament Divines, his Majesty did not conceive, that the Additions granted by the favour of His Royal Progenitors for the enlarging the power and priviledges of Bishops, did make the Government substantially to differ from what it was, no more than Arms and Ornaments make a Body really different from it self, when it was naked and devested of the same. Whereas they besought His Majesty to look rather to the Original than to the succession of Bishops, he thought it needful to look at both, the latter being the best *Clue* in such intrinsick cases to find out the former. Lastly, he professed himself unsatisfied in

their

their answer, concerning the perpetual and unalterable substantials of Church-government, as expecting from them a more particular Resolution therein, than what he had received. Eleven days after the Parliament Divines put in their answer to his Majesties last paper. Herein they affirmed, they saw not by what warrant the Writ of Partition of the Apostles Office was taken forth, that the Governing part should be in the hands of the Bishops, the Teaching and Sacramentizing in the Presbyters. They also said that some Fathers acknowledged, that Bishops were different from Presbyters onely in matter of Ordination. They also returned, that His Majestie's Definition of Episcopal Government, is extracted out of the Bishops of later date than Scripture-times.

Fuller's Chur. Hist. The darkness of the History of the Church in the times succeeding the Apostles (said they) had an influence on the Catalogue makers; who derived the Series of succession of Bishops, taken much from Tradition and Reports. And it is a great blemish of their evidence, that the nearer they come to the Apostles times (wherein this should be most clear to establish the succession at the first) they are most doubtful and contradictory one to the other.

They granted, that a succession of men to feed and govern those Churches, by Ecclesiastical Writers in compliance with the Language of their own times, were called Bishops, but not distinct from Presbyters. So that if such a succession from the Primitive times, *Seriatim* were proved, they would either be found *more* than Bishops, as Apostles and extraordinary persons; or *less*, as meerly first Presbyters, not having the three Essentials of Episcopal government insisted on by His Majesty. They humbly moved His Majesty, that the Regiments of Humane testimonies on both sides might be discharged the field, and the point of dispute tried alone by dint of holy Scripture.

They affirmed also, that the power of Episcopacy under Christian and Pagan Princes is one and the same, though the exercise be not but acknowledging the subordination thereof to the Sovereign Power, with their accountableness to the Laws of the Land. They conclude with thanks to His Majestie's Condescension in vouchsafing them the Liberty and Honour in examining his Learned Reply, praying God, that a Pen in the Hand of such Abilities might ever be employ'd in a subject worthy thereof. Some dayes after His Majesty returned His last paper, wherein he not onely acknowledgeth the great pains of these Divines to inform his judgement, according to their perswasions, but also took special notice of their Civilities of the Application, both in the Beginning and Body of their supply. However he told them, they mistook his meaning about a *Writ of Partition*, as if His Majesty had Cantoned out the Episcopal Government, one part to the Bishops, another to the Presbyterians alone: whereas his meaning was, that the Office of

Teaching

Teaching is common to both alike; but the other of Governing peculiar to Bishops alone.

The Lords and Commons vote their Commissioners return from the Treaty. The Commons debate of his Majesties Propositions, and agree.

I. *That he be in Honour, Safety, and Freedom, according to the Lawes.*

II. *That he have his Revenue as before, excepting the Dedications of such Forts and Garrisons, as were of old accustomed to be allowed maintenance.*

III. *That he have compensation for the Court of Wards.*

IV. *That an Act of Oblivion be past.*

The King having granted the Parliament to dispose of all great Offices for ten years, they vote it satisfactory.

On *November* 26. was presented a Declaration of the Army to the House of Commons, which was the day before subscribed by the General; it contained twenty six sheets of paper, shewing (as they termed it) the misgoings of King and Parliament severally, also in all Treaties betwixt them, especially, that they are now in. They desire, that the Parliament would reject those demands of the King, especially concerning his Restitution, and coming to *London*, with Freedom, Honour and Safety, and that they proceed against the King in way of Justice, &c. The Army on *December* 2. enter the lines of Communication, and at *Whitehall* quartereth the General, and the rest of the Army at the *Mews*, *St. James's*, *York-house*, and divers other places about the City. The King is taken from *Newport*, convay'd to *Hurst-castle*: on *December* 6. the Trained bands are discharged the Guard to the Parliament, and and *Pride's* and *Riche's* Regiments take it upon them. Many of the Members coming to the House are seized and kept in custody by the General's command in the Queen's Court, and Court of Wards. These were removed to the King's-Head Inn near *Charing-Cross*, and to the Swan Inn in the *Strand* under Guards of Souldiers.

The Army put forth a new Representative, called, *The Agreement of the People*. The King is brought up to *London*, arraigned before a select Committee for that purpose, called *An High Court of Justice*, indicted; and upon his refusal to own their Authority, finally condemned.

Having received the sentence of death, Dr. *Juxon*, Bishop of *London*, Preached privately before him at St. *James's* on the *Sunday* following: his Text *Romans* 2.16. Next *Tuesday* being the day of his dissolution, in the morning alone he received the Communion from the hands of the said Bishop. At which time he read for the second Lesson the 27th chapter of St. *Matthew*, containing the History of the death and passion of our Saviour. Sermon ended, the King heartily thanked the Bishop for selecting so seasonable and comfortable a portion of Scripture, seeing all Humane hope and happiness is founded on the sufferings of our Saviour: The Bishop answered, He had done it meerly following the direction of the Church of *England*, whose Rubrick appointeth that Chapter the second Morning-lesson for the thirtieth of *January*. At ten of the Clock, in the forenoon, he is brought on Foot from St. *James's* Palace over the Park to *Whitehall*, guarded with a Regiment of Foot-souldiers, part before, and the rest behind him, with Colours flying, and Drums beating, his private Guard of Partizans about him, and Doctor *Juxon* Bishop of *London*, next to him on one side, and Colonel *Tomlinson* on the other. He bid them go faster, saying, *That he now went before them, to strive for an Heavenly Crown, with less sollicitude, than he had oftentimes bid his Souldiers to fight for an earthly Diadem*. Then passeth he to the Scaffold, where he defendeth his Innocency: howbeit he acknowledgeth God's justice, pardons his enemies, takes pity on the Kingdom. He shews the Souldiers how much they are out of the way, and tells them, *They would never go right, till they give God his due, the King his due, and the people their due*.

You must (said he) *give God his due, by restoring his worship and Church rightly regulated* (*which is now out of order*) *according to his Word. And a National Synod freely called, freely debating among themselves, must settle this, when every Opinion is freely and clearly heard.*

For the King, said he, (*that is my Successor*) *Indeed I will not, the Laws of the Land will clearly instruct you for that: For the People, I must tell you, That their liberty and freedom consists in having Government under those Laws by which their Lives and Goods may be most their own. It is not in having a share in the Government, that pertains not to them. A Soveraign and a Subject are two different things.* He prayed God, they might take those courses that are best for the good of the Kingdom, and their own Salvation.

Then having declared, *That he died a Christian according to the profession of the Church of* England, *as the same was left him by his Father*; He said, *I have a good Cause, and a gracious God*; and gave his *George* to the Bishop, bidding him, *Remember to give it to the Prince*. Then, said He, *I go from a Corruptible to an Incorruptible Crown, where no disturbance can be, but peace and joy for evermore.* Then lifting up his eyes and hands to Heaven, having prayed secretly, stooping down to the block, he received the fatal stroak. On the *Wednesday* sennight after, his Corps embalmed, and Coffined in Lead, was delivered to the

care.

care of some of his Servants to be buried at *Windsor*. That night they brought the Corps to *Windsor*. The Vault being prepared, a scarff of Lead was provided, some two foot long, and five inches broad, therein to make an Inscription, which was

KING CHARLES 1648.

The Plummer souldred it to the Coffin, about the Breast of the Corpse. Then was the Corpse brought to the Vault, being born by the Souldiers of the Garrison: Over it a black Velvet Herse-cloth, the four Labels whereof the Duke of *Richmond*, the Marquess of *Hertford*, the Earls of *South-hampton*, and *Lindsey*, did support. The Bishop of *London* stood weeping by. Then was it deposited in silence and sorrow in the vacant place in the Vault, near to the Coffin (as it was thought) which contained the Corps of King *Henry* the Eighth (the Herse-cloth being cast in after it) about three of the Clock in the afternoon: and the Lords that night (though late) returned to *London*.

Prince *Charles* eldest Son to King *Charles* the first, by unquestionable right succeeded to the Crowns of *England*, *Scotland*, and *Ireland*, in the eighteenth year of his age. Proclamation and Coronation could not now have their due course. The Ruling part of the House of Commons, who usurped the Government with violence on the person of the late King, immediately published an Act even against Kingly Government. Yet this Inhibition did not deter many Loyal Subjects from doing their duty: and on *February* 2. a Proclamation in the name of the Noblemen, Judges, Knights, Lawyers, Gentlemen, Free-holders, Merchants, Citizens, Yeomen, Seamen, and other Freemen of *England*, did Proclaim Prince *Charles* King of *England*. The Proclamation was Printed, and scattered about the Streets of *London*.

The House of Peers continued yet sitting, and in regard the Commissions of the Judges were determined by the death of the King, they send to the Commons for a Conference about it, and other matters relating to the setling of the Government.

But Monarchy and the House of Lords are declared useless by the Commons.

The Peers in general resent these indignities put upon them by a small part of the House of Commons; they assert their own Priviledges, and the Fundamental Laws of the Nation; and disclaim and protest against all Acts, Votes, Orders, or Ordinances of the said Members of the Commons House, for erecting of new Courts of Justice, to try or execute the King, or any Peer or Subject of the Realm; for altering the Government, Laws, Great Seal, &c.

Hereupon the Army set a Guard upon the door of the House of Lords, and in further prosecution of the late Votes of Commons against Monarchy. An Act was passed by that House for the Exhæredation of the Royal Line, the Abolishment of Monarchy in this Kingdom, and the setting up of a Common-wealth, which they ordered to be published and Proclaimed in all parts of the Kingdom. But Alderman *Reinoldson*, then Lord Mayor of *London*, refused to publish this Act in *London*, and He with three of the Aldermen of his Judgment were sent prisoners to the Tower.

But on *February* 3. the King was Proclaimed at the Cross at *Edinburgh*. In the beginning of *March*, the Duke of *Hamilton*, the Earls of *Holland* and *Norwich*, the Lord *Capel*, and Sir *John Owen*, were tried and condemned by an High Court of Justice erected for that purpose: of which the Duke of *Hamilton*, the Earl of *Holland*, and the Lord *Capel*, were executed *March* 9. but the Earl of *Norwich*, and Sir *John Owen* were pardoned.

The Commons set forth a Declaration to justifie their proceedings. They promise the establishment of a firm and safe Peace, the advancement of the true Protestant Religion, the liberal maintenance of a godly Ministry, &c.

They pass an Act for propagating the Gospel in *Ireland*, *March* 8.

April 10. 1649. An Act was passed by the Commons for the sale of Deans and Chapters Lands, and for the abolishing of Deans, Deans and Chapters, Canons, Prebends, &c. and Tithes of or belonging to any Cathedral or Collegiate Church in *England* and *Wales*: but it was provided, That this should not extend to the Colledge of St. *Mary* in *Winchester*, nor to the Colledge of *Eaton*; nor to any of the Mannors, Lands, Tenements, and Hereditaments to them belonging.

June 2. 1649 An Act was passed for the better maintenance of Preaching Ministers, and School-masters (out of the Lands of Deans and Chapters) throughout *England* and *Wales*, in such places where maintenance is wanting, and for other good uses to the advancement of true Religion, Piety, and Learning. And the Commissioners of the Great Seal of *England* issued forth Commissions under the Great Seal, into all the Counties of *England* and *Wales*, to such persons as by the Parliament were nominated, giving them power by the Oathes of good and lawful men, &c. to find out the true value of all Parsonages and Vicarages presentative, and all other Ecclesiastical Livings, with care of Souls within such Cities and Counties, and to certifie into the Chancery what each of them were really worth *per Annum*; the names of the Incumbents, Proprietors, and Possessors thereof, and of such as receive the profits; who supplies the Cure, what he hath for his Sallary; how many Chappels are belonging to one Parish, and how situate, and fit so be united: and how the Churches and Chappels are supplied by

Preaching

Preaching Ministers, that so a course be taken for the providing both for Preaching and maintenance, where the same should be found to be needful.

About this time some Dissenters in the Army called *Levellers*, drew together five thousand Horse and Foot at *Burford*. Colonel *Reinolds* fell in upon them with a greater Body than they had, and routed them, taking nine hundred Horse, and four hundred Foot prisoners: whereof one *Thomson* and two more principal Leaders, were immediately shot to death, who died resolutely. Cornet *Den*, an Army-preacher, expressing his grief and sorrow, was reprieved at the Instant of execution, which their Fellows beheld from the leads of the Church. The Rest by *Cromwells* mediation were all pardoned, and sent home to their own houses. This proved the utter suppression of that faction, and rendred the Army entirely at his Command: so that they presently submitted to the lot which Regiments should be sent to *Ireland*, then almost reduced to the King's obedience by the Marquess of *Ormond*. Cromwell was ordained Commander in chief of the Forces appointed for *Ireland*, and tituladoed with the style of Lord Governour of *Ireland*, while the Lord *Fairfax* was left here to attend the Parliament. He with a potent Army landed at *Dublin*.

Flagellum, or the life and death of O. C. p. 83.

The Marquess of *Ormond* had besieged *Dublin*, but the siege was raised by Colonel *Michael Jones*, Governour of *Dublin*, with the utter defeat of the Marquesses Army. And the siege of *London-derry* was raised by Sir *Charles Coot* sallying out of the Town. *Cromwel* takes *Drogheda* by Storm, and puts all in it to the Sword. After this, in less than a year most of the Cities and Towns in *Ireland* were taken, and that whole Kingdom in a manner subdued to the power of the Common-Wealth of *England*; and the Marquess of *Ormond*, and all that oppose their Authority, withdrew themselves. But a little before, Colonel *Rich* received a Brush from my Lord *Broghil* in the County of *Cork*, where the Bishop of *Rosse* being taken was hanged.

July 19. 1649. An Act was passed by the Parliament of the Common-wealth of *England*, for the promoting and propagating the Gospel of Christ in *New England*. And a general Collection was made in and through all the Counties, Cities, Towns, and Parishes of *England* and *Wales*, as the foundation for so pious an undertaking, &c.

King *Charles* the Second being now at *Jersey*, part of the English Fleet was sent to attacque that Island, which put the King upon a speedy remove from thence into *France*, where he resided till the time appointed for the Treaty at *Breda*, which drew near, and then he repaired thither.

The Committee of the Estates of *Scotland* having concluded with the King at *Breda*, all correspondence with the English was by Proclamation forbidden, and all manner of provision stopped from being carryed into *England*, though the *Juncto* at *Westminster* had used all Artifices to keep

1650. keep the Scots from closing with the King. During the Treaty at *Breda*, the Marquess of *Montrosse* landed in the Isles of *Orkney* with fifteen hundred Armes, and five hundred German Souldiers: and after he had gathered more strength, he was defeated by Colonal *Straughan*, taken, and brought to *Edinburgh*, where he is brought to his Trial, condemned and executed.

The rigorous prosecution of the Marquess of *Montrosse* in that violent manner, was chiefly from the instigation of the Kirk, by which long before he had been Excommunicated. Concerning which he spake to the people in this manner upon the Scaffold.

> *What I did in this Kingdom, was in obedience to the most just Commands of my Sovereign, for his defence in the day of his distress; against those that rose up against him. I fear God, and honour the King, according to the Commandments of God, and the Law of Nature and Nations, &c. It is objected against me by many, even good people, that I am under the censure of the Church: this is not my fault, since it is onely for doing my duty, by obeying my Prince's most just Commands, for Religion, his Person, and Authority: yet am I sorry they did Excommunicate me; and in that which is according to God's Laws, without wronging my Conscience or Allegiance, I desire to be relaxed. If they will not, I appeal to God, who is the Righteous Judge of the World: and who must and will, I hope, be my Judge and Saviour.*

The King was much troubled at the Scots severity against this Noble Marquess.

After this the King lands in *Scotland*, and is Proclaimed King at *Edinburgh* Cross. But his Majesty had not been long among the Scots, but they began (according to their usual manner of Kirk Authority and Discipline) to obtrude upon the King such curbing conditions, as but ill-suited with Regal dignity.

Then the Common-wealth of *England* sent an Army against *Scotland*, and *Cromwel* is made General of the Parliament's Forces instead of Lord *Fairfax*: and about the end of *June* he marched towards *Berwick* in order to his advance into *Scotland*. The Scots raise an Army, and in the mean-time send many Expostulatory Letters to Sir *Arthur Haslerigg* then at *Newcastle*, urging the breach of Covenant, and the union between the two Nations, which availed nothing.

The Scots having been routed at *Muscleburgh*, they came to a Battel at *Dunbar*, where the whole Army was defeated by *Cromwel*: of the Scots there were slain in the Battel four thousand, and nine thousand were taken prisoners, with all their Ammunition, bag and baggage, and ten thousand Armes. The Scots after this loss quitted *Lath* and *Edinburgh*,

burgh, whereof the next day *Cromwel* took possession, and the King retired to St. *Johnstons*, where the Committee of Estates were assembled. The Scots ascribed this overthrow of the Army to their admitting the King into *Scotland*, before he had given full satisfaction to the Kirk in what they required of him; and began very much to impose upon him, and remove from his Person the most Faithful and Loyal of his Servants. The King departs secretly from St. *Johnstons* in discontent to the Lord *Dedup's* house near *Dundee*. The Estates at St. *Johnstons* send Major General *Montgomery* to fetch the King back: the King returns with him to St. *Johnstons*, where a grand Convention is held, and divers of the Royal Nobility are received into the favour of this Assembly.

Cromwel fortifieth *Lieth*, and lays close siege to *Edinburgh* Castle. Mr. *John Guthry*, Mr. *Patrick Gelespy*, Mr. *Samuel Rutherford*, with many other Ministers, withdrew from the Assembly at St. *Johnstons*, and in print remonstrated, in the name of themselves and the Western Churches, against the present proceedings; and with these Colonel *Ker*, *Straughan*, the Laird of *Warreston*, Sir *John Chiefly*, and Sir *James Stuart*, and others, Confederated. By this division *Cromwel's* Conquest was made very easie: and his fomenting that Rent in their Church, made their subjection to his Authority more lasting than otherwise it would have been.

The King was desirous to compose this disorder, or (at least) to prevent the dividing so great a Force, as was under *Ker* and *Straughan* from his Service: and to that end the Earl of *Cassels*, the Lord *Broody*, and Mr. *Robert Douglas* the Minister, were sent to treat with them; but they were somewhat averse to a composure; yet they declared against any conjunction with *Cromwel*, professing equally against Malignants (as they called the King's Loyal Subjects) and Sectaries. Soon after Colonel *Ker*, being defeated, was taken prisoner by Major General *Lambert*. Mr. *Rutherford* wrote divers consolatory Letters to him during his imprisonment both in *Scotland* and in *England*.

Edinburgh Castle was surrendered, by *Dundasse* the Governor, Son in Law to old *Leven*, upon conditions, unto *Cromwel*, on *December* 24. 1650. Shortly after all the Forts on this side of *Sterling* were taken by the English. The King was solemnly Crowned at *Scoone*, near unto St. *Johnstons* (the accustomed place of the Coronation of the Kings of *Scotland*) his Coronation being celebrated with loud Acclamations, Bonfires, shooting off of Guns, and with as much pomp and Ceremony as the present State of things would permit.

About the beginning of *June* the Parliament of *Scotland* ended, having before their dissolution given large Commissions and Instructions for the pressing of men in all parts of the Kingdom beyond *Fife*, and in the Western parts for a new Army, which was to consist of 15000 Foot, and 3000 Horse and Dragoons.

Addition to Sir *Richard's* Chron.

The

Then was the intended rising in *Lancashire* unfortunately disapointed, *Anno* 1651. by the taking of a Ship at *Ayx* in *Scotland*, which had been bound to the Earl of *Darby* in the Isle of *Man*, and the seizing of Mr. *Birkinhead* an Agent in the business, by whose Letters all was detected; and thereupon were apprehended Mr. *Thomas Cook* of *Grays-Inn*, Mr. *Gibbons* a Tailor, and Mr. *Potter* an Apothecary, together with Mr. *Christopher Love*, Mr. *William Jenkin*, Mr. *Thomas Case*, Dr. *Roger Drake*, and some other Presbyterial Ministers, who were brought before a High Court of Justice, and tried for their lives, and about the latter end of *July*, *Potter*, *Gibbons*, and Mr. *Love*, were sentenced to death; and a while after, *Gibbons* and *Love* were executed.

After the defeat of Sir *John Brown* by *Lambert*, and the taking of *Brunt-Island* and *Inchgarvy-Castle* by the English; *Cromwel* resolved to set upon St. *Johnstons*, which after one day's siege he gained. Hereupon the King leaves *Scotland*, and enters *England* with his Army by the way of *Carlile*, on *August* 6. 1651. At his first entrance upon English ground he was Proclaimed King of *Great Britain*, at the Head of the Army, with great Acclamations, and shooting off the Canons, on *August* 22. he came to *Worcester*. The Earl of *Darby* coming with Forces to the King, was routed by Colonel *Lilburn*. *Cromwel* having with the conjunction of the Militia of divers Counties, drawn together an Army of fifty thousand men, surroundeth the City of *Worcester*. Duke *Hamilton* (who behaved himself with undaunted courage) received a shot on his thigh, whereof presently after he died. The King's Army being over-powred, they were forced to retreat into the City, and many of *Cromwel's* Army got in with them. About seven at night the *Cromwellians* gained the Fort Royal, at which time his Majesty left the City, passing out at St. *Martin's* gate, accompanied with about Sixty Horse of the chiefest of his Retinue. The Town was taken, and miserably plundered.

There were slain in the Field, in the Town, and in Pursuit some two thousand; and about eight thousand were taken prisoners in several places; most of the English common men escaping by their *Shibboleth*. But at *Newport* there were taken in the pursuit, the Earls of *Lauderdale*, *Rothes*, *Carnworth*, *Darby*, *Cleveland*, *Shrewsbury*; the Lord *Spyne*, Sir *John Pakington*, Sir *Ralph Clare*, Sir *Charles Cunningham*, Colonel *Graves*, Mr. *Richard Fanshaw*, Secretary to the King, and many others: Six Colonels of Horse, eight Lieutennant Colonels of Foot, six Majors of Horse, thirteen Majors of Foot, thirty seven Captains of Horse, seventy two Captains of Foot, fifty five Quarter-masters, eighty nine Lieutenants. There were taken also some general Officers with seventy six Cornets of Horse, ninety nine Ensignes of Foot, ninety Quartermasters, eighty of the King's Servants, with the King's Standard, which

he

he had set up when he summoned the Countrey, the King's Coach and Horses, and Collar of S S. but the King's person God wonderfully preserved, delivering him from the Hand of all his Enemies, and after many difficulties he is safely transported, from *Bright-helmston* in *Sussex*, into *France*, by *Tatterfall*.

Cromwel comes with his prisoners to *London*, and having left Lieutennant General *Monk* in *Scotland*, *Sterling* with the Castle was surrendred unto him, and *Dundee* was taken by Storm; and soon after St. *Andrews*, *Aberdeen*, with other Towns, Castles, and Strong places, either voluntarily submitted, or rendred upon summons.

The Earl of *Darby* was beheaded at *Bolton* in *Lancashire*. The Isles of *Man* and *Jersey*, &c. are surrendred to the Parliament. The Isle of *Barbadoes* is yielded up to Sir *George Ascough*. Now the Parliament of *England* resolves upon an union of *England* and *Scotland*, and an incorporating of both Nations into one Common-wealth. This was much opposed and remonstrated against by the Scotch *Kirk*, but in vain.

Anno 1652. began the War with *Holland*: An Act was passed, entitled, *An Act against unlicensed and scandalous Books and Pamphlets, and for the better regulating of Printing*.

Anno 1653. The Officers of the Army consult about change of Government: on *April* 20. *Cromwel*, *Lambert*, *Harison*, and eight Officers more of the Army, entred the House of Commons, and after a short speech made by *Cromwel*, shewing some reasons for the necessity of their dissolution, he declared them dissolved, and required them to depart: but the Speaker would not leave the Chair till *Harison* pulled him out by the Arm. Then *Cromwel* commanded the Mace to be taken away, and no more to be carried before him. Then they caused the doors of the Parliament House to be locked up, and placed a Guard thereon to prevent the reassembling of the Members.

The first thing done after this change, was to constitute a Council of State of the chief Officers of the Army. These agreed upon the several persons all over *England* to form a new Representative, and a summons was sent to every one of them in the name of *Oliver Cromwel*, Captain General of all the Forces, *&c.* to take upon them the trust to which they were summoned, and to meet at *Whitehall*, on *July* 5. These assembled at the time appointed, and went to the Parliament House, and chose Mr. *Rouse* (made by the late Parliament Provost of *Eaton*) to be their speaker.

This mock-Parliament, called by some the little Parliament, aimed at the new modelling both of Magistracy and Ministry: but the Ministry and the maintenance thereof by Tithes, they arraigned as an Antichristian Constitution. Having passed an Act about Marriages, Births, and Burials, on *December* 12. *Rouse* the Speaker told the House, *That their fitting was no longer necessary;* and presently went out of the House with the Mace before him, and (many others following him) he came to *White-hall,* and there resigned to *Cromwell* the Instrument by him formerly delivered to them at their first sitting.

About four dayes after the Officers of the Army had prepared an Instrument, or Systeme of Government, on which the foundation of a new Dominion was to be erected, and they entreated *Oliver Cromwell* to accept of the Government under the Title of *Protector of the Commonwealth of* England, Scotland, *and* Ireland. He accepted it, and was that day, at one of the clock in the afternoon, Installed at *Westminster.* The Protector's Council being chosen and established, he makes a peace with the *Dutch,* and with the Queen of *Sweden;* Spain, Portugal, *and* France, seek *Cromwel's* friendship.

As to the state of Religion at this time in *England,* one thus describes it.

Flagellum, or the life and death of *O. C.* p. 144.

The *Orthodox Protestants were wholly suppressed, and yet some Reverend persons, as Doctor* Usher, *Archbishop of* Armagh, *and Doctor* Brownrigg, *the Bishop of* Exeter, *received some shews of respect and reverence from the Protector, which he more manifestly declared afterward in the Funeral-expence of the Learned Archbishop* Usher, *and this to captate a reputation of his love to Scholars, and the meek, modest, and vertuous Clergy.*

The Presbyterian *was rather tolerated than countenanced; and yet such of them as would comply with his Court-greatness became his Favourites, for others of them he cared not, pleasingly expressing himself, how he had brought under the pride and arrogance of that Sect, making those that would allow no liberty to others, to sue for it themselves.*

The Independents, *and* Anabaptists, *he loved, and preferred by turns, and was most constant to them, as the men that would support his Usurpation. Only he could by no means endure the* Fifth-Monarchy-men, *though by their dotages he had raised himself to this height. Therefore* Feak *and* Rogers, *Preachers, were by him committed to prison;* Feak *to* Windsor, *and* Rogers *to* Carisbrook *in the Isle of* Wight. *But it is said, he set Mr.* Kiffin, *the* Anabaptist *(whom he had taken out of design into his favour with the party) at variance with* Feak, *to the raising of a feud between them; the ballance of his security in the Government. The like he did between the* Presbyterian *and the* Independent, *a subdivided Schism from the Church of* England, *as the other were from* Independency. *And it was observed, that in most great Towns and Cities in* England, *he placed an* Independant *Minister, and a* Presbyterian *together, that the one might ballance the other.*

The *Kirk of* Scotland at this time had the wings of her Authority very much clipped, if not quite taken away by the dissolution of the General Assembly, which was done by Colonel *Morgan* at *Aberdeen,* where they were assembled; Mr. *Andrew Cant,* and the rest of them in vain

protesting

protesting against the Action. The like disturbance they had afterwards at *Edenburgh* from Lieutenant Colonel *Cotterel*.

The Marquess of *Argyle*, to keep up his Reputation with the Church of *Scotland*, seemed much troubled at this proceeding against the Assemblies, and interceded with the Protector for the liberty of the Church, wherein he had good success: and the Church of *Scotland* was indulged with the exercise of Religion, and a great part of their Jurisdiction and Discipline. They were restrained in little more than the power of keeping General Assemblies (their Presbyteries being permitted to convene) and the rigour of Excommunication; for whereas before persons excommunicated were not only excluded from the communion of the *Kirk*, but had all their Estates confiscated till their reconciliation. This latter part was not now to be executed; but to please the Ministers for the restraint of their power, the maintenance of Scholars in Universities of *Scotland* was encreased, and many priviledges were granted to them.

The Government and security of the Kingdom of *Ireland* was the next care of the Protector, and his Son-in-law, Lieutenant General *Fleetwood*, is made Deputy of *Ireland*.

About this time an Ordinance was published for the Trial and Approbation of Ministers, wherein Doctor *Thomas Goodwyn*, *Philip Nye*, *Hugh Peters*, Mr. *Manton* and divers others were named Commissioners. It was ordained, That every person who should after March 25. 1654. be presented, nominated, chosen, or appointed to any Benefice (called a Benefice with cure of Souls) or to preach any publick Lecture in England or Wales, should before he be admitted to such Benefice or Lecture, be adjudged and approved of by the Persons forenamed, to be a Person for the Grace of God in him, his holy and unblameable Conversation, and also for his knowledge and utterance, able and fit to preach the Gospel. And that after the said twenty five of March, no person, but such as should upon such approbation be admitted by the said persons, should take any publick Lecture, having a stipend legally annexed thereunto, or take or receive any such Benefice as aforesaid, or the profits thereof.

Hughs Abridgement of all Acts and publick Ordinances. part. 2.

On *June* the twenty third following, by the Protector, with the advice of his Council, it was further ordained, That in case any person, who since April the first, 1653. hath been proved in any publick Benefice or publick Lecture, should not before the twenty fourth of June, 1654. obtain approbation and admittance in manner as in the said Ordinance is expressed, that then the person, or persons, who have right thereunto, should and might present and nominate some other fit person to that place.

It was ordained also, That the said Commissioners in that Ordinance be authorized to give approbation and admittance to any person concerned in that clause

clause of the said Ordinances, at any time before the twenty third day of July, 1654. and that in the mean time no person should present, or nominate, any person to any Benefice, or publick Lecture, in the place of any such person, for the want of such approbation by the time aforesaid. But if such approbation and admittance should not be by the said twenty third of July obtained by the said persons therein concerned, then such person, or persons, as have right thereunto, might present or nominate some other fit person to such place, according to the said Ordinance.

August the sixteenth, 1654. an Ordinance was passed against ignorant and scandalous Ministers, in all the respective Counties within *England* and *Wales*: in which it was declared.

1. That such Ministers, and Scholars, should be accounted scandalous in their lives, as should be proved guilty for holding such blasphemous and Atheistical Opinions, as are punishable by an *Act of Parliament*, entitled, An Act against several Atheistical, Blasphemous, and Execrable Opinions, derogatory to the Honour of God, and destructive to Humane society: or guilty of cursing, swearing, or subornation of perjury.

2. Such as hold, or teach any of those Popish opinions, required in the Oath of abjuration, to be abjured: or be guilty of adultery, fornication, drunkenness; &c. carding, dicing, profaning of the Lord's day, or allow the same in their Families.

3. Such as have publickly, and frequently received and used the Common-prayer-book, since the first of January last, or shall at any time hereafter do the same.

4. Such as do encourage, or countenance, by word, or practice, any Whitsun-ales, Wakes, Morris-dances, May-poles.

5. Such as have declared, or shall declare, by writing, preaching, or otherwise, their disaffection to the Government.

6. Such Ministers were to be accounted negligent, as omit the publick Exercises of Preaching, and Praying, on the Lord's-day (not being hindered by necessary absence, or infirmity of sickness) or that are or shall be non-resident.

7. Such School-masters should be accounted negligent, as absent themselves from their Schools, and do wilfully neglect their duties in teaching their Scholars.

8. Such Ministers, and School-masters, should be accounted ignorant, and insufficient, as should be so declared, and adjudged, by the said Commissioners, five or more of them, together with five, or more, of the Ministers particularly named in the Ordinance for the several and respective Counties of *England* and *Wales*, Assistants to the said Commissioners.

August the thirtieth, 1654. It was ordained; That Sir Hugh Owen Baronet, and divers other persons particularly named in the Ordinance for all
the

the several Counties in the Dominion of Wales, be Commissioners in their several limits, and that the said Commissioners, or any three of them, therein are authorized by their Warrants under their hands and seals to call before them all such persons, who by authority and colour of an Act of Parliament, made February the twenty second, 1649. entitled [An Act for the better Propagation, and Preaching of the Gospel in *Wales*, *&c.*] have intermedled in the receiving, keeping, and disposing the said rents, issues, and profits of all or any of the Rectories, Vicarages, portion of Tenths, and other Ecclesiastical livings, Impropriations, and Glebe-lands within the said Counties: and to give a true and perfect account upon Oath (which Oath the Commissioners are impowred to administer) of all such rents, issues, and profits, which they, or any of them, have received. And if any of them shall refuse to give a true account, to commit him, or them, so refusing to the Gaol of the County, there to remain, till they conform themselves. The moneys found in their hands to be paid into the hands of such Treasurer as the respective Commissioners should nominate and appoint for that purpose: which Treasurer should within three months pay in the same into the Exchequer.

September the second, 1654. It was ordained, That the Ordinance, entitled, An Ordinance for bringing in the publick Revenue of this Commonwealth into one Treasury, to be paid into the Receipt of the Exchequer; nor any thing therein contained, shall extend, or be construed to extend to any the Rents, Profits, or Revenues, by Acts of Parliament, of Rectories impropriate, appropriate Tythes, &c. or any of them setled in the Trustees in the said Acts named.

That all and every the Rectories, Impropriations, Tithes appropriate, Donatives, Oblations, Obventions, First-fruits, Tenths, Pensions, Portions of Tiths. by the said recited Acts vested in the Trustees, and not exposed to sale by an Act, entitled, [An Act for the sale of Mannors, of Rectories, and Glebe-lands, belonging to Archbishops, Bishops, Deans, Deans and Chapters] shall from henceforth be setled in the possession and seizin of W. Steele, Serjeant at Law, and other persons particularly named in the Ordinance, Survivor and Survivors of them, and their Heirs, to the uses, and upon the Trusts in the said Acts expressed, &c.

That they shall sue for, recover, collect, and gather the Rents, Issues, and Profits thereof, as Owners in Trust, and manage the Revenue in such way and manner as shall be most advantageous for the carrying on of this service.

That the said Trustees shall have power to make unions of two Parishes, or more, into one, and the whole Ecclesiastical Revenues, Tithes, and Profits belonging to the said Parishes so united, to be supplied for a provision for one godly and painful Minister, to preach in such of the said Parish charge, where such union shall be made, as the said Trustees shall judge convenient.

The said Trustees also shall appoint, where the meeting of both the said Parishes, for the worship of God, shall be, &c.

The said Trustees also shall have power to sever and divide Parishes, where they shall conceive it needful, and fix such maintenance out of the profits of the said Church, so to be divided, as they shall think fit, to be approved of by the Parliament, and in the Intervals of Parliament by the Protector and his Council, &c.

This year died that famous and learned Antiquary, Mr. *John Selden*, and was buried in the *Inner-Temple* Church in *London*.

Addition to Sir *Rich. Baker's* Chron.

Anno 1655. the Duke of *Savoy*'s Souldiers having committed many cruel outrages upon the Protestants in *Piedmont*, *Cromwel* took this occasion to ingratiate himself with the Protestants abroad, and appointing a solemn day of Humiliation to be kept, he caused a large contribution to be gathered for them throughout the Nation, and sent his Agents abroad to mediate for them. Alderman *Viner* and *Pack* were made Treasurers for this Money, which amounted to a very large sum: but how much came to the hands of those for whom it was pretended to be collected, I know not. The French King accommodated the business, the Duke of *Savoy* refusing to admit *Cromwel*'s mediation.

Upon the tendring of certain Proposals, to the Protector, by *Manasseh Ben-Israel*, a Jewish Merchant, in the behalf of his Hebrew Nation, for their free admission to Trade, and exercise of their Religion in *England*, a Conference was held about it, several dayes at *White-hall*, by the Members of the Council, and certain Divines of the greatest note among them: and many Arguments being urged *pro* and *con*, those against their admission so far prevailed, that the Proposals took no effect. Mr. *Prynne* wrote a Book, at the same time, against their admission.

Then was an Ordinance made by the Protector, with the advice of his Council, for the Relief of Ministers put into sequestred Livings, against Molestations, and Suits, by Parsons sequestred and ejected.

On *September* the seventeeth, 1656. a Parliament assembled at *Westminster*, and chose for their Speaker Sir *Thomas Widdrington*. Now *The Humble Petition and Advice* was framed, which was a Module of Government, with which they several times waited on the Protector at *White-hall*, to desire him to take the chief Government of the Nations upon him, with the Title of *King*; of which the power he already had, the name only he wanted. He finding his Officers averse to it, at last returned answer, *That he could not take the Government upon him with that Title.*

Now was *James Nailor*, the great Ring-leader of the Sect called *Quakers*, brought to his Trial, who having spread his Doctrine, and gained many Proselites to it in divers parts of the Nation, was more especially taken notice of at *Exeter*, *Wells*, and *Bristol*, and from

Bristol

Briſtol was brought up to *London*, attended by several Men and Women of his Opinion, who all the way they came ſtrewed Gloves and Handkerchiefs in his way, and ſang *Hoſannah*'s to him, and (blaſphemouſly) are ſaid to have uſed the ſame kind of expreſſions toward him, as anciently the people of the Jews did to our Saviour, when he rode in triumph to *Jeruſalem*. *Nailor* being convented before the Parliament, was charged of Blaſphemy, for aſſuming to himſelf Divine honours, and ſuch Attributes as were due to Chriſt only. He was ſentenced by the Houſe to be (firſt at *London*) publickly whipt, pillored, and ſtigmatized, and bored through the Tongue with a red hot Iron, as a Blaſphemer: then to be conveyed to *Briſtol*, there to be alſo whipt; laſtly, to be brought back to *London*, to remain in *Bridewel* during pleaſure; which Sentence was inflicted upon him.

At this time the viperous brood of Sects, and Hereſies, ſwarmed through all parts of the Nation. Then the Ranters began to multiply, and the Socinians, who denied the Divinity of Chriſt; and one *Biddle* was infamous for theſe Opinions; and *Erbury*, formerly a Miniſter in *Cardiff* in *Wales*, degenerated unto Ranting.

The Compiler of this Treatiſe once heard this *Erbury* ſpeak in a publick Congregation, near *Bath* in *Sommerſet-ſhire*, of a threefold Diſpenſation of God to his Church and People. *There hath been* (ſaid he) *a twofold diſcovery of God to his People, or a two-fold Diſpenſation, namely, the Diſpenſation of the Law and the Goſpel, and God diſcovered himſelf to his People in both Diſpenſations diverſly. Under the Law God diſcovered himſelf to his people in a way of fear: therefore God was called the great and fearful God, and the delivery of the Law to Moſes was in a fearful manner.* Now when the Apoſtle ſpeaks of the Miniſtry of the Goſpel, he ſaith, You have not received the ſpirit of bondage again to fear, but the Spirit of Adoption, &c. *that is* (ſaid he) *now when the Goſpel came, men knew God to be a Father, and they in the Spirit of Adoption cried*, Abba, Father.

He added, *That under the Law God was known as a Lord, and Maſter, to keep his People in work; and as they had their work, ſo they had their wages; and if they did not work, they had terrors upon their ſpirits to affright them. But under the Goſpel, God was diſcovered to be a Father full of Light and Love, ſo that now we converſe with God in a loving manner, and ſerve him as a Son ſerveth his Father.*

He proceeded to tell us, *That there is a third Diſpenſation yet to come in the laſt dayes, wherein God will diſcover himſelf in a more fearful way, and yet in a way more full of light and love than in former times*.

He added, *That then there will be a fuller diſcovery of God, than hath been both under the Law and Goſpel: and the ignorance of this* (he ſaid) *hath been the cauſe of all the confuſions, and contentions, among the People of God*.

He

He said, *That the Apostles waited for this Dispensation, another state more glorious than any they had yet attained unto.* This glorious Dispensation (he told us) St. Paul *calls,* The Glory to be revealed in us, the glorious liberty of the Sons of God ; *and that St.* Peter *calls it*, The new Heaven, and new Earth, *and St.* John, The new Jerusalem.

He said, *That the Mystery of the Gospel, which was preached by the Apostles, was hid from men; they knew not the mystery of it : but the time will come, that this mystery of the Gospel will come forth in a fuller discovery than hath been heretofore made known.* But I shall trouble the Reader no further with him.

On *April* the nineteenth, 1657. at a certain House in *Shoreditch*, were apprehended a discontented party, formerly in the Army, that went under the same of. Fifth *Monarchy-men,* such as taking upon them to be the Champions of Christ s Monarchy on Earth, renounced all Monarchy besides : the chief of whom were *Thomas Venner*, a Wine-Cooper, Predicant, *Ashton, Hopkins, Gowler,* and *Gray* their Scribes. They had appointed to have rendezvouz that night at *Mile-end-Green*, and thence to have marched into some other Counties, to joyn with others of their party, that were ready to shew themselves upon the first opportunity. There was taken with them a great quantity of Arms, and certain printed Papers that were to be dispersed, and a Standard with a *Lion couchant, Gules, in a Field Argent*, having this Motto, *Who shall rouze him up ?*

There was also taken Major General *Harison,* Captain *Lawson,* late Vice-Admiral, Colonel *Rich, Carew* and *Courtney*, and Major *Danvers*; whereof the first was committed to the Serjeant at Armes, and the rest were sent to remote Castles and Prisons. General *Monk* had order to seize Major General *Overton*, and the Majors *Bramston* and *Holmes*, and cashier them after Fines and good Security for their behaviour. *Overton* was sent up to the Tower, and his Regiment conferred on Colonel *Morgan* : Colonel *Okey*'s Regiment was also taken from him, and given to a sure Confider : and one Major *Wildman*, a great Leveller, was taken at *Marleborough*, enditing and drawing Declarations against the Protector ; so the danger from the Army was soon suppressed.

About the same time a Book was published, called *Killing no Murther*, wherein it was urged, *That it was most lawful, just, necessary, and honourable to kill the Protector* ; and this printed with the name of one *Allen*, a disbanded Leveller, but so politely written, that it intimated a more exact and curious hand that framed it. Whosoever was the Author, it scared *Cromwel* almost out of his Wits. This made him most suspitiously fearful, so that he began to dread every person, or strange face he saw, (which he would anxiously, and intently, view) for an Assassinate, that Book perpetually running in his mind. It is said, it was his constant custom

stom to shift and change his Lodging, to which he passed through twenty several Locks, and out of which he had four or five wayes to avoid pursuit.

June twenty six, 1657. Then followed the Protector's Instalment, in a more solemn manner, in *Westminster-hall*, than before: and the Speaker of the Parliament, Sir *Thomas Widdrington*, in the name of the Parliament, presented to him a Robe of Purple-velvet, a Bible, Sword, and a Scepter, and having made a Speech thereupon, the Speaker took the Bible, and gave the Protector his Oath. Mr. *Manton*, Minister then of *Covent-Garden*, made a Prayer, wherein he recommended the Protector, Parliament, Council, the Forces by Sea and Land, Government, and People of the three Nations, to the protection of God. Which being ended, the Heraulds by Trumpets proclaimed *Cromwell* Protector of *England*, *Scotland*, and *Ireland*, and the Dominions thereunto belonging, requiring all persons to yield him due obedience.

Then were the attempts of the Royal Party, in behalf of his Majesty, betrayed, and discovered to the Protector, and Sir *Henry Slingsby*, Doctor *Huet*, Minister of St. *Gregories* by *Pauls* in *London*, Mr. *Mordant*, and others are imprisoned, and brought to trial before an High Court of Justice, set up under the Presidentship of Commissioner *Lisle*. Sir *Henry*, and the Doctor, were the two first that were brought to trial, and both of them sentenced to die as Traitors: the first upon the bare testimony of those three men, who had so treacherously circumvented him, which in vain he pleaded: the other, as a Mute, disowning the Authority of the Court, and thereupon denying to plead. On the eighth of *June*, 1658. they were beheaded on Tower-hill. Afterwards, on *July* the seventh, Colonel *Edward Ashton*, and *John Bettley*, were hanged and quartered, the first in *Tower-street*, the other in *Cheap-side*.

Cromwell was now again adorned with another success, and triumph, by the defeat of the Spanish Army, and surrender of *Dunkirk* into his hands, *Lockart* his Kinsman, and General of the English Forces, being made Governor thereof.

In *August*. 1658. the Protector was taken sick at *Hampton-court*, having not been well in mind some time before (troubled with the last distracted words of his beloved Daughter *Cleypole*, who died on the sixth day of *August*) which went near to his heart. After a weeks time his Disease began to shew very desperate symptomes: wherefore he was removed to *White-hall*, where his Chaplains kept Fasts for his recovery: but having declared his Son *Richard* his Successor, he died on Friday, *September* the third, at three of the Clock in the Afternoon.

The deceased Protector's Will, concerning his Successor, being imparted to the Council, and chief Officers of the Army, they all consent to the election of his Son *Richard*, and the President, and whole Council, went at once to congratulate him, and to condole his Fathers death. Then was he proclaimed by the City of *London*, and chief Officers of the Army. After the Proclamation, the Lord Mayor presented his Sword to him, which he presently returned: and after some Ceremonies passed, (the Council, and many Officers of the State, and of the Army being present) *Nathanael Fiennes*, one of the Commissioners of the Great Seal, administred an Oath unto him.

A Gentleman was sent into *Ireland*, who was chief Governor of that Kingdom, to acquaint *Henry Cromwell* with the present posture of Affairs in *England*: and Mr. *Thomas Clarges* was sent into *Scotland*, to General *Monk*, to see how he stood affected to *Richard*'s advancement. Then Addresses were made to the Protector from all parts of the Nation: and the Army of *Scotland* submit to what was was done in *England*. Addresses were also made to the young Protector from all the Regiments of the Army in *England*, *Scotland*, and *Ireland*, and other parts.

After the pompous solemnity of the Funerals of the late Protector, the new Protector summoned a Parliament, to meet at *Westminster*, on *January* twenty seven; he endeavours to new model his Council; but the Army grows jealous of him, and censure him, and the factious part of the Army had many seditious meetings, and he is perswaded to resign the command of the Army to *Fleetwood*, which he refuseth. The General Council of Officers (as they called themselves) met in *Fleetwood*'s House, where they acted with as much formality, as if they had been the supreme Legislators of the three Kingdoms. At length things came to this issue, the young Protector was forced to sign a Commission to Commissioner *Fiennes*, for the dissolving of the Parliament, and a Proclamation came forth, in the Protector's name, to publish the dissolution of the Parliament.

Soon after, whilst many of the Superiour Officers of the Army met at *Wallingford-house*, in further consideration of a Module of Government, the inferiour Officers being the most numerous, assembled in the Chappel at St. *James*'s, having Doctor *Owen*, and other Independent Ministers, to assist at their Devotion, and at last declared their forwardness to restore the latter part of the long Parliament, and to restore *Lambert*, and the rest of the Officers to their Commands; who had been displaced by *Oliver Cromwel* for disaffection to him.

Several Colonels were removed from their Regiments, and others put in their rooms; as likewise Governours of Towns and other Officers. *Lambert* being thus brought again into the Army, recovereth much of his former power.

Then a Declaration of the Officers of the Army was drawn up, which invited the Members of the long Parliament, who had sate till *April*,

Supplem. to Sir Rich. Baker's Hist.

the Church of GREAT BRITAIN.

April the twentieth, 1653. to return to the exercise and discharge of their trust. They accept of the Invitation, and take their places in the House.

General *Monk* seems to consent to what was done in *England*.

They publish their Intentions by Declaration, *viz.*

That they are resolved, by God's assistance, to endeavour to secure and establish the property and Liberties of the people, without a single Person, Kingship, or House of Peers: and shall vigorously endeavour the carrying on of Reformation, so much desired: to the end there may be a godly and faithful Magistracy, and Ministry upheld and maintained in the Nations, &c.

The Officers of the Army presented an humble Address to the Remnant Parliament, on *May* 12. 1659. by *Lambert* and others. *Richard*, the late Protector, sends his submission to the Parliament. All Commissions to the Officers of the Army are ordered to be signed by the Speaker: and *Henry Cromwell* is called from the Government of *Ireland*: *Fleetwood*, *Lambert*, and others, receive their Commissions in the House from the Speaker. The Governour of *Dunkirk* submits also to the change of our Government. General *Monk* likes not the *Junto's* designs of modelling his Army, and useth his utmost industry to obstruct it. Commissioners are appointed for the Goverment of *Ireland*.

In the mean time Captain *Titus*, and others, sent as Commissioners from the King, are active for his Majesties service in *London*, and in the Countrey. Sir *George Booth*, with several others, appear in a considerable Body; they take possession of *Chester* City, but the Castle holds out against them. *Chirk-Castle* is delivered to them by Sir *Thomas Middleton*. Collonel *Ireland*, and several others, at the same time declare for them at *Leverpool*, and Mr. *Brook*, one of the Members of the House of Commons.

Lambert is sent against Sir *George Booth*. Mr. *Nicholas Monk*, a Minister, and the only Brother to General *Monk*, is sent into *Scotland* from Sir *Hugh Pollard*, Sir *Thomas Stukely*, and other of his Majesties Friends in the West of *England*; He sollicits his Brother to embrace his Majesties Interest.

The King wrote a Letter to General *Monk*, and another to Sir *John Greenvill*, concerning the owning his Cause. Major General *Massey* was active in *Glocester-shire*, and the Lord *Herbert*, Son to the Marquess of *Worcester*, and others. The Lord *Herbert* was taken: so was Major General *Massey*, with others: but all the rest of the Prisoners, except the Lord *Herbert*, and *Massey's* Servant, make an escape.

A a a 2 *Lambert*

Lambert marcheth against Sir *George Booth*, and Sir *George* is defeated by *Lambert*, and soon after was seized at *Newport-pannel*, in a disguise, as he was riding to *London*.

After this defeat General *Monk* sends a Letter to the House, signifying his willingness to be dismissed from his Command. The Army begin to contrive the recovery and advancement of their power. The Officers of the Army, promoted by *Lambert*, dislike some proceedings of the *Juncto*. They conclude to draw up their desires in a Petition. Sir *Arthur Haslerig* vehemently opposeth the Armies proceedings: and incenseth the House against them and *Lambert*. *Fleetwood* endeavours to justifie the Officers of the Army, but in vain. *Ashfield*, *Cobbet*, and *Duckenfield*, presented the Petition of the Army to the House, thus directed.

T.a. the *Supreme Authority of these Nations, the Parliament of the Commonwealth of* England, &c.

The humble *Petition, and Proposals, of the Officers under the Command of the Right Honourable the Lord.* Lambert *, in the late Northern Expedition*.

The House signifie their displeasure, and vote against the effect of the Petition. Then the Officers resolve upon more moderate Proposals. Another Petition is brought into the Council of Officers more high than the former. General *Monk* writes his sence of it in a Letter to *Fleetwood*; and offers himself to march into *England*, to the assistance of the Parliaments Party.

October the fifth, Colonel *Desborow*, with many other Officers of the Army, present a Representation, and Petition of the Officers of the Army to the Parliament; who at first dissemble their distaste of these proceedings of the Army. The Council of Officers perceiving, that the Parliament labour to alter the Constitution of the Army, labour, to get Subscriptions to their Representation, and Petition. They send a Letter to General *Monk* concerning their Representation. He resolves to admit of no Subscriptions in *Scotland*. General *Monk* is courted by the Parliament, and complemented by Letters, with gratulatory Expressions for his good service.

The House takes the Armies debates into consideration, and answers them one by one. Mr. *Nicholas Monk* arrives from *Scotland* with private Orders from the General to Mr. *Clarges*. The house ordereth, That the Commissions of *Lambert*, and others be made void. They appoint Commissioners for governing the Army, and remove *Fleetwood* from the chief command thereof. Colonel *Morley*, and *Mosse*, are ordered with their Regiments to guard the House.

But

But *Lambert*, with the Regiments that adhere to him, stop the passages to the Parliament House, and having enforced the Speaker to return, they dissolve the Remnant Parliament, by hindring the Members from coming into the House.

The next day divers of the chief Officers of the Army met at *Whitehall*, and chose ten Army-Officers to be managers of the State Affairs *pro tempore*. They agree, that *Fleetwood* should be Commander in chief of all the Armies, and that *Lambert* should be the next chief Officer under him, and Colonel *Desborow* Commissary General of the Horse; and that all the Officers to be constituted in the Army, should be nominated by Sir *Henry Vane*, *Fleetwood*, *Lambert*, *Desborow*, *Ludlow*, and *Berry*. They dispatch Colonel *Cobbet* to General *Monk* with a large Narrative of the Reasons of their proceedings.

Now was Mr. *Armorer* sent by the Lord *Mordant* to the King, to inform him how matters went in *England*. The Council of Officers consult about a frame of Government. They nominate twenty three persons to take upon them the Government, under the Title of *The Committee of Safety*; and they invite them to sit, giving them Powers and Instructions.

General *Monk* writes to *Fleetwood*, and *Lambert*, complaining of their violation of Faith to the Parliament, declaring his resolution to endeavuor to restore them to their power, against all opposition whatsoever.

Mr. *Clarges* is dispatched away into *Scotland* by the Grandees of the Army, together with Colonel *Talbot*, to sollicit General *Monk* to a Treaty. *Monk* keeps in all the displaced Officers in their respective Commands, which causeth them to adhere unto him, and removes those whom himself distrusteth. He signifies his resolution to several of his Officers to march into *England*, to re-establish the Parliament, and hath their consent and encouragement.

He marcheth to *Edinborough*, and there orders all things to his best advantage.

Captain *Johnston* secures *Berwick*; Captain *Witter* takes possession, for the General, of the Cittadel of St. *Johnstons*, and is made Major of the Regiment. *Robson* gets possession of the Cittadel at *Ayre*, and is made Colonel of the Regiment. *Smith's* Regiment at *Innerness* is given to Colonel *Man*. The General marcheth to *Leith* to settle the Cittadel and Regiment there. Captain *Hatt* and *Dennis* bring off *Cobbet's* Regiment to the General; and *Cobbet* was detained prisoner at *Berwick*; as he was coming into *Scotland* with his Regiment, he was brought with a Guard to *Edenborough* Castle, and kept there.

At *Linlithgow*, at a Council of Officers, it was advised, that some way should be used to draw off the Independent Churches in *England* from favouring the English Army, which would have much weakened that party, if it had succeeded; for most of the Inferiour Officers were of that perswasion. For the effecting of this, a Declaration was framed, agreed to, published and dispersed all over *England:* and at the same time another *Declaration* was also made to satisfie the Kingdom in general with his proceedings.

General *Monk* invite's *Ludlow* in *Ireland* to a Conjunction with him. Colonel *Lilburn* at *York* with what forces he could draw together, makes all possible opposition against General *Monk*, and intercepts the General's Letters to Major General *Morgan*. *Talbot* and *Clarges* come to *Edinburgh Novem.* 2. and are well-received by the General.

General *Monk* take's hold, for his advantage, of *Lambert's* overture for a Treaty. Colonel *Clobery*, Colonel *Wilks*, and Major *Knight*, are chosen to be the General's Commissioners in this Treaty. They meet *Lambert* at *York*, who opposeth the proposal touching the restitution of the Parliament. The Army of Horse and Foot with *Lambert* amounted to neer twelve thousand, and *Monk* had not above half the number: but General *Monk* paid all his men, which the other did not.

Major General *Morgan* take's his journey into *Scotland* to General *Monk*, and his joyning with the General was a matter of great importance. He privately delivers a Letter to the General from Mr. *Bowles* a Minister of *York* a very eminent man of those parts, and of great credit with the Lord *Fairfax*. Mr. *Clarges* is sent to the Lord *Fairfax*, Colonel *Rossiter*, and others, to engage them to General *Monk*. Colonel *Talbot* is prevailed upon by *Lambert* to take part with him.

Colonel *Whaley*, Colonel *Goffe*, Captain *Dean*, and Mr. *Caryl* the Minister, are sent by *Fleetwood* to General *Monk*. *Fleetwood* by Letters Court's *Monk* to side with him.

The ruling Faction in *Ireland* declare their resolution not to joyn with General Monk. But Sir *Charles Coot*, Sir *Theophilus Jones*, and a considerable part of the Army resolve to assist him. Mr. *Clarges* returns from *Scotland*, and secretly confers with Mr. *Bowels* at *York*, to whom he brought a letter of Credit. *Bowels* negotiates with the Lord *Fairfax*, Colonel *Bethel*, and others in General *Monk's* behalf, who promise to assist him.

In the mean-time the Commissioners for the Independent Churches, which were sent into *Scotland*, were sollicitous to divert *Monk* from the prosecution of the War: there was a conference appointed with them at *Holy-rood-house*, where were present to treat with them General *Monk*, Colonel *Fairfax*, Colonel *Syler*, Dr. *Barrow*, the Judge Advocate of the Army, and Mr. *Gumble* one of the General's Chaplains, and Mr. *Collins* (who had been one of the Preachers to the late Council in *Scotland*) was admitted to be present there as a Newter.

Mr. *Caryl*

Mr. *Caryl* was the first that spake, and said, That they all came, not to declare their own sense of the General's proceedings, but the sense of the Churches (for so upon every occasion he called the Independent Congregations.) That the Churches had not given them Commission to enter into the merits of the cause, nor to debate whether *Lambert's* Action of turning out the Parliament were justifiable or not, but onely to present it to his Lordship, as their opinion, That though that Action could not be justified, yet his Lordship had not a call to appear against it in that manner that he then did, That his Lordship had onely in charge to keep *Scotland* in quiet, and was not bound to take notice of any differences in *England*. He proceeded to show reasons why the General should proceed no further, telling him, that it would put a strife among those that hitherto had been Brethren engaged all along in the same cause, partakers in the same dangers, and the same successes, among those that still in their Papers and all their Addresses, called and owned one another for Brethren; and that at a very unseasonable time, whilst the Canaanites and Perizzites were in the Land. He insisted on all the advantages the King and his Party would reap by this quarrel, and all the dangers the people of God (for so he called his own party) might run into. At last he told the General, that what Inconveniences soever should happen would be laid at his door, in regard he would appear to have been the beginner of the War.

At this the General interrupted him, shewing that the war was already begun by *Lambert* and his party, who had offered violence to those from whom they had all received their Commissions: not sparing largely to lay open their restless Instability, which would not suffer the three nations to enjoy any setled Government at all, but kept them in a perpetual circumvolution, till they were in danger to be brought to utter ruine; and Declaring, That if they continued in that course, he was resolved to oppose them to the uttermost, and would (to repeat his own words) lay them on their backs.

The Treaty ended between the Commissioners of the two Armies, who came to an agreement, which consisted of nine Articles, on *Novem.* 15, 1659. But General *Monk* consults how he might, with the most handsome pretence, refuse his Assent to these Articles. And it was proposed by Dr. *Barrow*, and agreed to by the General and the rest, That they should not declare a positive dissent to what their Commissioners had done, but urge, that there was something untreated of, further to be agreed upon, &c. and that therefore it should be desired, that two more might be allowed to be added to their Commissioners, to meet a like number of theirs to be thereunto authorized, to put a more absolute period to their differences.

Mr. *Atkins* and Colonel *Markham* are sent by the General with a Letter to the City of *London*, which so much incensed the Committee of Safety, that the Gentlemen who delivered it are Imprisoned.

On *November* 19. Nine of the Old Counsellors of State privately meet in *London*, and sent one Captain *Elmes*, with *Horton*, a servant of Sir *Arthur Hazlerig's* with a letter into *Scotland* to General *Monk*. This was a great encouragement to the Officers in *Scotland*.

Colonel *Whetham* at *Portsmouth* generously declared for General *Monk* with that Garrison, after the Council of State had framed a Commission, wherein they Constituted General *Monk* Commander in Chief of all the Armies in *England* and *Scotland*, which was dated *November* 24. sealed with their seal, and left in the hands of Mr. *Clarges*, till a safe messenger might be sent with it unto him. *Hurst-castle*, and the Isle of *Wight* are kept for the Parliament.

Commissioners from the several Shires and Burroughs of *Scotland* wait upon the General at *Berwick*, and the General and they part with a mutual respect. The General prepares to make defence against *Lambert*, if occasion were. There were many great differences between the City of *London*, and *Lambert's* party there. The Souldiers are affronted by the Apprentices not without some bloodshed. Oppositions from all parts encrease against *Lambert's* faction. *Lambert* was daily alarum'd with the success of the Commissioners at *Portsmouth*, and his party dayly decrease. *Fleetwood* submits, and desires the Members of Parliament to sit again. They take their Seats again in the Parliament House; and Order seven Commissioners for the management of the Army. Colonel *Morley* upon this change had his Regiment restored, and with it the Government of the Tower conferred on him. The *Irish* Brigade was brought off to General *Monk* by *Redman* and *Bret*. *Dublin-castle* is surprized: and Sir *Charles Coot* reduceth all *Connaught* to a compliance with the present Design. The Lord *Fairfax*, and several of *Monk's* party joyning with him, rise in *York-shire*.

Now General *Monk* begins his march into *England*. By that time he came to *Morpeth*, he was informed that *Lambert's* whole party was of themselves dispersed into several quarters in submission to the Parliament's Orders. There he receive's an Address from the City of *London* by Mr. *William Man*, their Sword-bearer, as likewise from the Gentry of the Countrey in all parts as he marched along.

The new restored Members on *January* 2. name 31. Counsellors of State, passing an Act for their Constitution, and several Instructions for them to Act by: among which it was provided, that none should sit, but such as should take an Oath of Abjuration of the King, His family, and Government. The Oath was opposed by divers of the House. *Scot* and *Robinson* are sent from the House to complement and attend General *Monk* upon his journey. Mr. *Clarges* gives him an account how affairs stand at *London*: he sends a letter by Mr. *Clarges* to the House from St. *Albans*. Several addresses are made to him in his March, pleading for a free Parliament. He marcheth with his forces

into

into the City of *London*. Being come to the Council of State, the Oath of Abjuration was tendred to him, which he refuseth to take. He is conducted with much Ceremony into the House, where he receives the gratulations of the House. The City continued malecontent, whereupon the General is Ordered by the Council of State to march into the City, and pull down the Gates and Percullices of the City, which he unwillingly caused to be done. The same day a Factious party of Citizens presented a Petition to the House by one *Praise-God Barebone* to countenance the Action.

The General sends a letter to the House signed by Himself and several Officers, complaining against the admission of *Ludlow* and others into the House, that had been by Sir *Charles Coot* accused of high Treason: and that they had countenanced too much a late Petition, to exclude the most sober and conscientious both Ministers and others by Oaths, from all employment and maintenance: he requested them, that by Friday next they should Issue out Writs to fill up their House, and when filled, should rise in some short time, to give place to a full and free Paliament. *Scot* and *Robinson* are sent from the House to the General with their answer to his letter.

The General excuseth his late proceedings in the City before the Lord Mayor and Common Council of the City. He tells them what he had written to the House touching a free Parliament: The City joyfully receives the news of a free Parliament.

The Council of State write to him to desire his presence with them: but he excuseth his stay in the City for some longer time, till the minds of the Citizens were more composed. The City, and Chief Officers of his Army disswade him from going to *White-hall*. The General is sollicited from all parts to admit the secluded Members. He admits of a conference before him, of the sitting with some of the secluded Members. The Officers of the Army consent to the admission of the secluded Members upon certain conditions: The General and the Officers at length agree upon their admission: and on the Tuesday morning following they were guarded to the House, and took their places in the Parliament.

Then was a letter signed by the General and his Chief Officers drawn up, and Copies of it sent to all the Regiments and Garrisons in *England*, and to the Commanders in Chief of the Armies in *England*, *Scotland*, and *Ireland* to acquaint them with what he had done.

The Parliament repealed the Act for the Council of State and the Oath of Abjuration, and passed an Act for another Council, consisting of one and thirty persons, most of them men of integrity, and well-affected to Kingly-government.

Then the General sends Colonel *Fairfax* to take possession of *Hull*, and Colonel *Overton* submits to his Orders. The Army in *Scotland* were

were well-satisfied with the General's Actions. About the thirteenth of *March* the Parliament abrogated the Engagement appointed formerly to be taken by each Member of Parliament, in these words, *viz.* [*I do declare and promise, That I will be true and faithful to the Common Wealth of England, as the same is now established without King, or House of Lords,*] and appointed it should be taken off the file, and made Null.

The Common Wealth Faction desire the General rather to take the Government upon himself, than to bring in the King; and treat with him about it. The General refuseth their offer. Then the Republicans attempt to make a mutiny in the Army. The long Parliament was now dissolved. The King removes to *Breda*.

The Council of State appointed by the late Parliament set forth a Proclamation for the preventing of tumults.

Lambert escape's out of the Tower. Colonel *Ingoldsby* and Colonel *Streater* march against *Lambert*, defeat his party, and take him prisoner. Colonel *Lambert*, Colonel *Cobbet*, and Major *Creed*, are sent prisoners to the Tower. Hereupon several seditious Pamphlets were published in Print, and dispersed to deprave the mindes of the people; and Tickets were thrown into the Courts of Guard in the night to divide the Souldiers. But none of them was penned with more virulency and malice, than that suppositious paper, carrying in it's Frontispiece, *A letter from* Bruxels, *&c.* Several letters were also sent to the General from unknown hands. Then came forth a Declaration of the Nobility and Gentry that adhered to the late King, residing in and about the City of *London*.

A new Parliament met at *Westminster, April* 25. 1660. The Lords chose the Earl of *Manchester* to be their Speaker; and the House of Commons Sir *Harbottle Grimston*. On *April* 27. Sir *John Greenvil* presents the General with a Commission from His Majesty, to Constitute him Captain General of all the Armies of *England, Scotland,* and *Ireland*; and a letter for the Council of State. The Letter had a Declaration in it, which were both read in the House. After the reading thereof the House of Lords voted, That according to the Antient and fundamental Laws of this Kingdom, the Government is, and ought to be, by King, Lords, and Commons.

The Officers of the Army present an Address to the General in compliance with His Majestie's Letter and Declaration: it is read by the Commons, and approved. Commissary *Clarges* is appointed by the General to wait upon the King with this Address. Six of the Lords and of the Commons, and divers Aldermen, and divers Episcopal and Presbyterial Divines, and some other eminent Citizens are sent to attend on his Majesty at *Breda*. His Majestie's Letter and Declaration to the Fleet, by the diligence of General *Mountague*, had the same success
there,

the Church of GREAT BRITAIN.

there, as that in the Army, being gratefully received by all the Commanders in the Fleet.

Three days after, the Lords and Commons having agreed upon a Proclamation to that purpose, His Majesty was Proclaimed with great solemnity in the Cities of *London* and *Westminster*, the Lords and Commons, and the Lord Mayor and Aldermen of *London* being present. Mr. *Clarges* carrieth the happy tidings hereof with a Letter from the General to His Majesty at *Breda*. Thereupon M. *Clarges* is Knighted by His Majesty. The Parliament's and Cities Commissioners have their audience from His Majesty at the *Hague*. The King afterwards landed at *Dover* with the Dukes of *York* and of *Glocester*, and many Noblemen and Gentlemen. There the General met him, upon whose motion for His going to *Canterbury*, the King hastned to His Coach, in His passage to which he was met by the Mayor and Aldermen of the Town, with Mr. *Reading* the Minister, who presented His Majesty with a large Bible with Golden Clasps. At His entrance into *Canterbury*, he was met by the Mayor and Aldermen, and Mr. *Lovelace* the Recorder, who made an eloquent speech to Him: the Mayor also presented Him with a Tankard of Massie Gold, and then conducted Him to the Palace, where He remained till Monday. From *Canterbury* He marcheth magnificently attended to *London*. When he came to S. *George*'s fields, the Lord Mayor and Aldermen on their Knees Reverenced His Majesty, and the Lord Mayor presented His Sword unto Him, which His Majesty gave back to him: from thence He was in a Triumphant and Glorious manner attended and conducted through the City of *London* to *White-hall*, On *May* 29. 1660. being His birth-day.

The Lord Mayor having taken leave of Him, He went to the Lords, where He was entertained with a grave and eloquent speech of the Earl of *Manchester*; and from thence to the Banquetting-house, where the whole House of Commons attending Him, the Speaker in their names expressed the joyful sence they all had to behold His Majesty return'd in safety, and thereby an end was put to that Tyranny and Slavery His good people had endured. His Majesty in brief expresseth his gracious intentions to them. Then His Majesty gave thanks to God in His Presence-chamber, for all His deliverances and mercies toward him. *May* 31. He sets forth a Proclamation against debauchery and profaneness. The Chief Officers of State, and of the King's Houshold, and the Lords of His Majestie's Privy Council, are constituted. The Commons set upon the Act of General Pardon. On *June* 4. the Oaths of Supremacy and Allegiance were taken by both Houses of Parliament, the King's Servants, and Officers of His Houshold. His Majestie's arrival is congratulated by the People from all parts of the Nation, and by several of the Nobility and Gentry both of *Scotland* and *Ireland*. The King on *July* 5. is magnificently entertained with the Dukes of *York* and *Glo-*

Bbb 2 *cester,*

cester, the Lords of the Privy-council, the two Houses of Parliament, and the Chief-officers of State, by the Lord Mayor and the Grandees of the City.

General *Monk* was created Duke of *Albemarle*, General *Mountague* made Earl of *Sandwich*, and the Marquess of *Ormond* made Duke of *Ormond*. The Chief Ministers of State are constituted in *Scotland*. Notwithstanding the late unanimous concurrence of the people at *Edinborough* (as well as other places) in the publick Proclaiming of His Majesty; yet soon after there began to discover it self a spirit of discontent among many Scotch Ministers, some of the principal sticklers of the Kirk-party, as appeared by their meeting together at a place appointed for the drawing up a Remonstrance concerning things wherein they thought themselves aggrieved: which the Committee of Estates having notice of, sent forthwith to apprehend them, and clapt them up in Prison; and for the prevention of the like disturbances for the future, set forth a Proclamation against all unlawful meetings, and seditious Papers.

The Marquess of *Argyle*, notwithstanding he came to Court with others of the Nobility and Gentry of *Scotland*, under pretence of tendring his service to His Majesty, yet was he charged with high Treason, and sent prisoner to the Tower: and together with him were committed the Marquess of *Antrim*, Sir *Henry Vane*, and Sir *Arthur Hazlerig*, with several others that followed. Sir *Arthur* died soon after of a Fever in the Tower. *Argyle* was sent back into *Scotland*, and their tried, condemned, and beheaded.

On *August* 19. among other Acts, an Act was passed by the King and Parliament for a perpetual Anniversary Thanksgiving on *May* 29. the day of His Majestie's Nativity and Restauration. An Act also was passed for a general Pardon, Indempnity, and Oblivion, in which among other things that were excepted, all accounts of the Revenues of Churches in *Wales* and *Monmouth-shire*, and all judgements of discharge, or *Quietus est* thereupon had.

This Exception as to the Churches in *Wales*, was inserted by the Parliament in this Act, upon information, that some factious people had, in the time of the late usurpation, procured to themselves an Authority to Sequester all those Revenues, upon pretence to employ them more equally to illiterate Preachers, for the better propagation of the Gospel in those parts, but kept the greatest part to their own use, leaving most of the Churches unsupplied.

All offences also done by any Popish Priest, Seminary, or Jesuite, contrary to the Statute of the 27 *Eliz.* were excepted.

Many of the late King's judges were excepted from pardon. All Trustees in a pretended Act made *Anno* 1649. concerning Tithes appropriate Fee-farm rents, and First-fruits, &c. and their heirs, were to be accomptable for such of the same as had not been employed according to the said Act: nevertheless, no Minister or School-master, or other person, for whose benefit the said Act was made, were to be accomptable.

The King on *September* 13. 1660. came to the House of Lords, and signed fourteen private, and eight publick Acts, among which one was an Act for the Confirming and Restoring of Ministers. This Act stopt the clamours of many Ecclesiastical Persons that had defective titles to their Cures: and the goodness of His Majesty was very much celebrated by His consent to it. It enacts, That every Ecclesiastical Person, or Minister, ordained by any Ecclesiastical Persons before the twenty fifth of *December* last past, and was then in possession, and received the profits, being in the King's gift, or of His Father, or of any Archbishop, Bishop, Dean and Chapter, Prebend, Archdeacon, Body Politick or Corporate, or other Person, other than such hereby restored, is declared lawful Incumbent.

Every Voluntary Resignation of a Benefice to the Patron, or any Pretended Power since the said first day of *January*, to be good, as if made to the Competent Ordinary.

No presentation is to be construed to be an usurpation in Law, to the prejudice of any that shall have right to present.

Every Ecclesiastical Person formerly Sequestred or ejected after Lawful presentation and reception of the profits, that hath not subscribed any petition to bring the late King to Trial; or by any Act endeavoured or justified the murther of the said King, or declared his judgement against Infant-baptism, by Preaching, Writing, Printing, or constant refusal to Baptize, shall be restored to the possession thereof, at or before the twenty fifth day of *December* next ensuing; and every Ecclesiastical person to be removed, may enjoy the profits to that day.

On *December* 29. following, on which day the Parliament was dissolved, 32 Acts more were passed by the King. Among which one was an Act for Confirmation of Marriages during the time of the late Usurpations. Another was for making the Precinct of *Covent-garden* Parochial. And an Act for the disappropriating of the Rectory appropriate of *Preston*, and uniting and consolidating of the said Rectory, and of the Vicarage of the Church of *Preston*, and for the assuring of the Advouson and right of Patronage of the same unto the Master, Fellows, and Scholars of *Immanuel-colledge* in *Cambridge*. And an Act for Confirmation of Grants and Leases from Colledges and Hospitals.

Now some sixty Fifth-monarchy men under the conduct of one *Thomas Venner*, a Cooper, broke forth into Rebellion. This *Venner* was a Preacher to a Conventicle of that opinion in *Coleman-street* in *London*. Such was the madness of these men, that they believed, that They and the rest of their judgement were called by God to reform the world, and make all the earthly powers (which they called *Babylon*) subservient

to

to the Kingdom of *Jesus*: and in Order thereunto never to sheath their swords, till the carnal powers of the world were subdued. They were taught and believed, that one of them should subdue a Thousand, making account when they had done their work in *England*, to go into *France, Spain, Germany*, and other parts of the world, there to prosecute their pretended holy design. The place where they plotted and continued their conspiracy was the meeting-place for their devotion, and thither they had at several times convayed arms. On Sunday *January* 6. which was the day before their excursion, they were very late at their Assembly, which made one *Martin*, the Landlord of the House, inquisitive after their doings. He peeping through a chink in their door, saw them arming themselves with Back, breast, and head-piece, and thereupon immediately gave notice to the next Officers. Half an hour after they came down, and first marched to S. *Thomas* the Apostle, to call some of their party, from thence to *Bishops-gate*, and after to *White-cross-street*. They escaped to S. *John's Wood*, and from thence to *Cane-wood*, betwixt *High-gate* and *Hampsted*. On Wednesday morning the Rebels came again into *London*, and divided themselves into two parties, one whereof about five or six in the morning appeared about *Leaden-hall*, and from thence marched to little *East-cheap*, where they fought desperately, but were dispersed by the trained bands. *Venner*, and another party came to my Lord Mayor's house, thinking to have taken him Prisoner, but missing him they marched into *Woodstreet*, where Colonel *Corbet* and nine of his party charged through the Rebels, and broke them. They fought with admirable courage, and if they had not been hindred from encreasing their numbers, a Thousand men so resolved might have done much mischief. *Venner* himself was much wounded before he was taken, and about five or six were killed that refused quarter. About eight or ten dayes after *Venner* with about sixteen or seventeen of the most notorious, were arraigned at *Justice-hall* in the old *Baily*, found guilty and executed in several parts of *London*.

About this time there was a conference at the *Savoy* between divers Episcopal and Presbyterian Divines about the Church discipline, but to little effect.

A new Parliament was called, which assembled at *Westminster*, *May* 8. 1661. In the first Session whereof an Act was passed, Entitled, *An Act for disenabling all Persons in Holy Orders to exercise any temporal jurisdiction or Authority*, Repealed. The Bishops were brought to sit again as Peers in the House of Lords, and their Ecclesiastical jurisdiction restored to them.

The Parliament explained a clause contained in an Act of Parliament, made in the seventeenth year of King *Charles* the first, Entitled, *An Act for Repeal of a branch of a Statute* Primo Elizabethæ, *concerning Commissioners for causes Ecclesiastical*.

At

the Church of Great Britain.

At the second Session of this Parliament, an Act was made against Quakers, and others, denying to take a Lawful Oath, with several penalties to be inflicted on them for several offences.

An Act was also passed for Uniformity of publick Prayers, and Administration of Sacraments, and other Rites and Ceremonies; and of ordering, and consecrating Bishops, Priests and Deacons in the Church of *England*.

The King's Majesty according to his Declaration of the 25th of *October* 1660. had granted his Commission under the Great Seal of *England*, to several Bishops and other Divines, to review the Book of Common-Prayer, and to prepare such additions and alterations, as they thought fit to offer. And afterwards the Convocations of both the Provinces of *Canterbury* and *York*, being by His Majesty called and assembled; His Majesty was pleased to Authorize and require the Presidents of the said Congregation, and other the Bishops and Clergy of the same, to review the said Book of Common-Prayer, and the Book of the Form and manner of making and Consecrating of Bishops, Priests, and Deacons, &c. Since which time upon full and mature deliberation, they the said Presidents, Bishops, and Clergy of both Provinces having accordingly reviewed the same Books, and made some alterations which they thought fit to be inserted to the same; and some additional Prayers to be used upon proper and emergent occasions: and having presented the same unto His Majesty in Writing, in one Book, entitled, *The Book of Common-Prayer, and other Rites and Ceremonies of the Church, according to the use of the Church of* England, *together with the Psalter or Psalms of* David, *pointed as they are to be sung or said in Churches; and the form and manner of making, Ordaining, and Consecrating of Bishops, Priests, and Deacons*. All which His Majesty having duly considered, fully approved and allowed the same, and recommended to this present Parliament (then sitting and yet continuing to sit) that the said Book of Common-Prayer, &c. be the Book which shall be appointed to be used by all that officiate in all Cathedral and Collegiate Churches and Chappels, and in all Chappels, or Colledges and Halls in both the Universities, and the Colledges of *Eaton* and *Winchester*, and in all Parish-Churches and Chappels within the Kingdom of *England*, Dominion of *Wales*, and Town of *Berwick* upon *Tweed*, and by all that make, or consecrate Bishops, Priests, or Deacons, in any of the said places under such sanctions and penalties as the Houses of Parliament shall think fit.

And accordingly it was Enacted by the King's Majesty and both Houses of Parliament, That Morning and Evening Prayers in the said Book contained, should upon every Lord's day, and upon all other days and occasions, and at the times therein appointed, be openly and solemnly read by all and every Minister and Curate, in every Church, Chappel,

pel, or other place of publick worship within this Realm of England, and places aforesaid.

It was also Enacted by the Authority aforesaid, That every Parson, Vicar, or other Minister whatsoever, who then had and enjoyed any Ecclesiastical Benefice, or Promottion, within this Realm of England, &c. should in the Church, Chappel, or place of publick worship belonging to his said Benefice or Promotion, upon some Lord's day before the Feast of St. *Bartholomew*, which should be in the year of our Lord God, one thousand six hundred sixty two, openly, publickly, and solemnly read the Morning and Evening Prayer, appointed to be read by and according to the said Book of Common-Prayer, at the times thereby appointed, and after such reading thereof, openly and publickly before the Congregation there assembled, declare his unfeigned Assent and Consent to the use of all things in the said Book contained and prescribed, in these words and no other.

I A. B. do here declare my unfeigned Assent and Consent to all and every thing contained, and prescribed in, and by the Book entitled, The Book of Common Prayer and Administration of the Sacraments, and other Rites and Ceremonies of the Church, according to the use of the Church of England, *together with the Psalter, or Psalmes of David, pointed as they are to be sung or said in Churches; and the form or manner of making, Ordaining and Consecrating of Bishops, Priests, and Deacons.*

And that all and every such Person, who should (without some lawful impediment to be allowed and approved of by the Ordinary of the place) neglect or refuse to do the same within the time aforesaid, &c. should within one moneth be deprived, *ipso facto*, of his spiritual promotions: and that thenceforth it should be lawful to and for all Patrons, and Donors of all and singular the said spiritual Promotions, or of any of them, according to their respective Rights and Titles, to present, or collate to the same, as though the person or persons so offending were dead.

And it was further Enacted, That every Person henceforth to be promoted to any Ecclesiastical Benefice, should read the Common-Prayer, and declare his Assent and Consent thereto within two moneths next after that he shall be in actual possession of the said Ecclesiastical Benefice or Promotion: and upon neglect or refusal to be deprived as aforesaid. And that Incumbents of Livings, keeping Curates, shall read the same once every moneth, upon pain to forfeit the sum of five pounds to the use of the poor of the Parish for every offence.

It was also Enacted, That every Dean, Canon, and Prebendary of every Cathedral, or Collegiate Church, and all Masters and other

Heads, Fellows, Chaplains and Tutors of, or in any Colledge, Hall, Hospital: and every publick Professor and Reader in either of the Universities, and in every Colledge else-where; and every Parson, Vicar, Curate, Lecturer, &c. and every School-master keeping any publick or private School; and every person instructing or teaching any youth in any House or private family, as a Tutor or School-master, &c. should before the Feast of St. *Bartholomew* in the year aforesaid, subscribe the Declaration following, *scilicet*.

> *I A. B. do declare, that it is not lawful upon any pretence whatsoever, to take up Arms against the King: and that I do abhor that traiterous position of taking Arms by his Authority against his person, or against those that are Commissioned by him: and that I will conform to the Liturgy of the Church of England, as it is now by Law established: and I do declare, that there lies no obligation upon me, or on any other person, from the Oath commonly called the Solemn League and Covenant, to endeavour any change or alteration either in Church or State: and that the same was in it self an unlawful Oath, and imposed upon the Subjects of this Realm against the known Laws and liberties of this Kingdom.*

The penalty for failing in subscribing, was for Deans, Vicars, School-masters to be deprived of their Ecclesiastical promotions, Schools and Lectures to be void, as if such person so failing were naturally dead.

Provided always, That from and after the 25th day of *March*, which shall be in the year of our Lord God, 1682. there shall be omitted in the said declaration so to be subscribed, and read (it being enjoyned to be openly and publickly read by every Minister, &c. upon some Lords day within three moneths after his subscription in the presence of the Congregation there assembled) these words following, *scil.*

> *And I do declare, that I do hold, there lies no obligation upon me, or on any other person, from the Oath commonly called the Solemn League and Covenant, to endeavour any change or alteration of Government either in Church or State, and that the same was in it self an unlawful Oath, and imposed upon the Subjects of this Realm against the known Laws and liberties thereof.*

So as none of the persons aforesaid, shall from thenceforth be at all obliged to subscribe, or read any part of the said declaration or acknowledgement.

It was further Enacted, That persons not ordained Priests or Deacons, according to Episcopal ordination, shall not hold any Ecclesiastical promotion: nor shall consecrate and administer the holy Sacrament of the Lord's Supper, upon pain to forfeit for every offence the sum of one hundred pounds; one moyety thereof to the King, the other moyety thereof to be equally divided between the poor of the Parish where the offence shall be committed.

It was also Enacted, That no other Form, or Order of Common-Prayers, Administration of Sacraments, Rites or Ceremonies should be used openly in any Church, Chappel, or publick place: *And it was further Enacted*, That if any person who is by this Act disabled to Preach any Lecture or Sermon, shall, during the time that he shall continue and remain so disabled, Preach any Sermon or Lecture, that then for every such offence, the Person and Persons so offending shall suffer three moneths imprisonment in the common Goal, without Bayl or Mainprize.

It was also Provided, That at all and every time and times when any Sermon or Lecture is to be Preached, the Common-Prayers and Service, in and by the said Book appointed to be read for that time of the day, shall be openly, publickly, and solemnly read by some Priest or Deacon, in the Church, Chappel, or place of publick worship, where the said Sermon or Lecture is to be Preached: and that the Lecturer then to Preach shall be present at the reading thereof.

It was further Enacted, That the Laws and Statutes formerly made for Uniformity of Common-Prayer should continue to be in force, and to be executed for punishing offendors against this Law. Hereupon many hundred Ministers, with divers Lecturers and School-masters, left their places, refusing to conform.

Another Act was also passed for restoring of all such Advousons, Rectories, Impropriate Glebe-lands and Tithes to his Majesties loyal Subjects as were taken from them, and making void certain charges imposed on them, upon their compositions for delinquency by the late usurped Power.

Another Act was passed for preventing Abuses, in printing Seditious, Treasonable, and Unlicensed Books and Pamphlets, and for regulating of Printing, and Printing-presses. Pamphlets and Books prohibited to be Printed, Published, or Sold, were Heretical, Seditious or Shismatical Books or Pamphlets; wherein any Christian Doctrine or Opinion shall be asserted or maintained which is contrary to Christian Faith, or to the Doctrine or Discipline of the Church of *England*; or which shall or may tend, or be to the scandal of Religion, or the Government or Governours of the Church, State, or Common-wealth, or of any Corporation, or particular person, or persons whatsoever: none shall import, publish, sell, or dispose any such Book or Books, or Pamphlets;

phlets; nor shall cause or procure any such to be published or put to sale, or to be bound, stitched or sewed together.

In the fifteenth year of his Majestie's Reign, an Act was passed for relief of such persons, as by Sickness, or other Impediment, were disabled from subscribing the Declaration in the Act of Uniformity, and explanation of part of the said Act.

In the sixteenth year of his Majestie's Reign, an Act was passed for suppression of Seditious Conventicles, under pretence of exercise of Religion. *Wherein it was Enacted,* That if any person being of the age of sixteen years and upwards, being a Subject of this Realm, at any time after the first day of *July* 1664. shall be present at any Assembly, Conventicle, or Meeting, under colour or pretence of any exercise of Religion, in any other manner than is allowed by the Liturgy or practice of the Church of *England,* in any place within the Kingdom of *England,* Dominion of *Wales, &c.* at which Conventicle, Meeting, or Assembly, there shall be five persons or more assembled together, over and above those of the same Houshold: then it shall and may be lawful to, and for any two Justices of the Peace of the County, limit, division, or liberty wherein the said offence aforesaid shall be committed, *&c.* and they are hereby required and enjoyned upon proof to him or them respectively made of such offence, either by confession of the party, or Oath of witness, or notorious evidence of the fact, to make a Record of every such offence under their hands and seals respectively. And that thereupon the said Justices, *&c.* shall commit every such offender so convicted, as aforesaid, to the Gaol, or house of Correction, there to remain for three moneths without Bayl or Mainprize, unless the said offender shall pay down to the said Justices or chief Magistrate such sum of money not exceeding five pounds, as the said Justices or Chief-magistrate (who are hereby thereunto authorized and required) shall fine the said offender at, for his or her said offence: which money shall be paid to the Church-wardens, for the relief of the poor of the Parish, where such offender did last inhabit. Upon every second offence the offender to be imprisoned six moneths, and to be fined ten pounds. And upon the third offence, the offender to be transplanted beyond the Seas to any of his Majesties Forreign Plantations (*Virginia* and *New England* onely excepted) there to remain seven years.

It was further Enacted, That the Lieutennants, or Deputy-lieutennants, or any Commissioned Officers of the *Militia,* or any other of his Majestie's Forces, with such Troops, or Companies of Horse and Foot: and also the Sheriffs, Justices of Peace, and other Magistrates and Ministers of Justice, or any of them joyntly or severally, within any of the Counties or places within this Kingdom of *England,* Dominion of *Wales, &c.* shall repair unto the place where such Conventicles are held, and by the best means they can, shall dissolve, and dissipate, or prevent all such unlawful meetings, and take into their custody such of those persons so unlawfully assembled, as they shall judge to be the leaders and seducers of the rest, and such others as they shall think fit to be proceeded against according to Law for such offences.

Every person who shall willingly suffer any such Conventicle, to be held in his or her house, out-house, barn, yard, &c. shall incur the same penalties and forfeitures, as any other offender against this Act ought to be proceeded against.

In the seventeenth year of His Majestie's Reign, an Act was passed for restraining Non-conformists from inhabiting in Corporations. *Herein is was Enacted,* That all Parsons, Vicars, Curates, Lecturers, and other persons in holy Orders, or pretended holy Orders, &c. who have not declared their unfeigned assent and consent as aforesaid, and subscribed the Declaration aforesaid, and shall not take and subscribe the Oath following.

> *I A. B. do swear, that it is not lawful upon any pretence whatsoever, to take Armes against the King; and that I do abhor that traiterous position of taking Armes by his Authority against his person, or against those that are Commissioned by him, in pursuance of such Commissions: And that I will not endeavour at any time any alteration of Government, either in Church or State.*

And all such persons, as shall take upon them to Preach in any unlawfull Assembly, Conventicle, or Meeting, under colour or pretence of any exercise of Religion, contrary to the the Lawes and Statutes of this Kingdom, shall not at any time from and after the 24th of *March* 1665. unless onely in passing upon the Road, come or be within five miles of any City, or Town Corporate, or Borough, that sends Burgesses to the Parliament, within His Majesties Kingdom of *England*, Principality of *Wales*, &c. or within five miles of any Parish, Town, or Place, wherein He or They have been, since the Act of Oblivion, Parson, Vicar, Curate, Lecturer, &c. or taken upon them to Preach in any unlawful Assembly, &c. under colour or pretence of any exercise of Religion, &c. before He or They have subscribed or taken the Oath aforesaid before the Justices of the Peace at their quarter Sessions to be holden for the County or division next unto the said Corporation, City or Borough, place or Town, in open Court (which said Oath the said Justices are thereby impowred there to administer) upon forfeiture for every such offence the sum of forty pounds of lawful English money: the one third part to his Majesty and his Successors; the other third part to the use of the poor of the Parish, where the offence shall be committed; and the other third part thereof to such person or persons as shall or will sue for the same by Action of Debt, Plaint, Bill,

Bill, or Information, in any Court of Record at *Westminster*, or before any Justices of Assize, *Oyer* and *Terminer*, or Gaol-delivery, &c.

Provided also, That it shall not be lawful for any person or persons restrained from coming to any City, Town Corporate, Borough, &c. or for any other person or persons as shall not first take and subscribe the said Oath, and as shall not frequent Divine Service established by the Laws of this Kingdom, and carry him or her self reverently, decently and orderly there, to teach any publick or private School, or take any Boarders or Tablers that are taught or instructed by him or her self, or any other, upon pain for every such offence to forfeit the sum of forty pounds, to be recovered and distributed as aforesaid.

The offender also to be committed for six moneths to prison, by two Justices of the Peace of the respective County, without Bayl or Mainprize, unless upon or before such commitment, he shall, before the said Justices of the Peace, swear and subscribe the aforesaid Oath and Declaration.

An Act was also passed for uniting Churches in Cities and Towns Corporate; which was judged necessary by reason of the great ruine of many Churches and Parishes in the late ill times, and otherwise. The Parishes to remain distinct as to all Rates, Taxes, Parochial rights, charges and duties, and all other Priviledges, Liberties, and respects whatsoever, notwithstanding any such union to be made by vertue hereof.

It was *Enacted*, That the Patrons of such Churches and Chappels so united, shall present by turns onely to that Church which shall remain and be presentative from time to time, &c. Provided, That Parishes having an hundred pounds maintenance *per Annum*, may not be united. Incumbents of such united Parishes must be Graduates in some University. Owners of Impropriations may bestow and annex maintenance to the Churches where they lye, and settle it in trust for the benefit of the said Parsonage or Vicarage, without any licence of *Mortmain*.

It was further *Enacted*, That if the setled maintenance of such Parsonage, Vicarage, Churches and Chappels so united, &c. shall not amount to the full sum of one hundred pounds *per Annum*, clear and above all charges and reprizes, that then it shall be lawful for the Parson, Vicar and Incumbent of the same, and his Successors, to take, receive, and purchase to him and his Successors, Lands, Tenements, Rents, Tithes, or other Hereditaments, without any licence of *Mortmain*; any Law or Statute to the contrary notwithstanding.

This year 1665. was a great Plague in *London* and in the Suburbs thereof; of which there died above an hundred thousand persons.

Anno 1666. On *September* 2d. a Great Fire arose in *London*, which consumed a great part of the City, whereby her beauty was defaced, and

and her glory stained: yea the Houses of God themselves became a heap of ruines, and a sad spectacle of desolation. The Citizens had not been long returned to their Houses which the late devouring Plague had driven them from, but now the fire swalloweth up all their habitations: and they that had so lately escaped the grave, do now see the City it self (as it were) buried in it's own ruines.

In *October* 1667. a Judicature was erected for determination of differences, touching Houses burned or demolished, by reason of the late fire which hapned in *London*.

An Act was passed for Re-building the City of *London*. And that the said Citizens and their Successors for all the time to come, may retain the memorial of so sad a desolation, and reflect seriously upon their manifold iniquities, which are the unhappy causes of such Judgments.

It was Enacted, That the second of *September* (unless the same happen to be the Lord's day, and if so, then the next day following) be yearly for ever hereafter observed, as a day of publick Fasting and Humiliation within the said City and Liberties thereof, to implore the mercies of Almighty God upon the said City, to make devout Prayer and Supplication unto him, to divert the like calamity for the time to come.

And the better to preserve the memory of this dreadful visitation; *It was further Enacted*, That a Column, or Pillar of Brass, or Stone, be erected on, or as near unto the place where the said Fire so unhappily began, as conveniently may be, in perpetual remembrance thereof, with such Inscription thereon, as hereafter by the Mayor and Court of Aldermen be directed.

It was also further Enacted, That the Parish-churches to be Re-builded within the said City of *London*, in lieu of those which were demolished by the late fire, should not exceed the number of thirty nine, to be set out and appointed by and with the advice and consent of the Lord Archbishop of *Canterbury*, and Bishop of *London* for the time being.

It was also Provided, That the Sites and Materials of such Churches as by this Bill are not to be rebuilt, together with the Church-yards belonging to such Churches, shall be, and are hereby vested in the Lord Mayor and Aldermen of the City of *London*, for the time being, to the end so much of the said ground, as shall not, upon the re-building of the said City, be laid into the Streets, be sold and disposed of by the Lord Mayor and Aldermen, or the Major part of them, with the consent of the said Archbishop and Bishop of *London* for the time being: and the money raised by such sale, shall be, by the said Mayor and Aldermen, or the major part of them, with the consent of the said Archbishop and Bishop, disposed of, and employed for and towards the rebuilding of such Parish-Churches as by this Act are intended to be rebuilt, and for no other use or purpose whatsoever.

Provided

Provided always, That any thing in this Act contained, shall not extend, or be taken to vest, or settle the Church of St. *Pauls,* and St. *Faiths,* or any part thereof, or the Church of St. *Gregory* by St. *Pauls,* or any of them, or the Church-yards to any of them belonging or appertaining, in the Mayor, Aldermen, and Commons of the City of *London,* or any of them, any thing in this Act notwithstanding.

An additional Act was also made for the rebuilding the City of *London,* uniting of Parishes, and rebuilding of the Cathedral and Parochial Churches within the said City. An Imposition was charged upon every Tun or Chaldron of Coales; and it was provided, That three fourth parts of all the moneys, which from and after the first day of *May* 1670. and before the 24th day of *June* 1677. shall be raised or payable upon the receipt of the said imposition of two shillings for every Chaldron or Tun of Coals; or in case of concealment thereof, shall be employed, and disposed for, and towards the rebuilding, erecting or repairing of the said Parish-Churches respectively, according to such order and direction, as by the Lord Archbishop of *Canterbury,* the Lord Bishop, and Lord Mayor of *London* for the time being, or any two of them, shall be given in that behalf: and the same shall from time to time be issued out, and paid accordingly unto such person and persons, as they or any two of them shall, by Warrant under their hands and seals for that purpose, direct and appoint. And that one moyety of all the moneys which from and after the said 24th day of *June* 1677. shall be raised, or payable upon the Imposition of three shillings the Chaldron or Tun of Coales; or in case of concealment thereof as aforesaid, shall be employed for and by such order and direction *&c.*

It was also Enacted, That it shall and may be lawful for the Lord Archbishop of *Canterbury,* the Lord Bishop of *London,* and the Lord Mayor for time being, *&c.* to employ or dispose, for and towards the building, repairing the Cathedral Church of St. *Paul,* one fourth part of the money by this Act given and appointed for the building, erecting or repairing the Parish-Churches. The profits of the impositions may be engaged to raise a present stock of money, to any persons that will advance any sums of money upon that security. All which moneys so to be borrowed shall be employed for and towards the rebuilding, and erecting or repairing of the said Cathedral and Parish-Churches respectively according to the true intent and meaning of this Act.

It was also further Enacted, That the number of Parishes to be setled, and of Parish-Churches to be rebuilded within the said City of *London,* shall be fifty one. The foresaid Act or any thing therein contained to the contrary, notwithstanding. The same Parish-Churches shall be rebuilt according to the modules appointed by the Lord Archbishop of *Canterbury,* Lord Bishop and Lord Mayor of *London,* with the King's approbation. The Parishes of *Alhallows Lumbard-street,* St. *Bartholomew-Exchange,*

change, St. *Brides*, *Bennet-Fink*, St. *Michaels Crooked-lane*, St. *Christophers*, St. *Dionis Back-Church*, St. *Dunstans* in the East, St. *James Garlick-hithe*, St. *Michael Cornhil*, St. *Bassishaw*, St. *Margaret Loathbury*, St. *Mary Aldermanbury*, St. *Martin Ludgate*, St. *Peter's Cornhil*, St. *Stephens Coleman-street*, and St. *Sepulchers*, shall remain and continue, as heretofore they were. And the respective Parish-Churches to each of the said Parishes belonging shall be rebuilded, and continued for the use of the said Parishes, and the other Parishes shall be respectively united, two Parishes into one; that is to say, the Parishes of *Alhallows Bred-street*, and St. *John Evangelist*, shall be united into one Parish, and the Church heretofore belonging to the Parish of *Alhallows Bred-street*, shall be rebuilded, and shall be the Parish-Church of the Parishes so united. The Parishes of St. *Albans Wood-street*, and St. *Olaves Silver-street*, shall be united into one Parish; and the Church heretofore belonging to St. *Albans Wood-street*, shall be the Parish-Church of the said Parishes so united. The Parishes of St. *Austin's* and St. *Faiths*, shall be united into one Parish, and the Church of St. *Austins* shall be the Parish-Church of the said Parishes so united. The like order is to be observed in all the rest of the Parish-Churches that are to be united.

It was further Enacted, That any Place and Goods heretofore belonging to any of the Church-Wardens of any of the Parishes burnt down, which are not to be rebuilt, shall be enjoyed by the Church-Wardens of those and their successors of the respective Parishes of such Churches to be rebuilded, whereunto the said other Churches burnt down, are united by this Act. *Provided*, That the Sites of the Churches to be demolished, and the Church-yards belonging to the same, shall be enclosed with Brick or Stone-walls, for burial, for the Parishes formerly belonging to the same, and the Parishes to which they are united as aforesaid, and not used or employed to any other purpose whatsoever; excepting such of the Sites and Church-yards, or parts of Sites and Church-yards of the said Parish-Churches so demolished as aforesaid, as are already laid into the Streets and Market-places set out for that purpose, *&c.* Notwithstanding the union, yet the Parishes to all Rates, Charges, and Priviledges, are to remain distinct. The present Incumbents of Churches not to be rebuilded, shall not be deprived of the Tithes, or other profits heretofore belonging to their respective Churches, so long as they shall assist in serving the Cure; and other offices belonging to their duty in the Parish-Church, whereunto their respective Parishes shall be united, and annexed by this Act according direction of the Ordinary, *&c.* saving to the King's Majesty, his heirs and successors, the Tenths and First-fruits of all such Parish-Churches as by force of this present Act shall be united and consolidated, *&c.*

Yet

Yet the said Parsons and Vicars are hereby indemnified from the payment of all First-fruits, Tenths, and Pensions due, and which shall be due to his Majesty: and from all dues to the Ordinary and Archdeacon, and all other dues whatsoever chargeable upon them respectively, untill such time as they shall receive the profits arising from the same, as formerly. And no Process shall be issued out of any Court whatsoever, against the persons aforesaid, for their non-payment of First-fruits, Tenths, Pensions, or any other the dues aforesaid, &c. They are indemnified for not reading the 39. Articles, or not doing other things enjoyned by Law, untill such time as the said Churches be re-edified, or made fit for publick worship. The said Parsons and Vicars are impowered to let Leases of their Glebe-lands, with the consent of the Patron and Ordinary, for any Term not exceeding forty years, and at such yearly rents, without fine, as can be obtained for the same: and that no lapses incurred upon any non-presentation in due time of any of the Patrons of the said livings since the said fire, shall any ways prejudice, or make void the Presentations that the said Patrons have since made, whereupon any Incumbent is since instituted and inducted, any Law or Statute to the contrary in any wise notwithstanding.

Ddd   A

A Catalogue of the Bishops of ENGLAND and WALES.

The Archbishops of Canterbury.

1. Augustine.
2. Laurence.
3. Mellitus.
4. Justus.
5. Honorius.
6. Deus Dedit.
7. Theodorus.
8. Brethwald.
9. Tatwyn.
10. Nothelmus.
11. Cuthbert.
12. Bregwyn.
13. Lambert, alias Jainbert.
14. Athelard.
15. Wifred.
16. Theologild.
17. Celnoth.
18. Athelred.
19. Plegmond.
20. Athelmus.
21. Wilfelm.
22. Odo Severus.
23. Dunstan.
24. Ethelgar.
25. Siricius.
26. Alfricus.
27. Elphege.
28. Liunig.
29. Agelnoth.
30. Eadsin.
31. Robert Gemeticensis.
32. Stigand.
33. Lanfrank.
34. Anselm.
35. Rodolphus.
36. William Corbel.
37. Theobald.
38. Thomas Becket.
39. Richard.
40. Baldwyn.
41. Reginald Fitz-Joceline.
42. Hubert Walter.
43. Stephen Langton.
44. Richard Wethershed.
45. Saint Edmond.
46. Boniface.
47. Robert Kilwarby.
48. John Peckham.
49. Robert Winchelsey.
50. Walter Reinolds.
51. Simon Mepham.
52. John Stratford.
53. Thomas Bradwardine.
54. Simon Islip.
55. Simon Langham.
56. W. Wittlesey.
57. Simon Sudbury.
58. William Courtney.
59. Thomas Arundel.
60. Henry Chichley.
61. John Stafford.
62. John Kemp.

63. Tho.

the Church of Great Britain.

63. Thomas Bourchier.
64. John Morton.
65. Henry Deane.
66. William Warham.
67. Thomas Cranmer.
68. Reginald Pool.
69. Matthew Parker.

70. Edmond Grindal.
71. John Whitgift.
72. Richard Bancroft.
73. George Abbot.
74. William Laud.
75. William Juxon.
76. Gilbert Sheldon.

Archbishops of York.

1. Paulinus.
2. Cedda.
3. Wilfrid.
4. Bosa.
5. John of Beverley.
6. Wilfrid.
7. Egbert.
8. Albertus.
9. Eanbaldus the First.
10. Eanbaldus the Second.
11. Wulfius.
12. Wimundus.
13. Wilferus.
14. Ethelbald.
15. Redward.
16. Wulstan.
17. Oskitel.
18. Athelwold.
19. Oswald.
20. Aldulf.
21. Wulstan.
22. Alfricus Putioc.
23. Kinsius.
24. Eldredus.
25. Thomas the First.
26. Gerard.
27. Thomas the Second.
28. Thurstan.
29. Henry Murdac.
30. Saint William.
31. Roger.
32. Geoffry Plantagenet.
33. Walter Gray.

34. Sewal.
35. Godfry de Kinton.
36. Walter Gifford.
37. William Wickwane.
38. John Roman.
39. Henry Newark.
40. Thomas de Corbridge.
41. William de Greenfield.
42. William de Melton.
43. Le Zouch.
44. John Thursby.
45. Alexander Nevil.
46. Thomas Arundel.
47. Robert Waldby.
48. Richard Scroop.
49. Henry Bower.
50. John Kemp.
51. William Booth.
52. George Nevil.
53. Laurence Booth.
54. Thomas Rotheram.
55. Thomas Savage.
56. Christopher Baimbridge.
57. Thomas Wolsey.
58. Edward Lee.
59. Robert Holgate.
60. Nicholas Heath.
61. Thomas Young.
62. Edmond Grindal.
63. Edwyn Sandys.
64. John Piers.
65. Matthew Hutton.
66. Tobias Matthew.
67. George

67. George Mounteign.
68. Samuel Harſner.
69. Richard Neile.
70. John Williams.
71. Accepted Frewin.
72. Richard Stern.

Archbiſhops of London.

1. Thean: *He is ſaid to have built St.* Peter's *Church in* Cornhil.
2. Elvanus.
3. Cadar.
4. Obinus.
5. Conan.
6. Palladius.
7. Stephen.
8. Iltut.
9. Dedwyn.
10. Thedred.
11. Hilary.
12. Reſtitutus.
13. Guitelnius.
14. Faſtidius.
15. Vodinus.
16. Theodorus.

Biſhops of London *after the comming of* Auguſtine, *when the Archbiſhoprick was tranſlated to* Canterbury.

1. Mellitus.
2. Ceadda.
3. Wina.
4. Erkenwald.
5. Waldher.
6. Ingwald.
7. Egwulf.
8. Wighed.
9. Eadbright.
10. Eadgar.
11. Kenwalch.
12. Eadbald.
13. Hecbert.
14. Oſwyn.
15. Ethelnoth.
16. Ceolbert.
17. Ceorulf.
18. Swithulf.
19. Eadſtan.
20. Wulffius.
21. Ethelward.
22. Eliſtan.
23. Theodred.
24. Wolſtan.
25. Brithelm.
26. Dunſtan.
27. Alfſtan.
28. Wulfſtan.
29. Alhun.
30. Alwy.
31. Elfward.
32. Robertus.
33. William.
34. Hugh de Orival.
35. Mauritius.
36. Richard Beavoys the Firſt.
37. Gilbertus Univerſalis.
38. Robertus de Sigillo.
39. Richard Beavoys the Second.
40. Gilbert Foliot.
41. Richard Fitz-Neal.
42. William de Sancta Maria.
43. Euſtachius de Fauconbridge.
44. Rogerus Niger.
45. Fulco Baſſer.
46. Henry de Wingham.
47. Richard Talbot.
48. Henry de Sandwich.
49. Henry

the Church of GREAT BRITAIN.   389

49. Henry Chishul.
50. Richard de Gravesend.
51. Ralph Baldock.
52. Gilbert Seagrave.
53. Richard Newport.
54. Stephen Gravesend.
55. Nicholas Byntworth.
56. Ralph Stratford.
57. Michael Northbrook.
58. Simon Sudbury.
59. William Courtney.
60. Robert Braibrook.
61. Roger Walden.
62. Nicholas Bubwith.
63. Richard Clifford.
64. John Kemp.
65. William Gray.
66. Robert Fitz-hugh.
67. Robert Gilbert.
68. Thomas Kemp.
69. John Marshal.
70. Richard Hill.
71. Thomas Savage.
72. William Warham.
73. William Barnes.
74. Richard Fitz-James.
75. Cuthbert Tonstal.
76. John Stokesley.
77. Edmond Bonner.
78. Nicholas Ridley.
79. Edmond Grindal.
80. Edwyn Sandys.
81. John Elmer.
82. Richard Fletcher.
83. Richard Bancroft.
84. Richard Vaughan.
85. Thomas Ravis.
86. George Abbot.
87. John King.
88. George Mounteign.
89. William Laud.
90. William Juxon.
91. Gilbert Sheldon.
92. Humphrey Hinchman.

Bishops of Winchester.

1, Birinus
2, Agilbertus
3, Wina
4, Eleutherius
5, Headda
6, Daniel
7, Humfridus
8, Kimhardus
9, Athelardus
10, Egbaldus
11, Dudda
12, Kineberthus
13, Alhmundus.
14, Wigtheinus.
15, Herefrid
16, Edmond
17, Helmstan
18, Swithunus
19, Adferthus
20, Dumberr
21, Denewulsus
22, Athelmus
23, Frithstan
24, Brinstan
25, Elphegus Calvus
26, Elsinus
27, Brithelinus
28, Ethelwald
29, Elphegus
30, Renulphus
31, Brithwold
32, Elsinus
33, Alwynus
34, Stigandus
35, Walklyn
36, William Gifford.
37. Henry

37, Henry de Bloys
38, Richard More
39, Godfrey de Lucy
40, Peter de la Roche
41, William de Raley
42, Ethelmarus
43, John Gernsey
44, Nicholas de Ely
45, John de Pontissara
46, Henry Woodloke
47, John Sandal
48, Reginald Aserius
49, John Stratford
50, Adam Tarleton
51, William Eddendon
52, William Wickham
53, Henry Beaufort
54, William Weinfleet
55, Peter Courtney
56, Thomas Langton
57, Richard Fox
58, Thomas Wolsey
59, Stephen Gardiner
60, John Poynet
61, John White
62, Robert Horn
63, Iohn Watson
64, Thomas Cooper
65, William Wickham
66, William Day
67, Thomas Bilson
68, James Mountague
69, Lancelot Andrews
70, Richard Neile
71, Walter Curle
72, Brian Duppa
73, George Morley

Bishops of Ely.

1, Hervæus
2, Nigellus
3, Galfridus Rydal
4, William Longchamp
5, Eustachius
6, Iohn de Fontibus
7, Geoffry de Burgo
8, Hugh Norwold
9, William de Kilkenny
10, Hugh Balsam
11, Iohn de Kirkby
12, William de Ludo
13, Ralph Walpool
14, Robert Oxford
15, Iohn de Keeton
16, Iohn Hotham
17, Simon Montacute
18, Thomas Lyld
19, Simon Langham
20, Iohn Barnet
21, Thomas Arundel
22, Iohn Fordnam
23, Philip Morgan
24, Lewis Lushborough
25, Thomas Bourchier
26, William Gray
27, Iohn Morton
28, Iohn Alcock
29, Richard Redman
30, Iames Stanley
31, Nicholas West
32, Thomas Goodrich
33, Thomas Thirlby
34, Richard Cox
35, Martin Heron
36, Lancelot Andrews
37, Nicholas Felton
38, Thomas Buckeridge
39, Francis White
40, Matthew Wren
41, Benjamin Laney

The

The Bishops of Dorchester.

The *Bishop of that Diocess, whereof* Lincoln *is now the See, sate first at* Dorchester *in* Oxford-shire. *His Diocess, and Jurisdiction, was all that Country, which now belongeth unto the Bishops of* Winchester, Lincoln, Sarum, Oxford, Bristol, Wells, Litchfield, Chester, Exeter. *He was called the Bishop of the* West-Saxons.

These were Bishops.

1. Birinus.
2. Agilbert, a French-man.

In his time Kenwalchus, *King of the* West-Saxons, *caused this huge Diocess to be divided into two parts, one of which he left to* Agilbert, *the other unto*

3. Wina, *appointing* Winchester *to be his See, and all the West-countrey his Jurisdiction.*

After Agilbert *there was no other Bishop of* Dorchester *a long time. He departing into* France, Wina, *and his Successors governed that See also.*

Not long after Oswy, *King of* Mercia, *erected an Episcopal See at* Litchfield, *and placed one* Diuma *in the same. He had all mid-England for his Diocess. So had six or seven of his Successors, until the year* 678. *at what time a Bishop was placed at* Sidnacester, *named* Eadhed. *He died within one year, then* Ethelwin *succeeded.*

Then these.

Embert, *who assisted* Beda *in writing his Ecclesiastical History.*
Alwigh Eadulf Ceolulf. *After him the See continued void many years.*

Anno 872. Brightred *became Bishop.*

In the mean time, sc. Anno 737. *another See was erected at* Legecester, *now called* Leicester : *but soon after removed to* Dorchester, *and one* Tota *made Bishop there.*

Then these.

Edbert.
Werenbert.
Unwona.
Rethun.
Ceolred.
Halard.
Ceolulfus.
Leofwyn.

Unto him the Diocess of Sidnacester *was also committed, (which had now continued void almost eighty years) and his See for both again was established at* Dorchester. *He was a great Benefactor to the Abbey of* Ramsey.
Alnoth : Anno 960.
Ascwin.
Alfhelin.
Eadnoth, *Provost of* Ramsey, *slain by the* Danes *in battel,* Anno 1016.
Eadheric.
Eadnoth.
Ulf, a Norman.
Wulffin.

Bishops of Lincoln.

The last Bishop of Dorchester, and first Bishop of Lincoln, was
1. Remigius
2. Robert Bloet
3. Alexander
4. Robert de Chifney
5. Walter de Conſtantiis
6. Saint Hugh
7. William de Bloys
8. Hugh Wallys
9. Robert Groſthed
10. Henry Lexinton
11. Benedict Gravefend
12. Oliver Sutton
13. Iohn de Aldarby
14. Thomas Beake
15. Henry Burwaſh
16. Thomas le Beck
17. John Synwel
18. John Bokingham
19. Henry Beaufort
20. Philip Repingdon
21. Richard Fleming
22. William Gray
23. William Alnwike
24. Marmaduke Lumley
25. John Chadworth
26. Thomas Rotheram
27. John Ruſſel
28. William Smith
29. Thomas Wolfey
30. William Atwater
31. John Longland
32. Henry Holbech
33. John Tailer.
34. John White
35. Thomas Watſon
36. Nicholas Bullingham
37. Thomas Cooper
38. William Wickham
39. William Chaderton
40. William Barlow
41. Richard Neile
42. George Mounteign
43. John Williams
44. Thomas Winniff
45. Robert Saunderſon
46. Benjamin Laney
47. William Fuller.

Bishops of Coventry and Litchfield.

1. Diuma
2. Cellach
3. Trumhere
4. Jaruman
5. Cedda
6. Winfrid
7. Saxulf
8. Headda

After Saxulf the Dioceſs was once more divided, and a Biſhop placed at Leicester, whoſe name was Wilfrid.

Headda, *that before was Biſhop of Litchfield, recovered the juriſdiction again.*
9. Aldwyn
10. Witta

The Countrey of Mercia was then again divided, and made three Biſhopricks. One was continued at Litchfield, *another was appointed at* Leicester, *the third at* Dorchester.

Litch-

the Church of GREAT BRITAIN.

Litchfield *was given to* Witta: Leicester *to* Tota: Dorchester *to* Eadhead

After succeeded these.

11. Hemel
12. Cuthfri
13. Berthun
14. Aldulf.

Offa *King of* Mercia *procured the Pope to make this* Aldulf *an Archbishop, and gave him authority over the Sees of* Winchester, Hereford, Leicester, Sidnacester, Helmham *and* Dunwich.

15. Humbert
16. Herewin
17. Hegbert
18. Ethelwold
19. Humbertus
20. Kinebert
21. Cumbert
22. Bumfrith
23. Ella
24. Alfgar
25. Kinsy
26. Winsy
27. Elseth
28. Godwin
29. Leosgar
30. Brithmar
31. Wilsius
32. Leofwyn
33. Peter

This man removed his Episcopal See to Chester.

34. Robert de Limesey:

He translated his See from Chester *to* Coventry, *where he was buried.*

35. Robert Peche, *buried at* Coventry.

36. Roger de Clinton.
37. Walter Durdent
38. Richard Peche
39. Girardus Puella
40. Hugh Novant
41. Geoffry de Muschamp
42. Walter de Gray.
43. William de Cornhul
44. Alexander de Savensby
45. Hugh de Pateshul
46. Roger de Welcham
47. Roger Longspee
48. Walter de Langton
49. Roger Northborough
50. Robert Stretton
51. Walter Skerlaw
52. Richard Scroop
53. John Burghil
54. John Keterich
55. James Cary
56. William Helworth
57. William Booth.
58. Nicholas Close
59. Reginald Butler
60. John Hales
61. William Smith
62. John Arundel
63. Geoffry Blithe
64. Rowland Lee
65. Richard Sampson
66. Ralph Bayn
67. Thomas Bentham
68. William Overton
69. George Abbot
70. Richard Neile.
71. John Overal.
72. Thomas Morton
73. Robert Wright
74. John Hacket
75. Doctor Wood.

Bishops of Sherborn.

After the death of Headda, the fifth Bishop of Winchester, Ina, King of the West Saxons divided his Diocess, which before contained all the Countrey of the West-Saxons, into two parts. The one of them he committed unto Daniel, allotting unto him Winchester for his See, and that Diocess, which now doth, and ever since hath belonged unto the same. The other part containing the Counties of Dorset, Sommerset, Wilts, Devon, and Cornwal, he ordained to be governed by a Bishop, whose See he established at Sherborn.

These Bishops were.

1. Adelm
2. Fordhere
3. Herewald
4. Ethelwold
5. Denefrith
6. Wilbert
7. Ealstan, a famous Warriour: he subdued unto King Egbright, the Kingdom of Kent, and the East-Saxons: he overcame the Danes in many battels: he much augmented the Revenues of the Bishoprick.
8. Edmond
9. Etheleage
10. Alfry
11. Asserius, the first publick Reader in the University of Oxford.
12. Sigelm
13. Ethelward, younger Son to King Alfred.

After Ethelward the See of Sherborn stood void seven years by reason of the Danish wars.

Anno 905. three Sees, newly erected, were taken out of the Diocess of Sherborn. One had jurisdiction over Cornwall; another over Devonshire; and a third over Sommerset-shire. Soon after that, a fourth was placed in Wilt-shire; having his See (some say) at Ramsbury in Wilt-shire (others) at Sunning in Berk-shire.

But to return to Sherborn.

14. Werstan
15. Ethelbald
16. Sigelm
17. Alfred
18. Wilfrin
19. Alfwold
20. Ethelrick
21. Ethelsius
22. Brithwin
23. Elmer
24. Brinwin
25. Elfwold

Bishops

Bishops of Wilt-shire.

1: Ethelstan; *he had his See at Ramsbury.*
2: Odo, *that became the Archbishop of Canterbury, Anno 934. was Bishop of VVilton.*
3: Osulf, *buried at VVilton.*
4: Alfstan
5: VVolfgar
6: Siricius, *translated to Canterbury.*
7: Alfricus; *he succeeded his Predecessor in Canterbury.*
8: Brithwold, *a Monk of Glastonbury, a great Benefactor of that Abbey, as also of the Abbey of Malmesbury; he was buried at Glastonbury.*
9: Herman, *Chaplain to King Edward the Confessor, was the last Bishop to this petty See.*

Bishops of Salisbury.

1: Herman
When VVilliam the Conqueror commanded that all Bishops should remove their Sees from obscure Towns to the fairest Cities of their Diocess, Herman made choice of Salisbury, and there laid the foundation of a Church, which he lived not to finish.
2: Osmond, *a Knight, and a Norman, came into England with the Conqueror, and was made by him Chancellor of England, and, after Herman's death, Bishop of Salisbury. He finished the building begun by his Predecessor, and added a Library, which he furnished with many choice Books. He was the first Author of the* Ordinale secundum usum Sarum.
3: Roger, *the rich Bishop of Salisbury.*
4: Joceline
5: Hubert
6: Robert
7: Richard Poor; *he forsook old Sarum, and began the foundation of a new Church in a place called Merifield, it was scarce finished thirty years after his departure.*
8: Robert Bingham
9: VVilliam of York
10: Giles de Bridport
11: VValter de la VVyle
12: Robert de VVikehampton
13: VValter Scammel
14: Henry Braunston
15: Laurence de Hawkborn
16: VVilliam de Comer
17: Nicholas Longspee
18: Simon de Gaunt
19: Roger de Mortival
20: Robert VVyvil
21: Ralph Erghum
22: John VValtham
23: Richard Metford
24: Nicholas Bubwith
25: Robert Halam
26: John Chandler
27: Robert Nevil
28: VVilliam Aiscoth
29: Richard Beauchamp
30: Lionel

3: Lionel VVodvill
31: Thomas Langton
32: Iohn Blythe
33: Henry Dean
34: Edmond Audley
35: Laurence Campegius
36: Nicholas Shaxton
37: Iohn Salcot
38: Iohn Iuel
39: Edmond Gheaſt
40: Iohn Piers
41: Iohn Coldwel
42: Henry Cotton
43: Robert Abbot
44: Martin Fotherby
45: Robert Townſon
46: Iohn Davenant
47: Brian Duppa
48: Humfrey Hinchman
49: Iohn Erle
50: Alexander Hide
51: Seth VVard

Biſhops of Bath *and* Wells.

1: Adelm, *Abbot of* Glaſtonbury, *was ordained Biſhop of Bath and* VVells, *and had* Sommerſet-ſhire *allotted him for his Dioceſs.*
2: VViſelinus
3: Elfeth
4: VVilfhelm
5: Brithelm
6: Kinewaldus
7: Sigar
8: Alwyn
9: Burwold
10: Leoningus
11: Ethelwyn
12: Brithwyn
13: Merewith
14: Dudoco
15: Giſo
16: Iohn de Villula.
This man procured his Epiſcopal See, which hiterto had been ſeated at VVells, *to be removed to* Bath, *whereas all his Predeceſſors had been called Biſhops of* Wells, *he renouncing* Wells *entitled himſelf Biſh. of* Bath, *where he was buried.*
17: Godfrey, *a Dutch-man, for a time Chancellor of* England, *he was buried at* Bath.
18: Reginald Fitz-Ioceline: *He built the Hoſpital of* St. Iohn's *in* Bath, *and gave certain Prebends unto the Church of* VVells. *Moreover, he gave unto the City of* VVells, *a Corporation, and Priviledges, which by his gift they enjoy to this day.*
19: Savaricus
20: Ioceline de VVells
21: Roger, *who died within ſix years after he came to that Biſhoprick: he is the laſt of thoſe Biſhops that were buried at* Bath.
22: William Button
23: Walter Giffard
24: William Button, *Nephew to the former of that name.*
25: Robert Burnel
26: William de Marchia
27: Walter Haſelſhaw
28: Iohn Drokensford
29: Ralph of Salop
30: Iohn Barnet
31: Iohn Harewel
32: Walter Skirlaw
33: Ralph Erghum
34: Henry Bower
35: Nicholas Bubwith

36: Iohn

the Church of Great Britain.

36: Iohn Stafford
37: Thomas Beckinton
38: Robert Stillington
39: Richard Fox
40: Oliver King. *He pulling down the old Church of the Abby of Bath, began the foundation of a fair and sumptuous building, but at the time of his death left it unperfected.*
41: Hadrian de Castello
42: Thomas Wolsey
43: Iohn Clerk
44: William Knight
45: William Barlow

46: Gilbert Bourn
47: Gilbert Berkley
48: Thomas Goodwyn
49: Iohn Style
50: Iames Mountague. *He gave a thousand pounds towards the reparation of the Abbey-church of Bath, and lies there interred.*
51: Arthur Lake
52: William Laud.
53: Leonard Maw.
54: Walter Curle
55: William Piers
56: Creeton
57: Mews.

Bishops of Devonshire, Cornwal, *and* Crediton, *&c.*

Two hundred years the West Countrey was subject unto the Bishop of Sherborn, *viz. from the year* 705. *to the year* 905. *at which time one Bishoprick was erected at* Wells *in* Sommerset-shire, *another in* Cornwal, *a third in* Devonshire.

1: *The See of* Athelstan, *Bishop of* Cornwal, *was for a while at St.* Petrocks *in* Bodmyn, *and afterwards St.* Germans. *The Successors of* Athelstan *in* Cornwal *were these.*

2: Conanus
3. Ruyodocus
4: Aldredus
5: Brytwyn
6: Athelstan; Anno 966.
7: Wolfi
8: Woronus
9: Wolocus
10: Stidio
11: Aldredus
12. Burwoldus.

Bishops of Devonshire.

1: Werstan; *He placed himself first at* Tawton, *but soon after removed to* Crediton, *now called* Kyrton.
2: Putta
3: Eadulphus
4: Ethelgarus
5: Algarus
6: Alfwold
7: Sydemanus
8: Alfredus
9: Alwolfus.
All these sate, and were buried, at Crediton.
10: Luyngus.
This man upon the death of Burwoldus, *Bishop of* Cornwal, *his Unkle*

kle, procured the County of Cornwal to be added unto his Dioecss, and afterwards became Bishop of VVorcester.

Bishops of Excester.

King Edward the Confessor coming to Excester, together with his Queen, took order that the Monks of St. Peter's, in that City, should be placed at VVestminster, and removed the Episcopal See from Crediton to Excester.

1. Leofricus was the first Bishop. The King taking the Bishop by his right hand, and the Queen by the left, led him up unto the Altar of his new Church, and there placed him in a Seat appointed for him. He obtained of the same King much good Land, and many Priviledges for this Church.
2. Osbert, a Norman
3. William VVarewest; a Chaplain both to the Conqueror, and his two Sons, VVilliam and Henry.
4. Robert Chichester
5. Robert VVarewest
6. Bartholomew Iscanus, so called of Isca, which is one of the antient names of this City.
7. Iohn, the Chaunter of this Church, and Subdean of Sarum.
8. Henry Marshal
9. Simon de Apulia
10. VVilliam Brewer
11. Richard Blondy
12. VValter Bromscomb
13. Peter Quivil
14. Thomas Bitton
15. VValter Stapleton
16. James Berkley; of the Noble house of the Lord Berkley.
17. John Godly
18. Thomas Brentingham
19. Edmond Stafford, Brother to Ralph, Earl of Stafford.
20. Iohn Keterich
21. Iames Cary
22. Edmond Lacy
23. George Nevil, Brother to Richard the Great Earl of VVarwick, by whose help especially Edward the Fourth obtained the Crown.
24. Iohn Booth
25. Peter Courtney
26. Richard Fox
27. Oliver King
28. Richard Redman
29. Iohn Arundel
30. Hugh Oldham
31. Iohn Vosei; Of 22. Lordships, and Mannors, which his Predecessors had left unto him, of a goodly Revenue, he left but seven, or eight, and them also leased out. And whereas he found fourteen Houses well-furnished, he left only one House bare, and without furniture; and yet charged with sundry Fees and Annuities.
32. Miles Coverdale
33. Iames Turbervill
34. VVilliam Alley
35. VVilliam Bradbridge
36. Iohn Wolton
37. Gervase Babington

38. Wil-

the Church of GREAT BRITAIN.

38. William Cotton
39. Valentine Cary
40. Ioseph Hall
41. Ralph Brownrigg
42. Iohn Gauden
43. Seth Ward
44.   Sparrow.

Bishops of the East-Angles.

Sigebert, *King of the East-Angles, returning out of France (where he lived in banishment) and obtaining his Kingdom, brought with him one Felix, a Burgundian, with whom he had lived familiarly, during the time of his Exile, and made him Bishop of the East-Angles, who converting the people to the Faith of Christ, had his See at* Dunwich.

Bishops of Dunwich *were these.*

1. Felix
2. Thomas, *his Successor.*
3. Bregilsus
4. Bisus. *He waxing old and crazy, divided his See into two parts; one part he appointed to be the Jurisdiction of a Bishop that should have his See at* Elmham; *in the other he continued, as also did divers of his Successors; which were these following.*
5. Acca
6. Astwolphus
7. Eadfarthus
8. Cuthwenus
9. Aldberthus
10. Eglasius
11. Herdredus
12. Aelphunus
13. Tydferthus
14. Weremundis
15. Wyredus.

Bishops of Elmham *were these.*

1. Bedwyn
2. Northbert
3. Headulacus

4. Edelfridus
5. Lanferthus
6. Athelwolph
7. Humferthus
8. Sybba
9. Alherdus
10. Humbiretus.

By *reason of the great troubles of those times in the Danish wars, these Sees stood void almost an hundred years.* Anno 955. *in the time of King* Edwy.

1. One Athulfus *was ordained Bishop of the East-Angles at Canterbury, and had his Seat at* Elmham.

After him succeeded these.

2. Alfidus
3. Theodredus the First
4. Theodredus the Second.
5. Athelstan
6. Algarus
7. Alwynus
8. Alfricus
9. Alyfreius
10. Stigandus
11. Grin-

11. Grinketellus
12. Egelmare.
All these, until the time of King William *the Conqueror, had their Sees at* Elmham.

Bishops of Thetford.

1. Arfastus *was the first Bishop, who was Chaplain to the Conqueror.*
2. William Herbert *was the second and last Bishop of* Thetford.

Bishops of Norwich.

1. William Herbert *translated that See from* Thetford *to* Norwich, *and was the first Bishop of* Norwich. *He built there the Cathedral Church at his own charge, which he dedicated to the holy Trinity, endowing it with great Lands and Possessions, Books, and all other necessaries; and on the North-side of the Church he founded a stately Palace for himself.*
2. Everard
3. William Turbus.
In his time the Cathedral Church at Norwich *was burnt with fire.*
4. John of Oxford.
This man finished the Church which Herbert *left unperfected, and repaired that which by fire was lately defaced.*
The same year he died the Church was again defaced with fire.
5. John de Gray.
After the death of John de Gray *the See was void for seven years.*
6. Pandulfus, *the Pope's Legat. After his death the See was void three years.*
7. Thomas de Blundevil
8. Radulphus
9. William de Raleigh.

The Bishoprick was then void by the space almost of three years.
10. Walter de Suffield.
He founded the Hospital of St. Giles *in* Norwich, *endowing it with Lands and great Possessions. He built also the Chappel of our Lady in the Cathedral Church, and in the same Chappel was also buried.*
11. Simon de Wanton
12. Roger de Skyrwing.
In his time was a dangerous Sedition between the Citizens of Norwich, *and the Monks of the Cathedral Church.*
13. William Middleton
14. Ralph de Walpool
15. John Salmon
16. William Armyn
17. Anthony de Beck.
He used his Monks too rigorously, and was poysoned by his own Servants.
18. William Bateman.
He forced the Lord Morley *to carry a burning Taper in his hand, through the streets of* Norwich, *unto the High Altar, for killing certain Deer in one of his Parks, and beating his Keepers: In his time happened a great Plague in* England. *In* Norwich *then there died*

the Church of GREAT BRITAIN. 401

died (*besides Religious men*) to
the number of 57104. *persons be-*
tween the first of January, *and*
the first of July, 1348.
19. Thomas Piercy
20. Henry Spencer
21. Alexander
22. Richard Courtney
23. John Wakering
24. William Alnwick
25. Thomas Brown
26. Gualter Hart
27. James Goldwel
28. Thomas Jan
29. Richard Nyx
30. William Reps

31. Thomas Thirlby
32. John Hopton
33. John Parkhurst
34. Edmond Freak
35. Edmond Scambler
36. William Redman
37. John Jegon
38. John Overal
39. Samuel Harsnet
40. Francis White
41. Richard Corbet
42. Matthew Wren
43. Richard Mountague
44. Joseph Hall
45. Edward Reinolds.

Bishops of Worcester.

Ethelred *divided* Mercia *into five Dioceses, whereof one was* Worcester. *For the first Bishop of* Worcester, *choice was made of one* Tarfrith, *a learned man, who died before he could be consecrated. After his decease,*

1. Boselus *succeeded.*
2. Ostforus
3. S. Egwyn.
This man went to Rome *with* Offa, King *of Mercia. He built the Abbey of* Evesham.
4. Wilfridus
5. Milredus
6. Weremundus
7. Tilherus
8. Eathoredus
9. Devebertus
10. Hubert
11. Alwin
12. Werebertus
13. Wilfreth
14. Ethelhune, *Abbot of* Berkley.
15. Wilferth
16. Kinewold
17. S. Dunstan.

18. S. Oswald
19. Aldulf
20. Wulstan
21. Leossius
22. Briteagus *Abbot of* Parshor.
23. Living.
24. Aldred
25. S. Wulstan
26. Sampson
27. Theulphus
28. Simon
29. Alured
30. John Pagham
31. Roger, *Son to the Earl of* Gloucester.
32. Baldwyn, *Abbot of* Ford.
33. William de Northale
34. Robert, *a Canon of* Lincoln, *Son unto* William Fitz Ralph, *Seneschal of* Normandy.

F f f   35. Henry,

35. Henry, *Abbot of* Glaston-bury.
36. John de Conſtantiis
37. Mauger.
He was one of them that excommunicated King John, *and interdicted the Realm, and thereupon fled the Realm.*
38. Walter Gray.
39. Sylveſter
40. William de Bleyes
41. Walter Cantilupe, *Son of* William *Lord* Cantilupe
42. Nicholas, *Archdeacon of* Ely, *and Chancellor of* England.
43. Godfry Giffard, *Archdeacon of* Wells, *and Chancellor of* England.
44. William de Gainsborough
45. Walter Reynolds, *ſometime School-maſter to King* Edward *the Second; firſt Treaſurer, then Chancellor of* England; *became Biſhop of* Worceſter.
46. Walter Maidſtone
47. Thomas Cobham
48. Adam Tarlton
49. Simon Montacute
50. Thomas Henibal
51. William de Bransford
52. John Thorsby
53. Reginald Brian
54. John Barnet
55. William Wittleſey
56. William de Lynne
57. Henry Wakefield
58. Tideman de Winchcomb
59. Richard Clifford
60. Thomas Peverel
61. Philip Morgan
62. Thomas Poulton
63. Thomas Bourchier
64. John Carpenter
65. John Alcock
66. Robert Morton
67. John Gyglis
68. Sylveſter Gyglis
69. Iulius Medices
70. Hieronymus de Nugutiis
71. Hugh Latimer
72. Iohn Bell
73. Nicholas Heath
74. Iohn Hooper
75. Richard Pates
76. Edwyn Sandys
77. Nicholas Bullingham
78. Iohn Whitgift
79. Edmond Freak
80. Richard Fletcher
81. Thomas Bilſon
82. Gervaſe Babington
83. Henry Parry
84. Iohn Thornborow
85. Iohn Prideaux
86. George Morley
87. Iohn Gauden
88. Robert Skinner
89. Walter Blandford

Biſhops of Hereford.

An Epiſcopal Seat being eſtabliſhed at Hereford,
1. Putta *was made the firſt Biſhop thereof.*
2. Tirhtellus
3. Torteras
4. Walſtodus
5. Cuthbert
6. Podda
7. Ecca
8. Ceadda
9. Albertus
10. Eſna
11. Ceolmundus
12. Utel

the Church of Great Britain.

12. Utellus
13. Wulfhardus
14. Benna
15. Edulf
16. Cuthwulf
17. Mucel
18. Deorlaf
19. Cunemund
20. Edgar
21. Tidhelm
22. Wulfhelm
23. Afrike
24. Athulf
25. Ethelstan
He builded the Cathedral Church from the ground. He was a holy man, and blind thirteen years before his death.
26. Leovegar, *Chaplain to Duke* Harold.
Matthew Westminster *gives this testimony of him, that he was undoubtedly* Dei famulus in omni Religione perfectus; Ecclesiarum amator, viduarum & orphanorum defensor; oppressorum subversor, virginitatis possessor.
Griffin, *King of* Wales, *assaulted the City, took it, slew the Bishop, and seven of the Canons of the Church, spoiled it of all the portable Relicks, and Ornaments, and then fired both Church and City.*
27. Walter
28. Robert Lozing; *An excellent Mathematician.*
29. Gerard
30. Roger, *the Queens Chancellor.*
31. Geoffry de Glyve, *Chaplain to King* Henry *the First.*
32. Robert Bertune, *Prior of* Lanthony, *a man much employed by the Pope in all his businesses within the Realm.*

33. Gilbert Foliot, *Abbot of* Glocester.
34. Robert de Melun
35. Robert Foliot
36. William le Vere, *a great Builder.*
37. Giles de Bruse, *Son of* William Bruse, *Lord of* Brecknock.
38. Hugh de Mapenor
39. Hugh Foliot
40. Ralph de Maidstone.
He resigned his Bishoprick, and became a Franciscan *Frier,* Anno 1239.
41. Peter Equeblank.
He caused King Henry *the Third to lay such Taxes on the Clergy, as almost beggared them,* An. 1255. *The Barons arrested him in his own Cathedral, seized on his goods, divided his Treasure unto their Souldiers before his face, and long kept him in prison in the Castle of* Ordeley.
42. Iohn Breton, *a great Lawyer.*
43. Thomas Cantilupe; *Of an ancient House. He was by the Pope Sainted after his death. All the Bishops of* Hereford, *since his time, do bear his Coat of Arms, as the Coat of their Sea.* G. three Leopards heads jesant, three Flower de luces O.
44. Richard de Swinfield
45. Adam Tarlton
46. Thomas Charlton: *He was Lord Chancellor, and chief Justice of* Ireland.
47. Iohn Trilleck
48. Lewis Charlton
49. William Courtney
50. Iohn Gilbert
51. Iohn Tresnant.
He was sent to Rome, *to inform the*

Po e of the Title of King Henry the Fourth to the Crown.

52. Robert Mascal.

He was Confessor to Henry the Fourth. He built the Quire, Presbytery, and Steeple of the White-Friers in London; gave many rich Ornaments to that House; died, and was buried there. He was often Ambassador to many Forreign Princes. He, with two other Bishops, was sent to the Council of Constance.

53. Edmond Lacy
54. Thomas Polton
55. Thomas Spofford
56. Richard Beauchamp
57. Reynold Butler
58. Iohn Stanbery
59. Thomas Milling
60. Edmond Awdley
61. Hadrian de Castello
62. Richard Mayo: *President of Magdalen Colledge for the space of twenty seven years, and Almoner to King Henry the Seventh. Anno 1501. he was sent into Spain, to fetch the Lady* Katherine, *to be married to Prince Arthur.*
63. Charles Booth, *Chancellor of the Marches of* Wales.
64. Edward Fox, *a learned man, and secretly a favourer of the true Religion. Mr.* Bucer *dedicated his Comment upon the Evangelists to him. Himself also wrote divers Books yet extant. He was Provost also of Kings Colledge as long as he lived.*
65. Edmond Bonner.
66. Iohn Skyp
67. Iohn Harley
68. Robert Warton
69. Iohn Scory
70. Herbert Westphaling
71. Robert Benet, *Dean of Windsor. He repaired the Bishops Houses of* Hereford *and* Whirburn.
72. Francis Godwin, *Bishop of* Landaff.
73. George
74. Nicholas Monk.
75. Herbert Crofts.

Bishops of Selsey.

1. Wilfrid, *Archbishop of* York, *being banished by* Egfrid, *King of* Northumberland, *preached the Gospel to the* South-Saxons. Ediwalch, *the King of that Countrey, had a little before received the Faith of Christ, by the perswasion of* Wulphur *K. of* Mercia. *He made much of* Wilfrid, *and assigned him an habitation in* Selsey, *a place all compassed about with the Sea, except one way, all that Land, containing eighty seven housholds, this King gave unto* Wilfrid *for his maintenance: He built a Monastery, and established his Cathedral See in the same. He converted, and baptized, great numbers of people, and was first Bishop thereof.*

2. Eadbert
3. Eolla
4. Sigga, or Sigfrid
5. Alubrith

6. Bo-

the Church of GREAT BRITAIN.

6. Bofa
7. Gilelher
8. Tota
9. Wigthun
10. Ethelulph
11. Beornege
12. Cenred
13. Guthard
14. Alfred
15. Eadelm
16. Ethelgar
17. Ordbright
18. Elmar
19. Agelred
20. Grinketel
21. Heka, *Chaplain to King Edward the Confeffor.*
22. Agelrike, *a man skilful in the Laws, and Cuftoms of the Land. He was appointed by King William the Conqueror to affift Gofrid, Bifhop of* Conftantia, *in judging a great controverfie between* Lanfrank *the Archbifhop,* and Odo, *Earl of* Kent, *the King's Brother, in a Convocation holden at* Windfor.

Bifhops of Chichefter.

1. Stigand, *Chaplain to the Conqueror, tranflated his Sea from* Selfey *(an obfcure place, and now eaten up by the Sea, fo that every high water covereth it) unto* Chichefter, *of old called* Ciffan-cefter. *So he was the firft Bifhop of* Chichefter.
2. William
3. Ralph, *a man of a very high ftature, and no lefs of a very high mind. He built the Cathedral Church at* Chichefter *from the ground. It was fcarcely finifhed, when as May* 5. 1114. *it was defaced, and a great part of the City confumed with cafual fire. He repaired it by the liberality of the King, and fome others. He was a great Houfe-keeper, and Alms-giver, and a painful Preacher, yearly vifiting his whole Diocefs, preaching in every place thrice, reprehending, and punifhing fin feverely.*
4. Seffridus, *Abbot of* Glafton.
5. Hilary
6. John de Greenford.
7. Seffridus the Second. *In his time, fcil.* October 19. 1187. *the Cathedral Church, together with the whole City, was cafually confumed with fire: the Church, and his own Palace, he both re-edified in good fort.*
8. Simon de Wells
9. Richard Poor
10. Ralph de Warham. *He gave to the Church a Windmill in* Bifhopfton.
11. Ralph Nevil, *Chancellor of* England. *He built Lincolns-Inn from the ground, to be an Houfe of Receipt, for himfelf and his Succeffors, when they fhould come to London. After his time it came to the poffeffion of* Henry Lacy, *Earl of* Lincoln, *who fomewhat enlarged it, and left it the name which now it hath.*
12. Richard de la Wyche. *He was born at* Wych *in* Worcefterfhire;

-shire: he was a holy and learned man, diligent in preaching: and canonized seven years after his death.

13. John Clypping: He built the Mannor-house of Drungwick, and gave it unto his Church.
14. Stephen de Barksted.
15. Gilbert de Stoleo fardo
16. John de Langton, sometime Chancellor of England. He built a costly Window in the South part of that Church.
17. Robert Stratford, *Brother to* John Stratford, *Archbishop of* Canterbury: *He found means to drive away Scholars from* Stamford, *that began to settle themselves there.*
18. William Lulimer
19. William Read. *He built the Castle of* Amberley, *and the Library of* Merton-colledge, *where he left his Picture, and many Tables, and Astronomical Instruments.*
20. Thomas Rushock
21. Richard Mitford
22. Robert Waldby
23. Robert Read
24. Stephen Patington
25. Henry Ware
26. John Kemp
27. Thomas Polton
28. John Rikinpale
29. Simon Sidenham
30. Richard Praty
31. Adam Molines
32. Reginal Peacock; He *was deprived of his Bishoprick.*
33. John Arundel
34. Edward Story
35. Richard Fitz-James
36. Robert Sherborn
37. Richard Sampson
38. George Day; *Deprived* Anno 1551. *restored by Queen* Mary, *after he had long lain prisoner in the Fleet. He was Brother unto* William Day, *long after Bishop of* Winchester.
39. John Scory: *By Queen* Mary *he was displaced, and by Queen* Elizabeth *preferred to* Hereford.
40. John Christopherson. *He was deprived by Act of Parliament, in Queen* Elizabeths *reign. He gave unto* Trinity-colledge *many Books, Greek, Hebrew, and Latin.*
41. William Barlow
42. Richard Curteise
43. Thomas Bickley. *He bequeathed unto* Merton-colledge, *in* Oxford, *an hundred pounds, to* Magdalen-colledge *forty pounds, and gave divers other sums of money to other good uses.*
44. Anthony Watson
45. Lancelot Andrews
46. Samuel Harsenet
47. George Carleton
48. Richard Mountague
49. Henry King
50. Peter Gunning.

Bishops of Rochester.

Augustine *having laid some good foundation of Christian Religion at* Canterbury, *for the further propagation of the same, thought good to ordain Bishops unto other Cities near adjoyning, and therefore in one day consecrated two, viz.* Mellitus *unto* London, *and* Justus, *a Roman, unto* Rochester, Anno 604.

The Bishops of Rochester were.

1. Justus
2. Romanus; *Travelling to* Rome *he was drowned.*
3. Paulinus.
Being driven from York *he was content to take charge of* Rochester.
4. Ithamar
5. Damianus
After his death the See long continued void.
6. Putta
7. William
8. Godwyndus
9. Tobias
10. Aldulfus
11. Duina.
He was present at a Provincial Council held by Rochester.
12. Eardulf.
Offa *King of* Mercia, Ecbert *King of* Kent, *and* Ethelbert, *another King of* Kent, *were benefactors to him and his Successors.*
13. Diora
14. Weremund
15. Beornredus
16. Tadnoth
17. Bedenoth
18. Godwyn the First
19. Cutherwulf
20. Swithulf
21. Buiricus
22. Cheolmund
23. Chineferth
24. Burrhicus
Unto him Edmond, *the Brother of King* Athelstan, *gave the Town of* Malling, Anno 945.
25. Alfstane
26. Godwyn the Second
27. Godwyn the Third
28. Siward
29. Arnostus Lanfrank
30. Gundulph
31. Ralph, *Abbot of* Say
32. Earnulph
He wrote an History of the Church of Rochester.
33. John, *Archdeacon of* Canterbury.
34. Ascelinus.
35. Walter, *Archdeacon of* Canterbury.
The Archbishop was wont, till this time, to nominate to this Bishoprick whom pleased him.
April 10. 1177. *the whole City, and Church of* Rochester *were consumed with fire.*
36. Gualeran
37. Gilbert Glanvyl
He deprived the Monks of Rochester of all their moveable Goods, all the Ornaments of their Church, Writings, Evidences, yea, and of great part of their Lands,

Possessions, and Priviledges. He built the Hospital at Stroud near Rochester, *and endowed it with fifty two pounds yearly revenue.*
38. Benedictus.
39. Henry de Sandford.
This man preaching at Sittingburn, *before a great Audience, declared openly,* That God had revealed unto him now three several times, how that on such a day the Souls of King *Richard* the First, *Stephen Langton,* late Archbishop, and another Priest, were delivered out of Purgatory.
40. Richard de Wendover
41. Laurence of St. Martin
42. Walter de Merton, *Lord Chancellor of England. Before he was a Bishop he built* Merton-colledge *in* Oxford.
43. John de Bradfield
44. Thomas Inglethorp
45. Thomas de Woldham
46. Haymo, *Confessor to King* Edward *the Second.*
47. John de Sheppey
48. William Wittlesey
49. Thomas Trillick
50. Thomas Brenton
51. William Boltsham
52. John Boltsham
53. Richard Young
54. John Kemp
55. Iohn Langdon
56. Thomas Brown
57. Iohn Wells.
58. Iohn White
59. Thomas Rotheram
60. Iohn Alcock
61. Iohn Russel
62. Edmond Awdley
63. Thomas Savage
64. Richard Fitz-Iames
65. Iohn Fisher
66. Iohn Hilsey
67. Nicholas Heath
68. Nicholas Ridley
69. Iohn Poynet
70. Iohn Scory
71. Maurice Griffin
72. Edmond Guest
73. Edmond Freak
74. Iohn Piers
75. Iohn Young
76. William Barlow
77. Richard Neile
78. Iohn Buckeridge
79. Walter Curle
80. Iohn Bowles
81. Iohn Warner
82. Iohn Dolben.

the Church of GREAT BRITAIN.

Bishops of Oxford.

About the year 730. Didan, Duke of Oxford, by the request of his Daughter, built a Monastery there for Nuns, and appointed her the Abbess. Anno 847. in the time of King Ethelred, certain Danes flying into this Monastery, to save their lives from the cruelty of the English pursuing them, the Monastery was burnt, and they all burnt in the same; but it was shortly after re-edified by the said King, and further enriched with divers Possessions

This Monastery was neglected, but Anno 1110. Guimundus, Chaplain to King Henry the First, became Prior of this renewed Monastery, repaired its ruines, and, by the favour of the King, recovered unto it what Lands soever had been given heretofore unto the Nuns.

In this state it continued, until Cardinal Wolsey got licenso to convert it into a Colledge, Anno 1524. calling it Cardinals-colledge.

He leaving it unperfect, King Henry the Eighth gave it a foundation, the stile whereof he first appointed to be, Collegium Regis Henrici Octavi: but afterwards he entitled the Church, Ecclesia B. Mariæ de Osney. He translated that See to the foresaid Colledge, placing in it a Bishop, a Dean, eight Prebendaries, a Quire, and other Officers, and finally stiled it, Ecclesia Christi Cathedralis Oxon, ex fundatione Regis Henrici Octavi.

The Bishops were,

1. Robert King
2. Hugh Curwyn
3. Iohn Underhill
4. Iohn Bridges
5. Iohn Howson
6. Richard Corbet
7. Iohn Bancroft
8. Robert Skinner
9. William Paul
10. Walter Blandford
11. Nathanael Crew, *Son to the Lord Crew.*

Bishops of Glocester.

Osrike, *King of* Northumberland, *founded a Nunnery in the City of Glocester, in the year* 700.

Kineburg, Eadburg, and Eva, *Queens of* Mercia, *were Abbesses of this Monastery one after another: it was destroyed by the Danes, and lay waste until* Aldred, *Archbishop of* York, *re-edified the same*, Anno 1060. *and replenished it with Monks, and erected from the very foundation that goodly Church, which is now the Cathedral See of that Diocess.*

Being given into the hands of King Henry the Eighth by Parliament, he allotted the Revenues of it unto the maintenance of a Bishop, a Dean, six Prebendaries, and other Ministers.

The Bishops were.

1. John Wakeman, *Abbot of* Tewksbury; *he was consecrated the first Bishop of this new erection,* September 7. 1541.
2. John Hooper. *He was burnt at* Glocester, *for the profession of the Gospel, in Queen* Maries *dayes.*
3. James Brooks.
4. Richard Cheiney.
5. John Bullingham.
6. Godfry Gouldsborough.
7. Thomas Ravis.
8. Henry Parry.
9. Giles Thomson.
10. Miles Smith.
11. Godfry Goodman.
12. William Nicholson.
13. Prichard.

Bishops of Peterborough.

Penda, *the Son of* Penda, *the first King of* Mercia *that was a Christian, began the foundation of a Monastery there,* Anno 656. *but was taken away, by Treachery, before he could finish the work. But this Monastery was afterward built up in stately manner by his Brother* Wolpher. *This Monastery he dedicated to* St. Peter, *and appointed one* Saxulf *to be the first Abbot thereof.*

Two hundred years after it was destroyed by the Danes, and having lain desolate one hundred and nine years, Ethelwold, *Bishop of* Winchester, (*a great Patron of Monkery*) *re-edefied it.* King Edgar *assisted the Bishop much in this foundation, and* Adulf, *Chancellor to the said King, who became Abbot there.*

After him Kenulph, *another Abbot, compassed this Monastery with a strong wall, about the year of our Lord* 1000. *through the liberality of divers Benefactors it grew to that greatness of wealth, as that all the Countrey round about belonged to it.*

King Henry *the Eighth converted it into a Cathedral Church, and the Revenues upon the maintenance of a Bishop, a Dean, six Prebendaries, and other Ministers.*

The Bishops were;

1. Iohn Chambers, *Doctor of Physick, he was last Abbot of* Peterborough, *and first Bishop thereof,* Anno 1541.
2. David Pool, *Doctor of Law.*
3. Edmond Scambler.
4. Richard Howland.
5. Thomas Dove.
6. William Peirs.
7. Augustine Lindsel.
8. Iohn.
9. Benjamin Laney.
10. Ioseph Henshaw.

the Church of GREAT BRITAIN.

Bishops of Bristol.

Robert, Sirnamed Fitz-Harding, because his Father (that was Son unto the King of Denmark) was called Harding; this Robert (I say) being a Citizen of Bristol, founded the Monastery of St. Augustines, and placed Canons in the same, Anno 1148.

This Foundation was afterwards confirmed, and augmented, by King Henry the Second, who preferred the Author of the same to the marriage of the sole Heir of the Lord Berkley. Of them are descended all the Lords Berkley.

In that place King Henry the Eighth erected an Episcopal See, and converted the Revenues of the same unto the maintenance of a Bishop, a Dean, six Prebendaries, and other Officers.

1. Paul Bush was the first Bishop of Bristol.
2. Iohn Holyman
3. Richard Cheiney.
4. Iohn Bullingham
5. Richard Fletcher
6. Iohn Thornborough
7. Nicholas Felton
8. Rowland Searchfield
9. Robert Wright
10. George Cook
11. Robert Skinner
12. Iohn Westfield
13. Gilbert Ironside
14.   Carlton

Bishops of Chester.

King Henry the Eighth converted the Monastery (the Church whereof there first built by that famous Earl Leofricus, and dedicated unto St. Wergburg) into a Cathedral Church, erected a new Bishoprick there.

The Bishops were,

1. Iohn Bird: He was deprived in Queen Maries dayes.
2. Iohn Coates
3. Cuthbert Scot
4. William Downham
5. William Chadderton
6. Hugh Bellot
7. Richard Vaughan
8. George Lloyd
9. Thomas Morton
10. Iohn Bridgeman
11. Iohn Walton
12. Henry Fern
13. George Hall.
14. Iohn Wilkins
15. Iohn Pearson.

Bishops of S. Davids.

1. David, *Unkle to King* Arthur, *removed his See from* Caerleon *to* Menevia, *which ever since, from him, is called St.* Davids. *He sate sixty five years, and died, Anno* 642. *having first built twelve Monasteries in the Countrey thereabout, being now one hundred forty six years of age.*
2. Cenauc, *who was first Bishop of* Patern.
3. Teilaw
4. Cenew
5. Morwal.
6. Haerunen
7. Elwaed
8. Gurnuen
9. Lendivord: *Anno* 810. *the Church of St.* David *was burnt by the* West-Saxons.
10. Gorwyst
11. Gorgan
12. Elvoed
13. Anian
14. Elvoed
15. Ethelmen
16. Elanc
17. Molscoed
18. Sadermen
19. Catellus
20. Sulhaichnay
21. Nonis
22. Etwal.
23. Asserius, *called in the Chronicle of* Wales, *Archbishop of all* Wales. *He died, Anno* 906. *he was Unkle to* Asserius, *Bishop of* Sherborn.
24. Arthwael
25. Sampson.

Henceforth the Bishops of St. Davids *never subjected themselves unto* Canterbury, *until the time of King* Henry *the First, King of* England.

26. Kucline
27. Rodheric
28. Elquin
29. Lywarch
30. Nergu
31. Hubert
32. Everus
33. Morgenu

This man of all the Bishops of St. Davids, first refused to eat flesh, saith Giraldus.

34. Nathan
35. Ievan: *He continued only one night.*
36. Argustel.
37. Morgenveth
38. Hernun, *a godly and learned man.*
39. Carmerin
40. Ioseph
41. Bleithud
42. Sulghein
43. Abraham
44. Rythmarch
45. Wilfrid
46. Bernard
47. David Fitz-Gerald.
48. Peter.

His Church had been often destroyed, in former Ages, by Danes, *and other Pyrats; and in his time was almost ruined. He bestowed much in re-edefying the same; and may in some sort be said to have built the Church which now standeth.*

49. Sylvester Giraldus: *He was commonly called* Giraldus Cambrensis.

the Church of GREAT BRITAIN.

brenſis. He *was Son unto* Giraldus de VVindſor, *that built the Caſtle of* Pembrock, *and* Neſta, *the Siſter of* Griffith ap-Rice, ap-Theodore, *Prince of* VVales. He *wrote a deſcription of* England, Ireland *and* VVales. *Of many* Books *that he wrote you may find the Catalogue in* Iohn Bale.

50. Edward, *an Abbot.*
51. Aſſelmus
52. Thomas, *Archdeacon of* Lincoln.
53. Richard Carren
54. Thomas Beck
55. David Martin
56. Henry Gower
57. Iohn Thorsby
58. Reginald Brian
59. Thomas Falſtaf
60. Adam Houghton
61. Iohn Gilbert
62. Gray Mohun, *Keeper of the Privy Seal: he was for a while Lord Treaſurer of* England.
63. Henry Chichley
64. Iohn Keterich
65. Stephen Patrington
66. Benet Nichols
67. Thomas Rodburn, *a great Mathematician, and Hiſtoriographer.*
68. VVilliam Lynwood, *Doctor of Law.*
69. Iohn Langton
70. Iohn Delabere
71. Robert Tully
72. Thomas Langton.
73. Hugh Pavy
74. Iohn Morgan
75. Robert Sherborn
76. Edward Vaughan
77. Richard Rawlins
78. VVilliam Barlow
79. Robert Ferrars.

He *was burnt at* Carmarthen *for the Truth,* March 30. 1555. *in Queen* Maries *dayes.*

80. Henry Morgan.

He *pronounced the ſentence of death againſt his Predeceſſor, and invaded his Biſhoprick: he was diſplaced in the beginning of the reign of Queen* Elizabeth.

81. Thomas Young
82. Richard Davies
83. Marmaduke Middleton
84. Anthony Rudd
85. Richard Milborn
86. VVilliam Laud
87. Theophilus Field.
88. Roger Manwaring
89. VVilliam Lucy.

Biſhops of Dandaff.

1. Dubricius
2. Telian
3. Odoceus
4. Ubylwynus
5. Aidan
6. Elgiſtil
7. Litnapeius
8. Comergen.
9. Argiſtwil
10. Gurvan
11. Guodoloin
12. Edilbiu
13. Grecielus
14. Berrygwyn
15. Trychan
16. Elgovus

17. Cat-

17. Cargwaret
18. Cercennir
19. Nobis
20. Galfridus
21. Nudd
22. Cimelianc
23. Libian
24. Marchhuth
25. Pater
26. Gogwan, *consecrated by Dunstan.*
27. Bledri
28. Ioseph, *consecrated by Agolnoth.*
In his time Kilthereh, *King of Wales gave many priviledges to his Church.*
29. Herewald: *he sate fifty eight years.*
30. Urbanus.
R. Hoveden *saith,* He was consecrated Bishop of this Church, *Anno* 1108. His See being spoiled, and the Church ruined, he obtained Letters of the Pope from the Council of *Rhemes,* to the King and Archbishop for a supply to repair it: which he obtained, and began to build the Church of *Landaff,* as now it is. He seeketh to recover divers Lands, taken from his See by the Bishop of St. *Davids,* and dieth in his way to *Rome.*
31. Uhtrid
32. Geoffry
33. Nicholas ap Gurgant
34. William de falso Marisco
35. Henry, *Prior of* Burgavenny.
Until this man's time the Bishoprick and Chapter *was one body, and their possessions not severed.*
36. William, *Prior of* Goldcliff.
37. Elias de Radnor
38. William de Burgo
39. John de la Ware
40. William de Radnor
41. William de Brews
42. John de Monmouth
43. John de Egglescliff
44. John Pascal
45. Roger Cradock
46. Thomas Rushock
47. William de Bottlesham
48. Edmond de Bromfield
49. Tideman. *Abbot of* Beaulieu
50. Andrew Barret
51. Iohn Burghil
52. Thomas Peverel
53. John de la Zouch
54. Iohn Wellys
55. Nicholas Ashby
56. John Hunden
57. John Smith
58. John Marshal
59. Iohn Ingleby
60. Miles Salcy
61. George de Arthegua, *a Spaniard, and Dominican*
62. Robert Holgate
63. Anthony Dunstan, *or* Kitchin
64. Hugh Iones
65. William Blethin
66. Gervase Babington
67. William Morgan
68. Francis Godwyn
69. George Carleton
70. William Murrey
71. Morice
72. Hugh Lloyd
73. Davies.

Bishops of Bangor.

1: Hervæus
2: David
3: Maurice
4: William, *Prior of St. Augustines*
5: Guianus
6: Albanus
7: Robert of *Shrewsbury*
8: Caducanus
9: Howel
10: Richard
11: Anianus
12: Caducanus
13: Gruffin
14: Lewes
15: Matthew
16: Thomas de Ringsted
17: Gervase de Castro
18: Howel
19: Iohn Gilbert
20: Iohn, *called* Episcopus Clovensis
21: Iohn Swaffham
22: Richard Young
23: Lewes
24: Benet Nichols
25: William Barrow
26: Nicholas
27: Thomas Cheroton
28: Iohn Stanberry
29: Iames, *called* Episcopus Achadensis
30: Thomas Ednan
31: Henry Dean
32: Thomas Pigot
33: Iohn Penny
34: Thomas Skevington.
He built all the Cathedral Church from the Quire downward, excepting that the two sides were partly standing. He was consecrated Iune 17. 1509.
35: Iohn Salcot
36: Iohn Bird
37: Arthur Bulkley
38: William Glyn
39: Rowland Merrick
40: Nicholas Robinson
41: Hugh Bellot
42: Richard Vaughan
43: Henry Rowland
He gave four Bells to the Church of Bangor: he gave also two fellowships to Iesus-colledge in Oxford
44: Lewes Baily
45: David Dolben
46: William Roberts
47: Robert Morgan
48: Humphtey Lloyd.

The History of

Bishops of St. Asaph.

About the year 560. Kentigern, *Bishop of* Glascow *in* Scotland, *being driven out of his own Countrey, erected a Monastery for himself, and his company, between the Rivers of* Elwyd *and* Elwy ; *where, in process of time, having built a Church, and some other Edifices fit for his entertainment, there flocked unto him such multitudes of people, as the number of his Monks amounted to no less than six hundred and sixty. His Church was first built of timber, and afterwards of stone.*

Malgocunus, *a British King, allowed the same Church to be an Episcopal See, and endowed it with divers Lordships, Mannors, and Priviledges. The Bishop of that See was then called* Elvensis, *of the River near which it standeth, and this* Kentigern *became the first Bishop of the same. After many years he was called home into* Scotland, *whereupon he gave over this Bishoprick unto a Disciple of his, called* Asaph. *In the time of King* Edward *the Second there were five Mansion-houses belonging to it, in which the Bishops used to reside,* scil. Lanelwy, Altmaliden, Landeglia, Nauverg, *and* St. Martins : *of all which there now remaineth to them* Lanelwy *only. Great havock was made of this Church in the reign of King* Henry *the Fourth by* Owen Glendover, *since which time the Canons Houses were never repaired.*

2. St. Asaph.
Of him the Cathedral Church was ever after, even unto this day, called Ecclesia Asaphensis. He was a man of great learning and vertue. Who succeeded him for some hundreds of years after we find not.

3. The next that is mentioned, is Geoffry of Monmouth, *the Historian.* Of a Benedictine Monk he became Bishop of St. Asaph, Anno 1151.

4. Adam, a Welch-man
5: Reynerus
6: Abraham
He gave half the Tithes of Wrexham to this Church.
7: Howel Ednevit

8. Anianus the First
9: Anianus the Second: *a Dominican, Confessor to Edward the First.*
Iohn, *Earl of* Arundel, *gave much Land to him and his Successors, and (after him)* Iohn, *his Son, added more.*
10: Lewellin de Bromfield
11: David ap Blethin
12: Ephraim
13: Henry
14: Iohn Trevor
15: Llewelin ap Madoc, ap Elis
16: William de Spridlington
17: Laurence Child, *a Monk of the Abbey of* Battel.
18: Alexander Bach
19: Iohn Trevor
20: Robert

the Church of GREAT BRITAIN.

20. Robert
21. John Low
22. Reginald Peacock
23. Thomas
24. Richard Redman
25. David ap Owen
26. Edmond Birkhead
27. Henry Standish
28. William Barlow
29. Robert Warton
30. Thomas Goldwel
31. Richard Davies
32. Thomas Davies
33. William Hughes
34. William Morgan
35. Richard Parry
36. John Hanmer
37. John Owen
38. George Griffith
39. Henry Glemhsm
40. Isaac Barrow

Bishops of Lindisfarn.

1. Aidan, who chose for his See a little Island, called Lindisfarn, now called Holy Island, where he, and divers of his Successors led their lives. He travelled up and down the Countrey on foot to preach the Gospel, giving whatsoever he could get unto the poor. He died August 31. Anno 651. for grief of the death of King Oswald, who was traiterously slain twelve dayes before.
2. Finan. He first built a Church for his See in the Island all of timber, and covered it with reed.
3. Colman. He gave over his Bishoprick, and returned into Scotland.
4. Tuda
5. Eata
6. St. Cuthbert, Bishop of Lindisfarn; he is famed for his Sanctity.
7. Wilfrid
8. Eadbert. He covereth the Church with Lead.
9. Egfrid
10. Ethelwold
11. Kenulfus
12. Higbald. In his time the Danes spoiled the Church, and Monastery, and the Monks forced to leave it.
13. Egbert
14. Eanbert
15. Eardulph.

In the mean time the Bishops of Haguftald were.

1. Aca
2. Fritherbert
3. Athmund
4. Titherus
5. Ethelbert
6. Heanred
7. Eanberthus
8. Tidferthus.

Hhh Bishops

Bishops of Chester on the Street.

1. Eardulph

Upon the burning of Lindisfarn, *removed his See to* Chester on the Street, *anciently called* Cuneceſtre. *And by* Elfred, *and* Guthred, *Kings of* Northumberland, *all the Countrey between* Tine *and* Tiſean *were given to the ſame See.*

2. Cuthardus
3. Milred
4. Withred
5. Ughtred
6. Sexhelm.

He being covetous, was ſo terrified with a Viſion of St. Cuthbert, *that he was forced to leave the See.*

7. Alſius, *or* Elffig.

He was the laſt Biſhop of Lindisfern, *or* Cheſter *on the Street*.

Bishops of Durham.

1. Aldhunus, *or* Aldvinus, *was conſecrated Biſhop, Anno* 995. *He with his Monks came to* Durham, *or rather* Dunholm; *which is compounded of two Saxon words,* Dun *ſignifying an Hill, and* Holm *an Iſland in a River; a place full of Woods. He with the help of* Uthred, *Earl of* Northumberland, *cauſed the Woods to be cut down, cleanſed the place, and in ſhort time made it habitable. A Church was finiſhed there in the time of this Biſhop. He was School-maſter unto the Children of King* Ethelred, Elfred, *and* Edward, *that afterward reigned, and is called* Edward the Confeſſor.

2. Edmond.

The Monks and Prieſts contending about a Succeſſor to Aldhunus, *this* Edmond *came among them, and (jeaſtingly) offered himſelf to be their Biſhop; and they choſe him againſt his will, he having a better mind to a Tennis-court than a Monks Hood,* Malmsb. lib. 3. de Pont. *He much adorned his Church, and the City with buildings.*

3. Eadred
4. Egelrick.

He builded a Church at Cuneagece-ſtre: *in digging the foundation of this Church, he found ſo much money, that he cared not for the Biſhoprick, but reſigned it unto* Egelwyn *his Brother, and returned to the Monaſtery of* Peterborough, *whence he came. He made the Cawſey from* Deeping *to* Spalding. *He was afterward accuſed to the Conqueror of Treaſon, and taken out of his Monaſtery, and impriſoned at* Weſtminſter, *where he died.*

5. Egelwyn.

He was Biſhop at the coming in of the Con-

the Church of GREAT BRITAIN.

Conqueror, he forsook Durham, and carried his Clergy with him unto the Church of Landisfarn, but he was not long before they returned again.

6. **Walcher, or Walter.**

He was so rich, that he bought the Earldom of Northumberland of the King. He and many of his Retinue were slain in the Church of Durham, May 14. 1080. and the Church burnt with fire, because two of his Servants had murdered Leulfus, one of the Ancestors to the now Lord Lumley. R. Hoved.

7. **William Kairlipho**, *Abbot of St. Vincent.*

He was consecrate at Glocester in the presence of the King, and divers of his Nobles. He procured license of Pope Gregory, to translate the Monks of Yarrow to Durham. He expelled divers married Priests out of his Church and suffered only Monks to dwell there, He pulled down the Church of Durham, that Aldhunus had built there, and began to erect another far more magnificent, but lived not to finish it.

8. **Ranulph Flambard**

9. **Geoffry Rufus**, *Chancellor of England.* He built the Castle of Alnerton.

10. **William de Sta. Barbara.**

11. **Hugh Pudsey**

He built a fair House at Derlington, as also the Church there. He founded the Priory of Finchal: He bought Sadbury of King Richard the First, and gave it unto his See: He built the Bridge of Elvet, and the Gallery at the West-end of his Cathedral Church, in which he placed the bones of Venerable Bede. He built two Hospitals, one at Allerton, another called Sherborn. Unto Sherborn he gave liberal maintenance for sixty five poor Lazers, and a certain number of Priests. For a great sum of money King Richard made him Earl of Northumberland-

12. **Philip de Poictiers.**

This Bishop, by the license of King Richard the First, set up a Mint at Durham, and began to coyn money there, Anno 1196.

13. William de Marisco.
14. Richard Poor
15. Nicholas de Fernham.
16. Walter de Kirkham.
17. Robert Stitchel
18. Robert de Insula.
19. Anthony Beake
20. **Richard de Bury.**

He was soon after Lord Chancellor, and within two years after that Lord Treasurer of England. He was often employed in Ambassages of great importance.

What time of leisure he had, he spent either in Prayer, or conference, with his Chaplains (whereof he had many about him, and those very learned men) or else in study. His Study was so well furnished with Books, that it is thought he had more Books than all the Bishops in England. Many Letters passed between him and Francis Petrarch, and other learned men in those dayes. Thomas Bradwardine was then one of his Chaplains, afterward Archbishop of Canterbury: Richard Fitz-Ralph

Ralph, *afterward Archbishop of Armagh,* W Burley, J. Mandut, R. Holcot, R. Killington, *Doctors of Divinity,* Richard Bintworth, *and* W. Seagrove; *the one afterward Bishop of London, the other of* Chichester. *He was very liberal to the poor.*
21. Thomas Halfield.
He built Durham colledge in Oxford, now called Trinity-colledge.
22. John Fordham
23. Robert Nevil
24. Laurence Booth
25. William Dudley
26. John Sherwood.
27. Richard Fox
28. William Severus
29. Christopher Bambridge
30. Thomas Ruthal.
31. Thomas Wolsey, *Cardinal.*
32. Cuthbert Tonstal
33. James Pilkinton
34. Richard Barnes
35. Matthew Hutton
36. Tobias Matthew
37. William James
38. Richard Neile
39. John Howson
40. Thomas Morton
41. John Cozens.

Bishops of Carlile.

Carlile *being destroyed by the* Danes *in the year* 900. *it happened King* William Rufus *passing that way,* Anno 1090. *re-edified it, and built a strong Castle in the same City.*

The Government of this new erected City was committed to a certain Norman Priest, named Walter, *that came into* England *with the Conqueror. This man being very rich, began to build there a Church to the honour of the blessed Virgin, but he died before he could perfect the work.*

Adelwald, *the first Prior of St.* Oswald, *and Confessor to King* Henry *the First, perswaded the said King to employ the Revenues that* Walter *left behind him, in the foundation of a Colledge of Regular Canons, to be annexed unto the Church forementioned. He did so, and moreover bestowed upon the said Colledge six Churches, with their Chappels, to be impropriated to the same use.*

The Bishops of Carlile *were.*

1. Adelwald, *the Prior forementioned.*
2. Barnard
3. Hugh, *Abbot of* Battell.
4. Walter Malcleck
5. Sylvester de Everdon
6. Thomas Vipont
7. Robert de Chause
8. Ralph de Ireton
9. John de Halton
10. John de Rosse
11. John de Kirkby
12. Gilbert de Welton
13. Thomas de Appleby
14. Ro-

the Church of GREAT BRITAIN.

14. Robert Read
15. Thomas Merkes
16. William Strickland
17. Roger Whelpdale
18. William Barrow
19. Marmaduke Lumley
20. Nicholas Close
21. William Piercy
22. John Kingscot
23. Richard Scroop
24. Edward Story
25. Richard, *Prior of* Durham.
26. William Sever
27. Roger Laburn
28. John Penny
29. John Kite.
30. Robert Aldrich
31. Owen Oglethorp, *that crowned Queen* Elizabeth.
32. John Best
33. Richard Barnes
34. John May
35. Henry Robinson
36. Robert Snowdon
37. Richard Milborn
38. Richard Senhouse
39. Francis White
40. Barnaby Potter.
41. Richard Stern
42. Edward Rainbow.

Of the manner of Installation of Bishops here in England in former times.

THe Installation of Bishops was a Ceremony of great solemnity in former Ages, the particularity whereof we find in *Walter Stapleton*, Bishop of *Excester*, in the beginning of the Reign of King *Edward* the Second, who was Consecrated *March* 18. 1307.

When he came to *Excester* to be Installed, at the East-gate he alighted from his Horse, and went on foot to St. *Peter*'s Church. All the way, where he should pass, being laid and covered with black Cloath, on each hand he was conducted by a Gentleman of great worship, Sir *Hugh Courtney* (who claimed to be Steward of his Feast) going next before him. At Broad-gate he was received by his Chapter and Quire in their Ornaments, with *Te Deum*, and so carried into the Church.

The usual Ceremonies being performed there, at his Palace a great Feast was prepared for the entertainment of such Noble-men, and other Persons of account, as repaired thither at that time. It is incredible, how many Oxen, Tuns of Ale and Wine are said to have been usually spent at this kind of Solemnity, even so much as the whole yearly Revenue, at this time, would not suffice to pay for.

Of those Englishmen that have been Cardinals of the Church of Rome.

1. THE first Leader of this Band is Pope *Joan*, called by *Sabellicus*, and some others, *John* the Seventh, but by *Platina* and other Writers, *John* the Eighth; who being but a Woman, became not onely Cardinal, but Pope of *Rome*: She was born at *Mentz* in *Germany*, the Daughter of an English Priest, who having a Wife whose Parents dwelt at *Mentz*, bringing his said Wife to see her friends, stayed there so long, till she was delivered of this Feminine Prelate, named in her Baptism *Joan*, as most say; *Gilberta* as others; or as *Fulgosius* delivereth, *Agnes*. In her youth she fell acquainted with an English Monk of the Abbey of *Fulda*, with whom travelling in Man's apparel to diverse Universities and Monasteries, as well Greek as Latin, she setled in the end at *Athens*, where she became Famous for Learning, and continued there with him untill the death of her said Paramour. Then coming to *Rome*, and, by Reading, Disputing, and other Exercises, having purchased to her self the reputation of a great Clerk, upon the death of *Leo* the Fourth, she was chosen Pope, *Anno* 855. and held that place two years five moneths and three days; in which mean time she was gotten with child by a certain Cardinal: and going in Procession hapned to be delivered of her burden in the open Street, in which place she instantly died, *viz.* between the *Colisco* and St. *Clement's* Church: the shame and turpitude of which disgrace unto that holy See, hath moved all the Bishops of *Rome* since that time to lengthen a little the walk of their Procession, and to go away much farther about, rather than they will endure to pass by that place. And to prevent the like inconvenience in time to come, they have ordained every Pope after his election to be searched by the Junior Deacon in a Marble-chair, made hollow for the same purpose. *Spectatur adhuc (saith Sabellicus) in Pontificia domo marmorea sella circa medium inanis, qua nobis Pontifex continuo ab ejus creatione residat, ut sedentalis Genetalia ab ultimo Diacono attrectentur.* This History (howsoever impugned of late by the Papists) is delivered by *Marianus Scotus*, and *Martin* of *Poland*, who lived *Anno* 1320. *Sabellicus, Fasciculus Temporum, Petrarch*, and divers others. And *Platina* recounting this Story, saith, *Quod onnes fere affirmant*; that it is observed almost by all Writers.

Bish. *Godwyn*.

2. The next in time is one *Ulricus*, an English-man, who being Cardinal, came into *England* as the Pope's Legate, *Anno* 1109. and brought the Archiepiscopal Pall unto *Thomas* the younger Archbishop of *York*,

and

and caused him to consecrate *Turgod* Prior of *Durham* unto the Bishoprick of St. *Andrews* in *Scotland*.

3. *Robert Bullen* of *Puley*, a very Learned Man in his time; unto him the University of *Oxford* is much beholden: for whereas in the Reign of King *Harold* it had been so wasted, as that for many years it lay desolate and forsaken of Scholars, he was a means to draw them thither again: and leaving the University of *Paris*, took great pains in Reading, Disputing, and Writing divers Learned Books; whereby he became so famous even in Forreign Nations, as by Pope *Innocent* the Second he was sent for to *Rome*; by *Celestine* the Second, made Cardinal *Sancti Eusebii*, *Anno* 1144. and by *Lucius* the Second, appointed the Pope's Chancellor; he died *Anno* 1150.

4. Two years after the preferment of *Bullen*, *Nicholas Breakspear* was made Bishop, Cardinal of *Alba*, and a while after Pope: he was born in *Hartford-shire* at *Abbots-Langley*, near unto St. *Albans*; a younger brother of the house of *Breakspear*, and the Son of one *Robert* a married Priest, the which *Robert* waxing old, and having lost his Wife, became a Monk in St. *Albans*, at which time his Son *Nicholas* was but a tender youth, resorting to his Father for relief and maintenance; the old man out of a superstitious conceit that the next way to Heaven was to renounce all care of Friends, Children, and all things else, save what by the rule of their Order was enjoyned, in a rude and churlish manner cast him off, willing him to try his fortune abroad, without expecting from him any manner of succor. He being thus turned off to the wide World without all means of livelihood, went over into *France*, and travelling through the Countrey found no entertainment till he came to *Valentia* in *Provence*, where the Monks of the Abbey of St. *Rufus* seeing him a beautiful and towardly child, witty, and for his age very industrious, took him in, and in process of time not onely admitted him into their fraternity, but also chose him first Prior, and afterward Abbot, having in the mean time by painful study attained to much learning.

But many differences grew between him and his Monks, who accused him of many things unto the Pope, that then was *Eugenius* the third. He after examination of the cause acquitted the Abbot, and sharply reprehended the Monks as froward fellows, charging them hereafter to yield unto him as their Governour all dutiful obedience, notwithstanding which after a little while they renewed their complaints. And as before, so now, the Abbot answered all their accusations, and that with such eloquence, discretion and modesty, as the Pope taking a great liking of the man, he told his Accusers they were unworthy of him; and therefore willing them to seek for some other for his place, with whom they might better agree; he created him Bishop, Cardinal, of *Alba, Anno* 1146. Soon after which time, upon experience of his great Wisdom and Learning, he sent him as his Legate into the Countries of *Denmark* and *Norway*,

the Church of Great Britain.

Norway, the Inhabitants whereof being then Pagans, he converted unto Christian Religion. At his return out of those parts *Anastatius* the Pope, who (*Eugenius* being dead in the mean time) had succeeded him, together with his Cardinals, received him with great honour, much approving his doings. It hapned that within a few moneths after his return, the said Pope died also: and this man also taking upon him the name of *Hadrian* the Fourth, was chosen Pope in his room. This was He that brought under his entire obedience the Citizens of *Rome*; that compelled the Emperor *Frederick Barbarossa* to hold his Stirrup, and appointed the Abbot of St. *Albans* to be the first Abbot of *England*, as St. *Alban* to whom the Abbey was dedicated, was the first Martyr of *England*. Having sate four years nine moneths, he died at *Anagnia*, being choaked by a fly in his drink.

5. Some report, that *Geoffry* of *Monmouth*, the Author of the British History, was a Cardinal at *Rome*. This can hardly be made good, but this is evident, he was consecrated Bishop of St. *Asaph*, *Anno* 1151.

6. *Busa* an English-man, saith *John Bale*, Nephew unto Pope *Hadrian*, was made a Cardinal, and the Pope's Chamberlain, *Anno* 1155. his Titles were first *SS. Cosma & Damiani*, then *S. Crucis* in *Jerusalem*, afterwards *S. Pudentiana*. Through his endeavour chiefly *Alexander* the Third was chosen Pope, by the voices of nineteen Cardinals: yet another Antipope was set up against him, having four voices onely: Under him, the said *Alexander*, he lived in great authority and favour, and died *Anno* 1180.

7. The book entitled, *Antiquitates Britannicæ*, ascribed to the late most Reverend Archbishop *Matthew Parker*, reporteth, how that *William Corbet*, Archbishop of *Canterbury*, being deceased, *Henry de Bloys* Bishop of *Winchester*, and Brother unto King *Stephen*, procured himself to be made a Cardinal, and appointed Legate *a latere* from the Pope.

8. *Herebert*, born at *Bosham* in *Suffex*, brought up in *Oxford* (where he proceeded Doctor in Divinity) was Secretary unto *Thomas Becket*, Archbishop of *Canterbury*, at the time of the said *Becket's* slaughter; the History whereof he wrote (besides divers other works) mentioned by *John Bale*. Pope *Lucius* the Third made him Cardinal, *Anno* 1178. and bestowed upon him the Archbishoprick of *Beneventum*.

9. *John Cummin*, an English man, and Archbishop of *Dublin*, was created a Priest-cardinal by Pope *Lucius* the Third, at *Velitrum*, *Anno* 1183. as testifieth that vertuous, learned, and eloquent man *Giraldus Cambrensis*.

10. *Stephen Langton*, afterwards Archbishop of *Canterbury*, was created Cardinal *S. Chrysogoni*, 1212.

11. *Robert Curson*, a Gentleman well descended, and an *Oxford-man*, was made Cardinal of *S. Stephen in Cœliomonte*: he was a good Divine, and eminent Preacher. From *Oxford* he went to *Paris*, where he proceeded

ceeded Doctor of Divinity: *Anno* 1219. he was with King *Lewis*, the French King, at the taking of *Damiata* in *Egypt*; after that, in the time of *Honorius* the Third, he was here as Legate in *England*: he left behind him a sum of Divinity, and a Discourse touching the salvation of *Origen*, certain solemn Lectures, and some other Works much esteemed.

12. *Robert Somerscot* made Cardinal of *S. Eustachius, Anno* 1234. he was a man (saith *Matthew Paris*) *discretus & circumspectu omnibus amabilis merito & gratiosus*. He was to have been elected Pope, after Pope *Gregory* the Ninth, but that some of the Cardinals caused him to be poisoned in the Conclave, where the Cardinals were assembled to make the election.

13. *Matthew Paris* maketh mention of an English Cardinal, called *John*, that when the Pope was very angry, because King *Henry* the Third withstood a certain exaction of His, and threatned to do great matters against him, sought by many effectual reasons to divert him from his publick course, but to no purpose, till at length the King for fear of his thunderbolts, was fain to yield. This man died at the Council at *Lyons, Anno* 1274.

14. *Atcherius*, Archdeacon of *London* (where *John Bale* saith he was born) was created Cardinal of *S. Praxedis, Anno* 1261. He died at *Rome, November* 1. 1286. and was buried in the Church to which he was entitled.

15. *William Bray* Doctor of Divinity; an English-man, between whom and the said *Archerus* had been a long continued Band of friendship even from their childhood. Being Archdeacon of *Rhemes* he was created by the same Pope, Cardinal of *S. Mark, Anno* 1262. He died at *Civita Vecchia, Anno* 1282. in the time of the vacancy.

16. *Robert Kilwarby*, being Archbishop of *Canterbury*, resigned his said Archbishoprick, to be Bishop, Cardinal of *Portus*, whereunto he was appointed by Pope *Nicholas* the Third.

17. *Hugh de Evesham*, being a Physician of the greatest renown of any then living in the Christian World, as also well seen in the Mathematicks (especially in Astrology) was sent for to *Rome*, by Pope *Martin* the Fourth, to give his opinion in certain doubts, and questions of Physick, which he performed so learnedly and readily, as gave great satisfaction. He was created Cardinal of St. *Laurence* in *Lucina, Anno* 1280. and was poisoned.

18. *John Bale* reporteth of one *Theobaldus* an English man, that (as he saith) was created Cardinal *S. Sabina in Aventino*, by Pope *Martin* the Fourth, *Anno* 1289.

19. A Catalogue of English Cardinals, in the History of Archbishop *Parker*, mentioneth one *Bernard de Auguiscello*, that being Archbishop of *Arles*, was made Bishop, Cardinal, of *Portus, Anno* 1281. and died 1290.

20. In

20. In the said Catalogue we find also one *Berardus* made Bishop, Cardinal, of *Præneste*: *Anno* 1268. he was sometime Canon of *York*: he died in *June* 1291.

21. The Register of *Ralph Baldock*, containing a Catalogue of the Deans of St. *Paul's*, reporteth, that one *Arnoldus de Cantilupo*, Dean of *Pauls*, was a Priest Cardinal, *Anno* 1306.

22. One *Leonardus Guercinus*, is likewise mentioned in the same Catalogue, he was made a Priest Cardinal by Pope *Clement* the Fifth, *Anno* 1310.

23. Pope *Benedict* the Eleventh, who himself had been a Friar-preacher, and General of that order, made *William Macklesfield* a Friar-preacher (a Batchelour of Divinity at *Paris*, and Doctor at *Oxford*) a Cardinal *S. Sabinæ*, *Anno* 1303. whereas he had been dead then four moneths before. His Cardinals hat notwithstanding was carried to *London* where he was buried, and with great solemnity set upon his hearse. He was born near *Coventry*.

24. Upon the news of *Macklesfield's* death, the Pope ordained in his place, and to the same title one *Walter Winterburn*, born in *Sarum*, a Friar-preacher (as was the other) a Doctor of Divinity, Confessor to King *Edward* the Third, and Provincial of his Order. He enjoyed his honour not past fifteen moneths, died in the eightieth year of his Age, *Anno* 1305. and was buried at *London*. A man of great learning, whereof he left some Monuments in writing not yet perished.

25. *Thomas Joyce* the next Provincial, of the Friars-preachers in *England*, succeeded *Winterburn* not onely in the place, but in his Cardinalship too; being likewise Doctor of Divinity, and Confessor to the King: being employed in an Ambassage to the Emperor, he died on the way, *Anno* 1307. and was buried in the Church of the Friars-preachers in *Oxford*, where he had been brought up. He had six brethren Preachers. by the same Mother, whereof one named *Walter*, became Archbishop of *Armagh*: Diverse of his works are remembred by *John Bale*.

26. *Sextorius* a Britan, that in his youth became a Franciscan Friar, of which Order he was chosen the nineteenth General, *Anno* 1339. Then by Pope *Innocent* he was appointed first Bishop of *Marsilia*, after that Archbishop of *Ravenna*; then Patriarch of *Grado*, and lastly Cardinal: *September* 17. 1361. but he died the same moneth. He wrote a Commentary upon *S. Augustine de Civitate Dei*, Expositions upon divers parts of the Bible, Sermons, Lectures, and divers other discourses.

27. Pope *Urban* the Fifth, named *William Grisant*, was (as *Thomas Walsingham* affirmeth) an English-man: he was the Son of a famous English Physitian, named also *William Grisant*, brought up in *Merton-colledge*. He died *December* 19. *Anno* 1370.

28. The first Cardinal created by the said *Urban*, was one *Anglicus Grimaldi de Grisacco*, who was supposed to have been an English man:

but all acknowledge that he was the Pope's brother's son, and so English by descent. He was Cardinal *S. Petri ad Vincula* at first and afterwards Bishop Cardinal of *Alba*: he died at *Avignon*, Anno 1387. having held in *Commendam* many years the Deanary of *York*.

29. *Bale* supposeth *John Thoresby*, Archbishop of *York*, to have been created a Priest-cardinal *S. Sabinæ*.

30. *Simon Langham*, Archbishop of *Canterbury*, was created a Priest-cardinal by the aforesaid *Urban* in September 1368. and afterward presented to be Bishop Cardinal of *Præneste* by *Gregory* the Eleventh.

31. *Adam Easton*, a Benedictine Monk of *Norwich*; born in *Hereford-shire*, proceeded Doctor of Divinity in *Oxford*, wrote much; a man of great wisdom and learning: he was created Cardinal *S. Cæciliæ*. Pope *Urban* apprehended at one time no less than seven Cardinals (this Cardinal being one) and after long imprisonment, caused five of them to be sowed up into sacks, and with barbarous cruelty to be thrown into the Sea. But this man (whose good fortune it was to escape) he committed to close prison, till, by the earnest entreaty of King *Richard* the Second, he was allowed some more liberty, all his Livings being taken from him. In that poor estate he continued five years even untill the death of *Urban*. His next successor *Boniface* the Ninth, set him quite at liberty, and restored him to all his preferments again; which thing was solemnly declared to the Estates assembled in Parliament at *Westminster*, Anno 1390. after which time he lived seven years in great prosperity, and died September 19. 1397. and was buried in his own title, where he hath a Monument of Marble with his Armes and Picture, and this rude Epitaph.

Artibus iste pater famosus in omnibus Adam,
Theologus summus, cardique nalis erat.
Anglia cui patriam, Titulum dedit ista Beatæ
Cæciliæq; ——— *morsq; suprema polum.*

Anno 1397; mens. Septemb.

He left in writing above twenty several Volumes, whereof the greatest part were either written in Hebrew, or Translations out of Hebrew; or at least some discourses concerning the Hebrew Tongue. Among the rest it is said, that he Translated all the Old Testament out of Hebrew into Latin.

32. *William Courtney*, then Bishop of *London*, was also made Cardinal by the same *Urban*.

33. *Philip Repingdon*, sometime Abbot of *Leicester*, consecrated Bishop of *Lincoln*, March 29. 1405. having been heretofore a great defender of the Doctrine of *John Wickliff*, was created Cardinal, *S S. Nevei & Achillei*, September 18. 1408. by Pope *Gregory* the Twelfth, who

before

the Church of Great Britain.

before had taken a folemn Oath to make no more Cardinals, till the controverſie concerning the Papacy was ended: but being forſaken by all his Cardinals except onely five, the better to ſtrengthen himſelf, he created ten in one day, whereof this man was one.

34. *Thomas Langley*, Biſhop of *Durham*, was created a Prieſt-cardinal, *June* 6. 1411. by Pope *John* the Twenty ſecond. He died *Anno* 1437.

35. *Robert Halam*, Biſhop of *Sarum*, was alſo created a Prieſt-cardinal, the ſame day he died, in the Caſtle of *Gotlieb* near *Conſtance*, being at the General Council there, *September* 4. 1417. having ſate Biſhop of that Church nine years.

36. *Henry Beaufort*, brother to King *Edward* the Fourth, and Biſhop of *Winchester*, was created Cardinal of *S. Eufebius* by Pope *Martin* the Eighth. *June* 23. 1426. He died *April* 11. 1447. and was buried in his own Church.

37. *Henry Chichely* was created Cardinal, *Anno* 1428. ſaith the Author of *Antiquit. Britan.*

38. *John Kemp*, Archbiſhop of *York*, was ordained Cardinal of *S. Eufebius*, *August* 9. 1439. long after being Archbiſhop of *Canterbury*, he was removed to the Title of *S. Ruffinus*.

39. *Thomas Bourchier*, Archbiſhop of *Canterbury*, was created by Pope *Paul* the Second, Cardinal *S. Syriaci in Thermis*, *Anno* 1464. He died *March* 30. 1486.

40. *John Morton*, Archbiſhop of *Canterbury*, was, by Pope *Alexander* the Fifth, created Cardinal *S. Anaſtaſii*, *Anno* 1493. He died *Anno* 1500.

41. *Chriſtopher Bainbrigg*, Archbiſhop of *York*, was made a Cardinal *S. Praxedis*, *Anno* 1511.

42. *Thomas Wolſey*, Archbiſhop of *York*, was created Cardinal *S. Cæciliæ*, *September* 7. He died *November* 29. 1530.

43. *John Fiſher*, Doctor of Divinity, and Biſhop of *Rocheſter*, was made Cardinal *S. Vitalis*: for refuſing the King's ſupremacy, and diſallowing his marriage with the Lady *Anne Bolen*, he was beheaded on the Tower-hill, 1535.

44. *Reginald Pool*, afterward Archbiſhop of *Canterbury*, was created Cardinal by Pope *Paul* the Third, *May* 22. 1536. and had three ſeveral Titles: the firſt *S. Nerei & Achillei*; then *S. Maria in Coſmedin*; and laſtly *S. Priſcæ*. He died *November* 7. 1558.

45. *Peter Petow*, a Friar, was made Cardinal by Pope *Paul* the Fourth, *June* 13. 1557. and alſo nominated by him unto the Biſhoprick of *Sarum*; and all to croſs and diſgrace Cardinal *Pool*. He died in *France* within the compaſs of the ſame year, and might never ſet Foot in *England*, to make ſhew of his red Hat, as (doubtleſs) he greatly deſired to have done.

46. *William*

46. *William Allen*, born in *England*: He raised a great combustion in our Church. This fugitive was born in *Lancashire*, and brought up in *Orial* Colledge; he ran away beyond the Seas, for his treasonable practices against his Countrey: he was by the Pope and other Enemies of the same, promoted to divers Ecclesiastical preferments; and lastly had a Cardinal's hat bestowed upon him in *August* 1587. He died a Priest-cardinal *S. Martini in Montibus* 1594. and was buried in the Church of the English Colledge at *Rome*.

Of the several Orders and Monks that have been in England.

Ex Fuleri *Ecclef. Hist.* 1.

*M*Athew *Paris* tells us, that in his time, *Tot jam apparuerunt ordines in* Anglia, *ut ordinum confusio videretur inordinata*; there then appeared so many Orders in *England*, that there seemed to be an inordinate confusion of Orders.

1. The *Benedictines*, or black Monks, the primitive Monks in *England*, so called from St. *Benedict* or *Bennet*, an Italian, first Father and founder of that Order. *Augustine*, the Monk, first brought them over into *England*; and these black Monks first nested in *Canterbury*, whence they have flown out into all the parts of the Kingdom. For (as *Clement Reyner* observeth rightly) all the Abbies of *England* before King *William* the Conqueror (and some while after) were filled with this Order: and though the *Augustinians* were their Seniors in *Europe*, yet they were their Juniors in *England*. The same Order was afterwards set forth in a new edition, corrected and amended under the names of.

First, *Cluniacks*, These were *Benedictines* refined, with some additionals invented and imposed upon them, by *Odo* the Fourth of *Clugny* in *Normandy*, who lived *Anno* 913. But these *Cluniacks* came not into *England*, till after the Norman Conquest, and had their richest Covents at *Barnstable* in *Devon-shire*, *Pontefract* and *Meaux* in *York-shire*, &c.

Secondly, *Sistercians*, so called, from one *Robert* living in *Cistercium* in *Burgundy*. He the second time refined the drossie *Benedictines*; and *Walter Espick* first established their Order, in *England*, at *Rival* in *York-shire*; besides which they have had many other pleasant and plentiful habitations at *Warden* and *Woburn* in *Bedford-shire*, *Buckland* and *Ford* in *Devon-shire*, *Bindon* in *Dorset-shire*, &c. The *Bernardine* Monks were of a younger house, or under-branch of the *Cistercians*. King *John* built an Abbey of the Cistercian Order at *Beaulieu* in *Hant-shire*.

Thirdly,

the Church of GREAT BRITAIN. 431

Thirdly, Of *Grandmont*, which obferved St. *Bennet's* rule. Thefe were brought into *England*, *Anno* 1233. and were principally fixed at *Abberbury* in *Shrop-shire*.

Thefe *Benedictines* with their feveral branches were fo numerous, and fo richly endowed, that in their revenues they did match all the Orders in *England*, efpecially if the foundations of *Benedictine* Nuns be joyned in the fame reckoning.

2. The *Auguftinian* Monks fucceed; it is conceived that *Eudo* the *Dapifer*, or *Sewer* to King *Henry* the Firft, firft brought them into *England*, *Anno* 1105. and that St. *Johns* at *Colchefter* was the prime place of their refidence. Doctor *Fuller* faith, that *Waltham Abbey* (for *Benedictines* at the firft) had it's Copy altered, and beftowed on *Auguftinians*. Thefe *Auguftinians* were alfo called *Canons Regular*. This Order in *England* brought forth feventy eminent Writers, and one in *Germany* worth them all in effect: I mean *Martin Luther*, who gave a mortal wound to all thefe Orders, yea to the root of the Romifh Religion.

3. *Gilbertine* Monks, a mongrel Order, obferving fome felect rules, partly of St. *Bennet*, partly of St. *Auguftine*, fo named from *Gilbert* (fon to *Joceline* a Knight) Lord of *Sempringham* in *Lincoln-fhire*. Being backed with the Authority of Pope *Eugenius* the Third, he ordained a Sect confifting of men and women, which fo grew and encreafed, that himfelf laid the foundations of thirteen Religious houfes of this Order. *Camden in Lincoln-fhire.*

4. *Carthufian* Monks, much famed for their mortified lives, and abftinence from all flefh. *Bruno* firft founded them in the *Dolphinate* in *France*, *Anno* 1080. and fome fixty years after they were firft brought over into *England*. *William de longa Spata*, Earl of *Salubury*, founded the firft houfe of *Carthufian* Monks at *Heltrop*; whofe wife *Ela* after his death founded the houfe of Nuns at *Lacock* in *Wilt-fhire*, and there continued her felf Abbefs of the place. The Books of the Englifh *Carthufians* were many, there being no lefs than eleven hundred Authors of them, their writings tend much to mortification; and out of them *Parfons* the Jefuite hath collected a good part of his refolutions.

Of the *Benedictine* Monks, there is reported to have been of that Order, twenty four Popes of *Rome*, one hundred eighty two Cardinals, one thoufand four hundred fixty four Archbifhops and Bifhops, fifteen thoufand and feventy Abbots of renown. Pope *John* the Twenty fecond faith, there have been of this Order five thoufand fix hundred fifty fix Monks Canonized, and made Saints.

The cloathing and rule of the *Cluniacks* was according to the appointment of St. *Benedict's* rule.

The *Ceftercians* wear red fhooes, and white rochets on a black coat: they are all fhorn fave a little circle.

The

The Order of those of *Grandmont*, is to lead a strait life (as Monks use to do) to give themselves to Watching, Fasting and Prayer; to wear a coat of Males upon their bodies, and a black cloak thereupon.

The *Augustinians*, or *Regular Canons*, their cloathing, by their first foundation, was a white coat, and a linnen rotchet under a black cope, with a scapular to cover their head and shoulders.

The *Gilbertines* may boast, that whereas *Benedictines* are by original Italians, *Augustinians African*, *Carthusians* French, *Dominicans* Spanish, *&c.* they are pure English by the extraction of their Order.

The life of the *Carthusians* was outwardly full of painted holiness, in forbearing flesh, in fasting from bread and water every Friday, in wearing hair-clothes next their body; they were addicted to much silence and solitariness, never going abroad, refusing all women's company, with other like ceremonies.

Of the several sorts of Friars that have been in England.

HEre it will be necessary to premise, what was the distinction between the Monks and Friars. The most essential difference is this: Monks had nothing in propriety, nor in common, but, being Mendicants, begged all their subsistence from the charity of others? Indeed they had houses or cells to dwell in, or rather to hide themselves in, but they had no means thereunto belonging.

But it may be Objected, That many Convents of Friars had large and ample Revenues, amounting to some hundreds (though never thousands) by the year. I Answer, That from the beginning (of the Institution of Friars) it was not so. These additions of Lands unto them was of latter date: not of their seeking, but of their Benefactors casting upon them.

We begin with their four elemental Orders. *Wickliff* commonly inveigheth against Friars under the name of C. A. J. M.

C. *Carmelites*,   J. *Jacobines*,   or   *Dominicans*,
A. *Augustinians*, M. *Minorites*,   *Franciscans*.

An uncharitable Rythmer thus lets fly at them.

Per decies binos Sathanas capiat Jacoboinas,
Propter & errores Jesu confunde Minores,
Augustienses, pater inclyte sterne per enses,
Et Carmelitas tanquam falsos Heremitas,

Sunt

The Church of GREAT BRITAIN.   433

Sunt Confeſſores Dominorum, ſeu Dominarum,
Et ſeductores ipſrarum ſunt animarum.

1. Of these, the *Dominicans* were the first Friars which came over into *England*, being but twelve in number, with *Gilbert de Fraxineto* their Prior; first landed at *Canterbury*, fixed at *Oxford*, but richly endowed at *London*. They were commonly called Black Friars, Preaching Friars, and *Jacobine* Friars. They took their name from St. *Dominick*, born at *Calogora* in *Spain*: and *Hubert de Burgo*, Earl of *Kent*, was their chief Patron, bestowing his Palace in the Suburbs of *London* upon them, which afterwards they ſold to the Archbiſhops of *York* reſiding therein; till by ſome tranſactions between King *Henry* the Eighth, and Cardinal *Wolſey*, it became the Royal Court, now known by the name of *Whitehall*. Afterwards by the bounty of *Gregory Rockſtey* Lord Mayor of *London*, and *Robert Kilwarby* Archbiſhop of *Canterbury*, they were more conveniently lodged in two Lanes on the bank of *Thames*, and ſtill retaining the name of Black Friars; no fewer than eighty Engliſh writers are accounted of this Order at this day. As beyond the Seas they are much condemned for being the ſole active managers of the cruel Spaniſh Inquiſition; ſo they deſerve due commendation for their Orthodox Judgements, in maintaining ſome controverſies in Divinity of importance againſt the Jeſuites.

Anno 1221

2. *Franciſcans* follow, commonly called *Gray Friers*, or *Minorites*: either in alluſion to *Jacob's* words, *ſum minor omnibus beneficiis tuis*; or from ſome other humble expreſſions in the New Teſtament. They received their name from St. *Francis*, born in the Dutchy of *Spoletum* in *Italy*; Canonized by Pope *Gregory* the Ninth; about two years after whoſe death the Franciſcans came over into *England*, and one *Diggs* (Anceſtor to Sir *Dudley Diggs*) bought for them their firſt ſeat in *Canterbury*, who afteward were diffuſed all over *England*. They were well-skilled in School divinity, and had a curious Library in *London* (built by *Richard Whittington*) in that age coſting five hundred and fifty pounds.

One *Bernard* of *Siena*, about the year 1400. refined the *Franciſcans* into *Obſervants*. King *Edward* the Fourth, firſt brought them into *England*, where they had ſix famous Cloyſters; ſince which time there have been a new Order of *Minims* begun beyond the Seas, *Recollects*, *Penitentaries*, *Capuchins*, &c. ſeeing they had their riſe ſince the fall of Abbies in *England*, they belong not to our preſent enquiry, &c. This Order afforded in *England* a hundred and ten Learned Writers.

3. *Carmelites*, or *White Friars*, come next; ſo named from Mount *Carmel*; brought over into *England*, in the Reign of King *Richard* the Firſt, by *Ralph Freeborn*; and placed at *Alnwick* in *Northumberland*, in a wilderneſs moſt like unto *Carmel* in *Syria*, whoſe Convent at their

K k k   diſſolu-

dissolution, in the Reign of King *Henry* the Eighth, was at low rates in that cheap County, valued at one hundred ninety and four pound and seven shillings *per Annum*; by which we may see, that even Mendicant Friars had houses endowed even with Revenues. *Hi cum primis Monachis Britonum & Scotorum ex Ægypto & Palestina in Britanicas Insulas Monachatum intulerunt.* It is said in the praise of our *Carmelites*, that they were most careful in keeping the Records of their Order. Let them thank *John Bale* herein once of them, who in his youth made the Catalogue out of love to his Order, and in his old age preserved it out of his affection to Antiquity. This Order was vertical, and in the highest exaltation thereof in the Reign of King *Edward* the Fourth, under *Nicholas Kenton* their twenty fifth Provincial. They reckoned no fewer than one thousand five hundred of their Order. But when *John Milverton*, his successor, began, in favour of Friary, furiously to ingage against Bishops, and the Secular Clergy, the Carmelites good Masters and Dames began to forsake them, and they never recovered their credit till they were utterly dissolved. *John Bird*, the one and thirtieth Provincial of this Order, zealously impugned the Pope's Supremacy in his Sermons, for which he was made the first Bishop of *Chester*, and was ejected that See in the Reign of Queen *Mary*, because he was married. The *Carmelites* boast very much of one *Simon Stock* of their Order, a Kentish boy, which being but twelve years old, went out into the Woods, and there fed on roots and wild fruit, living in the trunk of an hollow Tree, whence he got the Sirname of *Stock*. Having a revelation that soon after Some should come out of *Syria*, and confirm his Order, which came to pass when the Carmelites came hither, he afterwards became Master General of their Order (to whom the respective Provincials are accountable) and is said to be famous for his miracles.

Speed's Catal. *p.* 795.
Reyner de Apostolatu Benedictinorum. p. 164.
Vide the Catalog. in *Fullers* Church Hist. *l.* 6. *p.* 272

Stow's Survay of *London*, *p.* 321.

4. *Augustinian* Eremites, they entred *England*, *Anno* 1252. and had their first habitation at St. *Peters* in the Poor in *London*; These probably taking the denomination of poverty (otherwise at this day a very rich Parish in the City) because the said *Augustinian* Eremites went under the notion of begging Friars. Mean time what a mockery was this (as Doctor *Fuller* observeth) that these should pretend to be Eremites, who instead of a wide Wilderness, lived in *Broad-street London*, where their Church now belongeth to the *Dutch* Congregation. These *Augustine* Friars were good Disputants.

Beacon's Relicks of *Rome*.

The Order of the *Dominicans* is without all shame to beg, and forsake little by wilful poverty, that they may obtain much, and to wax rich of other mens labours, they themselves being idle, lazy and unprofitable drones of the Earth. Their coat is white, their cope and coule is black. The new guise of their vesture made Pope *Innocent* to wonder. But Pope *Honorius* the Third by his Bull honourably admitted the black Order of the Black Friars.

The

the Church of GREAT BRITAIN.

The Gray Friars, or Franciscans, go barefooted, as *Francis* their founder did, and gird themselves with a cord, wearing a little coule, whence some think they are called *Minorites*. Some of them be called Friars *Observants*, and are counted of more holiness than the common sort of Gray Friars are, which are called *Minorites*. At first the colour of their cope was russet, but afterward was turned into white by Pope *Honorius* the Third. This Order (saith the Dutch Chronicle) is to begg, to take of every man, and to do nothing again for it. They lye, dissemble, and beguile the people with flattering words under the pretence of long prayer.

William Duke of *Aquitain*, and Count of *Lectavia*, invented or rather renued the Order of the *Augustine* Friars, which had been before long decayed. This *William* first dwelt in the Wilderness with his Brethren, chastised his flesh, and subdued it with a coat of male on his bare Body, Praying, Watching, and Fasting night and day, so that he was called a Father and Restorer of that Order. Thus much for the four principal sorts of Friers.

The following Orders were but additional Descants upon the former, with some variations of their Founders, among whom were.

1. THE *Trinitarians*, for whom *Robert Rooksley* built first an house at *Mottingden* in *Kent*: they were called also *de Redemptione Captivorum*; whose work was to beg money of well-disposed people for the ransoming of Christians in captivity with the Pagans.

2. The *Crouched* Friars, who came over into *England* 1244. with the Pope's Authentick and this unusual priviledge, that none should reprove their Order, or upbraid them, or command them under pain of excommunication. Some say, they carried a cross on their staves, others on their backs, called, in French, a Crouch, the place of Crouched Friars in *London* still retaineth the Name.

3. The *Bonhomes*, or good men, being also Eremites brought over into *England*, by *Richard* Earl of *Cornwal*, in the Reign of his Brother King *Henry* the Third, so stiled because of their signal goodness. These *Bonhomes*, though begging Friars (the poorest of Orders) and Eremites the most sequestred of begging Friars, had two, and it is believed, no more Covents in all *England* (Monks onely excepted) the one at *Asheridge* in *Buckingham-shire*, now the mansion of the Right Honourable the Earl of *Bridgewater*: it was valued, at the dissolution, yearly at four hundred forty seven pound eight shillings half-penny. The other at *Eddingdon* in *Wilt-shire*, the late habitation of the Lady *Beauchamp*, valued, when dissolved, at five hundred twenty one pound twelve shillings half-penny.

In the year 1257. arose two new Orders, both of them were fixed in *Cambridge*: the first, the brethren, *De pœnitentia Jesu* (otherwise *Fratres Saccati*, brethren of the Sack) whose Cell is since turned into *Peter-house*. *Matthew Paris* gives this account of them, at their first coming into *England*; *Eodem tempore quidam novus ordo fratrum Londini apparuit, & incognitus. Papale tamen autenticum palam ostendens, ita ut tot ordinum confusio videretur; qui, quia saccis incedebant induti, Fratres Saccati vocabantur.* It is most likely, that this avaritious Pope *Alexander*, instituted this new Order to help fill his bag and Sachel by these *Fratres Saccati*, employed to promote his rapines and revenues, as the Friars *Minorites*, and *Predicants* were.

The other were the *Bethlemites*, dwelling somewhere in *Trompington-street*, and wearing a Star with five raies on their backs.

I will conclude with the *Robertines*, who owe their original to one *Robert Flower*, who had been twice Mayor of *York*, who forsaking the fair Lands left him by his Father, betook himself to a solitary life about the rocks in *Nidsdale* in *York-shire*, and it seemeth) at *Knaresborough* the first and last house was erected for his Order.

Of the Templars, and Hospitallers.

THE Inner Temple and Middle Temple, in *London*, do now stand in the very place, where, in times past, in the Reign of King *Henry* the Second, *Heraclius Patriarch* of *Jerusalem* Consecrated a Church for Knights Templars, which they had newly built according to the form of the Temple, near unto the Sepulchre of our Lord at *Jerusalem*. For, at their first institution, about the year of our Lord 1113. they dwelt in part of the Temple hard by the Sepulchre, whereof they were so named; they vowed Poverty, Chastity, and Obedience, to defend Christian Religion, the holy Land, and Pilgrims going to visit the Lord's Sepulchre against all Mahometans and Infidels: whereupon all men most willingly and most cordially embraced them: so that through the bounteous liberality of Princes and devout people, having gotten in all places very fair possessions, and exceeding great wealth; they flourished in great reputation for Piety and Devotion; yea and in the opinion, both of the holiness of the men and of the place, King *Henry* the Third, and many Noble men, desired much to be buried in their Church among them: some of whose Images are there to be seen with their leggs across; for so they were buried in that age, *That had taken upon them the Cross* (as they then termed it) *to serve in the holy Land*, or had vowed the same.

Stow's description of London.

But

But in procefs of time, when with unfatiable greedinefs they had hoorded up great wealth, by withdrawing Tithes from Churches, appropriating fpiritual livings to themfelves, and other hard means, from Almes-men they turned Lords: and though very Valiant at the firft (for they were fworn rather to die than to fly) afterwards they grew lazy, they laughed at the Rules of their firft Inftitution, as at the fwadling-clothes of their Infancy, neglecting the Patriarch: at length, partly their vitioufnefs, and partly their wealth, caufed their final extirpation. Pope *Clement* having long fojourned in *France*, had received many real Courtefies from King *Philip the Fair*; At laft *Philip* requefted of the Pope all the Lands of the Knights Templars through *France*, forfeited (as was pretended) by reafon of their horrible Herefies, and licentious living. The Pope was willing to gratifie him in fome good proportion for his favours received: and therefore being thus long the King's Gueft, he gave him the Templars Lands and Goods to pay for his entertainment. On a fudden all the Templars in *France* are clapt in prifon, damnable fins are laid to their charge, and they moft cruelly burned to death at a ftake, with *James* the Grand Mafter of their Order. All *Europe* followed the Copy that *France* had fet them. Here in *England* King *Edward* the Second, of that name, fuppreffed the Order, and put them to death. So by vertue of a Writ fent from him to Sir *John Wogan*, Lord Chief Juftice in *Ireland*, were they ferved there: and fuch was the fecrecy of the contrivance of the bufinefs, that the ftorm fell upon them ere they were aware of it.

Fullers Supplement of the Hift. of the Holy War, *l.* 5. *c.* 1.

In *England* their poffeffions were by Authority of Parliament affigned to the Hofpitaller-Knights of St. *John of Jerufalem*; leaft that fuch Lands given to good and pious ufes, againft the Donour's will fhould be given to other ufes. At the North-fide of the City of *London*, *John Brifet*, a rich and devout man, built an Houfe for the Knights Hofpitallers of St. *John of Jerufalem*, which in time grew fo great, that it refembled a Palace, and had in it a very fair Church, and a Tower-fteeple raifed to fo great height, with fo fine workmanfhip, that while it ftood, it was a fingular beauty and ornament to the City. Thefe Knights Hofpitallers, at their hrft Inftitution, about the year 1124; and long after, were fo lowly all the while they continued poor, that their Governor was ftiled fervant to the poor fervitors of the Hofpital of *Jerufalem*, like as the Mafter of the Templars, who fhortly after arofe, was termed, *The Humble Minifter of the poor Knights of the Temple.*

The Hofpitallers ware a white Crofs upon their upper black Garment, and by folemn profeffion were bound to ferve Pilgrims and poor people in the Hofpital of St. *John* at *Jerufalem*, and to fecure the paffages thither; they charitably buried the dead, they were affiduous in prayer, mortified themfelves with watchings and faftings; they were

courteous

<small>Camd. descrip. of London.</small> courteous and kind to the poor, whom they called their Masters, and fed with white bred, while themselves lived with brown, and carried themselves with great austerity: whereby they purchased to themselves the love and liking of all sorts, and through the bounty of good Princes, and private persons, admiring their piety and prowess, they rose from this low degree to so high an Estate, and great riches, that they did after a sort wallow in wealth and riches. For about the year of our Lord 1240. they had within Christendom nineteen thousand Lordships, or Mannors, like as the Templars nine thousand. And this estate of theirs grown to so great an height made way for them to as great Honours, so as their Prior in *England* was reputed the prime Baron of the Land (called the Lord of St. *Johns*) and able with fulness and abundance of all things to maintain an honourable Port, untill that King *Henry* the Eighth gat their Lands and livings into his own hands, like as he did of the Monasteries also.

They outlived all other Orders, yet at last they fell into a *Præmunire*: for they still continued their obedience to the Pope (contrary to their Allegiance) whose Usurped authority was banished out of the Land.

<small>Weavers Monum. p. 114.</small> They were forced to resign all into the King's hands: He allowed to Sir *William Weston*, Lord *Prior* of the Order, an annual pension of One thousand pounds. But he never received a penny thereof, but died instantly, struck to the heart when he first heard of the dissolution of his Priory, and lyeth buried in the Chauncel of *Clarkenwell*, with the pourtraiture of a dead man lying on his shroud, most artificially cut in Stone: others had rent assigned them of two hundred pound, one hundred pound, sixty pound, fifty pound, twenty pound, ten pound; according to their several qualities and deserts.

Queen *Mary* sets up the Hospitallers again, and Sir *Thomas Tresham*, of *Rushton* in *Northampton-shire*, was the first and last Lord Prior after their Restitution: for their nests were plucked down, before they were warm in them, by the coming in of Queen *Elizabeth*.

Of the English Nuns.

I Come now to Nuns, almost as numerous in *England*, as Monks and Friers, as having (though not so many Orders) yet more of the same Order. The weaker sex hath ever equalled men in their Devotion, often exceeded them in their Superstition.

At *Liming* in *Kent* the Daughter of King *Ethelbert* took the veile, and became the first English Nun.

There was an *Hermophrodite* Order (as is aforesaid) admitting both Men and Women under the same roof, and during the life of *Gilbert* their first founder, for seven hundred Brethren there were one thousand one hundred Sisters entred into that Order. Doctor *Fuller* divides the Nuns into three sorts.

> *First*, The Antientest.
> *Seconaly*, The Poorest.
> *Thirdly*, The latest Nuns in *England*.

1. Of the first sort, he accounteth the *She Benedictines*, commonly called black Nuns. *Bennet* the Monk, after he had placed himself and his Monkish Brethren in a certain Noble and Famous Cloyster upon the Mount *Cassinus*, raised up also an Order of Nuns, and made his Sister *Scholastica* Abbess over them. The apparrel of these black Nuns is a black coat, cloak, coule, and veyl: and least the Scripture should deceive her and hers, it was commanded, that none of that Order should read the Holy Scripture, without consent or permission of their Superior.

2. The poorest follow, being the strict Order of St. *Clare*, a Lady living at the same time, and in the same Town with St. *Francis*; she assembled and gathered together a Congregation of poor Women, and gave them an Order of life, like unto the rule that Frier *Francis* gave his Covent. Their garment is gray, their Order admitteth none but women-kind, except it be to say Mass.

3. The Nuns of St. *Bridget* were the latest in *England*, first setled here in the second year of King *Henry* the Fifth, *Anno Domini* 1415. dissolved with the rest, *Anno* 1538. so that they continued here onely one hundred twenty three years. *Bridget*, Queen of *Sweden* gave them their name and Institution, Men and Women living under the same roof; the VVomen above, the Men beneath. They were seated at *Sion* in *Middlesex*; which King *Henry* the Fifth (having expelled from thence the Monks *Aliens*) built for Religious

Virgins,

Virgins, to the Honour of our Saviour, the Virgin *Mary*, and St. *Bridget* of *Sion*. In this *Sion* he appointed so many Nuns, Priests, and Lay-brethren divided apart within their several Walls, as were in number (forsooth) equal to Christ's Apostles and Disciples, viz: eighty five.

    I. *Sisters*, Sixty.
   II. *Priests*, Thirteen.
  III. *Deacons*, Four.
  IV. *Lay-brethren*, Eight.

Walsingh. in Henric. I°.   Having bestowed sufficient maintenance upon them, King *Henry* provided by a Law, that contenting themselves therewith, they should take no more of any man: but what overplus soever remained of their yearly Revenue, they should bestow it upon the poor. Thomas *Walsingham* saith: if afterwards the whole World should proffer them Farmes and possessions, it was utterly unlawful for them to accept any thing thereof. This Order had but this one Covent in *England*: and so wealthy it was, that at the dissolution it was valued yearly worth one thousand nine hundred forty four pounds eleven shillings eight pence farthing. This Order constantly kept their Audit on *All Saints Eve*, *October* 31. and the day after *All Souls*, being the third of *November*.

Speeds Catal. of Religious Houses, p. 793.   No Covents of *England* more carefully kept their Records than the Priory of *Clarkenwel*, to whose credit it is registred. There is a perfect Catalogue, from their first foundation to their dissolution, of all their Prioresses, defective in all other houses.

Sir *Thomas Chaloner* not long ago built a spatious house within the close of that Priory, upon the frontispiece whereof these Verses were inscribed.

> *Casta fides superest, velatæ tuta sorores*
> *Ista relegata deseruere licet.*
> *Nam venerandus Hymen hic vota jugalia servat,*
> *Vestalemq; focum mente fovere studet.*

> Chast Faith still stay's behind, though hence be flown
>   Those veiled Nuns who here before did nest:
> For reverend Mariage wedlock-vowes doth own;
>   And sacred flames keep's here in Loyal breast.

Here I shall say little of the Houses for Leprous people; though indeed they deserved more charity than all the rest. *Burton-lazars* of
Leicester-

Leicester-shire was the best endowed house for that purpose: for so they used to tearm people infected with the Leprosie. Here was a rich Spittle-house, or Hospital; under the Master whereof, were, in some sort, all other Spittle-houses, or Lazar-houses in *England*, like as himself also was under the Master of the Lazars in *Jerusalem*. *Camden* in *Leicester-shire*.

It was founded in the first age of the Normans, by a common contribution over all *England*; and the *Mowbraies* especially did set to their helping hands. But as that Disease came into *England* by the holy War, so it ended with the end thereof.

FINIS.

FINIS

THE TABLE.

A

Abbey of *Battel* founded by K. *William* the Conqueror Page 37
Abbey of *Cnobsherburg* by whom founded 17
Abbey of *Crowland* founded 21
Abbey of *Peterborough* burnt by the *Danes*, with an excellent Library therein 25
Abbey at *Glastonbury* founded by King *Ina* 21
Abbey of St. *Edmond* founded and endowed by King *Canutus* 34
Abbeys and Religious Houses dissolved 149
Adelme, the first *English*-man who wrote in *Latine* 20
Pope *Adrian* the fourth an *English*-man 44
Pope *Agatho* composeth the differences betwixt the two Archbishops 17
Alcuinus, Scholar to Venerable *Bede*, and Tutor to *Charles* the Great 23
S. *Alban* the *Proto-martyr* of *Britain*, pag. 5. he is Canonized 23
Altars taken down by publick Authority 71

King *Alfred*, *England*'s deliverer from the *Danish* Tyranny: his Story from pag. 26. ad pag. 30.
Abbey of *Val-royal* in *Cheshire* founded by King *Edward* the first 105
All-souls Colledge in *Oxford*, by whom founded 130
King *Athelstan* a great Benefactour to the Church of S. *John* of *Beverley*, pag. 31. he commands the payment of Tithes, Ib.
Anne Ascough, her Martyrdom 157
An Act passed for restoring the Tenths and First-fruits to the Crown 209
An Act for the Dissolution of all such Monasteries, Covents, &c. as had been founded by Queen *Mary* 209
Articles passed in the Convocation in the first year of Queen *Elizabeth* 210
Abbey of *Westminster* converted to a Collegiate Church 221
The thirty nine Articles composed 227
Arthur King of *Britain* 10
St. *Asaph* 11
Aurelius Ambrosius King of *Britain* 10

Ll 2   Duke

The Table.

Duke of *Anjou* cometh into *England*   242
   Alanus Copus   243
Annates, or First-fruits when brought into *England*   103
Richard Armachanus Primate of *Ireland*   112
   Anabaptists Convicted and Censured   171, 172
Thomas Arundel, Archbishop of *Canterbury*, his lamentable end   125
Augustine the Monk sent into *England*. Thousands Baptized by him in one day.   12
He is the first Archbishop of *Canterbury*, his death   14
Archbishop *Abbot* Confined 299
Abbey of *Evesham* founded and endowed by King *Offa*   21
The Assembly at *Glascbow* pass Acts for the overthrow of Episcopacy, the Service-book and the Canons, &c.   313
Aihunus Bishop of *Holy-Island*, removeth his See and Covent to *Durham*   33
A new Representative, called the Agreement of the people   345
Alexander Alesius, a Learned *Scot*.   169

B

Abirgton's Conspiracy, page 248
Bacon a good School-man and Mathematician   107
Bertha wife to King *Ethelbert*   12
John Baconthorp, a Learned *English-man*   111

Thomas Becket, Archbishop of *Canterbury*, his story   45, 46, 47
His translation and enshrining   70
John of *Beverley*, who gave Education to *Bede*   21
Bede, Sirnamed *Venerable*, his Birth, Learning, Writings, and Death   22
Birth of our Saviour   1
Birinus converteth the *West-Saxons*   16
Bodies when first brought to be buried in Churches   23
Bernard Bishop of S. *David's* denies subjection to the Archbishop of *Canterbury*   42
Hubert de Burgo, Earl of *Kent*, his story   75
Brazen-nose Colledge in *Oxford*, when and by whom founded   138
Biddle a Socinian   359
Thomas Bradwardine Archbishop of *Canterbury*, his story, and writings   33
Christian *Britan's* Celebrated the Passover contrary to the Constitutions of the *Romane* Church   4
How long the *Britans* remained under the *Romane* yoke   4
Britans driven into *Britain* in *France*, *Wales* and *Cornwal*   9
Britans escaped all the persecutions of the Heathen *Roman* Emperours, except the last under *Dioclesian*   5
British Bishops in the Councils of *Arbes*, *Nice*, *Sardis* and *Ariminum*   6
When Bishops Seats were altered

The Table.

tered from Villages to great Cities 38

Bishops Imprisoned by King *Stephen* 43

Robert Brus King of *Scotland* 105

The Battel at *Bannocks-borough* 106

Beginning of the Broyls between the two Houses of *Lancaster* and *York* 131

Bainham a Martyr 147

Bilney burnt 146

Henry Beauford and Cardinal, the Founder of S. *Crosses* Hospital 131

The Popes Bulls of Provision for Ecclesiastical promotions 103

Archbishop *Boniface*, his making way for Popes Appropriating First-fruits unto themselves 80

The Bishoprickes of *Westminster*, *Oxford*, *Peterborough*, *Bristol* and *Chester*, erected by *Henry* the eight 154

Bishoprick of *Westminster* dissolved 221

Protestant Bishops placed in the Sees of the Popish Prelates 212

Bernard Gilpin refuseth the Bishoprike of *Carlile* 215

Bishops with other Divines met at *Lambeth*, resolved on divers Articles 258

Earl *Bothwel* married to the Queen of *Scots*, fleeth out of *Scotland* 232

Twelve Bishops Impeached, and sent to the Tower 238

The Counterfeit Boy of *Bilson* 282

Dr. *Bastwick*, *Prynne*, and *Burton* Censured 305

Brown and *Harrison* inveigh against Bishops, &c. 245

Bishops of S. *Andrews*, and *Glascow*, and Abbot of *Scone*, put in Iron-chains, and Imprisoned in *Port-chester* Castle 104, 105

The King's Palace of *Bridewel* given to the City of *London* for a work-house 177

The Bible Translated in the Reign of King *Henry* the eighth, King *Edward* the sixth, and Queen *Elizabeth* 161

Bible Translated in King *James* his Reign 273 ad 276

D. *Bound's* Book about the Sabbath 257

The first Bailiffs of *London* 348

Every Parish when bound to provide a Bible in *English*, and a Register-book to be kept there 150

Bishop *Bonner*, a cruel Persecutor, doomed to perpetual Imprisonment 212

M. *Bucer*, his coming into *England*; he takes the Chair at *Cambridge*, his death 169

Buckingham-shire Martyrs many before *Luther's* time 139

Benedictus Biscopius; the first Glass in *England* was his Gift 17

The Fatal Vespers at *Blackfriers* 291

A Bill Signed against Bishops Voting as Peers in Parliament 229

Walter Burley a Great Philosopher. 113.

C

The Table.

C.

Aurſines, what they were, when they firſt came into *England* page 74.

The Book of Canons made 269

Cadwallader, the laſt King of the ſtock of *Britans* 19

Caerleon in *Wales*, the Court of King *Arthur*: the See of an Archbiſhop: a Colledge of two hundred Philoſophers 11

Cadocus, Abbot of *Llancarvan* in *Glamorgan-ſhire*, his charity and liberality 11

Caranſius made a League with the *Britains*, and expelled the *Romans*, and made himſelf King 5

Congel, Abbot of *Bangor* 11

Columkil, a famous Seminary of learning 16

Mr. *Thomas Cartwright*. Articles tendred to him: his impriſonment 253

Col. *Edward Aſhton*, and *John Betley* executed 361

Colledges erected beyond the Seas for Engliſh youth to be educated therein 234, 235

Cridda firſt King of *Mercia* 9

Cerdicus firſt King of the Weſt Saxons 10

Conſtantius Chlorus, Emperor of *France*, *Spain*, and *Britain*: he died, and was buried at *York* 5

Conſtantine the Great, born, made King, and Emperor, firſt in *Britain* 6

A Council called at *Hartford* 18

A Council called at *Cliffe* in *Kent* by King *Ethelbald*, and *Cuthbert* Archbiſhop of *Canterbury* 22

A Council at *Harſield* 19

A Council at *Becanceld*. Another held at *Berghamſteed*, by *Withred* King of *Kent* 20

A Council held by *Wolphred* Archbiſhop of *Canterbury* at *Celichyth* 24

A Council aſſembled at *Alncæſter* to promote the building of *Eveſham-abbey* 21

A Council of Saxon and Britiſh Biſhops aſſembled under an Oak in the borders of *Worceſter* and *Hereford-ſhires* 12

A Council at *Intingford* 30

Divers Councils kept in the Reign of King *Athelſton*, viz. at *Exceter*, *Feverſham*, *Thunderfield*, and *London*; and at *Great Lea* 31

Three Councils held in the time of *Dunſtan*, viz. at *Wincheſter*, *Cartlage* in *Cambridge-ſhire*, and *Caln* in *Wilt-ſhire* 32

Chelſey-colledge founded 277

A National Council held by *Hoel. Dha*, for all *Wales*, at *Tyquin* 32

A Council of Biſhops called by King *William* the Firſt, at *Winton* 37

A Council againſt Appeals to *Rome* 117

A Conference held at St. *Albans* 7

The Univerſity of *Cambridge* founded by King *Sigebert* 15

Cambridge waſted by the Danes 25

Conference between Dr. *White*, and Dr. *Featly*, Proteſtants; and *Fiſher*, and *White*, Jeſuites 291

Iſaac Cauſabon, his Exercitations and death 280, 281

Conſtellation of *Caſſiopeia* 238

Con-

The Table.

Conference at *Hampton-Court* 261, *ad* 269

A Convocation wherein the Lord *Thomas Cromwel* sate in State above all the Bishops 149

King *Charles* the First, his story from 292, *ad* 347

A Council summoned by Archbishop *Anselm*, at *Westminster*, where all married Priests were excommunicated 41

A Council called at *Westminster*, by *Albericus* Bishop of *Hostia* 43

A Council at *Westminster* in the Reign of King *Henry* the Second 48

A Council held at *Oxford* 71

A Council held at *Lambeth*, by *Iohn Peckham* Archbishop of *Canterbury* 90

He summoneth another Council at *Reading* 96

A Council called by *Thomas Arundel* Archbishop of *Canterbury*, at St. *Pauls London*. 119

A Convocation in *London*. 126

A Council called by Archbishop *Morton*, to redress the luxury of the *London*-Clergy in Cloathes, and frequenting Taverns 137

King *Charles* the Second, his story from 347, *ad* 385

Sir *Iohn Old-castle*, Lord *Cobham*, his story from 123, *ad* 127

The persecution of the Lady *Eleanor Cobham* 129

Christ-church Colledge in *Oxford*, founded by Cardinal *Wolsey* 143

Miles Coverdale Bishop of *Exeter*. 172

Iohn Colet, a learned Englishman; the founder of the Free-School of St. *Pauls London* 142

Canons and Converts of the Order of *Sempingham*, turn Apostates 91

Contention between the two Archbishops of *Canterbury* and *York* 48

Alexander Cementarius his story 58, 59

Sir *Geoffry Chaucer*, when he flourished 113

Archbishop *Cranmer* his subscription to Popery for fear of death: he retracteth his retractation: he is burnt to ashes 202

Lord *Thomas Cromwel*, his story from 149, *ad* 155

The Canons made by the Convocation, Anno 1640. 318

D.

*D*Avid, Unckle to King *Arthur*, kept a Synod against the Pelagian error: he removed his Archiepiscopal seat from *Caerleon* to *Menevia*, now called St. *Davids* page 11

Danes, when they first invaded *England* 23

Earl of *Darby* beheaded at *Bolton* 353

Iohn Duns Scotus, or *Dunensis* 107

Dubitrius, his Academy near the River *Wye* in *Monmouth-shire* 9

Diuma first Bishop of *Mercia* 17

Dioclesian and *Maximian* resign their Ensignes of Command 59

Davids Psalms, when and by whom first translated into English metre 172

Lord *Darby* married to the Queen of *Scots*: his death 230, 232.

Dif-

The Table.

Disputation between the Protestants and Papists   211
The Synod of *Dort*   283, 284
University at *Dublin* founded   254
Dorchester in *Oxford-shire*, the seat of *Birinus* his Bishoprick   16
Dunstan, Archbishop of *Canterbury*, his story   31, 32
Dooms-day Book, when made   37
Battel of *Dunbar*   350

E.

Elvanus built a library near St. *Peter*'s Church in *Cornhil*   page 3
Eleutherius Bishop of *Rome*, his letter to King *Lucius*   ib.
Ella first King of the *South-Saxons*   9
Kingdom of the *East-Saxons* what it contained, and when it began. *Exchenwin* first King thereof   9
Kingdom of the *East-Angles*, what it contained, when it began their conversion advanced by King *Sigebert*   15
Edmond King of the *East-Angles* murdered by the *Danes*   26
Ethelbert King of *Kent* embraceth Christianity   12
Ethelfred King of *Northumberland* killeth one thousand two hundred Monks of *Bangor*: he is slain by the *Britains*   13
Egbert King of the *West-Saxons*, made himself sole Monarch of *England*   23
Erkenwald a Bishop, founder of the Monasteries of *Chertsey* in *Surrey*, and *Barking* in *Essex*   19
Edilwalch King of the *South-Saxons* is baptized   19
Edwyn the son of *Ethelfred* becometh a Christian   14
Ethelwolph King of the *West-Saxons* granteth the Tenth of all his Lands to God and his Ministers, &c. his story   24
Kind *Edward* the Elder restoreth the University of *Cambridge*, expells the *Danes*, &c.   30
Elphege Bishop of *Canterbury* stoned by the *Danes*   33
Eaton Colledge founded by King *Henry* the Sixth   131
Edward the Confessor, his Ecclesiastical Laws: his hereditary vertue left to his successors to cure the Kings Evil   35
England freed from the *Danes* 35
England interdicteded for six years in the Reign of King *Iohn* 57
Edmond Archbishop of *Canterbury* Canonized   80
King *Edward* the First, his story from   86. ad 105
Edward the Second, his story from   105. ad 109
Edward the Third, his story from   109. ad 114
Edward the Sixth, his story from   154. ad 179
Queen *Elizabeth*, her troubles during her Sister's Reign   190
The story of her Reign from   206. ad 261
Edinburgh Castle surrendred to O. *Cromwel*, by Colonel *Dundasse*   351

Paulus

F.

Paulus *Fagius* and *M. Bucer*, their bodies taken out of their Graves, and burnt 203

The Sect of the Family of Love 239

Flamines and Archflamines, their places turned into Bishopricks and Archbishopriks by King *Lucius* 3

Finan converted the East-Saxons 16

Focaria, Concubines to the Canons: they are imprisoned in the Tower

John Frith, a learned man, burnt in *Smith-field* 148

First-fruits Office, when set up in *London* 150

John Fisher Bishop of *Rochester*, beheaded 148

Mr. *John Fox* with some others settle themselves at *Basil* in Queen *Maries* days 200

His death 250

Fifth Monarchy-men apprehended 360

John Ficknam made Abbot of *Westminster* 196

The troubles of *Franckford* 197, 198

Robert Farrars, Bishop of St. *Davids*, imprisoned in King *Edward's* days, and burnt in Queen *Maries* days 175

Florentius, first Bishop of *Argentine*, or *Strausburg* 17

G.

G*asper Haywood*, the first Jesuite, that ever set foot in *England* 246

Gospel first planted in *Britain* 1

Britain first received the Gospel by publick Authority 2

Germanus Bishop of *Auxerre* is sent for into *Britain* to suppress Pelagianism 7

Gospel first planted by *Augustine* among the Saxons 12

Five Grammar Schools erected in *London* 129

Stephen Gardiner Bishop of *Winchester* he fell sick the same day that Bishop *Ridley* and *Latimer* were burnt: his sad end 194

A Gun shot at Dr. *Pendleton* preaching at *Pauls* cross 193

Lady *Jane Gray* proclaimed Queen of *England* 179

She and her husband, the Lord *Guilford Dudley*, and her Father the Duke of *Suffolk* are beheaded 188

Gutblake the first Saxon Eremite in *England* 21

Robert Grosthed Bishop of *Lincoln* 80. 81

The Gun-powder plot 270. 271

Archbishop *Grindal*, a patron of prophecyings, and how they were modelled 241

Godfrey Goodman Bishop of *Glocester*, committed to the Gate-house for refusing to subscribe the Canons made, Anno 1640. 320

He dies a Papist ibid.

H.

H*arold*, the Son of Earl *Godwyn*, King of *England*: he is slain at Battel in *Suffex* 36

Hardiknout, the last of the Danish Kings in *England* 35

Alexander Hales an English-man,

The Table.

Master to *Thomas Aquinas*, and Bonaventure 107
Honorius Archbishop of Canterbury divided *England* into Parishes 16
Helvetia converted by *Gallus* ib.
Hengist Captain of the Saxons, invadeth Britain 8
He is King of *Kent* 9
An Heptarchy established in Britain 9
Swallowed up in the West Saxons Monarchy 10
Robert Holcot a learned English man 112
Duke *Hamilton*, Earl of *Holland*, and Lord *Capel* beheaded 348
Hubba the Dane killeth *Hedda* the Abbot of *Peterborough*, and eighty four Monks with his own hand 25
King *Henry* the Third, his story from 68. ad 86
Henry the Fourth, his story from 118. ad 123
Henry the Fifth, his story from 123. ad 127
Henry the Seventh, his story from 135. ad 140
Henry the Eighth, his story from 141. ad 157
Sir *Henry Slingsby*, and Dr. *Hues* beheaded 361
Hospital at *Greenwich*, founded by *William Lambert* 250
Hospitals of Christ-church in London, and St. *Thomas* in Southwark founded 176. 177
The Statute made *Pro Hæretico comburendo* 119
Death of Prince *Henry* 280
John Hooper and *John Rogers*, founders of Non-conformity 169
Bishop *Hall's* Book in defence of the divine right of Episcopacy 317
Dr. *Iohn Hacket* defendeth Deans and Chapters 325
A sad contest between Mr. *Rich. Hooker*, and Mr. *Walter Travers* 255
King *Charles* the First, his Dispute with Mr. *Alexander Henderson* 342

I.

King *James*, his birth page 230
His story from 261. ad 293
Impropriations bought in to maintain a preaching Ministry 301
The Impostures of *Hacket*, *Arthington*, and *Coppinger* 253
Ilsutus, a profound Scholar 111
Ina King of the West Saxon, sets forth his Saxon Laws 20
He first granted *Peter-pence* to the Pope out of this Kingdom 22
Iohannes Scotus Enigena, murthered in the Abbey of *Malmesbury* 30
Iohn King of England, his story from 51. ad 68
Jews crucifie a Child at *Oxford*; their punishment 85
Their banishment out of England ibid.
Ioachim Abbot of *Calabria* 49
Ida King of *Northumberland* 10
Images taken away in most places of England 160
Inquisitors appointed to search out for Hereticks, with all *Wickliffs* Books 123
Many Italians held the best Livings in England: a Statute made against it. Four Italians followed each other in the See of *Worcester* 137

Iohn

The Table.

Iohn Iewel chosen to pen the first gratulatory letter to Queen *Mary* by his enemies   page 184
He subscribeth the Popish Tenets   187
He bewails his fall in the Congregation at *Franckford*: he is made Bishop of *Sarum*   187
His chalenge   218
His Apology.   226
Such Irish Impropriations as were in the Crown, restored to the Church   304
Dr. *William Juxon* Lord Treasurer   ib.

K.

Colonel *Ker* taken prisoner by *Lambert*   351
Kingdom of the South Saxons, comprehending *Sussex* and *Surrey*, when it began   9
The beginning of the Kingdom of *Kent*   9
Kentigern, Bishop of *Elwy* in North *Wales*   11
John Kemp Archbishop of *Canterbury* built the Divinity School in *Oxford*, and *Pauls* Cross   132
Kenulphus, King of the West Saxons conferreth large priviledges on the Monastery of *Abingdon*   169
Kings of *England* of old sent their Crowns to St. *Edmond's* shrine 34
Kimbeline King of *Britain* at the birth of our Saviour   1
Kyngils King of the West Saxons is baptized by *Birinus*   16
Order of the Knights Templars abolished throughout Christendom   106
Their Lands in *England* conferred on the Knights of St. *John* of *Ierusalem*   ibid.
Iohn Knox at *Franckford* preacheth against the English Liturgy as imperfect and superstitious. He is rebuked by Dr. *R. Cox*. He is accused to the State for High Treason against the Emperor. *Knox* departeth the City.   199
And setleth himself at *Geneva*   200
Kets Rebellion   166
Kilian, the first Bish. of *Wortsburg* first instructed the people of East *France* in the Christian Faith   17
The Bishop of *Wortsburg* carried a Sword and a Priest's Gown in his Badge   ibid.

L.

Hugh *Latimer* resigneth his Bishoprick of *Worcester*, rather than he would yield to the passing of the six Articles   169
Iohn Lambert, his Martyrdom   153
Divers Liturgies in use in *England* till King *William* the Conqueror's time   39
Lollards, after Abjuration, forced to wear the fashion of a Faggot wrought in thread on their sleeves   141
The Scottish Liturgy translated into the Latin Tongue   317
An Apology for vindicating the Liturgy commended to the Kirk of *Scotland*   317
A publick Liturgy framed in King *Edward* his days   164
Iohn a Lasco, with his Congregation of *Germans* setled at *London*: the West part of the Church of

Austin-friars allotted them p. 170.
His Congregation dissolved 184.
John Lewis an Arrian burnt at *Norwich*. 246
Levellers routed by Colonel *Reinolds* at *Burford* 349
Latimer and *Ridley* burnt at *Oxford* 194
Adam Loftus, Archbishop of *Dublin*, and Chancellor of *Ireland* 255
Matthew Lenox made Regent of *Scotland* 236
Earl of *Leicester* goes over into the Low-countries with a great Army 248
Mr. *Love* and *Gibbons* beheaded 352
Bartholomew Legatt an Arrian burnt 279
London burnt 381
The Commissioners of the High Commission at St. *Pauls* violently assaulted by *Lilburn* and the *London* Apprentices 321
Archbishop *Laud* impeached and sent to the Tower 323
And beheaded on Tower-hill *ib.*
Lucius, the first Christian King of *Britain* 2
His story 3. & 4
Lupus Bishop of *Troys*, cometh into *Britain*, and refuteth the Heresie of *Pelagius* 7
English Liturgy translated into French, for the Isles of *Jersey* and *Guernsey* 309
The Liturgy translated into *Welch* 175
Luther, when he arose 142

M.

General *Monk* his story, from page 363. *ad* 371
Marquess of *Montrosse* defeated, condemned and executed 350
Queen *Mary*, her Reign, from 180. *ad* 206
Maximus a Christian Prince, Governor of *Britain* 9
Marianus Scotus 35
Walter Mapez his verses setting forth the Church of *Rome* in her colours 67
Thomas Merks Bishop of *Carlile* faithful to King *Richard* the Second 108
Medvinus sent to *Rome* 2
Kingdom of *Mercia*, why so called, and what Counties it contained 9
Mercia divided into five Bishopricks 19
The Goods of three Orders of Monks seized into the hands of King *Edward* the Third 110
The number of Monasteries suppressed in the Reign of King *Henry* the Eighth 153
The number of those that suffered Martyrdom for the Gospel in Queen *Maries* days 194
Peter Martyr sent for into *England*; made Canon of Christchurch in *Oxford* 169
Quits the Realm in Queen *Maries* days 184
His Letters to Queen *Elizabeth* 220
His Wives body taken out of her grave, and burnt after his departure 184

Bishop

The Table.

Bishop *Morton* contrives the Union of the two Houses of *York* and *Lancaster*   135

Nine hundred Monks slain in S. *Augustines* Abbey in *Canterbury*   33

Murrey Regent of *Scotland*   233
His Death   236
The *French* Massacre   238
The Millenary Petition   269
Richard Middleton, entitled, Doctor *Fundatissimus*   107
Sir *Thomas Moor* a Great enemy to the Protestants: he was beheaded the next moneth after Bishop Fisher   149
Moratus, an old *British* writer   3

N

The Names of those that were Archbishops of *London*   3
Numbers of the Bishops, Abbots, Priors, &c. that were deprived in the beginning of Queen *Elizabeth*'s Reign   213
George Nevil, Archbishop of *York*, his Prodigious Feast: his Estate seized, and his person Imprisoned   133
The Numbers of Colledges and Chaunteries Demolished in the Reign of King *Henry* the eighth   154
Kingdom of *Northumberland*, subdivided into two Kingdoms, *viz.* of *Bernicia* and *Deira*   10
Nuns of the Abbey of *Ambresbury* Convicted for Incontinency   51
Non-conformists in Queen *Elizabeth*'s time of two sorts   229, 231

James Nailor, the Ring-leader of the Quakers publickly whipped, pillored, and Stigmatized   359

O

Offa, King of *Mercia* founder of the Monastery of S. *Albans* bestoweth great lands upon it: he was buried at *Bedford*   23
Osmond, Bishop of *Sarum* deviser of that Service, which after was observed in the whole Realm: all Service Ordered to be *secundum usum Sarum*   39
Oswald, second son of King *Ethelfred*, converted by *Aidan*: he disdained not to Preach to his Subjects and Nobles in the *English* Tongue   15
Oswald, Bishop of *Worcester*: *Oswald's* Law   31
William Occham, the Author of the Sect called *Nominales*   112
The first use of Oaths in Ecclesiastical Courts in *England*   78
Oath of the King's Supremacy established   145
Writers for and against the Oath of Allegiance   272
The form of the Oath framed in the Convocation *Anno* 1640   319
The form of the Oath taken by every Student admitted into the Popish Seminaries   235
Oak of Reformation   167
Oliver Cromwel, his Sory from   350 *ad* 361
The form of the Oath taken unto the Pope by every Popish Bishop at the taking of his Pall   139
Ordal for the trial of guilty persons   35

P

The Table.

P

Patern Preacher at *Lanpatern* in *Cardigan-shire* 11
Pelagius born in *Britain* broacheth his Heresies publickly 7
Pelagianism condemned in *Britain* in two Synods 8
S. *Petrock* Captain of the *Cornish* Saints 11
Paulinus baptizeth King *Edwyn*, with all his Nobles and much people at *York* 15
Penda King of *Mercia* embraceth Christianity 16
Pleigmund Consecrateth seven Bishops in one day
Mathew Parker Consecrated Archbishop of *Canterbury*. Divers Bishops Consecrated him 212
Kellison's and *Parson*'s slandering him to be Consecrated at the *Nag's-Head-tavern* in *Cheap-side* 214
His Story 223
S. *Paul*'s Church and Steeple in *London* burnt 222
Pope *Pius* Excommunicates Q. *Elizabeth* 235
The first setled Presbytery in *England*, at *Wandsworth* in *Surrey* 237
Popish Priests and Jesuites executed 242
The Little Parliament 353
The Humble Petition and Advice Framed 358
Statute of *Præmunire*, when enacted 117
Players forbidden by Proclamation in King *Edward* the sixth his time 161
Piers Gaveston surprized by *Guy* Earl of *Warwick*, who caused him to be beheaded 106
The first Patent of a *Commenda Retinere* granted by the King to any Bishop Elect 84
Geoffry Plantaginet Archbishop of *York*, his Story 52, 53
Peruwigs and long hair forbidden in the Clergy 77
Priests forced to forgo their wives 42
When the Pope made his first encroachment on the Liberties of the *English* Crown 38
Cardinal *Poole*'s reception into *England* 191
He absolveth the Parliament, and whole Kingdom for withdrawing their obedience to the Church of *Rome* 192
Consecrated to the See of *Canterbury* next Sunday after *Cranmer*'s death 202
English Ambassadours sent to *Rome* arrived there on the first day of the Papacy of Pope *Paul* the fourth.
Pembrock-colledge in *Oxford* founded 296
Pinckney the Provincial of the *Augustine-friars*, and Dr. *Shaa* onely of all the Clergy, engage for King *Richard* the third 134, 135
Parsonages not exceeding ten Marks, and Vicaridges ten pounds, freed from First-fruits 152
King *Philip* Married to Queen *Mary* 190
A Great Plague in *London* 381
Hugh Pudsey Bishop of *Durham*, made Earl of *Northumberland* by King *Richard* the first 48
Penry, *Barrow*, and *Greenwood*, condemned and executed 256
John Piers, Archbishop of *York* derided

derided by *Martin Mar-prelate* 256

Q

Queen's-colledge in *Oxford*, when and by whom founded 111

Queen of *Scots* assumeth to her self the Style and Title of Queen of *England* 213

She flies into *England*, and endeth her doleful life at *Fatheringhay Castle*. She is buried in the Quire at *Peterborough*: and twenty years after removed to *Westminster* 249

Queen *Eleanor*: a solemn Anniversary instituted to be kept for her, by King *Edward* the first her Husband 97

R

Romans forsake the Isle of of *Britain* 7

Rumold, called *Mechlinensis Apostolus* 16

King *Richard* the first, his Story 48, 49, 50

George Ripley a great Mathematitian 140

John Rouse a great Antiquary 140

King *Richard* the second, his Story, from 114 *ad* 118

Philip Rippinton, of a Professour became a cruel persecutor of the Gospel. He is made Bishop of *Lincoln* 121

Master *John Rogers* burnt in *Smithfield*: the first Martyr in Queen *Marie's* 194

Cardinal *Richlieu* an Incendiary between King *Charles* the first and the *Scots* 313

When the word *Recusant*, first came up 236

Reformed Religion advanced in *Ireland* 217

The Rites of the Church of *England* for a time remained the onely form of Worship for the Kirk of *Scotland* 216

Thomas Rudbourn a Monk of *Winchester*, an old Writer 3

The *Remish* Translation cometh forth 247

Rogers, his exposition on the thirty nine Articles of the Church of *England* 247

Roger a Monk of *Chester*, and an *Historiographer* 113

Doctor *Fulk* and M. *Cartwright*, their answer to the *Rhemish* Translation 247

Richard Cromwel, his Story 361, 362

S

That cruel Statute *pro Haretico comburendo*, first hanselled on *William Sautre*, Priest 119, 120

See of *Sarum* had five Bishops in five years space 94

Scotland, when freed from the See of *York* 133

Secular Priests ejected 31

A Survay taken of all the Glebeland of the Clergy 110

Severus cometh into *Britain* and assisteth in condemning *Pelagianism* 8

Sampson, Scholar to *Iltutus*: being made Archbishop of *Dole*, he carrieth away the Monuments of *British* Antiquity 11

Sibert, King of *Essex* embraceth Chri-

Christianity by the Ministry of *Mellitus* 14

Sigebert King of *East-Angles* enters into a Monastery 21

Saxons invade *Britain* 8

South-saxons converted to Christianity the last of the seven Kingdoms 19

A Survay taken of all the Revenues and Dignities Ecclesiastical in *England*, returned in a Book to be kept in the Exchequer 152

John Spottiswood, Archbishop of *S. Andrews*, his death 314

John Story a great persecutor, executed 234

A Statute made that all Convocations should be called by the King's Writ 146

The bloody Statute for the six Popish Articles enacted 155

A Statute made for the recovery of Tithes 156

Edward Seymour Duke of *Sommerset*, Lord Protector of the Realm in the Reign of King *Edward* the sixth: his story from 159 ad 174

Sommerset-house how, and when erected 165

The Sweating-sickness 174

Richard Sutton the Founder of *Charter-house* Hospital 280

M. Antonius de Dominis, Archbishop of *Spalato*, his Story 281, 288, 289, 290

Stubs and *Page*, their right hands cut off with a Cleaver 242

The *Scots* erect a New Government for themselves, consisting of four Tables for the four Orders of the State, *viz.* the Noble-men, Barons, Burgesses, and Ministers, they enter into Covenant 308

They enter *England* in an Hostile manner 321

The first settlement of the Church under Queen *Elizabeth* 215

Seminaries beyond the Seas erected for *English* youth 234

Stone's discovery of the Presbyterian meetings 254

Lord *Wentworth* made Lord Lieutenant of *Ireland*, and Earl of *Strafford* 315

He is impeached of High Treason 223

Many under the notion of scandalous Ministers Sequestred 332

Many Silenced Ministers and Lecturers put into Sequestred Benefices 332

Sherwin, *Kirby*, and *Briant*, Priests, and *Campian* the Jesuite, Executed for Treason 242

T

MErchant-Tailors School in *London* when founded 224

S. Teliau, a Scholar to *Dubritus* 11

Thetford burnt by the *Danes* 25

Adam Tarlton, Bishop of *Hereford*, the Grand contriver of all mischief against King *Edward* the second, his Story 108, 109, 110

Tindals Translation of the New Testament burnt in *Pauls* Churchyard 147

John de Trevisa, a learned English-man 117

Mr. *Walter Travers*, his story 255, 256

Theodorus

Theodorus Archbishop of *Canterbury* erected a well-furnished Library 18

Theodore Abbot of *Crowland* murdered by the *Danes* 25

John Thrask, his errours and censure 283

The Treaty at *Uxbridge* 337

The Treaty and Dispute in the Isle of *Wight* 343, 344

William Tindal strangled, and burnt at *Filford* in *Flaunders* 150

Nicholas Trivet, a Black Friar, wrote two Histories, and a Book of Annals 113

William Tailor, Priest, burnt 127

V.

King *Vortigern* sendeth for *Germanus* and *Lupus* into *Britain*, to refute the Heresie of *Pelagius*. He afterward marrieth with a Pagan woman, and is deserted of his Nobles page 8

Vortimer the son of *Vortigern*, chosen King of *Britain*; he is poisoned ibid.

Vodinus Archbishop of *London* put to death by the command of *Vortigern* ib.

Uffa, first King of the East Angles 9

Polyder Virgil the Popes collector General of the *Peter-pence* in *England*. He wrote a Latin History of *Britain* 148

Uter-Pendragon King of *Britain* 10

Aubery de Vere, a learned Lawyer, Advocate for King *Stephen* 44

An Act for Uniformity of publick prayers, &c. 375

An Act for uniting Churches in Cities and Towns corporate 381

W.

Willibrod Reformer of *Frisia* 17

Bishop *Williams* censured and imprisoned 305

Wilfrid Archbishop of *York*, converteth the men of *Freezland* in *Belgia* to Christianity 19

After his expulsion from *York*, he is for a time made Bishop of *Leicester*; at last he is restored to *York*, and was buried in his Monastery at *Rippon* 20

King *William* the First, gave unto the Bishops an entire jurisdiction to judge all causes relating to Religion, before that time the Bishop and the Sheriff kept their Court together 38

This King laid wast thirty Parish Churches in the New Forrest, to make a Paradise for his Deer 40

William Witlesee, Archbishop of *Canterbury*, freed the University of *Oxford* from the jurisdiction of the Bishop of *Lincoln*, formerly the Diocesan thereof 113

John Wickliff, his story 113, 114, 115

His bones burnt, and the ashes cast into the River 128

William Wainfleet Bishop of *Winchester* founder of *Mary Magdalen* Colledge in *Oxford* 131

The miserable death of Dr. *Whittington* a great Persecutor at *Sadbury* 140

William Wickham founded New Colledge in *Oxford*, and the Colledge at *Winchester* 117

Nnn *Thomas*

Thomas Wallis, a Dominican Friar, a writer of many choice Books 113
Cardinal *Wolfey*, his story 143, 144, 145
Dr. *William Whitacre*, his Anſwer to *Campian*'s Chalenge 241
His death 259
William White Prieſt, burnt, who was a Scholar of *Iohn Wickliff*: with him were burnt *Iohn Waddon* Prieſt, and Father *Abraham* of *Colcheſter* 128

Y.

When, and by whom the *Yeomen* of the King's guard were Inſtituted 136

Z.

Baltazar Zanchez, a Spaniard, founded an Almes-houſe at *Totnam-high-croſs* in *Middleſex* 259

ERRATA.

PAge 3. line 33. read *names*: p. 7. l. 7. r. *Franks*: l. 13. r. *Virtutem*: p. 8. l. 5. r. *Britain*: p. 9. in marg. r. *Tinmuthens.* p. 9. l. 15. f. *at* r. *and*: l. 23. r. *remain*: p. 15. l. 4. r. *Cern.* l. 20. r. *died*: p. 16. l. 32. r. *propagated*: p. 26. l. 3. r. *Halesdon.* l. 29. r. *Danish.* p. 46. l. 21. r. *the Pope*: l. 35. r. *the Cathedral*: p. 47. l. 30. r. *history*: p. 49. l. 28. r. *whom*: p. 55. l. 7. r. *reddituum*: p. 81. l. 22. r. *monachorum*: l. 30. r. *Papæ & papalibus*: p. 84. l. 35. r. *the King issued*: p. 86. l. penult. r. *the first*: p. 103. l. 24. r. *Ecclesiæ*: p. 104. l. 7. r. *or Benefice*: l. 8. r. *Expectancy*: p. 131. l. 4. r. *Regalis*: l. 16. r. *fellows*: l. 32. dele *out*: p. 137. l. penult. r. *thrifty*: p. 138. l. 5. r. *the Pope*: p. 140. l. 14. *they to cover*: p. 143. l. 18. r. *the Gatehouse*: p. 165. l. 28. r. *all Fridays*: p. 168. l. 39. r. *was signified*: p. 172. l. 41. r. *who would not*: p. 173. l. 21. r. *she bare*: p. 176. l. 16. dele *in their companies*: p. 180. l. 11. r. *eight thousand*: p. 181. l. 9. r. *Framingham*: p. 182. l. 32. dele *but*: p. 186. l. 16. r. *convocation*: l. 40 r. *days*: p. 188. l. 7. r. *to be examined*: p. 200. l. 15. r. *the reformation*: p. 204. l. 20. r. *turned*: p. 207. l. 24. r. *her age*: p. 215. l. 9. r. *gowns*: p. 229. l. 20. r. *was required*: l. 38. r. *VVyat*: p. 232. l. 20. dele *w.us*: p. 237. l 6. r. *which made many*: p. 239. l. 39. r. *Bentham*: p. 241. l. 35. r. *the old continued*: p. 242. l. 20. r. *Gulphs*: p. 248. l. 40. r. *discoverer*: p. 253. l. 41. r. *Scory*: p. 256. l. 16. r. *privately*: l. 30. r. *Greenwood*: p. 257. in marg. r. *Pitzeus*: l. 31. 1596. p. 260. r. *first Protestant Bishop*: p. 261. l. 25. r. *Brother to the Lord Cobham*: p. 263. l. 25. r. *Lordships*: p. 270. l. 1. r. 1604. p. 300. l. 9. r. *were restrained*: p. 321. l. 14. r. *it was*: p. 322. l. 2. r. *of their*: p. 326. l. 26. r. *tremenda*: p. 333. l. 21. r. *Corbet*: p. 335. l. 33. r. *enjoyning*: p. 370. l. 22. r. *suppositious*.

www.ingramcontent.com/pod-product-compliance
Lightning Source LLC
Chambersburg PA
CBHW022058300426
44117CB00007B/501